DIRECTING

THE DOCUMENTARY

Fifth Edition

DIRECTING
THE DOCUMENTARY
Fifth Edition

Michael Rabiger

AMSTERDAM • BOSTON • HEIDELBERG • LONDON • OXFORD • NEW YORK
PARIS • SAN DIEGO • SAN FRANCISCO • SINGAPORE • SYDNEY • TOKYO
Focal Press is an imprint of Elsevier

Focal Press is an imprint of Elsevier
30 Corporate Drive, Suite 400, Burlington, MA 01803, USA
Linacre House, Jordan Hill, Oxford OX2 8DP, UK

Library of Congress Cataloging-in-Publication Data
Rabiger, Michael.
  Directing the documentary / Michael Rabiger.—5th ed.
      p. cm.
  Includes bibliographical references and index.
  ISBN 978-0-240-81089-8 (pbk.: alk. paper) 1. Documentary films—Production
  and direction. I. Title. PN1995.9.D6R33 2009
  070.1′8—dc22

                                                                    2008044539

British Library Cataloguing-in-Publication Data
A catalogue record for this book is available from the British Library.

ISBN: 978-0-240-81089-8

For information on all Focal Press publications
visit our website at www.elsevierdirect.com

09 10 11 12   5 4 3 2 1

Printed in the United States of America

Working together to grow
libraries in developing countries

www.elsevier.com | www.bookaid.org | www.sabre.org

ELSEVIER   BOOK AID International   Sabre Foundation

For all my students.

Thank you for teaching me so much.

CONTENTS

PREFACE TO THE FIFTH EDITION

You want to make documentary films? Most of what you'll need is here to encourage you. Using a hands-on, project-oriented approach and talking to you as an artist and colleague, the book guides you from beginning to advanced levels of competency. Many people are experiential learners and unsuited to absorbing masses of untried information, so the book accommodates several different kinds of learner. See if your profile is here:

- *I learn best from doing, not from a lot of intellectual preparation.* Jump in, do the projects, and use the text for problem-solving when solid issues take shape.
- *I like to feel prepared before I undertake practical work.* Each phase of production includes an introduction, practical hands-on information, and analogies from everyday life to help you adopt a documentarian's procedures and mindset.
- *I really want to direct fiction but think documentary skills might be useful.* Indeed they are. In Chapter 36, From Film School to Film Industry, you'll see how documentary experience develops the confidence to improvise, experiment, and capitalize on spontaneity.
- *I'm doing routine media craft work for a living and wonder whether I can direct documentaries.* Working on the technical side often saps people's confidence to direct, but this is an accessible manual that believes you can make the leap.
- *I have neither time nor money for schooling. Can I still learn to make documentaries?* Emphatically, yes! Many self-starters have used earlier editions of this book to get on their feet. This one should be better still.

This, the fifth edition, has been thoroughly revised and expanded to reflect changing technology and the torrent of fascinating new work. Its changes respond to developments in the learning style, knowledge, and enthusiasm that the Internet generation brings to the genre. It is now two complementary books, each designed to empower a different level of experience and learning. You will now start shooting with less prior reading, and its juxtapositional layout—illustrations, diagrams, boxes containing definitions and project suggestions—reflects today's preference for multilayered information. Bibliographic or Web site information appears where you need it in the text. Suggestions for practical projects appear wherever they are useful. A detailed table of contents precedes each part.

BOOK I: FUNDAMENTALS

For the beginner needing concise, practical information who wants to start getting films up on the screen without delay. Filmmaking is something you must do anyway before theoretical issues gain substance.

Part 1: You and Your Ideas. Recognizes the ambitions you bring to beginning documentary making; introduces what the life is like and helps you recognize formative experiences underlying your artistic identity (yes, it will show you that you already have one).

Part 2: Documentaries and Film Language. How documentaries, technology, and documentary language evolved symbiotically. At each stage, there is a project with which you can explore and internalize the particular language it offers.

Part 3: Preproduction. Creating a brief proposal; turning it into a shooting plan; basic budgeting; getting permissions to shoot; developing a crew.

Part 4: Production. Choosing equipment; camera controls and handling; two-person shooting; basic lighting; essential location sound; directing participants and crew; basic interviewing.

Part 5: Postproduction. Editorial housekeeping; viewings; getting the most from each editing stage; refining your cut; trying it out on trial audiences; preparing and mixing sound; titling; press kit; Web site; shopping your film around festivals where recognition awaits if your work is good enough.

Signposting at salient points in Book I directs you to Book II's information in greater depth, while Book II directs you back to missed or forgotten fundamentals in Book I.

BOOK II: ADVANCED ISSUES

For those ready for professional-level concepts and practices.

Part 6: Documentary Aesthetics. Introduces the notion of the documentary storyteller and what it takes to achieve an individual "voice" in your work. Explores point of view, reflexivity, types of discourse, plot and the three-act structure, the dramatic arc, structuring narrative time. Also, form and style, setting creative limits, using mixed forms such as the docudrama or reconstruction. Questionnaires help you find aesthetic options for any project.

Part 7: Advanced Production Issues. Addresses advanced challenges and difficulties that typically surface during the production cycle. Highlights are:

    Part 7A: Advanced Preproduction. Types of research; evidence and exposition; representation and speaking for others; mission and identity issues of the filmmaker; proposing advanced documentaries; the treatment; budget planning; the prospectus. Also, making a directing plan; ensuring dialectics; developing a storyteller's angle; scouting locations; scheduling; solving permission and legal issues.

    Part 7B: Advanced Production. Lens optics: space and perception; choosing lens types; perspective and image texture; controlling the look of the film. Drawing up the equipment list; camera settings; options; aesthetics. Advanced location sound: single or double systems; recorders; mixers; microphone types and handling. Organization of the larger crew; procedures; social and formal issues. Advanced directing: psychology of actors in relation to documentary participants; how the camera changes people; camera coverage options. Also, conducting interviews; camera placement and directing; strategies for interviewing in depth; inward journey monologues.

Part 7C: Advanced Postproduction. Making a script from transcripts; creating narration; improvising for spontaneity. Library music; working with a composer. Editing refinements and structural problems; rhythm and flow; subtexts; diagnostic methods for identifying further problems and solutions.

Part 8: Education and Starting Your Career. Planning a career; choosing a film school and type of degree; internships and creating contacts for life beyond graduation; finding or making a job; creating an identity in the film industry; searching for subjects and markets; applying to funds and foundations; job information and journals; documentary as a prelude to directing fiction.

Appendix. Thirty-two hands-on discovery projects in a common checklist format: Analysis Projects (8), Development Projects (6), Budgeting Projects (2), Shooting Projects (14), and Postproduction Projects (2).

THANKS

Over the last two decades many have contributed help and ideas to this book. My thanks to Peter Attipetty, Camilla Calamandrei, Dr. Judd Chesler, Michael Ciesla, Dan Dinello, Dennis Keeling, Tod Lending, Cezar Pawlowski, Barb Roos, Paul Ruddock, and Bill Yancey. For pictures and pictorial sources, my gratitude to Dirk Matthews and Milos Stehlik of Facets Multimedia.

Thanks to my esteemed teaching colleagues Chap Freeman, Madeleine Bergh, Rolf Orthel, and Otto Schuurman; to CILECT; and to all the teachers and students who made the VISIONS European documentary workshops the undertaking of a lifetime.

At New York University, thanks to Dean Mary Schmidt Campbell, Ken Dancyger, and George Stoney (doyen of the American documentary), as well as the film faculty and students at the Tisch School, for the rare privilege of working with them.

Most of the information for the music chapter came from Paul Rabiger, a composer for film and television. Joanna Rabiger, a documentary editor and researcher, helps keep me current in documentary development. Penelope Rabiger-Hakak, a teacher expert in learning styles, made me understand my early difficulties with traditional education and why I opted for other paths.

Thanks to Doe Mayer, Jed Dannenbaum, and Carroll Hodge for the inspiring exchanges, formal and informal, preceding the publication of their work *Creative Filmmaking from the Inside Out* (2003, Simon & Schuster). My thanks for their permission to summarize some of its ideas.

My greatest debt of gratitude is to Columbia College Chicago, which over three decades encouraged me to implement so many of my ideas. Through the support and vision of Bert Gall and Caroline Latta, the Film/Video Department was radically rethought, expanded, and rehoused during my tenure as chair. Over the years, the college and its Film/Video Department, now under the able leadership of Bruce Sheridan, have shown me great affection and trust.

This edition benefited particularly from generous criticism and suggestions by Ken Dancyger of New York University; Valerie Brown, University of Central Lancashire, U.K.; Michael C. Donaldson; Michael Farrell, University of Nebraska–Lincoln; Tom Fletcher of Fletcher Chicago; Daniel Gaucher, Emerson College; Susan Hogue, University of South Carolina; Mary Healey Jamiel, University of Rhode Island; Laura Kissell, University of South Carolina; Jan Kravitz, Stanford University; David Krupp; Andy Opel, Florida State University; Geoffrey Poister, Boston University; Jennifer Proctor, Grand Valley State University; Linda Sever, University of Central Lancashire, U.K.; Heidi Solbrig, Bentley College; and Shannon Silva, University of North Carolina at Wilmington. If only I was equal to implementing all their suggestions!

Warm thanks to filmmakers Tod Lending, Monica Ahlstrom, Melinda Binks, Evan Briggs, and Orna Shavitt, as well as to the Maine Media Workshops for permission to show Maine work on this book's Web site.

The Focal Press staff has always been a pleasure to know and work with. In particular I want to thank Elinor Actipis, Acquisitions Editor, and Michele Cronin, Associate Acquisitions Editor, for their outstanding encouragement, good humor, and professionalism.

Lastly, heartfelt thanks to my wife Nancy Mattei for her help, patience, and unfailingly kind and astute encouragement. With so much help from so many people, all errors and omissions are mine alone. I should perhaps add that I have no relationship of gain with any of the manufacturers, services, or institutions named in this book and that uncredited images are from my photographic or film work.

Michael Rabiger
Chicago, 2008

BOOK I

FUNDAMENTALS

Just think: You can collect little bits of reality—voices, actions, landscapes, images, people talking—weave them artfully into a story, and audiences will watch and wonder. If you are really skillful, they will laugh, be spellbound, or even weep. Your reward? Moving hearts and minds.

This book concentrates on what a documentary maker must think about, feel, do, and know at every stage. Film about actuality is now being used everywhere—on the Internet (most prominently on YouTube™), between friends via cell phone, and at special-interest Web sites, as well as in cinemas and on television via cable, satellite, and the airwaves. Today, anyone can aim to make actuality into cinema-quality documentaries because the equipment and resources are within the common person's reach. What you'll mostly need is a reservoir of ideas, the courage to go where angels fear to tread, and inventive ways of using the medium to tell gripping stories.

OBTAINING FILMS

Many documentaries are cited in this book. You can rent most of them from www.netflix.com, or purchase them from www.amazon.com or from other sources supplying new and used copies. The best-stocked supplier in America is the videothéque Facets Multimedia at www.facets .org, which holds copies of many obscure or international films. Occasionally a film is only available by tracking down its maker via the Internet.

Before you order a film, check that your equipment can play disks of its designated region. Computers generally play any DVD, but manufacturers of dedicated DVD players lock them to a particular region. Look for your player's unlock code via www.dvdexploder.com or by Googling "region free."

OF BOOKS, BOXES, BULLETS, AND BIBLIOGRAPHIES

Books: This, the fifth edition, contains much that is new, and it is now divided into two levels:

- *Book I: Fundamentals* supplies what you need to get into action and learn from actual filmmaking. Each subject area suggests chapters where more advanced information is available.
- *Book II: Advanced Issues* contains information in depth that would only impede beginners. Chapter references refer you back to the fundamentals in Book I, should you need them.

Boxes: Embedded in the text are "Remember Boxes" containing important ideas or definitions. These keep bedrock truths in sight while you work through the details. At salient points you will also find "Project Boxes" suggesting you try a particular hands-on project—always the best way to learn. Most of the projects are in the Appendix with any notes and illustrations, but a few are necessarily embedded in chapters. For simplicity, project descriptions tend to be brief, in a common checkbox format, and gathered under five headings:

- 1-AP Analysis Projects (8)
- 2-DP Development Projects (6)
- 3-BP Budget Projects (2)

- 4-SP Shooting Projects (14)
- 5-PP Postproduction Projects (2)

Bullets and icons: In the text you'll encounter bullet points and icons, each with a function that makes the book easier to navigate:

 Important fact or idea.

 Actions to take or questions to ask.

 Key concept to remember.

 Hands-on discovery project for you to make or do.

 Resource for greater information.

Bibliographies: Book and Internet sources are either embedded in the relevant text or under "Going Further" at the ends of chapters.

GETTING INFORMATION VIA THE INTERNET

This book's Web site: Go to this book's Web site (http://directingthedocumentary.com) for downloadable information such as documentary film examples, production cycle "don't forget" checklists, projects and useful forms, bibliography, list of films cited, etc.

If you are a teacher: See teachers' notes for using this book at the book's Web site. Consider downloading projects, forms, and project assessments so you can customize them for your own teaching purposes.

General information via the Internet: Here are some good resources:

- For *biographies*, *definitions*, or *working principles*, try starting with Wikipedia® at www.wikipedia.com.
- For *film information* such as personnel, year, medium, genre etc., try the International Film Database at www.imdb.com.
- For a film and video *resource directory*, links to *equipment providers, materials, software, facilities,* and *services* go to the nonprofit University Film and Video Association (UFVA) at www.ufva.org. Also an excellent source for up-to-date festival, conference, and workshop information too.
- Find *rare film copies or information* by entering the title and director's name in Google. This often leads to the film's Web site, either put up by its distributor or its maker.
- *See portions of films* by entering the title in www.YouTube.com, though the quality may be poor. Watch out that someone hasn't recycled a film's material to make his own statement. Usually it's evident when you're not seeing the genuine article.
- For *reviews and opinions* try Rotten Tomatoes at www.rottentomatoes.com or simply Google the title of a film in quotation marks plus the word "review."

Since Web users freely copy and exchange information, don't bet the farm on anything that could cost you in time and money without first cross-checking that you've got the straight dope.

Technical information:

- Manufacturer Web sites offer FAQ (frequently asked questions) sections.
- Large supply houses are often a mine of good explanatory information.
- At user groups, those freewill areas in which people exchange problems and solutions, you can enter key words associated with your equipment or problem in "Groups" at the Google menu.
- For video and digital technical information of all kinds, try http://video.thedveshow.com where you can also find video tutorials and links.

Production information: There are many documentary interest sites, but especially helpful is the one founded by Doug Block and Ben Kempas called The D-Word at www.d-word.com (Figure 0-1). Its archives are a mine; discussions include every level of maker and cover every aspect of production and postproduction. It's a work of enthusiasts—free, interactive, and with participants from all over the world.

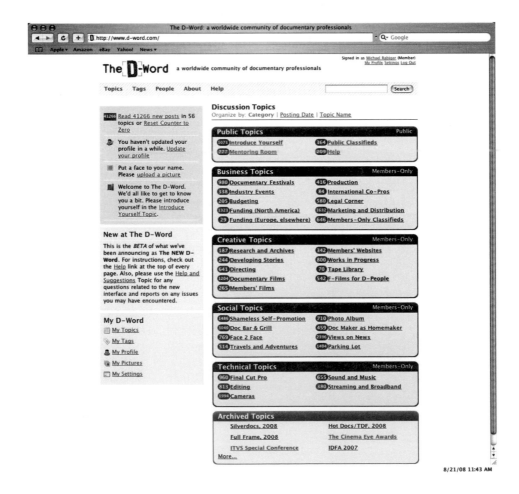

FIGURE 1

The D-Word portal of entry—a helpful, multifaceted, and free Web site for production enthusiasts.

PART 1

YOU AND YOUR IDEAS

Part 1 deals with the director's role as prime mover and source of film ideas, with the need for the self-knowledge to know what truly energizes you for the long haul, and with developing a plan for a short film.

CHAPTER 1

THE DIRECTOR'S ROLE

WHO MAKES DOCUMENTARY AND WHY

Go to any documentary festival and you will see that filmmakers are a varied lot—old, young, shy, outgoing, haunted, introverted, extroverted, large, and small. Most are friendly, unassuming, and very approachable. You quickly feel at home with them, because they say profound things through their films, yet remain unassuming and natural. Their films—long and short—take you on magic journeys into hidden or unexpected worlds. A 12-minute piece like Pawel Lozinski's *The Sisters* (1999, Poland; Figure 1-1) shows nothing more than two elderly ladies arguing on a courtyard bench. The elder wants the younger to walk

 Analyze aspects of a favorite documentary using any of **Projects 1-AP-1 Analyze Using Split-Page Script, 1-AP-2 Make a Floor Plan, 1-AP-6 Analyze Editing and Content,** or **1-AP-7 Analyze Structure and Style** (all in the Appendix).

and exercise her hip implant; the younger smilingly evades her every entreaty. Each complains conspiratorially to the camera about the other. The elder says their parents spoiled her sister and made her lazy. The younger says the elder has always been bossy. The film hits you with a poignant truth: Nothing changes between siblings. They need this daily ritual of argument, but time is running out. Soon one will be alone and a lifetime of comforting disputation will go silent.

A feature-length film such as Michael Moore's *Sicko* (2007, United States; Figure 1-2) brings the biting truth of caricature. It starts with horror stories from people who fell through the cracks in the American health care system. Then, through his specialty—hilarious, surreal confrontations—Moore builds a

FIGURE 1-1

Pawel Lozinski chronicling roles unchanged since childhood for *The Sisters*. (Photo courtesy of filmmaker Pawel Lozinski, pawel.lozinski@wp.pl.)

devastating case for the profit motive turning America's health care system into a travesty. He shows how Americans are brainwashed into believing that other countries have inferior socialized health services—meaning communistic. Then he shows what Canadians, French, British, and Cubans actually get and what millions of Americans—conditioned to believe their own society is superior—don't get.

Each film is funny and entertaining and leaves you pondering. Each works quite differently because there are so many ways a documentary can propose ideas about the real world to its audience. Today's documentary makers use every imaginable storytelling method to engage us with ideas about the actual: They can magnify a tiny backwater, explore intimate and unlikely relationships, chronicle large historical events, or rattle the teeth of a nation by speaking truth to power.

What do you get from making documentary? The process takes you below the surface of life into more mysterious regions where you start living life more profoundly. Documentary makers learn to value the joy, pain, compromise, and learning that come from being completely *alive*. No wonder they make such good company. They love to use the screen to explore what they find fascinating or scandalously unjust. Today you can do this without money, power, position, or even much in the way of special training. What you mostly need is courage, a passionate drive to solve mysteries, and the persistence to make what you've gathered into a story that will detonate in the minds of an audience.

FIGURE 1-2

Michael Moore in *Sicko* preparing to probe the American health care system. (Photo courtesy of The Kobal Collection/Dog Eat Dog Films/Weinstein Company.)

MAKING A LIVING

Now that nonfiction filmmaking is inexpensive to produce, there are many kinds of film that can bring its makers a little money, though usually not enough for a middle-class lifestyle. Directors often have to teach or make instructional or other workaday videos to earn their daily bread. At the glamorous and profitable end is the independent feature documentary that is shown in cinemas and is able to make big money. Luc Jacquet's *March of the Penguins* (2005, France; Figure 1-3) made $77 million in its first 20 weeks, while Michael Moore's *Fahrenheit 9/11* (2004, United States) grossed over $119 million. Disney is launching Disneynature, a new production unit that will produce and distribute documentaries for an initial cycle of four years. The young filmmaker just starting out can obtain local commissions, such as medical, training, wedding,

FIGURE 1-3————————————————————————————————

March of the Penguins: Sometimes documentaries hit the jackpot. (Photo courtesy of The Kobal Collection/Buena Vista/APC/Jerome Maison.)

birthday, Internet, local activist, and other films. There are news coverage, reality shows, and fundraising films for charities and nongovernmental organizations (NGOs), any of which could take you to the ends of the earth. You might work in travelogue or educational films, films about music, or films about a thousand other special interests. You could make industrial films or films for social scientists or anthropologists. There is no limit to the kind of films that people want. The trick is to make them ingeniously, inexpensively, and for money. There is, as you will see, a highly entrepreneurial aspect to surviving in this way of life.

Many people put off deciding how they should specialize as a future professional. If you mean to take up documentary as a way of life, it is a serious business; it means learning to walk the walk and talk the talk. Professional journals can draw you into the world of documentary by showing what the various jobs and interests lead to. *The Independent* (formerly *The Independent Film and Video Monthly*; see www.aivf.org), *International Documentary* (Figure 1-4), *American Cinematographer*, and *DV* are a mine of professional, critical, and technical information. You can get up-to-the-minute news on ideas and trends, new approaches in

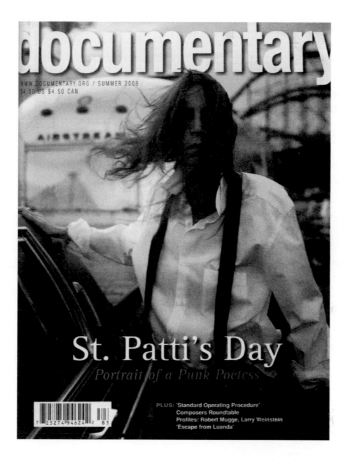

FIGURE 1-4

International Documentary, a leading documentary journal. (Photo courtesy of International Documentary Association.)

independent filmmaking, cinematography, postproduction, distribution, and festivals. *Variety* will tell you everything about the commercial film industry. Astute reading will soon enable you to think, act, and handle yourself like an insider.

The European Documentary Network (http://tv.oneworld.net) is representative of many special-interest Web sites. By Googling a combination of words that interest you (such as *documentary, festival, production, proposal, pitch, funding, center,* etc.), you can locate an enormous body of information on the Internet. Not everything is accurate or valuable, of course, but the whole scene is open for you to sightsee.

DOCUMENTARY IS . . .

Documentary's founding father John Grierson—to whom we shall return—defined documentary as the "creative treatment of actuality." He meant that if you use your creativity to organize pieces of recorded reality into a narrative, then you have produced a documentary, but this embraces all nonfiction forms such as

nature, science, travelogue, industrial, educational, social, and even
factually based promotional films.
Today, particular values and issues
seem to distinguish the documentary
from its nonfictional siblings.

Documentary according to
John Grierson is the creative treatment of actuality.

AN ORGANIZED STORY WITH A MEANING

A brief documentary might have as its sole character a large beetle trying to
climb a stalk in order to take wing. As a kid I once sat with my father watching
this happen, and we were both
entranced. Its efforts, and the
obstacles making its takeoff so
uncertain, gave its progress great
dramatic tension. When the bug
finally went buzzing on its way,
we'd seen a marathon in the insect
world, a whole documentary film
in a single shot.

To be successful, your
documentary must have
engaging characters,
narrative tension, and something to
say about the human condition.

Every compelling story, fictional or documentary, has characters striving to
accomplish something and overcoming obstacles from their circumstances. How
they do this and whether they succeed provides the dramatic tension that keeps
us enthralled. In *Winged Migration* (2001, France; Figure 1-5) by Jacques

FIGURE 1-5

In *Winged Migration*, the "characters" are birds struggling to survive. (Photo courtesy of
The Kobal Collection/Sony Pictures/Mathieu Simonet.)

Cluzaud, Michel Debats, and Jacques Perrin, the "characters" are different species of birds, each living under the compulsion of migratory survival. Each faces death as they expend every ounce of energy to overcome the challenges of distance, weather changes, and cold that sap their reserves. The sad truth is that the weaker or unfortunate ones do not complete the journey.

CHARACTERS TRYING TO GET, DO, OR ACCOMPLISH

Successful documentaries have engaging characters, narrative tension, and something to say about the human condition. Each active character is trying to get, do, or accomplish something. Similar elements show up in humanity's earliest narratives: nursery stories,

Try **Project 4-SP-10 Basic Interview: Camera on a Tripod** (in the Appendix) and see how fair you can be as an interviewer.

folktales, myths, and legends. The documentary thus continues the spirit of the oral tale.

A STORY THAT MEANS TO ACT ON ITS AUDIENCE

All narratives are workhorses—their work is to purposefully act on an audience. They delve into cause and effect to help us perceive what underlies human organizations and agendas. T.S. Eliot believed that the function of art is "to give us some perception of an order in life, by imposing an order on it."[1] Stories help to warn of danger, teach about the treacheries of human nature, urge us to live by our ideals, and so on. When the masterful storyteller takes us by the lapels, we welcome the embrace.

SOCIALLY CRITICAL

You can distinguish a documentary from other nonfiction forms by asking:

- *Does it show a range of human values?* Documentary is interested in the values and choices people make, and the consequences that flow from them. Its concerns go beyond the factual into moral and ethical spheres.

The documentary explores human predicaments and values and the consequences that flow from them.

- *Is it concerned with raising awareness?* The best documentaries are models of disciplined passion; they show us new worlds, or familiar worlds in unfamiliar ways, and raise our level of awareness. Advocacy documentaries such as Al Gore's *An Inconvenient Truth* (2006, United States) challenge us to turn understanding into action.

---

[1]Thomas Stearns Eliot (1888–1965), an American poet who migrated to England.

- *Does it imply social criticism?* Many nonfiction genres such as the travelogue, industrial, and (sad to say) educational films present a body of information without questioning the human values they document. They lack
  the very element of social criticism that characterizes the true documentary.
  A factually accurate film about the way workers manufacture razor blades
  would be an industrial film, but a film showing the effect on workers of
  repetitive precision manufacturing and *which invites the spectator to draw
  socially critical conclusions* can only be called a documentary—however
  well it also relays the physical process of manufacturing.

DOCUMENTARY INTENTIONS AND INGREDIENTS

THE WORK DOCUMENTARY DOES

Documentary films investigate, analyze, warn, indict, explore, observe, announce,
report, explain, educate, promote, posit, advocate, celebrate, experiment, expound,
propagandize, satirize, shock, protest, remember, revise, prophesy, chronicle, conclude, conserve, liberate, revolutionize. . . . Notice these are all verbs—that is, *doing*
words. Documentary lives in the real world, does active work, and means to act on
its audience.

ACTUALITY

Exploring actual people and actual situations is the documentary's specialty.
Where there is less certainty is over allied concerns; such as, what any given actuality really is, how to record it without injecting alien values, and how to honestly
and truthfully convey something that,
being more spirit than materiality,
you can only assess subjectively. Such
questions are not a fault in the genre:
rather, they echo the unavoidably
complex nature of human life itself.
As such, they are a sign of documentary's growing maturity.

 Central to documentary's
spirit is exploring actual
people and authentic
situations.

    To many people, actuality is something objective that we can see, measure,
and agree about. This is what the documentary theorist Bill Nichols calls *historical reality*, since it encompasses what can be proved and defended in court.
Films conveying large bodies of information often fall into this camp, though
facts can be contradictory and all the more interesting for it. Television has often
favored *monological* discourse; that is, actuality delivered in a linear way by specialists and authority figures who interpret, assign meanings, and decide what's
important for the rest of us.

    Many documentaries now take a *dialogical*—a multiple and critical—view.
They reject the stance of settled, paternalistic observation and reveal a reality
full of contradictory information, impressions, perceptions, and feelings.

Dialogical film deals better with the richness and changeability of real life, with the subjectivity of human experience and therefore memory, and with the arbitrariness or injustices of the *status quo*.

Under extreme pressure, human perception turns surreal and hallucinatory, as you see so memorably

 Dialogical documentary shows reality as contradictory; that is, it explores conflicting perceptions and feelings, and presents a complex, implicitly critical view.

in Errol Morris's *The Thin Blue Line* (1988, United States). Exceptional documentaries represent not just the outward, visible reality of those they film but also their inner lives. Our thoughts, memories, dreams, and nightmares also count as actuality since they are, after all, the interior dimension of outward existence. Writers have always been able to summon these dimensions, sometimes even including the storyteller's perceptions as part of the narrative. In his

postmodern novel *The French Lieutenant's Woman*, John Fowles admits he has lost control of his characters. He gets into a 19th-century train and travels with them for awhile and watches his main character Charles. Film, the most recent of the arts, is gradually learning to claim such freedoms for its own needs.

 Our interior life of thoughts, memories, dreams, and hopes are part of our reality. This, too, is something the documentary can show.

UNFOLDING EVIDENCE

The modern documentary differs from its earlier, more scripted and premeditated forms. Mobile technology allows us to easily record events in motion and to show an authorial consciousness at work *even as events unfold*. This captures the sensation of spontaneous living familiar from heightened moments in our own lives. Take, for example, Nicholas Broomfield and Joan Churchill's *Soldier Girls* (1981, United Kingdom; Figure 1-6). Ostensibly, it shows how the U.S. Army trains its women soldiers, but it also reveals many other formal and informal moments, including sadistic training and humiliations, that are all the more disquieting when imposed by authoritarian white male sergeants on black or

Hispanic women recruits. The film delays confronting its central paradox until late: Warfare is brutal and unfair, so a caring instructor cannot kindly train soldiers of either gender to survive. But, this argument wears thin after what we have seen and leaves us disturbed by larger questions about military

 Mobile camcorders capture events in motion, show life spontaneously unfolding, and help convey the filmmakers' responses even as the events take shape.

FIGURE 1-6 ——————————————————————————————————————

In *Soldier Girls*, minority women undergo sadistic training and humiliation in the U.S. Army. (Photo courtesy of The Kobal Collection/First Run Pictures.)

traditions and mentality—just as the film's makers intended. We share what moved or disturbed Broomfield and Churchill, but they never tell us what to feel or think. Instead, *by exposing us to evidence that is contradictory and provocative* they jolt us into realization and inner debate. A film that exposes us to compelling though contradictory evidence makes us jury members arbitrating not right versus wrong—which is easy to decide—but right versus right, which is not.

 Modern documentary avoids telling us what to feel or think. Instead, it exposes us to contradictory, provocative evidence that moves us to inner debate and realization.

 Right versus wrong is easy to decide—more interesting and challenging is right versus right.

TAKING MANY FORMS

A documentary's form is the way in which its story is presented. It can be controlled and premeditated, spontaneous and unpredictable, lyrical and impressionistic, starkly observational, or farcical. It can use commentary or no speech at all, interrogate or ambush its subjects, catalyze change, or muse out loud on its own unsatisfactory progress. It can narrate using words, images, music, or human behavior. It can employ literary, theatrical, or oral traditions and borrow from painting, music, song, essay, or choreography. Any of the arts, not just film, holds models of form for your future documentaries.

 A story's form is the way in which it presents its events and characters.

HOPE

All successful stories center on some aspect of human development, no matter how minimal and symbolic this happens to be. In a world convulsed with evil and pain, stories leave us with hope and some optimism, for unless we see the most important characters learn something and grow just a little, then watching their struggles produces a feeling of defeat that discourages us from taking any action of our own.

 Unless central characters learn, change, or develop in some way, a story will seem pointless.

THE OBJECTIVITY MYTH AND FAIRNESS

SUBJECTIVE/OBJECTIVE

Many people believe that documentaries are objective, but can a camera really record anything objectively? For instance, is there such a thing as an *objective* camera position, when someone must decide where to place the camera? How do you *objectively* decide when to turn a camera on and off? And, after viewing the material, how do you *objectively* spot the truth that you should use? Besides, you must turn what is lengthy and diffuse into something brief, focused, and meaningful. These are all decisions that you can only make subjectively.

The reason documentaries look objective is because television often speaks with authority and balances out opposing points of view. This is a tradition in journalism that sometimes goes very wrong. In the mid-1930s, reputable British newspapers depicted the trouble brewing in Germany as a petty squabble between Communists and Fascists, with each side equally at fault. In the world war that followed, millions lost their lives or became refugees. With hindsight, the reporting about the gathering forces of war was neither impartial nor responsible. You can't sit on the fence and report a conflict in this hands-off way. Indeed, few issues ever have two equal facets; most are a tangle of just and unjust forces at work. A documentary should not just relay counterpoised batches of information; it should try to *interpret* events and reveal their weighting in a way that history would vindicate. This means taking chances and being led by your most intelligent passions.

 Memorable documentary does not sit on the fence and balance opposites. It tries to value and *interpret* people and events in a way that history would vindicate.

So why do the media favor "balanced reporting"? Because corporations want to avoid being proved wrong or being accused of political bias. The "balanced perspective" stance is a smoke screen that allows staff and editorial perspectives to look like the opinion or conflicts of others, especially when cloaked in the uniformity of a "house style" of writing or filmmaking.

The shortest film can always reveal the complexity of human life and imply where the truth may lie. Longer and weightier works often have to lead us through a maze of contradictory evidence and let us come to our own determinations—just as the makers came to theirs. This, interestingly enough, is how courts put evidence before a jury of ordinary people—still the ultimate test of truth in a democracy.

DOCUMENTARY IS A SUBJECTIVE CONSTRUCT

You can't show events themselves, only a *construct* that sketches the key facts, logic, dynamics, and emphases—all of which you must select. Your unavoidably subjective work becomes worthy of trust if you can show a broad factual grasp of your subject, evidence that is persuasive and self-evidently relia-

 Since you must subjectively choose everything you show, your documentary can never be objective truth. Instead, it is a construct by which you convey the spirit of the truth.

ble, and the courage and insight to make interpretive judgments about using it.

Many editorial decisions involve ethical dilemmas that give you sleepless nights. Whatever you intend for your audience, the medium is also part of the message. Only by doubting what that message is and what impact your film actually delivers can you be confident that your construct delivers what you intend.

FAIRNESS

If you can't be objective, you can be fair. That means you don't stack the evidence and, where valid, you do show conflicting points of view. If, for instance, you tell the story of a malpractice accusation, it would be prudent to give equally careful and sympathetic coverage to the allegations of both surgeon and aggrieved patient. Like any good journalist or detective, you must cross-check everything independently verifiable, since matters are seldom as they seem. The accused is not always guilty, and the accuser or bystander is not always innocent. Weighing countervailing views helps to protect your interests, no matter whose part you take. Truthful as well as untruthful films make enemies, so you may have to defend yours in court. If your opponents can find a single error, they will seize on it to destroy your credibility. Michael Moore's critics took some questionable chronology in his first film, *Roger and Me* (1989, United States), and tried their damnedest to discredit him.

CLARIFICATION, NOT SIMPLIFICATION

What interests the documentarian is seldom clear-cut, but there is an ever-present temptation to render it so. Nettie Wild's *A Rustling of Leaves* (1990, Canada) is a courageous and sympathetic account of the populist guerrilla movement in the Philippines, but the partisan nature of her beliefs makes you feel guiltily skeptical throughout. Her left-wing peasants are heroic as they struggle against right-wing thugs, but soon both sides commit atrocities and the waters become too muddy to remain a story of moral rectitude. Being fair means exposing the ugly and paradoxical aspects of liberation through violence. Wild does this, for instance, by showing the trial and execution of a youthful informant by guerrillas, but you wonder if any trials exist once there are no cameras around.

A film may be accurate and truthful but fail unless perceived as such. This means anticipating the film's impact on a first-time viewer and knowing when the audience's skepticism requires you to build more into the film's line of argument. The more intricate the issues, the more difficult it will become to strike a balance between clarity and simplicity on the one hand and fidelity to the murkiness and complexities of actual life on the other.

THE DIRECTOR'S JOURNEY

The documentary director is essentially someone who:

- Investigates significant people, topics, or aspects of life.
- Does what is necessary to ethically record whatever is essential and meaningful.
- Lives to expose underlying truths and conflicts in contemporary life.
- Has empathy for humankind and develops a humane understanding of each new world.
- Orchestrates footage to make a story that is cinematically and dramatically satisfying.
- Deeply engages an audience in mind and feelings.

Many experienced directors operate from a gut recognition that is really a process of internalized logic. Working more by reflex than deduction, they recognize what works and will be effective. This is maddening to anyone trying to learn from watching them. Even professional crew members routinely harbor quite distorted ideas of what's going on. To them, directors make decisions in a remote and arty compartment of their brain. But directing really isn't a mystical process. Directors only appear inscrutable because it's a strenuous inner process that monopolizes their energies.

No film—indeed, no artwork of any kind—emerges except by conscious, responsible choices and decisions. Each new film will require you to enter a new world, decide what is significant in it, and crystallize what matters on film. This means:

- Being critically aware of each unfolding aspect of your film's world and characters.
- Retaining not only *what* you learned on your learning journey but also *how* you learned it.
- Using film freshly and inventively so your audience gets an equal or better learning journey than your own.
- Expressing ideas about the meaning and nature of actuality, not just showing it in a value-neutral way.

 Making each new documentary means entering a new world, deciding what's significant there, and crystallizing it on the screen.

The multilayered consciousness it takes to keep all these balls in the air is not a "talent"; it comes from the kind of practice a juggler employs. Expect to learn from many mistakes or miscalculations. This is all good learning. The *American Cinematographer*'s standard interview asks famous people, "Have you made any memorable blunders?" The answers make reassuring reading. At times everyone feels inept and defeated, but you pick yourself up and go on.

Making documentary is very, very rewarding. You enter people's lives, involve yourself in their issues and mysteries, and travel into new worlds with the best of traveling companions. Raising your own and other people's awareness, you never have to ask yourself whether you are using your one and only life wisely.

  Analyze how filmmakers begin their films. How do they handle the "setup" of vital information? How long before the story is under way? Try using **Projects 1-AP-5 Diagnose a Narrative** or **1-AP-6 Analyze Editing and Content** (both in the Appendix).

THE "CONTRACT," FILM OPENINGS, AND TALKING TO YOUR AUDIENCE

Intentionally or otherwise, every film signals its nature and premise within its first minute or two. Like a restaurant handing out an inviting menu, the wise storyteller sets terms in the opening moments so the audience can anticipate something compelling. This is the *contract* you strike with your audience and is a large part of your opening. By going to this book's Web site (http://directingthedocumentary.com) you can run 12 minutes each of two documentaries by Academy Award nominee Tod Lending—*Legacy* (2000, United States) and *Omar and Pete* (2005, United States)—to see how they are set up. You can also see four 5-minute student documentaries in their entirety. Each implies a promise to its audience and sets up the world of its central characters as economically and appealingly as possible. This task is called a story's *exposition* and often presents difficulties. How much should you lay out? How much factual material can the audience absorb before meeting the characters? Can you start the action (a lesson, an arrest, or, in the case of *Legacy,* a death) to give momentum during the initial exposition of the film? How much should you hold back to create dramatic tension?

 When providing a *contract* with the audience, the wise storyteller hints at the outset where the story is going and why.

Opening any dramatic work takes art and verve, or you lose your audience. The exposition and the discourse that follows depend on how you present evidence to the audience and how you acknowledge other points of view. I see three main types of communicator:

1. *Propagandist*: Wants to condition the audience and produces only the evidence to support a predetermined conclusion; wants the audience to buy the premise.

2. *Binary communicator*: Likes to give equal coverage to both sides while remaining neutral and shadowy as a narrative voice; sees the audience as empty vessels to be filled with knowledge and entertainment.

3. *Mature communicator*: Sees the audience member as an equal, willing to sift through contradictions and make thoughtful judgments; aims neither to condition nor divert the viewer but to share something from life with all of its contradictions and human mystery.

In the last category is Ira Wohl's deeply touching *Best Boy* (1979, United States; Figure 1-7). An elderly couple is uneasy about yielding their 50-year-old mentally handicapped son to an institution. Soon they won't be around to care for him, so the need is urgent. The film touches on all the humor, regret, and pain connected with the son's position as a handicapped member of a family, and it leaves the audience entranced. The film does not set out to celebrate, sell, or convert but rather to expand the viewer's mind and emotions. It succeeds by drawing us through a series of events that are fraught with emotion, meaning, and uncertainty. It lets us draw difficult conclusions about motives and responsibilities and takes us along as accomplices in a painful quest for answers. Like a good friend, a good film engages us actively; it never patronizes or manipulates its participants or its audience.

THE FILMMAKER AND THE MEDIA

Film students sometimes think that cinema is an alchemy that aggrandizes and ennobles whatever you put before the camera, but it's primarily a framer and magnifier: It makes truth look more true, and artifice more artificial. Small is big, and big is enormous. Along with any insights, every step exposes the makers' fallibilities. Content chosen and mediated by a string of human judgments is biased by the lenses, lighting, film stock, or video medium used and even by the context in which you see the movie (crowded cinema, motel TV, with your family, etc.). Rendering the spirit of the real takes knowledge of cinema and judgment.

FIGURE 1-7

Best Boy touches on all the humor, regret, and pain of a family with a handicapped son. (Photo by Ira Wohl.)

Today documentary makers mostly rely on television, satellite, or cable to show their work, although the Internet may soon change this. For those who currently control broadcasting, the notion that truth may reside more powerfully in the vision of two or three individuals than in the consensus of the boardroom is a prickly issue. Corporations are committed to audience figures and profits; they are top-down power structures that shape programming by subtracting what might offend a sector of the audience or hurt profitability. They are hypersensitive to sponsors, politicians, and self-appointed guardians of public morals. Getting anything unusual on television takes unending struggle. Paradoxically, though, it has been philanthropic endowments, enlightened corporations, or embattled individuals within them whose commitment to free speech has kept the documentary alive and (by extension) kept its contribution alive to democratic pluralism.

The diversification of messages via DVD, airwaves, cable, satellite, the Internet, and video facilities—with production and replay equipment becoming better and cheaper—is making ever more video presentations available on every imaginable topic. With more channels of distribution, more films get made, competition rises, and making a living becomes more difficult. If you are to live by filmmaking, it must be with outstanding screen work. This book hands you the keys.

FIGURE 1-8

A Sony HDR-SR12—all you need to begin making documentaries. (Photo courtesy of Sony Corporation.)

With the proliferation of digital camcorders (Figure 1-8) and desktop nonlinear editing, you can learn the basics of filmmaking rapidly and at low cost. You can shoot and edit basic material with a consumer camcorder and computer costing under $1200. Quite sophisticated work is possible with a package costing under $2500, and you can work to high-definition (HD) broadcast quality with a $10,000 package. This includes an HD camcorder, fast audio-visual computer with high-capacity hard drives, and video and sound editing software that outputs to a digital recording medium such as tape or DVD.

Digital editing, now ubiquitous, restores the flexibility of editing film while dispensing with all the drudgery of film splicing and manual filing (my first film industry job). A lab transfers film "dailies" via a film-to-digital transfer machine to a high-capacity hard disk. Origination is now in the digital domain using flash memory instead of tape cassettes, making the digital process ever more efficient. Using a computer, you can now assemble and manipulate any number of cut versions with the speed and efficiency of word processing.

The phone camera is even changing history by putting material on the Internet for worldwide consumption, as governments and police departments discover to their cost after they beat and kill their critics.

BEARING WITNESS

Ordinary people know virtually nothing about the lives and minds of their forebears. Search for your forebears in censuses and other records, and you'll find names, occupations, births, marriages, and deaths but little else about your genetic heritage. I would like to know more about the orphanage my father went to at 11 and about which he never said one word. I would like to know about the branch of his family who were village chimney sweeps near London. They left two pieces of oral information, evocative in their contradiction: that the boys had saltpeter rubbed into their torn knees and elbows to toughen their skin for the brutal job of climbing inside chimneys and that their family was illegitimately descended from the tutor of Queen Elizabeth I. The wound repair sounds grimly authentic, and the rest is surely delusions of grandeur. One universal fact stands out, though. The great mass of humanity has left nothing but what we glimpse in folk music, cautionary sayings, and marks on the landscape. Unless they tangled with the law or did something remarkable, they sank without trace. If anyone recorded their story, their masters did it for them—so the record isn't exactly unprejudiced.

You and I need not pass so silently from life or rely on others to tell the tale of our lives. The screen is now ours to chronicle what we see and feel. We can reinterpret history, bear witness to our times, and prophesy the future. Documentaries record the grassroots voices and visions of today, and the DVD and Internet transmit them. Those holding power can no longer ignore them (Figure 1-9). The consequences— for democracy, and for a more equitable tapestry of cultures—are incalculable.

 Now that digital equipment has democratized the screen, documentary is an ever more powerful conduit for grassroots vision.

DOCUMENTARY AS ART

COLLABORATION

Film, including the documentary genre, is a social art in every stage of its evolution. You work with others behind and in front of the camera. You direct, shoot, and edit a documentary collaboratively, and then another collective—the audience— reacts to the resulting work. This collective creative process has helped make film preeminently influential and successful in comparison with the other arts.

ART, INDIVIDUALITY, AND POINT OF VIEW

Émile Zola defined a work of art as "a corner of Nature seen through a temperament."[2] Let's borrow this and amend it: "A documentary is a corner of actuality seen through a temperament." This advances on Grierson's "creative treatment of actuality" because the characters and events in a memorable film *do* seem to arrive through a human mind and feelings. Even when a film's authorship includes a hundred people, you still see this unity because each

---

[2]Émile Zola (1840–1902), a French novelist writing in the literary school of naturalism.

FIGURE 1-9

Television and local activists cover an antiwar speaker during a Chicago antiwar demonstration. (Author photo.)

person in the team works for the good of the project. Each finds such satisfaction in their craft that they have no need to control the whole. Not even the director does this, for he or she coordinates the collaborative effort, never controls it. It is the passion to entertain and persuade that unites film artists; they aim to make visible what is only at the edge of consciousness for the rest of us. The human condition is what fascinates documentarians, and they revel in using their medium to explore it.

Most documentaries have a progenitor, someone who gets the whole process going and who, by common consent, directs the team. This means that your documentaries can only come through you. The chapters that follow concentrate on self-knowledge as a director's starting point.

 A documentary is a corner of actuality seen through a temperament, and this temperament can be individual or the collective identity of a group.

 The best documentaries arise from their makers' lifelong quest for knowledge and self-knowledge.

GOING FURTHER

Christopher Vogler and Michele Montez's *The Writer's Journey: Mythic Structure for Storytellers and Screenwriters* (2007, Michael Wiese) uses the foundation laid by the folklorist Joseph Campbell to show how much contemporary films share with more ancient forms of storytelling.

CHAPTER 2

DEFINING YOUR ARTISTIC IDENTITY

QUEST

By nature human beings are seekers, and the quest for those in the arts is to find meanings in life—a fundamental and noble drive if ever there was one. Documentaries are a superb vehicle for this work. Here are some questions for you to ponder:

How should you use your developing skills in the world?

What kind of subjects should you tackle?

How will you earn a living?

What are you avid to learn about?

Do you already have an artistic identity and can you articulate it aloud?

Do the work in this chapter, and even if you've never done anything artistic before, you'll find you already have an artistic identity. That is, you have an inner drive to create order and emotional meaning in connection with particular issues. You probably know intuitively that you have this, but it's tempting to set it aside as too grandiose, too pretentious for now. So most people take worthy subjects and put all their effort into the technical side of capturing them with the equipment. If you, too, do this, something will be missing. You. You will be missing in action from the beginning.

> Your artistic identity is your inner drive to create order and emotional meaning in relation to your own particular issues in life.

Every project, no matter how short or simple, is an opportunity to say something from the heart. "The only work really worth doing—the only work you *can* do convincingly—is the work that focuses on the things you care about. To not focus on those issues is to deny the constants in your life," say the authors of *Art & Fear*.[1] The respected actor and directing teacher Marketa Kimbrell adds, "To put up a tall building you must first dig a very deep hole." A fine work is always rooted, she believes, in a strong foundation of self-knowledge.

To make a name for yourself in documentary you are going to need strong, positive ideas. These won't appear when you need them: you will have to take a series of small steps. First you will need to look nonjudgmentally at whatever tensions, passions, and compulsions you carry, without labeling them "positive" or "negative," since that would be self-censorship. As an appetizer, try this modest quiz:

PROJECT 2-1: VALUES QUIZ

This is a private self-examination. With complete honesty, rate how true the following statements are for you:

	Not True (0 points)	Fairly True (1 point)	Very True (2 points)
I avoid imposing my values on other people's lives.			
I never pass judgment on friends and family.			
I have taken more knocks than I have delivered.			
I seldom see any need for confrontation.			
I need people to think well of me.			

Total.._____

If you scored:

- Above 5, read what follows carefully.
- Near 10, read what follows *very* carefully.
- Below 5, read what follows anyway, in case you're simply good at passing tests.

The quiz is meant to reveal how active and intrusive you feel in relation to your surroundings. It tests self-knowledge as it affects directing. Most people feel they know themselves intimately, but anyone who teaches screenwriting will tell you otherwise. Were this true, beginner's writing would never have the universal problem of the passive central character.

---

[1]Bayles, David and Ted Orland, *Art & Fear: Observations on the Perils (and Rewards) of Artmaking* (Saint Paul, MN: Image Continuum Press, 1993), p. 116.

ACTIVE AND PASSIVE

Why do we think of central characters in documentary as people *to whom things happen*? The explanation is, I think, that as the hero of our own story we mostly notice how people act on us, *not* how we act on others. This might be a survival mechanism or a mindset left over from the vulnerability of childhood. Passivity when directing documentaries blinds you to the many ways that participants actively make their own destiny. Instead, we see people as victims. Maybe this is why so many documentaries enshrine the "tradition of the victim."[2]

 Passive self-images disable storytellers because the central characters they depict emerge as passive, too.

To begin seeing yourself (and those with whom you identify) as assertive may require changing the habits of a lifetime.

"CHARACTER IS FATE"

Try applying the saying "character is fate"[3] to people you know well. Consider two or three people in your parents' generation: how have their characters steered their destinies? Seeing people as authors of their destiny is extremely helpful when you make character-driven films. Not everyone is a helpless victim. Most people do plenty to influence the direction of their lives.

CREATIVITY

You become creative in the arts, as in life, when you generate active, sustained inquiry, both inward and outward. Acquiring self-knowledge will forever be a work in progress, and each film will be a stage (in both senses of the word) of your development. Your documentaries will not touch people unless you are reaching for something that touches your own well-being.

 In the arts, you become creative when you generate an active, sustained inquiry that travels both inward and outward. To the degree that this touches you, it touches others through your work.

SELECTING SUBJECTS

Anyone marked by dramatic experience (say, of being an immigrant, living in the streets, or of family turmoil) has an easier time selecting subjects because

---

[2]See "The Tradition of the Victim in Griersonian Documentary," by Brian Winston, in Rosenthal, Alan, Ed., *New Challenges for Documentary* (Los Angeles: University of California Press, 1988).
[3]Heraclitus, c. 540–480 BC.

they seldom doubt where their work must go. But for those of us whose lives are less obviously dramatic, comprehending what motivates our sense of mission can be baffling. It's a conundrum; you can't make art without a sense of identity, yet identity is what you seek through making art.

Some choose the arts to express themselves, but this is usually seeking the therapy of self-affirmation. Therapy exists to help you acquire a sense of normality and well-being. It is self-directed and there's nothing wrong with that, but making art is other-directed. It's about needing to do useful work—in and for the world.

 Therapy is self-directed work that helps you find well-being. Art is other-directed work that you do in, and for, the world.

Documentary is a branch of drama, and for your dramas to be original and authentic you will need to develop a dialogue—with yourself and between yourself and your audience—through the stories you choose to tell. This will start happening as soon as you recognize your hot issues. Each will offer endless variations.

The work you have already done and the work you are going to do will form significant patterns, and these form part of the inner dialogue. Right now you need to establish what matters to you most, or you won't do your best work. The key to this is already inside you and close at hand. In the projects that follow, complete the provisional self-profiles—candidly and in private—and you'll begin to see your artistic identity. You may confirm what you expected, or you may be surprised (as I was) to discover what you have been overlooking for years.

HOW HAS YOUR LIFE MARKED YOU?

Finding your central issues begins by looking for your few strongly emotional concerns. Whatever unfailingly arouses you to strongly partisan feelings comes from the marks you carry left by the life that you've led. Finding and acting on the self-discovery material that follows means taking chances and trusting that it will lead somewhere. Most of us are shy and cautious, but film is an audience medium, and it's important to get accustomed to having people listen to you and reacting. Self-promotion is an unpalatable but necessary business. One way to minimize the discomfort is to become generous and supportive in your partnerships—in short, to promote mutual development in those around you. Then, what goes around, comes around.

The issues that mark you will be few and personal. Exploring them sincerely and intelligently through your films will deeply touch your audience and keep you busy for life. Here are some projects to help you begin digging.

 Whatever unfailingly arouses you to strongly partisan feelings comes from the incisions left by your life. Exploring these can deeply touch your audience.

PROJECT 2-2: THE SELF-INVENTORY

Discover your issues and themes (and thus what you are most qualified to give) by making a nonjudgmental inventory of your most moving experiences. This won't be difficult, since the human memory retains only what it finds significant. Think you already know them and don't need to do this? Make the inventory anyway—you may be surprised. Honestly undertaken, this project reveals the life events underlying your formation. There will only be a few, but acknowledging them will encourage you to explore the fundamental issues.

Here's what to do:

➤ **Note major experiences**—Go somewhere private where you can write rapid, short notations just as they come to mind. Name the major experiences in which you were deeply moved (to joy, rage, panic, fear, disgust, anguish, love, etc.). Keep going until you have ten or a dozen.

➤ **Arrange them in groupings**—Stand back and group them by type. (This, an important skill when making art, is called *clustering*.) Name each group and define any relationship or hierarchy you can find between the experiences. Some will seem "positive" (with feelings of joy, relief, discovery, laughter), but most will seem "negative"; that is, they have disturbing emotions attached to them such as embarrassment, shame, or anger. Make no hierarchy, for there is no such thing as negative or positive truth. To discriminate is to censor, which is just another way to prolong the endless and wasteful search for acceptability. Truth is *truth*—period!

➤ **Give yourself a role to play**—Examine what you've written as though looking at a fictional character's backstory. By objectifying your formation you should see trends, even a certain vision of the world, arising naturally from the experiences. Boldly develop this character's mission and push it to the point of caricature. Your job is not to psychoanalyze yourself or to find ultimate truth (which is impossible) but to fashion a role you can play with all your heart. Because it's only a role, not a straitjacket; it's temporary, and you can change it, evolve it, and improve it as you go.

Now without disclosing anything too private, write notes to help you make a presentation to a class or group:

➤ Describe the **main marks your life has left on you** as a result of formative experiences. Keep your description of the experiences to a minimum and concentrate on their effects, not their causes.

Example: "Growing up in an area at war, I had an early fear and loathing of uniforms and uniformity. When my father came home after the war, my mother became less accessible, and my father was closer to my older brother, so I came to believe I must do things alone."

➤ Describe two or three **themes** that emerge from the marks you carry.

Examples:

• "Separation breeds self-sufficiency."

• "Someone taking what you value can motivate you to fight for your rights."

• "Good work often starts out on the wrong foot."

> ➤ Describe several **different characters for whom you feel special empathy.** These can be people you know, types of people, or people who exist and whom you could contact.

Examples:

- A friend from an orphanage who had to overcome difficulty with intimacy
- A friend who vents his anger through antiglobalization protests
- An older woman who fought to regain the job that her boss gave to someone younger

> ➤ Invent two or three **biographical topics.** Make them different, but all reflecting your central themes. Displacing your concerns into other areas of life accomplishes two things: it avoids autobiography, and it lets you explore new worlds with authority. Be sure to choose worlds that reflect the concerns to which you are already committed.

Examples:

- Someone whose existence is complicated by having to keep their identity secret (such as a gay person in the military)
- Someone overcoming a situation where she has been made to feel unacceptably different
- Someone forced into a lesser role and who must find ways to assert they still have value

PROJECT 2-3: USING DREAMS TO FIND YOUR PREOCCUPATIONS

Keep a notebook next to your bed and make a log of your dreams. Here the mind expresses itself unguardedly and in surreal and symbolic imagery. Over a period, common denominators and motifs begin showing up. Awake gently so you can hold onto the dream long enough to write it down. If you really get interested in this work, a good dream will wake you automatically so you can write it down. Needless to say, this won't be popular with a bedroom partner.

 Dreams often project a series of forceful and disturbing images. Those that recur often hold the key to your deepest concerns.

Dreams often project a series of forceful and disturbing images. Make sure to write the dream down as it is. You can interpret and reinterpret as you amass material. Recurring images are often the best keys to your deepest thematic concerns.

PROJECT 2-4: ALTER EGOS

Some believe we have a single true self; others that we are made of multiple personalities, each evoked by particular circumstances. The latter view is convenient for storytelling. In this exercise you uncover those characters or situations to which you resonate. This lets you supplement the previous project with additional and maybe new self-characterizations.

> Authoring a story means choosing a particular storytelling role to play. This is something you take on, like an acting part, that heightens your storytelling style.

➤ List six or eight **fictional characters** from literature or film with whom you feel a special affinity. Welcome those with darker and less tangible qualities. Rank them by their importance to you.

➤ Do the same thing for **public figures**, such as actors, politicians, or sports figures.

➤ Make a list of **influential friends or family** who exerted a strong influence on you at some time. Leave out immediate family (often too complicated because they are too close).

➤ Take the strongest in your three lists above and note any **dilemma or predicament they have in common** and any **mythical or archetypal qualities** you can see they represent.

➤ **Invent an authorial role** for yourself and describe **what kind of documentaries this author should be making.** Don't be afraid to be brash and bold with your imagination here.

PROJECT 2-5: WHAT IS THE FAMILY DRAMA?

Prepare notes so that you can speak for around four minutes on:

• The **main drama in your family.** If there are several, pick the one that affected you most (*Examples:* The impact of the family business going bankrupt, discovering that Uncle Wilfred is a cross-dresser, or the effect on your mother of her father wanting all his children to become musicians).

• **What you learned** as a result of the way the family drama played out.

• What kind of **subjects your family drama has qualified you to tackle** as a result.

> The family is the great crucible for drama— which is why the gods of Greek mythology were all related to each other.

Making a self-profile brings you closer to what's inside you that is trying to complete unfinished business. Your mission is to understand the marks you carry and express what they signify in terms that others will understand.

PROJECT 2-6: SUMMARIZING YOUR GOALS

If you've done more than one of the projects in this chapter, you have covered considerable ground. Summarize where you are now by finishing these prompts:

➢ The theme or themes that arise from my self-studies are . . .

➢ The changes for which I want to work are . . .

➢ The kinds of subject for which I feel most passionately are . . .

➢ Other important goals I have in mind are . . .

 Bring a magnifying glass to someone's life by interviewing them using **Project 4-SP-10 Basic Interview: Camera on a Tripod.**

FINDING YOUR ARTISTIC IDENTITY

Your life, especially at its darkest, has equipped you to understand particular forces and the ways they work in the world. This is your artistic identity. It asks that you work to show those forces at work and to express your human feeling about them.

IF YOU LOSE YOUR WAY

Filmmaking has risks that arise from its social nature. You depend on the approval of those you like and respect, but you will sometimes lose sight of your point of view in the face of criticism. We make and view films collectively; to hold on to the purpose behind your work, you must develop a resilient sense of purpose. Never, ever alter more than small details of your work before spending considerable time in reflection.

You will lose your way—and find it again, over and over. This is the apprenticeship for learning to trust your innate instincts and intelligence.

PROGRESS AND THE ARTISTIC PROCESS

When you make documentary—or anything in the arts—the work's process releases fresh dimensions of understanding. This is the creative process at work, something cyclical and endlessly fascinating that brings us closer to other human hearts and minds. At the beginning you get clues, clues lead to discoveries, discoveries lead to movement in your work, and movement leads to new clues and a new piece of work in which to evolve them. Your work—whether a piece of writing, a painting, a short story, a film script, or a documentary—is therefore both the evidence of movement and the source of inspiration to continue. Help in all this comes in mysterious ways. "Coincidences" occurred in my filmmaking career that were inexplicably lucky. Goethe said, "The moment one definitely commits oneself, then Providence moves too. All sorts of things occur to help one that would never otherwise have occurred." Luck favors the prepared mind.

 The artistic process is like a cycle of nature—involvement leads to discovery, and discovery leads to further involvement and understanding that you want to share with others.

PRIVACY AND COMPETITION ISSUES

If you take the bull by the horns and decide to work in the arts, you cannot remain private. In any group you'll see how the people of courage, even though shy by nature, go out on a limb while others who make a show of self-assurance are actually too afraid to show themselves. Opening your deeper self to creative partners is important, for we cannot urge liberation on others without first freeing ourselves.

HOSTILE ENVIRONMENTS

The best study situations are nurturing yet demanding; they help people flower by challenging them to leave their comfort zone and evolve. Some educational environments, however, seem hostile. The personal chemistry is wrong, or competitive personalities dominate. Usually it's because someone in authority is holding out perquisites, operating a patronage system, or passing other advantages to favorites. Common and deplorable though this is, regard it as a challenge put there by destiny to test your mettle. Sooner or later you'll encounter it in the workaday world anyway.

Important work arises out of conflict, never from comfort and contentment. Don't wait for better circumstances. Bloom where you're planted. Choose work partners carefully; with good ones you can handle anyone and anything.

GOING FURTHER

Try my *Developing Story Ideas* (2006, Focal Press) or Anne Lamott's very enjoyable *Bird by Bird* (1995, Anchor Books). Both are about plumbing the depths for the stories that connect to the truths one carries within.

CHAPTER 3

DEVELOPING YOUR STORY IDEAS

IDEATION

This chapter continues the work of ideation (choosing and developing ideas) by making use of all the story resources at hand. You never need to wait for inspiration, since potential film ideas are all around you. The aim is to experiment while finding and developing a strong film idea. Here, making documentary and writing fiction have something in common. Writers wear several hats, but the two they wear the most use quite different parts of the mind:

- *Story discovery*—You use play, imagination, and intuition to look for the subject or topic that brings you a "shock of recognition."

- *Story development and editing*—Here, you logically analyze, test, and structure the material you've generated, aiming to shape and improve the tale it yields for the screen.

 As a writer you wear different hats and use different parts of your mind. You generate story materials by freeing your mind to make associations, but story development and editing take logic, analysis, and order.

Writer's block sets in when the logical mind at its most negative keeps barging into the play area, censoring and belittling what's on paper. Many people had writing ruined earlier in life by overly prescriptive teaching that made them start with an outline. The insistence on order at such an early stage blocks the heart and imagination, which needs to be free to play during the ideation stage of any project. Logic, intellect, order, and control will have plenty to contribute later.

Let's see where to look for ideas for documentaries.

COLLECTING RAW MATERIALS

You may already be using some of what I'm about to describe—ways of collecting and sifting material for a story, *the* story, you need to tell next. Examine your collection diligently, and you will actually see the outlines of the collector, the shadowy self that is implacably assembling what it needs to represent its preoccupations. Nowhere is this more evident than in your journal.

JOURNALS

Keep a journal and note down anything that strikes you, no matter what its nature (Figure 3-1). This means always carrying a notebook and being willing to use it publicly and often. Copy incidents into a simple database in your computer. The act of copying gives you time to think, consider the incidents, and to group and rearrange your observations. Invent thematic or other keys so you can call up material by particular priorities or groupings. A computer isn't inherently better than, say, index cards, except that it lets you juggle and print your collection as well as experiment with different structures. Also, of course, things somehow detach from you and look better in print.

Reading over your journal notes becomes a repeatable journey through your most intense ideas and associations. The more you note what catches your eye,

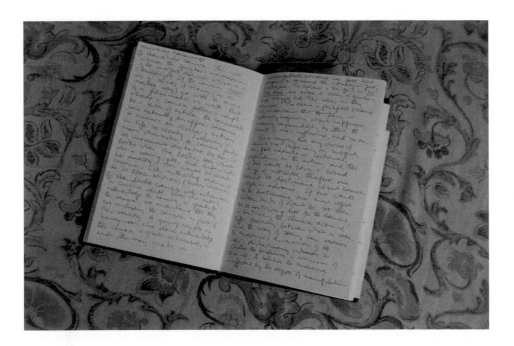

FIGURE 3-1 —————————————————————————

A journal is a log of everything you find significant. Later, by clustering the material in groupings, you find underlying patterns in your preoccupations. (Author photo.)

the nearer you move to your current themes and underlying preoccupations. You may think you know them all, but you don't.

NEWSPAPERS AND MAGAZINES

Real life is where you find the really outlandish tales. Keep clippings or transcribe anything that catches your interest and classify them in a system of your own. Categorizing things is creative busywork because it helps you discover the underlying structures in your life and your fascinations.

Newspapers are a cornucopia of the human condition at every level, from the trivial to the global. Local papers are particularly useful because the landscape and characters are accessible and reflect local economy, local conditions, and local idiosyncrasies. The agony columns, the personals, even the ads for lost animals can all suggest subjects and characters. With every source, you have possible characters, situations, plots, and a meaning to be found.

INTERNET

Here is a fount of possibility. By using the community Web site www.craigslist .com and going to my own locality, I found these samples. The writers being local, I could approach any of them to propose I do a film with them. I have removed names to protect their identities:

- Peace Corps: My Daughter just informed me that she has been accepted, Medical and FBI part left to do. For god's sake how safe is it really? She wants to go to Africa and work on AIDS/HIV education. Seriously, why do I feel like my child is going off to war? Is this a normal reaction? Don't get me wrong . . . I am very proud of her but scared as well.

- Documentary Filmmakers Wanted: "InnerViews" is a series of short films being created at L—— Geriatric Centre in S—— to document the life stories of our residents. Each of these films will chronicle the life of a resident from infancy to childhood to adulthood and through his or her senior years. The only prerequisites to volunteering for this project are computer literacy and an interest in documentaries and filmmaking.

- Stop smoking/volunteer to be hypnotized: Hypnotists in training seeking volunteers to be hypnotized. You can have a free session! Contact instructor L—— W—— to schedule your session! Indicate the issue you are seeking help with when calling or emailing.

The first might lead to a film about an anxious mother/daughter relationship, the second to a film about (probably very amateur) filmmaking with old people, and the third could be about desperate smokers seeking help. Any of these could be full of humor.

HISTORY

History doesn't happen; it gets written. Look at *why* someone makes a record or *why* someone writes a historical overview, and you see not objective truth but someone's wish to interpret, mark, and persuade. History is all about point of view—which is why they say that historians find what they look for.

Every area has its local history department and its enthusiasts researching the past. You might make a film about amateur historians or about some feature in your locality that has stories attached to it. You may find people reenacting history; that is, playing parts in some drama that took place in a particular place or landscape. There are thriving societies that put on shows in which they fight battles in authentic costumes and according to the best of their knowledge.

You may find the pursuits of archeology fascinating—detective work aimed at reconstructing the past. There is even a television series called *The History Detectives* that shows this kind of work (www.pbs.org/opb/historydetectives). The show often takes an artifact or piece of information handed down in a family and researches its significance or authenticity. Here are three "teasers" from their Web site:

Bonnie & Clyde Bullets

Could five .45 caliber bullets owned by a woman in a small Wisconsin town be responsible for the demise of the notorious Bonnie Parker and Clyde Barrow?

Movie Palace

Is it possible that a theater in the small town of Baraboo, Wisconsin, could have been the country's first great movie palace?

Sears Home

Might an Ohio couple's residence be a long-forgotten Sears home?

If history excites you, maybe your job is to disinter stories that have force and meaning for you. Do it well, and you will move people and even persuade them to act a little differently.

MYTHS AND LEGENDS

Legend is inauthentic history; by taking a real figure and examining the actuality of that person in relation to the legend built around him or her, you can see how humankind refashions the actual in order to catch public imagination. This is the subject of Mark Rappoport's hybrid production, *From the Journals of Jean Seberg* (1995, United States; Figure 3-2), which uses a look-alike actress to play the part of a hypothetical Jean Seberg. Rappoport's film, instead of allowing her to die at 40, makes her look back questioningly over the parts she played through her life.

Every culture, locality, community, or family has icons to reflect its sense of saints, fools, demons, and geniuses. When you can find them or resurrect them, they make powerfully emblematic film subjects. Myth is useful because it expresses particular conflicts that humans find enduringly insoluble and which we must therefore accommodate. The human truths in Greek mythology (for instance) do not lead to easy or happy resolution, but instead leave the bittersweet aftertaste of fate and prove to be unexpectedly uplifting. Yes, we think, *that's* how it is! In Martin Doblmeier's biography *Bonhoeffer* (2001, United States; Figure 3-3), for instance, we meet the intriguing young German

FIGURE 3-2 ————————————————————————————————————

The iconic actress Jean Seberg, around whose roles and life Mark Rappoport wove an improvised fiction film. (Photo courtesy of The Kobal Collection/Columbia Pictures.)

theologian who worked his way around to justifying an assassination attempt on Hitler, and who was then horribly executed when the attempt failed. At this remove in time his courage as a pacifist, weighing one evil against a larger one, makes him a mythical figure, a David who loses the battle against Goliath.

FAMILY STORIES

All families have favorite stories that define special members. My grandmothers seem like two figures from fiction. My family said of Granny Bird that she "found things before people had lost them." Conventional in most ways, she had mild kleptomania, especially where fruit and flowers were concerned. At an advanced age, during breaks in long car journeys, she would hop over garden walls to borrow a few strawberries or liberate a fistful of chrysanthemums. How a family explains and accommodates such eccentricities is a tale in itself.

Granny Rabiger began life as a rebel in an English village. She married an alcoholic German printer who beat her and abandoned her in France, where she

FIGURE 3-3

Martin Doblmeier shooting *Bonhoeffer* in the Berlin jail where the dissident pastor was once imprisoned. (Photo courtesy of Journey Films.)

stayed the rest of her life. Her life and those of her three children are too fantastic to be credible in fiction but would make an interesting documentary if any of the primary witnesses were still alive. Family tales can be heroic or they can be very dark, but as oral history they are always vivid or they don't survive.

  Shoot an interview as in **Project 4-SP-10 Basic Interview** but make the subject a family story or a story from childhood. Preinterview so you find a story that holds a strong meaning for the interviewee. If illustrative material—photos, family film, or video—is available, use it.

CHILDHOOD STORIES

Everyone emerges from childhood as from a war zone. If you did the creative identity exercises in the previous chapter, you surely wrote down traumatic events from your childhood that have become thematic keys to your subsequent life.

One that springs to mind as I write this is when, at the age of seventeen, I overheard on the studio set a misogynistic comment about my editor. On returning to the cutting room, I naively repeated this to her as something absurd, but she flushed scarlet and sped out of the room to find the commentator. I died several deaths waiting for what I felt sure would be murder and mayhem. What a lesson in the price of indiscretion.

The incident has rich thematic possibilities: We are sometimes spies, sometimes guardians, sometimes defenders, sometimes denunciators. When life hands us power, how should we use it? So many invisible influences direct our destiny. How far have you explored yours? What happened to blast you into a new consciousness?

SOCIAL SCIENCE AND SOCIAL HISTORY

Social science and social history are excellent resources for documentarians. If the way the privileged exploit the poor moves you, you can find excellent studies of farm, factory, domestic, and other workers. Each will contain a bibliography listing what other studies exist. The more modern your source, the bigger the bibliography. Some books now contain filmographies, too.

Case histories are a source of trenchant detail when you need to know what is typical or atypical. They usually include both observation and interpretation, so you can see how your interpretations compare with those of the writer. Social scientists are disciplined chroniclers and interpreters; their work can inform you because they usually work from a large and carefully considered knowledge base. You can also draw on their work to confirm whether your feelings and instincts have support.

FICTION

Just because you are working with actuality, don't discard fiction. Novels and short stories are often superbly observed and give inspiring guidance in a highly concentrated form. Jane Smiley's *A Thousand Acres* is not only an excellent novel that reinterprets *King Lear* in a rural Midwest setting, but it is also a superbly knowledgeable evocation of farmers and farming. To read it in association with an intended work on, say, the depopulation of the land as agribusiness swallows up family farms is to find reminders at every level of what a documentary maker should seek.

TESTING A SUBJECT

SELF-QUESTIONING

Testing the power of a subject idea takes research (to find out what is really there) and some self-questioning (to make sure it's for you). Most important is to ask at the outset, "Do I *really* want to make a film about this?" Silly question? Beginners often attach themselves to subjects for which they have no knowledge or emotional investment. Making a documentary is a long, slow process, and initial enthusiasms easily dim over the long haul. To avoid this, see how you answer these questions:

> ➢ In what area am I most knowledgeable and even opinionated?
> ➢ Is there an aspect of it that I could cover well?
> ➢ Do I feel a strong and emotional connection to doing it—more so than to any other?
> ➢ Can I do justice to the subject?
> ➢ Do I have a drive to learn more about this subject?

Answered honestly, these questions will flush out your level of commitment. Commitment low? Keep searching, and you'll eventually hit on a subject or idea that feels really right. The best sign that your interest and energy will stay high is when you feel a strong desire to learn more.

NARROWING AND INTENSIFYING

Everyone initially bites off more than they can chew. Simple economics will keep you out of many topics because they are only open to large companies. For example, a biographical study of a movie actor would be impossible without corporate backing because the actor's work is only visible in heavily copyrighted works.

Another kind of inaccessibility arises when you choose an institution as your subject. Some make fascinating film topics, but filming the police or the army, for instance, would be insurmountably difficult without very high-level approval. Even a local animal shelter may be hedged around with politics and suspicion. Most institutions have nothing to gain from letting you in, because for all they know you might dig up (or manufacture) sensational and damaging evidence in their disfavor. Other institutions are unremarkable; a film merely confirms what commonsense would expect. And what use is that?

Narrow your sights, pick a manageable subject area, and take on what matches your capabilities and budget. Not for a moment need this confine you to small or insignificant issues. If, for instance, you are fascinated by the roots of the war in Afghanistan but have no access to combat or archival footage, you might find that a local plumber is a military veteran with a fascinating and representative experience. He has a network of friends with snapshots, home movies, and mementos. Now you can tell your tale about Everyman who goes to war in the belief that he's defending freedom.

Initial ideas that one has are usually those that anyone would have, so prepare to reject the obvious. This is an important habit if you are to refine subjects so they become compelling. Try asking yourself:

> What is this subject's underlying significance to me?
> What do most people already know, and what don't they know?
> What would I—and most people—really like to discover?
> What is unusual and interesting about it?
> Where is its specialness really visible?
> How narrowly (and therefore how deeply) can I focus my film's attention?
> What can I *show* (as opposed to narrate)?

Discovering the personal connection of a subject, rather than trying to see it from an imagined audience perspective, usually takes you into new and exciting areas. Clarify—on paper, if you can—what you want to show and what you really want to avoid.

Let's say you want to make a film about inner-city life. Trying to cover too many aspects will lead to lots of thinly supported generalizations, which any mature viewer will reject. On the other hand, profiling a particular café from dawn to midnight might reveal much, and in very specific terms.

Think small. Think local. Any number of good films exist within a mile of where you live. Most people do not think of exploiting their own turf.

 Think small, local, and *short*. Developing your skills on fragments allows you to inquire in depth and avoids the discouragement that comes from overload.

LOCATING THE STORY PRESSURES AND RAISING THE STAKES

In every story, something is at stake for the central character or characters, those folks *who are trying to do, get, or accomplish something.* Raising the stakes might mean:

 Consider analyzing a film that raises the stakes using **Project 1-AP-6 Analyze Editing and Content.**

- Sending canoeists through the banks of a river narrows where the water runs faster and more dangerously.
- Reducing the rations for a long journey—the travelers have less to carry but less margin for delay or accidents.
- Seeing rain beginning to fall on mountain climbers.
- A stock market plunge for a business that is in danger of going broke.
- An emotional setback for somebody taking an important exam.
- The snowstorm for Nanook.

 Interesting characters are always trying to do, get, or accomplish. Once you know what someone is trying to get, think about what is at stake and how to show this at its most extreme.

You get the idea. "Raising the stakes" is a screenwriters' expression derived from gambling, and it means considering (and sometimes contriving) what would make things more challenging for your characters in struggle. A skilled storyteller looks for *what would make the central characters play for higher stakes.* The more there is at stake, the more the players care about succeeding, and the more compelling and important the game becomes for all concerned. The source of tension for the striking coalminers in Barbara Kopple's *Harlan County, USA* (1976, United States; Figure 3-4) is over establishing the right to a union and bargaining for more humane conditions. The stakes rise when company thugs snipe at the crew in the dark, eventually killing one of the dissident miners.

New circumstances provide greater pressure, more hazards, more tests that the hero in folk stories must always face while he or she undertakes the epic journey.

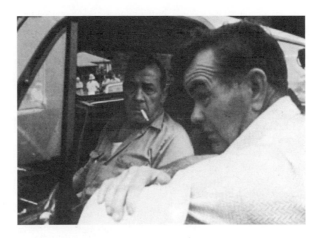

FIGURE 3-4————————————————————————

Harlan County, USA: real-life violence in the making. (Photo courtesy of Krypton International Corp.)

As you plan a film, ask what might legitimately raise the stakes for your central characters before our very eyes. Consider:

➢ What obstacles your protagonist(s) might face

➢ Whether this will happen spontaneously or whether you must assist

➢ Whether you can legitimately arrange things to optimize your chances

➢ How to get your camera in the right place at the right time

➢ How to film appropriately and with the greatest credibility

Contriving to make things happen can get you into trouble. In John Schlesinger's lyrical *Terminus* (1961, United Kingdom)—a "city symphony" documentary about the events and rhythms in a great London train station—a small boy's mother fails to return as he waits with his suitcase. This is every child's nightmare, and his fright and misery are palpable as a policeman leads him to the stationmaster's office to await his mother. But Schlesinger had contrived the situation with the mother's agreement, and later when this emerged, he was condemned for improving his film at the cost of a child's misery (Figure 3-5). Coincidentally, *Terminus'* camera assistant Nick Hale met the boy again as an adult. He said the experience had done him no harm and was amused that people had worried on his behalf.

To raise the dramatic temperature and make your audience care about your characters:

➢ Be sure to establish all pressures the central characters experience

➢ Anticipate your audience's questions and shoot whatever will answer them

➢ When important situations fail to develop or resolve, be ready to help things happen by contriving events or confrontations, *but only if it's ethical*

FIGURE 3-5

Rigged moment at a train station: a small boy discovers he has lost his mother in *Terminus* (frame from film).

> ➤ Raise the stakes only when (a) you have the permission of those involved, or (b) you can obtain their agreement afterwards that your intercession was legitimate
> ➤ Don't risk alienating participants or the audience by injecting what is false. There may be no way back into favor
> ➤ Set ethical lines that you won't cross, but don't forgo all experimention. Political correctness should not prevent the occasional gamble. You don't have to show everything you shoot. Nothing ventured, nothing gained.

USING THE MEDIUM TO STIR FEELINGS

THE SHOCK OF RECOGNITION

My late BBC producer Stephen Peet asserted that the best documentaries deliver an emotional shock. This might peak in a single memorable scene or become the sum of a whole film, as in Werner Herzog's *Grizzly Man* (2005, United States; Figure 3-6). His study of Timothy Treadwell is a biography of someone literally consumed by his interests. An animal rights advocate, he identified with grizzly bears and, wishing to protect them, convinced himself that they loved him as much as he loved them. Herzog draws on the 100 hours of video footage Treadwell left behind to plumb his notion of what animals feel and to warn against sentimentalizing the forces of Nature. Like all Herzog's work, the film transcends facts and opinions, delivers an emotional impact, and illuminates ideas about the human condition.

FIGURE 3-6

Grizzly Man is a cautionary tale about a man who thinks that bears reciprocate his feelings for them. (Photo courtesy of The Kobal Collection/Discovery Docs.)

PRIMARY EVIDENCE

"What can I show?" is the key issue because the screen isn't like other forms of communication. Film persuades when it shows people and situations in action, so we want primary evidence, things seen in motion. Doing and feeling is more interesting, more inherently credible, than talk about doing or feeling.

Can you position yourself to collect primary evidence? Can you get feelings from your participants and not just information? Can you film material and tell a story with minimal narrating speech?

B-ROLL BLUES

Documentary units often go out to "collect B-roll" footage. This means shooting a supply of cutaways as illustrative material. Frankly, I detest the whole idea of B-roll. By presuming that images exist to enhance words, the B-roll idea is alien to screen art and belongs in the lecture hall, hack TV show, and government agency. Besides, slotting words and pictures together is show and tell, and instinctively we distrust any technique so readily manipulated.

LECTURING LACKS IMPACT

True, some subjects can only be talking heads. I made two films about World War I conscientious objectors. They were very brave men—preferring to be shot rather than shoot someone else. (Now think what *that* takes in moral courage!) So subversive were these gentle men to the war effort that the authorities allowed no camera near them, so I had no stills or movie footage of them resisting, only photos of them as young men and photos of a prison or other facility. Now, under the right circumstances, a talking head film can be very dramatic, and these old gentlemen were quiet dynamite. But most topics are best explored when talking heads are kept to a minimum.

Why do we turn so readily to people talking instead of imagery and people in action? Probably because it's emotionally safe; the events are in the past and the speaker can safely go there and take you along. Or, maybe schooling and television indoctrinate us with show and tell; we begin from an abstraction ("It was really awful") and then reach for an illustration. Imagine Flaherty's seminal documentary,

Nanook of the North (1922, United States), made as a talk show. A reporter would narrate a film based on interviews with B-roll of snow, dogs, and igloo shots. The real power of the cinema to show action and behavior would go unused.

 Test any film idea by *imagining you must make it as a silent film.* What action, behavior, and imagery will you need?

TESTING FOR CINEMATIC QUALITIES

So, are you thinking like a journalist or like a filmmaker? Being the latter means trying to chronicle and narrate with imagery rather than with recorded speech. Show us behavior, action, and interaction, and then we'll think, feel, and make judgments. Whenever you are successful, the action of each shot scene will convey a clear, strong feeling and imply a foundation of ideas.

MOOD MATTERS

Good cinematography and strong action create a strong *mood*. Viewers enter your movie wholeheartedly and open their hearts to your film's thematic thrust. Free your film from the tyranny of the interview + B-roll approach, and it can become sensual, lyrical, and sensitive to atmospheres, lighting, and small but significant details. All of these build that strong aura of subjectivity that viewers recognize from personally felt experiences of their own.

LOCAL CAN BE LARGE

Aim not to parochially capture the attention of your peer group or locality but of people at large. Make films that are thematically large. You can do this by taking the most localized material and, through making your eye wise, finding the universal truths within. This is not easy. But if you push yourself and use those around you as sounding boards, there is always more to envision and further to go.

SUBJECT-DRIVEN VERSUS CHARACTER-DRIVEN FILMS

One way to avoid the didactic film, which lectures or illustrates concepts like a school text, is to avoid messages as a starting point and look instead for characters of spirit and energy who are trying to get or do something. Nathaniel Kahn's pained search for the truth about his enigmatic and aloof father, *My Architect* (2003, United States), is dominated by the spirit of the great architect who, sadly, was far from being a great human being.

The essence of drama is effort expended against some kind of opposition. The lives and behavior of people with these qualities always suggest ideas and thematic meaning once you dig into what they are doing. Energetic characters, ones making waves, always come with strong issues attached. These may be connected with blood relations, regaining something, revenge, justice, redemption, letting go, taking back . . . anything. You have to uncover what the person's issues are and conceive a film that clarifies their nature, reveals them in action, and implies their significance. A whole, nicely structured film can come from the imperatives of character.

SUBJECTS TO AVOID

Many subjects that come easily to mind are current and being pumped up by the media. It's usually good to stay away from:

- Worlds you haven't experienced and cannot closely observe.
- Any ongoing, inhibiting problem in your own life (see a good therapist— you won't find solutions while trying to direct a film).
- Anything or anyone "typical" (nothing real is typical, so nothing typical will seem real).
- Preaching or moral instruction of any kind.
- Problems for which you already have the answer (so does your audience).

DISPLACE AND TRANSFORM

Every film I have ever made has been about trying to escape imprisonment, but it was years before I realized this. A colleague said that underlying all his films has been the search for a father (his own died when he was young). Each of us is marked in particular ways and each deeply moved and motivated by this. Direct autobiography is inhibiting, but it is liberating and fascinating to pursue situations that are analogous to one's own.

After careful inquiry and reflection, take your two or three best subjects and, even though they seem temporary and subject to change, assume they are viable. If you are working too closely from events and personalities in your own life, look for other people in similar situations. This permits you some distance, which:

- Frees you from self-consciousness.
- Lets you tell all the underlying truths, not just those palatable to friends and family.
- Allows you to concentrate on dramatic and thematic truths instead of getting tangled in issues of autobiographical accuracy.

GOING FURTHER

In addition to my *Developing Story Ideas* (2006, Focal Press) mentioned previously, you will find more on developing stories for films in my *Directing: Film Techniques and Aesthetics* (2008, Focal Press). This, the fiction counterpart to the book you are holding, is useful for making comparisons with the fiction process and useful, too, if you are considering the move from documentary to fiction.

Highly recommended are Jed Dannenbaum, Carroll Hodge, and Doe Mayer's *Creative Filmmaking from the Inside Out: Five Keys to the Art of Making Inspired Movies and Television* (2003, Fireside). It considers the creative process under the categories of Introspection, Inquiry, Intuition, Interaction, and Impact and interviews prominent creative figures on their beliefs and approaches in both fiction and documentary. It's particularly good on "embedded values"; that is, the way that filmmakers embed inculcated values and ethics in their work that contradict their conscious intentions.

CHAPTER 4

PROPOSING AND PITCHING A SHORT DOCUMENTARY

This chapter covers developing an initial documentary idea to the point where you can *pitch* it to other people. The term, which comes from baseball, signifies giving a brief, orally delivered description from which other people can "see" your film and react to it. From this you can get an audience reaction to your film even before you've made it and learn what changes your idea needs in order to become really striking.

WHY YOU NEED A PROPOSAL

People making their first documentary often do so with little or no preparation. They feel they have a compelling subject and must shoot immediately. So they shoot . . . and shoot, and shoot. The problem is that, when you run the camera without focused ideas, everything looks potentially significant, so what you shoot is . . . everything. Later at the computer, you face hours of footage with no narrative thread or point of view. The lesson is *you must focus your ideas ahead of shooting, so you can look for particular material.* That's directing as opposed to archiving.

 Shape your ideas and clarify your intentions by developing a proposal. If you don't, you will probably shoot everything that moves. This leads to misery when you edit.

But, you protest, shouldn't I shoot with an open mind and not decide beforehand what's going to happen? Yes and no. What you need is a plan that narrows and deepens your quest. Armed with this, you either see what you hope for as you shoot or you'll register new aspects. With plans in mind, you know whether to incorporate the new or discard it.

Here are the preparation steps:

1. Write a *working hypothesis*. This crystallizes your intentions for the filming.

2. Develop a *film proposal* on paper.

3. Develop an oral *pitch* of your film. An audience assesses your likely film, and you get an audience reaction to help you go further.

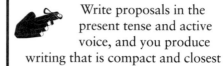

> Write proposals in the present tense and active voice, and you produce writing that is compact and closest to the viewing experience.

FILM WRITING IS DIFFERENT

Film scripts or proposal materials are always in the present tense and active voice. This produces compact writing that is closest to the viewing experience. First, you'll probably write, "He will be shown digging his garden." Realizing you've put this in the future tense, passive voice, you change it to the present tense, active voice: "He is digging his garden." Better yet would be "He digs his garden." See how compact and purposeful these four words are, compared with the original seven? Because passive constructions are indispensable to our "I'm not responsible—don't blame me" culture, you may have to do what I do, which is set your word processor to spot them and prompt you when you come off the rails.[1]

PROJECT 4-1: DEVELOPING A BRIEF WORKING HYPOTHESIS

Use the eight prompts below to develop any documentary idea into a working hypothesis, which is really a delivery system for your documentary's convictions:

• Prompt 1 asks for your conviction as the starting point.

• Prompts 2 through 6 are the body of ideas, purposes, and concepts that make your film persuasive to an audience.

• Prompts 7 and 8 are the target—an audience member's heart and mind.

On the following page is the eight-stage Working Hypothesis Helper. The examples in the right-hand column help you answer the prompts on the left. Work to compress your answers until you have the briefest, most compact and

---

[1]In newer versions of Microsoft® Word® for the PC, click on the Review tab and in the Proofing group, click on Spelling & Grammar. At the first passive sentence in your writing, the program should report "passive voice." If not, click "Options…" in the Spelling and Grammar pane and set the writing problems for which you'd like alerts. It's good but not infallible, by the way.

comprehensive statements you can manage. For the more advanced version, go to **Chapter 23, The Advanced Proposal.**

Working Hypothesis Helper

Prompt	Answer should include
1. In life I believe . . .	a. Your convictions that made this topic so attractive b. Any truths or "laws of the universe" that bear upon your central person or subject c. The theme you want to explore in your film *Example:* In life I believe one is always tempted to avoid failure by not trying, but life keeps facing you with tests of courage. Once you try to overcome something, you feel great—even though the problem remains.
2. The world where I will show this in action is . . .	Brief description of the "corner of nature" in which your conviction will come to life *Example 1:* A grade school full of noise, activity, and boisterous kids at a swimming lesson *Example 2:* Breeding kennel where puppies develop in a run with their mother, competing for food and space *Example 3:* A busy building site with its daily cycle of activities both great and small
3. My central character is . . .	A person, creature, or thing *Example 1:* Timid foreign schoolboy still learning the language of his peers *Example 2:* The runt in a litter of puppies, smaller and weaker than the others *Example 3:* A small, feisty Bobcat earth pusher on a building site, rushing headlong amid cranes and other behemoths
4. My film's main conflict is . . .	The main competing forces that your film wants us to consider—be really careful, as it's easy to choose superficially and not discover the deeper levels until later *Example 1:* The struggling individual boy vs. the tribal cruelty and pack mentality of young children *Example 2:* The disadvantaged creature vs. those better endowed to survive (without human intervention, the weak are eliminated in Nature's pitiless competition) *Example 3:* Big, heavy, slow-moving construction machines versus our small, crazily active earth pusher

(Continued)

Prompt	Answer should include
5. I expect my film's structure and viewpoint will be determined by . . .	The thrust of time or movement around which you can organize your film—you want it to generate a strong storytelling momentum. Also, whose viewpoint will we share? *Example 1:* The preparation for, process during, and aftermath of a school swimming lesson seen from the frightened child's perspective *Example 2:* The repeating cycles in which puppies suckle, sleep, explore, and then compete for the mother's breast—through seeing several such cycles from the smallest puppy's experience, we understand that the runt of the litter routinely gets elbowed out *Example 3:* A day in the life of the construction site in which small must avoid large, yet all contribute according to their means to the greater effort. We are led to identify with the smallest and most active machine.
6. Possible resolutions are . . .	A conclusion that may take more than one path. This is a chance that the filmmakers (and the audience) take. Prepare if you can for different outcomes (resolutions) and different meanings. *Example 1:* The boy has a bad time and can't swim; the boy manages a little swimming and feels good about it; the boy does poorly but someone (friend, teacher?) encourages him to continue. *Example 2:* The bigger dogs exclude the central character and deny her food. This is a miserable conclusion. A human hand could remove the largest, most aggressive pup and obtain advantage for the weakling. This would show that human intercession can rectify injustice. *Example 3:* At the end of the day, the construction workers descending from their machines all look equal, as if all have contributed equally. Or, they all descend and ignore the Bobcat driver, who remains an outcast.
7. Ultimately I want my audience to feel . . .	The prevailing mood (or succession of moods) that you want your audience to experience since hearts and minds change because of feelings, not facts *Example 1:* The sense of being alone and surrounded by others who are stronger because they all belong together *Example 2:* That Nature's purpose is effective but heartless *Example 3:* That size matters; the large lord it over the small

Prompt	Answer should include
8. and to understand that . . .	What you want your audience to realize intellectually, during and after your film *Example 1:* Children prosper if someone encourages them. *Example 2:* Nature cares about survival, humans about justice. *Example 3:* Though size creates a hierarchy, in the end everyone's work matters.

ONE CONVICTION, MANY FILMS

Examples 1 to 3 in the Working Hypothesis Helper table show that different film ideas can emerge from the same conviction. This I could paraphrase more proactively as:

> You can avoid failure by not trying, but life keeps facing you with tests. Overcome even something minor, and you feel great.

The same principle turns up in three different interpretations: one involving a boy at school, another a disadvantaged puppy in a kennel, and a third in the shape of a contemptibly small machine in a mechanized jungle. Many, many more are possible.

PROJECT 4-2: PITCHING A SUBJECT

You will have to repeatedly sell your current project when you go looking for crew, finance, or other support. By pitching your film, you rehearse with audiences until you can explain its essentials rapidly and attractively. In professional situations, you may get 10 minutes to convey a feature-length documentary, so you should be able to pitch a 5- to 20-minute film in 3 to 5 minutes. You can pitch ideas at all stages of their evolution as a check on how the idea is developing.

Pitching is seldom easy or comfortable. Be enthusiastic and use colorful language so you convey a clear pictorial sense of what the film will be like and why you and nobody else should make it. What you must convey is your passion and belief in the special qualities of the story. Rehearse before a mirror or camcorder so you can make a well-judged presentation. There is no set formula, and part of the challenge is to present your idea in whatever narrative steps best suit its nature. Here's what you might cover for a short, event-driven documentary.

Make notes so you can explain:

1. *Background* of the topic
2. *Character or characters* and what makes them special
3. *Problem* or situation that puts the main character(s) under revealing pressure
4. *Style* of the coverage and the editing

5. Any *changes or growth* you expect during the filming

6. *Why it's important that this film gets made* and *why you are the person to make it.*

A TYPICAL PITCH

Here is a pitch worked out from using (1) through (6) above:

Step	Pitch statements
1. Title and setting	The title of this documentary is *The Swimming Lesson,* and the setting is a rough-and-tumble grade school in a settled urban district with few if any minority or foreign kids. The buildings are old and run down, and the kids are hard to discipline.
2. Genre (that is, type or family of documentary)	This will be an observational documentary in which the camera will accompany the main character, sharing his situation and predicaments with us.
3. Main character and other characters	The main character is 9-year-old Mohsen, a sheltered and introverted Iranian boy whose English is still limited. His raucous and lively classmates come from an Irish–American area of Chicago. His experienced, overworked 50-year-old class teacher views him with concern. Mohsen's other teacher is a dedicated African–American swimming teacher in his 30s.
4. Problem or predicament the main character faces	Mohsen is new to the school, new to the country. He speaks little English, so life at school is overpoweringly confusing. He is always watching the other kids and imitating what they do because he cannot understand.
5. Main character's drive (what he or she is trying to get, do, or accomplish)	He wants above all to fit in with the other kids, to be accepted, and not to feel different.
6. Obstacles main character must overcome (why these obstacles matter and what is at stake)	He faces the ordeal now of going on a bus to the local swimming pool. He hates taking his clothes off and shivers in the cold air. The staff will separate the kids into those who can swim and those who can't. He must go through the ordeal of learning to swim. His swimming teacher, Terry, is likeable and treats the kids considerately and sympathetically.

Step	Pitch statements
7. Changes the main character undergoes	Mohsen already feels like an outsider and very much wants to learn to swim. He will try hard but is afraid of failing. The film will concentrate on the relationship between Terry and Mohsen as the teacher aims to get the boy's trust and to get him to take a few strokes with his foot off the floor.
8. Expected resolution or outcome of the film	Mohsen may make the first strokes, in which case he will be very happy. If he doesn't, we will return to see whether Terry can coax him into his first swimming strokes the next time. Terry is sure he will succeed; sooner or later Mohsen will make the advance that means so very much to him.
9. Cinematic qualities that make the film special	The camerawork and editing will give us a strongly subjective feeling of the way Mohsen sees and feels. There will be no interior monologue—everything we learn we learn from watching, as he has to do in his new surroundings. In a waterproof housing, the camera will be at water level and might even briefly go underwater if Mohsen does by mistake. In the early classroom sequence, other kids will seem distant, distorted, and almost jeering at him. The noise at the indoor swimming pool is at first hellishly deafening and confusing. Gradually as Terry calms him and gets him to concentrate on overcoming this first big test, the noise recedes and other kids turn out to be aware of him and even encouraging.
10. Theme the film is handling	*The Swimming Lesson* deals with the lonely terrors of being in a new element and of having to win acceptance.
11. Premise underlying the film	The key to earning your peers' respect is taking the first steps. It helps to have someone who supports you.
12. Why I must make this film	I went to four different schools between the ages of 9 and 11, and so was the new kid on the block four times over. As a result, my stomach still gets knotted up at the sound of a school yard. I'd like to exorcize these memories by revisiting the situation as an adult, and making a film sympathetic to a boy in a predicament I know only too well.

This is your chance to show your intentions for a film and get a first audience response. It is normal to be imaginative and propose what you hope to capture, even though the reality may turn out different. After you finish, listen to the comments, take notes, and say as little as possible. Your film idea has had its chance to communicate; now open yourself to its effects so that you can redraft it for another pitch to another audience.

➤ Several days later, pitch your film again, taking into account all the critique that you found useful.

➤ Pitch it a third time and see what your audience thought of the latest version. Even if the idea hasn't improved, your delivery probably has.

When your early audiences light up, you have the ingredients for a good film. Where they don't, keep changing your approach until your experience shows that every aspect is masterful. Pitch a new documentary idea every week to anyone willing to listen and respond. You'll be amazed at how many good ideas you can come up with and how much you learn from pitching them. Afraid that someone will steal your idea? You won't be, when you have too many.

EXPANDING THE PITCH TO A PROPOSAL

Here are samples of pitches expanded into three formal proposals. Each film now suggests a distinct area of endeavor in the human or natural worlds.

1. The Swimming Lesson

In a noisy, inner-city schoolroom the children boisterously finish up their work. As they get ready for an outing they yell excitedly in spite of their teacher's plea to be quieter. The camera concentrates on a timid, foreign-looking boy who watches the others to see what he should do. He is new and unsure what is expected. When he must interact he speaks haltingly with a foreign accent. At the swimming pool, his confusion turns to fear: He is with the few who are learning to swim. One by one the nonswimmers have to take their feet off the floor and thrash forward a few paces. Our boy looks more and more concerned as it gets nearer his turn. Other kids seem to laugh at him, but the instructor is patient and understanding. He helps him until he has swum a few strokes. The other kids applaud. His face goes pink with pride and relief. He has survived. In the event that he fails, we will follow further visits until the experienced and sympathetic instructor helps this boy, as he does other children, to finally swim.

2. The Litter

A breeding kennel is in the distance. Unseen dogs of every age bark maniacally in every register. The owner carries food from pen to pen, talking freely to us about the dogs and their puppies. Most litters, he explains, have a runt—a puppy that somehow got less in the womb and enters the world undersized and underequipped to compete. The owner exits, leaving us alone with a litter of puppies. In extended observation and montage, we see that every puppy fights for a teat, feeds aggressively, goes wandering, gets tired and sleeps, then awakens to fight for a teat again. This cycle repeats. The poor little runt has a bad time, getting elbowed out of competition and having neither the energy nor curiosity of the larger pups to go exploring its pen. It's a sad business until a human hand in close-up disconnects the most aggressively successful feeder and replaces him with the runt. In equally large close-up, we see a concerned human face (the owner? someone else?) ready to mediate if the smallest is threatened.

3. Bobcat

The sun is rising at an urban building site. Concentrated together, huge cranes, cement delivery trucks, bulldozers, and giant hole-borers are all furiously at work with construction people yelling or talking into walkie-talkies. Uproar changes to orchestral music in which the larger, heavier instruments of the orchestra accompany the action of the larger, heavier machines in an extended ballet. Bobbing and weaving at the feet of all the huge machines is a small four-wheeled Bobcat earth pusher. It changes its direction not by steering but by skidding one set of wheels. This gives it crazy, jerky, frenzied movements that are quite different from all the other machines. The music has a fast, high, repeating melody that syncs comically with the Bobcat, which has to constantly defer to, or avoid, its more ponderous brethren. As the sun sinks, the machines all come to a halt and drivers leave their cabs. The Bobcat is the last to stop. Its driver gets out and joins the other men. As the music resolves to a harmonious close, the construction men joking with each other and picking up their lunch pails all look the same. End the film on a montage of heroic, static machines, including the Bobcat, framed to make it look as large as the other machines.

The first is a drama, the second a tragedy, and the third a Chaplinesque comedy realized through machines. All three depart from the same philosophic starting point, yet they arrive in rather different destinations. You could get another hundred films from that one conviction.

PROPOSALS FOR SOME ACTUAL FILMS

As models, here are short proposals for some films made at the International Film & Video Workshops at Rockport, Maine (see www.theworkshops.com for information about the school and go to http://directingthedocumentary.com to see the films online). They are from a month-long class taught by myself and Chandler Griffin, who now leads Barefoot Workshops (see www.barefootwork-shops.org). Our 14 students, whose ages spanned from the 20s to the 50s, learned from scratch to conceive and propose a short documentary, to shoot using an advanced Panasonic® camera, and to edit using Final Cut Pro®. Working in groups of three, each person directed and edited a 5-minute film and crewed on two others. Rockport is a small coastal town where all the students were outsiders, so each had to pound the pavement to find a local subject. All succeeded, with only one subject backing out and needing replacement. There being insufficient time for formal written work, the students delivered their proposals orally. I have therefore written the kind of proposal that led to the film you see. Needless to say, each film sprung surprises on its makers and didn't necessarily reflect the pitch they made. Most, however, surpassed expectations.

Dreaming of Blueberries (2005, Evan Briggs; Figure 4-1)
Jestine Bridges is 17 and lives with her family on their farm in Maine's blueberry country. She dreams of becoming the Blueberry Queen in a local beauty competition. We shall follow her through the stages of preparation and learn what it feels like to be a shy young woman on the threshold of her life, getting ready to try her chances at the fair. This event-centered film will end after the judges have announced the winner.

The Writing on the Wall (2005, Melinda Binks; Figure 4-2)
Tom Jacobs, visiting his mother's grave, tells how he came to care for her during her last, long illness—Alzheimer's disease. Interwoven is his account of what being a caring son is like while the beloved patient gradually loses all mental capacity. In fact, they exchange roles: He becomes the parent, she the child. Tom thinks it a small sacrifice but now faces having to do the same all over again for his father, also diagnosed with Alzheimer's. The film will evoke the feeling of her continuing presence in the little wooden house, and the camera will feature the empty chair that she used to sit in.

Blaikie Hines (2005, Orna Shavitt; Figure 4-3)
Blaikie is a painter and Civil War historian whose life at one time was heading on a downward path. At the lowest point in his life he had a moving encounter with God and later found salvation in learning to paint.

FIGURE 4-1 ——————————————————————————————

In *Dreaming of Blueberries*, Jestine tries her luck in a Maine beauty contest (frame from film).

FIGURE 4-2

A man recounts his mother's journey to dementia in *The Writing on the Wall* (frame from film).

FIGURE 4-3

A Vietnam draft dodger becomes a religious man, then a painter and Civil War expert in *Blaikie Hines* (frame from film).

He believes that the keys to the present lie in the past, so he not only writes about history but also dresses up in authentic costume to teach it.

The Yellow House (2005, Monica Ahlstrom; Figure 4-4)
William Anderson lives alone and seems to own the only house in Rockport that isn't painted the regulation white. At 30 years of age, during a Concord

FIGURE 4-4

Photographer William Anderson in *The Yellow House* looks at his granddaughter (frame from film).

reenactment, he lost his hands in a cannon accident. As a follower of the Transcendentalists who loves walking, he made the choice to live by and for photography and refused to let the damage to his hands stop him from searching for the beauty in nature and in his grandchildren. The film will relate this during one of his walking trips.

MY COMMENTARY

Dreaming of Blueberries is a *process film*—that is, it introduces Jestine and takes as its forward movement her process after she decides to enter the competition. Its momentum and modest tension come from wondering whether she will win. Impressionistically it builds a lyrical, rather ornate picture of its shy 17-year-old central character. Its director was a young woman looking forward to getting married, and the film reflects the safety and pleasure to be found in loving family relations. The director went on to study documentary at Stanford University.

Tom Jacobs in *The Writing on the Wall* makes a circular journey of reminiscence that starts at his mother's graveside. He tells how he repaid his dues as a son once his mother began losing her memory. The journey became dark and troubled as his mother became ever more fearful and alienated. Against pictures of him as a child with his mother, he recounts how he became the parent and she the child. The film, starting and ending by looking through a rain-drenched window at Tom next to his mother's grave, gives the effect of looking through a veil of tears. His account, delivered without self-pity and in the gloom of her cottage from one of his parents' two chairs, is almost an interior voice that speaks for them. At the end we learn that now, with a weary heart, he faces the same one-way journey with his father toward senility and death. The director Melinda Binks began as assistant to a famous wildlife photographer and now makes documentaries for aid and other organizations worldwide.

Blaikie Hines is an autobiographical memoir, its structure hinging at the moment of redemption that is its turning point. Blaikie's autobiographical account takes us on his downward path when, as a Vietnam draft dodger, he sank into drink and drugs on the run in England. He reached a state of feeling he was "buried alive." Failing to reach his sister during an emotional crisis, he began praying and found God. After this his life and art came miraculously together. Returning to the present, we find him readying himself in Civil War uniform to give a history presentation. In his final incarnation as a painter and Civil War historian, he repays a debt to the lost young men of the 1860s. The director is an Israeli genetic scientist whose life was indelibly scarred as a young girl when her beloved father was killed during the Six Day War in Israel and his body lost on the battlefield for a week. She and her daughter are now working on a film about this.

The Yellow House is more of an *event-centered* film that makes effective use of connotation in its images. Its structure uses William Anderson's circular journey up to, and then back from, the water's edge where he takes photographs. During this circuit we learn of the terrible accident that changed his life when his hands were blown off by a cannon. His yellow house is his starting and ending point. Note how it was abandoned and needed fixing up and that he rebelliously painted it yellow instead of the locally approved white. The film has made the house into a metaphor for Anderson himself—a solitary, dissident personality who elected to study and record the beauty of the world in spite of (or because of?) his damaged hands. The film's director, Monica Ahlstrom, specializes in search-and-rescue operations for those lost in the Canadian wilds.

Three of the films give older men's viewpoints; the fourth, that of a girl approaching womanhood. For comparison I have made a graph superimposing the rise and fall of optimism in each story (Figure 4-5). Passing through highs

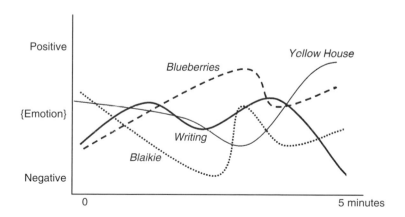

FIGURE 4-5 ————————————————————————————————

Graph superimposing the arcs of *Dreaming of Blueberries*, *The Writing on the Wall*, *Blaikie Hines*, and *The Yellow House* to show how hope fluctuates through their stories.

and lows, the curve for each is different through its span. Possibly they reflect what's characteristic for their subjects' place on life's great road, but the trajectories are also intrinsic to the way their makers have chosen to tell their stories. The more common graphing for stories—by intensity of feeling—produces the *dramatic arc* or *dramatic curve*, which you can read about in **Chapter 18, Time,** **Development, and Structure,** under "Drama and the Three-Act Structure."

The next chapter looks at the range of film language that documentaries use and how it developed in parallel to the technology available to filmmakers.

PART 2

DOCUMENTARIES AND FILM LANGUAGE

This part looks at how documentary language evolved because of its reliance on technology. The film language that emerged from this is as much your heritage as the mother tongue you use every day. Becoming fluent in film language allows you to make films that your audience will long remember. Technology and, with it, film language, are still changing.

CHAPTER 5

DOCUMENTARY LANGUAGE

TECHNOLOGY AND SCREEN LANGUAGE

People made the first moving pictures in the mid-1890s from what was immediately around them. As they developed the tools—cameras, film stocks, sound facilities, and editing equipment—film's language and its ability to move hearts and minds improved, too. All this time the audience's grasp of screen language was evolving, so filmmakers needed an ever more sophisticated narrative shorthand. It is this evolution rather than the enormity of documentary history that we explore in this chapter.

In just over a dozen excellent films—ones today's audiences still find moving—you will get the sweep of how technology and documentary developed in response to filmmakers' need to say something impassioned. To some, old documentaries are dinosaurs from which there is nothing to learn, but this is not true. Every advance in screen language, every technical and ethical issue, remains vibrant today. With each groundbreaking film I have paired a modern example that uses the pioneer language for a modern purpose. You can explore this for yourself by doing any of the hands-on projects that I've suggested. Because some of my own and my family's history has threads in this century-long tapestry, I'll mention this, too. Cinema is a human art made of intertwined human lives—an important message for documentary making.

Key films or film anthologies are in ***bold italic*** print. You can view passages from many of them on your computer by entering titles in YouTube™ (www.YouTube.com); however, beware personalized versions where someone has re-edited the original.

BEGINNINGS

In 1895, the French brothers Auguste and Louis Lumière (Figure 5-1) laid the foundations of the cinema. It all began when their painter and photographer father, who owned a photographic business in Lyon, saw Edison's Kinetoscope during a business trip to New York (Figure 5-2). It was a moving image in a box, and he thought his sons could get the image out of the box and up onto a public screen. They lived up to their dad's confidence. With a hand-cranked camera (Figure 5-3) whose film advance mechanism they borrowed from the intermittent action of the sewing machine, they filmed subject matter from their daily lives and began showing 50-second movies. Their technique was to plant the camera on a tripod, stills-camera fashion, and let the action pass in and out of frame. On the DVD *The Lumière Brothers' First Films* (1895–1897, remastered in 1996 from the originals), their work is as fresh as in its infancy. The Lumière employees go to lunch in *Workers Leaving the Factory*, and the family

FIGURE 5-1

Auguste and Louis Lumière. (Photo courtesy of Institut Lumière.)

FIGURE 5-2

Edison's Kinetoscope—moving images in a box. (Photo courtesy of The Kobal Collection.)

FIGURE 5-3

The Lumière Brothers' hand-cranked camera. (Photo courtesy of Institut Lumière.)

FIGURE 5-4 ——

Passengers in the Lumière brothers' film at La Ciotat railway station have no idea they
are making history. (Photo courtesy of The Kobal Collection/Institut Lumière.)

gardener becomes victim of a hosepipe prank in *The Sprinkler Sprinkled*. *Arrival
of a Train at La Ciotat* records an everyday scene at a station. The passengers
who glance at a camera while alighting are unaware that they are making history (Figure 5-4).

Each little narrative, structured
around an observed or contrived
event, has no cuts or camera movements. Some participants know
they are being filmed; Auguste and
his wife in *Feeding the Baby* enjoy
showing off their daughter, and the
family gardener plainly enjoys ham-
ming it up for his employers. These
are the world's first home movies,
naïve but beautiful. Notice that film
is always *now*. True, *A Boat
Leaving the Harbor* happened over
a century ago, but each time a film
starts we are right there in the here
and now.

 To use a camera is thrilling and makes you see
with new eyes. This is
palpable in the Lumière brothers'
films.

 Film is forever in the
present tense. Even
though each shot was
taken a hundred years ago, its
events are always happening now.

By coupling their ingenious little wood and brass camera with a light source, the Lumières made it double as projector and printer. Soon Lumière operators swarmed across the world shooting exotic or newsworthy events, their films founding the new paying business called the cinema. Soon somebody broke company rules and took a moving shot from a Venetian gondola. Others followed, shooting from carriages and trains. The race to develop film language was on.

Early footage still turns up. In the 1990s, someone found two unknown Lumière films in a French sanatorium attic—left there in a biscuit tin after entertaining inmates a century earlier. In northern England, workmen demolishing a factory found barrels containing 28 hours of footage from the early 1900s. See selections in the DVD *Electric Edwardians: The Lost Films of Mitchell & Kenyon* (2005, Great Britain). The two photographers filmed busy street scenes and held shows the same night. On YouTube™ you can see tradesmen jogging past in horse-drawn carts and others idling in the street, mugging at the camera, or running errands by bike. The footage contains one of the earliest shots of someone directing. In a market, one of the photographers moves into shot, plainly instructing people what he wants them to do. My great-uncle Sidney Bird, a Portsmouth cinema projectionist in 1909, may have projected material like this.

 Consider making your own Flaherty-style movie using **Project 4-SP-4 Flaherty-Style Film**, or document an event using **Project 4-SP-7 Document an Event** (both in the Appendix).

BIRTH OF THE DOCUMENTARY

Between 1895 and 1920, cinema audiences saw a vast amount of news footage, including the unfolding tragedy of World War I. But not until Robert Flaherty's **Nanook of the North** (1922, United States; Figure 5-5) did they see an actuality story with a deliberately imposed, overarching meaning. Flaherty was an American mining engineer whose boyhood was spent prospecting with his father in northern Canada, where he learned to love and respect the Inuit people. In 1915, he began an ethnographic record of an Eskimo family using a 16 mm camera. Back in Toronto, editing his film, he discovered that nitrate film and chain smoking don't go together well. His 30,000 feet of negative went up in flames, and he was lucky to escape with his life.

Seeking the funds to reshoot, he was compelled to screen his surviving workprint many times over. He saw that his film was flat and pedestrian and resolved to shoot another that told more of a story.

Setting out again with his hand-cranked camera and insensitive film stock that needed artificial light and shooting in appalling weather conditions, Flaherty often asked his subjects to do their actions in special ways. By now his main character Nanook (not his real name) really liked Flaherty; both men felt they were making a record of a vanishing culture. Flaherty's Inuit cast was actors demonstrating a way of life: They watched *dailies* (material from the previous

FIGURE 5-5

Nanook warming his son's hands. (Photo courtesy of The Museum of Modern Art/Film Stills Archive.)

day's shooting) and contributed ideas and guidance to the story. Thus, Flaherty came to shoot a factual film in real surroundings but "acted" as though it were a fictional story (Figure 5-6).

Even by the standards of his day Flaherty's shooting style is basic, but his cast is delightful and

 Assembling his own families and having them do typical things, Flaherty made an idealized recreation of reality. Each of his films nevertheless tells a story with a meaning.

the Arctic majestically beautiful. His *participants* (as I shall call those who take part in documentaries) came to trust him so completely that they are free of all self-consciousness. Though the film seems ethnographically authentic, Nanook's

clothing and equipment actually come from his grandfather's time. The igloo has no roof (to allow in light for filming), and the hunting spears are antiques, since the Inuit were already using rifles. Flaherty was in fact reconstructing a way of life already swept aside by industrial society and its technologies.

 What makes Flaherty's work special is his underlying awareness of mankind's ancient and deadly struggle to survive. This makes Nanook a timeless and universal figure.

FIGURE 5-6

From *Nanook of the North*—a family to feed. (Photo courtesy of The Museum of Modern Art/Film Stills Archive.)

Audiences did not know it, but Nanook, shown cheerfully biting a phonograph record after hearing it play, was no isolated native. He was Flaherty's astute collaborator who assembled their lighting and filming equipment and developed the footage for screenings.

Generations of critics have debated the ethics of Flaherty's artifice, but what makes the film special is that Flaherty's vision of a family surviving in the Arctic respects its subjects and builds a larger theme—that of mankind's ancient and deadly struggle for survival against the forces of Nature. Their daily life shows how a traditional Eskimo family is a tightly interdependent unit whose very survival depends on everyone carrying out their functions. Nanook, their leader, is a human dynamo; with irrepressible humor, he improvises housing, hunts food, teaches his children, and tackles each new obstacle along their increasingly isolated and perilous journey. Flaherty does not return the family to safety; instead, the film leaves them huddled in the Arctic wastes, a snowstorm threatening to engulf their all-important huskies. Life at its most elemental, says Flaherty, depends on human resourcefulness, cooperation, and optimism.

 Exposition is the factual framework or background that supports each story. Without it, the audience can neither understand nor sympathize. Artful storytellers keep the story moving forward so exposition does not stand out.

Tragically, while New York audiences lined up around the block to see the film, its subject died hungry during a hunting accident. Who can imagine a sadder or more ironic validation of the truth in Flaherty's vision?

Directly in the Flaherty tradition is *The Story of the Weeping Camel* (2003, Germany; Figure 5-7), directed by two Munich film students, Luigi Falorni and Byambasuren Davaa. In collaboration with Mongolians living in yurts in the Gobi Desert, the directors made a partly scripted, partly improvised film about Mongolian family life and the annual birth of the Bactrian camels on which they depend.

NAMING THE DOCUMENTARY AND FACING ITS PARADOXES

The word "documentary" surfaced during a mid-1920s conversation between Flaherty and John Grierson, a Scots social scientist interested in the psychology of propaganda. Critiquing a cut of Flaherty's *Moana* (1926, United States), Grierson said he thought it was "documentary" in intention, and so, retrospectively, was *Nanook*—today acknowledged as the genre's seminal work. Laurels didn't come easily to Flaherty, who came under attack for creating lyrical archetypes. This is undeniably true, for Flaherty was a romantic who never forgot his

FIGURE 5-7

The Story of the Weeping Camel—a modern tale from the Gobi Desert that is directly in the Flaherty tradition. (Photo courtesy of The Kobal Collection.)

wilderness boyhood. Many of his films even use a boy as their central character. Though his critics admired his humanism and poetic photography, they thought it deplorable that he assembled his own photogenic families rather than filming real ones. In *Man of Aran* (1934, United States; Figure 5-8), he incensed his critics by leaving out the large house of the Aran islanders' absentee landlord, who was mostly responsible for the islanders' deprivations. It was their fight with Nature that excited Flaherty, not their victimization by an extortionate social system.[1]

The charges leveled at Flaherty still resound today: What is documentary truth? How objective is the camera? Is what we see literal truth or does what we see represent the *spirit* of truth? And whose truth should you show? If you juxtapose material to create new meanings, what makes your edited version less

FIGURE 5-8

In *Man of Aran*, Flaherty assembled a photogenic family rather than use one already existing. (Photo courtesy of The Kobal Collection/Gainsborough Pictures.)

---

[1]Included with the DVD of *Man of Aran* is George Stoney and Jim Brown's *How the Myth Was Made* (1978). On Aran they investigated Flaherty's processes with some of the film's surviving cast.

or more truthful? Can you be objective like a social scientist? When can you use poetic and emotive means, as Flaherty did, to evoke feeling? What part should aesthetics play in persuading an audience?

THE RUSSIANS ARE COMING

After the 1917 Revolution, the Bolshevik government found itself administering a vast federation of nations whose least educated citizens could neither read nor understand each other's tongues. Among those working for the revolution was the poet, musician, and film editor Dziga Vertov, busily compiling newsreels for the Agitprop regional train screenings. Seeing how imaginative editing and camerawork affected audiences, he produced his Kino-Eye manifesto—a prescription for recording life without imposing on it. His silent masterpiece *Man with the Movie Camera* (1929, U.S.S.R.; Figure 5-9) is a visual symphony. It begins in a movie theater and dashes into the streets to spin many strands of simultaneous narrative—in homes, in the streets among the homeless, in workshops and factories, on the beach—during a tumultuous day among the citizens of Moscow and Odessa. The film works virtually without titles and revels in

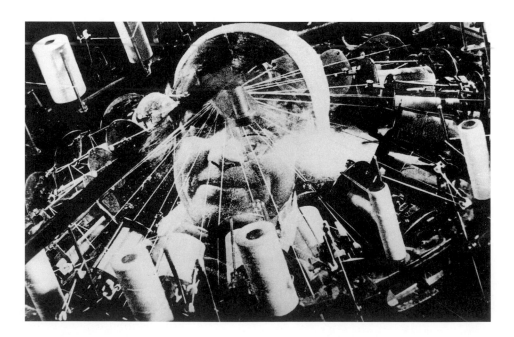

FIGURE 5-9

Dziga Vertov tried to create a specifically cinema eye in *Man with the Movie Camera*. (Photo courtesy of The Kobal Collection/VUFKU.)

showing its ubiquitous cameraman on flying trucks, clambering up bridges, or standing on towering buildings. In his gallery of playful illusions, Vertov includes every form of trick photography. At the end, its virtuoso performance complete, the camera takes a bow on animated, striding tripod legs.

Try your own montage skills using **Project 4-SP-5 Vertov-Style Montage Film** or reveal the mood and drama in a place through **Project 4-SP-8 Dramatize a Location** (both in the Appendix).

The DVD of *Man with the Movie Camera* (significantly enriched by Michael Nyman's obsessive, minimalist score) divides the film into chapters with titles that suggest its ambitiousness: Awakening, Locomotion, Assemblage, Life Goes On, Manual Labor, Recreation, Relaxation, and Cinematic "I" (a play on Kino-Eye). Making the camera reflexively aware of its own capacities, the movie pays homage to the unending possibilities of filmmaking. Through juxtaposing so much action and so many points of view, Vertov believed he had freed the screen from all viewpoints except that of the all-seeing camera. In fact, it is Vertov's mind and personality delivering what we see, a virtuoso experiment that demonstrates how each action, movement, and shot has its own inherent rhythms. In its form and content, so creatively edited together at a time when no editing viewers existed, we see a music for the eye. Today's equivalent is MTV and music videos. You will find a creative re-edit of *Man with the Movie Camera* to a big-band score at www.youtube.com/watch?v=vvTF6B5XKxQ.

FROM SILENCE TO SOUND: THE ESSAY FILM

The cinema's first quarter century produced a richly expressive language of action, movement, and imagery. Accompanied by live music, silent film liberated the audience's imagination by telling stories and developing ideas visually. Electrically driven cameras freed the operators to be even more mobile and inventive, but when synchronous sound arrived in the late 1920s this momentum petered out. The cinema, including documentary, adopted the more theatrical discourse of words, music, and sound effects.

Sound equipment's size and power limitations mostly confined shooting to studios. I first saw a sound camera (as they were called) as a 9-year-old visiting my make-up man father in England's Pinewood Studios in the late 1940s. From the brightly lighted Technicolor® stage we went to a darkened truck nearby. There in perpetual gloom sat the behemoth that recorded sound photographically on 35 mm film, its unlucky operator linked to the shooting stage by wires and headphones. A year earlier, my father, a recently demobilized sailor, had somehow become a make-up trainee for David Lean's classic Dickens adaptation, *Oliver Twist* (1948, United Kingdom). His first assignment was putting a black patch over the eye of Bill Sykes' dog. One evening at home he tried to get my baffled, 8-year-old self to play Oliver asking the orphanage masters for more

FIGURE 5-10

Oliver asking for more in David Lean's grimly realistic *Oliver Twist* (frame from film).

food (Figure 5-10). Decades later I realized he was reliving his own orphanage youth. So often what moves us comes from the scars in early life.

The documentary could never afford studios and sync sound, so its makers continued shooting silent (Figure 5-11) and fitted sound afterward during editing. Two of my earliest editing assignments—one concerning international marriage customs; the other, the 1966 soccer World Cup—were shot and cut in this way. Though laborious, editing was satisfying and creative because you had to create an audio "score" of narration, music, and sound effects. Outstanding films can still be made this way.

In *Land Without Bread* (1932, Spain), Luis Buñuel, the renegade son of a privileged Spanish family, contends that the medieval poverty and suffering in a remote region of Spain results from his own caste's neglect. The ragged, stunted, inbred villagers we see are ignorant of the waterborne illnesses that are killing them. Buñuel drives us to angry incredulity that church and state could be so indifferent to souls in their care.

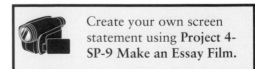

Create your own screen statement using **Project 4-SP-9 Make an Essay Film.**

Using a detached travelogue narration and a grandiloquent symphony as musical accompaniment, the film's flat gaze at its catalogue of horrors drives even a modern audience to outrage. Buñuel is a satirist; he makes us angry by showing surreally

FIGURE 5-11 ——

Flaherty shooting silent footage for *Louisiana Story* (1948, United States). Sync sound remained impractical on location for documentaries until the 1960s. (Photo courtesy of The Museum of Modern Art/Film Stills Archive.)

awful events through the pseudoscientific cant of the travelogue. Like Flaherty, he was not above rigging the evidence—look carefully at the death of the goat when it falls from a ravine and you'll see a puff of gun smoke. Everything else, however, seems genuine. One of the crew even steps into the frame to help a child who died the next day (Figure 5-12). The dead baby floating down a stream in her little coffin while the grieving family makes its way to the graveyard is indelibly tragic.

Harry Watt and Basil Wright's **Night Mail** (1936, United Kingdom), made by the Post Office Film Unit led by Grierson, features postal workers working overnight sorting letters picked up in London for delivery in Edinburgh. The bucolic vision of fields, cows, rabbits, and ancient churches is an island of tranquility between two grimy industrial heartlands. What you see is a metaphor for a society in flux—wealth and poverty, town and country, night and day, past and present. By orchestrating the beat of words, images, repetitive work, and train rhythms, the film creates a driving sense of forward movement. Key to this are Benjamin Britten's score and a striding narration by the poet W.H. Auden:

> This is the Night Mail crossing the border,
> Bringing the check and the postal order,
> Letters for the rich, letters for the poor,
> The shop at the corner and the girl next door . . .

FIGURE 5-12

Poverty, sickness, and death owing to indifference by the ruling caste in *Land Without Bread* (frame from film).

Night Mail has brief sync dialogue exchanges that may have been *post-synchronized*; that is, spoken lines could have been recorded and fitted to simulate sync dialogue. Equipment limitations meant filming the letter-sorting and dialogue sequences on a set. The postmen reenacted their work in a replica sorting carriage that was rocked to simulate the train's movement (Figure 5-13).

The film builds dramatic tension out of the fundamental situation—working against the clock to complete tasks before the journey ends—and out of charged scenes such as the high-speed mailbag drop and pickup along the way. The film's temporal spine comes from its subject—an epic journey from the smoky metropolis, up England's backbone through the bucolic countryside, and arriving as the sun rises over Edinburgh, its citizens dozing in their beds:

> They continue their dreams,
> And shall wake soon and long for letters,
> And none will hear the postman's knock
> Without a quickening of the heart,
> For who can bear to feel himself forgotten?

Notice how the commentary, which started on a quick, sharp, repetitive beat, ends now on a slower, loping beat as the train slows majestically for arrival. *Night Mail* shows what's possible with a stirring subject, great photography and narration, and first-rate music. It also shows that film *is* music.

Color film was expensive and came late to documentary. Alain Resnais' ***Night and Fog*** (1955, France; Figure 5-14) integrates black and white with color and must be the most haunting documentary ever made. In 31 minutes, the film tours what remained of the Auschwitz death camp and imagines the terrified

FIGURE 5-13

Mail sorters reenacting their work on a set for *Night Mail*. (Photo courtesy of The Kobal Collection/GPO Film Unit.)

FIGURE 5-14

Resnais' impassioned plea for humane watchfulness in *Night and Fog*. (Photo courtesy of Films, Inc.)

daily existence of the prisoner. What, it asks, lies beneath the brackish water in the ponds, now that it's all over? Much of the film's power comes from the restrained, evocative narration by the French poet Jean Cayrol, himself a death camp survivor, and the astringent, ironic score by Hanns Eisler, a German wounded in World War I. Playing against stereotype, the film never dramatizes or heightens. Instead, its questioning narration is in a dry, distanced monotone while the score counterpoints delicate, playful woodwind themes or high, trilling violin notes against archival footage of casual horror. Every mute object in this film speaks, and the film ends by questioning who among us will step forward next time to torture and kill in exchange for a little power. *Night and Fog* is a pinnacle in documentary filmmaking. It shows that nonsync shooting, coupled with brilliant writing, composing, and editing, can raise a screen essay to the level of a major requiem in meaning and emotion. Today the possibilities of this wonderful technique are little used.

SHOOTING GOES MOBILE

Evolving technologies gave filmmakers the tools to capture actuality as it happened. Magnetic tape recording in the 1950s allowed sound shooting with a portable audio recorder. Film stocks had been getting faster, so cameras could more often shoot in available light. Though camera and sound recorder (eyes and ears) were free to move at will, they remained connected by an "umbilical" wire that occasionally tripped up the crew or corralled members of the unsuspecting public. Then in the early 1960s came crystal-sync technology, which allowed a camera and recorder to maintain sync without connection. With the Éclair NPR camera in 1963 came a 16mm self-blimped (mechanically quiet) camera.[2] It was balanced for off-the-shoulder shooting and had 10-minute magazines that could be changed in seconds (Figure 5-15). For sound recording there was the ultra-reliable, portable Nagra® tape recorder from Switzerland (Figure 5-16).

These advances transformed every aspect of location filming, from newsgathering and documentary to improvised dramatic production. A film's subjects were free now that a two-person handheld unit could follow wherever their action might lead. The result was immediacy and unpredictability on the screen, and event-driven or character-driven stories replaced scripted and contrived subject-driven ones.

This affected the fiction cinema. I was lucky to work on one of the first British fiction films shot wholly on location. *A Taste of Honey* (1962, United Kingdom; Figure 5-17) was adapted from an autobiographical play about a girl whose mother abandons her after she gets pregnant. Its director, Tony Richardson, came from the theater and had participated in the Free Cinema Movement, a loose grouping of individuals from several countries who made groundbreaking documentaries about gritty British working-class life in protest against the mediocre, studio-dominated feature films of the day. It was thrilling

---

[2]For a short history, see the Éclair enthusiast's Web site (http://members.aol.com/npr16mm).

FIGURE 5-15

Eclair NPR self-blimped camera wielded by the author. (Photo courtesy of Aran Patinkin.)

FIGURE 5-16

Portable sync sound—a Neopilot version of the Nagra III from the 1960s. (Photo courtesy of Nagra, a Kudelski Group Company.)

FIGURE 5-17————————————————————————————————————

A British fiction feature made entirely on location, *A Taste of Honey* was shot by documentary cameraman Walter Lassally. (Photo courtesy of The Kobal Collection/British Lion Film Corporation/Woodfall Film Productions.)

to see Walter Lassally's black-and-white photography of sooty, post-industrial Manchester—a city of canals and decaying industrial might. Richardson's documentary experience of working fast and informally and his actor-centered directing brought a new but short-lived standard of excellence to British cinema.

 Direct cinema, now called *observational cinema*, minimizes the camera's intrusion. Its adherents shoot like ethnographers, aiming to capture events just as people live them.

DIRECT CINEMA AND *CINÉMA VÉRITÉ*

In documentary the new immediacy sparked opposing philosophies concerning the camera and its human subjects. In North America, the Maysles brothers, Fred Wiseman, Allan King, and others favored what they called *direct cinema* (now called *observational cinema*). Like ethnographers, they shot unobtrusively and by available light, aiming to capture the spontaneity and uninhibited flow of events as people lived them.

FIGURE 5-18

The Maysles brothers in *Salesman* filming Paul selling to people who can't afford to buy.
(Photo by Bruce Davidson, courtesy of Maysles Films.)

OBSERVATIONAL CINEMA

The intrepid Maysles brothers, Albert and David, and their editor, Charlotte
Zwerin, made the landmark documentary **Salesman** (1969, United States;
Figure 5-18). They had taught themselves filmmaking and even cobbled their
own equipment together. The film follows a sales drive by hard-nosed Bible
salesmen—really a pack of hunters tormented by sales-figure quotas. For each
sale a salesman must gain entry, befriend the householder, give a demonstration,
and make a killing by getting an
order signed. To sell Bibles they lie
and use all manner of tricks, but
their victims live poor and cramped
lives and don't need lavishly illustrated Bibles.

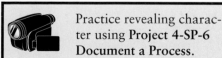 Practice revealing charac-
ter using **Project 4-SP-6
Document a Process.**

Here is the reality that Arthur Miller wrote about in his classic play *Death of a Salesman*. It's the tragedy of the salesman who must choose between compassion for his clients and fleecing them to support his family. Paul, the kindest and funniest of the salesmen, cannot bring himself to extort from these pitiable families. Like Miller, the Maysles brothers put a frame around the man of heart and conscience who is doomed to fail. No two works expose the cost of the American dream with more deadly wit and accuracy.

In form, *Salesman* breaks into three parts that follow the classic three-act dramatic structure (about which there's more in **Chapter 18 Dramatic Development, Time, and Story Structure**):

- Act I (Boston, snow) is the exposition that introduces the characters and their work, shows their working-class origins, and delineates their "problem" (hunting sales to stay alive).

- Act II (Chicago, packed conference hall) is the sales conference that escalates their "problem." It announces the goals, pressures, and values and puts the group on notice. Stragglers will be eliminated for "refusing" success.

- Act III (Florida, heat) is the extended race for survival during which Paul, the most likeable of the bunch, falls behind and confronts defeat. This leaves us conflicted: Paul has failed at predation, is suffering, and will somehow have to remake himself elsewhere. Can he find a more constructive way to make a living, or is this all he knows?

Some claimed a certain purity for the "fly on the wall" observational documentary, but unless the camera is actually hidden—ethically dubious at best—participants know it's there and adjust accordingly. Really, *every* form of observation produces some change in those under scrutiny, whether it's a visiting child or a camera crew. An observational film makes us feel like privileged observers, but we are seldom seeing life unmediated as *transparent* films suggest. This is appearance more than reality, for an editor has subtracted everything that breaks the illusion, such as people turning to the camera or putting on special behavior because they know they are on camera.

 Observational films are seldom as unmediated as *transparent* filmmaking suggests. People usually know they are being filmed and adapt accordingly, but never in a way that is out of character.

For a recent "fly on the wall" observational documentary, see Yoav Shamir's *Checkpoint* (2003, Israel; Figure 5-19). It is its director's first film and records without comment what happens at Israel Defense Force (IDF) checkpoints, where Shamir once served as a guard. In this embattled region Palestinians must constantly pass checkpoints. Some soldiers carry out their policing function with tolerance and even humor, but it is always demeaning for Arabs to wait in line for hours in order to get to a

 Try some "fly on the wall" filming with **Project 4-SP-12 Make an Observational Film.**

FIGURE 5-19

Checkpoint, an observational film revealing how power corrupts when soldiers control a population (produced by Amythos Films – Eden Productions).

nearby hospital or go to work. The IDF scrutinizes every pedestrian, car, truck, school bus, and ambulance. Each at some time has been a conduit for bombs that killed and maimed Israelis in markets, buses, restaurants, and night clubs.

Some of the uniformed, gun-toting, 19-year-olds who wield absolute power behave with sadistic disregard; while "following orders" they plainly enjoy subjecting Palestinians to senseless aggravation. Every story that Arabs tell them is suspect, no matter how credible and evident the reason for needing to cross. As the film proceeds, the cases get worse and you feel a growing hopelessness and outrage. The film uses no commentary or interior monologues; its points emerge simply from faces, behavior, body language, and by the way it stays for minutes, say, on some elderly man trying in vain to get his sick wife to a medical appointment. You share a deepening sense of rage and frustration on behalf of the humiliated—which is what this Israeli film wants you to feel. How strange that the scrutiny meant to protect a nation is worsening the conditions that threaten it. The film doesn't need to put this into words; it gathers like a thunder cloud.

Checkpoint's structure is a series of repeating cycles, with each crossing worse than the last. The whole business feels like the advancing screw-thread in a torture device. Ironically, the IDF now uses the film to train guards what *not* to do.

 Facts alone don't change hearts and minds, but emotions do.

PARTICIPATORY CINEMA

Europeans favored the alternative approach, then called *cinéma vérité*. Because the term degenerated into a catchall for spontaneous filming, it's now called *participatory cinema*. It gets at truth on film by drawing any significant participation—before or behind the camera—into the process of making the documentary record. The idea came from the French ethnographer Jean Rouch who found, while documenting life in Africa, that filming invariably provoked important off-camera relationships with participants. He felt that the only honest way to acknowledge this was to share the making of his film on-camera. He and his codirector Edgar Morin in *Chronicle of a Summer* (1961, France) encouraged interaction among participants, the directors, and the crew while asking ordinary Parisians the deceptively simple question, "Are you happy?"

The torrent of impassioned replies includes many that are touchingly personal and confessional. Some, shown their replies, went further—all of which Rouch and Morin filmed. In a gesture to Vertov they called their method *cinéma vérité*, or "cinema truth" (a translation of his *Kino-Pravda*).

By making documentary a collaboration, *cinéma vérité* directors could catalyze or even provoke events and thus probe for truth rather than simply await its appearance. Rouch particularly prized what he called "privileged moments"—those special times when a human truth emerges plainly and miraculously like an egg from a chicken.

Participatory cinema seeks documentary truth by drawing everyone into the process of making the record. This gives different results from observational cinema, which aims to remove all evidence of filming.

"Privileged moments" is what Jean Rouch called those times when human truth detonates from the screen.

An excellent participatory film mentioned briefly in Chapter 1 is Ira Wohl's *Best Boy* (1979, United States). A family in Queens, New York, faces crisis because the aging Pearl and Max can't let go of their 52-year-old mentally handicapped son. Wohl sets out to film his lovable cousin Philly and also to press his aging uncle and aunt into recognizing that Philly must gain autonomy and move into an appropriate institution. We see the process of Philly being tested by a psychologist, many scenes of him at home doing chores for his mother, and Philly singing "If I Were a Rich Man." Max, worn out after an operation, dies, leaving his wife Pearl bereft. How can she let go of her "best boy" now? But relinquish him she must, and Philly begins to flourish among challenging responsibilities in a residential home. Pearl, always so open, tells with heartbreaking candor how very alone she now feels. This, we realize, is the price she must pay for her son's comfort.

Catalyze human truth through **Project 4-SP-13 Make a Participatory Film.**

The family was very aware of the filming, and the camera's presence seems to bring out the best in everyone, not least because of a director who cares so deeply for his family. The DVD contains a follow-up film with the ever-cheerful Philly, now age 70. *Best Boy* shows that when shooting people under duress

 Keep the camera running when people go silent. Your patience will often be rewarded: The slower a person reacts, the greater their interior journey.

you must keep the camera running and wait. People need time to process anything major. Impatient filmmakers blow these moments by chivvying their subjects onward. Wohl (who went on to become a psychotherapist) is always willing to wait and see. Time and time again his patience is repaid when the tension of awaiting someone under pressure is followed by a release. This arc of pressure that gathers, peaks, and then releases is called the *dramatic arc* or *dramatic curve*.

WHICH APPROACH IS BEST?

In *Documentary: A History of the Non-Fiction Film* (1974, Oxford University Press), Eric Barnouw summarizes the differences between the two documentary approaches:

> The direct cinema documentarist took his camera to a situation of tension and waited hopefully for a crisis; the Rouch version of *cinéma vérité* tried to precipitate one. The direct cinema artist aspired to invisibility; the Rouch *cinéma vérité* artist was often an avowed participant. The direct cinema artist played the role of uninvolved bystander; the *cinéma vérité* artist espoused that of provocateur.

Documentary makers are artists; they make subjective judgments to reveal human truth on the screen. The differences between the two approaches pale when you realize that both depend on editing to abridge, shape, and intensify what time and space separate. By this token, the documentary shares much with the fiction film. Both documentary methods prize the unpredictably spontaneous and telling moment and jettison the essentially theatrical process of scripting and reenactment. In your filmmaking you need declare no allegiance to either approach; today's documentaries are eclectic and use whatever approach best serves the needs of the subject matter. Try applying the guidelines in the boxes. Science, nature, or historical documentaries that rely on archive

 Direct cinema stalks human truth using a wildlife camera; participatory cinema catalyzes truth and uses artifice when it must. Flaherty knew this: "One often has to distort a thing to catch its true spirit."

 Observational cinema works best when events claim most of participants' attention; often it's your only choice when shooting uncontrollable events. *Participatory cinema* allows you to interact with participants on camera and to challenge or catalyze whatever may be invisible or withheld.

footage or reenactment still need scripting, and being able to write for film is still a key skill that you should develop.

THE RISE OF EDITING

Both *vérité* approaches had similar drawbacks: their high film shooting ratios and uncertainty of outcome generated masses of footage, much of it unusable. Editors took on a new burden of directorial interpretation and rose to the challenge by inventing new forms of allusion and abbreviation (also called *ellipsis*). Editing began using freer and more intuitive forms; it counterpointed voice and effects tracks and used impressionistic, even hallucinatory cutting to abridge time and space. These innovations became part of feature film language, too. Somewhere Dziga Vertov sat on his cloud, chuckling.

VIDEO TECHNOLOGY

Video recording promised a cheaper and more immediate process when it arrived in the 1970s. At first it was poor quality and hard to edit, but once cassettes and small-format video arrived, filmmakers had easy shooting. Linear tape-to-tape editing, however, was slow; any editing changes required a ripple of changes throughout the tape. But once nonlinear (computerized) editing arrived, documentarians became free to shoot and edit with ease. The digital camera and computer software handed independent filmmaking the freedoms that word processing had given writers. Today digital technology allows us to title, freeze, text, or slow motion our footage. This means we can comment on actuality. More subjective and impressionistic, this unshackles the screen from the tyranny of real time and the banality of realism.

ECLECTIC FILMMAKING

From the 1980s onward, documentary makers began to more freely draw on allied art forms and disciplines and using mixed documentary forms. Here are just a few examples.

LONGITUDINAL STUDY

Michael Apted's *28 Up* (1986, United Kingdom; Figure 5-20) is a single episode in a series of longitudinal television studies. Every 7 years Apted steps away from his career as a feature film director to revisit the same original 14 English 7-year-olds. We see them grow from kids to young adults and become middle-aged citizens. Composed mainly from sensitive, probing interviews, the *Up*

 Develop superior interviewing skills with **Project 4-SP-10 Basic Interview: Camera on a Tripod** or **Project 4-SP-11 Advanced Interview: Three Shot Sizes.**

FIGURE 5-20 ————————————————————————————

Every 7 years Michael Apted steps away from his feature career to shoot another *Up* documentary episode. (Photo courtesy of The Kobal Collection.)

series concentrates on individual stories and sometimes on the dynamic of a group. Beginning in 1964 as *7 Up*, the series has now reached *49 Up*, with each succeeding film referring backward to an ever-growing bank of material shot when its subjects were younger.

 The *premise* is the fundamental concept driving a documentary's story. A good one means the film interprets its characters and events boldly and has something worthwhile to say.

The *premise* for the series (that is, its ruling idea) is that family and social class implant expectations that children realize in their subsequent lives. *7 Up* quotes the Jesuit saying, "Give me a child until he is seven, and I will show you the man." Alarmingly, it comes largely true, though not for everyone. Most disturbing in *28 Up* is Neil, who blames his home life for making him wind up as a penniless and solitary vagabond, plagued with psychological disturbances. For his sake alone you will want to see *35 Up*, *42 Up*, and now *49 Up*. The DVD for *49 Up* has an illuminating interview with Apted, who seems gloomily resigned to continuing the series until he keels over. Some participants are equally weary of putting their lives on record, but all seem aware that the series is the most embracing account ever made of growing up.

Structurally, each *Up* film is like an octopus. Each arm is a single story, but all are joined to the

 A film's *structure* is the order and logic in which it tells its tale.

body of a recorded past. The commanding determinants of class and race persist. Four decades later the original premise seems truer than ever, especially considering what we now know about the effect of advantages and disadvantages on children's self-image and expectations.

BRECHTIAN PROTEST

Through a series of imaginative, elliptical, and disturbingly urgent tellings and performances, Marlon T. Riggs' *Tongues Untied* (1989, United States; Figure 5-21) conveys what he and others, black and gay like himself, experienced growing up in a white, racist, homophobic society. Riggs, a journalist and poet, has produced a performance art film like Brechtian theater. Sidestepping all recognizable traditions, it hurls us from a finger-popping rap performance to the anguish of losing friends to AIDS; from a sad drag queen telling of her loneliness to stories of gay bashing and a white gay club refusing a black man entry due to his color. From archives come civil rights marchers and Eddie Murphy telling a homophobic joke.

There is no obvious through-line of argument or assertion, only a volley of forcefully stylish performances—everything from dance and body movement to inner monologue, street talk, and rap. Structuring the film's kaleidoscopic form is a driving, insistent sense of rhythm, as though Riggs is angrily drumming out the remains of his foreshortened life. The film received some national arts

FIGURE 5-21 ———————————————————————————

Marlon Riggs and Essex Hemphill in *Tongues Untied*. (Photo courtesy of Signifyin' Works/Frameline.)

funding and caused apoplexy among conservatives over the use of taxpayers' money. Riggs died of AIDS and the film is his last testament.

DOCUMENTARY NOIR

Errol Morris' *The Thin Blue Line* (1988, United States; Figure 5-22) is built traditionally on a foundation of interviews but makes imaginative use of music, reenactment, and clips from old detective movies. Creating its own trial structure, the film examines the course of Texas justice on behalf of a man who may be falsely imprisoned. Its Philip Glass score accompanies an opiate mix of fact and fiction that undermines the original trial. The crux is contradictory evidence from a number of witnesses concerning what happened one night during 30 seconds on a Dallas freeway. Someone stopped by Dallas police for driving without lights shot the cop walking over to inform him. We see this encounter reenacted differently according to each witness's account. Morris uses the lawyers, passersby, drawling Texas policemen, and the two men in the car—both in prison—to argue the flaws in each witness' version.

With its central characters on death row and so much of its action taking place at night, Morris jokingly classifies his film as a *documentary noir*. His rock-steady visual style, minimalist score, and obsessive reexamination of key details eventually pays off with new evidence pointing toward the actual murderer. Randall Adams escaped execution because of Morris' film.

FIGURE 5-22

Randall Dale Adams, convicted for a murder he did not commit, in Errol Morris' "documentary noir" *The Thin Blue Line*. (Photo courtesy of The Kobal Collection/American Playhouse/Channel 4 Films.)

DIARY

Agnes Varda, who directed *The Gleaners and I* (2000, France; Figure 5-23), is an experienced feature film director whose late husband, Jacques Demy, was France's most imaginative director of musicals. From paintings of gleaners in cornfields, she develops the theme of picking up and using what others have abandoned—a green habit by which she has furnished her cozy home. In what becomes a travel diary, she journeys to different regions of France in search of junk and more junk.

FIGURE 5-23

Agnes Varda, director of the intimate documentary journal *The Gleaners and I*. (Photo courtesy of The Kobal Collection/Stéphane Fefer.)

Along the way she meets a rich gallery of characters who glean for food, drink, or materials to make artworks or, as they relate with passion, in pursuit of ecological principle.

Like a travelogue, the film is incessantly having encounters. Everything Varda films she connects with states of mind—that is, with childhood, with her beloved husband Jacques, or with herself as an aging woman who sees in the mirror that she too must be dis-

 Make your own screen journal using **Project 4-SP-14 Make a Diary Film.**

 Denotation is what something is; connotation is the ideas and feelings it awakens.

carded—by life itself. In this tender, good-natured film, Varda's journeys become metaphysical, and denotation becomes connotation. By the end, this highly circular and autobiographical film conveys a rare sense of intimacy.

AMBUSH AND ADVOCACY

In a damning indictment of the American medical system, Michael Moore's *Sicko* (2007, United States) combines ambush journalism, satire, and leftist sympathy for the ordinary working stiff. Moore is always brilliant at Trojan horse stunts. In *Bowling for Columbine*, he organized wounded students to appear at the Kmart where the killers had purchased their ammunition, demanding they cease selling bullets. Taken aback, Kmart changed its policy.

 Adapt **Project 4-SP-9 Make an Essay Film** to try a little ambush journalism of your own.

Sicko trains its satirical crosshairs on the U.S. health care system and exposes an appalling litany of failure. Privatized insurance excludes over 50 million U.S. men, women, and children from medical coverage and won't cover anyone with a "preexisting condition." (Now, who doesn't have one of *those*?) By sampling other countries' health systems, Moore builds up a series of surreal comparisons that make you laugh in pained disbelief. After exposing the denial of health care to 9/11 first responders made sick by their rescue efforts, Moore loads them into a boat and cruises to Guantanamo Bay in Cuba. Calling up through a megaphone at some scary U.S. Army fortifications, he asks the military if his patients might get some of the medical care freely available to the "evildoers" imprisoned within. The reply, a warning siren blast, sends Moore scuttling off to Havana with his sad cargo, where they find medical care—free. Cubans, it seems, have better health and life statistics than Americans, and for a fraction of the cost.

Moore's preferred form for his films is the Everyman quest, for which he dresses in his signature baseball hat and baggy T-shirt (Figure 5-24). His first-person narration starts from a central question and then, as he proceeds, alternates between reasonable inquiry and astonished discovery. Simple disbelief propels him from one

FIGURE 5-24

Just a regular guy—Michael Moore in *Sicko* asking a few simple questions. (Photo courtesy of The Kobal Collection/Dog Eat Dog Films/Weinstein Company.)

anomaly to the next until he's forced to acknowledge, like a latter-day Candide, a compelling pattern of human greed, graft, and extortion—all underpinned by government policies secured in the first place by health care provider lobbyists. Pursuing analysis, advocacy, and provocation with deadpan effectiveness, Moore paints the American health care system as a theater of the absurd. Using stunts that juxtapose victims and perpetrators, he projects an appalling vision of the profit motive distorting what should be a basic human right.

ARCHIVE-BASED FILMMAKING

The American experimental filmmaker Jay Rosenblatt plucks the stereotypical moms, dads, and kids from mid-twentieth century films and uses them to represent the suffocating archetypal figures he grew up with—and was, himself. In **Phantom Limb** (2005, United States; Figure 5-25), he uses interviews and a range of archive material to make a 12-chapter meditation that confronts the most harrowing of personal stigma—the guilt and sorrow that he and his family suppressed after the death of his younger brother. Rosenblatt's work, and this film in particular, often feels like a muted scream at the suffering we endure while marching in lockstep with the notions of our era. *I Used to Be a Filmmaker* (2003, United States; Figure 5-26), however, celebrates filmmaking and fatherhood, and you sense a rebalancing between the poles of his emotional life.

Archive footage is a staple for History Channel and Discovery Channel productions, which specialize in factually accurate expositions of scientific and

FIGURE 5-25 ———————————————————————————————

Jay Rosenblatt behind his ill-fated brother Eliot in *Phantom Limb* (a frame from their father's 8 mm film, courtesy of the filmmaker).

FIGURE 5-26 ———————————————————————————————

Exploring the joy of parenthood in *I Used to be a Filmmaker*. (Photo courtesy of Jay Rosenblatt.)

historical material. A fine combination of testimony and archives is Ken Burns and Lynn Novick's impassioned series for PBS, *The War* (2007, United States). It features World War II eyewitnesses doing what battlefield veterans hate to do, which is to speak candidly about the atrocious and often pointless suffering they witnessed or caused, and the legacy of spiritual pain they must carry evermore.

GOING FURTHER

Visit the Lumière Museum online at http://www.institut-lumiere.org (click flags for different languages), and see a range of early cinema gadgets at www.victorian-cinema.net/machines.htm

For more types of documentary and the language they use, see **Chapters 17 to 20 in Book II, Advanced Issues.** For a lively and concise overview of documentary history, issues, and practices, see Patricia Aufderheide's excellent and pocket-friendly *Documentary Film: A Very Short Introduction* (Oxford University Press, 2007, 158 pp.). Histories of documentary include:

Barsam, Richard M. *Non-Fiction Film*. Bloomington, IN: Indiana University Press, 1992.

Barnouw, Erik. *Documentary: A History of Non-Fiction Film*. London: Oxford University Press, 1993.

Ellis, Jack C. and McClane, Betsy A. *A New History of the Documentary Film*. London: Continuum, 2005.

CHAPTER 6

ELEMENTS AND GRAMMAR

SCREEN LANGUAGE

People often think of screen language as professional packaging. Used as techno-wrapping, it can easily make a film mechanical and soulless, but whenever we see a sensitively shot and visualized film, we sense a questing human intelligence is at work. This is because the film's language arises from the maker's interests and sympathies, and he or she is using it in an emotionally integrated way. Let's see how this works.

Imagine you go to your high school reunion and afterwards find a little camcorder that someone has left behind. It has no name on it, so you run some of its footage to see to whom it might belong. You see what another former student filmed. The camera is his eyes and ears, and he recorded whatever he cared to notice. What he shot gives you such a characteristic idea of his personality that you are pretty sure of the owner. You see not only who he looked at and talked to but also how he spent time and how his mind worked. From his actions and reactions, you can see into his mind and heart, even though he says little from behind the camera and never once appears on-screen.

 Routine camera coverage often seems mechanical and dead, but in good documentary you sense a heart and mind at work.

 Make your own study of documentary imagery using **Project 1-AP-4 Analyze Picture Composition.**

A good documentary's handling of events and personalities creates the same overarching sense of a heart and mind doing the perceiving. Misused professionalism, on the other hand, replaces this quality with a soulless kind of instructional efficiency. This chapter explores how to shoot with soul.

INGREDIENTS

All documentaries are permutations of remarkably few elements. Their recombinant possibilities seem endless but are naturally limited by the conventions of screen language. Mere conformity won't, however, make your filmmaking distinguished, so this chapter supplies some analogies and practical guidelines to help raise your shooting above a formulaic approach. First, here are the basic ingredients that everyone must work with.

Picture

Action
- People
- Creatures
- Landscapes
- Inanimate things

Graphics
- Photographs
- Documents, titles, headlines
- Line art, cartoons, or other graphics

People talking
- Camera unobtrusive or hidden
- Consciously contributing to the camera's portrait of themselves

Interviews
- Interviewer present
- Interviewer off-camera
- Interviewer absent and questions edited out

Reenactments, factually accurate, of situations that are
- Past and were not, or could not be, filmed
- Suppositional or hypothetical

Archive
- Library material
- Material recycled from other films

Blank screen—makes us reflect on what we have just seen or give heightened attention to existing sound

(Continued)

Sound

Sound effects
- Spot (sync) sound effects
- Wild (nonsync) atmospheres

Narration
- Narrator
- Voice of the author
- Voice of a participant

Voice-over
- Audio-only interview
- Drawn from interview with picture discarded

Diegetic sound (synchronous sound shot while filming)
- Accompanying sound, especially of sound events
- Dialogue

Wild sound (nonsynchronous)
- Atmospheres
- Sound effects

Music
- Diegetic (part of actual sound)
- Composed and added to comment on scenes

Silence—a temporary absence of sound creating a mood change or causing us to look critically at the picture

You can combine these ingredients effectively by modeling your film visualization on everyday patterns of perception, a faculty that unconsciously integrates observation, feeling, and thinking so they turn into action. Ordinarily we know little about how this works, since it functions perfectly and automatically, much as our leg muscles coordinate while we walk. This chapter suggests ways to study your perceptual processes so you can improve your shooting and editing. It takes a high degree of concentration but no equipment, since you can practice anywhere that people congregate.

Let's work from what is familiar from the screen backward to its much less familiar human origins.

 Film language came from early filmmakers looking for "what worked." Intuitively they recreated what was already embedded and functioning in the human mind.

SCREEN GRAMMAR

Filmmaking, especially for documentaries, resembles the three-stage process we employ to process experience and consolidate its significance:

- Experiencing an event and storing the event's highlights in memory
- Inwardly reviewing what happened, giving it meaning, and making it into a story
- Telling that story to an audience to gauge its effect and validate our interpretation

Here are the life and cinema processes side by side:

Life process	Cinema process
(a) Experiencing an event and storing the event's highlights in memory	Shooting (using intelligence plus the camera's eyes, ears, and memory)
(b) Inwardly reviewing what happened, giving it meaning, and making it into a story	Editing (shaping, structuring, and abbreviating material using a computer)
(c) Telling that story to an audience to gauge its effect and validate our interpretation	Screening (for audience reaction and feedback)

Film equipment is like eyes and ears, and the operator plus director are its guiding intelligence. The storage medium (film, tape, or chip) is the cinema's memory. The editor dips into that memory and uses a computer, software and the grammar of film to restructure, consolidate, and compress the memory's essences. The aim is to produce a stylish, compelling narrative. At the screening, the filmmakers try their story on an audience to verify its effect and meaning, then further modify it for maximum impact.

 Film equipment is eyes and ears to which its operators provide heart and intelligence. What you record becomes a fund of experiences from which the editor brings meaning.

The event that becomes a story might be a dispute at work, a shockingly expensive day of shopping, an archeological discovery, or, as happened to me recently while walking our dog, something as mundane as a fall on an icy sidewalk. I was unhurt and enjoyed telling afterwards how it happened:

Tramp, tramp through the icy dark with Cleo on her lead. Then, the ominous sound of my foot sliding, a momentary vision of whirling horizon, the sound of teeth rattling in my head, and the thump and clatter of forehead and eyeglasses on icy concrete. Lifting nose from gritty ice, I lumber onto all fours, filled with rage at the neighbor who doesn't shovel after snowfalls. I'm still clutching the dog lead. She is shocked but excited that I plummeted to her level. I realize from the direction I'm facing that I must have spun round in midair before landing on forehead and kneecaps. I get up and move off, one knee and both hands aching fiercely. Under a street light a man watches, mute and expressionless.

Tales involve a succession of actions or events, each experienced in a particular way (many of mine were through sound). We structure them by chronology or some other priority, then organize them for brevity and effectiveness. Then we try them on somebody for effect to see how they react.

Let's look at how cinema language parallels human experience. This table gives a flavor and does not pretend to be comprehensive.

Film term	Meaning	Equivalent in life
Shot	Framed view	Watching, staring, expecting, enjoying, confronting—either close or at some distance
Pan	Camera pivots horizontally	Taking in one's surroundings; comprehending; discovering; revealing; escaping; assessing; fearing, expecting
Tilt	Camera pivots vertically	Assessing height or depth; looking up to; looking down on; threatening or feeling threatened
Crane	Camera travels vertically	Traveling up with; down with; getting up; sitting down; looking up at; looking down on
Dolly, track	Camera travels horizontally	Physically moving toward or away from something or someone; traveling alongside, behind, or in front of; attraction; repulsion; advance; retreat (perspective changes)
Zoom	Objects grow bigger or smaller	Looking more closely or retreating (but not physically moving because perspective is unchanging during a zoom)
Cut	Juxtaposing two images	Seeing something and looking immediately at something else (we often blink between them); comparing; transitioning; compiling impressions
Montage	Series of shots suggesting a mood or progression	Impressions piling up when we lose or cede control
Rhythm	Sensation of pace in an image texture or repetition in editing	Rate of change in one's surroundings; living fast or slowly or changing from one to the other

(Continued)

Film term	Meaning	Equivalent in life
Fade in	Going from an empty screen to an image	Transitioning from a tranquil state of mind to a situation
Fade out	Going from an image to an empty screen	Transitioning from a situation to a tranquil state of mind
Dissolve	Image B melts into, and replaces, Image A	A new situation forming while one is still thinking about the old one
Scene	What takes place in a single location	Sense of being in a place where events are unfolding
Sequence	Succession of scenes	Experiencing a series of events, one usually leading to the next

A film shot arises from two sources: what's physically in front of the camera and what's in the operator's mind behind the camera as he or she reacts, adapts, and adjusts. Should any action come too early or late, the shot communicates a lack of integration. Editing can make some adjustments, but most camerawork is unforgiving and allows just one opportunity to get it right. Unfortunately, whatever is imperfect is just as revealing.

MOTIVATION

Every edit and camera movement must feel *motivated* because in life something always initiates our actions. The camera's actions (moving aside, coming closer, reframing, backing away, altering focus, craning up) can imply anticipation, curiosity, appreciation, surprise, apprehension, intuition, dread, affection, anger—whatever the situation calls for.

Practice imagining the camera and editing equivalencies for these events:

- A voice behind you in a crowd motivates you to turn around to see who it is.
- While you are writing, footsteps approach. You lift your head to look at the door, anticipating who will enter.
- It's someone you find boring, so you turn back to your writing.
- In a ski lodge you open a door to the outside and find yourself facing a mountainside. You tilt your head back to see the peak.
- Your eyeline is obstructed by a tree, so you move sideways to see past it.

What the camera pursues, avoids, or finds exciting colors the "corner of nature seen through a temperament." We feel a focused heart and mind at work, one that sees opportunity, enigma, threat, obstruction, beauty, or horror as each new situation takes shape. Sometimes the camera is tired or drained and reacts passively. More often it is lively and draws us along with its active ideas and agendas. To

 To make memorable documentary, put your subjects and their goals in a larger and provocative context.

see all this in action, run the seminal direct cinema work *Primary* by Robert Drew, Terry Filgate, Richard Leacock, Albert Maysles, and D. A. Penncbaker (1960, United States). It's the classic film about the process by which John Kennedy sought the presidency, and you can clearly see the decision making during the filming.

Finding patterns and explanations—what T. S. Eliot called "imposing order"—is an important part of authorship.

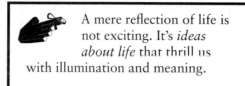

A mere reflection of life is not exciting. It's *ideas about life* that thrill us with illumination and meaning.

COVERING A CONVERSATION: THE ACTOR AND THE ACTED UPON

In a conversation we seldom know we are acting on those around us, but in fact *everyone acts upon those around them all the time,* even by adopting the strategy of passivity. Everyone has agendas, and you already know how to assess them. Try scrutinizing how your perception moves between two people talking. Sometimes you only look at whoever speaks. Naïve camera operators who cover a whole conversation like this produce what I think of as Dog Television. Man's best friend, lacking powers of interpretation, can only look hopefully at the source of sound.

Maybe the conversation you are watching becomes more intense. You notice that you look first at each speaker as she begins, and then in mid-sentence you switch to watching the listener. To understand what's going on here, think of watching a tennis game. At any given moment, one player will *act* (hit the ball), while the other is *acted upon* (receives the shot). Player A is set to launch an aggressive serve, but your eye jumps ahead of the ball, eager to know how Player B will deal with the onslaught. She runs, jumps, swings her racquet, and intercepts. The moment you know she's going to succeed, your eye flicks ahead of the ball to check whether Player A can handle her return.

A ball game suggests how initiative passes between people during any interaction. Each acts and reacts in swift alternation. We're fascinated by what remains hidden; that is, what each person is really trying to get, do, or accomplish.

We follow the actions and reactions in human relationships in this way because we know subconsciously that people are always *trying to get, do, or accomplish* something. A tennis game ritualizes this exchange as a competition for points, but a conversation can be just as structured and competitive. See how fast the "actor" and the "acted upon" switch roles. Your eyeline keeps probing their motivations, and your mind keeps building ideas about who wants what. That's what is behind film technique.

To get a better sense of control, try instructing your eyeline by talking it through "editing" the conversation. As soon as you see how A has begun acting, tell your gaze to switch in mid-sentence over to B to see how she is taking it. When you see how B is adapting and acting back, tell yourself to switch back to A. In television, a person acting as a switcher does this between multiple cameras covering the same event.

 Everyone acts upon others all the time, but few know what they are truly pursuing. It's your job to show this.

Can you pinpoint the moments of knowledge or realization that trigger—or should trigger—each move? Your perceptions are now hard at work, and dragging their lightning decisions into consciousness is how you study them. Human beings do all this searching because the clues to actions and reactions perennially fascinate us. From such clues we read character, mood, and motives.

 Knowing how we search for meaning unlocks secrets to intelligent camera coverage and editing.

Once you recognize this principle forever working in your daily life, the shooting and editing decisions that mimic it are easy. However, your decisions about motives also depend on one more principle. It's called the *subtext*.

 Beneath every human situation are *subtexts,* the hidden agendas that provide most of its tension.

SUBTEXT

Underlying the visible surface of any human situation is an invisible *subtext*— that is, the participants' hidden and usually unconscious agendas that provide most of the situation's tension. A married couple's argument isn't really about whose turn it is to take the car for servicing. You sense that there's a subtext, something present but unspoken. You don't know what it can be, so you eavesdrop until you pick up that he's hurt and jealous because she had lunch with an old boyfriend. Their acrimony isn't about whose turn it is to take the car in; it's about him being possessive and her needing to assert her autonomy.

 Look for the subtext to each situation, and you'll seldom waste your time.

 To find a subtext, look for the need that each person keeps hidden. Test and modify your hypothesis until you've got the key.

In theater and in fiction films, the director and actors put a lot of work into developing the subtexts, because they fuel the tensions that animate real life. In documentary you don't need to add subtexts because they already exist; your challenge is to identify what is at work and then to use cinema language to get the audience to look for what's under the surface.

PERCEPTION

Perception by a camcorder is a mechanical process; an imaging chip at the focal plane sends video signals to the recorder while the microphone diaphragm does the same by responding to the air-pressure changes by which sound travels. The result is a scientific fact—sound and picture that you can replay indefinitely. Perception by a human being is far more complex and ephemeral. As information comes to us, we scan it for meaning and decide what action is possible and justified: Doesn't she trust me? Should I offer help? What did she say that was different before? And so on. Confidence or self-doubt can help or hinder this, but perception usually makes us want to *do* something. For instance, we might want to:

- Interpret (Is this an insult, and if so, how should I react?)
- Formulate a subtext (I don't trust that kind of smile. What's really going on?)
- Test the information (Can this be true? What does it remind me of?)
- Commit what's significant to memory (That's interesting; I'll need it later.)
- Imagine consequences or alternatives (If . . . supposing . . . then . . .)
- Decide what to register (Can I show what I feel or should I hide it?)
- Fight or flight (Should I fight to change this situation? Keep watching? Take evasive action?)

In camerawork, framing and camera movement communicate as thought and feeling. Really sensitive, appropriate camerawork conveys a human heart, intelligence, and soul at work. It takes strong mental and emotional focus while you operate the camera. Sometimes your mind goes ahead of, or away from, the task in hand. You are admiring a composition, guessing the source of a shadow, or thinking associatively about something else. You're no longer in touch and the audience senses it straight away. Actors call this "losing focus."

 If you need to, focus your concentration as you direct or shoot with an inner monologue—rather like a sports reporter broadcasting a game.

Camera operators must maintain an unbroken interior life on behalf of the camera or it won't move, react, search, retreat, evade, or go closer as any lively human intelligence should. This motivation and reactivity are very obvious in handheld, spontaneous coverage but still present when the camera is on a tripod and producing more settled, formal coverage. You work from a tripod whenever you use a long lens and whenever you want shots to be steady. An unsteady camera during an interview, for instance, is simply a distraction unless we are in the back of a truck in a war zone, and the improvised nature of the exchange is fully justified.

DENOTATION AND CONNOTATION

A shot's content, as we said in an earlier chapter, is what it denotes, but what the shot *connotes* is a different matter. Imagine calm shots of a flower or a hand lighting a candle. The shots *denote* what their subjects "are"—that is, a flower and a candle. But in the right context each can connote or suggest "natural beauty," "devotion," or a host of other associations.

You trigger connotation in your audience's mind to make them follow you toward the poetic and philosophic, which is the domain of mature authorship. To practice for this exalted role, make a habit of assessing everything you shoot—images, sounds, words—as potentially a metaphor. Iranian cinema is powerful because it comes from a culture immersed in poetic thinking. Even a humble shepherd can recite poetry by heart and is trained through his religion to know that matters of the spirit are conveyed through symbols and metaphysical imagery. This is a way of seeing and of expressing that you can make your own.

 Every image and situation "is" something but connotes (represents) something, too, depending on context.

SHOTS IN JUXTAPOSITION

When you cut two images together in *juxtaposition*, you lead us to infer meaning from their relationship. The Kuleshov experiment of 1918 used the same reaction shot three times over. It was of a man looking out of frame rather expressionlessly. By cutting it against a plate of soup, a girl, and a coffin, audiences inferred he was hungry, feeling desire, or grieving. Clearly, juxtaposing shots not only suggests relationship but also stimulates ideas and interpretations.

 See in detail how editing works using **Project 1-AP-6 Analyze Editing and Content.**

The examples in Figure 6-1 illustrate an engaging disagreement between two early Russian editing theorists. Examples 1 to 5 illustrate the categories of juxtaposition posited by Vsevolod Pudovkin (1893–1953), which are essential for exposition and building a story narrative. This covers establishing the location's geography, the characters and what they are doing, and the central character's "problem"—whatever he or she is trying to get, do, or accomplish.

 Cover exposition (scene-building information) in multiple ways so you can choose the best later.

Examples 1 to 5: Pudovkin's Categories of Juxtaposition			
	Shot A	Shot B	B in relation to A	Type of cut
1	Woman descending interior stairway	Same woman walking in street	Narrates her progress	Structural (builds scene)
2	Man running across busy street	Close shot of his shoelace coming undone	Makes us anticipate his falling in front of a vehicle	Structural (directs our attention to significant detail)
3	Hungry street person begging from doorway	Wealthy man eating oysters in expensive restaurant	Places one person's fate next to another's	Relational (creates contrast)
4	Bath filling up	Teenager in bathrobe on phone in bedroom	Shows two events happening at the same time	Relational (parallelism)
5	Exhausted boxer taking knockout punch	Bullock killed with stun-gun in an abattoir	Suggests boxer is a sacrificial victim	Relational (symbolism)

Examples 6 to13: Eisenstein's Categories of Juxtaposition			
	Shot A	Shot B	B in relation to A	Type of cut
6	Police waiting at roadblock	Shabby van driving erratically at high speed	Driver unaware of what he's going to soon meet	Conflictual (still vs. the dynamic)
7	Giant earth-moving machine at work	Ant moving between blades of grass	Microcosm and macrocosm coexisting	Conflictual (conflict of scale)
8	Geese flying across frame	Water plummeting at Niagara Falls	Forces flowing in different directions	Conflictual (conflict of graphic direction)
9	Screen-filling close-up of face, teeth clenched	Huge Olympic stadium with a line of runners poised for pistol start	The one among the many	Conflictual (conflict of scale)
10	Dark moth resting on white curtains	Flashlight emerging out of dark forest	Opposite elements	Conflictual (dark vs. light)
11	Girl walking into carnival	Distorted face appearing in carnival mirror	The original and its reflection	Conflictual (original vs. distorted version)
12	Driver seeing cyclist in his path	In slow motion, driver	Event and its perception	Conflictual (real time vs. perceived time)
13	Driver geting out of disabled car	Same image, car in foreground, driver walking as a tiny figure in distance	Transition—some time has gone by	Jump cut

FIGURE 6-1

Examples of juxtaposed shots or cuts.

Examples 6 to 13 show categories favored by Sergei Eisenstein
(1898–1948). To him, the essence
of narrative art lay in dialectics and
in the meanings that emerge from
tension between what is dissimilar.
His editing confronts the viewer
with comparison, contrast, and
conflict—all juxtapositions that
argue as much as they inform.

 As you direct, search for
contrasts in scale, move-
ment, situations, and
images. You'll need these to suggest
the scene's conflicting forces or
ironical juxtapositions.

Most modern filmmaking contains most types of editing. For the building-
site film in the previous chapter you would need expository shots to establish
each machine, its purpose, and its driver, and you would also need to show how
their activities link together and how they interact. For contrasts, you'd want to
contrast the rushing Bobcat with the slowest and largest machine all in the same
shot; the jaws of a machine grabbing trash juxtaposed with a foreman pushing a
sandwich in his mouth, a truck halting for a bulldozer, and so on.

LINES OF TENSION, SCENE AXIS, AND CAMERA AXIS

Let's return to the idea of two people having an animated discussion. Figure 6-2
represents A and B under observation by O, who is a child. Children are good
for my example because they are highly observant, feel strong emotions,

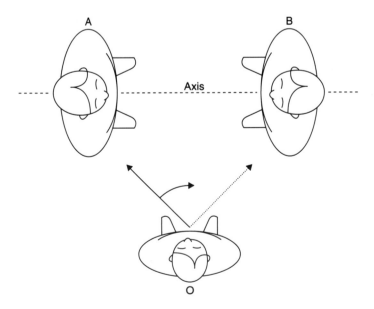

FIGURE 6-2

The Observer watching a conversation.

and often go unseen by their seniors. Imagine you are O, your eyeline moving back and forth between your parents, A and B, as they talk. Your awareness travels the *line of tension* between them; that is, the active pathway of words, looks, awareness, and volition. Known as the *scene axis*, it is really the subject-to-subject axis.

Apart from having one or more subject-to-subject axis, every scene also has an observer-to-subject axis, which my example shows at right angles to the axis between A and B. When the camera replaces the Observer, that axis becomes the *camera axis* or *camera-to-subject* axis. This may all sound rather technical, but it's really quite human. The Observer has a keen sense of relationship to each person (his axis), to the invisible connection between them (their axis), and to what passes between them.

In turning to look from person to person, the Observer can be replaced by a camera *panning* (i.e., moving horizontally) between the two speakers. In Figure 6-3 you can see what happens when O moves closer to A and B's axis. To avoid missing any of the action, the Observer must swerve his or her attention quickly between A and B.

Under this circumstance we momentarily blink our eyes to avoid the unpleasant blur between widely separated subjects. The brain reads this as two static images with no period of black in between. Cinema reproduces this familiar experience by cutting between two subjects, each taken from the same camera position. Historically this solution probably emerged when someone tried cutting out a nauseatingly fast pan between two characters. It "worked," as we've said earlier, because its counterpart was already inherent to human psychological experience.

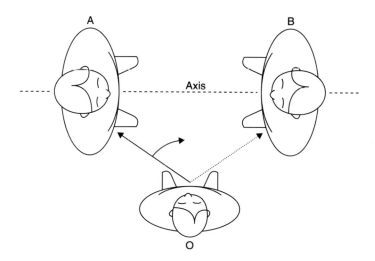

FIGURE 6-3

The Observer moves close to the characters' axis.

SCREEN DIRECTION

A subject's direction or movement through a composition is called his *screen direction*, and these have been formalized using left to right, right to left, up screen, and down screen (Figure 6-4). Where a subject's movement links several shots, as in a march, this becomes rather important. In successive shots all the action should cross the screen in the same screen direction (Figure 6-5). This

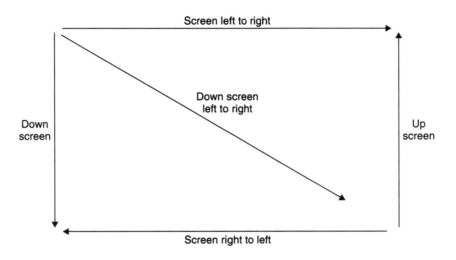

FIGURE 6-4 —————————————————————————————

A range of screen directions and their descriptions.

FIGURE 6-5 —————————————————————————————

Series of shots all maintaining right to left movement.

means you must shoot *characters and their movements from only one side of the scene axis.*

To explain why, let's imagine you take shots of a parade going screen left to right (L–R), then you run ahead of the parade so you can shoot it filing past a landmark. To get a better background, you cross the parade's path to shoot from the other side, something that feels quite unremarkable. However, when you try to intercut the R–L material with the L–R close-ups shot earlier, things go awry. The audience assumes there are two factions marching toward each other.

Cutting to a new camera position across the axis looks awful because we only see the "before" and "after," *not the transition where you crossed the scene axis.*

CHANGING SCREEN DIRECTION

You can, in fact, change the screen direction of a parade, chase, or character's path, but you *must show crossing the scene axis* on-screen. The two ways to do it are:

- By filming at an angle to a corner as in Figure 6-6: The marchers enter in the background going L–R, turn the corner in the foreground, and exit R–L.

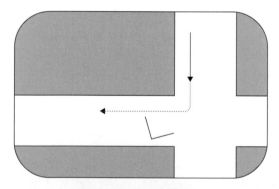

FIGURE 6-6

By shooting at a corner, a parade or moving object can be made to change screen direction.

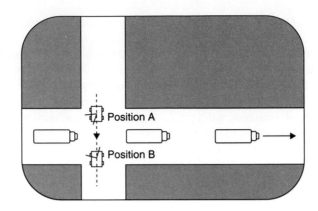

FIGURE 6-7 ————————————————————————————————————

Dollying sideways between floats in a parade changes the parade's effective screen direction, but the dollying movement must be shown.

In essence, they change screen direction. Subsequent shots must now show their action continuing R–L.

- By running the camera and dollying *visibly* across the subject's axis of movement during a gap in the parade (Figure 6-7): The audience sees and understands the change in screen direction. In subsequent shots, the action must maintain the new screen direction.

DURATION, RHYTHM, AND CONCENTRATION

You determine the duration of a shot by how much attention its content requires. A simple analogy is an advertisement on the side of a bus. If it's a simple image with four words of text, the bus can drive past quickly and you'll get the ad; but if the ad has four lines of text and a complicated diagram, the bus cannot go so fast.

Dissimilar shots edited together may be of different lengths yet seem similar in duration because the editor has timed them so each takes a similar degree of concentration to decode. Because each is present for the time you need to "read" it, their *visual rhythm* feels about equal.

Film language makes use of many rhythms that originate in the human mind and body. Our breathing and heart rate provide rhythms. We tap our feet to music or jump up to dance when the music takes us. The rhythms, duration, and capacity of our minds and bodies determine everything we do. Anything with a strong rhythmic structure helps audiences maintain concentration, which is why the entertainers of antiquity composed their epic stories as poems. Film makes use of every possible rhythm. Many sounds from everyday life—birdsong, traffic, the sounds from a carpenter's shop, or the wheels of a train—will contain strong rhythms that help you compose a sequence. Even pictorial compositions contain visual rhythms such as symmetry, balance, repetition, and opposition—all patterns that entertain and intrigue the eye.

When you shoot long dialogue exchanges, you'll become very aware of speech and movement rhythms. You will want to move your camera and edit within the characters' rhythmic framework. Pacing and cutting, as we saw in the exercises earlier, reproduce the way an onlooker's senses shift direction in search of meaning. A long reaction time, for instance, might suggest "she's uncertain how to answer," but a quicker reaction will imply "she's been waiting for him to suggest this." Different

 A sequence is the events that happen at a single location or during a single segment of time.

meanings emerging from different pauses! These scenes are exquisitely demanding to get right, either when moving with the camera during handheld coverage or later when you find you can edit complementary angles together. Enhancing subtexts requires you to orchestrate delicate nuances of behavior and coverage, and this is wonderfully challenging work.

SEQUENCE

How do you know what to shoot in a daylong process such as a marathon? In life there is an unending flow of events but only some that are significant. A short biographical film will reduce a whole lifetime to 30 minutes by showing only its significant moments bridged together. The building blocks are segments of time—the hero's visit to the hospital emergency room after a road accident, the two high points during his residency in Rome, the stages of building his own home while his wife became increasingly exasperated at the time it was taking. Each of these is a sequence.

Think of any time period as a middling waveform with a few high and low points (Figure 6-8). To represent it, you'd skim off the peaks and troughs, and the audience will understand that you have compressed that life by eliminating what was tedious and insignificant.

TRANSITIONS AND TRANSITIONAL DEVICES

The transitions between the building blocks (sequences) of a story are junctures that you can hide or show as the story demands. Most of the transitions we make in life—from place to place or time to time—are imperceptible because we are preoccupied and drive or walk automatically. Stories replicate this by minimizing the seams between sequences. An *action match* cut between a woman drinking her morning fruit juice and a beer drinker raising his glass in a smoky dive minimizes the scene shift by focusing attention on the act of drinking. A

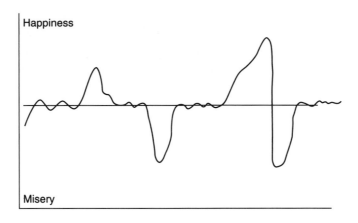

FIGURE 6-8 ───

A period—a day, maybe a month—during which someone's happiness fluctuates. By focusing on the extremes, biography condenses the record to what is significant.

dissolve from one scene to the other indicates (in outdated screen language) "and time passed." A simple cut from one place to the next invites the audience to fill in the blank.

If, however, the transition must surprise or shock, we emphasize the junctures. A teenager singing along to the car radio in a long, boring drive, followed by flash images of a truck, screeching tires, and the teenager desperately yanking the steering wheel, is intentionally a series of shock transitions. It replicates the violent changes we go through when taken nastily by surprise.

Sound can also function as a transitional device. Hearing a conversation over an empty landscape

 We are too preoccupied to notice most transitions in daily life—between places, people, or segments of time. Film can make them soft or hard, depending on what the audience should experience.

 Transitions are narrative devices that handle the need to move between discontinuous blocks of time and space. The right transition conveys an attitude or point of view in either the characters or their storyteller.

can draw us forward into the next scene (of two campers in their tent). Cutting to a shot of a cityscape while the birdsong from the campsite is still fading out gives the feeling of having moved to the city while the mind and heart lag behind in the woodland. Both examples imply an emotional point of view.

GOING FURTHER

In Part 6: Documentary Aesthetics, Chapters 17 to 20 take film language further and show how to use it in greater detail while you direct and edit. Daniel Arijon's *Grammar of the Film Language* (1991, Silman-James Press) is a formal primer.

PART 3

PREPRODUCTION

Research is the work you do to decide what and whom you intend to film. Some documentaries seem heavily researched and premeditated; others appear to spring fully armed from the moment. In fact, few stories simply take shape before the camera, and even those that do benefit from a great deal of strategic planning. Writing a proposal is putting this down on paper and using the writing process itself to help refine and sharpen what you intend to do. Other preparations during preproduction concern the logistics of filming, and marshaling the people and resources to carry it out.

CHAPTER 7

RESEARCH

Research means immersing yourself in your subject so you can decide who and what you might film. Growing familiarity and analysis reveal which people, situations, and materials you'd really like for your documentary. Then you can direct a film with shape and purpose.

 Direct intelligently by reaching preliminary conclusions before shooting. If you don't, everything will look equally useful. Afterwards your material will look like surveillance camera material—no weight, purpose, or inherent story.

CREATING RESTRICTIONS

You research not just to discover people and situations but also to decide the restrictions that will narrow and deepen what you shoot. The clay on the potter's wheel is a shapeless lump until the potter's hands begin containing and squeezing it. These constraints make the clay rise and take shape. Saying "I don't want to make a talking head film or shoot everything handheld" is already to apply creative pressure. Know what aspects of the subject you are *not* interested in, what coverage you *don't* want to shoot, and you can better decide what aspects you *do* want to concentrate on and what strategies you'll use to do them justice. In **Chapter 19, Form, Control, and Style,** you'll find more on setting limits for creative purposes.

RESEARCH METHODS ARE SUBJECT DRIVEN

The subject and type of documentary determine the kind of research you should do.

Example 1. You want to make an observational film about a street gang, so you use *networking* to make contact, declare your interests to them, and get them to accept your first visit. The idea behind networking is that everyone knows someone who knows someone else. A London journalist friend used to say, "Anyone can get to anyone else in the world in five or less phone calls."

Once you are preliminarily accepted by the gang—who are as curious to see themselves on the screen as anyone else—you may need to hang out with them over a period of weeks or months until they come to know you and thoroughly trust your motives. This is how the modest, kindly Hubert Sauper made *Darwin's Nightmare* (2004, Austria). The story concerns sick, starving Tanzanians trapped in a toxic ring of exploitative commerce. Lake Victoria's fishermen catch a predatory fish, then foreign merchants and middle men sell it to European gastronomes and local people get the rotting heads. Guess what the Russian transport planes bring in unmarked boxes on the return trip to Africa? Guns.

People saw that Sauper truly wanted to know them because he stayed around for months. The result is a series of amazingly candid, inwardly searching conversations with street urchins, weary Russian pilots, prostitutes who dream of education and a good job, and the guard of a research facility whose only weapon is a bow and poisoned arrows. Their inward-looking frankness makes this occasionally funny, often shocking film very special.

Example 2. You want to make a tightly argued film about a group of scientists, so you must research using books, libraries, interviews, and the Internet to master intricate patterns of scientific cause and effect. You'll also want to get well acquainted so you can profile the personalities and workplaces of the scientists themselves. You'll want to know how they relax, what their family life is like, what they fear, and what they hope for.

Example 3. You want to make a film about how children visit a zoo. Again, you must hang out, ask innumerable questions, and learn the regular, cyclical patterns by which each day follows the last. Wittily and economically your film should establish how everyone catches their breath at the stink when they enter the lion house, how grandparents and babies doze off after lunch, or how gaggles of boys taunt the unfortunate chimpanzees. These are obligatory scenes at which your audience will smile in recognition. By the time you are ready to shoot, you need to know what's typical and also what's unusual—and thus be ready to film it. There's that kid lying on his side so he can look the armadillo in its beady black eye. There's that depressed man in a raincoat and red woolen hat sitting with his back to a depressed baboon. Quick, shoot it!

COURAGE AND PUSH-UPS

The Chinese say that a long journey begins with a single step. It's hard when you start to break the innate barriers of modesty and reserve. You have to force yourself

 Your major concern is always whether you have a viable film. You can't make a film from ambitions or ideas, only from what you can capture with a camera.

to keep taking steps because we're all afraid of rejection, of the stinging or sarcastic rebuke. Yet take that step, and you'll find how welcoming and helpful most people are. You and your camera, after all, bring a little glamour. Taking those steps gets easier if you practice by walking up to a couple of new people each day and finding out about their lives. These encounters are the documentarian's push-ups.

 As you research, sketch any important physical circumstances using **Project 1-AP-2 Make a Floor Plan** and then develop a working hypothesis using **Project 2-DP-3 Basic Working Hypothesis Helper** (both in the Appendix).

THE WORKING HYPOTHESIS

A vital first step, when you first have an idea for a film, is to make a working hypothesis. This helps fashion a through line of logic to connect your initial convictions, your characters and their main issue, and the realizations, thoughts, and feelings that you want to engender in your audience. Project 2-DP-3 Basic Working Hypothesis Helper (in the Appendix) poses a series of prompts for you to fill in, so it ends up looking something like this:

1. In life I believe that [your life principle concerning this subject] sometimes you have to trust other people's authority and judgment in order to grow.

2. My film will show this in action by exploring [situations] the circumstances leading up to a young marine's first parachute jump, of which he is very afraid.

3. My central characters are [their characteristics] Louis, a rather sheltered young man; his protective mother, Zelda; and his sergeant, who drives the marine beyond what he feels capable of doing.

4. What each wants to get, do, or accomplish: Louis wants to prove himself but is afraid, his mother wants to save him from fear and danger, and his sergeant wants to show him he can do more than he thinks.

5. The main conflict in my film is between Louis' love and loyalty to his mother and his need to prove his manly independence.

6. I expect my film's structure to be determined by the pace and sequencing of marine training that leads up to the parachute jump.

7. Ultimately I want my audience to feel Louis' inner struggle to master his terror and his joy at overcoming it by floating like a bird in the air.

8. . . . and to realize that everyone has tests they must pass in life in order to gain self-respect.

As you research, as you shoot, and even as you edit, you will need to revise your hypothesis as a way to keep control over the meaning and direction of your evolving film. This is a fascinating exercise.

RESEARCH OVERVIEW

Your object during research is to assemble a shooting plan, budget, and rough schedule. Below are the common steps. Don't fret if you are forced to take them out of order or must tackle several at once. Explanations like mine must arrange things logically, but life is often messy and circular. During research consider the overall film and:

➢ Test the viability of your original idea by making a new hypothesis.

➢ Designate a purpose for each scene in the film's likely narrative.

➢ Imagine the different possible outcomes once you start filming.

➢ Think and rethink the possible meanings your film could deliver.

➢ Develop a detailed proposal that outlines your intended content, theme, style, and outcomes.

➢ Pitch your film to gauge its impact on an audience, raise funds, or otherwise gather support.

➢ Assemble all the human and material resources you need to begin shooting.

During research for particular scenes or situations:

➢ Analyze each situation for its significance and filmability.

➢ List the exposition (basic information) each scene must convey. Without this, your audience can't attain your level of understanding.

➢ Observe characteristic activity so you can:

- Figure out shooting that is characteristic, telling, and brief.
- Know when anything abnormal or potentially dramatic starts happening.
- Get to know participants.
- Explain your motivation and purposes for making the film.
- Become known and trusted.
- Understand roles people have adopted.
- Decide who represents what and narrow your choices.
- Decide who will be communicative and effective.

INVENTORY

From research and forming a film in your head, now make an inventory of materials you'll need to shoot. Use the list of sound and picture materials at the beginning of **Chapter 6, Elements and Grammar,** as a reminder. Your inventory—really a shopping list—for a short film might look something like this:

"Getting ahead" 10 minutes

Sequences

1. Garage Sequence—Kenny at work
2. School Sequence—Jean in the gym
3. Clinic—Maria getting an x-ray
4. Home—Family dinner, Jean doing homework
5. Letter carrier on rounds, delivers envelope to McPhersons
6. Maria interviewing for the new job

Archive

1. Parents' 8 mm film of Maria as child (beach, Christmas, Easter)
2. Parents' VHS of Jean as a child (beach, soccer, birthday parties)
3. Maria's VHS of her parents Jorge and Ana visiting from Mexico

Interviews

1. Jean regarding her mother's ambitions
2. Kenny regarding his money troubles
3. Maria concerning the low expectations of her parents and changes she's trying to make in her own outlook

Sound

1. Chihuahua folk song sung by Jorge
2. Playground atmosphere
3. Hospital atmosphere with announcements
4. Repair shop atmosphere
5. Christmas carols at local church

DRAMATIC CONTENT HELPER

Now try using **Project 2-DP-1 Dramatic Content Helper** (in the Appendix). It will help you locate the dramatic ingredients that all stories need and set you up to direct them well. There's no set formula for making good documentary, but successful ones often contain the elements of drama (characters, situation, conflict, confrontation, and resolution). The Helper's questions help you dig out those hiding in any film idea you have under consideration. You won't be able to answer all the questions, but merely trying will prod your imagination.

 Find and then direct the dramatic ingredients that all stories need using **Project 2-DP-1 Dramatic Content Helper** (in the Appendix).

THE OUTLINE

Now take your Working Hypothesis and the material generated by the Dramatic Content Helper and turn them into an outline. This is a narrative in the present tense, active voice that walks the reader, one sequence at a time, through the experience of seeing and hearing the intended film. You'll need to introduce the characters, the main character's situation and "problem," and then show by what situations the film develops and with what likely outcome. Where imponderables may affect the meaning of the film in different ways, write about these, too.

 Funding juries know that every documentary proposal contains conjectural elements. Write practically about what you expect and hope for, and be open about the twists and turns in the road—or it won't be a documentary.

DOCUMENTARY PROPOSAL

Anyone making documentaries spends considerable time and effort competing to get funding or other support for their projects. Writing a documentary proposal is the means by which you do this, and each is going to be different according to the film and the approach. Unfortunately, this means that there are no reliable models to emulate. You can, however, get a great deal of information about independent producers' past applications by thoroughly exploring the Independent Television Service's Web site (www.itvs.org/index.htm).

A basic documentary proposal has to say in as few as 2–3 pages what your documentary is about, who its characters are, what world they live in, and what issues they are struggling with. You must also indicate the film's approach, style, and likely outcomes. This is not easy when you intend to film anything that is uncertain of outcome, so you must guess at likely outcomes and say what development is likely to take place in your central characters. Most important is to describe your target audience and to establish why you have a passion to make this particular film. Any fund or foundation to which you apply will also ask for a rough budget.

Use **Project 2-DP-5 Basic Proposal Helper** to flush out the information, and then transpose and rewrite your materials until your writing:

- Progresses in logical steps
- Includes all the necessary fundamentals
- Is free of all repetition
- Reads effortlessly

In **Book II, Chapter 23: Proposing an Advanced Documentary** there is a more advanced proposal process that makes use of **Project 2-DP-6 Advanced Proposal Helper.**

STYLE AND CONTENT QUESTIONNAIRE

The **Project 2-DP-2 Style and Content Questionnaire** (Figure 7-1) will help you develop ideas for style and shooting. (You will find a blank to photocopy in the Appendix.) Aim to give each sequence a distinct mood, purpose, and meaning. Even interviewees need a meaningful setting and meaningful lighting. The challenge is to accentuate the intrinsic identities and contributions of each part of the material. Don't worry about the material's order, since that won't be final until editing. Include archive footage, too, even though it's a given and can only be altered in postproduction (hue, contrast, color saturation and balance, etc.). Archive material also contributes mood and information.

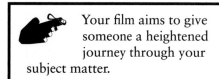 Your film aims to give someone a heightened journey through your subject matter.

If this looks too much like fiction, remember that it's only a set of ideals. You want to bring some vision and expectation to the shots you expect to cover, not just make do with whatever shapes up. Documentary planning is usually overly ambitious, given that some material may be grab shooting, but good things happen because you dream them into existence.

Sequence name and content	What it should convey	Style
Bus station: Parents put Ellen on bus and wave goodbye.	Ellen is fearful about traveling alone. The experience is troubling.	Handheld camera, emphasizing movement, instability, weird faces, disconnection, noise.
Small town bus-stop: Ellen gets off, looks for grandparents. She is surprised to find only Grandpa there. She asks where Grandma is.	Small figure in a big world; anxiety, then relief at arriving. But where is Grandma?	Tripod and long lens as bus arrives and a small Ellen gets off, then handheld as she searches for her grandparents and finds only Grandpa.
Hospital: Grandma is in bed after a stroke, asleep but could be dead. Ellen is scared until Grandma awakes and greets her. She seems tired but alright.	The hospital room has scary equipment, plastic tubes, electronic metering. Grandma looks very vulnerable until she awakes and smiles. By intercutting Ellen we get a strong sense of her concern, then of her relief.	Tripod-mounted camera, wide-angle shots to give unpleasant distortion. Perspectives stabilize as Ellen realizes that Grandma is going to be OK. Do POV close shots of the dials, readouts, and tube clamps, and record all of the sounds, especially Grandma's labored breathing.

FIGURE 7-1 ——————————————————————————

Specimen Style and Content sheet for first three sequences of a documentary about a child's visit to her grandparents. (See Project 2-DP-2 in the Appendix for a blank to photocopy.)

LUCK FAVORS THE PREPARED MIND

Plans for documentaries are full of imponderables, but defining what you'd ideally like often makes the gods smile. Being well prepared lets you see alternative possibilities as you shoot and also, rather mysteriously, often attracts extraordinary luck.

SCHEDULING

To schedule a short film, break your material into intended sequences and allot time for each. Expect to cover perhaps two lengthy sequences in a day of work, provided you can get from one to the other without too long a journey. Setting up lights rather than shooting under available light also slows things down.

Beginning directors often expect to cover too much in a given time and end up shooting for inhumanly long hours. After a few grueling days, work gets sloppy and the crew resentful. So err on the light side, because a crew in good shape is always ready to shorten a given schedule by working longer days, while a crew suffering from terminal fatigue may rebel at the idea of two extra hours. Treat your crew reasonably and they will rise to crises selflessly.

If you have exteriors that depend on a certain kind of weather, schedule them early and have interior shooting standing by in case you need it. If your film depends on a success with a particular scene or situation, plan to shoot it early in case it proves difficult or impossible and makes the rest of the film moot.

LOCATION AGREEMENT

For each privately owned location you will need a signed permission *before* you shoot. Called a location agreement (Figure 7-2), you'll need one to shoot in any building or on any piece of land that is not a public thoroughfare. Whether it's an empty church, a public park, or city transportation, each comes under the jurisdiction of a guardian body to which you are supposed to apply. This is to regulate shooting on their property and to protect yourself against being sued. Say you shoot someone on a bus who *just* happens to be running away with someone else's wife. Their shot *just* happens to appear on national television, and he sues the bus company for allowing you to invade his privacy. Guess who the bus company sues?

You obtain a signature on an individual release form *after* shooting. One appears in **Chapter 9, Basic Camera Equipment.** Fuller, more legally binding, and downloadable forms for location and individual release appear in **Chapter 24, Preparing to Direct.** They come from Michael C. Donaldson's excellent *Clearance and Copyright: Everything the Independent Filmmaker Needs to Know* (2003, Silman-James Press).

 Attach a price to the work you're doing right now with **Project 3-BP-1 Basic Budget.**

LOCATION AGREEMENT

Location of Property: _____

Description of Property: _____

Dates of Use: _____   Fee for Use: $_____

PICTURE: _____   PRODUCER: _____

In consideration of the payment of the above-indicated fee, the undersigned hereby grants to Producer, its successors and assigns the right to enter the area located as described above (hereafter "Property") on or about the dates listed above, for the purpose of photographing by motion picture, videotape, and still photography and to make sound recordings and to otherwise use for so-called "location" purposes (the results of which are hereafter collectively referred to as "Photographs"). If such photography is prevented or hampered by weather or occurrence beyond Producer's control, it will be postponed to or completed on such date as Producer may reasonably require. Said permission shall include the right to bring personnel and equipment (including props and temporary sets) onto the Property, and to remove the same therefrom after completion of work.

The undersigned hereby grants to Producer, its successors, assigns and licensees the irrevocable and perpetual right to use the Photographs of the Property taken by Producer hereunder in connection with motion picture, television photoplays or otherwise, and all the ancillary and subsidiary rights thereto of every kind and nature in such a manner and to such extent as Producer may desire. The rights granted herein include the right to photograph the Property and all structures and signs located on the Property (including the exterior and interior of such structures, and the names, logos and verbiage contained on such signs), the right to refer to the Property by its correct name or any fictitious name and the right to attribute both real and fictitious events as occurring on the Property and to fictionalize the Property itself. The undersigned hereby agrees and acknowledges that any and all Photographs made or to be made by Producer shall be Producer's sole and exclusive property and the undersigned shall have no claims thereto or rights therein or to the proceeds hereof.

Producer agrees to use reasonable care to prevent damage to the Property and to remove any and all property which Producer may place upon the Property in connection with its use thereof. Producer agrees to restore the Property as nearly as possible to its original condition at the time of Producer's taking possession thereof, reasonable wear and damage not caused by Producer's use excepted.

Producer hereby agrees to indemnify and hold the undersigned harmless from any claims and demands of any person or persons arising out of or based upon personal injuries and/or death suffered by such person or persons resulting directly from any act of negligence on Producer's part while Producer is engaged in the photographing of said Photographs upon the Property.

The undersigned hereby releases Producer and its licensees, successors, assigns, all networks, stations, sponsors, advertising agencies, exhibitors, cable operators and all other persons or entities from any and all claims, demands, or causes of action which the undersigned, its heirs, successors or assigns may now have or hereafter acquire by reason of Producer's photographing and using the Photographs taken of the Property, including, but not limited to, all buildings (exterior and interior), equipment, facilities and signs thereon.

The undersigned hereby represents and warrants that the undersigned is the _____ (fill in: owner, lessee or agent for the owner) of said Property and has the full right and authority to grant the license herein contained. The undersigned hereby indemnifies and agrees to hold Producer free and harmless from and against any and all liability, damages, claims, costs or fees, including but not limited to attorney fees, arising from, growing out of or concerning any breach by the undersigned of this warranty.

FIGURE 7-2 —————————————————————————————————

Location release form, courtesy of Michael C. Donaldson's *Clearance and Copyright: Everything the Independent Filmmaker Needs to Know* (2003, Silman-James Press). Download a copy from info@clearanceandcopyright.com.

BUDGET

As an eye-opener, assess what your film would cost if you had to rent equipment and pay everyone (see project box). Use your Internet research skills to find daily rates for professionals and their equipment. Allow a 5-day week of editing for every 10 minutes of final screen time. Give yourself a *shooting ratio* of 24:1, which means that you'll need *stock* on which to shoot (cassettes, disks, solid-state memory, etc.) that is 24 times your intended screen length of 10 minutes. Thus, you'll need 24 × 10 = 240 minutes, or 4 hours of stock.

Shooting ratio refers to the minutes of *stock* (cassettes, disks, solid-state memory, etc.) you'll need in relation to the minutes of final screen time.

Shocked at your budget grand total? Films cost big money, which is why surviving as a maker requires a practical mind equipped with basic business skills.

Documentary makers often detest all the time it takes to get projects funded and then, once

Proposing films, estimating what they will cost, and bringing good ones in—on time and on budget—are what make you a professional.

they're made, the further energy it takes to distribute them in order to recoup their cost. If you do well, you'll look for a producer who actually likes doing this kind of work. Believe it or not, they do exist. Few independent documentary makers achieve this level of success and come to accept—and even excel at—the job of finding and administering funds. Saving precious resources becomes a preoccupation for everyone in the crew.

Meanwhile, prepare to travel the festival circuit with any film of winning caliber so you can negotiate with distributors and make contacts over leveraging new projects.

This chapter's work should get you thinking about how to make a living from filmmaking. If you haven't yet studied **Part 8: Career Track,** now is the time to face reality and lay your plans.

GOING FURTHER

See Michael C. Donaldson's *Clearance and Copyright: Everything the Independent Filmmaker Needs to Know* (2003, Silman-James Press) to better understand the legal restraints that hedge the professional filmmaker. For research in more depth see **Chapter 21, Advanced Research,** and **Chapter 23, The Advanced Documentary Proposal,** for more information on defining a film's point of view. Also see:

Bernard, Sheila Curran. *Documentary Storytelling: Making Stronger and More Dramatic Nonfiction Films.* Boston: Focal Press, 2007.

CHAPTER 8

DEVELOPING A CREW

You "develop" rather than "choose" a crew because you should always do some trial shooting together. This verifies that equipment is functioning and that you understand each other's values, signals, and terminology. One operator's close-up is another's medium shot, so developing a brief and unambiguous communication is important, especially when you face "run and gun" shooting. Responding to a rapidly changing situation, with no possibility of rehearsal or repeats, allows wide margins for misunderstanding. Only if your crew understands your occasional whispered instructions do they achieve successful subject selection, framing, composition, speed of camera movements, and microphone positioning. Shoot exercise footage and expect to find wide variance in taste and skill levels. Look, too, for variations in responses, technical vocabulary, and interpretation of standard jargon. It's the director's job to unify the crew so it becomes like a many-armed individual.

DEVELOPING YOUR OWN CREW

In the worst-case scenario you live remote from centers of filmmaking and must train your own crew. Let's say you have access to a camcorder, microphone, and replay facilities. How many and what kinds of people will you need? What are their responsibilities?

Certainly ascertain technical expertise and experience, but also find out their feelings and ideas concerning documentary, books, plays, music, hobbies, and interests. Technical acumen matters, but a person's maturity and values matter more. You can negotiate many changes, but not with someone who is uninterested in your choice of subject or disdains your approach.

WHY CREW MEMBERS' TEMPERAMENTS MATTER

Today documentary crews are smaller than ever—two, maybe three persons. You depend utterly on your colleagues. They must have personalities that sup-port not only the project and each other but also those in front of the camera. Most documentary partici-pants have never experienced film-ing before, so the crew's interest and support are vital, especially if the shooting extends over days or months. Because of their exposure to the new and unfamiliar work, they are highly attuned to bad atmospheres.

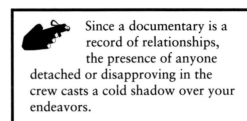 Since a documentary is a record of relationships, the presence of anyone detached or disapproving in the crew casts a cold shadow over your endeavors.

The BBC usually assigned me wonderful crews, but occasionally I got indi-viduals with problems. Typically it was forgivable lapses in mental focus, but more than once I got people who were actively subversive and one person who proved to be mentally ill. Being under pressure and far from home can further unbalance some people and exacerbate latent insecurities and jealousies. This is difficult to foresee and in documentary becomes an appalling liability because good relationships are everything.

Whenever potential crew members have done other film or team work, speak confidentially with their coworkers. Filming is intense, so work partners quickly learn each other's temperamental strengths and weaknesses. Assess new teammates according to their:

- Realism
- Reliability
- Ability to sustain effort and concentration over long periods and in discom-fort or danger
- Commitment to the processes and purposes of making documentaries
- Knowledge and appreciation of films or filmmakers that you particularly respect

In all film crew positions, beware of those who:

- Fail to deliver on what they've promised
- Forget or modify verbal commitments
- Habitually overestimate their own abilities
- Let their attention wander beyond their own field of responsibility
- Have only one working speed (it's usually medium slow; faced with a crisis, these people slow up in confusion or go to pieces)
- See you as a stepping-stone toward something more desirable

Be sure to assign areas of responsibility so each person knows which is theirs. Be on guard against areas mistakenly assigned to nobody or to two people, when each can think the other has taken care of the problem and neither does.

In a small crew in particular—camera operator, director, and sound recordist—each person ends up with important additional roles, such as prophet, visionary, scribe, or fixer. Someone is always the jester because every unit develops its own special inside jokes. The pleasure from working well together is the best intoxicant you can imagine. It becomes headiest under pressure and there's no hangover the morning after. Carefully selected partners make anything possible, because determined friends are unstoppable.

SMALL CREW ROLES AND RESPONSIBILITIES

Here is an outline of each crew member's responsibilities in a minimal crew and the strengths and weaknesses you might look for. Of course, in real life many of the best practitioners are the exceptions, so this list is fallible. Editors and their work are described under "Postproduction" in Chapter 13, Editing: From Start to First Assembly. For producers, production managers, gaffers, and grips found working on larger projects, look in **Chapter 28, Organization, Crew, and Procedures.**

DIRECTOR

The director is responsible for the quality and meaning of the final film. He or she must also:

- Assemble funding
- Conduct or supervise research
- Decide on content
- Assemble a crew
- Schedule shooting
- Lead the crew
- Direct participants during shooting
- Supervise editing
- Hustle distribution

A good director has a lively fascination with the causes and effects behind the way real people live. He or she has a mind always searching for links and explanations, is social, and loves delving into people's stories. Outwardly informal and easygoing, he or she is methodical and organized but quite able to throw away prior work when early assumptions prove obsolete. The best directors have endless patience in stalking the truth, and strong ambitions in doing it justice in cinematic terms. They are articulate and succinct, know their own minds without being dictatorial, and can speak on terms of respectful equality with other film craftspeople.

Directors are, however, very human. Many are obstinate, private, awkward, and even shy beings who do not explain themselves well, change their minds, or are disorganized and visceral. Most can be intimidated by bellicose technicians, have difficulty in balancing attention between crew and participants, and desert one for the other under pressure. During shooting, sensory overload catapults many into a state of acute doubt and anxiety in which all choice becomes pain-ful. Some cannot relinquish their original intentions and go catatonic or act like a captain at the wheel of a sinking ship. Directing can change normal people into manic–depres-sives chasing the Holy Grail. If that is not enough, the director's over-heated mental state can generate superhuman energy that tests crew members' patience to the limit.

 Directing a process that crystallizes life is a heady business. It often means living completely in the present, whether you like it or not. Initial success raises the bar. Thereafter, you fear failure more.

Like a mountaineer dangling over a precipice, the director often comes to depend on the adrenaline pumping from dread and exhilaration during the cine-matic chase. This, like stage fright for actors, is a devil that never really goes away. But aren't fear and excitement the portents of everything worthwhile?

DIRECTOR OF PHOTOGRAPHY (DP) AND/OR CAMERA OPERATOR

In the minimal crew, the director of photography (DP):

➤ Orders the camera equipment if it's hired,

➤ Tests and adjusts it,

➤ Masters all its needs and working principles, and

➤ Answers to the director but takes initiative when shooting handheld action footage.

He or she is also responsible for:

➤ Scouting locations to assess light and electricity supplies,

➤ Lighting aesthetics,

➤ Setting up lighting instruments,

➤ Deciding camera positioning in collaboration with the director, and

➤ Making all camera movements.

Handheld camerawork is a talent that all operators think they have, but which few do. Work on it using test footage and critique the results. A good operator:

• Is highly image conscious, preferably from training in photography and fine art

• Has a highly developed sense of composition and design

• Has an eye for the sociologically telling details that show in people's surroundings

- Is sensitive to the behavioral nuances that reveal so much about character
- Is interested in people, not just photography.

Experienced camera personnel sometimes hide in the mechanics of their craft at the expense of the director's deeper quest for themes and meanings. One such answered a question of mine with "I'm just here to make pretty pictures," and he might have added, "and not get involved."

You can direct the handheld camera up to a point, but usually

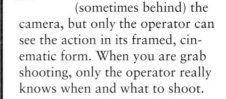

The director sees *content* happening in front of (sometimes behind) the camera, but only the operator can see the action in its framed, cinematic form. When you are grab shooting, only the operator really knows when and what to shoot.

you have to rely very much on your operator's discrimination. For this reason, a camera operator must be decisive, and mentally and physically dexterous. The best are low-key, practical, and inventive types who don't ruffle easily in crises. They enjoy improvising solutions to intransigent logistical, lighting, or electrical problems.

A narrow "tech" mentality is never good enough. Crew members must comprehend both the details and the totality of a project and see how to make the best contribution at any given moment. Look for the perfectionist who will cheerfully find the best and simplest solution when time runs short.

In a two-person crew, the director often handles the microphone. This is a recipe for bad sound because you have too much on your plate.

SOUND RECORDIST

Students often think sound recording is unglamorous and unimportant and leave it to whoever consents to do it, but poorly recorded sound fatally disconnects the audience. Capturing clear, clean, and consistent sound is highly specialized. The sound recordist is responsible for:

- ➤ Checking equipment in advance
- ➤ Choosing the right equipment for the situation
- ➤ Not causing shadows or letting the mike creep into frame
- ➤ Keeping the microphone close to the sound source even during handheld shooting
- ➤ Hearing sound inequities and curing them whenever possible
- ➤ Shooting atmospheres and sound effects on his or her own initiative

A good sound recordist needs patience, a good ear, and the maturity to be low person on the totem pole.

FIGURE 8-1

Wearing high-quality, ear-enclosing headphones is the only sure way to monitor sound quality. (Jason Longo and Byron Smith shooting for David Sutherland Productions.)

The camera position and lighting (if there is any) come first, so the sound recordist must hide mikes, cause no shadows, and yet try to achieve first-rate sound. For some, shooting becomes a series of aggravating compromises. Many professionals end up bitter that "good standards" are routinely trampled, but it's the disconnected craftsperson, not the whole filmmaker, who gags on necessary compromise.

 The art of sound recording is all about the selection and placement of mikes. You listen not to words but to sound *quality*. This means hearing all the buzzes, rumbles, or edginess that the novice unconsciously screens out.

With a camera that is handheld and on the move, sound work requires skill, awareness, and quietly agile footwork. The recordist must wear ear-enclosing, isolating headphones (Figure 8-1); when moving the mike, he or she must be able to hear the differences. Musical interests and musical training best equip people to judge. Once the material is edited together, *then* you begin hearing all the inequities (Figure 8-2).

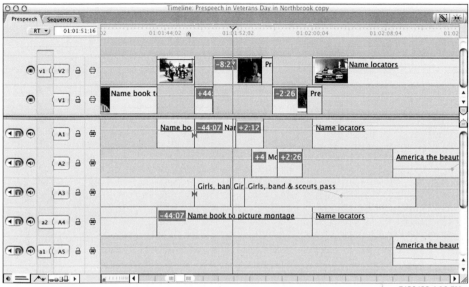

FIGURE 8-2 —————————————————————————————————

Sound mismatches emerge when you play the cuts between mike positions. A skilled recordist can minimize differences in the field.

GOING FURTHER

See **Chapter 28 Organization, Crew, and Procedures,** for notes on the larger unit needed to make more elaborate documentaries.

PART 4

PRODUCTION

This part concerns the documentarian's acquisition tools—the camera and sound recording equipment that commit scenes to a memory medium. At one time this was film or tape—increasingly, it is solid-state memory or hard drives, for few working parts and an easy interface with the computer that will handle the editing during postproduction.

Photography involves using lenses and lights, while sound involves the astute use of microphones. The techniques for using the eyes and ears of the documentary aims to bring the chosen subject up close—and make it visible and audible in its true nature. For the problems that intervene there is a range of solutions, and this is what makes documentary filming such an interesting challenge.

Finally, this part prepares you for your first experiences at directing a crew and at relating to your subjects. Participants will be self-conscious and self-doubting without some work on your part to involve and relax them in what they do.

CHAPTER 9

CAMERA EQUIPMENT

You can make good documentaries with the most modest equipment, especially when you are learning. There is so much excellent equipment today, so this chapter will highlight just the key features you should look for.

CAMCORDER

BODY

In documentary you often shoot material handheld, so the professional electronic newsgathering (ENG) *camcorder* (camera + sound recorder) has a side-mounted eyepiece and a body balanced to nestle on the operator's shoulder. This allows the camcorder to become part of one's head and shoulders (Figure 9-1). Smaller camcorders often record amazing sound and picture, but having the eyepiece at the rear means the camcorder is a free-floating appendage held ahead of your face (Figure 9-2). The lack of bodily contact produces stress in your arms, wrists, and hands when you must hold shots steady for minutes at a time. Usually, a pivoted liquid crystal display (LCD) unfolds from the side of a small camcorder so you can look into it from any angle. For low-angle shots, you look down into it; you can even face it forward so you can see framing as you speak to the camera (Figure 9-3). LCD screens work fine until you try shooting under sunlight—when the image becomes too dim to see. That's when you need the viewfinder eyepiece. Controls are miniaturized and fiddly for larger hands and not always placed where you want them. Never doubt, however, that if you work within their limitations, they are capable of serious work.

Practice controlling all of your camcorder's functions until their operation becomes second nature. This is your instrument; practice until you play like a pro.

FIGURE 9-1 ——

An ENG camcorder such as the JVC HD-250 sits nicely balanced on one's shoulder and against one's head. (Photo courtesy of JVC.)

FIGURE 9-2 ——

Hand-holding a small camcorder becomes stressful after a few minutes because you can't brace it against your face or body.

FIGURE 9-3

Fold-out color screen that will even face forward.

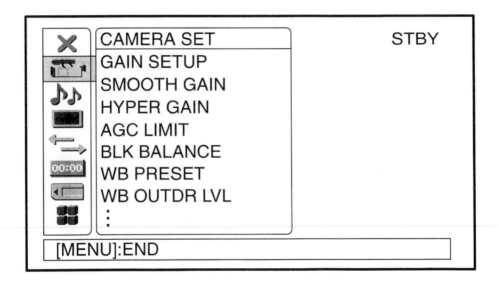

FIGURE 9-4

Typical instructions for accessing a camcorder's menus. (Photo courtesy of Sony Corporation.)

LEARNING YOUR OPTIONS

Consumer equipment offers variables in video and audio through tiny switches or thumbwheels. The menus these deploy look like verb tables for a foreign language (Figure 9-4). Learn what they offer, and run through all the options until you've used every one. Current choices show up in the viewfinder as icons, so these you must recognize, too—or discover later that all your participants have yellow jaundice because the winking saucer was trying to tell you, "Set white balance."

Most camcorders have multiple functions. In addition to serving as a movie camcorder, yours may become a stills camera, a player, or a line recorder (meaning you can use it to rerecord like a VCR or DVD recorder). A function knob routes you to the chosen option, whereupon you face more options. The manuals holding the key to these riches are often discouragingly cramped, so it's good to download a full-size manual from the manufacturer's site. To absorb the manual painlessly, turn it into flash cards so you and your crew can test each other. Tossing on the high seas in a trawler is no place to start looking for the manual sound-level control.

PROFESSIONAL OPTIONS

Professional equipment, being rugged and physically large, allows visible, easy-to-set controls, of which there are many. Expect professional and prosumer (midway between professional and consumer) camcorders to have a black level control and a gamma (color linearity) control, as well as manual exposure, focusing, and sound level settings. Also usual are genlock (ability to electronically lock sync with other cameras and recorders) and four sound channels.

COLOR BALANCE

WHITE BALANCE

In color work you aim to make flesh tones look natural, so the first move in digital camerawork is to set the correct *white balance*. This allows the camera to shoot white objects under a particular light source and show them as white onscreen, not pale pink, green, or orange. The reason is this: Although white light contains the whole spectrum, real-life light sources—including different kinds of skylight—are mixtures in which different colors predominate. Each bias is said to have a different *color temperature*. To compensate, you must set your camcorder's "white balance" for shooting under that particular source. If you don't, everyone under that supermarket fluorescent lighting turns out a bilious green.

 Every light source has its own *color temperature*.

Adjust a camcorder white balance by framing on white paper illuminated by the relevant light source. Press manual white balance control, then wait until the camcorder reports that balancing is complete. Anything under that light source will now be recorded with color accuracy.

Look for these white balance options on your camcorder:

Automatic—not good for all situations but a necessity for some. When, for example, you must follow someone through several lighting zones, let the automatic white balance and exposure make the adjustments as you go.

Manual—preferable under stable lighting situations. Here you want exposure and color to remain stable as the camcorder pans across differently lighted areas. Options include:

- *Preset white balance*—These are factory settings that usually offer typical sunlight (which has a blue bias), typical tungsten-filament bulb light (orange bias), and typical fluorescent light (green bias). Since no light is typical, presets are approximations that you use in an emergency only.

- *Manually set white balance*—Adjusting for an actual, rather than theoretical, light source is always best.

- *White balance memory*—This function retains a setting when the camcorder is turned off, its battery is being changed, or you need to shoot matching material days or months later under the same lighting situation.

White balancing balances the camcorder's response under a given light source's color temperature. It is no match for problems arising in a scene containing mixed color temperature sources.

SHOOTING UNDER MIXED COLOR TEMPERATURES

Outdoor and indoor color temperatures always vary. It's normal to use lighting between, say, 2800 and 3200°K (degrees Kelvin) indoors and then find that what's visible out of a window, being under 5600°K daylight, looks blue biased onscreen. You face a dilemma: White balance for the outdoor light, and the folks indoors look orange. Balance to indoor tungsten light, and the folks outdoors go bluish. Here are three approaches to shooting in mixed color temperature situations like these:

- *Solution A: Do nothing.* If the view out of the window is incidental and unimportant, just let it go blue. Conversely, if an incidental exterior includes a lighted room seen from outside, let it go orange. Audiences accept both as a convention of movies.

- *Solution B: Tape gel filter #85 (orange) over windows.* This will be invisible to the camcorder and holds back the excess blue in daylight. What light enters now matches tungsten light. White balance your camcorder to the indoor tungsten light, and colors seen outside will look normal. More significantly, daylight entering and adding to your tungsten light won't be the wrong color temperature. Fail to filter your windows, and highlight areas will go bluish. In documentary this is not a capital offense. Watch a range of documentaries for lighting and you'll see it.

- *Solution C: Place #80A filters (blue) over your 3200°K tungsten movie lights.* This holds back excess orange content so their light output now matches daylight color temperature. This method, however, at least halves the output from your lights—so they may not remain adequate. Filters for lighting get very hot and so are made of a special heatproof glass.

CAN'T I FIX IT IN POSTPRODUCTION?

Yes and no. Digital color correction in postproduction is remarkable. You can easily warm an overall cold color cast or change contrast and brightness, but changing only a single shade (a human face, for instance) without altering

FIGURE 9-5

Sunset silhouette shot enhanced through underexposure.

everything else takes advanced software and the skills of a colorist. Moral: Cure everything you can during the shoot.

EXPOSURE

MANUAL EXPOSURE CONTROL

Your camcorder probably offers manual exposure control. The link may be electronic or, in more expensive camcorders, a physical *lens aperture* (or *f-stop*) control. With this you can underexpose to simulate a sunset (Figure 9-5) or overexpose to see the features of someone backlit (Figure 9-6). Lockable exposure is vital if you don't want it to float every time a light or dark object crosses frame. The type and accessibility of the control (lever, knob, thumbwheel) are as important as its responsiveness. Positive and immediate control is good, floating and slow is not.

AUTOMATIC EXPOSURE

The camcorder normally adjusts by averaging light in the whole frame, which only answers some situations. Even when the camera samples chosen areas of the frame, it's easy to get undesirable effects. Don't get into the habit of relying on automatic exposure; it will let you down when you can least afford it. In circumstances of rapidly changing light, however, only automatic exposure can maintain acceptable results. Imagine, for instance, following someone out of a

FIGURE 9-6

Detail in features of a backlit subject achieved by increased exposure. Notice the "hot" background.

car at night and into a roadside café. You pass through a maze of lighting and color temperature situations and need all the help you can get. Here, switching exposure and white balance to automatic can help you do a better job.

BACKLIGHT CONTROL

A backlight control compensates exposure when a subject's major illumination is coming toward the camcorder and is thus backlit. Avoid using the preset; use manual exposure to set the exposure so you get the backlighting effect you want.

NEUTRAL DENSITY (ND) AND OTHER FILTERS

Many camcorders have inbuilt *neutral density (ND) filters*. These, when you activate them, act like sunglasses, lowering the amount of light reaching the imaging chip while remaining color neutral. A one-stop reduction is a .3 rating; two stops, .6; and so on. You may need ND filtering to avoid overexposure, or you can use it to force your lens into using a larger aperture. This makes it work at a shorter depth of field, which might be useful if you wanted to throw a background or foreground out of focus.

With the addition of a matte box (see Chapter 26) to hold filters in place, you can:

- Use a color correction filter
- Cool a hot (overbright) sky with a graduated ND filter
- Simulate fog or mist with a fog filter
- Reduce contrast with a diffusion filter
- Create sparkles on highlights with a star-effect filter
- Reduce glare of water and certain metal surfaces with a polarizing filter

PICTURE GAIN

Most camcorders have a *picture gain* control. This, calibrated in decibels, amplifies the camera's response so you can still shoot in really low light situations. Useful, but expect to pay with increased *picture noise* (electronic picture "grain"). After you've used it, remember to return the gain to normal.

LENSES

Camcorder lenses often have no visible calibration, but you can get tech specifications for your camera and make comparisons with others through the B&H Web site provided below. You can also run simple tests using a tape measure to determine your lenses' widest and narrowest angles of acceptance. Unless you are filming wildlife, a long telephoto end for the zoom lens won't be as useful as a truly wide-angle end. Wide-angle lenses make moving shots look steadier and they allow you to cover the action in a confined space such as a courtyard, car interior, or small apartment.

 Zoom lens ranges are expressed in millimeters from shortest to longest focal length. A 9 mm to 90 mm zoom has a 10:1 *zoom ratio* (divide the large figure by the small).

Below is lens information for a Canon® XL-2, which has a good wide-angle end. For other camcorder specifications, visit the B&H Photo-Video-Pro Audio Web site (www.bhphotovideo.com/c/shop/1881/Camcorders). B&H carries a huge range of equipment, and their Web site offers much excellent information.

Standard 20× Zoom Lens with Canon XL Mount

Information	Explanation
Focal Length	
5.4 to 108 mm 20× optical zoom No digital zoom	5.4 mm is wide at the end of the zoom range; 108 mm is telephoto—divide one by the other and you get 20× magnification. Focal lengths are related to the size of the imaging chip, so be sure you compare like with like. The XL mount means you can remove the lens and replace it with another of different characteristics. Some camcorders can magnify the image digitally, but it has little practical use.

Information	Explanation
Wide Aperture Range	
f/1.6–3.5 (depending on zoom)	Wide aperture describes the lens's light-gathering ability. f/1.6 is fine for the wide-angle end of the zoom, but f/3.5 at the telephoto end of the zoom range is about 2½ stops less. Since each stop-change halves or doubles light, f/3.5 admits only about one-sixth the light of f/1.6. This is normal, not an anomaly.
Filter Diameter	
72 mm	72 mm is the size of any filter you screw directly on the front element of the lens.
Minimum Object Distance	
20 mm macro mode 1 meter standard mode	Of the two focusing modes, standard lets you focus as close as 1 meter (3 feet, 3 inches) and macro as close as 20 mm (8.66 inches).

INTERCHANGEABLE LENSES

A camcorder body that accepts interchangeable 35mm stills-camera lenses looks like a wonderful idea. When the imaging chip is smaller than a 35mm format, however, much of the image gets wasted and the advantages are largely illusory. Look instead for a good-quality zoom to which you can add *diopters* (supplementary enlarging lenses) when you need to alter the lens's range. Diopter shortcomings usually show in the widest image as a softening of focus or a *vignetting* (darkening and cropping) at the image corners. This is especially obvious when using a large lens aperture in low light. A fixed (non-interchangeable) zoom lens has one other, less obvious advantage—it keeps the imaging chip sealed from dirt and damage.

 Depth of field (DOF) is the range of distances through which objects remain in acceptable focus. If you focus on a subject at, say, 10-foot distance, focus may be acceptable as near as 8 feet and as far as 14 feet—a DOF of 6 feet. DOF varies according to (a) focal length of the lens and (b) aperture (or area of the lens) in use. For more information, see **Chapter 25, Optics.**

FOCUS AND DEPTH OF FIELD (DOF)

The camera operator, especially during handheld movements, must often rapidly adjust focus. In well-lit surroundings, focus is not critical because small imaging

FIGURE 9-7

Manual focus got the kachina doll sharp, while automatic focus, sampling the center of the frame, placed the focus on the back of the composition.

chips, like the 8 mm film cameras of yesteryear, have a large depth of field (DOF; see definition in box). Under low light conditions, DOF shrinks, focus becomes critical, and maintaining focus may become a struggle. The large viewfinder and mechanically positive lens control of professional cameras make this easier, but focus control on small camcorders may be an imprecise electronic connection. Some even have a lag between adjustment and seeing any results. Most, however, have a useful *focus button* that temporarily engages autofocusing. Expect most camcorders to offer these focusing options:

Automatic focusing (autofocusing) is fast and accurate but depends entirely on which part of the image the optics are set to scan. Usually it's a small area in the center of frame, but if there's a choice, the last user may have set it differently. If so, the camcorder will duly misfocus (see Figure 9-7). Check that autofocus can be disengaged so the camcorder doesn't hunt for focus every time the picture composition changes. Autofocus won't usually work through glass. Either it hunts for focus or focuses on the glass instead of the subject.

Manual focusing is preferable, but without a large, lightproof eyepiece focusing can be hit or miss. High-definition (HD) video raises the stakes—you often see misfocused footage on the nightly news. To focus manually, zoom in quickly, run through focus before settling on what's visibly best, then quickly zoom out to the preferred image size. Try confining this procedure to unimportant action, such as a question during an interview.

Macro focusing allows you a short focus range that often permits focus within inches of the lens—really useful when shooting small objects or images.

LENS PROTECTION

For everyday use, keep an *ultraviolet filter* (UV) on the front element of your lenses. It protects the lens from damage and inhibits UV light scatter in large landscape shots, which the digital system sees as mist. Always use a *lens hood* to shield the front lens element from shafts of sun or other strong light. Even when coming from outside the lens's field of view, it strikes the lens's front element at an angle and causes *halation* (light bouncing internally between multiple lens elements). This degrades the overall picture with an admixture of white light.

SOUND

For all aspects of camcorder sound, see **Chapter 11, Location Sound**.

POWER SUPPLIES

Portable video equipment runs off rechargeable batteries. Chargers double as power converters, so you can run equipment indefinitely from an AC wall outlet. *Rechargeable batteries* seldom run equipment as long as you want, especially if incorrectly charged. Manufacturers' literature abounds with optimism, so estimate generously how many batteries you should take on location. Work each battery to its useable limit and then completely recharge, expecting it to take between 6 and 10 hours. Read manuals carefully in relation to conserving battery life, as wrong handling can shorten a battery's memory.

Buying or renting a large-capacity battery belt would seem to solve the dying battery problem, but many camcorders only work with batteries of a particular interior resistance. Sensing it's in bed with a foreigner, the camcorder will shut down automatically. Never assume anything will work unless confirmed by manufacturer's literature or reliable experience. This you can often find via the Internet. Locate user groups by Googling "groups" and your equipment's make, type, and model. Enthusiasts are often generous with their help and experience.

CAMERA SUPPORT SYSTEMS

TRIPOD AND ACCESSORIES

There's cold comfort here for the underfunded. The budget *tripod* and *tilt head* are a dismal substitute for the real deal. They may work fine for static shots, but try to pan or tilt and wobbly movements reveal why professionals use heavy tripods and hydraulically damped tilt heads. You can improve any camera movement by shooting with a wide-angle lens. Turning on the *image stabilization* may smooth your movements, but believe nothing until you've tested it.

A *baby legs tripod* is a very short one used for low-angle shots, and a *high hat* is a hat-shaped support for placing the camcorder on the ground or other solid surface. A serviceable alternative is a sandbag, which you pat into shape to allow a degree of angling.

A *spreader* or *spider* is a folding three-arm bracket that goes under the spike legs of a professional tripod (Figure 9-8). You lock the legs to the spreader so they don't splay and collapse. A spreader also guards against scratching or denting a

FIGURE 9-8

Vinten® tripod and spreader. (Photo courtesy of Vinten, a Vitec Group brand.)

floor and lets you pick up the camcorder and tripod as one unit so you can plunk it down rapidly elsewhere.

PAN/TILT HEAD SETUP

At each new setup, check the spirit-level bubble built into the *pan/tilt head* to see that it's level. If you don't, you'll pan only to find by the shot's end that horizontals are inclined. Better tripods allow quick leveling through a ball-and-cup system (Figure 9-9).

Adjust the head to give some drag when you pan or tilt to help smooth your movements. If your head permits, position the camcorder's center of gravity so you balance its weight equally over the pivoting point. If you don't, it may roll forward or back when you momentarily let go of the *pan handle*.

QUICK-RELEASE PLATE

This bolts to the base of the camera and in one movement mates instantly with the pan/tilt head (Figure 9-10). Later, if you switch to handheld operation, you can instantly free the camera by pulling a single lever. Take care that the camera is securely mounted; some quick releases are dangerously sensitive if your sleeve catches the lever.

FIGURE 9-9

Ball-mounted tripod heads make fast leveling easy.

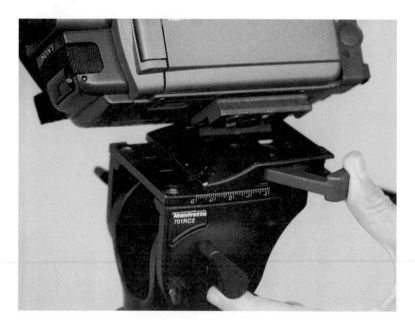

FIGURE 9-10

Quick-release plate screwed to underside of the camera allows it to instantly separate from the tripod head in one movement. This Manfrotto tripod head lets you center the camera's weight for balanced tilting.

MOBILE SUPPORT SYSTEMS

A practiced and well-coordinated human being makes an excellent mobile camcorder support. For a small-format camera during long-take shooting you may need a *shoulder brace* (Figure 9-11). For more ambitious work involving movement, try

FIGURE 9-11

VariZoom DV Traveler shoulder brace for comfortable extended handheld shots. (Photo courtesy of VariZoom Lens Controls.)

using one of the Glidecam (Figure 9-12; www.glidecam.com), VariZoom (www. varizoom.com), or Steadicam® (www.steadicam.com) systems. Heidi Ewing and Rachel Grady used one to good effect in *Jesus Camp* (2006, United States), their frightening film about the religious conditioning of young children. After grooming young children with a mixture of inspiration and fear, fundamentalist preachers whip them up in preparation for future leadership roles to "take back America for Christ." The gliding, swooping camera complements the kids' agitation as they reach a weeping, speaking-in-tongues fervor.

For a *dolly*, use a wheelchair with its tires a little underinflated. Professional dollies run on tracks like a miniature railroad. Your production must fully justify the outlay because they are heavy to transport, expensive to rent, and labor intensive to use. If your film is a historical reconstruction, for example, you may need all the equipment and expertise of a feature film crew. Before you get to this point, you can shoot perfectly good tracking shots:

- Backwards out of a car trunk or station wagon
- Forward or sideways off a tripod tied down inside a car with bungee cords and shooting through any window aperture
- Forward from a camcorder securely roped to the car hood with a towel under it to protect the car surface

FIGURE 9-12 —————————————————————————

Glidecam® Smooth Shooter. Capable of very sophisticated camera movements, such camera supports need a lot of practice. (Photo courtesy of Glidecam.)

Minimize movement and road vibration by using a wide-angle lens. You can also smooth a tracking shot during postproduction by applying a degree of slow motion.

MONITORS

Reliable color and framing come only with a properly adjusted field monitor, which can double as a jumbo viewfinder when you shoot off a tripod. This is your guarantee of color fidelity while shooting and a double-check on viewfinder framing, which can easily be misaligned. If you must make do with a domestic television, use the highest quality video inputs: digital, S, or component inputs are better than analog composite, where the signal is encoded and sent down a single wire. Monitors and televisions have abysmal sound quality, so feed the camcorder or DVD player sound into hi-fi headphones or into a stereo system during viewings. The improvement is truly dramatic.

CAMERA HANDLING

Novices tend to move the camera too readily and to overuse the zoom (it's called "firehosing"). Unless well judged, every camera movement becomes a problem during editing. Slow camera movements, especially uncertain ones or long, slow zooms, make editing difficult or even impossible. Shoot handheld material with a wide lens and using physical movement up to, or away from, the subject instead of zooms, which are always unsteady handheld.

  Develop zoom-and-compose skills using **Project 4-SP-11 Advanced Interview: Three Shot Sizes.**

Any material you shoot should be conceived in three boldly different sizes of image—wide shot (WS), medium shot (MS), and close shot (CS). For special moments, there's also big close-up (BCU). Only boldly different images of the same thing cut together well—two shots of a statue, for instance. If the size change is too small, a cut looks like an ugly jump cut. A good discipline while you're shooting a series of shots is to internally call each new composition and then go to it as quickly and naturally as possible. Handheld shooting should be a series of held compositions linked by efficient movements—each keyed, where possible, to movement within the frame, such as the movement of a character.

 Develop handheld camera skills with **Projects 4-SP-1 Skills Practice: Handheld Camera Steadiness, 4-SP-2 Skills Practice: Handheld Tracking on a Moving Subject,** and **4-SP-3 Skills Practice: Handheld Tracking Backward with Moving Subject.**

HANDHELD

Shooting handheld often means holding the camcorder in front of your face, so your steadiness deteriorates as your arms get tired. You may need a shoulder brace for long take work (Figure 9-11). Most camcorders incorporate image stabilization technology that somewhat compensates for unsteadiness, but this can introduce a weird movement lag.

Practice all the major controls until your fingers automatically find everything that matters—sound level, exposure, focus, zoom, and so on. Every camcorder you ever use will have limitations, so practice your instrument until you can always get professionally respectable results.

WHEN TO USE A TRIPOD

When deciding whether to use a tripod or go handheld, simply ask yourself what experience you want the audience to have. At a young children's birthday party, you'd get among the kids with a handheld camera, because this height and viewpoint augment their perception of themselves. The point of view of an uncle standing apart would be more grounded and best taken from a tripod, as would the kind of interview you see in Figure 9-13 where Nancy Schiesari is directing *Tattooed Under Fire* (a work in progress for a KLRU/ITVS production).

Sometimes your subject calls for complete mobility, so you sacrifice some stability for nimbleness. When the audience sees the need for compromise, it can well accept it. Other times, you want to use a telephoto lens and can only do so from a tripod mounted camera.

The worst misuse of a handheld camera is for wide shots of buildings or landscapes. Our perception of such things, unless we are inebriated or suffering an earthquake, is of things solid and secure, so common sense dictates that you place the camera on a stable support.

FOCUSING

Finding focus while the camera is running is an accepted part of filming actuality. To focus:

➤ Zoom in close
➤ Run focus back and forth to find its sharpest setting
➤ Zoom back to the size of shot you want

FIGURE 9-13

Typical setup using tripod-mounted camera for off-axis interviewing in *Tattooed Under Fire*. (Photo by Rebecca Adams, courtesy of Nancy Schiesari.)

VIEWFINDER AND MOVEMENTS

Rehearse with the recordist where your edges of frame are going to be in different sized shots. Once the camera is running, *run your eye periodically around the edges of your composition*. You want to assess your composition as a whole, not simply put your subject in the crosshairs like a rifleman. You also want to detect microphone or other intrusions straight away. Watch for telltale shadows (of the microphone, for instance). When you intend panning or tilting the camera to a new composition, momentarily open your closed eye to check where you mean to go, and then make the movement. When you are about to make a strong camera move, try to flash a hand or facial warning so you don't catch the recordist by surprise. He or she should constantly be checking your movements as well as those by the subject.

ERROR RECOVERY

If you under- or overshoot and alight on an incorrect framing, hold the erroneous composition for a few seconds and then imperceptibly "creep" the frame to its correct proportions. To acknowledge error by recovering too quickly makes the audience feel insecure.

Your composition will be better once you've done **Project 1-AP-4 Analyze Picture Composition.**

WALKING A CAMERA HANDHELD

When making a handheld tracking shot:

➤ Bend your knees a little so you glide rather than bob up and down.
➤ Turn your feet a little outward, duck fashion, and put your feet down in a straight line so you don't sway from side to side.
➤ Draw (not lift) each foot over the floor surface so you can:
    ↪ Make an imperceptible weight transfer from foot to foot, rather than stomping.
    ↪ Feel any bump or stair before having to deal with it.
➤ Use the camerawork projects listed earlier in this chapter to develop your skills

Here's how to develop the camera operator's Groucho Marx gliding walk:

➤ Pin 12 feet or more of string horizontally a few inches below your head height so you must flex your knees and lower your center of gravity to walk beneath its length.
➤ Practice moving along its length without a camera, until your body has learned how to glide in a straight line. With no swaying or bobbing, keep

your scalp just brushing the underside of the line. Note how much you've modified your habitual walk in order to achieve true straight-line travel.

➢ For an extra challenge, add low floor bumps.

➢ Now do it while the camera is running and rate your performance. Walking beside a brick wall at 2-foot distance gives a really revealing reference for steadiness.

BODY MECHANICS

Whatever camera movement you make, always try to:

➢ Position yourself when panning so you turn from an uncomfortable to a comfortable holding position.

➢ Stop in a position that allows you to move smoothly onward to the next composition.

➢ If you must kneel, sink on one knee only, or you won't be able to rise without jerking the camera.

➢ If you sit down, place one or both feet under you so you can rise without rolling forward.

EQUIPMENT CHECKOUT

Whoever checks out equipment should always assemble and test it before leaving its checkout point. Make "test and test again" your true religion. Leave nothing to chance. Make lists, then lists of lists. Pray.

GOLDEN RULE #1: BE PREPARED FOR THE WORST

Optimism and filmmaking are bad bedfellows. One blithe optimist left the sound tapes of a feature film in his car trunk overnight. The car happened to be stolen, and there being no copies, a vast amount of work was transformed instantly into so much silent footage. Imagination expended darkly at predicting the worst makes you carry spares, special tools, emergency information, first-aid kits, and three kinds of diarrhea medicine. A pessimist never tempts fate and, constantly foreseeing the worst, is tranquilly productive compared with your average optimist.

GOLDEN RULE #2: TEST IT FIRST

Whoever checks out equipment should arrive early and assemble and test every piece there and then. Nobody should ever assume that because the equipment is coming from a reputable company, everything will be all right. Murphy is waiting to get you. (Murphy's Law: "Everything that can go wrong will go wrong.") Expect him to lurk inside everything that should fit together, slide, turn, lock, roll, light up, make a noise, or work in silence. The whole Murphy clan lurks in every wire, plug, box, lens, battery, and alarm clock. Make no mistake; they mean to ruin you.

GOING FURTHER

For tips on scouting locations, see **Chapter 24, Preparing to Direct**; for more on lenses and their use, see **Chapter 25, Optics**; for more on camera equipment and camera supports, see **Chapter 26, Advanced Cameras and Camera Equipment**; and for books on camera usage and film techniques, see:

Artis, Anthony Q. *The Shut Up and Shoot Guide: A Down and Dirty DV Production*. Boston: Focal Press, 2007.

Ascher, Steven and Edward Pincus. *The Filmmaker's Handbook, Completely Revised and Updated*. New York: Plume Books, 2007.

Bernard, Sheila Curran. *Documentary Storytelling: Making Stronger and More Dramatic Nonfiction Films*. Boston: Focal Press, 2007.

Detmers, Fred, Ed. *American Cinematographer Handbook*. Hollywood: American Society of Cinematographers, 2004.

Groticelli, Michael, Ed. *American Cinematographer Video Manual*. Hollywood: American Cinematographer, 2004.

Hurbis-Cherrier, Mick. *Voice and Vision: A Creative Approach to Narrative Film and DV Production*. Boston: Focal Press, 2007.

CHAPTER 10

LIGHTING

Comprehensive lighting instructions are beyond the scope of this book, but you will need some basic points. In the notes for **Project 1-AP-3 Analyze Lighting** (in the Appendix) you'll find a brief illustrated description of lighting terms. Later in this chapter you will find a simple and reliable setup that can get you through a lot. Shooting in black and white requires great skill to give your imagery dimension, space, and textures, but color greatly simplifies the task by separating tones by hue. This means you need less elaborate lighting strategies to get pleasing results. Modern video cameras also make it easy to work in low light situations. The technology is on your side.

LIGHTING AND SPONTANEITY

Lighting in fiction films pays little attention to actors' comfort, since it's their job to adapt. Adding lighting to documentaries, however, risks making some participants self-conscious or even physically uncomfortable. Lights compromise some people's sense of normality, but others feel liberated by it. For boxers, actors, or conjurors, for instance, lighting confers an exciting sense of occasion and recognition. If somebody puts you on the public screen, you matter.

  Learn to assess lighting effects using **Project 1-AP-3 Analyze Lighting** (in the Appendix; this project also has notes, definitions, and illustrations).

The best way to learn about lighting is by learning to analyze its effects (see project box). You can study either fiction or documentary films. Include those shot by available light, as they show the kind of deficiencies that lit films labor to rectify.

WHY YOU MAY NEED IT

Digital camcorders can register good images by candlelight, so you would think lighting is unnecessary; however:

- An interior lit by daylight has bright highlight areas and impossibly dark shadow areas. (*Problem*: Contrast ratio of key to fill light is too high. *Solution*: Cut highlight illumination—difficult with sunlight—or boost shadow area lighting.)

- An interior lit by daylight with pools of artificial light does strange things to skin hues when people move around. (*Problem:* They are passing through mixed color temperature lighting. *Solution*: See previous chapter's advice on shooting under mixed color temperatures. Essentially, you filter one source to make it consistent with others.)

- An exterior where you must shoot in heavy shadow has a sunlit background that burns out. (*Problem*: A huge contrast ratio between sunlit and shadow areas. *Solution*: Use lighting or reflectors to raise light level in shadow area, or angle camera differently to incorporate a less "hot" background.)

 Film and video imaging systems reveal variations in light levels and color temperatures that the eye evens out. Documentary lighting often aims to remedy the lighting for screen images so they appear as the human eye would see them.

To produce the look of normality, you must rebalance light levels so that an evening interior shot appears as the eye sees it in life. Exposure or focus limitations may preclude using a naturally low overall light level because you'd have to work at a large lens aperture and thus a very reduced depth of field (DOF). This would require very precise focusing—difficult or impossible when camera and subject are on the move. By adding more overall light, you can now use a smaller lens aperture, get a greater depth of field, and have fewer focusing problems.

Consider using supplementary lighting when:

- The shadow area is too dark to get an exposure or detail where you need it.

- A scene or an object does not look its best under available light.

- Available light is too contrasty, creating "hot" (overbright) highlights and impenetrably murky shadow areas. See *lighting ratio* in box on the opposite page.

- You are working under mixed color temperature sources; that is, light sources having a mix of color biases.

AVOIDING THE OVERBRIGHT BACKGROUND

In small, light-colored spaces, the amount of light thrown back by the walls can overpower that reflected by your subjects. This at its worst gives dark humanoid outlines against a blinding white background. The low-end camcorder, having circuitry that adjusts for the majority of the image, is a prime offender. Color quality and definition all suffer.

The solution is to separate or "cheat" furniture and subjects away from walls so you can raise lighting on the foreground and lower it on background walls. Do this by sending light down from instruments raised high; this keeps light off the background and casts shadows low and out of sight.

 When your image lacks detail in shadow areas or has burnt-out highlights, you have an unmanageably high *lighting ratio*—say, 10:1. To fit the scene's range of brightnesses within your recording medium's *latitude*, either lower the highlight illumination or boost shadow area illumination with *fill light*.

CURING CONTRAST PROBLEMS

The need to reduce contrast—shadow areas too dark, highlight areas burning out—usually requires you to raise light levels in the shadow areas. You can provide fill light with a soft-light instrument or by *bouncing* light off a white card, silver reflector, white walls, or ceiling. Once you lower the lighting ratio to the range your camcorder can handle, your screen reproduces the picture you want—now with detail in both highlight and deep shadow areas, detail that would have been lost without carefully placed extra light.

HARDWARE

LIGHT QUALITY AND LIGHTING INSTRUMENTS

Figure 10-1 shows the kind of portable lighting kit that documentarians use. You can do acceptable interior work using only a 750-watt quartz *soft light*. Light is *diffused* or *soft* when it creates soft-edged shadows or no shadows at all. Diffused light has the same effect as scattered light arriving from a broad source. It throws shadows so soft that they are hardly noticeable. You can produce soft light from one of the spotlights on stands (see Figure 10-1) by shining its output through a large square of diffusing silk or fiberglass or by bouncing its light off an aluminized umbrella or a white wall or ceiling.

Open-face quartz lamps are light and compact for travel. Quartz bulbs have a long life and remain stable in color temperature, and their bulbs are small enough to provide fairly hard light. Their disadvantage is that light pours uncontrollably in every direction, making lighting a rather rudimentary exercise unless you have *barn doors* (adjustable flaps at the sides, top, and bottom, as shown in Figure 10-1) to stop light spilling in unwanted directions. If you are on a stringent budget, you can find useable, low-cost quartz worklights at hardware stores that function well to create bounce-light sources.

FIGURE 10-1 ————————————————————————————

Lowel® DV Creator lighting kit. (Image courtesy of Lowel-Light mfg, Inc.)

Light becomes *hard* or *specular* when it projects hard-edged shadows (Figure 10-2). Paradoxically, a candle, although of low power, creates hard light because its effective light source is small and it casts distinct, hard-edged shadows. If you want the kind of hard light associated with sunlight, you will need a *focusing lamp* or *spotlight* (Figures 10-3).

Safety warning: Lights that use quartz bulbs run very, very hot and involve safety issues:

➤ Let lamps cool before disassembling them after shooting.

➤ Use a wadded tissue to hold quartz bulbs. Never touch them; oil in your skin bakes into the quartz envelope, causing the bulb to discolor or even explode when it is turned on the next time.

FIGURE 10-2

The same object under soft light and hard or specular light.

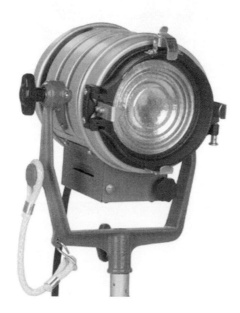

FIGURE 10-3

Molequartz® 650-watt Tweenie II Solarspot Fresnel spot lamp. (Courtesy of Mole-Richardson Co.)

➤ Never switch on an open-face lamp when someone is in range. This is when bulbs most often explode.
➤ Never let rain get to hot bulbs. Sudden cooling by water spots makes them explode.

LIGHT-EMITTING DIODES (LEDS)

Banks of LEDs are now quite powerful (Figure 10-4), and some are adjustable for color temperature or for changing light quantities without losing color temperature. They draw very little current, create no heat, and are safe and easy to use. You can carry a circle around the lens (Figure 10-5) for traveling shots

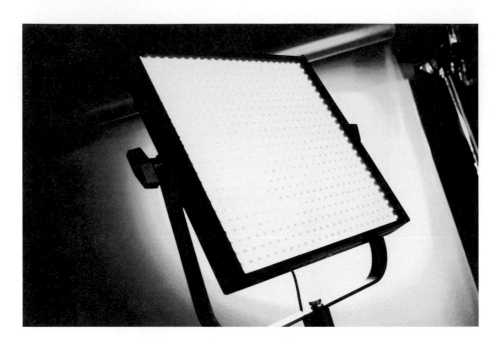

FIGURE 10-4

A 1 × 1 Litepanels™ LED bank. (Photo courtesy of Litepanels, Inc.)

FIGURE 10-5

The Litepanels™ Ringlite™ Mini, with LEDs circling a camera lens. (Photo courtesy of Litepanels, Inc.)

FIGURE 10-6

The Litepanels™ LP Micro LED panel on top of a camera. (Photo courtesy of Litepanels, Inc.)

that require some fill light. The Litepanels™ LP Micro panel clips to the top of the camera and is particularly useful for fill light while shooting inside a car (Figure 10-6; www.litepanels.com), but not all participants will take being lit in this way in their stride.

FLUORESCENTS

Though all fluorescents produce a broken spectrum, you can get tubes and compact fluorescent lamps (CFLs) from the hardware store that are marked with an approximate Kelvin temperature: warm white (3000°K or less), white or bright white (3500°K), cool white (4000°K), or daylight (upward of 5000°K).

Kino Flo produces banks of fill lights that give good light output, draw comparatively little current, and create minimal heat (Figure 10-7; www.kinoflo.com). Balanced to give daylight or tungsten color temperatures, they come on immediately, are silent (unlike the ballasts in most fixtures), and are even dimmable.

POWER REQUIREMENTS

The amount and type of lighting you will need depend on the size and reflectivity of the location space, how much available light you have (and its color

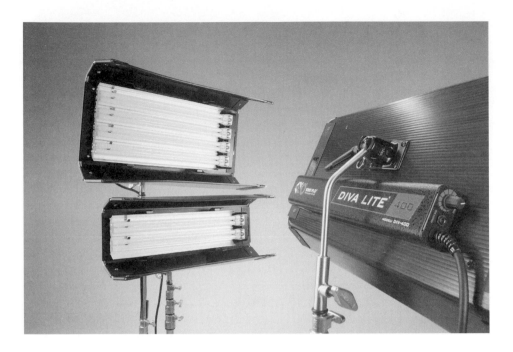

FIGURE 10-7——

Kino Flo® Diva-Lite 400 and 200 fluorescent banks produce cool soft light. (Photo Courtesy of Kino Flo, Inc.)

temperature), and what kind of lighting look you are aiming for. When in doubt, shoot digital photos or sample footage and view them on a good screen.

Both LED and fluorescent lamps are energy efficient and provide good soft-light output with little heat. For a harder, more *specular* (hard-edged, shadow-producing) light you'll need tungsten spotlamps or quartz movie lights. These are power hungry, run hot, and consume anywhere between 500 and 2000 watts each. A 2-kilowatt (2000 watts) soft light run from a 110-volt supply and consumes 19 amps (9 amps, if you are in a 220-volt-supply country). The basic North American domestic household circuit (110 volts at 15 amps) cannot power a 2-kW lamp, so you must locate a supply of 20 amps or better.

CALCULATING CONSUMPTION

To calculate power consumption in *amps* (rate of flow), divide your total desired *watts* (amount of energy consumption) by the *volts* (pressure) of the supply voltage. Here's how to calculate the unknown third factor when you have two that are known. I've assumed you are using a 110-volt working supply. To calculate:

Amperes (A): $W \div V = A$ (Example: $2000\,W \div 110\,V = 18.18\,A$)

Watts (W): $A \times V = W$ (Example: $25\,A \times 110\,V = 2750\,W$)

Volts (V): $W \div A = V$ (Example: $4000\,W \div 36.36\,A = 110\,V$)

When scouting locations for electrical supply, keep high current requirements in mind. Wherever you can, aim to spread heavy amperage loads over multiple circuits. Locate house fuse or breaker boxes, which will contain fuses or breakers for each circuit rated as 15 A, 20 A, 50 A, and so on. By killing one circuit at a time and mapping electrical outlets belonging to each circuit, you can plan to spread the electrical load; that is, you can power your lights from several circuits rather than overloading one. Make a note to bring the necessary lengths of heavy-duty extension cords.

An expensive mistake is to tap into a 220-V supply and blow one's lamps. Arm yourself with an inexpensive little multimeter (combining voltage, resistance, and current) from an electronics store so you can check supply voltages. Use it to measure voltages for any heavy-consumption lamp powered from a long extension cord. A lowered voltage can markedly lower color temperatures.

At each location, determine whether an appliance, such as a refrigerator or air conditioner, is going to kick in during shooting and trigger a circuit overload or make a noise that intrudes on the sound track. If you turn off a refrigerator while shooting, remember to turn it back on before you leave, or face having to replace the fridge contents. A recommended reminder is to leave your car keys in the fridge.

DEFINING SHADOWS: HARD AND SOFT LIGHT

Hard light, as we said earlier, casts hard-edged shadows, while a *soft light* source provides soft edges or virtually no shadows. Sunlight and the light of a candle, although of wildly different strengths, each cast hard-edged shadows and count as hard-light sources. Sunlight coming through a cloud layer, however, is light coming from the effectively large source and becomes a soft-light source. This can produce virtually shadowless light.

BASIC LIGHTING METHODOLOGY

ADDING TO A BASE AND USING A KEY LIGHT

In documentary you often have to work fast, so there is a simple and reliable solution to lighting interiors. Called *adding to a base*, it means first providing enough ambient soft light for an exposure, then adding some modeling by using a harder light source as a shadow-producing key. Here's what to do:

- **Baselight**—If the base light is insufficient, provide your own by using a soft light or by bouncing hard light off a reflective wall or ceiling. This provides a good overall illumination but used alone will give a rather dull and *flat* (that is, comparatively shadowless) look. This may be just right for some dull, flat situations (hospital, classroom, office, etc.).

- **Key light**—The light providing highlights and casting shadows is the key light. From its pattern of light and shadow, the audience infers time of day, mood, and even time of year. When you add key light it must be *motivated*; that is, it must appear to come from a logical source. In a bedroom scene,

FIGURE 10-8

A *practical* is part of the scene but usually contributes little to its actual lighting.

> for instance, you would position the key low and out of frame to produce the characteristic shadow pattern cast by a bedside lamp. For a warehouse scene lit by a bare overhead bulb hanging into the frame, the additional key light would have to come from above. In a pathology lab where the source is a light table, the key would have to strike the subject from a low angle. Using multiple key lights is a skilled business and without a lot of practice can lead to the dread trademark of amateur lighting—ugly, multiple shadows. When in doubt, keep it simple.

- **Cheating**—You can substantially *cheat* (creatively adjust) the angle of the key for convenience, for artistic effect, and for minimizing shadows on the background, providing you stay within the bounds of what looks credible. You can also cheat furniture and participants away from walls, so shadows are projected not on the walls but low and out of sight. To help with framing, you can cheat people closer together than looks normal in life—always providing you don't compromise your participants' sense of normality.

- **Practicals**—Lamps that appear in the picture are called *practicals*, but they seldom function to provide any of the lighting (Figure 10-8). Adjust a table lamp's output so there is enough to register as a light but not so much that you burn out that portion of the frame. You can seldom use a dimmer to lower a practical's output, as the tungsten filament turns very red. Instead, cut the light output by putting layers of paper or neutral-density (ND) filter around the inside of its shade.

FIGURE 10-9

A flat-lit subject and the same subject side-lit. (Photos by Dirk Matthews.)

KEY LIGHT DIRECTION AND BACKLIGHTING

Folklore about taking photos with your back to the sun suggests that light is best falling on the subject from the camera direction, but this ensures a minimum of shadow area and removes evidence of the subject's third dimension—depth. Interesting lighting effects on the human face begin when the key light's angle of throw is to the side of the subject or even relatively behind it (Figure 10-9). When shooting by available light, you may be able to light your participants more interestingly simply by reorienting the proposed action in relation to the ambient lighting or by altering the camera placement.

Backlighting creates a rim of light that helps separate subject from background and gives highlights and texture to hair (Figure 10-10). Achieving subject/background separation is important in black-and-white photography but less so in color, where varying hues help define and separate the different planes of a composition.

THREE-POINT LIGHTING

Three-point lighting is a more advanced setup that is ideal for lit interviews. See **Project 1-AP-3 Analyze Lighting** (in the Appendix) for a study project with notes, diagrams, and frames from a documentary to illustrate the different lighting approaches.

LIGHTING TESTS AND REHEARSALS

- *Lighting tests*—The only way to assess film lighting is to shoot test shots with a digital stills camera—preferably in the actual locations—and critique your results. If lighting is at all elaborate, a lighting rehearsal using a digital

FIGURE 10-10

Backlighting helps define a subject's outline and gives texture to hair.

stills camera can obviate embarrassingly lengthy location lighting sessions—
or worse, costly electrical failures.

- *Backgrounds*—Aim to shoot when possible against dark or book-covered
  walls. These absorb the light that would otherwise overpower light reflecting off your subjects. When this is impossible, keep light off the background walls, as we have said, by: (1) angling light; (2) using barn doors
  on your light sources to keep illumination off the subjects' backgrounds;
  and (3) cheating participants away from walls so you can better control
  shadow and background illumination problems. Moving them away also
  distances them from sound-reflective surfaces and reduces sound reverberation problems.

GOING FURTHER

Most of what's written about lighting, naturally enough, concerns the fictional
arena where the director of photography (DP) has full control. It's here, though,

that you'll learn the basic principles and practice. Documentary DPs accomplish what they can according to circumstances.

Box, Harry. *The Set Lighting Technician's Handbook: Film Lighting Equipment, Practice, and Electrical Distribution*, 3rd ed. Boston: Focal Press, 2003.

Carlson, Verne and Sylvia Carlson. *Professional Lighting Handbook*, 4th ed. Boston: Focal Press, 1993.

Ferncase, Richard K. *Film and Video Lighting Terms and Concepts*. Boston: Focal Press, 1995.

Fitt, Brian and Joe Thornley. *A–Z of Lighting Technology*, 2nd ed. Boston: Focal Press, 2001.

Gloman, Chuck and Tom LeTourneau. *Placing Shadows: Lighting Techniques of Video Production*, 3rd ed. Boston: Focal Press, 2005.

Millerson, Gerald. *Lighting for TV and Film*, 3rd ed. Boston: Focal Press, 1999.

Viera, Dave and Maria Viera. *Lighting for Film and Electronic Cinematography*, 2nd ed. Belmont, CA: Wadsworth, 2004.

CHAPTER 11

LOCATION SOUND

Picture gives information, but sound brings emotion, so your documentary needs a bold sound design and good, clean location sound as a foundation. Some sound theory and knowledge of basic equipment, as well as practice and a critical ear, will help you achieve this.

Unfortunately for sound recordists, documentary film shoots can't always accommodate their needs. In transparent filmmaking, microphones must stay out of sight and recordists adapt as best they can to the needs of the scene. The director can help by stabilizing speakers during a dialogue sequence or by concealing a useful microphone in that nice potted plant on the dining room table. Most of all, he or she can help by appreciating what is involved in sound acquisition and the pain recordists suffer when they can't always turn in first-rate work.

DIALOGUE COMPONENTS AND HOW SOUND BEHAVES

Imagine hitting a bunch of billiard balls; some go into the intended pocket, others ricochet off the cushions before finding their way into pockets. This illustrates the behavior of sound when you record a voice in a moderately sound-reflective room. The voice is *signal* and what accompanies it is *reflected* or *reverberant sound* (Figure 11-1). That is, some of the voice goes straight to the microphone, but some of it radiates outward and bounces off the floor, ceiling, walls, and that table in front of the speaker before reaching the mike. Reverb sound, making a longer journey, arrives fractionally later. Direct and reverb sound then combine at the microphone to muddy the clarity of the original. People think, "Oh, let's fix it in the sound mix," but once combined, sounds are no more separable than the eggs in an omelet.

In Figure 11-1, a person sits in a room talking to camera. The microphone is picking up not just signal and reverb but also background *presence* or *ambient* sound. Also called *atmosphere*, it might include distant traffic, the hum of a refrigerator, a dog barking, or in summer the whir of air conditioning. Ideal dialogue

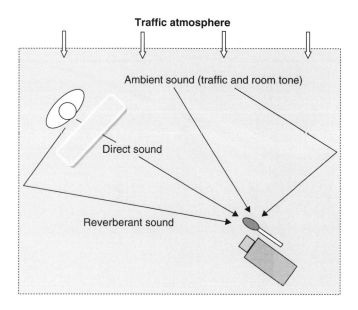

Traffic atmosphere

Ambient sound (traffic and room tone)

Direct sound

Reverberant sound

FIGURE 11-1 ————————————————————————————

Diagram representing a film interview and the three types of sound present in any recording situation: direct, reverberant, and ambient.

recordings have lots of signal (what you want) and very little noise (everything else). The world is not ideal for sound recordists, but there's always something you can do to improve matters. That mike in Figure 11-1 could go a lot closer to the speaker. Moving it won't affect ambience or reverb levels much, but it will dramatically raise the direct signal level in relation to them. For this reason, avoid using a deck mike (one mounted on the camera) if you can work with a partner using a *boom* or *fishpole* to get the mike in close (Figure 11-2). Reasons to abandon the deck mike are:

- It's nearly always too far away from source sounds.
- It points only along the camera axis when important sound in a discussion, say, will often come from off-axis.
- It's nicely placed to pick up the whine of the zoom motor and the bumping sounds of your hands fumbling for the camcorder controls.

 Location sound always has three main elements: (1) signal, (2) reverberation, and (3) ambience. The recordist tries to maximize signal while minimizing reverb and ambience. These can always be added later, but not subtracted.

We'll look at boom handling techniques a little later.

On-axis sound (also called *on-mike* sound) is sound arriving down the mike's most receptive axis. *Off-axis* or *off-mike* sound arrives from other axes.

FIGURE 11-2

A microphone on a fishpole can reach over people and equipment and get close to the sound source. Carbon-fiber models are the lightest. (Photo courtesy of K-TEK.)

Directional mikes favor on-axis sound and discriminate against that arriving off-axis. Most of the reverb and ambience in Figure 11-1 arrives off-axis, so the right mike can discriminate against them.

Sound perspective is the aural sensation of changing distances when a sound source (person, helicopter, horse) moves around.

A *resonant* space is one that has a note to which the room spontaneously resonates. You'll know this from singing in your shower and finding a frequency at which the room starts ringing and augmenting your voice. Resonances and sound reflectivity are bad news to sound recordists, as are noisy locations.

SOUND ENVIRONMENTS AND SIGNAL-TO-NOISE (S:N) RATIO

If you record someone speaking in a large, sound-insulated, carpeted room with heavy drapery, then you will have an excellent signal-to-noise ratio. Record that person in a medium-sized bathroom, with tiled

 Recordists test the acoustics of any recording space on entering by making a single loud hand clap and then listening critically to its aftermath. The space is either *live* (echoey) or *dead* (sound absorbent). The latter is nearly always preferable.

walls and floor and no soft furnishings, and you'll have a dreadful S:N ratio. In postproduction, you can always add atmosphere or reverb to a clean recording, but only under special circumstances can you subtract noise commingled with signal.

Speech-based filmmaking, therefore, calls for careful recording. Recordists aim to:

➤ Choose the microphone with the best pickup pattern for the circumstances.

➤ Get a high ratio of signal to noise by placing each mike as close as practicable to its intended signal (the speaker).

➤ Get sound that is *on mike*—that is, with the mike's most receptive axis pointing at the sound source.

The improvised nature of many documentary conditions often confounds these aims. Imagine you're filming your main character working out at a noisy health club, and this is where he chooses to tell you what's breaking his heart. Or he embarks on something just as important in a rattly truck cab. When your subjects are restless teenagers, staying on-axis gets difficult. Because the camera must have different shots to cover a sequence, the recordist must make fast mike position changes. The recordist must either adapt or appear momentarily onscreen with that deer-in-the-headlights expression.

Once you edit sound together, inequities become glaringly apparent. Adjusting playback levels can even out a speaker's voice level from angle to angle, but that leaves you with varying ambience levels at each sound cut. In postproduction, you can ameliorate these by loading up the quieter tracks with ambience, but the net result is, of course, more noise.

During production, reduce reverb by:

➤ Getting the mike as close to the source as possible, to optimize S:N ratio.

➤ Laying carpet or blankets on hard, sound-reflective surfaces that are out of camera sight; to fully dampen live (sound-reflective) surfaces, blankets must hang several inches away from the wall, not against it.

SOUND AND THE CAMCORDER

BALANCED AND UNBALANCED INPUTS

Professional mikes use *balanced line* cables with sturdy XLR connectors that lock into their sockets, and they use noise-canceling three-wire connections between mike and recorder (Figure 11-3). With these you can use 10- to 20-foot or longer microphone cables without picking up electrical interference. Consumer equipment uses the two-wire or *unbalanced* sound connections, easily identifiable by their two-contact jack plugs (Figure 11-4). These allow only short cable runs before noise and interference set in. Also, because mini-jack sockets are attached to camcorder circuit boards, a single yank on the cord can do

FIGURE 11-3

XLR plug on three-wire balanced cable and the locking socket it goes into.

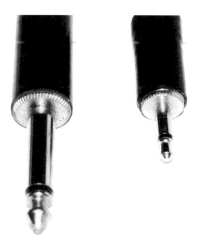

FIGURE 11-4

Phone jack and mini-jack plugs. Two-connector unbalanced lines like these tend to pick up hum and other electrical interference.

untold damage. Even in kinder circumstances, jack sockets quickly become unreliable unless you provide cable *strain relief*. This means anchoring the headphone or mike cable to the camera body so handling stresses do not reach the plug or its socket (Figure 11-5).

FIGURE 11-5

How a strain-relief measure protects a plug and its socket from the inevitable tugs on the cable.

CHOOSING MANUAL OR AUTOMATIC SOUND LEVEL

Whenever possible, set sound levels manually. This means, during a test, lowering the recording level as it registers on the volume unit (VU) meter or bar graph until no peak sound surpasses, say, –6 decibels. Check what your camcorder manual recommends and make test recordings of loud *transient* sounds such as hand claps or door slams to pinpoint the threshold where distortion sets in.

VOLUME UNIT (VU) METERS

In the typical stereo VU meters in Figure 11-6, the numbers run counterintuitively from minus to plus quantities. Low sound levels register as high minus decibel (dB) numbers. Then as sound levels rise, the safe or *sound saturation* point peaks at 0 dB. Beyond that you enter the red or danger zone of +dB levels where distortion can ruin the recording. Here beginneth wailing and gnashing of teeth.

AVERAGING AND PEAKING

Analog sound—the precursor to digital recording—was quite forgiving during overloads, but peaks beyond 0 dB in digital recording usually distort badly. Be aware that unless your equipment has a *peak reading meter*, your VU meter is *averaging* incoming signals and thus hiding the awful truth from the unsuspecting

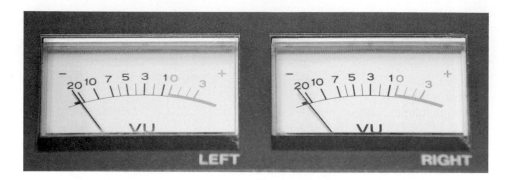

FIGURE 11-6

Typical sound volume unit (VU) meter layout. Camcorders usually supply a moving bar graph in the viewfinder.

FIGURE 11-7

Two-channel input box that can handle either microphones or amplifier (line) input. (Photo courtesy of BeachTek, Inc.)

user. By the time you've seen the peak red light come on, the damage is done. To guard against this, set levels for averaging meters to peak at –6 dB.

AUTOMATIC LEVEL

Using automatic sound-level spares you distortion, but during long gaps in an oral memoir, for example, the recording level may *hunt*—that is, record at louder and louder levels until your subject speaks again. The reason is that electronic circuitry has zero intelligence and does its job strictly according to level. Use automatic level whenever you are in a chaotic situation with soft sound punctuated by, say, door slams, screaming revelers, or other loud and transient peaks.

MICROPHONE INPUT BOXES

If your camcorder has a single mini-jack mike input, add one of the excellent proprietary input boxes (Figure 11-7). Because it is clamped under the camera body, the box and its beefy XLR sockets safely absorb the inevitable cable-handling stresses. Now you can plug in two balanced-line microphones and even adjust each for level. As the illustration shows, the box's output plugs into the camcorder mike input using a stereo (three-connector) mini-plug on a pigtail lead. Be aware that condenser microphones—in particular, shotgun mikes—either run on inbuilt batteries or draw current from *phantom power* supplied by some (but by no means all) camcorders and input adapter boxes. Phantom power is not as exciting it sounds. It's a tiny current at 48 volts fed to the mike through two legs of its three-wire cable.

STEREO

Virtually all camcorders have stereo (two-track) recording capability and can accommodate two inputs. If yours makes recordings that are well separated, then you can record, say, two people each wearing a lavalier (chest) microphone and end up with a clean, totally separate track for each. You might, for instance, use a telephone attachment to record a soldier speaking by phone from the Middle East in one channel and in the other his mother speaking into the phone in her front room. Being on separate tracks, you can adjust their levels in the sound mix.

 Don't assume you have two discrete camcorder sound channels until you've tested for channel separation. That is, record peak-level sounds on one channel and leave the other in silence. Play back the silent channel at high volume to be sure there is no recorded bleed-through. Reverse the procedure to test the other channel.

MICROPHONE HANDLING TECHNIQUES

LISTEN TO YOUR WORK

Whenever you shoot sound, monitor what you are recording through quality, ear-enclosing headphones (Figure 11-8). Not monitoring, or monitoring with a more stylish substitute like iPod® earbuds, will land you in trouble.

HANDLING THE FISHPOLE

Your best sound, as we've said, will come from using a directional mike angled on a fishpole. Position it above, below, or to one side of the frame line. Miking from above is preferable because a voice will then be louder than the speaker's footsteps and body movements. If this causes fishpole shadow problems, try coming in from the side of the frame. If all else fails, point the mike upward from below frame. This is least desirable because it privileges footsteps and body movements over voice levels.

WINDSCREENS AND SHOCK MOUNTS

Suspend your mike in a rubber *shock mount* to reduce the transmission of handling sounds to the mike. Figure 11-9 shows a common rubber-band model,

FIGURE 11-8

Videographer wearing ear-enclosing headphones—a necessity for proper sound monitoring. (Photo courtesy of Vinten, a Vitec Group brand.)

FIGURE 11-9

Two types of mike shock mount. The rubber-band type (left) is common but is likely to make sounds of its own. The K-TEK (right) is the more reliable design. (Photo courtesy of K-TEK.)

FIGURE 11-10 ——————————————————————————————————

Zeppelin type of microphone windscreen. (Photo courtesy of K-TEK.)

which I don't recommend, next to a more reliable design. Shield the mike from air-current interference, even indoors, with a *windscreen* (Figure 11-10). This is a rigid zeppelin wind guard, and to it you add a fuzzy fur mini-screen or windsock (Figure 11-11) to defeat outdoor air movement. Absent such shield-

 For an inexpensive but practical windsock, wind many layers of cheese-cloth around the mike and then pull a black tube sock over it to lower its medical associations.

ing, air currents shake the mike's diaphragm and produce earthquake quantities of wind rumble.

ACHIEVING ON-MIKE SOUND

Getting mikes close to participants without causing shadows takes coordination among recordist, camera operator, and director. Handheld sequences are

FIGURE 11-11 ————————————————————————————————————

Fuzzy fur mini-screen, or windsock, covering zeppelin. (Photo courtesy of K-TEK.)

the most challenging because the mike must not edge into the frame. Miking from a safe distance isn't an option because S:R ratios decline precipitously and you may wind up with extreme noise and intelligibility problems.

RELATIONSHIP OF RECORDIST TO CAMERA

Experienced, on-the-ball recordists constantly scan the subject, the likely edge of frame, and the camera operator for telling facial expressions or hand signals. These might signify, "Watch out, I'm going to swing in your direction," or "Back off—mike's edging into frame." Usually the recordist stands a little ahead and to the left of the camera, in the camera operator's left-eye sightline (Figure 11-12). The goal is to position the mike as close as possible to, and pointed at, each new speaker while staying just out of frame. Staying close to the sound axes of moving participants, yet keeping the mike from edging into frame, requires the recordist to predict who, between camera and participants, will move next and what direction they may take. With experience, camera and sound people learn to work in perfect balletic harmony—and even to exchange hand or eye signals during the take. It's a joy to watch.

Sometimes the recordist lifts the mike over the camera to allow the operator to pan left or back away from the subject. If a new sound axis calls for it, the

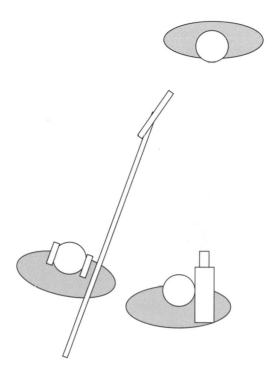

FIGURE 11-12

Diagram showing typical sound recordist's positioning during mobile shooting. (Also see photo in Chapter 9, Figure 9-13.)

recordist crosses the shooting axis behind the camera and positions the mike temporarily over the camera on the right (Figure 11-13). All the while the recordist tries to maintain eye contact with the camera operator—a choreography all to be managed in silence. Often the sound operator will lightly touch the camera operator's shoulder to ensure they don't collide or stumble over objects. Sometimes the director also uses touch to assist.

The ultimate challenge to the mobile documentary unit is a rapidly moving subject who whirls through a street market and then jumps into a taxi, all the while chatting to the camera. Keeping all this nicely framed on the screen and with no sign of the unit's frantic activity will stretch a crew to its limits, particularly when two extra people silently cram themselves and their equipment around a surprised taxi driver.

 Camera and sound subjects are often the same, but when they diverge, the alert recordist covers the sound subject until sound and camera subjects converge again.

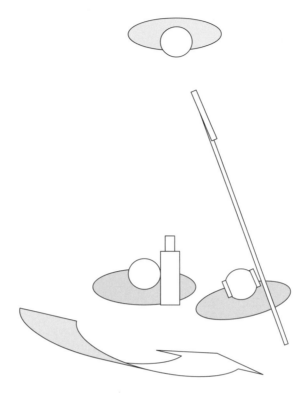

FIGURE 11-13

The recordist must sometimes cross behind the camera, mike still in place, to angle in from the right side of frame. The camera body may now block eyeline exchanges with the camera operator.

WHEN SOUND AND PICTURE SUBJECTS DIVERGE

In a group scene, the camera may dwell on someone's telling expression. Someone new starts speaking, so the mike cannot stay with the camera subject but must swing immediately toward the new sound subject (Figure 11-14). Mike placement can be:

- From either side of the frame, depending on which way speakers are facing.
- Above the frame, depending on sound needs and lighting (that is, shadow) considerations; absent shadow problems, miking from above is preferable.
- Below the frame when all else is impracticable.

RECORDIST AS SAFETY MONITOR

In a two-person crew when the camera must track backward, the recordist lightly touches the operator's back with her free hand to signal, "I'm here and I'm watching for your safety." This touch includes gentle steering—overzealous would rock the camera—so the operator clears furniture or doorways without looking around.

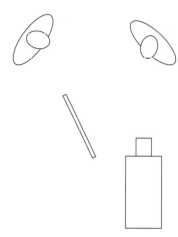

FIGURE 11-14

The camera shoots a reaction shot while sound covers the off-camera speaker. In everyday life, our eyes and ears often unconsciously separate like this.

It's quite marvelous to watch an experienced crew cover all eventualities with balletic precision and confidence. This is something you only get from much practice.

MICROPHONES

Film recording uses a variety of microphones made by Sennheiser, Schoeps, Audio Technica, and other manufacturers. With microphones, as with so much else, you get what you pay for. You also get better or worse performance depending on your knowledge of the strengths and weaknesses of various types of microphones. Your knowledge is a more powerful influence for good than the cost of the instrument. A friend who teaches sound even says, "There is no such thing as a bad microphone, only bad users."

POWER SUPPLIES

Many mikes require battery power, so carry backups and only use the alkaline variety. Other varieties run down and excrete a corrosive mess into the mike body. Some professional mikes require phantom power through a small voltage fed from the recorder via the mike cable. Many nonprofessional camcorders now supply it, but if a mike mysteriously refuses to function, then check the manual to see whether yours is not among them.

PICKUP PATTERNS

Inexpensive microphones, as we have said, don't necessarily do a poor job—you just have to use them judiciously. Most important is to know sound pickup

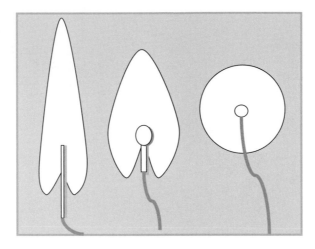

FIGURE 11-15 —————————————————————————————

Diagram indicating microphone pickup pattern differences among: (1) shotgun, (2) cardioid, and (3) omnidirectional mikes. A scientifically accurate polar pattern is shown in **Chapter 27, Location Sound.**

patterns for each type. The representation in Figure 11-15 of the pickup patterns of three different mikes indicates where, as you circle each type of mike, you'd expect to place a noise-emitting object (think of a cicada in mating mood!) to maintain an equal level recording. The omnidirectional mike is the simplest; it picks up sound equally from all around, so you'd place your cicada at the same distance all around it. To differing degrees the other mike types favor on-axis sound and discriminate that which is off axis. Here are some generalizations:

- *Omnidirectional mikes* give the most pleasing voice reproduction but tend to indiscriminately pick up unwanted sound reflected by surrounding surfaces.

- A *directional mike* (also called a *cardioid* because of its heart-shaped pickup pattern) helps cut down on off-axis reverberant and background noise. In practical terms this means that pointing the mike's axis at a speaker improves his S:N ratio.

The *hypercardioid* or *shotgun mike* (so-called due to its shape and menacing appearance; Figure 11-16) does the best job of discrimination. A favorite in documentary and electronic newsgathering (ENG) work, it is especially practical in noisy situations. Its drawback is a slight loss of sound warmth and fidelity. More than most mikes, it requires astute handling so it stays out of shot, doesn't cast shadows, and yet still points at the right speaker in a group. A BBC news crew using a shotgun mike in the jungle was astonished to find it had taken a prisoner during the Vietnam War. Many mikes have small switches that allow you to "roll off" (attenuate, reduce) a particular band of frequencies. A "lo-cut" is useful because it reduces traffic rumble during street dialogue scenes.

FIGURE 11-16————————————————————————————

Shure® SM89, an affordable shotgun microphone with two selectable low-cut frequencies. (Photo courtesy of Shure, Inc.)

FIGURE 11-17————————————————————————————

Wire looped under lavalier clip as strain protection for a delicate mike.

Use *lavalier* or lapel mikes (Figure 11-17) for interviews or speech recording in noisy surroundings. When clipping the mike in place, anchor its cord as the photo shows so as to leave a free loop under the mike. Then, if the cord is touched or yanked, handling noise or damage won't reach the mike. Participants wear these tiny omnidirectional mikes under upper clothing so they stay exceptionally close to the signal (speech) source. Place them at least a hand's breadth away from a speaker's chin or sound levels will vary too much when the speaker's head swivels.

Since you'll need one lavalier per speaker, multiple speakers require a location mixer (see Part 7: Advanced Production Issues, **Chapter 27, Advanced Location Sound**).

Body mikes are prone to picking up clothing rustles and body movements—especially when the user wears manmade fibers. These generate static electricity, which sounds thunderous. Ask participants to wear natural fibers, but if they don't, place adhesive tape between the mike and the offending surface. Lavaliers also excel at amplifying the intestinal activity that follows dining, and they love loose dentures in the elderly.

Lavalier mikes give lovely voice quality but lack all sense of *sound perspective*—the aural sensation of changing distances that we're so used to. Staying close to the speaker's mouth, they pick up little reverberant coloration and thus give no aural perspective changes even when a speaker is visibly on the move. You can emulate perspective changes later in the sound mix if you really need to.

WIRELESS MIKES

When they work, they're wonderful. Connect a lavalier mike to a personal radio transmitter, clip a small radio receiver to the camera, and, presto, everyone has complete mobility. Ah, but they have drawbacks. Like mobile telephones, even the most expensive may fade or pull in taxi radios. Be warned, too, that participants forget they are wearing them and may, without your intervention, broadcast their visits to the bathroom. A court used a recording made inadvertently by some of my students at a demonstration as evidence to indict a duplicitous police chief. See **Chapter 27, Advanced Location Sound**, for wireless mike recommendations.

WIRED MIKES

A wired lavalier, though limiting to your subject's mobility, is trouble-free compared with its wireless brethren. You hide the cable in the participant's clothing so it emerges from a pants leg or skirt bottom. Be aware that here, too, people forget they're wearing them. They walk away until, quite literally, they reach the end of their tether.

SPARES AND ACCESSORIES

Breakdowns often occur in cables and connectors, so carry backup cables. Mikes and mixers need batteries; be sure to carry the right alkaline spares. A basic toolkit of solder, soldering iron, pliers, screwdrivers, adjustable wrench, Allen keys, can of compressed air (for cleaning), flashlight, and an electrical multimeter can get you out of much trouble in the field.

 Analyze the sound design of an imaginative film using **Project 1-AP-1 Analyze or Plan Using the Split-Page Script Form.**

SOUND DESIGN AND SHOOTING ATMOSPHERES

While you shoot, close windows and doors to screen out exterior sound. Switch off any equipment that makes intermittent noise such as air conditioners and refrigerators. Leave your car keys there to ensure you switch them back on after shooting. Any location, interior or exterior, has its characteristic ambient sound:

- A playground has a distant traffic hum coming from one direction.
- A riverside location has the hum and intermittent rumbling of a coal-fired power station a quarter mile off.
- A storeroom has the intermittent sound of a trapped fly and the hum from a fluorescent fixture.

Ambient sound is only noticeable during silences, but each location and each mike position within that location has its own characteristic presence. One is unlikely to cut well with another.

AMBIENCE IN FILMS

In a finished film, the audience accepts some ambient atmosphere as part of each new sequence's reality. The ear identifies the ambient content, then screens it out. Such easy adaptation deteriorates, however, when irritating and intrusive "atmos" changes occur on cuts from angle to angle. To cure this, backgrounds have to be built and adjusted in editing to create a seamless auditory experience. This is how we experience ambience in everyday life, so we expect no less in films.

LOCATION PROCEDURE

Before calling for a wrap at any location, whether interior or exterior, let the crew record a *presence track* (also known as *atmosphere, room tone,* or *buzz track*). Do this in every location, every shooting day, because each occasion has its own changing ambience. The procedure is simple:

1. The recordist calls, "Everyone freeze: We need a presence track!"
2. Everyone stands completely silent.
3. The recordist makes a recording of the ambient sound from the current mike position, disturbing nothing in the location.
4. The recordist calls "Cut!" and everyone jumps into action, wrapping up for that location.

 In postproduction, you can never remove background atmosphere from dialogue tracks. You therefore must add background to quiet tracks so they match louder tracks. This is risky with any dialogue on the margin of intelligibility.

HOW THE EDITOR WILL USE PRESENCE TRACKS

The two minutes of presence recorded on the set, duplicated if necessary to make more, becomes the vital material from which to fill dead spaces in dialogue tracks. These might occur when, for example, you use a cutaway that was shot silent. Because post-production can only add, never remove, background atmosphere in dialogue tracks, the editor must work to make every angle's background become consistent. Tracks with quiet presence must match those in the angle having the loudest, if all angles are to end up having the same admixture of ambient sound.

 Scout locations for camera opportunities, but remember to look for sound problems. If you don't, participants walking on gorgeous autumn leaves will sound like elephants crunching cornflakes, and the expressway that was so quiet at 2 p.m. will rise to a throaty roar by rush hour.

LOCATION AMBIENCE PROBLEMS

Every shooting situation comes with problems, which you try to anticipate when scouting the location. Overhead wires turn into Aeolian harps, dogs bark maniacally, garbage trucks mysteriously convene for bottle-crushing competitions, and somebody starts practicing scales on the trumpet. The astute location spotter can anticipate some of these sonic disasters, but not all. In each case, choice of mike, the axis of directional mikes, and getting the mike in close to the desired signal can make a crucial difference. What would life be like without such challenges?

SOUNDS ON THE SET

During takes, the crew and any onlookers must be as stationary and silent as possible, and the camera must make no sound that the mike can pick up. Fluorescents like to buzz, filament lamps can hum, and pets come to life at inopportune moments. Mike cables placed in parallel with power cables may produce electrical interference through induction, and sometimes very long mike cables pull in cheery DJs via radiofrequency (RF) interference. Elevator equipment can generate alternating current magnetic fields, and the most mysterious hum sometimes proves to come from something on the floor above or below. Every situation has some degree of remedy, once you have located the cause.

SOUND RECONSTRUCTION

In film sound, you often have to provide what is appropriate and not what was present. To be true in spirit, you reconstruct some sound during postproduction. At the exquisite nature center near where I live in Chicago, there are deer, wildflowers, some prairie, a lake with a heron or two, and lots of wild birds. I have daydreamed about filming a year-long cycle of life there, but it's under the flight path for the world's busiest airport, and vehicles roar past only two blocks away. I would need to reconstruct every atmosphere and sync sound because no audience could concentrate on lyrically backlit meadow grasses to the ominous whine of sinking jetliners.

EFFECTS AND WILD TRACKS

A track shot independent of picture is called a *wild track*. When a participant flubs a sentence or some extraneous sound cuts across dialogue, the alert sound recordist asks for a wild, voice-only recording immediately after the director calls "Cut!" The participant repeats the obscured words just as he spoke them during the take. Because it's recorded in the same acoustic situation, the words can be seamlessly edited in.

An *effects track* (FX) or *atmosphere track* is a non synchronous recording of sounds that might be useful to augment the sequence's sound track later. The recordist might carry a small recorder to get tracks of that barking dog, as well as other sounds to help create a composite atmosphere. In a woodland location this might mean getting up early to catch bird calls, river sounds of water gurgling, ducks dabbling, and wind rustling in reeds. A woodpecker echoing evocatively through the trees is probably best found in a wildlife library, since getting near them is hard and background noise is usually high. A sound recordist needs initiative and imagination, and a high level of tolerance to frustration.

AESTHETICS, SOUND DESIGN, AND SOUNDSCAPES

In a highly stylized documentary such as Errol Morris' dreamlike *The Thin Blue Line* (1988, United States), the imaginative conventions set by the film itself allow great latitude for nonrealistic invention. Under similar circumstances you might conceivably recreate dialogue in a *looping* or *automatic dialogue replacement* session (see **Chapter 15, Editing: From Fine Cut to Sound Mix**), but it is always expensive in time and effort. Sound effects are a different matter; for a sequence in a muddy swamp that had trucks thundering past out of sight, you will have to reconstruct the swamp atmosphere and re-record footsteps in mud. Labor intensive, but creatively effective.

The most potent aspects of sound for film lie not just in faithful recording techniques but in *psychoacoustics*, a term describing how we perceive and interpret sounds. In this regard, the expert is Michel Chion, whose *Audio-Vision: Sound on Screen* (1994, Columbia University Press) explains ideas developed over three decades. Be warned that they are far from simple and require learning a specialized vocabulary.

In 1975, the World Soundscape Project began to research the acoustic ecology of six European villages. Sponsored by the Tampere Polytechnic Institute in Finland, the goal is to document acoustic environments in change over many decades. Go to www.6villages.tpu.fi. The Web site reveals the riches you discover when you set out to explore using your ears, something I started learning as a teenager in England from Brian Neal, a musician and great friend who is blind. Every place has its soundscape, and it takes an attentive ear to analyze what makes it individual and special.

To create with sound is to provoke imagination at the highest levels, much as music does. The most memorable soundscapes usually come from simplifying and heightening rather than from being literally true to everything in the location. In sound as in everything else, less is more.

Even the film industry relegates sound to a low priority, so it's little wonder that sound is the neglected stepsister in low-budget or film school filmmaking. Really, a movie sound track is an orchestral score, something to be designed from the outset so it furthers the aims of the movie you are making.

As you develop your documentary proposal, make a design for the sound you expect to shoot. What kind of world are you showing? What are its special features? What will you need to record, and how? What kind of impact should the sound track make on the audience?

GOING FURTHER

See **Chapter 24, Preparing to Direct,** for location scouting advice, including a hand-clap acoustics test you can apply to any interior. For more sound information, go to **Chapter 27, Advanced Location Sound.** An excellent Web site for all sound information is www.filmsound.org. Sound designer Randy Thom talks about feature films and the fact that even fiction directors (whose control is enviably embracing) often lack sound design consciousness. Find excellent information on a variety of sound techniques at Fred Ginsburg's Equipment Emporium Web site (www.equipmentemporium.com). This user-friendly company sells a wide range of modestly priced equipment and offers good, down-to-earth advice online for low-cost shooting solutions. Download their articles on current equipment such as mixing panels for production sound, an introduction to time code recording, production audio recording for digital video camcorders, reviews of editing systems, troubleshooting guides, and much else. A site with useful basics on effective placing of mikes and other sound-related information is www.soundinstitute.com/index.cfm. Good handbooks are:

Holman, Tomlinson. *Sound for Film and TV,* 2nd ed. Boston: Focal Press, 2001.

Rose, Jay. *Producing Great Sound for Film and Video.* Boston: Focal Press, 2008.

Yewdall, Lewis. *Practical Art of Motion Picture Sound.* Boston: Focal Press, 2003.

CHAPTER 12

DIRECTING

SHOOTING PROCEDURES

CREW ETIQUETTE

While shooting, the crew keeps movement to a minimum and stays out of participants' eyelines to avoid distracting them. Even when something funny happens, the crew tries to remain silent and expressionless. If you allow yourselves to behave like an audience, participants turn into entertainers. Every crew member has something vital to monitor:

- *Camera operator* watches for focus, compositions, framing, movements, and whether the mike is edging into the shot.
- *Sound recordist* listens for unwanted reverb or echo, ambient noise, mike handling sounds, and sound consistency from shot to shot. The last takes the most skill.
- *Director* monitors the scene for content, subtext, and emotional intensity. What does this add up to? What meanings are taking shape under the surface (*subtext*)? Where is the scene going? Is it what I expected? Does it deliver what I hoped, or is this something new?

  The scene proceeds until the director calls "Cut!"

WHO ELSE CAN CALL "CUT!"

Nobody but the director can call "Cut!" unless you've agreed to the right to do so beforehand. The camera operator, for instance, might abort the scene if some condition that only he or she can see makes it useless to go on. An arbitrary halt, however, may damage a participant's confidence, so it's nearly always best to keep filming. Sometimes a participant, unhappy with something said or done, may call

---

Personal Release Form

For the sum of $_____ consideration received, I give _____
Productions, its successors and assigns, my unrestricted permission to distribute and sell all still
photographs, motion-picture film, video recordings and sound recordings taken of me for the
screen production tentatively entitled _____

Signed _____

Name (Please print) _____

Address _____

_____

Date _____

Signature of parent or guardian _____

Name (Please print) _____

Witnessed by _____

Date _____

FIGURE 12-1————————————————————————————

Short personal release form suitable for student productions. A full-length release appears in Chapter 24, Figure 24-2, but its all-encompassing legalese may intimidate those contributing to modest productions.

"Cut!" and you may have no option but to comply. Do not encourage participants to take over your role.

SOUND PRESENCE

Make sure that you have a minute or two of silence for each location. This, variously called *presence*, *buzz track*, *room tone*, or *ambience*, is background atmosphere inherent to the location. All locations, even those indoors, have their own characteristic ambient sound, and you shoot a presence track at the same recording level as the rest of the scene. Recording some at every location ensures that the editor can always fill in spaces or make other track adjustments.

Warn participants that you have to shoot a presence track. When the time comes, everyone stands in eerie silence for a couple of minutes. You are uncomfortably aware of your own breathing and all the little sounds in the room until the recordist calls "Cut!" For more information, see **Chapter 11, Location Sound**, and **Chapter 27, Advanced Location Sound**.

GETTING THE PERSONAL RELEASE FORM SIGNED

Once you finish shooting with someone, you ask him or her to sign a legal release document. This gives you the right to make public use of the material in return for a symbolic sum of money, such as $1. It does not, however, immunize you against legal action should you misuse the material or libel the signatory. Some documentarians get a *verbal release* by asking participants to say on camera that they are willing to be filmed and that their name and address is such and such. This certainly guards against subsequent claims that they didn't know they were being filmed but does not fulfill what a lawyer would want. It does not, for instance, guard against people deciding not to participate later and rendering void months of work. The brief release version in Figure 12-1 will suffice for your first productions, but any work for broadcasting requires a release form whose pages of legalese make ordinary people go pale with alarm. Normally you won't have legal problems unless you allow people to nurture the (not unknown) fantasy that you are going to make a lot of money selling their footage. For full-length location and personal release forms, see the end of **Chapter 30, Conducting and Shooting Interviews**.

IT'S A WRAP

Once you have shot the scene and the editor has all necessary materials, it's time to strike (dismantle) the set. Check that you shot a presence track and then announce "It's a wrap!" Everyone moves to begin their own winding-up responsibilities:

➤ Lower the lights and roll up cables while hot lighting fixtures cool down.

➤ Strike the set; collect clamps, stands, and boxes.

➤ Replace furniture and household goods exactly as you found them.

➤ Take the camcorder off its support, dismantle it, stow all gear in protective travel boxes.

➤ Stow sound equipment in its own travel boxes.

➤ Whoever is supervising the schedule confirms the next day's shooting with those affected.

➤ Director makes sure that the location is undamaged and everything is left clean and tidy, and thanks participants and each person in the unit for a good day's work.

DIRECTING PARTICIPANTS

CREATING TRUST

You create trust by explaining why you want to shoot a particular scene or topic and by convincing participants that something about their lives is valuable for other people to know. You can film an old man feeding his dog and talking to it because he senses you feel it's a special part of a special life. A taxi driver will happily chat to the camera while cruising for a fare because that is his central reality and he enjoys sharing it. You may discreetly film a woman relaxing in her morning bath because it was in this very bath that she made the momentous decision to visit Egypt.

 When you film people, encourage them to pursue their normal activities, and your aims won't seem objectionable. You will, however, have to explain why other people would be interested.

You and your camera can plumb the depths of other people's lives whenever they sense that you and your crew personally accept, like, and value them. A *documentary is a record of relationships*, so success depends on what took place before the camera is ever switched on. For this reason I have always avoided topics or participants for which I feel little interest or empathy. Not always, though. I once embarked with very mixed feelings on a BBC film about Sir Oswald Mosley and his 1930s British Union of Fascists in *The Battle of Cable Street* (1969, United Kingdom). We set about tracing people from across the sociopolitical spectrum who had taken part in the decisive anti-Semitic street confrontation, particularly those who admitted to being his followers. As it happened, they were shockingly ordinary; no horns or cloven feet anywhere. They were anxious to present their case and even made a distorted kind of sense. All researcher Jane Oliver and I needed to do was play the part of younger people learning history from its protagonists. In the end, I interviewed Mosley himself. I knew him to be urbane, an upper crust swaggerer with a penchant for distorting everything connected with himself. I felt apprehensive—less over his followers' reputation for violence or my revulsion with their values than with his reputation for squashing interviewers. So, instead of trying to trick him, I encouraged him to explain the events for which his published views were most specious.

> A documentary is a record of relationships. How you prepared the ground prior to running the camera will show onscreen.

During the lengthy editing period, my editor and I grew increasingly fascinated and repelled. I wanted to relay his version of the 1936 events, yet show how delusional it was. This emerged through juxtaposing his account with those of other witnesses and participants and he hanged himself on the rope we gave him. The film pleased the left (who opposed the freedom Mosley was given to organize racial hatred) and even Mosley himself, since he had expected to have his account distorted.

IN SEARCH OF NATURALNESS

People often ask, "How do you get people to look so natural in documentaries?" Of course, you want to shake your head and imply many years spent learning professional secrets. Actually, it's much easier to achieve than is, say, a satisfactory dramatic structure, but it still takes some basic directorial skills. When participants are uniformly unnatural, as you sometimes see, it is mistaken directing. The key lies in the way you brief your participants, as we shall see.

Interviewing is just one way to direct a documentary, and some of the most gripping films are entirely made of people talking. In an oral history work where little but survivors provide imagery, this may be the only film you can make. Most directors, however, take pains to show people active in their own settings, doing what they normally do. This spares the audience the hypnotic intensity of being talked at for long periods. In any case, we like judging character and motivation more by what people do than by what they say. Actions do speak louder than words, and film is inherently behavioral, so we make sure participants have familiar things to do, things that set them at ease.

So you decide to shoot your subject with his family, at work collaborating with an employee, and in the neighborhood bar playing pool with cronies. These situations won't transcend the stereotypical unless you can make them yield something satisfying—about your subject or his milieu. There is also another slight hitch. He feels most normal when nobody is watching. Once he's under scrutiny, as you film, his sense of himself fragments. I once filmed in a glass-door factory, and a lady who had spent years passing frames through a machine completely lost control of her machine when we turned the camera on her. To her deep embarrassment, the frames began to jam or miss the jet of rubber sealer solution. It happened because she was *thinking* about her actions instead of just doing them.

In documentary we aim to capture people looking normal, and self-consciousness wrecks the process. The factory worker, feeling she must "act," lost automatic harmony with her machine, and all I could do was reassure her that this sometimes happens. So we waited until she managed a few rounds in her old rhythm. It was a memorable example of the mind impeding the body's habitual function and shows how important it is that you help people stay inside their own sense of normality.

GIVING PARTICIPANTS WORK

Make sure your participants have familiar things to do, even while they talk to the camera. For every action sequence, have some requests lined up in case you sense self-consciousness. I should have asked the lady in the factory to mentally count backward in sevens or discuss her shift with a colleague to get her mind off the idea of being filmed.

 Try your interviewing skills in **Project 4-SP-10 Basic Interview: Camera on a Tripod,** then judge your performance using **Project 5-PP-1 Assess Your Interviewing.** Do *vox populi* street interviews using **Project 4-SP-11 Advanced Interview: Three Shot Sizes.**

INTERVIEWING

If you interview, here are some brief hints. Make a point of being relaxed and natural, so you don't scare your interviewee. Prepare your questioning in advance so you know what you want to explore or find out. Make a list of questions but try not to use it, since working from a list will seem formal and even mechanical to your interviewee. Instead, keep it handy in case your mind goes blank, and simply have an interesting conversation that touches all the points you want to explore. Use your list as a checklist before you finish, so you don't forget anything important.

You will probably want to edit out your questions, so it's important not to overlap your voices. This means you need a clean start from the interviewee, with no overlap and no beginning that depends on your question. If, for instance, you asked "Tell me about your first job?" you might get the kind of answer that starts, "Well, it was in a school bus company, and my job was to. . . ."

This reply depends on the question, so you'd ask him to start over using the words, "My first job was. . . ." You can try asking interviewees ahead of time to incorporate your question's information in their answer, but they often forget. As the interviewer, it's your responsibility to ensure a clean start to each answer.

The other important thing is not to be afraid of silences. Be absolutely sure the interviewee has said all she wants to say before you come in with another question. If you think there's more to come, *wait*. With digital media it costs nothing, and you're going to edit the material heavily. A pause is not a failure— it's being considerate. Often you get gold when you wait.

Interviewing is a very productive skill, so **Chapter 30, Conducting and Shooting Interviews,** is devoted to the subject.

FILMING IN INSTITUTIONS OR ORGANIZATIONS

Organizations, especially those operating in extreme situations, are far more likely to be paranoid than are individuals. At any time they may want you to explain in writing why you are filming this topic or that scene. Keep explanations simple and uncontroversial. Your explanations should be consistent (because participants compare notes) but not so specific that you box yourself into a corner.

DIRECTING THE CREW

COMMUNICATION

Day-to-day direction while shooting should begin from a comprehensive printed schedule with timely updates in cases of change. Include travel directions and cell phone numbers in case of emergency or cars getting separated. Give everything of possible importance in writing since shooting is no time to test people's powers of recall.

 People become natural in a documentary whenever you give them things to occupy them that feel natural.

Ideally, the crew has been intimately involved in evolving ideas for the film, but when you shoot for television, you often get an assigned crew. Outline the intended filming for the day, and keep the crew abreast of developments—something I used to forget when the pressure mounted.

WHO'S RESPONSIBLE FOR WHAT

Be formal about the chain of responsibility at first, then once things are running well, you can afford to relax the traditional structure. If you start informally and then find you must tighten up, you will meet with resentment. Once the crew assembles at the location, privately reiterate the immediate goals. You might, for instance, want a store to look shadowy and fusty or to emphasize a child's view of the squalor of a trailer park. Confirm the first setup, so the crew can get the equipment ready. A clear working relationship with your director of photography (DP) will relieve you from deciding myriad details that might detract from your main responsibility, which is toward participants and the narrative coherence of the film. Now get busy preparing the participants.

WORKING ATMOSPHERE

The transition into shooting should hide the excitement and tension you may feel and instead be a time of relaxed but focused attention. Shooting should take place in as calm an atmosphere as possible, and the crew should convey warnings or questions to you discreetly or through signs. The recordist or camera operator, for example, may hold up three fingers to indicate that only three minutes of tape or memory remain.

In potentially divisive situations, only the director should give out information or make decisions. The crew must preserve outward unity at all costs and make no comment that undermines the authority of the director or each other. They should be particularly scrupulous about keeping any disagreements from the participants, who need a calm and professional atmosphere. When student films break down, it is usually because crew members are apt to consider themselves more competent than the person directing. As difficulties arise, well-meaning but contradictory advice showers down on the director. This propagates alarm and despondency in participants and crew alike.

 To get professional reliability from your crew, become a model of professionalism yourself.

 In private, the crew can be informal, but in public they must maintain formal lines of responsibility or the unit may look discordant and immature. Filmmaking, though collaborative, is seldom democratic.

MONITORING AND INSTRUCTING

- *Check the shot*—If the camera is on a tripod, make a habit of checking the cinematographer's composition before you shoot. Afterwards it will be too late. At the end, look through the viewfinder again to check the ending composition. Some camera operators may suggest that you don't trust them because of this. Insist, because you'll be held responsible, not them. After a while you'll find checking is seldom necessary.

- *Run-up*—Each time you give the command "Roll camera," allow a few seconds of equipment run-up time before saying the magic word "Action" to your participants. Most cameras hit speed almost instantaneously, but action immediately following a camera startup is not always usable because there may be color or picture instability problems. In **Chapter 28, Organization, Crew, and Procedures,** under "The Countdown to Shooting"

section, there is the more elaborate procedure you need when you start up a separate camera and sound recorder.

- *Positioning yourself*—If the camera is tripod mounted, stand next to, and to the left of, the camera so you can see as nearly as possible what it sees. If the camera is handheld, you may have to drop back a foot or two, in case the camera wheels around.

- *Communication with camera operator*—Relay minimal camera directions by whispering into the operator's ear, making sure, of course, that your voice will not spoil a recording. Be brief and specific: "Go to John in medium shot," "Pull back to a wide shot of all three," or "If he goes into the kitchen again, walk with him and follow what he does."

- *Communication with sound recordist*—Usually you have visual communication with the person holding the mike, and the two of you can communicate with hand or facial signals. If the camera is handheld, the recordist has to rapidly adapt to the action, do what the camera does, and stay out of frame. He will shoot you meaningful glances now and then. Listening for quality, he will grow agitated at the approach of a plane or the rumble of a refrigerator that has turned itself on in the next room. Wearing headphones, he won't know what direction the interference is coming from. I recall shooting an interview in a raucous London pub, and the incredulous look stealing over the recordist's face as a drinker in the next bar lost his investment, followed by the clank of clean-up operations with a bucket. The interviewee noticed nothing since all this took place the other side of a partition, but the recordist was looking around apprehensively and I wanted to howl with laughter. Often in such a circumstance a recordist will draw his finger across his throat and raise his eyebrows beseechingly, mutely asking you to call "Cut!" Should you?

- *Sensory overload*—You have to make a decision and your head pounds from stress. You are supposed to be keenly aware of ongoing content and yet must resolve through glances and hand signals all sorts of other stuff . . . problems of sound, shadows, escaped pets, or people who have done the unexpected(!). At such times, the director is blinded by sensory overload.

BREAKS

When participants are not present (during breaks, say), encourage the crew to discuss the production. From just listening you can learn a lot. At first you may be shocked by the crew's lack of all-around observation. The reason is simple: A good camera operator concentrates wholly on composition, lighting, shadows, framing, and camera movements. To the diligent sound recordist words are less important than voice quality, unwanted noise or echo, and the balance of sound levels. Neither can have a balanced awareness of film content.

Because crew members monitor a restricted area of *quality*, you should periodically reconnect them to the project as a conceptual entity. Not everyone will appreciate your efforts. In "the industry" there is often a hostile division between "arty types" and "techies." Your technicians may never have had their opinions sought outside their own area of expertise. Treated like factory hands, they may not have considered their work from a directing standpoint. Be ready to meet hesitant or even hostile reactions to your efforts. Persist. If you want a crew whose eyes, ears, and minds extend your reach, take pains to share your thinking with them.

Always acknowledge crew feedback even when it's embarrassingly off target. Make mental adjustment for any skewed valuations and be diplomatic with advice you can't use. Above all, encourage involvement, and don't retreat from communicating.

 Coffee and sandwiches produced at the right moment can work miracles on a weary crew's morale. On long shoots, crews need time off.

Something else to remember: When you direct, you are fully involved all the time and tend to overlook mere bodily interruptions, like hunger, cold, fatigue, and bathroom breaks. For a keen and happy crew, stick to 8-hour days and build meals and breaks predictably into the schedule. On long shoots away from home, allow time off so people can buy presents for their loved ones at home.

GOING FURTHER

For more information go to **Chapter 29, Advanced Directing,** and **Chapter 30, Conducting and Shooting Interviews**. For every aspect of directing documentary in the real world, go to The D-Word Web site at www.d-word.com and be prepared to search their extensive archives.

PART 5

POSTPRODUCTION

Editing a documentary is really the second chance to direct it. Seldom does a film follow the kind of scripting through time that determines shooting a fictional story. Often there's a considerable plasticity to documentary material, and I have finished shooting more than one film without any clear idea of how I should assemble it. What determines a film's structure—if you haven't been able to predetermine it—arises out of the nature and emphases in the material. Editing becomes like making a picture from found objects. Individually and in juxtaposition, they suggest what pictures are possible, and you start experimenting. Such searching and experimenting in the cutting room usually arises because shooting has taken its own pathways and turned out differently from what you expected. Life is random, and films about life often have to be shot opportunistically and *ad hoc*.

This part supplies a set of operations that will give you optimal conditions in which to search for the wood among the trees. Your film's identity and purpose will emerge as you work on it—a truly fascinating experience for most people. The process culminates in making a final sound track and adding titles. Now you have your first documentary and can show it to audiences for a reaction.

CHAPTER 13

EDITING: FROM START TO VIEWING THE FIRST ASSEMBLY

Editing a documentary is similar no matter whether the film is short or long. Of course, longer films require a more extensive filing system and are more difficult to structure successfully. Newcomers to editing, once they've mastered how to control the editing program, usually do very well. Most of the operations described here are the small-unit editor's responsibility. In larger productions, the operations are distributed among specialists. It's an excellent learning experience, though, to do most of the work yourself in the early stages of your learning.

 Editing a documentary is not just assembling to a plan; it's more like coaxing a successful performance from a jumbled and incomplete music score. While editing you must see, listen, feel, think, adapt, and imagine as you try to fulfill your film's emerging potential.

DIRECTOR–EDITORS

Under the rubric of economics, the director often becomes the editor. In the beginning, you should certainly get the experience of editing your own work, but for longer and more complicated projects a one-man band is hazardous. Every film benefits from the steadying, questioning point of view of an editor who questions the director's assumptions, supplies alternative ideas and solutions, and acts as proxy for the audience. I once worked most fruitfully with an

FIGURE 13-1————————————————————————————————

Avid® Media Composer, the film industry's preferred editing software. (Photo courtesy of Avid Technology, Inc.)

editor whose politics were the polar opposite of mine. Foregoing this tension never allows you to get a necessary distance from your material.

 Every film benefits from an independent, creatively skeptical editor—one who sees like an audience. The director's prior investment never allows him or her to be so objective.

EDITING: PROCESS AND PROCEDURES

Computerized editing software such as Avid®, Final Cut Pro®, and Adobe® Premiere®, among others, has become ubiquitous. The early established Avid system (Figure 13-1) remains the front runner in performance and user friendliness but has been legendarily expensive to maintain because of the company's habit of requiring frequent, expensive updates. A clear advantage of Avid's low-end product is that the keystrokes you learn remain the same throughout Avid's range, and this will be a benefit should good fortune take you upmarket.

Many independent filmmakers prefer Apple's Final Cut Pro (Figure 13-2), a stable and modestly priced program that handles everything you can expect of it

FIGURE 13-2

Apple® Final Cut Pro® editing software on a PowerBook® portable computer. (Photo courtesy of Apple, Inc.)

with aplomb. The Apple operating system seems better integrated than the PC, which depends on Windows® and its notorious peccadilloes.

POSTPRODUCTION OVERVIEW

Postproduction is the extremely creative phase of filmmaking when you transform sound and picture dailies, as well as graphics, text, photographs, etc., into a film for an audience. In documentary, the editor is virtually a second director. Postproduction is supervised by the editor, and the work of the editor and editing crew includes the following:

- Synchronizing sound with action (necessary if sound acquisition was via a separate "double-system" recording)
- Screening dailies for the director's and producer's choices and comments
- Logging material in preparation for editing
- Making an editing script, unless the director and/or writer makes one
- Making a first assembly
- Making the rough cut
- Evolving the rough cut into a fine cut
- Supervising, with the director, the recording of narration (if used)
- Preparing for and supervising, with the director, any original music recording

- Finding, recording, and laying component parts of multitrack sound such as atmospheres, backgrounds, and sync effects
- Supervising, with the director, the sound engineer's mix-down of these tracks into one smooth final track

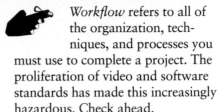

Workflow refers to all of the organization, techniques, and processes you must use to complete a project. The proliferation of video and software standards has made this increasingly hazardous. Check ahead.

- Progress chasing the making of titles and necessary graphics
- Supervising, with the cinematographer, the post-editor's color balancing as well as the rest of the postproduction finalization

On a large production under a deadline or in a large production facility, the work is distributed among specialists, but for a low-budget independent project the editor assumes much responsibility. Experience as an editor is therefore a fine preparation for directing, especially after you've acquired a reputation for adept handling of the structural and dramatic problems that always arise while editing documentaries.

First transfer all selected material to the hard drive of the editing computer. Particularly with reenactments requiring many takes, anything more than "pulled" or "circled" (that is, the best) takes would needlessly clog the storage system. To guarantee you can incorporate material from multiple sources (such as digital video, photographic files of various kinds, scanned film, etc.), check very carefully that your editing software can integrate them. Your workflow can become extremely complicated if you want to incorporate, for instance, NTSC (American standard video) at 30 frames per second (fps), film scanned from 25 fps PAL (European) video, along with stills in JPEG file interchange format as well as Windows BMP (bitmap) format. Add to this the fact that your main footage is in 24p high definition (HD), and your workflow becomes extremely complicated. See Part 7, Advanced Production Issues: **Chapter 34, Editing: Refinements and Structural Problems,** for further explanation.

Many systems are now so fast and have such large storage that you can edit on a laptop computer at full resolution. This abolishes all need for the two-pass, off-line, and on-line processes, with their extra time and expense.

Once you have digitized your material, organize it into bins containing each major sequence or classification of materials (Figure 13-3). Log the material by shots or sections so you are ready to lay a first assembly of segments along a time line. You will be able to lay multiple sound tracks opposite their picture and to predetermine sound levels so you hear a layered and sophisticated track as you edit (Figure 13-4).

Depending on the features of the nonlinear editing (NLE) system you use, postproduction may involve:

- *Digitizing* a low-resolution (inferior grade) image so that much material can be stored on a hard drive of limited capacity. Up-to-date systems have the capacity to work at full resolution and at good speed, although

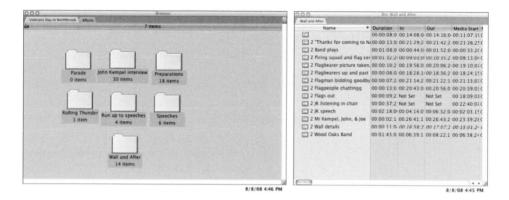

FIGURE 13-3 ————————————————————————————————

Final Cut Pro® project bins and the shots in one of them.

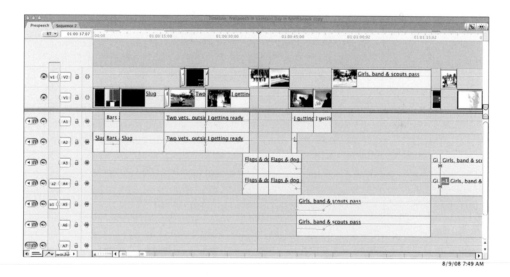

FIGURE 13-4 ————————————————————————————————

Final Cut Pro® time line with segments of picture and track sections laid below.

you may have to wait during *rendering*, the process by which the computer makes new files for shots with elements that overlap or combine in some way.

- *Synchronizing* sound to picture when a separate machine shot each of them. Line up the sound of the clapper board closing with the frame where the clapper closes in picture, thus ensuring that the whole take is in sync. Keep an eye open for creeping sync (drifting out of sync) over long takes.

- Sound finalization in the *audio sweetening* process uses sophisticated sound processing software such as the industry favorite, Digidesign's Pro Tools. This enables control over sound dynamics such as:
  - *Limiting* (sound dynamics remain linear until a preset ceiling, when they are held to that ceiling level)
  - *Compression* (all sound dynamics are compressed into a narrower range but remain equal in ratio to each other)
  - *Equalization* control (sound frequency components within the top, middle, and bottom of the sound range can be individually adjusted, or preset programs applied)
  - *Filtering* (for speech with prominent sibilants—for instance, one can use a de-essing program)
  - *Pitch changes* or *pitch bending* (Pro Tools has its roots in music and can be useful for surreal sound effects or creating naturalistic variations from a single source)
  - *MIDI integration* (allows you to integrate a keyboard-operated sampler or music setup)
- Using the *edit decision list* (EDL) after a low-resolution edit to redigitize only the material used in the cut
- *Reassembling* the edit at high resolution

Producing a video final print includes:

- Color correction
- Audio sweetening, as described above
- Copy duplication for release prints with master copies stored for future duplication

VIEWINGS

CREW DAILIES VIEWING SESSION

Even if everyone has viewed dailies piecemeal, let the crew see their work in its entirety after shooting ends. It's useful for everyone to see their patterns and mistakes, not just the successful material that makes it into the final edit. The editor might attend this viewing, but discussion is likely to be a crew-centered post-mortem that is not especially useful to editing.

EDITOR AND DIRECTOR'S VIEWING SESSION

If nothing has yet been edited, the director and editor should see all the dailies together. This reveals the general thrust of the material and the problems that you face for the piece as a whole. The longer and more ambitious the film, the more challenges and possibilities lie in the material. For you, the director, this is a stressful time. Often you are in the grip of depression over a sense of failed goals, and your mind is working furiously as you try to see a way out. What you mainly see is problems. Maybe you see irritating mannerisms in one of the participants that you never noticed, and these must be cut around if he is not to appear shifty. Or one of your two main characters is more interesting and articulate, and you must rethink your original premise.

View all of the material again, scene by scene. You can easily see digitized dailies in likely scene order rather than shooting order. Stop to discuss each scene's problems and possibilities.

TAKING NOTES

The editor or the editor's proxy keeps notes about the director's choices and any special cutting information. It's useful to have someone present whose only function is to take notes, but if you must write during a viewing, make large, scribbled notes on many pages of paper. That way your eyes never leave the screen. If you look away, you will undoubtedly miss important moments and nuances.

GUT FEELINGS MATTER

Note all emotional high points or unexpected outcomes. These contain the clues pointing toward a successful film. You must work out where they come from and what they signify. Almost certainly these moments of delivery are so significant that they represent the mainstays of the future film. Note any unexpected moods or feelings. If you find yourself reacting with, "She seems unusually sincere here" or "I can't believe that really happened," then note it down. One often doubts that gut feelings are really founded in anything, and you are apt to ignore, then forget, them. But seldom are these isolated personal reactions. What triggered them is embedded in the material and will strike any first-time audience. Later, all the spontaneous perceptions you recorded will be useful when inspiration lags from overfamiliarity.

REACTIONS

When the crew (or anyone else for that matter) sees dailies, there will be useful debates over the effectiveness, meaning, or importance of different aspects of the material. Crew members often harbor differing feelings about participants' credibility and motivation. During the filming they often develop partisan feelings about the participants and filming situations. Listen to their opinions but don't argue, because similar thoughts may occur to your future audience. At any viewing you will learn most from sitting at the back and watching viewers' body language. You need to know their thoughts, feelings, and observations, but keep in mind that crew members, like you, are far from objective. They are highly involved in their own discipline, tend to often overvalue its positive or negative effects, and don't see the film from a director's or editor's perspective. The sum of the dailies viewing is a notebook full of the director's and the editor's choices and observations and fragmentary impressions of the movie's potential and deficiencies.

THE ONLY FILM IS IN THE DAILIES

Now the director changes hats. No longer are you the instigator of the material; instead, you and your editor are surrogates for the audience. Purge yourself of prior knowledge and intentions; all understanding and feeling must arise wholly from the screen. Nobody in the cutting room wants to hear about what you intended or what you could have produced.

 Your film now lies somewhere in the dailies. Only what you can see and hear in the dailies is relevant. The proposal, working hypothesis, and treatment are historic relics, old maps to a rebuilt city. Stow them in the attic for your biographer.

PREPARING THE FOOTAGE

LOGGING THE DAILIES

The handwritten log of dailies should be cumulative, noting the *timecode* for each new scene, important action, or event. Timecode is the unique, time-related number assigned by the camera to each video frame at the time of shooting; it becomes the ID by which the editing program handles everything. Figure 13-5 shows the editing program's list of shots that your notes will give relevant

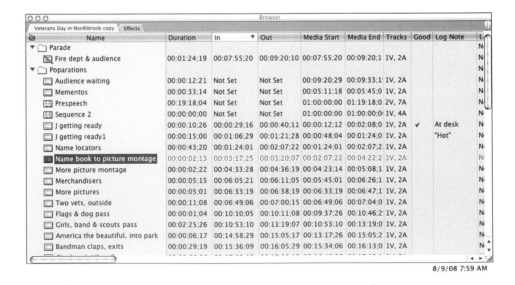

FIGURE 13-5 ——————

Examples of timecode listings.

details for. Keep descriptions brief—they need only remind you what to expect. For example:

01:00:00 WS [wide shot] of man at tall loom
01:00:30 MS [medium shot] of same man seen through strings
01:00:49 CS [close shot] of man's hands with shuttle
01:01:07 MS as he works; stops, rubs eyes
01:01:41 His POV [point of view] of his hands and shuttle
01:02:09 CS of feet on treadles (MOS)

The figures are hours:minutes:seconds. Timecode includes a frame count, but such hair-splitting accuracy in a content log is usually pointless. The example explains all the standard shot abbreviations except the last. In England, the expression for "shot without sound" is "mute," but America still enshrines its German immigrant directors' call of "Mit out sound!" which is abbreviated MOS.

Place each new sequence in a designated bin having a distinctive title, as in Figure13-3. If the software's log lacks space for qualitative notes, keep them on paper. Logs, bins, and shot descriptions exist to help you locate material quickly, so on a longer production you will want to design divisions, indexes, or color codes to assist your eye and save time. Inadequate filing always exacts its own revenge because Murphy (of Murphy's Law) loves to hide out in sloppy filing systems.

MAKING TRANSCRIPTS AND A WORKAROUND SOLUTION

Tedious though it sounds, *transcribing* every word your participants speak is invaluable to grasping what they mean. If your film is about court testimony, say, people's actual words will be paramount and transcribing them unavoidable. **Chapter 31, From Transcript to Filmscript**, describes how to make a whole first assembly from edited transcripts. Transcribing is not as laborious or unrewarding as people fear; it saves work later and helps ensure that you miss few creative opportunities. If you can't bring yourself to do this, then log *topic categories*. That is, instead of writing down actual words, summarize the topics covered at each scene or interview and then log these by approximate timecode in and out points. Now you have quick access to any given subject, but later you'll have to make decisions during editing by auditioning whole sections. Not making transcripts is a "buy now, pay later" situation, because making content and choice comparisons without a transcript is hard labor of a different stripe.

Using transcripts too literally has some dangers. You can place too much emphasis on words and thus make a speech-driven film. Then again, speech that looks significant on paper sometimes proves anemic on the screen. This is because the act of transcription always to some degree imposes an artificial and literary organization—the more so if the original scene took place impulsively and chaotically. Also, how something is said is quite as important as *what* is being said. When voices overlap, or people use special nuances or body language, transcripts often mislead by simplifying reality. What is lived and how someone transcribes it may carry quite different subtexts.

ASSEMBLING A VISUALLY DRIVEN FILM

The more that images and action drive your film instead of words, the more cinematic it will be. Experience has taught me that planning a film from transcripts leads to a film stuffed wall-to-wall with talking. If, however, you first assemble all of the film's usable visual and behavioral material, something different happens. By choosing a likely time structure and arranging the material in a loosely assembled flow, you start from a close scrutiny of behavior, action, imagery, and atmosphere. You will, of course, need words and language, and you'll have the opportunity to draw on what you need, but this way you start from the behavioral power of the cinema. If you build on words and then illustrate them, you won't escape the journalistic habit of privileging spoken language.

SEEKING A STRUCTURE

WHY STRUCTURE MATTERS

If you were able to realize your goals during the shoot, structuring the assembly may be straightforward. More often—since documentaries are usually improvisations about people improvising their way through life—what you shoot is not what you imagined. Your goals were frustrated or had to change, so now you need a new planning process that will make use of what you actually filmed. Editing is your second chance to direct.

 Documentaries—improvisations about people improvising their way through life—seldom run as planned. Editing is your second chance to direct.

TIME AND STRUCTURAL ALTERNATIVES

Identifying a structure for your footage means, first of all, deciding how to handle time, since temporal progression is an all-important organizing feature. In what order should you show cause and effect? Are there advantages in altering the natural or chronological sequence of events? Can you use parallel storytelling to run two narratives concurrently? All of this affects the *contract* you will strike with your audience.

THE CONTRACT

Yes, your audience expects a contract—an indication in the film's first moments of the story's premise, goals, and route. You may spell it out in narration or imply it in the logic of the film's development. You may signal it by the film's title or by something shown, said, or done at the outset.

You'll find longer film structural types with examples in Part 7, Advanced Production Issues: **Chapter 18, Dramatic Development, Time, and Story Structure.** The examples and discussion there may further help you decide what limitations or potential lie in your dailies. Ways to analyze your film and find alternative structures appear in Chapter 34, Editing: Refinements and Structural Problems.

 Progression through time is the all-important organizing feature of any documentary. How will you organize yours?

 At your film's opening, your audience needs a *sense of direction* and *an implied destination.* This contract implies how your tale will reward their time and attention.

STORY STRUCTURES NEED DEVELOPMENT

A problem for many documentaries is that, unless the film is shot over months or years, development must be implied rather than shown because most human change is too slow for an affordable shooting schedule. Michael Apted's *28 Up* (1986, United Kingdom) and the other longitudinal studies it has inspired are strikingly successful because they log progress over decades, and for once really explore each person's sense of goals and destiny.

Now that many documentarians have their own equipment, longitudinal films have become more feasible. Intermittent filming is also something that independents can do more easily than corporations.

How will your film imply that someone has grown or changed?

MICROCOSM AND MACROCOSM

Sometimes a subject is large and diffuse, and you have to imply what is happening through examples in microcosm. I once worked on a series that attempted to show aspects of France while Britain was joining the Common Market (now called the European Union). Our series, "Faces of Paris," showed aspects of the French by profiling interesting individuals.

Here we faced a paradox: I can't show all of France, so maybe I should confine myself to Paris, but "Paris" is too diffuse, so I should concentrate on representative Parisians to give my film some unity and progression. But how typical is any Parisian? Trying to represent the universal, one looks for an example in the particular, but this only demonstrates how triumphantly atypical all examples really are. Making generalizations in the relentlessly specific medium of film can be a real problem. Indeed, this may signal that you should bite the bullet and consider narration.

Writers faced, and solved, similar problems in previous centuries. One solution may be to find a naturalistic subject that carries strongly metaphorical overtones.

John Bunyan's *Pilgrim's Progress* is a journey of adventure, but it also functions as an allegory for the human spiritual voyage. The Maysles brothers' superb *Salesman* (1969), mentioned earlier in Chapter 5, shows every phase of door-to-door selling, which was something the brothers had done themselves at one time. It also dramatizes how moral compromise and humiliation can be the price of competing for a share in the American dream.

Another famous American director repeatedly uses an allegorical "container" structure. Fred Wiseman will take an institution and treat it as a complete and functioning microcosm of the larger society that houses it. Through the emergency room doors in *Hospital* (1970) come, for example, the hurt, the wounded, the drug-overdosed, and the dying in desperate search of succor. It yields a frightful vision of the self-destruction stalking American cities and threatening the American psyche. Yet, the same "institution as walled city" idea applied in *High School* (1968, United States; Figure 13-6) seems diffuse and directionless. The relationship Wiseman wants us to notice between teachers and the taught is too low key, repetitive, and unremarkable to build much sense of development. His noninterventional approach and lack of narration or interviews left him with no tools to develop and intensify what I presume is the vital issue—that an average American high school is extraordinarily autocratic and prepares young people better for the military than to participate in a democracy. He would retort, I think, that it's my job to work it out. This is true.

Don't imagine that today's technology has reduced a storyteller's apprenticeship. Your models for strong narratives lie in expertise developed over centuries in all the time arts. Understand their achievements and you won't have to reinvent the wheel.

FIGURE 13-6

High School—no place to learn democracy. (Photo courtesy of Zipporah Films, Inc.)

DEVELOPING THE STRUCTURE OF YOUR FILM

To summarize:

- Look for the best story in your dailies and the best way to tell it.
- Satisfying stories tend to deal with change or the need for it.
- Literary, poetic, theatrical, musical, and other disciplines have parallel examples to help you with the syntax of the story you are developing.

There are two common approaches to the first assembly. Most people, unaware they have options, take the verbal route and end up with a torrent of verbiage. The alternative, you'll recall, is image and action oriented and leads to the more cinematic solution. Which you use depends on how you approached directing the subject, what you were able to shoot, how you organize the editing, and how you want to relate to your audience.

FINDING AN ACTION-DETERMINED STRUCTURE

If you have plenty of action and visual sequences, put together an assembly using only observational material and then view it as a whole and without stopping:

1. What does this material convey? Does it, for example, tell a story, convey a mood, introduce a society, or set an epoch?
2. What time period do you know your material spans, and how well does the assembly convey that lapse of time? (It's always useful for events to happen in a set period of time.)
3. What memorable interchanges or developments did you capture on camera? This, of course, is probably your strongest and most persuasive "evidence."
4. What would your film convey if it were a silent film? (This is the acid test by which to see whether any film is cinematic rather than literary or theatrical.)
5. How many phases or chapters does the material fall into, and what characterizes each?
6. What verbal material, as yet unused, could you use that adds new dimensions to the "silent film" assembly above?
7. What new dimensions does the original action-based and behaviorally based film acquire? (Make a new working hypothesis.)
8. How little speech material do you need to further shift the film toward something you want?

Beginning from visual and behavioral evidence lets imagery suggest the story. Beginning from words means that words take control. But by bringing few words to your behavioral assembly and perhaps by using voice-over rather than "talking heads," you are developing characters who seem to be speaking from their interior lives rather than addressing an interviewer.

FINDING A SPEECH-BASED NARRATIVE STRUCTURE

If you start by assembling interviews, your film is probably a historical retrospective or one about the present that scans many people's viewpoints. You will find the best word-driven structure through making a paper edit from transcripts (see Part 7, Advanced Production Issues: **Chapter 31, From Transcript to Film Script**).

THE FIRST ASSEMBLY

Whichever approach you used to develop a structure, you can now roughly assemble the useable material. Don't agonize over the consequences of what you are doing. Leave everything long and expect repetition. You have two different accounts of how the dam broke? Slap them both in and decide based on the evidence which one to rely on.

 Every story needs someone who learns or something that develops if the story is to seem satisfying and worthwhile.

Putting the material together for the first time is the most exciting part of editing. Don't worry at this stage about length or balance. It's important to *see an assembly as soon as possible before doing detailed work on any sections*. Only then can you make far-reaching resolutions about its future development. Of course, you will want to polish a favorite sequence, but fixing details is often a way to avoid defining your film's overall identity and purpose.

 The first assembly auditions the best material and launches the denser and more complex film to come. As a show, it is long and crude, yet its artlessness often makes it affecting and exciting.

SCREENING THE FIRST ASSEMBLY AND RETURN TO INNOCENCE

To judge a first assembly, try to purge all foreknowledge from your mind or you won't see with the eyes of a first-time viewer. This unobstructed, audience-like way of viewing is necessary *every* time you run your film. To this end, it's always helpful to have one or two people present for whom the movie is new. As we said earlier, sit behind them and study their body language for clues. Even when they don't utter a word, newcomers somehow give filmmakers fresh eyes.

 You can no more premeditate a complete film from its dailies than plan a journey to shore on a surfboard.

During the first assembly, and certainly after it, your material will start telling you where and how to cut. This signals a welcome and slightly mysterious change in your role from proactive to reactive. Formerly, you had to expend energy to get anything done, and now the energy starts to come from the film itself.

DECIDING AN IDEAL LENGTH

As your creation comes to life, you will find the process profoundly exciting. First viewings will yield important realizations about the character, dramatic shape, and best length of the film. You should have a particular length in mind, depending on the medium. Television usually has quite rigid specifications; for example, a 30-minute PBS or BBC slot requires a film (including titles) of about 28 minutes, 30 seconds, to allow for announcements at either end. Television documentaries usually appear as a series because audiences come to associate a particular time with particular programs. Films are thus either funded as packages and coproductions or acquired for showing under a series title, such as "Independent Lens" or "POV." If your movie were to appear on commercial television, it would have to be broken up into segments of perhaps 5 minutes with so-called natural breaks to allow for commercials.

Thus, the outlet for your film determines its length and structure:

- Classroom films are normally 10 to 20 minutes.
- Television uses 30-, 40- (in Europe), 60-, and 90-minute slots.
- Short films that say a lot have a better chance of acceptance on the festival circuit, where reputations are created. They also appeal to those who browse the Internet.
- Internet videos such as those on YouTube™ are usually under 10 minutes. Most exhibit the interests, skills, and naïveté of home movies—which is essentially what they are. Home movies can still be an art form.
- When the Internet is able to deliver full fidelity, longer and more substantial pieces will inevitably take over; however, only those developing commitment, storytelling, and craft sophistication will find large audiences.
- Newspaper videos (see www.mefeedia.com) are often just 45 seconds and are generally amateurish in every respect. See the *Digital Journalist* article for pointers regarding what *not* to do (www.digitaljournalist.org/issue0805/how-not-to-do-newspaper-video.html). The skills you develop from using this book diligently should put you way ahead.

 Before each viewing, empty your mind of everything you know about your film. Only by emulating an audience's innocence can you make judgments on its behalf.

Look to the content of your film for guidance on length. Sit on a jury, and you'll see that most documentaries are at least a third too long. Your immersion while shooting makes you a poor judge of length, so seek advice. A film's natural span depends on the richness and significance of its content, and, to a lesser extent, the expectations people will have depending on where they see it. Audiences for television, cable, community cable, cinema, or YouTube bring different expectations. Where does your project really belong? If you can recognize that your film has 10 minutes of content, then you can get tough with that earnest 25-minute assembly and shape it for its most likely audience.

DIAGNOSTIC QUESTIONING

Immediately after viewing an assembly, scribble a list of material that made the most impact. You're going to use this a little later. Dealing with your film in its crudest form, you must now elicit your own dominant reactions. After the first viewing, ask:

> ➤ *Does the film feel dramatically balanced*? That moving and exciting sequence in the middle of the film may be making the rest of the film seem anticlimactic. Or your film may circle around for a long while before it really starts moving.
> ➤ *When do you sense a story unfolding, and when not*? This helps locate impediments in the film's development and sets you analyzing why the film stumbles.
> ➤ *Which parts of the film seem to work, which drag, and why*?
> ➤ *Which participants held your attention and which didn't*? Some may be more congenial or just better on camera than others.
> ➤ *Was there a satisfying alternation of types of material*? Or was similar material clumped indigestibly together? Where did you get effective contrasts and juxtapositions? Can you make more? Variety is as important in storytelling as in dining.
> ➤ *Does the audience get too much or too little expository information*? Sometimes a sequence fails to work because the ground was not properly prepared, or because it fails to contrast in mood sufficiently with the previous sequence.
> ➤ *Exposition*
>   ↻ *Can it be delayed*? Too much too early deluges viewers with information about people and issues they don't yet care about.
>   ↻ *Is there too much*? This reduces the will to concentrate by removing all anticipatory tension in the viewer.
>   ↻ *Is it too clumped*? Consider thinning or holding back expository material until it's really needed. Make the audience work—they enjoy it.
> ➤ *What kinds of metaphysical allusions does your material make*? Could you make more use of connotation and metaphor? Are you signaling the film's values and beliefs sufficiently?

WHAT WORKS, WHAT DOESN'T

Take your impact list made immediately after the first viewing and compare it with a full sequence list. The human memory discards what it doesn't find meaningful, so you forgot all that good stuff in the full list because it fails to deliver. This doesn't mean it can never work, only that it's not working yet. Common reasons for material to misfire:

- *Two or more sequences are making the same point.* Repetition does not advance an argument unless there is escalation. Make choices, ditch the redundant.

- *A climax is in the wrong place.* If your stronger material is early, the film becomes anticlimactic.

- *Tension builds then slackens.* Plot your movie's rising and falling emotional temperatures; if it inadvertently cools before an intended peak, the viewer's response is seriously impaired. Sometimes transposing sequences works wonders.

- *The film raises false expectations.* A film, or part thereof, fails when you don't deliver what the viewer has been led to expect.

- *Good material is somehow lost on the audience.* We read into film according to the context. A misleading setup or a failure to direct attention to the right places can make material fall flat.

- *You have multiple endings.* Decide what your film is really about and prune accordingly.

 New directors find it hard to say a lot through a little. Result? Zeppelins—that is, films that are slow and distended because people assume that length means importance.

THE DOCUMENTARY MAKER AS DRAMATIST

If this looks like a traditional dramatic analysis, that's because it is. Like a playwright watching a first performance, you are using your lifelong addiction to drama to sniff out faults and weaknesses. This is difficult because you can't make any objective assessments. All you can do is dig for *feelings* about the dramatic workings of your material. Where does the instinct for drama come from? We're trained by the entertainment we consume. It's a drive present since antiquity that leaves us with a compulsion to hear and tell stories. Think of the Arthurian legends from the Middle Ages; they're still being adapted and updated, still giving meaning and pleasure after a thousand years!

PLEASING YOUR AUDIENCE

Because the documentary is a tale consumed at one sitting, it carries on the oral tradition. It succeeds whenever it connects with the audience's emotional and imaginative life. You must be concerned not only with self-expression, which can be narcissistic, but also with entertaining and therefore serving your audience. Like all entertainers, the filmmaker has a precarious economic existence and either fulfills the audience or goes hungry. In *Literature and Film,*[1] Robert Richardson argues that the cinema's high vitality and optimism is due to its collaborative authorship and its dependency on public response. Of course, it would be absurd and cynical to claim that only the applause of the masses matters, but the enduring presence of folk art—plays, poetry, music, architecture, and traditional tales—should alert us to how much we share with the tastes of our forebears. The truth is that the ordinary person's tastes and instincts—yours and mine—are highly acculturated. In everyday life we seldom make conscious use of them, so we lack confidence when it comes time to do so.

 The human memory is a great editor: It forgets whatever made no impact. Whatever you forgot from a screening isn't delivering. Figure out why.

AFTER THE DUST SETTLES, WHAT NEXT?

After the first assembly, fundamental issues emerge. Maybe you see your worst fears: Your film has no less than three endings—two false and one intended. Your favorite character makes no impact at all beside others who seem more spontaneous and alive. You have to concede that a sequence in a dance hall, which was hell to shoot, has only one really good minute in it. A woman you interviewed for a minor opinion actually says some striking things and is upstaging a "more important" contributor.

 Documentary succeeds when it connects with the audience's emotional and imaginative life.

Avoid trying to fix everything you now see in one grandiose swipe. Forswear the pleasures of fine-tuning or you soon won't see the forest for the trees. Wait a few days and think things over. Then you'll be ready to tackle the major needs of the film.

GOING FURTHER

Digital Video magazine (www.dv.com) has excellent articles and reviews on everything for digital production and postproduction. Try Googling "groups" to locate users of your particular software; often this yields answers at the dead of

---

[1]Richardson, Robert. *Literature and Film.* Bloomington: Indiana University Press, 1969, pp. 3–16.

night when you're ready to tear your hair out. Here are some books. After swallowing my pride, I found Kobler's *Dummies* guide particularly helpful:

Angell, Dale. *The Filmmaker's Guide to Final Cut Pro Workflows*. Boston: Focal Press, 2007.

Dancyger, Ken. *The Technique of Film and Video Editing*. Boston: Focal Press, 2006.

Kauffman, Sam. *Avid Editing*. Boston: Focal Press, 2006.

Kobler, Helmut. *Final Cut Pro HD for Dummies*. New York: John Wiley & Sons, 2004.

Osler, Jason. *Final Cut Pro Workflows*. Boston: Focal Press, 2008.

Young, Rick. *The Focal Easy Guide to Final Cut Pro 6*. Boston: Focal Press, 2007.

CHAPTER 14

EDITING: THE PROCESS OF REFINEMENT

Editing techniques are hard to grasp from a book, but you can learn about them from films you admire. Work out for yourself how they suggest eyes, ears, and intelligence working together as they dig for subtextual meanings. At the beginning of **Chapter 34, Editing: Refinements and Structural Problems**, there is an important analogy linking editing to the way human consciousness works. It's in the advanced editing section because you'll probably prefer to make your own editing discoveries first.

Lay bare your favorite documentary's techniques using **Project 1-AP-6 Analyze Editing and Content** and **Project 1-AP-7 Analyze Structure and Style** (both in the Appendix).

UNIFYING MATERIAL INTO A FLOW

After running your first assembly two or three times, it increasingly strikes you as clunky blocks of material having a dreadful lack of flow. First you may have some illustrative stuff, then several blocks of interview, then a montage of shots, then another block of something else, and so on. Sequences go by like a series of floats in a parade, each separate from its fellows. How do you get that effortless flow seen in other people's films?

Once you have found a reasonable order for the material, you will want to combine sound and action in a form that takes advantage of counterpoint techniques. In practice, this means bringing together the sound from one shot with the image from another. To show, say, a teacher with superb theory and poor performance, you could shoot two sets of material, one of relevantly structured interview and the other of the teacher droning away in class.

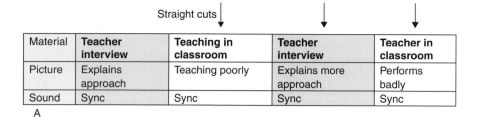

Straight cuts ↓		↓	↓

Material	**Teacher interview**	**Teaching in classroom**	**Teacher interview**	**Teacher in classroom**
Picture	Explains approach	Teaching poorly	Explains more approach	Performs badly
Sound	Sync	Sync	Sync	Sync

A

Overlaps |———| |—| |—|

Material	**Interview**	**Classroom**		**Interview**	**Classroom**	
Picture	Teacher explains approach	Teacher teaching poorly		Explains more approach	Performs badly	
Sound	Sync	V/O	Sync	V/O	Sync	V/O	Sync

B

FIGURE 14-1————————————————————

(A) First assembly of material using a straight cutting boxcar approach compared with (B), an overlap edit, which allows abbreviation and a simultaneous counterpoint of idea with actuality.

We edit these materials into juxtaposition. The conservative, first-assembly method would alternate segments as in Figure 14-1A: a block of interview in which the man begins explaining his ideas, then a block of teaching, then another block of explanation, then another of teaching, and so on until the point is made. This is a common, although clumsy, way to accomplish the objective in the assembly stage. After a little back-and-forth cutting, technique and message are predictable. I think of it as *boxcar cutting* because each chunk goes by like boxcars on a railroad.

Instead of alternating the two sets of materials, you can integrate them as shown in Figure 14-1B. Start with the teacher examining his philosophy of teaching and then cut to the classroom sequence, with the classroom sound low and the teacher's explanation continuing over it (this is called *voice-over*). When the voice has finished its sentence, we bring up the sound of the classroom sequence and play the classroom at full level. Then we lower the classroom atmosphere and bring in the teacher's interview voice again. At the end of the classroom action, as the teacher gets interesting, we cut to him in sync (now including his picture to go with his voice). At the end of what was Block 3 in Figure 14-1A, we continue his voice but cut—in picture only—back to the classroom, where we see the bored and mystified kids of Block 4. Now, instead of having description and practice dealt with in separate blocks of material, description is laid against practice, and ideas against reality, in a harder hitting counterpoint. The benefits are multiple. The total sequence is shorter and sprightlier. Talking-head material has been kept to a decent minimum, while the behavioral material—the classroom evidence against which we measure the teacher's ideas—is now in the majority.

By counterpointing essentials the interview can be pared down, giving what is presented a muscular, spare quality, usually lacking in unedited reminiscence. And there is a much closer and more telling juxtaposition between vocalized theory and actual teaching behavior. You challenge your audience to use its own judgment about the man's ideas and what he actually does.

Counterpoint editing cannot be worked out in a script or paper edit, but you can quite confidently decide which materials will intercut well. You have to work out the specifics from the materials themselves.

THE AUDIENCE AS ACTIVE PARTICIPANTS

A more demanding texture of word and image places the spectator in a more responsible relationship to the "evidence" presented by expecting active rather than passive participation. The contract is no longer just to absorb and be instructed. Instead, the invitation is to *interpret and weigh what you see and hear*. Sometimes the film uses action to illustrate, other times to contradict, what has seemed true. The teacher is an *unreliable narrator* whose words you cannot take at face value. Whatever makes any of us an unreliable narrator is always going to be interesting.

 No audience likes stories made too easy. We prefer to interpret and weigh information as we do in everyday life. An "unreliable" character is particularly interesting because he or she challenges us to use our judgment.

Other ways to juxtapose and counterpoint stimulate the imagination by changing the conventional coupling of sound and picture. For instance, you might show a street shot in which a young couple goes into a café. We presume they are lovers. They sit at a table in the window. We, who remain outside, are near an elderly couple discussing the price of fish, but the camera moves in close to the window. We see through the glass the couple talking affectionately to each other but hear an old couple arguing over the price of cod. The effect makes an ironic comment on the two states of intimacy; we see courtship but hear the concerns of later life. With great economy of means, and not a little humor, a cynical idea about marriage is set afloat—one that the film might go on to dispel with more hopeful alternatives.

 To hook those who normally turn away from documentary, we must find ways to be as funny, earthy, and poignant as life itself. How else to get audiences contemplating the darker aspects of life?

By juxtaposing material that demands interpretation by the audience, film can counterpoint antithetical ideas and moods with great economy. At the same time, it can kindle the audience's involvement with the dialectical nature of life.

THE OVERLAP CUT

DIALOGUE SEQUENCES

Another contrapuntal editing device useful to hide the telltale seams between shots is the *overlap cut* (also known as *lap cut* or *L cut*). The overlap cut brings sound in earlier than picture or picture in earlier than sound and thus avoids the jarring level cut, the underlying cause of all clunky boxcar editing.

Figure 14-2 shows a straight-cut version of a conversation between A and B. Whoever speaks is shown on the screen. This quickly becomes predictable and boring. You can alleviate this problem by slugging in some reaction shots (not shown).

Now look at the same conversation using overlap cutting. A starts speaking, but when we hear B's voice, we wait a sentence before cutting to him. B is interrupted by A, and this time we hold on B's frustrated expression before cutting to A, driving his point home. Before A has finished and because we are now interested in B's rising anger, we cut back to him shaking his head. When A has finished, B caps the discussion, and we make a level cut to the next sequence. The three sections of integrated reaction are marked in Figure 14-2 as x, y, and z.

When should you make overlap cuts? Usually it's done later in editing, but we need a guiding theory. Let's return for a moment to human consciousness, our ever-reliable model for editing. Imagine you are witnessing a conversation between two people; you have to turn from one to the other. Seldom will you turn your head at the right moment to catch the next speaker beginning—only an omniscient being could be so accurate. Inexperienced or bad editors often make neat, level (and omniscient) cuts between speakers, and the results have a packaged, sterile look that destroys the illusion of watching a spontaneous event.

In real life you can seldom predict who will speak next. The intrusion on our consciousness of a new voice in fact tells us where to look. To convince us a conversation is spontaneous, the editor should mostly follow shifts or anticipate

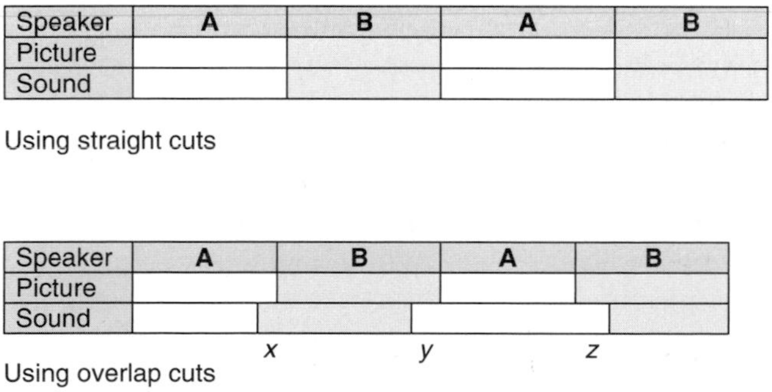

Speaker	A	B	A	B
Picture				
Sound				

Using straight cuts

Speaker	A	B	A	B
Picture				
Sound				

　　　　　　　　　x　　　　*y*　　　　*z*

Using overlap cuts

FIGURE 14-2 ————————————————————————————

Intercutting two speakers to make use of overlap cutting. Overlaps x, y, and z function as listening, reacting shots. This technique reduces the sound gaps between speakers without speeding up apparent pacing.

them. This replicates the disjunctive shifts we unconsciously make as our eyes follow our hearing or our hearing focuses in late on something just seen.

Effective cutting always mimics the needs and reactions of an involved observer, as if we were there ourselves. Listening to a speaker as she begins making her point, we often switch to consider the effect of the point on her listener. Even as we ponder, that listener begins to reply. A moment of forcefulness causes us to switch attention to the listener, so we glance back at her. The line of her mouth hardens, and we know she is disturbed.

We are getting complementary impressions—the speaker through our hearing and the listener through our vision. We listen to the person who acts but look at the person on whom she acts. When that situation reverses and our listener has begun his reply, we glance back to see how the original speaker is reacting. Always we are looking for visual or aural clues—in facial expressions, body language, or vocal tone—to the protagonists' inner lives.

 Editing often must hint at the subtext—that is, the hidden agenda that's going on under the surface. Subtexts make drama more rich and layered.

Good editing does this. It engages the spectator, not just in hearing and seeing each speaker as he utters (which would be tedious) but also in *interpreting what is going on inside each protagonist* through catching key moments of action, reaction, or subjective vision. In dramatic terms, this is the *search for subtext*, for what is going on beneath the surface.

For the ambitious editor the message is clear: Be true to life by conveying the developing sensations of a critical observer. Do this, and sound and picture changeover points are seldom level cuts. Overlap cuts achieve this important disjunction, allowing the film to cut from shot to shot independently of the "his turn, her turn, his turn" speech alternations in the sound track.

SEQUENCE TRANSITIONS

A transition from one sequence to the next may also be a staggered cut. Imagine a scene where a boy and girl discuss going out together. The boy says he is worried that the girl's mother will try to stop them. The girl says, "Oh don't worry, I can convince her." The next scene is of the mother closing the refrigerator with a bang and saying firmly, "Absolutely not!" to the aggrieved daughter.

A level cut is like a fast theatrical scene change. More interesting would be to cut from the boy/girl scene to the mother at the refrigerator while the girl is still saying ". . . I can convince her." While she is finishing her sentence, the picture cuts forward in time to show the mother slamming the fridge door—which carries metaphorical force. Then she caps it with her line, "Absolutely not!"

Another way to avoid the staccato level cut and merge one scene into the next would be to hold on the boy and girl, have the mother's angry voice say "Absolutely not!" over the tail end of their scene, and use the surprise of her incoming voice to motivate cutting to the mother's picture as the scene continues.

Either of these devices serves to make the "joints" between one sequence and the next less noticeable. Sometimes, of course, you want to bring a scene to a slow closure, perhaps with a fade-out, and then gently and slowly begin another, this time perhaps with a fade-in. More often, you want to keep up the momentum and get to the next scene. A level cut often seems to jerk the viewer rudely into a new place and time, while a dissolve integrates the two scenes, but dissolves insert a rest period between scenes and dissipate the carryover of momentum.

The overlap cut is the answer. It keeps the track alive and draws the viewer after it, so the transition seems more natural than forced. You have surely seen this done with sound effects: The factory worker rolls reluctantly out of bed, then as he shaves and dresses, we hear the increasingly loud sound of machinery until we cut in picture to him at work on the production line. Here *anticipatory sound* drags our attention forward to the next sequence. Because our curiosity demands an answer to the riddle of machine sounds in a bedroom, we do not find the location switch arbitrary.

 In L-cuts or lap-cuts, *anticipatory sound* arrives ahead of its accompanying picture, while *holdover sound* runs on after its picture has ended and a next one has arrived. These techniques are useful to soften or blur the transition between scenes.

Another overlap cutting technique makes sound work the other way; we cut from the man working on the assembly line to him getting some food out of his home refrigerator. *Holdover sound* of factory uproar subsides slowly as he exhaustedly eats some leftovers.

In the first example, the aggressive factory sound draws him forward out of his bedroom; in the second, it lingers even after he has gotten home. Each lap cut use implies a psychological narrative because each suggests that the sound exists in his head. It suggests how unpleasant his workplace is to him. At home he thinks of it and is sucked up by it; after work the din continues to haunt him.

Overlap cuts soften transitions between locations or suggest subtext and point of view by implying the inner consciousness of a central character. You could play it the other way, and let the silence of the home trail out into the workplace, so that he is seen at work, and the bedroom radio continues to play softly before being swamped by the rising uproar of the factory. At the end of the day, the sounds of laughter on the television set could displace the factory noise and make us cut to him sitting at home, relaxing with a sitcom.

Use sound and picture transitions creatively, and you transport the viewer forward without the ponderousness of optical effects like dissolves, fades, and (God help us) wipes. You can also scatter important clues about your characters' inner lives and imaginations.

MONO- AND BIDIRECTIONAL ATTENTION

In life we either probe our surroundings monodirectionally (eyes and ears on the same information source) or bidirectionally (eyes and ears directed at different sources). Our attention also moves in time—forward (anticipation and imagination) or backward (memory). Look for these facets in the films that inspire you and work out for yourself how they suggest eyes, ears, and intelligence working together while they dig for subtextual meanings.

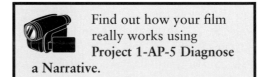

Film language can signify many aspects of shifting consciousness. Such shifts become associated with the characters, the storyteller, or both.

REGAINING YOUR OBJECTIVITY

After considerable editing, a debilitating familiarity sets in and your ability to make judgments seems to go numb. This is most likely to cripple director–editors who have lived with the intentions for the footage since their inception. Soon every alternative version looks similar, and all seem too long. Two steps are necessary. One is to make a flow chart of your film like a block diagram so you can see its ideas and intentions anew. The other is to show the working cut to a trial audience of a chosen few.

DIAGNOSIS: MAKING A FLOW CHART

Whenever you need a better understanding, it helps to translate it into another form. Statisticians wield the full implications of their figures by making a graph, pie chart, or other proportional image. In our case, we are dealing with the mesmerizing actuality of film, which, as we view it, embraces us within its unfolding present to the detriment of any overview. Luckily, a block diagram will give you a fresh perspective (see box) and make a radical analysis of your film easy.

Find out how your film really works using **Project 1-AP-5 Diagnose a Narrative.**

To use a block diagram:

➤ Stop your film after each sequence.
➤ Briefly describe the sequence's content in the box. A sequence might contribute:
  ● Factual information
  ● Information on or an introduction to a new character
  ● A new situation and a new thematic strand
  ● A location or a relationship that will be developed later in the film
  ● A special mood or feeling
➤ Describe what the sequence contributes to the film's development as a whole.
➤ Add timings (optional, but helpful for making decisions about length).
➤ Give each sequence an impact rating of 1 to 5 stars (helpful at seeing how well strong and weak materials are distributed).

Now you have a flow chart that lets you see, dispassionately and functionally, what is subconsciously present for an audience. What does the progression of contributions add up to? As with the first assembly, there are more problems hiding in the bushes:

- Lack of early impact or a pedestrian opening that makes the film a late starter (fatal on television)
- Redundancy, especially of expository information
- Necessary information inconsistently supplied
- Holes or backtracking apparent in progression
- Type and frequency of impact poorly distributed over the film's length (resulting in uneven dramatic progression)
- Similar thematic contributions made several ways (choose the best and dump or reposition the rest)
- Material that fails to advance the film (be brave and kill your darlings)
- The film's conclusion emerging early, leaving the remainder an unnecessary recapitulation
- Multiple endings (three is not uncommon—choose)

As each ailment emerges from the analysis, it suggests its own cure. Put these into effect, and you can feel rather than quantify the improvement. It hard to overstress the seductions film practices on its makers. After housecleaning, expect a new round of problems to surface. Make a new flow chart even though you feel it's unnecessary. Almost certainly you'll find more anomalies.

Over your career, much of this formal process will become second nature and occur spontaneously. Even so, filmmakers of long standing invariably profit from subjecting their work to this formal scrutiny.

A FIRST SHOWING

Knowing what every brick in your movie's edifice must accomplish, you are ready to test run your movie on a small audience. In a media organization, this may be the people you work for—producers, senior editors, or a sponsor—so the experience will be grueling. If you can, show the film first to half a dozen whose tastes and interests you respect. The less they know about your film and your aims, the better. Warn them that, as a work in progress, it is still technically raw and has materials missing—music, graphics, sound effects, end titles, whatever. Incidentally, placing a working title at the front helps because it signals the film's identity.

Before each public showing, the editor should check the film purely for *sound levels*. Even experienced filmmakers misjudge a film when sound inequities make it inaudible or overbearing. Present your film at its best, or risk getting misleadingly negative responses.

Your work with the flow chart has given you an agenda to explore with your first audience. You know the likely strong and weak points, so now you can find out.

SURVIVING YOUR CRITICS AND MAKING USE OF WHAT THEY SAY

After the viewing, ask for impressions of the film as a whole. You are about to test the film's working hypothesis and prove the "what it contributes" part of your analysis form. Don't be afraid to focus and direct your viewers' attention, or someone may lead off at a tangent. Listen carefully, but retain your bearings toward the piece as a whole. Say no more than strictly necessary; never *explain* the film or *explain* what you intended, as it will only compromise your audience's perceptions. A film must stand alone without explication from its authors, so concentrate on getting what your critics are really saying. If these people are your employers, you must be extremely silent.

 At screenings for a trial audience, never *explain* the film or *explain* what you intended. Your film is supposed to do that. Instead, turn any questions around and solicit the audience's perceptions. These will tell you how your film is actually functioning. Listen carefully and keep notes.

It takes great self-discipline to sit immobile and take notes. Hearing negative reactions and criticism of your work is emotionally battering. Expect to feel threatened, slighted, misunderstood, and unappreciated and to come away with a raging headache. Following is a typical order of inquiry. Note that it moves from large issues down to the component parts:

- What do audience members think are the film's theme or themes?
- What are the major issues in the film?
- Did the film feel the right length or was it too long?
- Which parts were unclear or puzzling?
- Which parts felt slow?
- Which parts were moving or otherwise successful?
- What did they feel about . . . [name of character]?
- What did they end up knowing about . . . [situation or issue]?

Depending on your trial audience's patience, you may get useful feedback on most of your film's parts and intentions. Allow for the biases and subjectivity that emerge in your critics. An occasional irritation is the critic who insists on talking about the film *he* would have made, not the film you have just shown. When this happens, diplomatically redirect the discussion. If several people report the same difficulty, wait. Further comments may cancel each other out and no action be called for. Resolve to make no changes without careful reflection, and keep

 Never under any circumstances will you be able to please everyone in any audience, so don't even be tempted to try. Instead, listen for any general agreement that you can usefully act on. Hold onto your deepest intentions for the film, though.

this in mind: When you ask people for criticism, they look for possible changes—if only to make a contributory mark on your work.

Most important is to *hold onto your central intentions*. Never revise them without strong and positive reasons to do so. Meanwhile, *act only on those suggestions that support and further your central intentions*. This is a dangerous time for the filmmaker and indeed for any artist. It is fatally easy to let go of your work's underlying identity and lose your sense of direction. Keep listening, and don't be tempted by strong emotions to carve into your film precipitously.

After one of these sessions it's quite normal to feel that you have failed, that your film is junk, and that all is vanity. The fact is that works in progress always look fairly awful. Audiences are disproportionately affected by a wrong sound balance here, a shot or two that need clipping, or a sequence that belongs earlier.

 At this stage, it's quite normal to feel that you have failed, that your film is junk, and that all is vanity. This is the low point of the artistic process. Be patient and you will recover!

Wait two or three days for the criticism to settle. Now you can look at your film with the eyes of the three audience members who never understood the boy was the woman's son. Yes, their relationship is twice implied, but there's a way to insert an extra line where the boy calls her "Mom." Problem solved. You move on to the next one, and solve that, too. This is the artistic process.

EDITING PITFALLS

Here are some traps that emerge during editing that you'll want to avoid:

- *Misidentified sources*—Allowing reenacted or reconstructed material to stand unidentified in a film made of otherwise original and authentic materials will get you in trouble. Identify the material's origin by narration or subtitle. Identify speakers, too, if they need it, with subtitles.

- *Spatial errors*—If you don't check essential geography, you can edit actions to suggest that the kitchen is next to the bathroom, and London is near Madrid.

- *Temporal mistakes*—Show events in a chronology that is demonstrably wrong, and your critics will try using it to discredit the film, as happened to Michael Moore with *Roger and Me* (1989, United States).

- *Elision judgments*—Documentary editing involves compression; long statements can be plundered to serve the film but misrepresent the speaker's original pronouncement. Any participant who runs his own audio recording while you film (as happened to me when filming the leader of the British Union of Fascists) may be preparing to sue you.

- *Bogus truth*—You can make truth and meaning by juxtaposing unrelated events or statements. Even though something you've done is invisible and insignificant to you and even a general audience, participants may be scandalized. They are shocked that you have compressed buying a house into three shots, so be ready to defend and justify each aspect of your narrative flow.

- *Participant fears*—Sometimes you face a participant's fear/fantasy when, after weeks of anguish, she wants to retract an innocuous statement vital to your film. You have her signature and the legal right to use it, and you know it can bring her no harm. Can you, *should* you, go ahead and override her wish? Your good name and career may suffer, and at the very least your conscience will prick you for violating someone's trust. Then, again, you may have a lot of time or money invested. Maybe a trusted third party can talk her out of her fears?

- *Informed consent*—A liability to a participant may emerge only at the editing stage. You find, let's say, that you must either release a significant film that causes pain or danger to someone who trusted you or remove something vital to your film's effectiveness. At stake is "informed consent." If you work for a media organization, they will have an explicit policy that you should know intimately. It's designed to protect the integrity of the organization of which you are a part. Participants should understand how their material will be used and sign a release in good faith indicating that they understand the consequences. You have a right to imply a critical view of someone's behavior or function but seldom to deceive them and cause them harm. Public figures may be fair game, but private people often merit your diligent protection.

Listening to your conscience is good, and consulting with responsible friends, colleagues, and a lawyer is usually better. Documentaries are critical, they are not made to please people. Real dilemmas do not lie in choosing between right and wrong, but between right and right. Seek advice—and don't feel that ethical dilemmas are ever something you must solve alone. You may have to level with your participant and see what he feels.

PARTICIPANTS' VIEWINGS

When should a participant have the right to see and veto a cut? This seems like an easy and natural thing to agree to, but it's a mine-field. Your work, like that of a journalist, also counts as free speech and you have rights that you shouldn't give away without good cause.

So, if you:

- Have made a film that might land you or your participants in legal trouble, then get legal

 You secure a personal release from participants so you have the right to edit as you see fit. When they want to see your film before it's finished, you can use the argument that nobody interviewed by a journalist expects to see the reporter's notebook or to vet the article before publication. Sometimes, of course, an ethical or moral right will override your authorial privileges and you must bend (gracefully, if you can).

advice. Be aware that lawyers look on the dark side, because their job is to look for snags and to err on the side of caution.

- Agreed at the outset that you would solicit participants' feedback, then this is their right.
- Did *not* work out a consultative agreement with your subjects, then it's a bad idea to embark on one now without very strong cause.
- Agree to show a work-in-progress cut to participants, then do so only after clearly explaining the limitations to their rights.
- Are willing to take advice but not instruction, then be really clear or expect much bad feeling.
- Think a participant may feel upset or betrayed by something in your film, then prepare him or her in advance so he does not feel humiliated in the presence of family and friends. Fail to do so, and that person may henceforward regard you as a traitor and all film people as frauds.

Participants see themselves with great subjectivity. To overcompensate in the hope of pleasing them is to abandon documentary work for public relations. Sticky situations at public showings usually go best if you have some general audience members *and* the person's friends and family present. Their enjoyment and the approval of the majority usually override the subject's momentary sensitivity and leave him or her feeling good about the film as a whole.

THE USES OF PROCRASTINATION

Whether you are pleased or depressed about your film, it is always good to cease work for awhile and do something else. This might be taking a week away from the film, or, if you are under deadline, going to a birthday party instead of working all night. If this anxiety is new to you, take comfort: You are deep in the throes of the creative experience. This is the long, painful labor before giving birth. When you pick up the film again after a judicious lapse, your fatigue and defeatism will have gone away, and the film's problems and their solutions will seem manageable again.

 After sustained editing work, try putting your film away for a week or two. When you return, your energy and optimism will have recovered, and making changes no longer seems so monumentally difficult.

TRY, TRY AGAIN

A film of substance that requires a long editing evolution will need several new trial audiences. Try the last cut on the original audience to see what progress they think you've made. Having a lot of editing in my background, I believe you really create a documentary in the editing process. Magic and miracles happen in an alchemy that is unknown even to crew members unless they have lived through it.

CHAPTER 15

EDITING: FROM FINE CUT TO SOUND MIX

THE FINE CUT

With typical caution, filmmakers call the end result of the editing process the fine, not the final, cut, since there may still be minor changes and accommodations. Some of these arise out of laying music or other sound tracks in preparation for *locking* the picture ready to make a master mixed sound track.

CHECK ALL SOURCE MATERIAL

Before picture lock, review all dailies to make sure you've overlooked nothing useful. This is tedious and time consuming, but almost invariably there will be some "Eureka!" discoveries by way of compensation. If there aren't, you can rest easy.

  If you haven't yet analyzed an imaginative film for its sound, consider using **Project 1-AP-1 Analyze or Plan Using the Split-Page Script Form** either to study an existing film or for planning sound in yours.

SOUND

Especially if you have given thought to your film's sound design all along, the sound mix will be a special and even exhilarating occasion. Sound is an incomparable stimulant to the audience's imagination, but only rarely does sound design get due attention. Usually it languishes on the back burner until the "audio sweetening" session is in view, an expression I dislike for its rescue connotations. Better terms are *sound design*, *sound editing*, and *sound mix*.

Finalizing sound is of course another computer operation. On your first films you can do a good job using the audio suite supplied with your editing program, but for more advanced work it's usual to use Digidesign Pro Tools® with a first-rate amplifier and speaker system that replicates a good cinema's sound environment. Few cinemas approach the state of the art, but good sound, as Dolby® cinemas know, is good business, so sound may yet get its day. Currently, most people see documentaries on television sets, so it's important to check how your track sounds on television. More about this later.

SOUND DESIGN DISCUSSIONS

If sound design has been a concern from the inception of the film, this part of the process will be one of finalizing. Mostly film sound just evolves, so an overview discussion near the end of editing is a good way to ensure you are tackling the big picture. Although film sound is composed of dialogue, atmospheres, effects, and music, it is a mistake to think of them separately. How and why you intend using music, and what music rights may complicate your choice, also require careful discussion. For more information see **Chapter 33, Using Music and Working with a Composer**.

Decide the sound profile for the whole film before the editor goes to work reorganizing dialogue tracks and laying in missing sound effects. Assign each sequence a particular sound identity. This might be loud and noisy, mysterious, lyrical, building from quiet to a crescendo—all sorts of patterns and moods might apply. You should also agree on how to tackle known sound problems. This is a priority, as dialogue reconstruction—if it's needed—is an expensive, specialized, and time-consuming business, and no film can survive having it done poorly (see "Postsynchronizing Dialogue (ADR)" on the following page).

Though documentary leads the way in narrative inventiveness, feature films use far more resources to develop their sound tracks, and documentarians can learn much from them. Walter Murch, the doyen of editors and sound designers, makes a practice of watching a film he is editing with the sound turned off, so he has to imagine what the sound might be. Other functions of sound, listed in Randy Thom's "Designing a Movie for Sound," (www.filmsound.org/articles/designing_for_sound.htm) are to:

- Indicate a historical period
- Indicate changes in time or geographical locale
- Connect otherwise unconnected ideas, characters, places, images, or moments
- Heighten ambiguity or diminish it
- Startle or soothe

It's not the quantity or complexity of sound that makes a great sound track, but rather the psychological journey it leads you on. This is the art of *psychoacoustics*. Usually sound does this most effectively when you use simple and subjective sound rather than complex and naturalistic. By "subjective" I mean that you use sounds for their emotional or narrative significance—either to the characters or to the viewer—rather than the full, numbing panoply of sounds often present in contemporary locations.

SOUND CLICHÉS

Sound clichés result from loading up a movie with stereotypical sounds instead of responding creatively to the narrative needs of the movie. A cat seen walking across a kitchen does not call for a cat meow, unless said cat is visibly demanding its breakfast. This is a sound cliché. For a hilarious list of them, look up www.filmsound.org/cliche. Here all bicycles have bells; car tires always squeal when a car pulls away, turns, or stops; storms start instantaneously; wind always whistles; doors always squeak; and much, much more. The message? Less is more in sound, too.

POSTSYNCHRONIZING DIALOGUE (ADR)

Postsynchronizing dialogue, very rare in documentary, is used to remedy poor dialogue tracks and means asking participants to become actors lip-syncing to what they said in an existing shot. You'll see its full horrors in second-rate fiction filmmaking where it's variously called *dubbing, looping,* or *automatic dialogue replacement* (ADR). Actors in a studio watch a screen or monitor and rehearse portions of their lines to picture until given the okay to record. Long dialogue exchanges must be broken into small increments. Voices invariably sound flat and dead in contrast with live location recordings, and this is not because they lack background presence, which can always be added, or even because sound perspective and location acoustics are missing. What kills ADR is the artificial situation. The poor actor is flying blind as he labors to reconstitute ten seconds of dialogue. He is completely in the hands of whoever is directing each few sentences. Actors hate it.

However good the whole, it invariably lowers the impression of actors' performances so they hate ADR with a passion. Luckily, documentary audiences are tolerant of rough sound recording, which they understand is the trade-off for capturing reality. So never consider ADR unless the original is incomprehensible. For marginal recording, the usual documentary solution is to add subtitles.

RECREATING SOUND EFFECTS IN THE FOLEY STUDIO

You can, however, fit sound effects to your film, whether shot on location or more recently in a Foley studio, and they will work fine. The Foley process was named after its intrepid inventor, one Jack Foley, who realized back in the 1940s that you could mime all the right sounds to picture if you had a sound studio equipped with a range of resources, materials, and props. A Foley studio has a variety of surfaces—concrete, heavy wood, light wood, carpet, linoleum, gravel, and so on. To this collection, Foley artists may add sand, paper, or cloth to modify footsteps so they suit what's on the screen. My job in an appalling Jayne Mansfield comedy (*The Sheriff of Fractured Jaw*, Raoul Walsh, 1959, United Kingdom) was to make horse footsteps with coconuts and steam engine noises with a modified motorcycle engine. It was great fun. We also shot all the footsteps, body movements, and horse harnesses jangling.

It takes some ingenuity to create the right sound for a particular shot. Baking powder under compression in a sturdy plastic bag, for instance, makes the right scrunching noise for footsteps in snow, and for a film about boxing you might have to experiment with punching a cabbage or thumping a sandbag to get a decent range of body blows. Paradoxically, many sounds must be contrived because the genuine article sounds phony. A door closing that sounds like someone kicking a cardboard box destroys the level of illusion on which all films depend. Making them sound authentic is an art.

Create sounds to fit a repetitive action such as knocking on a door, shoveling snow, or footsteps by recording their action a little slower. Then, on the computer, remove some frames before each impact's attack. More complex sync effects (two people walking through a quadrangle) will have to be postsynced to picture, paying attention to the different surfaces that the feet pass over (grass, gravel, concrete, etc.).

You can see Foley work in Luigi Falorni and Byambasuren Davaa's *The Story of the Weeping Camel* (2003, Germany), where they have recreated many spot effects. Some of the most important action with camels was shot with long lenses. The mike being distant meant sound was unusable. Films on nature subjects commonly contain a lot of sound recreation.

A grueling postsync session makes one understand two things: that location recordists who procure good original recordings are worth their weight in gold and that the best feature sound and editing crews are really top notch at their jobs. On a complex production with a big budget, the cost is fully justified. For the low-budget filmmaker, improvisation can cut costs. What matters is that sound effects are appropriate and that they are in sync with the action onscreen. Where and how you acquire them are not so important providing they feel authentic. You can find appropriate sound effects in sound libraries, but never assume from a printed list that an effect is usable until you've seen it against picture. Googling "sound effects library" will turn up many sources of sound libraries. Some even let you listen or download effects. Try Sound Ideas at www.sound-ideas.com/bbc.html.

One caution: Sound libraries sometimes have material shot long ago, and effects may come with a heavy ambience or system hiss. Loud or exotic sounds like helicopters, Bofors guns, and elephants rampaging through a Malaysian jungle are no problem. It's nitty-gritty noises like footsteps on grass, door slams, or "small dog growling" that are hard to find in a useable version. At one time, only *six* different gunshots were in use throughout the film industry. I heard attempts at recording new ones. Authentic guns sounded like ruptured air hoses—not at all what you expect. And meeting expectation is the key to getting it right.

 Equalization (EQ) is the filtering and profiling of each individual track either to match others or to create maximum intelligibility, listener appeal, or ear comfort.

EQUALIZATION (EQ) AND WHAT THE SOUND MIX CAN DO

The culmination of the editing process is to mix the component sound tracks. Balancing tracks is not just a matter of adjusting levels; it also takes *equalization* adjustments. Each sound track contains a variety of frequencies, and each group of frequencies is adjustable by level relative to other groups. For instance, in a busy street we see two people talking, but their conversation is on the margin of intelligibility due to a heavy traffic background. Their voices are in the frequency range of 500 to 3000 Hz (hertz, or cycles per second), but most of the traffic is below 200 Hz. By "rolling off" (or *attenuating*) frequencies in the bass area you lower the volume of the band of frequencies below the speech range. Voices now emerge louder and clearer because the competition is weaker (Figure 15-1).

Equalization has other uses. A voice recorded from two mike positions doesn't match when you cut the tracks together, but by tweaking the different bands of component frequencies they can perhaps become indistinguishable. You can also use EQ to make sound effects more comfortable on the ear, or more striking, and you can use it to prevent background sounds on one track from competing with the foreground on another, which might be speech or music. Sound and sound mixing deserve a very large book all to themselves, so what follows is a list of essentials along with some tips.

You are ready to mix down tracks into one master track when you have:

- Finalized the content of your film
- Fitted music
- Split dialogue tracks, grouping them by equalization and level commonality:
  - A separate track for each mike position used in dialogue recording
  - Sometimes a different track for each speaker, depending on how much EQ is necessary for each mike position on each character
  - *Filled in backgrounds* (missing sections of background ambience, so there are no dead spaces or abrupt background changes)
- Recorded and laid narration (if there is any)
- Recorded and laid sound effects and mood-setting atmospheres
- Finalized sound time line contents

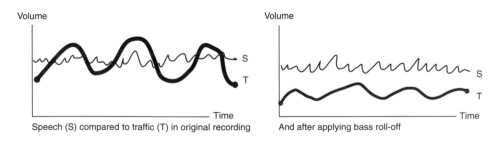

Speech (S) compared to traffic (T) in original recording   And after applying bass roll-off

FIGURE 15-1———————————————————————————

Representation of recorded voices in a heavy traffic atmosphere, first as recorded then using bass attenuation or "roll-off."

The mix procedure determines the following:

- *Sound levels* (say, between a dialogue foreground voice against a background of noisy factory sounds if, and only if, they are on separate tracks)
- *Equalization for consistent quality*
- *Level changes* (fade up, fade down, sound dissolves, and level adjustments to accommodate sound perspective and such new track elements as narration, music, or interior monologue)
- *Sound processing* (adding echo, reverberation, telephone effect, etc.)
- *Dynamic range* (a compressor squeezes the broad dynamic range of a movie into the narrow range favored in TV transmission; a limiter leaves the main range alone but limits peaks to a preset maximum)
- *Perspective* (to some degree, EQ and level manipulation can mimic perspective changes, thus helping create a sense of space and dimensionality through sound)
- *Multichannel sound distribution* (if you are developing a stereo track or 5.1 surround sound treatment, a sound specialist will send different elements to each sound channel to create a sense of horizontal spread and sound space)
- *Noise reduction* (Dolby and other noise-reduction systems help minimize any appreciable system hiss during quiet passages)

SOUND MIX PREPARATION

Track elements appear below in the common hierarchy of importance, but that order may vary; under some circumstances, for instance, music might occupy the foreground and dialogue be purposely inaudible. As you cut and lay sound tracks, consider using the program's audio waveform option (Figure 15-2). It displays sound modulations and saves you from cutting off the barely audible tail of a decaying sound or clipping the attack. Sound editing should be done at high volume, so you hear everything that's there—or that isn't there when it should be. Laying tracks with a digital sound editing program such as Pro Tools means you can edit with surgical precision, even within a syllable. The layout is visibly logical, and you can hear your work immediately.

NARRATION OR VOICE-OVER

If you lay narration or interior monologue, you will need to fill gaps between narration sections with room tone so the track remains live, particularly during a quiet sequence. If you're writing narration, see **Chapter 32, Creating Narration.**

DIALOGUE TRACKS AND THE PROBLEM OF INCONSISTENCIES

Digital editing systems can handle many tracks, but it is prudent to premix groups of tracks so you leave final control of essentials till last. First, you will have to carefully divide dialogue tracks. Because different camera positions occasion different mike positioning, a sequence's dialogue tracks played "as is" will

FIGURE 15-2

Waveform option in Final Cut Pro®, which allows easier sound editing by displaying frequency and amplitude (or volume) of a chosen track segment.

change in level and room acoustics from shot to shot. The result is ragged and distracting when your film calls for the seamless continuity familiar from feature films. Your painstaking, labor-intensive sound work will be as follows:

➤ *Split the dialogue tracks*; that is, lay them on separate tracks according to speaker and mike positioning. For instance:
  ↪ In a scene shot from two angles and having two mike positions, all close shot sound goes on one track and all the medium shot sound goes on the other.
  ↪ With four or five mike positions, expect to lay at least four or five tracks
  ↪ Tracks may have to be subdivided according to character, especially if one is louder than the other. This is because they may require different EQ settings.
  ↪ Determine EQ settings roughly during track laying, but leave final settings until the mix. Aim to make all voices consistent and to bring all tracks into acceptable compatibility. The viewer usually expects sound perspective to match the different camera distances.
➤ *Clean up background tracks* of extraneous noises, creaks, and mike handling sounds—anything that doesn't overlap dialogue and can be removed. Any resulting gaps will sound like drop-out unless filled with the correct room tone.

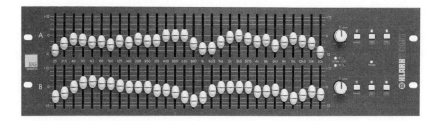

FIGURE 15-3

Graphic equalizer. When each slider is midway, all tracks play "flat" (as recorded). Improve a troublesome track by raising or lowering the volume of particular frequency bands. The resulting slider positions then draw out a graph of the equalizer's settings. (Photo courtesy of Klark Teknik.)

Inconsistent Backgrounds

Frequently when you cut between two speakers in the same location, the background to each is different in level or quality. The microphone may have been angled differently, or perhaps background traffic or other activities changed over time. The cure is to:

- Use the location presence track to augment the lighter track so it matches its heavier counterpart.

- Consider using a graphic equalizer to filter out an intrusive background sound (Figure 15-3). A high-pitched whine occupying a narrow band of frequency or traffic rumble can be lowered. Graphic equalization lets you tune out the offending frequency, but by losing the offending frequency you also lose all sounds in that frequency band, including that frequency in your character's voices.

- Join dissimilar backgrounds or room tones as a quick dissolve behind a commanding foreground sound. The new foreground distracts the audience's attention from noticing the change. The worst place to make a nasty sound change is in the clear.

Inconsistent Voice Qualities

When speakers' voice qualities vary, your audience experiences strain and irritation from adjusting to irrational changes. The causes can include:

- Varying acoustical environments in the location
- Different mikes
- Different mike working distances

These variations play havoc with consistency; however, intelligent sound filtering at the mix stage plus some additional background tracks can greatly improve consistency.

LAYING MUSIC TRACKS

Laying music is not difficult, but acquiring it legally may be (see **Chapter 33, Using Music and Working with a Composer**). To make library music conclude at a certain point, back-lay it from the known ending point, then fade it up at the starting point. If the music is only a little too long, you can commonly find repeated sections, so try cutting one out. Conversely, if it's a little short, copy a section and repeat it.

In and Out Points

Cut in music or any prerecorded sound just before the first sound attack so we don't hear atmosphere first. Arrow A in Figure 15-4 represents the ideal cut-in point; to its left is unwanted presence. To the right of A are three attacks in succession that lead to a decay down to silence at arrow B.

Attack–Sustain–Decay Cutting

The sound profile in Figure 15-4 appears in many sound effects (footsteps, for instance). By removing sound between x and y we could reduce three footfalls to two. This editing strategy has many uses.

SPOT SOUND EFFECTS

Spot sound effects are those that sync to something on-screen, like a car door closing, a coin placed on a table, or someone picking up a house phone from its cradle. Important sound is often unavoidably poor in the location recording. A chapel interior, for instance, may have the heavy drone of trucks from outside, so you must replace atmospheres and footsteps. These must be synchronized and have the right perspective. You can hide an unavoidable background change by making the transition behind a commanding foreground effect, such as a doorbell ringing. Otherwise, bring a new background in or out by fading it up or down; don't let it thump in and out as cuts because *the ear registers a sudden sound change far more acutely than one that is gradual.*

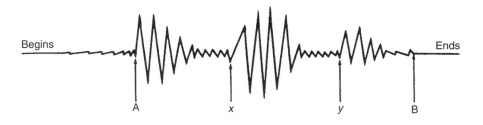

FIGURE 15-4

Diagram of sound attack and decay for a recording of three footsteps. Points A and B are ideal in and out cutting points. Points x and y are alternative in points.

ATMOSPHERES AND BACKGROUND SOUND

You lay atmospheres to create a mood. It might be morning birdsong over a valley or singing and tire irons jangling from within a garage. Some notes to remember:

- Obey screen logic by laying atmospheres to cover the entire sequence, not just a part of it.
- When a door opens during an interior scene, the exterior atmosphere (children's playground, for instance) will rise for the duration that the door is open.
- When you create a sound dissolve, lay the requisite amounts to allow for the overlap.
- Listen for inequities hiding in the overlaps, such as the recordist quietly calling "Cut."

SOUND MIX STRATEGY

PREMIXING

One sequence of a feature-length documentary might require 40 or more sound tracks, so you must premix tracks in groups. Do this *in an order that leaves control over the most important elements until last*. Since intelligibility means audible dialogue, keep control over the dialogue-to-background level till the last stage of mixing. Documentary sound may already be on the margin of intelligibility, and were you to premix dialogue and effects early, any added effects or music would uncontrollably augment and compete with that dialogue.

TAILORING

Many tracks, played as laid, enter and exit abruptly and leave an unpleasantly jagged impression on the listener. People respond less well to your subject matter, so you want to achieve a seamless effect whenever you are not deliberately disrupting attention. Cutting from a quiet to a noisy track, or vice versa, can be minimized by tailoring—that is, by building in a quick fade-up or fade-down so the louder track meets quieter on its own terms. The effect on-screen is still that of a cut, but not one that assaults the ear (Figure 15-5).

COMPARATIVE LEVELS: ERR ON THE SIDE OF CAUTION

Mix studios use first-rate speakers, but the resulting mix can be misleading, since most people will see your documentary on a domestic television set, which has a small, inexpensive speaker. The unlucky home viewer loses not only frequency and dynamic ranges but dynamic separation (that is, between loud and soft) as well. Foregrounds nicely separated from backgrounds in the mix become swamped on the home television. Be conservative, therefore, when you add a heavy background to a dialogue scene; keep foregrounds and backgrounds well separated. A mix suite will obligingly play your track through a television set, if you ask, so you can check what the home viewer will hear.

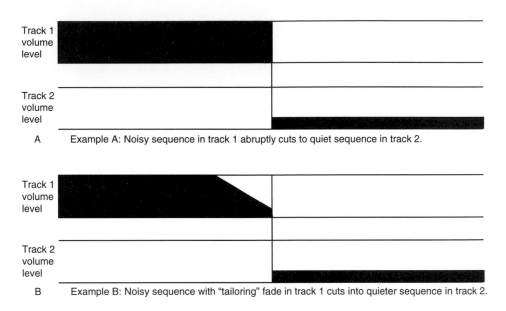

Track 1
volume
level

Track 2
volume
level

A   Example A: Noisy sequence in track 1 abruptly cuts to quiet sequence in track 2.

Track 1
volume
level

Track 2
volume
level

B   Example B: Noisy sequence with "tailoring" fade in track 1 cuts into quieter sequence in track 2.

FIGURE 15-5

Abrupt sound cut tailored by quick fade of outgoing track so it matches the level of the incoming track.

REHEARSE, THEN RECORD

When you mix in a studio, you as the director must approve each stage. You and your editor must know whether each sequence meets your expectations. To your requests, and according to what the editor has laid in the sound tracks, the mix engineer will offer alternatives from which to choose. Mixing is best accomplished one section at a time, building sequence by sequence from convenient stopping points. At the end, *listen to the whole mix without stopping*, just as the audience will. Usually there's an anomaly or two to put right.

SAFETY COPIES

A sound mix being a long and painstaking process, professionals immediately make backup copies on a durable medium to be stored in multiple buildings in case of loss or theft. Follow the same backup principle for picture; that is, keep media masters, safety copies, or film negatives and internegatives in different places so all trace of your work doesn't vanish. An unlucky Chicago group suffered irreparable losses in a fire, and a friend in New Orleans found 10 years of work wiped out by Hurricane Katrina. More usually it's thieves walking off with a computer. Expect the worst and you're not always wrong.

MUSIC AND EFFECTS TRACKS

In case your film makes an international sale, make a transcript of the whole film. A foreign festival can then make a simultaneous translation for people to hear through headphones. Also make a music- and effects-only mix, which is often called an *M & E track*. This allows a foreign language crew to dub the speakers and mix the new voices in with the original atmosphere, effects, and music tracks.

GOING FURTHER

For structural and other dramatic or conceptual problems, see **Chapter 34, Editing: Refinements and Structural Problems**. An excellent source of information for all aspects of sound in film is www.filmsound.org. These books are also helpful:

Purcell, John. *Dialogue Editing for Motion Pictures*. Boston: Focal Press, 2007.

Rose, Jay. *Audio Postproduction for Film and Video*. Boston: Focal Press, 2008.

Sonnenschein, David. *Sound Design: The Expressive Power of Music, Voice and Sound Effects in Cinema*. Studio City, CA: Michael Wiese, 2002.

Wyatt, Hilary. *Audio Postproduction for Television and Film*. Boston: Focal Press, 2004.

Yewdall, David Lewis. *The Practical Art of Motion Picture Sound*. Boston: Focal Press, 2007.

CHAPTER 16

TITLES AND ACKNOWLEDGMENTS

TITLES

Although every film acquires a working title, its makers often pluck the final title late during an agony of indecision. Your film's title may in fact be the only advertising copy your audience ever sees, so it should be short and snappy and epitomize the film's allure. Because TV listings and festival programs rarely have space to describe their offerings, the title you choose may be your sole means of drawing an audience:

- *Style*—Form follows function. Documentary titles are usually plain and unfussy. Find examples among TV documentaries or video rentals. Some of the most artistically ambitious films use brief and classically simple white-on-black titles. You could do a lot worse.

- *Font, layout, and size*—Choose font for clarity and size, and avoid small lettering. Anything too small or too fancy disappears on the television screen, where most work appears. Because differently adjusted televisions often clip the edges of the image, keep titling well within a safe area. Be aware, too, that images shot in 1.33:1 aspect ratio will likely be cropped top and bottom to make the film fit today's 1.78:1 ratio. Any titles, especially subtitles, that you place there would be lost.

 In your titles, don't let the same name appear too often, even if you did do nearly all the work. Keep thank-yous brief, and check and recheck spelling.

- *Overladen titles*—A sure sign of amateurism is a film loaded with a long and egocentric welter of credits. Don't let the same name crop up in multiple key capacities, and keep acknowledgments eloquently brief.

- *Contractual or other obligations*—Participants often grant favors in return for an acknowledgment in the titles, so be sure to honor your debts to the letter. Funding sources may stipulate acknowledgments in prescribed wording, so double-check this and all such agreements before you lock your titles down. A television release will often have a contract specifying the titles and closed captions that you must provide.

- *Spelling*—Check titles and subtitles scrupulously for spelling and use at least two highly literate, eagle-eyed checkers. The proper spelling for people's names should receive special care, since a mistake indicates for all time that you cared too little about someone to get his or her name right.

 Time the on-screen duration of a title by reading the contents of each screen aloud one-and-a-half times.

- *Title lengths*—See box for title length calculations. Long *rolling* or *crawl titles* (titles that slide up or across the screen) must run fast, or TV stations chop them off. Check the speed of other people's titles.

 Keep titles and fonts classically simple and you can't go wrong. Aim for legibility and to ensure that anyone viewing your film in another aspect ratio won't miss titles or subtitles.

- *Digital titling*—Good-looking titles are not difficult in digital postproduction. Editing software comes with basic titling, but you may need a plug-in program for refinements. You should have the choice of a large array of typefaces with drop shadow, movement, crawl, and other exotic behaviors. Resist the temptation to exult in your new freedom; keep titling classically simple—unless of course your film's topic and treatment call for something more in keeping. Digital postproduction is WYSIWYG (What You See Is What You Get) so you can keep experimenting until everything looks right. Superimposed lettering, colored or white, is more legible when you add a black outline, and this is especially true for subtitles. Often they run over a light or dark background, and the black outline is crucial in keeping them legible.

FOREIGN MARKETS: SUBTITLES AND TRANSCRIPT

As mentioned in the previous chapter, a foreign festival may ask for a typed transcript of all dialogue in the film (for simultaneous translation), and they may also stipulate a subtitled print in a particular language. This is straightforward although time-consuming to do. Here are some guidelines:

1. Make an *abbreviated* transcription of dialogue you want to appear as subtitles. Compress dialogue exchanges down to essentials—you don't want the audience so busy reading that it doesn't see your film.

2. Get the text translated by a literate, native speaker (not that friend who took several Spanish classes). Have it typed up with all the appropriate accents and then checked by at least two other people who are literate native speakers.

3. Make a copy of your film ready to lay in superimposed subtitles.

4. Pick a clear typeface in yellow with black edging. Your subtitles must be clearly legible no matter how light or dark the background. Use a size of font that is easy to read on a TV screen and place subtitles well into the TV safe area so nothing gets lost on a differently adjusted set.

5. Place every sentence within a continuous shot. This is because we read the title all over again if it overhangs the next shot. This is very irritating and unnecessary.

6. To accommodate this, break long sentences into short sections, indicating anything that is run-on with an ellipsis (...), as in this example, which is spread out over four shots:

How are you?	Shot 1
I feel OK just now . . .	Shot 2
. . . but I am hoping you can . . .	Shot 3
. . . give me some advice.	Shot 4

7. *Copyright*—At the very end of the titles, remember to include your name and the © symbol, with the year as a claim to the copyright of the material. To file for copyright in the United States, look up the U.S. Copyright Office at www.loc.gov/copyright and follow the directions. If you reside in another country, be sure to check out the correct copyright procedure with professionals.

LEGAL OMISSIONS

If and when you come to sell your film, legal omissions can be costly or even paralyzing. Be sure you have the legal right to use everything in your film, especially contributions by participants and all music that was not a legitimate part of a location's sound. No television channel will transmit your film unless you have documentary proof that all contents are legal for them to transmit.

PRESS KIT AND WEB SITE

Now your film is complete, you can enter it in festivals. People who see or read about your work may look for you on the Internet, so develop a Web site for your film where they can reach you or buy copies. To help you market your work at festivals, carry press kits to give out. This might be a folder containing a leaflet promoting the film, quotations from any praise or reviews it has received, brief details on the careers of the makers, and good quality photographs. Everything printed should include your e-mail and Web site address, phone number, fax number, and mailing address.

FESTIVALS

Find festivals via the Web sites cited in **Chapter 36, From School to Film Industry**. At last, you get to experience the ultimate rite of passage: seeing your film in the company of your true masters—a paying audience. This can either be thrilling or chastening. Whichever comes your way, it's the final reckoning, the last phase of learning, and represents closure on that project. Go to all the festivals you can afford and go armed with press kits and business cards. You will be surprised what develops from serendipitous encounters at screenings and conferences.

Now what film will you make next?

BOOK II

ADVANCED ISSUES

PART 6

DOCUMENTARY AESTHETICS

Having done some documentary work, you are now ready to go further. Maybe you sense you aren't yet using the screen to its utmost, or you want to make films that are more cinematic. Perhaps you want better subjects or to more effectively liberate the heart and soul of your participants and what they represent.

Part 6 explores several aspects of *aesthetics*. The word itself suggests choice when in documentary one often feels handcuffed by subject matter. In a film about a primary school, for instance, you may want to intercut classroom material with interviews with teachers and children, then add visuals of kids in the playground and at home. This is a norm that arises from one's conditioning by television. It's the result of flying visits by well-educated, sociologically inclined people whose habit is to illustrate recent trends and surveys through speech-driven filmmaking. Is this you, or do you want something different?

Imagine instead that you are Vietnamese or Lithuanian and speak little English. You have free rein to shoot in an English-speaking school. Everything strikes you as different: the children's faces, clothes, schoolbooks. What they eat, the architecture of their school, the schoolroom layout, the children's body language—everything feels particular, significant, and special. What you hear is not the meaning of their language but a vocal composition mixed with birdsong from an open window. You are feverish to record this new world's textures and imagery. Later, the school sees your film and is astonished at the sheer otherness of what you've found in the familiar.

How to bring this anthropological freshness and sensitivity to our own tribe? Radical vision comes from purging oneself of the cultural packaging that muffles actuality, but it's a tough undertaking. Picasso said he took three years as a child learning to draw like Raphael, then many, many years to draw as children do. More individual vision will come from choosing outside the obvious, default aesthetic options. Doing this rigorously is in effect to deprogram oneself. The resources to do this lie within you and are the subject of Part 6. Every chapter in this Part contains practical ideas not only for conceptualizing your documentary but also for directing, camera operating, and editing it.

CHAPTER 17

POINT OF VIEW AND THE STORYTELLER

This chapter is particularly relevant to anyone operating a camera or directing. It deals with an aspect of documentary making—point of view—that is hard to conceptualize and uncertain to control. Differing points of view—those of the characters and that of the film—are the mark of mature filmmaking minds.

 Film is always in the present tense and makes the spectator *infer cause and effect even as events are happening.* Like music—which Ingmar Bergman considered film's nearest relative—the screen grasps the spectator's heart and mind with existential insistency.

FILM, LITERATURE, AND POINT OF VIEW

Point of view as a concept comes from literature, but film and literature are very different. Reading is a pensive activity during which you create the narrative in your mind's eye. Film you experience as an onslaught of events in the here and now. Literature can direct the reader into the past or in the future, but film grips the spectator in its relentlessly advancing present so that even a flashback quickly turns into another ongoing present. Watching a really engrossing film is thus rather like dreaming. What a difficult medium to control! Yet control is possible.

Documentary realism strives to make us feel we are seeing unmediated reality, but analysis soon reveals that its makers and their values dominate any documentary. Like the fiction films they resemble, documentaries are authored constructs, and this will become abundantly clear if you analyze one (see box on the following page).

When you collect the evidence from which your film will be made, you have more control than you know. For the different filming situations discussed in this chapter I have provided explanatory diagrams. The camera outline symbolizes a recording eye and ear, but to

See how a film projects its point of view and those of its characters using **Project 1-AP-8 Assessing a Director's Thematic Vision.**

this you must add the human hearts and intelligences guiding their attention as they collect evidence. The lines connecting the camera, director, and participants represent their awareness of, and relationship to, each other. If you view the film examples (as I hope you do) you will quickly realize that any diagram is a simplified view of a subtle and complex range of realities.

COLLECTING EVIDENCE: OBSERVATIONAL OR PARTICIPATORY APPROACH

Your first and most fundamental choice is between the two approaches you will recall from Chapter 5, Documentary Language: one being to observe without interceding and the other allowing the director and crew to intercede and interact.

The first major ideas concerning the camera in relation to everyday truth arose, as we have said, in Russia with Dziga Vertov's *Kino-*

Use either **Project 4-SP-12 Make an Observational Film** or **4-SP-13 Make a Participatory Film** as hands-on practice at collecting documentary evidence, or use **Project 1-AP-6 Analyze Editing and Content** to examine how evidence has been used in an existing film.

Pravda, or "cinema truth." In France of the 1960s, Jean Rouch revived this approach under the equivalent name in French, *cinéma vérité*. But because English speakers corrupted the term to connote spontaneous shooting, documentary using these intercessional methods is now called *participatory*.

Figure 17-1 represents how filmmakers collecting evidence with an observational camera do their utmost to remain onlookers with minimal effect on the proceedings. Figure 17-2 represents participatory cinema, in which camera and crew are avowedly present and inquiring, ready to catalyze, if necessary, an interaction between participants or between participants and themselves. Few films take a purist attitude—most use whatever strategy is effective. With each new sequence you film, you will have to choose between these two polarities.

The distinguished American documentarian Fred Wiseman, a former lawyer, only ever uses the camera observationally. To minimize compromising his intentions, he uses no lighting, no directing of participants, and no questioning. He shoots massive amounts of footage and makes his films from the evidence he collects. If you are an ethnographer or have similar convictions about the worth of observation, then you may well use this approach. But, should you want to film an

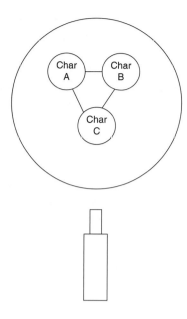

FIGURE 17-1

Diagram representing direct or observational cinema, in which the camera records life and intercedes as little as possible.

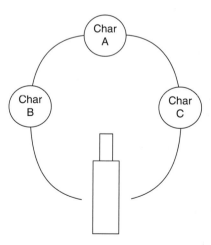

FIGURE 17-2

Diagram representing *cinéma vérité* or participatory cinema, in which the camera and crew may alternately be discreet onlookers or catalyze responses and situations.

interview, then merely asking questions and leading the conversation means you've catalyzed the record—even though all the questions are subsequently edited out.

A modern example of observational cinema is Yoav Shamir's *Checkpoint* (2004, Israel), discussed in **Chapter 5, Documentary Language**. It has no central characters and concentrates on observing without comment the social process of filtering human beings at arbitrarily created boundary points. An example of participatory cinema is Ross Kauffman and Dana Briski's *Born into Brothels: Calcutta's Red Light Kids* (2004, United States), a film they started during a photography project in India. You see them invite the stigmatized and impoverished children of prostitutes in the Red Light District and teach them how to document their surroundings using photography (Figure 17-4). The children learn not only remarkable camera skills but also how to pursue their own observations and values, and ultimately to respect themselves—which was the underlying hope for the project. (See the children's pictures at http://kids-with-cameras. org/kidsgallery/, and read how the project has since spread to other countries.) The film chronicles growing skills and relationships and ends with the kids giving a gallery show. Some go on to get an education but others return to their dead-end environment.

Whether to use participatory or non-intercessional shooting is usually a commonsense decision. Where 15 fire engines are hard at work putting out a fire, you won't need to exert any formative pressures by interceding. But if a naked environmentalist has chained himself to the Ministry of Agriculture's railing, you will have to question him, or the filming won't get beyond a single enigmatic image.

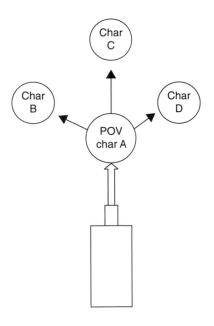

FIGURE 17-3

Diagram representing a single point of view (seeing through a character in the film).

FIGURE 17-4————————————————————————————————

Born into Brothels grew out of teaching Red Light District children to document their surroundings. (Photo courtesy of The Kobal Collection/HBO/ThinkFilms Company, Inc.)

POINT OF VIEW (POV)

We often associate *point of view* (POV) with, say, a Marxist political or Freudian psychological outlook used as tools of social or psychological analysis. In fact, cinematic point of view describes something rather more intangible that is intrinsic to films with a mature identity. When POVs are strongly present you know, because you get that enormously exciting sense of temporarily vacating your own existence and entering someone else's emotional and psychological experience. How this works almost defies explanation, and filmmakers able to convey it seem to practice it more viscerally than conceptually.

 Experiencing a character's or storyteller's point of view means temporarily leaving your own existence to enter someone else's and to experience their emotional and psychological reality.

It begins from this: As a film storyteller you must aim not only to convey your perception of your characters but also to get us emotionally involved in their perceptions and feelings. It is hard to believe you can control any of this during a shoot and hard even to locate these qualities in a finished film except in an intuitive way. Maybe you can see now why throughout this book I have stressed that all film technique came from human experience. When practiced from the head, it becomes an intellectual design, or just commercial packaging. If you want to change hearts and minds (in that order), your heart will have to rule over the tools of your trade. I don't mean you must inject sentimentality; I mean you must recognize and share in the emotion that's present. Everyone while growing up arms himself against feeling vulnerability and pain by denying his emotions. That's why it took Picasso half his lifetime to paint with the emotional receptivity and openness of a child. Making documentary will help you undo this damage, and your films will directly reflect where you have got to. See the Maysles brothers' *Grey Gardens* (1975, United States; Figure 17-5) for a film that fully accepts, and never patronizes or mocks, its highly eccentric mother and daughter subjects. This is a filmmaking team for whom "nothing human is alien."

FIGURE 17-5

The Maysles brothers' *Grey Gardens*—eccentric characters taken on their own terms. (Photo courtesy of The Kobal Collection/Portrait Films.)

Such empathy and points of view begin spontaneously emerging whenever the filmmaking team:

- Has a clear and guiding purpose for telling the tale
- Knows at every point what they want the audience to feel
- Relates empathically, not just intellectually, to the characters and their story
- Is fully mature in its embrace of other human beings, however different

 A surveillance camera can have no POV because it has no empathy. You, however, are making a film and relating to the participants, shot by shot, day by day, issue by issue. Your involvement translates to the kind of understanding that transforms any film.

Points of view begin to arise during ideation (elaborating the central idea) and continue to solidify during creation (researching, writing, shooting, and editing). They will strengthen as you crystallize your film's identity and purpose and make it serve what you feel. This happens most tangibly during editing.

The clearer and stronger your inner attitudes are—both to your participants and to the film's purpose—the more your film acquires heart and soul. That's why this book insists on, first, self-exploration as the foundation of creative identity and, second, creative identity as the springboard to purposeful and inspired filmmaking. Maintaining this empathic involvement will help counteract the endless distractions that come with using cinema tools. Picasso was lucky; he could work alone in silence with a brush or pencil. You, however, must often work in a hubbub of equipment, lights, and people. No wonder inspired cinema is rare.

 The uniqueness and force of a film's major POV depend on its tension with other, minor POVs. In art, as in life, everyone needs something to push against.

The next major question a dramatist asks is, Who is my central character? This is where developing your skills as a dramatist will help. With whom do we empathize, and whose story is it? This can lead to a variety of very interesting answers that we will examine, beginning with the simplest and moving toward more complexity.

SINGLE POV (CHARACTER IN THE FILM)

From Figure 17-3, you can see that the film is being channeled through, or perhaps even narrated by, a main character. This person, who is observing, recounting, participating in, or reenacting events, may be a bystander or major protagonist. This type of film is often a biography or, if the central character talks in the first person, an autobiography.

The seminal single point-of-view documentary is *Nanook of the North* (1922, United States), with its heroic central figure struggling to uphold his

family unit and survive. Though the
film is silent, it nevertheless leaves a
strong sense of intimacy with the
father of the family and establishes
that POV emanates from what
someone does just as powerfully as
from anything he might say.

> POV is established mainly through what a person does rather than what he says. Actions speak louder than words.

Vesting a film's point of view in
a leading character tends to restrict its scope to what that person can legitimately
know, understand, and represent. Flaherty implies that Nanook stands for the Inuit
nation and so places a heavy onus on a single delegate. He also represents the
heroic, unspoiled native fighting as part of an endangered species. The man who
played Nanook had a strong historical sense of his people and probably approved
of these representations. Flaherty's noble savage idealizations became more uncomfortably visible in *Man of Aran* (1934, United States) onwards. George Stoney and
Jim Brown's *How the Myth Was Made* (1978, United States) is a sympathetic documentary accompanying a DVD version of *Man of Aran*. It revisits the scene of the
film, talks with participants in Flaherty's film, and makes clear the apolitical selec-
tivity of Flaherty's gaze. In his later work, Flaherty declined to collaborate, and by
Louisiana Story (1948, United States) the passion in Flaherty's storytelling had
become sentimentality and his dramatizing manipulation.

A rather different biographical documentary is Werner Herzog's *Land of
Silence and Darkness* (1971, Germany; Figure 17-6). It has such a strange and

FIGURE 17-6

Through its character-within-the-film point of view, Werner Herzog's *Land of Silence and
Darkness* shows that for the deaf–blind, contact with the rest of the world is by touch
alone. (Photo courtesy of New Yorker Films.)

fascinating subject that it can use non-intercession most of the time. It follows Fini Straubinger, a deaf–blind woman who lay in an institution for 30 years until taught the deaf–blind tactile language. She takes a journey around Germany to locate others as isolated and despairing as she once was herself. As the film progresses, her eerie, prophetic simplicity gives you the shivers; you realize how we take human contact for granted and how devastating its absence or loss is to those whose senses have shut down. She emerges as a gauche angel who personifies the love and nobility latent in the human spirit. Because the film includes interviews, it also uses participatory elements.

Pernilla Rose Grønkjær's *The Monastery: Mr. Vig and the Nun* (2006, Denmark; Figure 17-7) chronicles the interaction between two central characters. The main POV comes through Grønkjær's fondness for and fascination with an eccentric old man nearing the end of a very long life. He happens to own a dilapidated castle and has always wanted to start a monastery. When he offers it to the Russian Orthodox Church, Moscow sends a lovely and very business-like nun. She sets about organizing both the project and the exhausted Mr. Vig. This delicately beautiful film, set around a huge, crumbling building that is

FIGURE 17-7————————————————————————————

The Monastery: Mr. Vig and the Nun—an unlikely love story. (Photo courtesy of Danish Film Institute Stills & Posters Archive/SF Film.)

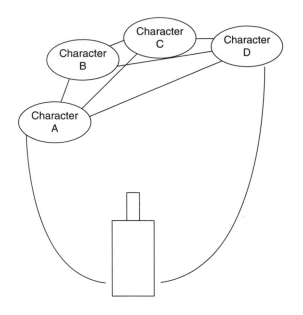

FIGURE 17-8

Diagram representing the multiple point of view. We may "see" anyone by way of anyone else's perspective.

returning to Nature as Mr. Vig must soon do, tells the story of a growing respect between two very unlikely people. Grønkjær mostly observes with her camera, but she sometimes interacts with her subjects from behind it. To see the film's trailer, go to www.imdb.com (the vast database of world film information).

MULTIPLE CHARACTERS' POVs WITHIN THE FILM

The viewpoints represented in Figure 17-8 are of multiple characters, in which none tends to predominate. The combination of camera and editing may look *at* the other characters, or *through* each individual's consciousness of the others. Through what each seer sees, we intuit what he or she is feeling.

 The multiple-character POV approach, excellent for demonstrating a social process, its actors, and outcomes, works with either observational or participatory approaches. It particularly suits a cross-section film, revealing cause and effect within a collective such as a family, team, business, or class of society.

Of the key films discussed in **Chapter 5, Documentary Language,** the Maysles brothers' *Salesman* (1969; United States) is such a film, and so are Michael Apted's longitudinal study films in the *Up* series (1964 to present, United Kingdom).

Barbara Kopple's classic *Harlan County, USA* (1976, United States; Figure 17-9) covers a strike by impoverished Kentucky coal miners. The film has

FIGURE 17-9

Barbara Kopple's *Harlan County, USA*. Music as an expression of suffering and protest adds to the multiple characters' viewpoints. (Photo courtesy of Krypton International Corporation.)

prominent characters but no ruling point of view, because the central issues are exploitation and class conflict between workers and big business. Ironic protest songs often carry the narrative forward, and these laments, creating a powerful aura of folktale and ballad, help make the film live on powerfully in one's memory afterward. Shot mostly as observational cinema, there are moments—most memorably when company goons shoot at the crew one night—when the filmmakers become participants in the events.

 When each character represents a different thread in the social tapestry, you can build a texture of different, counterbalancing viewpoints.

Andrew Jarecki's *Capturing the Friedmans* (2003, United States) and Doug Block's *51 Birch Street* (2005, United States; Figure 17-10) are each about the extraordinary dynamics within a family. The first concentrates on the closet homosexuality of the father, and the second on the unfulfilled love life of the mother. By exploring their family's multiplicity of views and allegiances, each looks at the emotional sources for each aspect of "questionable" behavior. *51 Birch Street* must be one of the most revealing journeys yet made into the hidden pain of a normal, outwardly comfortable, middle-class family. Block's diary style creates an intimate portrait of himself as well as the complex crucible of his family

FIGURE 17-10

The Block family during the 1970s in *51 Birch Street*—concealing their stresses like any normal family. (Photo courtesy of Doug Block.)

while he grew up. We come to understand, as he does, the intolerable burden that women carried—and perhaps carry still—and the cost to normal women in terms of personal fulfillment. Best of all, the film's outcome is amazingly constructive and positive. Here is the emotional liberation that intelligent documentary can bring its participants—and the ultimate posthumous tribute to Block's mother.

OMNISCIENT POV

Omniscience is comparable to the eye of God, who (I'm told) looks down on us, is everywhere, and knows everything. The limitations of my diagramming (Figure 17-11) suggest that omniscience is mostly free camera movement. Certainly the camera is no longer limited to what one character can see or know, and the eye of the omniscient storyteller does indeed move freely in time and space. In the hands of corporations and government agencies, this POV becomes an impersonal mirror whose purpose is authoritarian instruction, but in better examples the storyteller makes witty and entertaining use of omniscience's agility to convey a decided outlook and moral purpose.

 The omniscient viewpoint is really the all-knowing intelligence of the storyteller transporting us magically to any place and time in pursuit of the story. Typically in the third person, the narrative often expresses a collective rather than individual viewpoint.

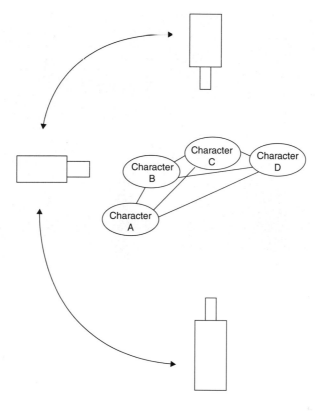

FIGURE 17-11 ————————————————————————————————

Diagram representing the omniscient point of view, in which the camera moves freely. Because POV comes from the storyteller, not a particular character, it's free to roam in time and space.

Typically narrated in the third person, the omniscient documentary often expresses a collective rather than individual viewpoint. The central organizing vision may be institutional or corporate or that of the filmmaker, who as storyteller need make no apology or explanation.

The early documentary seems to have acquired its stance of omniscience from the gentleman's slide lecture of earlier times. For modesty, he (rarely she) avoided speaking in the first person by presenting his material as science or ethnography. Older documentaries adopting this stance don't always have such humility. Leni Riefenstahl's *Triumph of the Will* (1935, Germany; Figure 17-12) and *Olympia* (1938, Germany) used an omniscient camera to camouflage a proudly partisan view of Hitler and Nazi Germany. Her masterly use of narrationless documentary serves to ascribe power and inevitability to her subject, and this should warn us that "art for art's sake" is a dangerous mask.

 All film seeks to persuade, but films that hide their subjectivity by glossing over the paradoxes and conflicts in the world they reflect intend to condition more than enlighten.

FIGURE 17-12

A Hitler mass rally in Leni Riefenstahl's *Triumph of the Will*. (Photo courtesy of the Museum of Modern Art Film Stills Archive.)

Pare Lorentz's *The Plow That Broke the Plains* (1936, United States; Figure 17-13) and *The River* (1937, United States) use poetic narrations that turn each film into a long, elegiac ballad—a folk form that legitimizes the films' omniscient eye and seemingly egoless passion. Their powerfully aesthetized imagery and ironic montage establish an unforgettable vision of a land plundered through ignorance and political opportunism. This is propaganda at its best, though my late friend and mentor Robert Edmonds, author of *Anthropology on Film* (1974, Pflaum Publishing), contended that all documentaries are propaganda because all seek to persuade. He liked to be provocative; all documentaries argue for something, but one that simplifies the evidence to make its conclusions unavoidable is seeking to condition, not argue. This is undoubtedly propaganda.

Few documentaries are set in the future, but Peter Watkins' *The War Game* (1966, United Kingdom; Figure 17-14) appropriates a news program style to posit the nuclear bombing of London. Here the omniscient POV, appropriating the authoritarian voice of the newsreel, relocates the facts of nuclear bombing in Japan and the fire-bombing of Dresden to a hypothetical present with devastating effect. With grim impartiality it constructs an infernal, incontestable vision of nuclear war, all the more mesmerizing for its veracity. Passionately seeking to

FIGURE 17-13 ————————————————————

In his omniscient classic *The Plow That Broke the Plains,* Pare Lorentz uses stark imagery and ironic montage to set up a haunting vision. (Photo courtesy of the Museum of Modern Art.)

FIGURE 17-14 ————————————————————

Peter Watkins' *The War Game,* a frightening view of nuclear disaster that was kept from the public. (Photo courtesy of Films, Inc.)

persuade, it shuns heroics and avoids the personalizing normal in screen treatments of disaster. Somehow this forces us to include ourselves and our loved ones among the doomed. As a new parent when I first saw it, I found it nearly unbearable.

Omniscience seems appropriate for complex and far-reaching subjects like war or race relations in which an individualized point of view would seem parochial. Al Gore in his extended slide lecture *An Inconvenient Truth* (2006, United States, directed by Davis Guggenheim) takes a magisterial overview of a world choking under the assault of human intervention.

PERSONAL POV

Here the point of view is unashamedly and subjectively that of the director, who sometimes narrates the film. The director can alternatively supply filmmaking skills for someone in front of the camera. In the 1960s, I made a film about the peace-campaigning pediatrician Dr. Spock in a BBC essay series called *One Pair of Eyes*. The personal film may thus present its views in the form of a first-person or third-person essay. There are no limits to the personal point of view beyond what the author/storyteller can demonstrably see and know. In Figure 17-15, the director is behind the camera but can step forward into the visible world of the film.

Barbara Sonneborn's *Regret to Inform* (1998, United States) is a personal journey to the place in Vietnam where her first husband lost his life when they were both young. Undertaken as an exorcism, the ten-year journey to make the film put her in touch with both American and Vietnamese war widows, and the result is a searing examination of what war does to those left behind.

Mark Wexler's *Tell Them Who You Are* (2004, United States; Figure 17-16) is a first-person account from behind the camera of growing up in the shadow of his peppery and famous father, the Hollywood cinematographer Haskell Wexler. What makes it unlike a retrospective is that the two filmmakers couldn't avoid playing out their tensions as they filmed. Nothing of the friction and pain between them is resolved, but it was the engagement that probably mattered, and this is sometimes uncomfortably revealing.

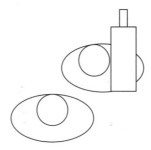

FIGURE 17-15 ———————————————————————————————

Diagram representing the personal point of view, in which the author/storyteller is the point-of-view character.

FIGURE 17-16

Filmmaking father and son battle it out in *Tell Them Who You Are*. (Photo courtesy of The Kobal Collection/Wexler's World, Inc.)

ENTER THE STORYTELLER

Under the largely discredited *auteur* theory of filmmaking, the authorship of each movie is the director's, but controlling how a collective (the film crew) creates such a complex perceptual stream is simply beyond any one person's control. I therefore personify this as the role of the *Storyteller*. The whole crew helps fulfill its purpose, which is to give the tale a narrative identity or "voice," as they call it in literature. For different films, the Storyteller might be grave, saucy, brazen, nonplussed, sarcastic, resigned, pleading—whatever the nexus between story and audience calls for. Part of Michael Moore's force is the playful charm his films exert through the persona of his storytelling voice.

Screen language at its most compelling implies, as we have said, *the course of a particular intelligence at work as it grapples with the events in which it participates.* While the characters grapple with their situation, the Storyteller highlights the implications of their story so the audience is entertained, and learns something.

 In a sometimes dark and hopeless world, we need stories reminding us of the constructive options that are always present. This is the role of the Storyteller and represents a power for good.

Nobody will recognize you and give you the storytelling authority you long to exert. You must take it. Choose the Storyteller role your film needs to adopt, and play it to the hilt. We expect stories with meaning, humor, style from you . . . stories that reverberate with meaning. You won't entertain us by reflecting reality. Holding up a mirror is seldom enough. You need to give us a reality that is heightened, unusual, and marked with purpose and personality.

 Documentary storytelling means *assembling pieces of reality with verve and style and saying something about what it means to be alive*. Nothing else is enough. Only those of large heart and large mind and willing to do a large amount of work can carry this out. Today, with so many people making documentaries, only the outstanding can prosper at it.

Werner Herzog has always entertained with a purpose. In *Grizzly Man* (2005, United States) he took the tapes that Timothy Treadwell made of himself and used them to tell how Treadwell came to identify with grizzly bears. Like the *Titanic* on track for its iceberg, Herzog shows us Treadwell heading for a gruesome destruction of his own making—and taking with him his unfortunate girlfriend. The span of Herzog's fable is complete when the incoming pilot spots the human ribcage on the ground below. This is no exploitative tale of mistakes or bad luck; its message is about granting human feeling to dangerous animals and, more important still, of sentimentalizing the blind forces of Nature.

Balseros (2002, Spain, directed by Carlos Bosch and Josep Maria Domènech) has a strong storytelling voice, but since it is a largely observational film the voice is implied, not personal. The film follows several Cubans who escape the geriatric Castro revolution for the Promised Land whose fulsome enormity begins in Florida. It then shows in merciless detail what befalls each of them. Loneliness and homesickness in the face of a sybaritic culture send most down paths of self-destruction. Though they have survived all sorts of hardship, prospering amid plenty takes skills for which paternalistic Cuba never equipped them. This film shows people unprepared for Nature of a different stripe—human nature.

 To become an outstanding Storyteller, study how your psyche interacts with the world, then apply your findings to filmmaking. Develop instincts for what your audience makes of what you give it, knowing that answers lie not in film theory or audience studies but in shared instincts concerning human judgments and human truth.

REFLEXIVITY AND REPRESENTATION

Reflexive documentaries are those that acknowledge and even investigate the effect of filmmaking itself. Figure 17-17 shows that the filming process can now monitor the directing, shooting, and editing in the filmmaking process itself. This I have symbolized, not too confusingly, I hope, by a mirror. The anthropologist

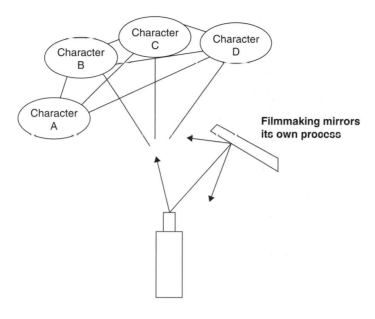

FIGURE 17-17

Diagram representing the reflexive point of view, one able to share salient aspects of the filmmaking process with the audience.

Jay Ruby, whose specialty is assessing the cultural content of photographs, film, and television, says that:

> To be reflexive is to structure a product in such a way that the audience assumes that the producer, the process of making, and the product are a coherent whole. Not only is the audience made aware of these relationships, but it is made to realize the necessity of that knowledge."[1]

By dispensing with the conceit that we are watching unmediated life, reflexivity acknowledges that films are "created, structured articulations of the filmmaker and not authentic, truthful, objective records."[2] You can find Jay Ruby's long essay, "Exposing Yourself: Reflexivity, Anthropology, and Film," at http://astro. temple.edu/~ruby/ruby/exposing.html. As he says, the investigation of documentary language began with Vertov in the 1920s, whose *Man with the Movie Camera* (1929, U.S.S.R.) is discussed in **Chapter 5, Documentary Language**. Like documentarians everywhere, Vertov aspired to show "life as it is," but he had also become fascinated by the mysterious processes of cinema itself. His life-embracing Kino-Eye manifesto, not exactly a hit with the Russian authorities at the time, prepared the ground for *cinéma vérité* 40 years later. Vertov believed that the dynamics of camera and montage transcended human agency, and though we often see shots of the cameraman at work, he seems more the camera's servant

[1]Ruby, Jay. "The image mirrored: Reflexivity and the documentary film," in *New Challenges for Documentary*, Alan Rosenthal, Ed. Berkeley: University of California Press, 1988, p. 65.

[2]*Ibid*, pp. 717–775.

than its master. To deny personal authorship, Vertov vested film truth in the apparatus itself—an ebullient mystification that he didn't quite pull off while trying to have his ideological cake and eat it.

A film that exposes the paradoxes of its own evolution draws the audience into issues dogging all documentary. For instance:

- How often are we really seeing spontaneous life rather than something instigated by or for filmmaking itself?

- How much of a film's purview is inhibited by ethical concerns for its participants?

- Do the participants know how we will judge them?

- Does the film reflect reality or does it manufacture it?

Reflexivity allows the filmmakers to open a window on filmmaking itself and to share thoughts about whatever ambiguities arise during the process. Ethnographic filmmaking, supposed to be uncontaminated by the filmmaker's own cultural assumptions, is a prime candidate for such scrutiny.

 Explaining one culture for the benefit of another is inherently hazardous. From trying to do it you learn important lessons about one person's right to represent another.

Jay Rosenblatt is an experimental filmmaker unlike most because he has real mastery of the subtleties of the medium and its history. *I Used to Be a Filmmaker* (2003, United States; Figure 17-18) is ostensibly about film practice and film terminology but is suffused with the joy of discovering his infant daughter Ella. Playfully, the film bridges two essential relationships— with one's child and with one's art. The interplay compares the development of a medium with the development of a human being—even the development of a new love.

 The art of documentary is itself a work in progress, a question mark. No longer is it a closed system only good for pumping knowledge or opinions into vacant heads.

Aside from investigating film's boundaries, its distortions, subjectivity, or misinformation, there are further issues to concern us:

- Under what circumstances do we as an audience suspend disbelief or withhold believing?

- When does the medium deceive its makers?

- What may or may not be ethical?

SELF-REFLEXIVE

The ultimate in reflexivity is the self-reflexive film, which not only reflects on its own process but also incorporates its authors' thoughts, doubts, and self-examination, as well (Figure 17-19). This can become the snake that eats its own tail or the pool in

FIGURE 17-18 ——————————————————————————————

Jay Rosenblatt faces the new force in his life in *I Used to Be a Filmmaker*. (Photo courtesy of the filmmaker.)

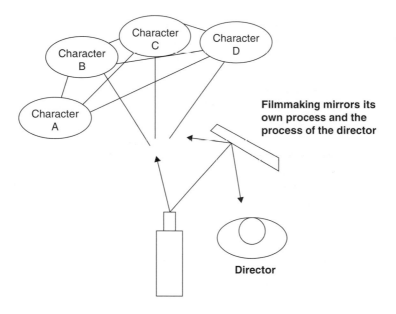

FIGURE 17-19 ——————————————————————————————

Diagram representing the self-reflexive point of view. This allows examination of both the film's process and that of its makers. Approach this form cautiously, because little separates self-reflexivity from self-indulgence.

which a certain young man drowned. Treacherous and difficult though it is to pull off, it can be wonderfully rich in the hands of someone with the maturity to evade its seductions.

Michael Rubbo's *Sad Song of Yellow Skin* (1970, Canada) is an Australian/Canadian filmmaker's search to define Vietnam amid the flux of that war-torn country's tragic paradoxes. By confining his attention mostly to city street kids and the young American dissidents working with them, Rubbo exposes the seamy side of a peasant civilization torn apart by its wealthy, technocratic, and self-involved occupiers. Rubbo's ironic view of himself and the world saves his films from sentimentality.

Alan Berliner in *Nobody's Business* (1996, United States; Figure 17-20) uses documentary to approach his crabby father in the hope of achieving a better understanding. He is roundly repulsed—hence the film's title—when Berliner

FIGURE 17-20

Nobody's Business by Alan Berliner—a son challenges his irascible father to reveal himself. (Photo by D.W. Leitner.)

senior is adamant that he is an ordinary man with nothing to say. This, a challenge to any documentarian, sends the son to family film, photographs, and letters in search of the father he hardly knows. His dad being the son of an immigrant Jew, the quest broadens by association to include ethnicity, ethnic identity, and even America as the melting pot that failed, thank goodness, to alloy its citizens into one culture. What emerges more than justifies the intrusion it takes to get there. This film shows, as do all those that really illuminate family life, that the most important doors never open until the director pushes and pushes. Power (that is, vital information that tells you who you are) is never given. You take it when you decide to grow up.

Explore authorial voice using **Project 1-AP-8 Assess a Director's Thematic Vision.**

THE AUTHORIAL VOICE

Today's movement toward a more confident, individual "voice" confirms that documentarians no longer have to suppress the ambiguities and contradictions they encounter along the way. Digital technology liberates you to subtitle, freeze, or otherwise break out of actuality's hypnotic advance. By slowing the image, playing it backwards, filtering it, superimposing or interleaving texts at will, you can invite us to question, doubt, and reflect—not simply accept as heretofore.

Digital technology lets you comment on actuality, rather than simply reproduce its appearance and hope the audience will look deeper. More subjective and impressionistic, this freedom of treatment unshackles the screen from servitude to real time and its byproduct, realism.

FINDING NEW LANGUAGE

Your greatest challenge as a filmmaker will always be finding fresh film language. You'll do this best, I contend, by journeying inward to comprehend your own emotional and psychic experience and finding equivalencies to render it on the screen. Only in this way can you connect us convincingly with other realities—those of your subjects and those of yourself and your associates. Perhaps someone will see your work and echo André Malraux's words about the French novelist Louis-Ferdinand Céline—that he wrote "not about reality, but about the hallucinations raised by reality."

Documentary is a young genre in the young art of cinema; it has only scratched the surface of its potential. You are entering a time when documentaries no longer have to pretend to present objectivity or transparency. The only restraint is still that documentaries must relay aspects of actuality (past, present, or future) and imply a critical relationship to the fabric of social life.

QUESTIONS TO ASK YOURSELF ABOUT POV

Each possible POV offers a different way of entering the people and their world. Switching POV creates a vital contrast between what different characters see and feel as they navigate their predicaments. Seeing through eyes other than our own, we retain our values and have a double experience that helps us define both ourselves and others. Of your film, ask yourself:

How many POVs are possible in my film?

Which POV should predominate . . .

- Throughout?
- Through different parts of the documentary?
- Through one or two parts?

What is my brief description of each POV in relation to the . . .

- Character's agenda?
- Character's limitations and blind spots?
- Overall development of the story?

What must I shoot to serve each necessary POV?

- How should I shoot each so I complement the character's nature and biases?

How do I, as the Storyteller, want to color the story?

- What role does my Storyteller play in order to further the nature of the story?
- What should I shoot to show the Storyteller's POV?
- How should I shoot to imply the Storyteller's POV, so I build the storytelling atmosphere and emphases?

Should my audience be able to take into account . . .

- Aspects of the filmmaking that surfaced during production?
- My experiences during the filmmaking that are significant to what the audience will think and feel?

CHAPTER 18

DRAMATIC DEVELOPMENT, TIME, AND STORY STRUCTURE

Aiming to change our hearts and minds, documentaries are stories that organize their characters, events, and pressures toward some revelatory purpose. They do this to increase or challenge our knowledge and to alter our emotional frame of reference. This chapter looks at the relationship between the chronology of documented events, their organization into a satisfying dramatic form, and the way a story's dramatic needs may lead you to reorganize events to give a story more impact.

PLOTS AND HEROES

PLOT AND THE RULES OF THE UNIVERSE

The filmmaker and philosopher Michael Roemer has made the intriguing suggestion that plot is really the rules of the universe at work.[1] This explains why the most fascinating characters are often those contesting—heroically, and sometimes unsuccessfully—the way things simply *are*. The legion of films about civil rights leaders or returning soldiers overcoming terrible injuries falls under this category.

 Plot is the organization of situations, circumstances, and events that pressure a story's characters.

---

[1]Roemer, Michael. *Telling Stories: Postmodernism and the Invalidation of Traditional Narrative.* Lanham, MD: Rowman & Littlefield, 1995.

Heroes and Heroines

Heroes are central characters writ large—characters of magnitude who challenge what people consider normal and thus seem to contest the rules of the universe. In 1955, Rosa Parks did this in Montgomery by refusing to yield her bus seat to a white person, an action that helped precipitate the civil rights movement. Conscientious objectors who risk torture and imprisonment by refusing to kill and those who choose prison for racial equality, as Nelson Mandela did, are all plainly the stuff of heroism. In documentary, the hero will often be someone obscure whose special qualities mean they will strug-gle to accomplish something. The dramatic tension you generate comes from getting us involved with this person (or people) and making us care whether they prevail. Human qualities, principles, and will come under test, and we watch a trial of strength. From this we learn some-thing, and the values by which we live may be a little changed, renewed, or vindicated.

 A dramatic hero may be flawed and even pitiable. He or she may contest the way things are from outrage, self-righteousness, ignorance, inno-cence, obstinacy, conceit, or a host of other reasons.

What do you want your audience to make of your central figures? What are you saying through them? What do you want to say about human nature, human folly, or noble human aspiration?

DRAMA AND THE THREE-ACT STRUCTURE

Plots often have common denominators in their organization. To explain this, the ancient Greeks devised the *three-act structure*, which remains an invaluable tool for organizing story elements today and was introduced in **Chapter 5, Documentary Language**, in relation to the Maysles brothers' *Salesman* (1961). See the three-act structure as an aid to your thinking, not a formulaic strait-jacket:

Act I   Establishes the *setup* (establishes characters, relationships, situation, and the dominant *problem* faced by the central character or characters).

Act II   Escalates the *complications* in relationships as the central character struggles with the obstacles that prevent him or her from solving the main problem.

Act III Intensifies the situation to a point of *climax* or con-*frontation*, when the cen-tral character then *resolves* it, often in a climactic way that is emotionally satisfy-ing. A resolution isn't nec-essarily a happy ending; it might be a boxer accepting defeat.

 The three-act structure is an invaluable tool for organizing story material. Apply it on a micro or a macro level—that is, to a single scene or to the way scenes flow in an extended story.

The three-act structure is plainly visible in a survival program such as *Pioneer Quest: A Year in the Real West* (2003, Canada) made for Life Television Canada. A group trying to live like pioneers on the prairie has a problem—winter is coming and they must make their own shelter. Constructing a cabin, they must work through all the obstacles that make hand building from local materials so difficult. The resolution is a viable (if drafty) cabin. Next, they struggle to keep warm during the coldest winter in 120 years.

In recent years, many reality-based "time traveler" programs have explored what earlier generations lived through. One I like—because it illuminates my English wartime childhood, I suppose—is *The 1940s House* (2003, United Kingdom, directed by Caroline Ross-Pirie and shown on PBS). The director, who specializes in historical reality experiments, gets a volunteer family to live with the restricted food and clothing, primitive sanitation, self-entertainment, and daily radio war bulletins that a typical London family knew during the outbreak of World War II. The unspoken question it poses is, "How would *we* handle the problems and conditions those people encountered?" This is a central question for anyone exploring the past, especially as you awaken to how little you know about the relatives you have lost.

Social experiments make wonderful material for documentary makers. Their situations run on the fundamentals of character, problem, obstacle, struggle, and outcome or resolution. Even at the simplest level you show similar dramatic problems—whether it's someone opening a front door with their arms full, trying to button a 1940s school uniform, or the family pet figuring out how to open the back door. Dramatists call this cycle of character/problem/escalation/crisis/resolution the *dramatic curve* or *dramatic arc*, and its build, peaking, and fall look rather like a fever patient's temperature chart (Figure 18-1).

 The *dramatic curve* is an invaluable tool when you direct because with it you can interpret the unfolding action you're filming and decide how to shoot it.

THE DRAMATIC CURVE

It's seldom straightforward to forecast how documentary shooting will turn out. Applying the traditional dramatic curve to your ideas, however, is useful during research. It's vital to your judgment as action unfolds in front of your camera, and it's outstanding as an analytic tool during editing, which is really the second chance to direct.

The dramatic arc concept comes from ancient Greek drama and represents how most stories first state their problem, develop tension through scenes of increasing complication and intensity, then arrive at an apex or "crisis." Following this comes change and resolution—though not, let me say quickly, necessarily a happy or peaceful one. In Broomfield and Churchill's *Soldier Girls* (1981, United States/United Kingdom), the crisis is probably the point at which Private Johnson, after a series of increasingly stressful conflicts with authority, leaves the army dishonorably but in a spirit of relieved gaiety. The film's resolution, after this major character quits the stage, is to examine more closely what soldiers need during training to survive battle conditions.

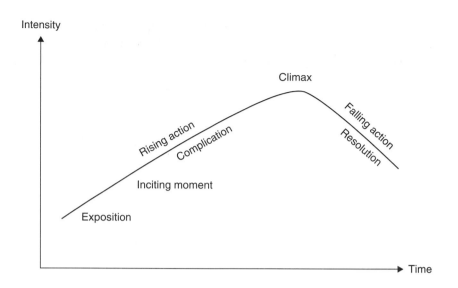

FIGURE 18-1 ⎯⎯⎯⎯⎯⎯⎯⎯⎯⎯⎯⎯⎯⎯⎯⎯⎯⎯⎯⎯⎯⎯⎯⎯⎯⎯⎯⎯⎯⎯

The arc of changing pressures fundamental to all drama.

In the Maysles brothers' *Salesman* (1969, United States; discussed in **Chapter 5, Documentary Language**), most people think the story's apex is the

moment when Paul Brennan, the salesman who has been falling steadily behind the pack like a wounded animal, sabotages a colleague's sale. In the film's coda, his partners have distanced themselves as if deserting a contagious man. The resolution is Paul gazing offscreen into a void, as if staring at his oncoming fate.

 Pinpoint the apex or crisis of a scene, and the rest of the dramatic convention arranges itself naturally before and after the peak of the curve.

No matter what drama you analyze—whether a scene or a whole epic—once you pinpoint the apex or crisis, the rest of the dramatic convention begins to fall into place before and after the peak of the curve. Often you can then divide the piece into the classic three-act structure. Three categories or units precede the climax, and one follows. Let's examine the idea in more detail so you can apply it to your research:

- ACT I
  1. The *introduction or exposition* establishes the *setup* by laying out main characters and their situation and giving enough necessary factual information about time, place, period, and so on to get started. Modern drama often lacks a captive audience, so it cannot afford to delay the major *committing action*. The main conflict, or struggle between opposing forces, will probably be established early in the documentarian's

contract with the audience. Signaling the scope and focus of the film to come, the introduction aims to secure their interest for the duration.

2. The *inciting moment* is whatever sets in motion the opposition of interests. In the military, the onset of basic training sets in motion a battle between the homogenizing goals of the army and the self-protecting individualism of the recruit. The army aims to break down individual identity and replace it with a psyche trained to unthinkingly obey. In *Soldier Girls*, the inciting moment is when Sergeant Abing sees Private Johnson smirking after he has rebuked her. This triggers a long and unequal struggle between them. Because a white male is imposing his will on a black female, the situation abounds with disquieting overtones of slavery and colonialism.

- ACT II
    1. *Rising action* or *complication* usually shows the basic conflicts being played out as variations having surprise, suspense, and escalating intensity. In *Soldier Girls*, the army's expression of will and the misfits' expression of cowed resistance are repeatedly raised a notch to more serious and offensive levels. Seeing protagonists and antagonists engaged in such a revealing struggle, we come to understand the motivations, goals, and background of each, and during this period we choose sides. Our sympathies vacillate in the face of ambiguity.

- ACT III
    1. In the final *confrontation* comes the *climax* or apex of the curve, a point of irreversible change.
    2. The *resolution* or *falling action* is what the piece establishes as the consequence. This includes not only what happens to the characters but also what interpretation for the last scene or scenes suggest for the whole work. How the audience last sees your characters—in a documentary as in other story forms—can alter the impact of an entire film.

Few documentaries fall neatly into this shape, but some memorable ones do. Hollywood uses the three-act formula with awful fervor; some screenwriting manuals even prescribe a page count per act, with page numbers at which "plot points" should take the story lurching off at an unexpected tangent. Documentary is too wayward to enable such control, but it still needs to be dramatically satisfying. This remains true for essay, montage, or other forms of documentary, not just those that are obviously about struggle. Indeed, you find this escalation of pressure up to a crisis then lowering down to resolution in songs, symphonies, dances, mime, and traditional tales, because it is as fundamental to human existence as breathing or sex.

THE BEST SCENES ARE DRAMAS IN MINIATURE

What is fascinating is that a successful documentary scene is a drama in miniature; it follows the same curve of pressures building to a climax before releasing into a new situation. During the shoot, the documentary director often sees a scene develop, spin its wheels, and refuse to go anywhere. Then, perhaps with some *side coaching* (verbal inquiry or prompts by the director from off-camera), the characters lock onto an issue and struggle over it until something significant changes.

This fulcrum point of change, called in the theater a *beat,* is the basic unit of any scene containing dramatic interchange. Even compilation montage films that lack foreground characters, such as Pare Lorentz's *The River* (1937, United States), follow the same cyclic sequencing of building pressure, then releasing.

 A documentary scene can be a drama in miniature, following the curve of pressures that build to a climax then release into a new situation.

LOOK FOR BEATS AND DRAMATIC UNITS

When you see someone go through a moment of irreversible change of consciousness, such as realizing his love is recognized or being faced with incontrovertible evidence that he lied, you are seeing a *beat.*

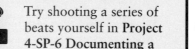 Try shooting a series of beats yourself in **Project 4-SP-6 Documenting a Process.**

Other characters in the scene may not notice anything, but that character (and the informed onlooker) registers that moment of change, and knows that he must now take a different course of action. Two men maneuvering a refrigerator through a narrow hallway will yield a series of beats. Their progress might look like this:

 A *beat* is when someone in a scene registers an important and irreversible change. Often it's when participants realize they have lost or gained an important goal. A beat signals a new phase of action, so you must film them astutely since they are your film's most intense and dramatic moments.

1. They puff and pant getting fridge to doorway.

2. Obstacle A—It's too big to go through. *Failure.*

3. Strategy—They confer, measure it, realize it'll go through if they remove the door (delay while they find tools). Remove door, take out all the shelves.

4. Try again—It's lighter. *Success.* They rejoice when it goes through the doorway.

5. Obstacle B—Now it won't go under a rigid light fixture.

6. Strategy—Too complicated to dismantle fixture, so must lie fridge down lengthways.

7. They back it into the doorway, roll it forward, get it under the fixture. *Success.* They move forward

8. Obstacle C—The fridge is too long to get past the bottom of a protruding staircase.

9. Strategy—They must roll the fridge upright again. They are getting tired and fractious.

10. They try this and it works. They can maneuver the fridge into the kitchen. *Success at last*. Mission accomplished.

Each new obstacle poses a problem that they attempt to solve with a strategy. If it fails, they must come up with a new one. If it works, that particular problem is solved and you have a beat (beats are italicized as *failure* or *success* above). Solving a problem leads onward to a new obstacle, and so on. With two people cooperatively trying to do something, each dramatic unit includes:

- Following an agenda, the central characters face an issue.
- They encounter complications that raise the stakes.
- They reach the apex of the problem.
- They develop a strategy to solve the problem.
- It either works or doesn't, leading to a *beat*—which is a point of irreversible realization.
- Success or failure is the resolution.
- Resolution leads into a new issue or problem.

A scene may have one dramatic unit or several. As you learn to recognize them taking place all around you in daily life, you mentally practice how you'd film them. For the example above, how much attention should your camera give to the fridge? How do you show the obstacles? How much do you dwell on one or other of the two men? What character traits does each manifest during this revealing interaction, and how can you bring them out?

Divide an existing documentary into its parts using **Project 1-AP-7 Analyze Structure and Style.**

Being able to recognize this dramatic breathing action, being able to cover it sensitively with the camera as it takes place, is the preeminent skill for directors in fiction or in documentary.

A successful progression of beats hikes the *dramatic tension*. It sets up questions, anticipations, even fears in your audience. Never be afraid to make them wait and guess.

Wilkie Collins, father of the mystery novel, said about readers, "Make them laugh, make them cry, but make them wait." Your films need dramatic tension, so make your audience wait—but not too long.

THE DIRECTOR AND THE DRAMATIC ARC

As a director or camera operator, you must be able to see the dramatic arc unfolding in everyday activities around you. Often you will be filming spontaneously unfolding life events. Your central figures will grapple with problems and face complications, each from the perspective of his or her own agenda. As the scene develops, it helps greatly to envision your characters' purposes and estimate how far they are along the dramatic curve. This is an indispensable skill, for it prepares you to catch what matters. Seeing ahead of the characters, you are ready to adapt to what they do. You have become a dramatist and not just a wide-eyed onlooker.

 Directing or shooting, you are always trying to see ahead and discern each character's agenda. How to cover the scene only emerges once you have clues and a hypothesis.

Other times, as you mentally log your characters' progression, the scene stalls instead of resolving into the change you expected. Perhaps somebody's aspiration leads to failure or goes off at a tangent, only to initiate a new cycle of problem, complications, and escalation. Perhaps the scene simply hangs up. If you are shooting participatory cinema, you can try breaking the log jam by asking questions or making suggestions about options. You might even cut the camera and confer with them about their options before proceeding.

 Generating momentum—and therefore anticipation—will be your most valuable storytelling skill.

TIME AND STRUCTURE

All stories need a sense of forward movement if they are to satisfy. The key lies in the agendas of the main characters, and the *givens* (inbuilt certainties) of the subject matter. Because of givens, you can shoot intelligently whenever you plan to cover particular circumstances, such as the effect of a destructive fire on a family. You won't know who the family is until the fire engine goes roaring away on its mission, but fires have a predictable course and the givens (in this case, causes and effects) are inevitable, so you can practically guarantee that your story will include:

- How the fire started
- How people tried to stop it
- How it spread
- What neighbors did—heroic or otherwise—to save the victims
- How far the fire got before being brought under control by firefighters
- What the consequences are for the lives thereafter

You can even see where each element might belong in the three-act structure. By shooting astute coverage, you can practically guarantee the elements of a satisfying story.

Most narratives tell their tale in chronological order. Some do otherwise because there is a compelling

 All subjects for films (that is, events, lives, processes, issues, problems) have stages that the documentary dramatist can make into narrative stages.

reason to organize them differently or because basic chronology is weak, absent, or unimportant to the angle of the story. Most important is to envision what range of outcomes to expect, as these represent the all-important developments that will rescue your film from becoming static.

EACH STORY NEEDS CHANGE AND DEVELOPMENT

Because so much human development is slow, documentaries often fail to show any real change—especially those shot on a short schedule. The power to abridge and to compare past and present is thus important for narrative art to assert that growth and change are indeed possible. In a BBC series called *Breakaway*, setting out to avoid making any more "non-event films," we specifically looked for people about to plunge into a major life change.

   Use **Project 5-PP-2 Story Structure Helper** to make any set of story materials into playing cards. With them you'll discover alternative narrative organizations—perhaps for your next film. To test the potential of different structures for your film, place its major sequences on cards, lay them out in different orders, and narrate each new story line to listeners. To make this more interesting, go to **Project 5-PP-2 Story Structure Helper** in the Appendix.

Following are some common documentary categories whose examples should suggest how you might structure your intended film. The list merely illustrates the relationship between time and structure; it's not meant to be definitive or embracing.

TIME CHRONOLOGICALLY PRESENTED

The Event-Centered Film

The stages of the event become the vertebrae in the film's temporal spine. Expectation and its predictable or unexpected stages provide the sense of forward movement. Once the event has gained momentum you can afford to plug in sidebars like ribs along the spine, knowing that the audience is always ready for the story to revert to the event's next stage. These digressions might be sections of interview, pieces of relevant past, or even pieces of the imagined future.

Some events, such as a marathon race or a political rally, move fast or have many facets unfolding

 Every documentary needs some consuming, ongoing process that generates momentum. This, called the *through line* in drama, is the spine of your film, the forward movement of quest and revelation that is central to the film's purpose. Once you have one, you can attach the digressive elements of your story along the spine like so many ribs. Each digression in the story holds the promise of returning to the through line.

FIGURE 18-2————————————————————————

The beauty of sports as seen through a National Socialist sensibility in *Olympia*. (Photo courtesy of The Kobal Collection/Olympia-Film.)

simultaneously. Leni Riefenstahl's dark classic, *Olympia* (1938, Germany; Figure 18-2), relays the Berlin Olympic Games in this way and with seductive virtuosity places Adolf Hitler, godlike, at the center.

When multiple strands of narrative happen simultaneously, you may need several cameras. I once directed a unit among several covering a pheasant shoot, and my team concentrated on the gamekeeper. As always, plan your shooting around what is predictable because you need to anchor the film in its event's stages. Knowing you can deliver these liberates you to record the unexpected along the way.

 Using multiple cameras takes foresight and good organizing. Without, cameras tend to stray into each others' scenes, duplicate some coverage, and miss others.

The Process Film

This type of documentary chronicles a sequence of events during which something is produced or accomplished. Ordinary events such as making a meal, building a shed, taking a journey, or getting married can become fascinating if you treat them

 Parallel storytelling lets you advance multiple story lines, abbreviate each to its essentials, and create tension between them via astute juxtapositioning.

as archetypal or metaphorical. Process films are usually modular with each event or unit, having a clear beginning, middle, and end. Usually they follow chronological sequencing but can use parallel storytelling by cutting between multiple events. A father may be at work in a factory, for instance, while his daughter is in school getting the education that allows her *not* to work in a fac-

 The more familiar the steps of an event or process, the more you can condense it to essentials. This achieves narrative compression and allows you to open up other, more significant parts of your film to deeper exposure.

tory. As each sequence advances by steps, the characters and their predicaments develop in a linear fashion.

David Sutherland's three-year study, *The Farmer's Wife* (1998, United States; Figure 18-3), chronicles the effects of relentlessly growing economic pressure on a Nebraska family farm couple. The process in question is slow starvation. Blow by blow and in extraordinary intimacy we see what Darrel and Juanita Buschkoetter must endure to stave off bankruptcy. The worst casualty is their marriage. During the six 1-hour episodes, Darrel doggedly works multiple jobs while Juanita holds the family together, finishes college—and this is the series' development—and matures from girl to woman. It's through her strength of character that they pull through and survive—hence the series title. Culled from 200 hours of footage, the film's essence lies in many poignant, lonely episodes that play out as sustained interactions. Each is filled with tension, and many are real dramatic experiences such as you hope for in the theater.

FIGURE 18-3

Strength and faith to survive in *The Farmer's Wife*. (A David Sutherland Film. Photo by John Schaefer © WGBH.)

Emile Ardolino's *He Makes Me Feel Like Dancin'* (1983, United States) shows the dancer Jacques D'Amboise teaching New York schoolchildren how to let go and dance; it gives careful attention to the methods and encouragement that he lavishes on his students. He also gives a class for adult nondancers which includes a brave New York cop hoofing it with the rest. Everyone revels in their new ecstasy of movement, and you can see why. Though it deals with a series of processes, you hardly notice because it makes such masterful use of montage and rhythmic editing. This is a film about dancing that dances—form and content perfectly matched.

Les Blank's *Burden of Dreams* (1982, United States; Figure 18-4) chronicles the shooting of Werner Herzog's *Fitzcarraldo*, a fiction feature about a real-life opera impresario who contrived to bring a river steamer over the Andes. Through Herzog's own struggle to get a steamer up a jungle mountainside, Blank reveals Herzog's dictatorial obsessiveness and how a cherished project can become more important to its director than the physical dangers faced by his

FIGURE 18-4

Werner Herzog and the boat he hauls up a hillside in Les Blank's *Burden of Dreams*. (Photo by Maureen Gosling.)

workers. The objectives and values revealed by the process become metaphors for the ruthlessness that often lurks under the guise of making art.

The Journey Film

Journeys promise change and development. Ross McElwee's *Sherman's March* (1989, United States; Figure 18-5) sets out to follow General Sherman's destructive journey during the American Civil War and then, growing bored with its self-imposed task, switches to a parallel and more personal journey by its director. In a witty and extended bid to end his status as a single man, McElwee encounters old and new girlfriends on the road. At the end, starting a promising relationship, he finds that the General is still with him but as a cautionary metaphor. Shot solo using 16 mm film and embodying many hoarse, late-night confessionals, McElwee's wry and self-reflexive movie triggered an avalanche of imitations—not one of which matched the tone or sophistication of the original.

 They say in the film industry that no film about a train has ever failed. The journey's allure, with its metaphoric overtones, characters in transition who face tests and obstacles, and all the inbuilt rhythms of movement add up to fertile ground for documentary.

Luc Jacquet's *March of the Penguins* (2005, France; Figure 18-6) shows the epic journey that emperor penguins make in the Antarctic in order to breed. Some

FIGURE 18-5

Sherman's March, a road movie of encounters between a man and all the women he might marry. (Photo courtesy of The Kobal Collection/McElwee Productions/Guggenheim Fellowship.)

FIGURE 18-6

Shooting *The March of the Penguins*. (Photo courtesy of The Kobal Collection/Bonne Pioche/Buena Vista/APC/Jerome Maison.)

do not finish the journey, find a mate, or manage to guard their chicks, so the film has a dramatic tension that made it immensely popular. The struggle to survive has such anthropomorphic resonances that the film exemplified "family values" for some. Apparently, the French version had a set of voices speaking as if for the penguins (which sounds truly awful). More conventionally, the English version uses the omniscient, voice-over narration beloved by the National Geographic Society, which coproduced. The film is gripping and worth study for its editing alone, which orchestrates much mass action and movement culled from a year of shooting. Luckily penguins do similar things and all look alike, so you get extraordinarily detailed coverage of each stage of their long and arduous journey.

Jorge Furtado's 13-minute *Isle of Flowers* (1989, Brazil) was once voted one of the most important short films of the twentieth century. By following the brief life of a tomato, it starts at the growing site, follows its being made into sauce, and then watches its dregs finishing up in the municipal dump. Because tomatoes here are metaphors for human beings, the film shocks audiences with its message about the despicable way we treat each other. Another film to see for its virtuoso montage.

In Lars Johannson's *The German Secret* (2005, Denmark), the filmmaker chronicles his wife, Kirsten Blohm, crossing Europe in search of the Nazi father

FIGURE 18-7

Mother and daughter in *The German Secret*. Who was my father? Why won't you tell me? (Photo courtesy of Lars Johansson.)

(as they think) whose identity her mother refused to discuss until near death. Amazingly, 50 years later there are still people alive along the route who remember the beautiful, haughty blonde with the strangely neglected child (Figure 18-7). Piece by piece, the two establish the truth, which shapes up to be far from what they expected. Her hopeful, occasionally funny, and often vividly painful journey delivers only partial liberation from a heritage of doubt and anger. This is a tender and masterful film full of intimate reflection and intense, sustained encounters.

The Historical Film

Strictly speaking, all film is history because as soon as it's recorded every frame is history. Film ought to be a good medium for historical films but is not always so. More than most story forms, histories

 Historical subjects are foreclosed whenever their outcomes are familiar. If you must forfeit the elements of anticipation and surprise that create dramatic tension, try instead to focus more on the processes of history instead of their outcomes.

must often digress to build their tributary chains of cause and effect. Imagine a film about a plane crash in which all six of an airliner's safety features failed. You have a known outcome, but your film must spend most of its time explaining what each safety feature is supposed to do, how it failed, and how its breakdown contributed to the disaster. Here time is a minor player in the tale of causality.

Even the makers of screen history themselves aren't always satisfied, as Donald Watt and Jerry Kuehl have pointed out.[2] Many history films, they say:

- Bite off more than they can chew.
- Commandeer specific images as backdrops for generalizations.
- Are inherently unbalanced whenever archive footage is lacking for important events.
- Fail to recognize that the screen is different from literature or an academic lecture.
- Are often dominated by unverifiable interpretations.
- Try to sidestep controversy as school textbooks do.
- Fail to enlighten their audience about strings attached to funding.
- Suffer because their makers wanted to build a monument.
- Suggest consensus opinion and paper over vital disagreements.
- Fail to acknowledge that historians find what they look for.

To this we can add that the screen history, by its realism and ineluctable forward movement, discourages contemplation and often glides over anything it can't illustrate. Historical meanings are in any case abstractions, and the screen is inherently better at showing the concrete.

We should be cautious when a film uses omniscience to obscure its sources. The all-knowing narrator guiding us through tracts of history is worrisome, especially in those History Channel series that use archive footage to cover vast thematic and factual territory. In Britain, Thames Television's *The World at War* of the 1970s and, in America, WGBH's *Vietnam: A Television History* in the 1980s both echo the textbook emphasis on facts rather than questions and issues that arise today. Even Ken Burns' *The Civil War* (1990, United States; Figure 18-8), which counterpoints contemporary accounts and photographs, seems overwhelmed by the repetitive minutia of its period.

 The ambitious scope, authorial impersonality, and apparent finality of many history series make them highly suspect. Who is speaking to whom, for whom, and representing whom? Why do they sometimes suffocate historical curiosity rather than awaken it?

[2]Watt, Donald and Jerry Kuehl. "History on the public screen I & II," in *New Challenges for Documentary*, Alan Rosenthal, Ed. Berkeley: University of California Press, 1988, pp. 4318–4453.

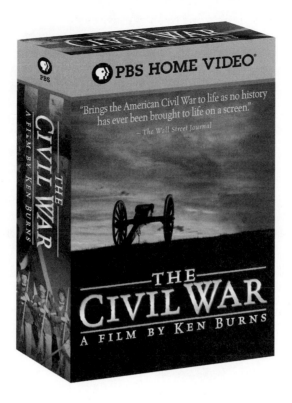

FIGURE 18-8

The American tragedy captured in the groundbreaking history series *The Civil War.* (Photo courtesy of PBS.)

Some screen histories succeed, of course. An openly critical one-off film like Peter Davis' *Hearts and Minds* (1974, United States) argues by analogy that the American obsession with sports provided a deadly and misleading metaphor for the tragically mistaken U.S. involvement in Southeast Asia. Here the viewer is on a clearer footing and can engage with the film's propositions rather than go numb under a deluge of suspiciously uninflected information.

Eyes on the Prize (1990, United States), a PBS series from Blackside, Inc., chronicled the development of civil rights in America and managed to tread a fine line between historical omniscience and personal testimonies that were imbued with commitment. Though crew members were carefully chosen for racial balance, you are never in doubt that the film speaks on behalf of black people so egregiously wronged in equality-proclaiming America.

The War (2007, United States; Figure 18-9), directed by Ken Burns and Lynn Novick, is an oral history whose excellently chosen witness/participants tell their stories with multiple voices and viewpoints. Unlike Burns' earlier, seemingly more linear and event-bound histories, its voice is free from patriotic hubris. The series adds up to a fervently non-nationalistic, antiwar perspective, a

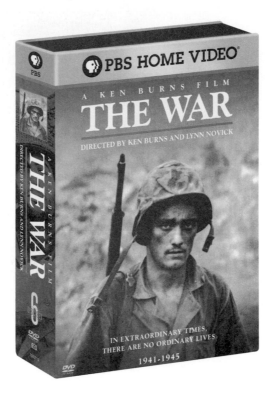

FIGURE 18-9

The War—as close as you'll get to the realities of trying to stay alive in battle. (Photo courtesy of PBS.)

timely corrective when embedded journalism presents so many fighting "heroes" during the good-versus-evil simplifications of wartime.

The Biographical Film

Following a single character through time is a variation on the hero's journey paradigm of the folklorist Joseph Campbell.[3] Point of view plays a significant part, since the central character's sense of events is often in tension with those around him or her. The progression in which the main character grows up, develops, and meets test after test also generates the kind of momentum that easily allows sidebar excursions along the way.

    Stevie (2002, United States; Figure 18-10) is a biographical film about an antihero, an abused boy to whom its director, Steve James, had been a Big Brother a decade earlier. Tracking down the shy rural kid he'd once known,

---

[3]For the best, movie-oriented explanation, see Christopher Vogler's *The Writer's Journey: Mythic Structure for Storytellers and Screenwriters* (1992, Michael Wiese).

FIGURE 18-10

An abused boy becomes an abusing adult in *Stevie*. (Photo courtesy of The Kobal Collection/Kartemquin Films.)

James finds Stevie moving on a downward path through a fog of alcohol and petty crime. During the period of filming Stevie graduates to child molesting and goes to prison. Unjudgmentally the film helps us understand that Stevie was a victim himself until he sexually abused a young girl relative. Once roles are reversed, the abuse gets kicked forward another generation. By the end of this subtle and sympathetic film you understand in detail how so many lives get ruined. There's not much cause for optimism here but a lot to understand.

Errol Morris' *The Fog of War: Eleven Lessons from the Life of Robert S. McNamara* (2003, United States; Figure 18-11) gives the former U.S. Secretary of Defense a self-serving platform in his old age. From telling of his apprenticeship presiding over U.S. policy in Vietnam, he now dispenses pearls of wisdom for reducing future warfare, such as: "In order to do good, you may have to engage in evil." Along the way he magnanimously admits to a few mistakes. Morris gives MacNamara such a long rope that he is hoisted by his own petard.

Taggart Siegel's *The Real Dirt on Farmer John* (2006, United States; Figure 18-12) profiles a third-generation Midwest farmer. As a young man, he took over the family land, foreswore agribusiness chemicals, and turned his farm into a thriving commune growing vegetables named Angelic Organics. If that didn't rile the farming neighbors, then driving his tractor in a feather boa and frolicking with very young girls did. He was fire-bombed as a devil worshiper.

FIGURE 18-11 ─────────────────────────────

The Fog of War: Eleven Lessons from the Life of Robert S. McNamara. (Photo courtesy of Fourth Floor Productions.)

FIGURE 18-12 ─────────────────────────────

Bees at play in *The Real Dirt on Farmer John.* (Photo courtesy of Slava Doval/Angelic Organics.)

Playfully shocking and great fun, the film darts around in time during its self-presentation by this dada agriculturalist. Its apex is the point where he lost the farm before making a comeback.

NONCHRONOLOGICAL TIME

Poetic Time

This category is seldom event- or character-driven and more likely to pursue imagery and metaphor in exploration of an observation, mood, or belief. All the best documentaries have poetic elements, of course, but too few rely mainly on powerful imagery. Some are discussed in **Chapter 5, Documentary Language**, the most memorable being *Land Without Bread* (1932, Spain), *Night Mail* (1936, United Kingdom), *The Plow That Broke the Plains* (1936, United States), and *The River* (1937, United States; Figure 18-13). Humphrey Jennings, "the only real poet that British cinema has yet produced,"[4] made documentaries during World War II while his country was under siege, notably *Listen to Britain* (1942, United Kingdom), *Fires Were Started* (1943, United Kingdom; Figure 18-14), and *Diary for Timothy* (1945, United Kingdom). Their use of emotively loaded imagery and sounds resonated for people at the time but won't mean much to

FIGURE 18-13 ——————————————————————————————

Soil erosion in an early ecology masterpiece, *The River*. (Photo courtesy of the Museum of Modern Art Film Stills Archive.)

———————————

[4]According to the British director Lindsay Anderson.

FIGURE 18-14

Making *Fires Were Started*, an early dramadoc that brought together grim firefighting footage with dialogue scenes improvised between the firemen. (Photo courtesy of The Kobal Collection/Crown Film Unit.)

younger people today. In *Fires Were Started*, Jennings mixed appallingly vivid firefighting footage with firehouse scenes using rather stilted improvised dialogue.

The common denominator—perhaps a very significant one—is that all these filmmakers shot silent and put imagery first. They composed sound separately and later and based it on inspiration provided by images. How you do things determines what you end up with.

More recently, Godfrey Reggio's *Koyaanisqatsi or Life Out of Balance* (1982, United States; Figure 18-15), about the rape of the environment by humankind, is realized through music allied to imagery that is original and from archives and that has no relation to time progression. When it first appeared, its premise about humanity causing environmental catastrophe seemed romantic and apocalyptic, but time has proven Reggio prophetic.

Some biographical films I specially admire are difficult or impossible to find. Orod Attapour's *Parnian* (2002, Iran; Figure 18-16) profiles an ill-fated family of Tehran archaeologists. Both mother and son suffer from an incurable wasting disease that is killing the mother. The father cares for them while they probe Iran's rich history with obsessive, desperate energy. Every image in the film carries rich metaphorical overtones, and every sequence and every image has an

FIGURE 18-15

Koyaanisqatsi or Life Out of Balance—an apocalyptic vision that time has vindicated. (Photo courtesy of The Kobal Collection/Institute for Regional Education.)

FIGURE 18-16

In *Parnian*, a young archeologist suffering a wasting disease taunts destiny (frame from the film).

analogical relationship to others. Skillfully the film implies, like the Persian poetry that plainly influences it, a wheel of life binding us to those who lived and suffered before us. We too must live and suffer as they did, and so we lead the way for those who will follow. Compressed into its austere half hour is a whole vista of time, repeated destiny, decay, and renewal.

Vincent Dieutre has structured his poetic first-person narrative *Lessons of Darkness* (2000, France) by his thoughts, memories, and feelings. He is a gay man falling out of love while journeying between three European cities and find-ing solace in the erotic solidity of the men in Caravaggio's paintings. The narrative weakness in any poetic film is likely to be that it for-goes the dramatic tension and momentum of plot for the intensity and resonance of imagery and moment. When we are in masterful hands, as here, this is no sacrifice, but in those of lesser ability it can produce work that is wandering and arbitrary.

 Any film led by mood, metaphor, and imagery risks forgoing dramatic tension and momentum for the intensity and resonance of the moment. This is no loss if the film holds our interest and leaves us with a larger vision.

Time Reordered

A common rearrangement of time is to show an event and then backtrack to analyze the interplay of forces that led up to it, as in Joe Berlinger and Bruce Sinofsky's *Paradise Lost: The Child Murders at Robin Hood Hills* (1996, United States). The film opens with the tragic sight of three murdered 8-year-old boys and then focuses on the trial of the three local teenagers accused of killing them in a satanic ritual. The film casts doubt on the validity of the evidence, rather as the filmmakers did in their earlier *Brother's Keeper* (1992, United States), which told of some reclusive rural brothers accused of mercy killing a sibling. Both films examine the arguments for and against each allegation, deconstruct them and their key events, and then invite us to draw likely conclusions. Berlinger and Sinofsky's films are interested in character as much as facts, and this takes their films further than the conventional investigation.

The Personal Film

Four distinguished films probe family secrets and find surprises and heartache behind "successful" lives. Each film develops along the line of new information as it surfaces. In *My Architect* (2003, United States), Nathaniel Kahn recreates the father he hardly knew by building a picture of the distinguished and elusive architect Louis Kahn. Mostly he does this through the generous women whom Kahn made use of while leveraging his career. Here is a ruthless, driven man who used whomever was willing in his single-minded pursuit of architectural innovation. The consequences emerge through those who maintain or critique his architecture, the women who loved him, and the son who searches to define and hold him.

FIGURE 18-17——

A family harboring molesters in *Capturing the Friedmans*, or a miscarriage of justice? (Photo courtesy of The Kobal Collection/HBO Documentary/Notorious Pictures.)

Andrew Jarecki's controversial *Capturing the Friedmans* (2003, United States; Figure 18-17) follows up the arrest of a respectable Long Island teacher and one of his sons for alleged sexual crimes against children. The film gathers all available family perspectives, looks at the 8 mm home movies of the archetypal suburban family at happy play, and finds in the end that all is mystery and nothing adds up. So often, families are strangers to each other.

In Doug Block's *51 Birch Street* (2005, United States), as mentioned in the previous chapter, a son begins searching out the truths behind about his parents' long but blighted marriage, hoping to reach his father after his mother suddenly dies. In the writing she left behind, he is astonished to discover that the mother he had felt so close to had maintained a secret love life. The father he always found remote suddenly marries his secretary of 40 years earlier, then emerges as warmer and far more understanding of his wife than Block had ever imagined. The miracle—which no documentarian can ever forget—is that truth does indeed set people free, as the film shows.

Where the previous three biographies analyze lives largely completed, the next film crackles with misplaced father/son hopes and resentments whose roots go back decades. Mark Wexler shot *Tell Them Who You Are* (2005, United States) hoping to get closer to his famous Hollywood cinematographer father, Haskell. Few films have explored the psychic wounds between generations more nakedly, painfully, and obstinately, and seldom do family relations seem more irreconcilable.

Each of these four biographies begins from some basic questions that, pursued through a labyrinth of ambiguous discovery, unfold like a detective story. Following clues and pursuing hypotheses, their protagonists lance at layers of protective myth and stereotype. Family members hold partisan views, each fixed in subjectivity, and nowhere is this truer than of children in relation to their parents. All four films reveal their main characters' development over time, and these emerge through multiple perceptions, but it is the hierarchy of discovery that determines the films' structures. Though all pursue a crooked course, high intelligence and sophistication make each seem to have taken the only path possible.

 A well-structured film usually seems so inevitable that you cannot imagine it following any other path.

The Walled-City Film

Societies, institutions, and tribal entities define their boundaries, close in upon themselves, and develop self-perpetuating codes. Films profiling them are often impressionistic, since boundaries usually contain many simultaneous activities. Juxtaposing these by theme, mood, or meaning can imply polemic using the light hand of montage. The 10-hour PBS special *Carrier* (2008, United States) aspires to be the mother of all such endeavors, although its subtitle ("One Ship, Five Thousand Stories") may seem more like a warning. Conceived by Mitchell Block and its director Maro Chermayeff, it draws on 1600 hours of superb filming during 6 months' residence aboard the nuclear-powered U.S. aircraft carrier *Nimitz*. Each hour-long episode handles a theme ("controlled chaos," "show of force," "rites of passage"), and each is bookended with title sequences redolent of recruiting films. Most episodes are diffuse, high on testosterone (the average age aboard is 19), and punctuated with upbeat songs that seem suspiciously like narrative aids. Even so, the series is worth seeing from beginning to end as a thorough study of a military society riddled with contradictions and conflicts. Sailors of both sexes and all ranks are remarkably candid, and the series' connective tissue becomes the evolving personal stories of 15 central characters. We come to see a rare camaraderie that for many compensates for the turmoil and pain wrought by dysfunctional family origins. Most suffer excessively because of long periods of separation from their loved ones, as do the families they leave on land.

 The walled-city type of film explores a microcosm in order to imply criticism of the macrocosm—the larger world that spawned it.

The sheer enormity of the series in relation to its enlightenment leaves you feeling ambiguous. Unintentionally, I think, it glamorizes military life and celebrates the gunboat diplomacy for which the *Nimitz* was built. The unspoken issues—why America chooses military might over social justice, adequate health and education, and a modern infrastructure for its citizenry and why military might makes ideological enemies rather than beats them—remain outside the pale. As with many documentaries, you are left wondering what restrictions the filmmakers accepted—or imposed on themselves—as the price of entry.

Most of Frederick Wiseman's documentaries—at long last available on DVD—are walled-city films, most notably two of his earliest—*Titicut Follies* (1967, United States) and *High School* (1968, United States). The Titicut Follies is a revue presented by the staff and inmates in a Massachusetts prison for the criminally insane. Wiseman makes it function as a backbone for the film and also a grimly nihilistic metaphor. When there are no interviews or narration you cannot retreat from scenes that are grippingly horrific, as if retrieved from the eighteenth century. In stark, Daumier black-and-white imagery we see the inmates' degrading spectrum of daily experience—from induction, psychiatric evaluation, nakedness, forced feeding, to burial. In one sequence, a seemingly sane Hungarian tries desperately to extricate himself from the institution's nightmarish embrace. In another, a psychiatric doctor with an ash-laden cigarette on his lower lip rams a feeding pipe down a half-dead prisoner's nose. Each digression from the ongoing revue is so engrossing that the revue itself becomes a mocking commentary. Wiseman and his cameraman Bill Brayne lead us into a living hell and at the same time define what observational documentary means.

Two films by Nick Broomfield—*Soldier Girls* (1981, United States/United Kingdom, with Joan Churchill) and *Chicken Ranch* (1982, United States/United Kingdom, with Sandi Sissel; Figure 18-18)—qualify as walled-city films but differ significantly in approach from narrated and observational approaches. The first looks at women soldiers in basic training, while the second is about the women, their relationships, and their customers in a brothel. Both explore social ghettoes and find their structure in a series of events that spontaneously occurred during a stay by the filmmakers. Each shows how those who rule institutional life set about conditioning and controlling their inmates. Each leaves us more knowledgeable and critical.

Neither, however, pretends to be neutral or unaffected by what it finds. By letting us see a discharged woman soldier embrace the camera operator, by including the brothel owner's tirade at the crew for filming what he wants kept confidential, each scene admits where the filmmakers' sympathies lie and hints at the liaisons and even manipulation that went into their shooting. Broomfield has since made *Battle for Haditha* (2007, United Kingdom; Figure 18-19), a documentary-style enactment of the 2005 event after a marine was killed by a roadside bomb in Iraq. His colleagues went to find the perpetrators, resulting in 24 Iraqi civilians dead in a frenzy of killing that the military tried to conceal. Over time, a director's themes emerge, and Broomfield seems concerned with the way that inferiors are manipulated into serving the interests of their masters.

 Documentarians sometimes graduate to docudrama or fiction in order to hypothesize what cannot be established in acceptable documentary terms.

FIGURE 18-18

The ladies in Nick Broomfield's *Chicken Ranch* pose with their madame. The documentary led to a musical. (Photo courtesy of First Run Features.)

FIGURE 18-19

Battle for Haditha—docudrama can sometimes say what documentary cannot. (Photo courtesy of The Kobal Collection/Channel 4 Films/Barney Broomfield.)

The Thesis Film

This is any film that uses the essay form to educate, analyze, or elaborate on a thesis. Exposés, agitprop, experimental, or activist films are often structured by the stages of an extended process, but more often they use montage to display ideas for the audience to consider. Let's suppose you want to convince the audience that poor immigrants, far from draining the local economy, add economic value to a large American city. You must establish how and why the immigrants came, what work they do, what city services they do or don't use, what their enemies say about them, and so on. You must build an argument and advance the stages of a polemic in order to convince the skeptics in your audience.

 Thesis films must marshal facts and impressions and build a careful sequence of logic if they are to persuade. They are demanding films to plan and shoot and require sustained effort to edit.

 Of the films mentioned in **Chapter 5, Documentary Language**, both Buñuel's *Land Without Bread* and Resnais' *Night and Fog* advance passionate arguments about the mechanisms of human cruelty. The Pare Lorentz ecology duo, *The Plow That Broke the Plains* and *The River* convey strong messages about the rape of the land. Michael Moore's *Fahrenheit 9/11* (2004, United States) argues that the Bush Administration, supported by the corporate media and its embedded journalists after 9/11, used the wave of public feeling to further its prior agenda for invading Afghanistan and Iraq. Hubert Sauper's *Darwin's Nightmare* (2004, Austria/Belgium/France/Canada/Finland/Sweden; Figure 18-20) draws connections between the export of fish from Lake Victoria, the neglect and starvation of

FIGURE 18-20

Darwin's Nightmare creates a rare intimacy with poor Africans living on the edge of starvation. (Photo courtesy of The Kobal Collection/Saga Films/Coop 99.)

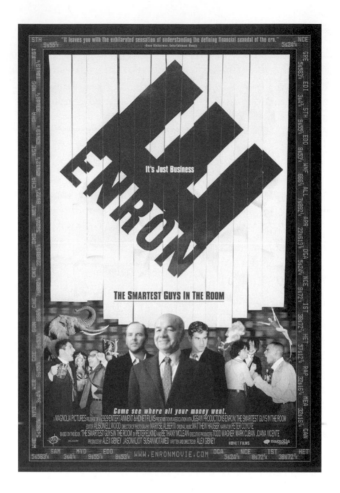

FIGURE 18-21

A house of cards collapses in *Enron: The Smartest Guys in the Room*. (Photo courtesy of The Kobal Collection/HDNet Films/Jigsaw Films.)

its native Tanzanian population, and the import of munitions used to fuel wars over Africa's mineral resources. Alex Gibney's *Enron: The Smartest Guys in the Room* (2005, United States; Figure 18-21), built on work by *Fortune* reporters, explains how the energy company built a house of cards and why it collapsed.

These are the independent voices of democratic reason that shine light in dark places. Their freedom to argue today rests squarely on the growth of accessible digital equipment but remains limited by the fact that most film archives are corporately controlled and very expensive. Meanwhile, the Internet is developing as an uncontrolled arena for the exchange of information and opinion. History will probably judge public discourse to have changed radically at this time.

TIME AS NONRELEVANT

The Catalogue Film

The catalogue film is a type of documentary whose main and enthusiastic purpose is to examine something comprehensively rather than critically. A film about harpsichords, steam locomotives, or dinosaurs might organize their appearance by size, age, structure, or other classification. Unless the film takes the stages of a restoration or archeological dig as its backbone, time probably won't play a centrally organizing role.

Joris Ivens' *Rain* (1929, Netherlands; Figure 18-22) is a silent, highly atmospheric 12-minute film shot in Amsterdam over two years. It reveals the beauty of rain in a cityscape. A year earlier, Ivens had shot another equally lyrical 11-minute classic, *The Bridge*. These films will stand for all time as defining portraits of city life in 1920s Holland. Soon Ivens and Henri Storck turned to social justice with *Borinage* (1932, Belgium), in which concern for the misery of exploited miners replaced Ivens' earlier interest in aesthetics. By showing how the men and their families lived from day to day, the film exposed a hidden and desperate part of European society to the rest of the world.

Les Blank's films, usually described as celebrations of Americana, are really catalogue films. There is *Garlic Is as Good as Ten Mothers* (1977, United States), *In Heaven There Is No Beer* (1984, United States), and the delightful *Gap-Toothed*

FIGURE 18-22

Amsterdam under umbrellas in *Rain*. (Photo © European Foundation, Joris Ivens Archives.)

Women (1987, United States). All are good-natured forays into special worlds, and were they not so innocent they would probably appear voyeuristic. The travelogue, diary film, and city symphony are frequently montage-based catalogue types.

When No Time Structure Predominates

There may initially be no obvious time structure. A film about stained glass windows may have no time structure inherent in the footage. You could posit a structure from the dating of particular windows, technical developments in glass, the region of the artifacts, or the origin and idiosyncrasies of the glassmakers. Which option you take depends on what you want to say and what your material best supports. Anthology films that chronicle a particular year take this approach.

Surreal Documentary

Surreal documentary is a rare form well suited to a playful handling of the outlandish or appalling. Terry Zwigoff's *Crumb* (1994, United States; Figure 18-23) profiles the 1960s underground comic artist Robert Crumb, best known for Fritz the Cat. So weird was his upbringing that he and his family seem dangerously dysfunctional (he was suicidal and an older brother killed himself). His comic strips explore sexual obsessions and revolve around personal, confessional

FIGURE 18-23 ————————————————————————————————

In *Crumb*, we meet the comic artist, his family, and his inspiration. (Photo courtesy of The Kobal Collection/Superior Pictures.)

FIGURE 18-24 ———————————————————————————————————

Deborah Hoffmann and her mother in *Complaints of a Dutiful Daughter*. (Photo by Frances Reid, courtesy of Deborah Hoffmann.)

observations about abnormality. It's hard to tell whether it is Zwigoff's film or the subject matter that is more surreal.

As Deborah Hoffmann's mother descends into Alzheimer's disease, *Complaints of a Dutiful Daughter* (1995, United States; Figure 18-24) uses dark humor to explore what would otherwise be a crushingly sad situation. The film's progression is organized by the daughter's journey—from early consciousness of her mother's growing eccentricity, to fearing that her mother will turn into the pathetic shell of her former self, to realizing that her mother is actually becoming more her essentially humorous self.

MONOLOGICAL VERSUS DIALOGICAL FILMS

Though old habits of disseminating improving tracts to the unwashed masses die hard, documentary is becoming less monological and more dialogical. Slowly documentary is acquiring the complexities of language, thought, and purpose once confined to older art forms such as literature and theater. The newer documentaries are willing to

 A new generation is supplying films that provoke an active inner dialogue rather than feeding a diet of facts intended for passive consumption. The older form speaks monologically; the newer, dialogically.

investigate people's innermost thoughts and feelings and do not lecture their audience.

QUESTIONS TO ASK YOURSELF REGARDING STRUCTURE

Whether you are planning a film or confronting the dailies of one already shot, the structure you choose must accommodate a few central concerns. Your options may not be as limited as you think. To find alternatives, try answering these questions:

What is your film's inbuilt chronology?

- Event or process?
- Elapse of time?
- Journey?
- Other?

What do you gain, and what do you lose, by sticking to that chronology?

- Can you hold back your major sequences, or must you blow them early?
- Does chronological order dissipate or focus the main issue?
  What stakes are your participants playing for?
- What can you do to raise them?

What other aspects might structure your film?

- Catalog order (by physical size, age, complexity, color, etc.)?
- By significance (in complexity, consequences, energy, noise, etc.)?
- By significance to a main character (the order of recall, effect, consequence, etc.)?
- Narration (which might come from a character in the film)

How soon can your film gain momentum?

- How little exposition can you get away with to get it moving?
- Should you bunch the exposition (risky) or can you mete it out gradually?

What is the film's likely turning point, or climax?

Where can you place the film's climactic scene(s) on the dramatic arc? Can it happen:

- At the beginning?
- At the end?
- Two-thirds through?

What proportion of your movie's screen time should you ideally devote to:

- Getting to the climax or turning point?
- Dealing with all the consequences that make up the resolution?

How do you want your film to act on its audience?

- Mostly inform them?
- Take them through an experience whose outcome is unimportant?
- Make them think about causes rather than effects?
- Keep them guessing as long as possible?

Whose point of view is the film channeled through, and how might this lead you away from the obvious structural solution?

- The main character?
- A subsidiary character?
- Multiple characters?
- The Storyteller?

Who or what changes during your film?

- The POV character?
- Someone else?
- A situation?

Where does this change probably happen?

- Is it the film's climax?
- Is it gradual and in the background?
- Is it sudden, precipitous, and in the foreground?

Where will your film's dramatic tension come from?

- An overall situation that is long in developing?
- A volcanic, climactic moment? (Can you delay it and raise the stakes?)
- An impending change or crisis (such as a heart operation)?

Answering these questions probably won't produce ready solutions but will lead you to think hard about your story's essentials, which is the spade work of creativity.

CHAPTER 19

FORM, CONTROL, AND STYLE

This chapter may be heavy going unless you've had experience in other narrative art forms. If it seems foreign, skip to the table of prompts at the end and use them for your next film. Once you've made one or two films, you'll recognize the path you've been on, and ideas about form and style will begin to complement your own thinking.

FORM

Flaherty was original enough to single-handedly invent the genre of documentary because he saw that documentary needs narrative compression and storytelling techniques to engage its audience. This is disturbing to the ethnographer, or any purist for whom manipulation is suspect. But our experiences and meanings pursued through documentary won't get across unless you can make an audience *feel* them. This reconnects with the notion of a film's contract with its audience. It must promise something, deliver what it promises, and remain consistent while doing so. Only the director can decide how to do this, but the nature of your subject is a powerfully deciding force.

 A large and enthusiastic public now exists for the best documentaries, but you will have to devise strong narrative approaches if your films are to rise above the average.

The inbuilt limitations that come with your subject provide a useful spur to creativity. They insist you concentrate on the essentials of what you're doing. The most pervasive are in time, personnel, equipment, travel, shooting days, and resources. They help concentrate the mind so you shoot no more than necessary. Film schedules have tightened ever since digital shooting and editing sped up production. These are the realities, and like the rules limiting any game, they make filming finite and challenging. Whether you can work fruitfully within them decides whether you survive—financially and professionally. Accordingly, you plan and schedule in detail, breaking tasks into bite-size pieces so you can tell where you have under- or overscheduled.

There are also limitations you set yourself, ones you choose that give you *something meaningful to push against* and that force you to find creative solutions. Let's briefly examine how setting their own aesthetic rules galvanized a couple of visual movements.

SETTING LIMITS AND THE DOGME GROUP

In America of the early 1930s some photographers banded together under the name Group f/64. They felt that photography could never realize its potential unless it stopped emulating high-art forms like painting, sketching, and etching. From that consciousness came a fantastic movement in photography that gave us the groundbreaking work of Edward Weston, Imogen Cunningham, Ansel Adams, and Willard Van Dyke.

In Denmark of the mid-1990s, the founding members of the Dogme 95 cinema group arrived at similar conclusions and went on to produce landmark fiction films. *The Celebration* (1998, Denmark, directed by Thomas Vinterberg; Figure 19-1), *Breaking the Waves* (1999, Denmark, directed by Lars von Trier; Figure 19-2), and *The Idiots* (1999, Denmark, directed by Lars von Trier) were

FIGURE 19-1

The Celebration—a Dogme fiction film that jettisons many fiction conventions in favor of more informal and immediate shooting techniques. (Photo courtesy of The Kobal Collection/Nimbus Film Productions.)

FIGURE 19-2————————————————————————————————————

Improvisation, fine performances, and a documentary approach give *Breaking the Waves* an impassioned urgency. (Photo courtesy of The Kobal Collection/Zentropa.)

all shot digitally and handheld. Their starting point is a playful manifesto explicitly rejecting the embrace of Hollywood and that moves their methods toward the norms of documentary. It appears in various versions and translations, so I have taken the liberty of putting it in vernacular English:

A Vow of Chastity

- Shooting must be done on location. Props and sets must not be brought in, but shooting must go where that set or prop can be found.

- Sound must never be produced separately from the images or *vice versa*. Music must not be used unless it occurs where the scene is shot.

- The camera must be handheld. Any movement or immobility attainable by handholding is permitted. The action cannot be organized for the camera; instead, the camera must go to the action.

- The film must be in color. Special lighting is not acceptable, and if there is too little light for exposure the scene must be cut, or a single lamp may be attached to the camera.

- Camera filters and other optical work are forbidden.

- The film must not contain any superficial action such as murders, weapons, explosions, and so on.

- No displacement is permitted in time or space; the film takes place here and now.

- Genre movies are not acceptable.

- Film format is Academy 35 mm.
- The director must not be credited.

Furthermore, I swear as a director to refrain from personal taste. I am no longer an artist. I swear to refrain from creating a "work," as I regard the instant as more important than the whole. My supreme goal is to force the truth out of my characters and settings. I swear to do so by all the means available and at the cost of any good taste and any aesthetic considerations.

Signed _____ [member's name]

The last clause is really intriguing: By rejecting a leadership hierarchy and even personal taste, the manifesto strikes at the narcissism of ego. The effect of deemphasizing leadership and film techniques was to hand their actors a rich slice of creative control, to which they responded handsomely. About their manifesto, Thomas Vinterberg said:

> We did the "Vow of Chastity" in half an hour and we had great fun. Yet, at the same time, we felt that in order to avoid the mediocrity of filmmaking not only in the whole community, but in our own filmmaking as well, we had to do something different. We wanted to undress film, turn it back to where it came from and remove the layers of make-up between the audience and the actors. We felt it was a good idea to concentrate on the moment, on the actors and, of course, on the story that they were acting, which are the only aspects left when everything else is stripped away. Also, artistically it has created a very good place for us to be as artists or filmmakers because having obstacles like these means you have something to play against.[1]

 Contradictions always arise from trying to live according to beliefs, but the Dogme Group's work and the superb involvement it called forth from actors demand respect for their spirit and achievements.

Their guiding values helped catapult Danish film to the forefront of international cinema. The moral? Filmmakers decide what matters by rejecting what intrudes. In documentary, some limitations come with the subject but others you must choose.

So, what creative limitations will you set yourself?

 Creatively inspired limitations—no matter whether you encounter them or impose them on yourself—are valuable because they give you something meaningful to push against.

---

[1]Interview by Elif Cercel for *Director's World*; see http://stage.directorsworld.com

CONTENT INFLUENCES FORM

Most of those working in the arts—musicians, writers, and painters, for instance—control their own content and form. The documentarian, however, is more like a mosaic artist who works from the idiosyncratic, chance-influenced nature of found materials. Each documentary depends on acts, words, and images plucked from life—all elements largely outside your control. This means that, unless your film is of the highly malleable essay type, its source materials already restrict your options. Also limiting you are your ethics, interests, and ideas about what work the documentary should do. They will shape your work and give it a *style* that is yours and nobody else's.

 No documentary succeeds unless you can turn your footage into a compelling narrative. Memorable films are thus each one of a kind, so you can't treat the best as prototypes.

Fiction films create characters and situations in the service of ideas, but documentary discovers meanings hiding inside lived reality. That's why it's so fascinating—you have to present the world as it really is, not as you wish it to be.

STYLE

The documentarian begins work very practically, by selectively shooting and editing in order to direct the audience's attention at what is meaningful and would otherwise go unnoticed. Getting your meaning across will be easier if:

- The subject is gripping.
- The treatment (that is, form and style) is imaginative.
- Point of view comes from an emotional response rather than one that is intellectual.
- The film makes use of imagery, metaphor, and symbolism to suggest there is more going on than meets the eye.

 Examine a documentary's style in detail using **Project 1-AP-7 Analyze Structure and Style.**

All the conventions of the cinema are at your service as you transform actuality into a story with style, point of view, and the meanings that you and your associates come to know are present.

 Jean-Luc Godard said, "To me, style is just the outside of content, and content the inside of style, like the outside and inside of the human body—both go together; they can't be separated."[2]

---

[2]Roud, Richard. *Jean-Luc Godard.* Bloomington: Indiana University Press, 1970.

However, every film treads a fine line between drowning in realism on the one hand and over-imposing order and meaning on the other. You navigate between extremes. Stamp your work too heavily and you will crush the personalities, events, and subtexts subtly present in the dailies. Withdraw all interpretive effort from the tale, and the point of telling it evaporates.

The word "style" is often and confusingly interchanged with "form." There are in fact two aspects of style—what you can choose and what you can't.

STYLE YOU CAN'T CHOOSE

Happily, you can't choose aspects of your films' style that arise from your tastes and identity. If this seems a little foggy for an art that is so collaborative, you can still recognize the authorship in a Michael Moore or a Werner Herzog documentary, even when you don't particularly care for their films. Contributing to this are:

- Choices of subject
- Camera handling
- Forms that each director favors
- Marks of personality and taste
- Methods and messages.

A film's genre, its voice, meanings, and its style overlap during production and are difficult to see separately afterwards. If you overreach during production, you can quite easily upset the balance so that stylizing actuality (that is, intensifying its essential nature) turns into *stylized* actuality. The ultra-fragmented, MTV camera-waving style of Daniel Myrick and Eduardo Sánchez' fake documentary, *The Blair Witch Project* (1999), and the overcomposed look of Errol Morris' biography of Stephen Hawking, *A Brief History of Time* (1991, United States; Figure 19-3), both suffer, in my view, from an overemphasis on a stylistic "statement." The film on Hawking, although it argues his complex theories brilliantly, was shot not in authentic locations but on specially constructed sets.

So what to do? Working simply, sincerely, and intelligently is most likely to make an audience connect emotionally with your work. Simplicity is wise anyway, since you have a long developmental curve ahead as you acquire the technical and conceptual skills to serve what you have to say.

Because you can't choose your identity, some of your film's style will take care of itself. Audiences

 Trying to strike a style or project an artistic identity leads rather easily to watch-me gimmickry. More important is to develop your deepest interests and be guided by the marks left on you by formative experiences.

 Expressiveness through cinema is no easier to learn than expressiveness through a musical instrument. You will never stop learning and growing.

FIGURE 19-3 ————————————————————————————————————

A Brief History of Time profiles the life and ideas of the paralyzed theoretical physicist Stephen Hawking. It conveys the agility of his mind with a dizzying and stylized treatment. (Photo courtesy of The Kobal Collection/Triton Films.)

and critics may even tell you what your style is. Beware! You'll be tempted to play safe by imitating your reputation.

STYLE YOU CAN CHOOSE

Films about a children's author, a tree disease, or early submarines all occupy different worlds, belong in

 Serve the controllable aspects of your films well over a period, and people will come to recognize something in your films that they'll call your style.

different documentary genres, and call for different approaches. A film about a Talmudic scholar should look very different from one about a skateboarder simply because each occupies an utterly different physical and mental reality. One might call for low-key (large areas of shadow) lighting, rock-steady indoor compositions, and a Vermeer palette of dark colors. The other is more likely to have high-key (mainly bright) lighting and be shot outdoors with an adventurously handheld camera.

 The nature and meaning of whatever you film always give clues on how you should film it. Good stylistic choices can help us more easily join your characters in their particular world.

PROMPTS TO HELP YOU MAKE STYLISTIC CHOICES

As you decide a shooting and editing style, try completing these prompts in writing:

Meaningful limitations I will impose on myself for this film are . . .

The contrasts or differences between my main characters and their worlds are . . .

My POV character(s) is trying to get, do, or accomplish . . .

His/her/its environments are composed of . . . and suggest . . .

The different rhythms my film contains are . . .

The main change and development during my film is of:

- Place
- Pace or rhythm
- Season or country
- Palette
- Other _____

The film's contents suggest a preponderance of:

- Warm, close, intimate photography
- Cool and distanced views
- Static frames with action choreographed within them
- Contained, measured movement
- Fast, unstable, or subjective movement
- Other _____

Characteristic colors in each of my film's sequences are . . .

- Each suggests . . .
- Their progression through the film suggests . . .

The main conflict my film handles (between . . . and . . .) suggests that contrasting or complementing visual and aural elements might be . . .

The editing style in my film should aim to be:

- Slow, deliberate, unhurrying
- Alternating between . . . and . . .
- Fast, glancing, and impressionistic
- Other _____

- Slow or fast motion, freeze frames, and other optical treatments would achieve . . . in my film.
- Narration in my film might come from . . . [character or type of narrator]
- The difference between the start of my film and its end suggests that editing and photography need to change from . . . to . . .
- Soundscapes in my film include . . .
- Aspects of sound design that my film will emphasize are . . .

CHAPTER 20

REENACTMENT, RECONSTRUCTION, AND DOCUDRAMA

REENACTING EVENTS

A controversial aspect of the documentary is its ability to conjecture. You do this on a minor scale when you ask questions, expose contradictions, or juxtapose opposites in order to make the audience find answers to the tension you have created. Conjecture on a larger scale often means reconstructing bygone situations. Perhaps some vital episode in your subject's life happened before you began filming—a crucial career interview, say, for a job that your reformed criminal main character has already begun. The company decided to take a chance and hire him, and this has changed his life. For him the encounter was pivotal, so you need to represent it in the film. Your participants are ready and willing to reenact the scene, but can you—should you—film it? Will your audience need to know it's a reconstruction? If so, how do you let them know? To pass the scene off as the real thing would be highly misleading. You would rightly be accused of faking, and this could seriously damage your credibility—even your career. Some films run a "Scene reenacted" subtitle, but this seems like overkill if narration or voice-over makes this clear in spirit by using a distancing past tense.

 By constructing future or bygone situations or by creating "what might have been," documentary can conjecture. You need valid reasons for doing this, or your audience will look for what's inauthentic.

In *The New York Times* (http://morris.blogs.nytimes.com/2008/04/03/lplay-it-again-sam-re-enactments-part-one/), Errol Morris writes in fascinating detail about the way he used reenactment to scrutinize witness testimony in *The Thin Blue Line* (1980, United States). He

When all else is authentic, it's wise to clearly identify any reenacted footage that might lead us to draw formative conclusions.

includes telling comment on the misuse of reenactment as well as archive footage. There is, for instance, only one set of shots showing Jews being put on a train to the death camps, yet the same footage is used for any film (including one of my own) for deportations in any part of Europe. Those familiar with a period's archives are distressed to see footage transposed in time and place to serve a multitude of historical narratives. Today, cropping or altering images is only a mouse-click away and offers a seductive solution for problems of narrative or missing coverage. If this is done in plain sight to serve the spirit of the truth, it may not be a problem. But whenever the audience is deceived into accepting what it sees as reliable evidence, then it can only be called deception. For a full exploration of the problems, read Morris' article and the train of correspondence it evoked.

The dividing line is one of good faith; there is nothing controversial about showing that a participant got caught shoplifting, if factually this is what happened. But if he maintains that the store police entrapped him, it matters very much whether we see the actual arrest or a reenactment. Several people's integrity is up for judgment.

TRUTHFUL LABELING

In Amsterdam, some talented film students in the 1990s made an explosive documentary. It showed dropout kids playing a deadly game where they lay their arms between the wheels of railroad wagons. As the engine started in the distance, they would wait as long as possible while the clink–clink–clink of the couplings got nearer before jumping clear. The film culminates with a horrific hospital scene in which the smallest boy has lost both arms. Lodewijk Crijns' *Kutzooi* (1995, Netherlands; Figure 20-1) turned out to have been wholly and

masterfully fabricated—indeed, not a documentary at all, but a mockumentary. Like those with whom I saw it (mostly documentary teachers), I was irate with the film for bamboozling us, as I think any audience would be,[1] for we had trusted what it seemed to be—recorded actuality.

When someone swaps the labels between fiction and documentary, we feel our trust has been abused. Being uncertain which one is watching is just as worrisome.

---

[1] I am indebted to enlightening discussions of docudrama and false documentaries led by Otto Schuurman and Elaine Charnov at the "Sights of the Turn of the Century" documentary conference at the Centro de Capacitación Cinematográfica in Mexico City, 1996.

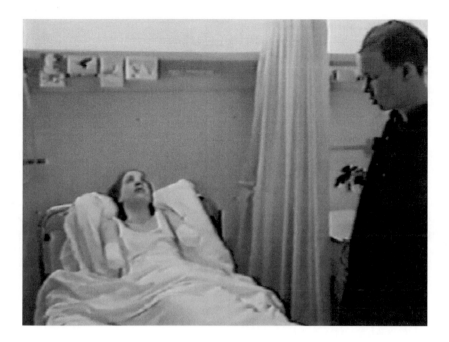

FIGURE 20-1

The youngest boy after losing both arms in the mockumentary *Kutzooi* (frame from film).

The point is that when someone swaps the labels we feel manipulated—indeed, Otto Schuurman showed the film to make this very point. Ironically, we would have praised it to the sky had the makers shown it as a Ken Loach type of fiction film drawn, as it truly was, from Dutch working class life.

USING ACTORS

Some documentaries recreate biographical material using actors, or even create someone representative but imaginary. Historical biographies routinely use actors when no archive footage exists of their subject, but this is still an acceptable way to explore history if it is identifiable as such. Eric Stange, himself a producer of history films, wrote:

> Documentary reenactments are almost always shot without dialogue, through fog or haze, or in a shadowy half-light. The camera often focuses only on close-up details—a hand on a quill; feet running through the woods; a sword being buckled on—and almost never on an actor's face. . . .

> These visual clues send several important messages: that the reenactment is not *fictional* (if it were, there would be dialogue); that the reenactment is only a "suggestion" of what happened (signified by the ambiguous fog or haze); and that the actors are not portraying specific people so much as representing them. (From "Shooting Back," *Common-Place*, April 2001; see www.common-place.org/vol-01/no-03/stange)

Such material can stimulate the audience's imagination or fill significant gaps in the narrative. It can also, as the rest of the article suggests, rapidly become money-saving clichés. See any episode of the PBS series *Secrets of the Dead* (2001–2008, United States) for plentiful examples. The producers deserve plaudits for tackling so many fascinating riddles of history, but their visual material is often stretched perilously thin.

 When you direct a reenactment, you'll get better results if you encourage participants or actors to approach their task not as acting but as an exercise in reliving the spirit of what actually took place.

Errol Morris in *The Thin Blue Line* (1988, United States) uses reenactment to show six different versions of the shooting of a Texas traffic cop, each based on a witness's account in the trial. Part of the film's purposes is to show just how unreliable witnesses' memories are and to prove—as it does conclusively—that not one of their accounts was accurate.

WHOLESALE RECONSTRUCTION

When reconstruction involves several scenes or even a whole film, the sources on which their veracity rests can be eyewitness memories, documents, transcripts, photographs, or hearsay. Large-scale reconstruction that draws on several sources must carefully identify what it's using or risk alienating its audience. British television once showed an acted reconstruction directed by Stuart Hood of the trial of the anarchists Sacco and Vanzetti. Adapted from court transcripts of the famous 1920s trial, it proved intelligent, restrained, and austerely memorable. Actors portraying the accused, the lawyers, and the judge used only the words and ideas preserved in court records. This made it trustworthy and undoubtedly documentary in spirit.

 When you cannot show actuality it's fine to represent the spirit of the truth. Be sure your audience knows where you get the authority to do so.

Usually included with the documentary genre is Peter Watkins' *Culloden* (1964, United Kingdom)—a beginning-to-end reconstruction of a 1746 battle in the Scottish Highlands. It shows how feudally Bonnie Prince Charlie's army was raised and how cruelly the British crushed his Jacobite cause. Apart from the costumes, tactics, and location, there's little other pretense of historical accuracy, since what the officers and foot soldiers say in Watkins' "interviews" are a modernist guess at what they might have expressed at the time. The film nevertheless conveys respect for the distant historical actuality and much empathy for its unlucky participants. Yes, it deals with politics and the abuse of power, but its deepest sympathies lie with the humble folk so easily made into cannon fodder during the ideological and turf struggles of their masters. Those currently fighting on both sides in Iraq and Afghanistan would understand its message perfectly.

 Nobody really knows how to divide documentary from fiction. Filmmakers are always trying to push the boundaries and critics are quick to challenge them.

THE DOCUDRAMA

There is a yet more imaginative—some would say fanciful—use of the real, known as *docudrama* or *dramadoc*, a hybrid straddling two genres that is most common in Britain. Two notable examples must suffice; one successful and one not. Jeremy Sandford's *Cathy Come Home* (1966, United Kingdom) dramatized the plight of Britain's homelessness at a time when it was new and shocking. Working from case histories, Sandford and his wife, Nell Dunne, constructed a "typical" blue-collar couple that overspend, encounter bad luck, and plunge down the social scale until the welfare state dismembers the family "for the good of the children."

Coming on the heels of the seductive Conservative reelection slogan, "You never had it so good," the British public was appalled to discover that the drama was true to life in all its particulars. *Cathy*'s effectiveness lay in its superb acting and documentary presentation; the furor it aroused effected a change in the law—rare for a film of any kind.

 Premise, style, and fidelity to actuality influence how we assess anything proffered as "true to life."

Anthony Thomas' *Death of a Princess* (1980, United Kingdom) set out to show how a Saudi princess had been publicly humiliated and executed for a sexual offense. It raised a storm of critical reaction on all sides, though less for using actors and reconstruction than for taking liberties. One was with the truth, which was insufficiently determinable. Another was with the portrayal of Islamic culture and assumptions, both plainly outside the producers' realm of sympathy or expertise. Linking the film's inquiry, and further undercutting it, was a romanticized journalist figure serving as a proxy for its director and his journey of investigation. Though Thomas had undoubtedly researched among weird and dubious characters, transmuting his own role into that of a suave, James Bond-ish investigator gave the film an irritatingly self-involved central character and left *Death of a Princess* seeming contrived. Apparently more concerned with entertainment values, it was docudrama having too much drama and not enough doc.

SUBJECTIVE RECONSTRUCTION

Someone recounting how he found an unexploded bomb in a plowed field as a boy might return as an elderly man to reenact, in the same place, how he found it. You could half bury a bomb casing for him to find and shoot his actions as he remembers them, laying his voice over the actions. The audience would be in no doubt that the sequence represents memory, not actuality. Alternatively, he could talk to the camera as he relives the actions of finding the bomb. There are fertile possibilities for these techniques, especially when memory is unclear and a person has to run through several possibilities to find the most likely. Plainly you are exploring not only what happened but also the instability of human memory itself, as Alain Resnais did on a massive scale in his baroque fiction *Last Year in Marienbad* (1961, France).

Documentary may be the better tool for investigating the psychology of memory. Lars Johansson's *Traveller's Tale* (1994, Denmark) accomplishes this masterfully: An old man during the middle of the twenty-first century looks back on the material he shot when the walls of Communism fell in Central Europe and outsiders could visit. The film is a meditation on the past showing the virtually medieval world that Johansson himself had captured on such a journey, guided by three different women he encountered along the way.

Occasionally a complete reconstruction is notable for persuading us to accept the authenticity of its central subject. A lovely BBC biographical documentary is Chris Durlacher's *George Orwell: A Life in Pictures* (2003, United Kingdom). It happens that no voice recordings or archive footage exist of Orwell, so the producers used an actor, Chris Langham, to create a facsimile. Looking like Orwell, he speaks words culled from Orwell's letters, diaries, novels, and essays. Drawing plentifully on period archive footage, the film intercuts "interviews" in which Langham plays Orwell with interviews by people who knew him. The effect is eerily authentic, for it gives you the feeling that you are traveling on a rigorous personal retrospective with the great anti-authoritarian author. Mixed in, and not at all intrusive, is a library of home movie footage created in authentic places—again with Langham. The effect is a sustained, imaginative portrait that one trusts throughout, even though strictly speaking much of its material is faked.

The authority on docudrama, and tireless champion of its merits, is the distinguished political filmmaker and documentary historian Alan Rosenthal. His *Why Docudrama? Fact–Fiction on Film and TV* (1999, Southern Illinois Press) is a comprehensive survey of docudrama's history and possibilities.

FAKE DOCUMENTARIES OR MOCKUMENTARIES

Mitchell Block's renowned short film about a female rape victim, *No Lies* (1973, United States; Figure 20-2), shows how dangerous documentary can become in amoral hands. The pressure we see the director apply to the victim is disturbing, yet we go along because the revelations he pries from his subject are fascinating. Then the film turns on its heel to confront the audience with the fact that both are actors, and the exploitative relationship a calculated performance. The film was made, apparently, to "cinematically . . . demonstrate and commit rape—and it does so in such a way as to make the experience of being the unwary, unprepared victim of an aggressive assault on one's person, on one's pride, and on one's expectations of and security in familiar activity in familiar surroundings a very

FIGURE 20-2

The documentary process as violation in *No Lies*. (Photo courtesy of Mitchell Block.)

real experience accessible to anyone of *either* sex who views the film."[2] The film rubs our noses in the way we voyeuristically enjoyed the fruit of exploitation.

Ken Featherstone's *Babakiueria* (1987, Australia) works differently. It reports how Aboriginal colonists discovered Australia back when the country was thinly peopled by primitive whites ritually cooking

 Like any form of expression, documentary becomes amoral and even dangerous when its makers think the ends justify the means. Leni Riefenstahl's promotion of Nazi values should alert anyone who thinks there can be art for art's sake.

flesh in places called barbecue areas (hence, the film's title). A nervously compliant white family tries to cooperate with the black colonizers' social workers who have decided to split the family up for their own good. By inverting Australian racial values and farcically inverting white treatment of blacks, the film pushes home what it must feel like to have liberal paternalism forced on you by another race.

In Larry Charles' *Borat: Cultural Learnings of America for Make Benefit Glorious Nation of Kazakhstan* (2006, United States), the inimitable Sacha Baron Cohen travels around America making people think he is an outrageously crass Kazakh journalist. Made from improvised situations based on a journey framework, this *Candid Camera* offshoot rejoices in springing practical jokes on the unwary. Borat's aim is to be murderously funny—and this it is, in scenes that sometimes defy belief. It's not a documentary, but it uses documentary methods

---

[2]Sobchack, Vivian C. "No lies: Direct cinema as rape," in *New Challenges for Documentary*, Alan Rosenthal, Ed. Berkeley: University of California Press, 1988, p. 332.

to capture many spontaneous encounters catalyzed by a highly skilled comedian. If it levels any critique, it is that some Americans are alarmingly credulous. As a caveat, see Wikipedia® on resulting lawsuits.

SOME QUESTIONS TO ASK

When considering the reconstruction of an action or scene:

- What are you really trying to get across to the audience?
- Is there any way you can avoid reconstruction—say, by making your point through narration?
- What makes a reconstruction valid or invalid from the audience's point of view?
- Are you implying that what you show is typical or that it is particular and pivotal? (Typical is probably okay, but reconstructing a pivotal moment could backfire.)
- Are you using the original participants or actors playing them? How will the audience know?
- What do the participants feel about reenacting something bygone?
- How should you cover the scene to avoid injecting histrionics?

When considering docudrama:

- What is the film's premise and why does it need to be a docudrama?
- Why not make a fiction film avowedly based on real events?
- How will you justify "faking it" to the audience?
- What additional values will you put in play to justify taking so much control?

When considering mockumentary:

- Is the target of your satire (if that's what it is) some practice, custom, event, etc., or is it documentary itself?
- If you are lampooning documentary (which can always use some house cleaning), are you sure you have enough knowledge, ideas, and material to work with?
- How can your piece develop? (Many ideas for this form are one liners and not adequate for an extended piece.)
- What is your purpose, if you mean to deceive your audience and then undeceive them? If your audience perceives your underlying purpose as constructive, it will probably applaud. But, if you mean to mock their trust, then you are attacking the very foundations of audience participation and had better have a compelling reason to do so.

PART 7

ADVANCED PRODUCTION ISSUES

PART 7A

ADVANCED PREPRODUCTION

Part 7 revisits in greater depth key aspects of the three main stages of filmmaking—preproduction, production, and postproduction. Sustaining an audience's interest through extended and complicated issues in longer documentaries takes greater foresight and planning. Story lines become more convoluted, and more rests on the credibility of what an extended chain of participants might do and say. You'll need sophisticated thinking all around to bring your longer films to a professional level of depth and resonance. Part 7 advances many ideas and techniques at each major stage to help you.

PART 7A PREPRODUCTION

This part goes into greater depth with the written proposal and includes defining a point of view and what makes evidence persuasive. The ethical choices you make are part of the value system driving the heart of your filmmaking, and you want them to stand up to scrutiny. Out of this comes a more detailed proposal of the kind you might submit to a funding organization. It includes genre, film dialectics, and defining the all-important Storyteller role that gives a film its individual "voice." Part 7A concludes with a round-up of the logistical preparations for an organized shoot.

CHAPTER 21

ADVANCED RESEARCH

The guidelines that follow will help you prepare most film subjects, but you might want to review the fundamentals in **Chapter 7, Research.** Most films stand or fall depending on the depth of thought that has gone into their conception. The rest of this chapter expands key aspects

Help yourself during research by using **Project 2-DP-1 Dramatic Content Helper** to flush out what your story may still need.

of research, but don't treat them as holy writ. Adapt them to your tasks and treat them as a guide, not a straitjacket.

OVERVIEW OF STEPS

INITIAL STAGES

1. **Make a working hypothesis.**
2. **Begin site research;** that is, familiarize yourself with:

A documentary is only as good as the thinking that goes into it, and this is where most people feel insecure. The key is a solid working hypothesis and periodic revision.

- *People and situations* that you are thinking of using. Take time to get to know each other and trust each other's motives.

- Find out what's *typical* in the world you are going to film.

- Find out *what's unusual*, unexpected, and particular.

- *Stay loose.* Keep explanations to potential participants broad and tentative so you don't paint yourself into a corner.

3. **Do background research;** that is:
   - Use the Internet to find useful references and ideas.
   - Study *publications* such as magazines, newspapers, professional journals, and even fiction. Any of these may offer useful ideas and observations.
   - See all other *films* on your subject, but maybe only after you have formulated your own approach.
   - *Talk to experts.* Documentarians routinely depend on the expertise of specialists, on those devoted to or involved in what you're filming. Often they have an extensive network of contacts and their word on your authenticity can act like a passport. Be aware that experts rarely know what a lay audience needs.

4. **Develop trust:**
   - *Communicate.* Make yourself, and a broad version of your purposes, known to whomever you may want to film. Let them question you on your values and purposes and answer briefly but truthfully.
   - *Learn.* Parry some questions with questions of your own. Put yourself in the position of learning from them, the experts. *Hang out* with likely participants.

5. **Make reality checks** to ensure that:
   - You have *multiple perspectives* on each person, fact, or facet, especially when there are ambiguities.
   - *What you want to film is accessible.*
   - *People are amenable* and cooperative.
   - *Releases and permissions* will be forthcoming.
   - The *resources* you will need are not beyond your means.

 Since you are always a surrogate for a first-time audience, not being an expert in the film's subject is a positive advantage. Experts seldom understand what a lay audience needs—that is your expertise.

 Never commit yourself to anyone or anything in the early stages of research, however strongly you feel it's a foregone conclusion. Things can still change.

 Spending lots of time with participants before filming starts is invaluable; it lets you absorb what you need to know and lets people develop trust in your character and purposes.

 Using **Project 2-DP-2 Style and Content Questionnaire** (in the Appendix) will help you round up your content and intentions so you miss nothing important.

ADVANCED WORKING HYPOTHESIS

The advanced working hypothesis in **Project 2-DP-4** (Figure 21-1) is similar to the basic one in **Project 2-DP-3** referred to earlier in the book but with the crucial addition

 Develop your authorial voice by using **Project 2-DP-4 Advanced Working Hypothesis Helper.**

of (1) point of view and (2) point of view's influence over style. This capitalizes on important discussions in **Part 6: Advanced Documentary Aesthetics,** and helps you more fully develop the foundation for your next film.

RESEARCH METHODS

Documentary makers often observe lives they intend filming over a period of time. The two main categories of research they use, in the field or in the library, are quantitative and qualitative.

QUANTITATIVE RESEARCH

(See definition in box.) Information of this kind can weigh a film down, but knowing the factual and numerical framework lets you assert, for instance, that many accountants take early retirement, or cite other causes and effects. If birth

---

ADVANCED WORKING HYPOTHESIS

a) In life I believe that (*your philosophy regarding the life-principle that your film will exemplify*) _____

_____

b) My film will show this in action by exploring (*situation*)

_____

c) My film's main conflict is
between _____ and _____

d) My film's point of view, or its POV character, will
be _____

e) I expect my film's structure to be determined by

_____

f) The subject and point of view suggest a style that is

_____

g) Ultimately I want the audience to
feel _____

h) … and to understand that

_____

FIGURE 21-1 ———————————————————————

Prompts to help create an advanced working hypothesis.

complications rise sharply after a county has dismissed all its mid-wives, but not in the counties that retained them, you can argue persuasively that midwives are useful and deserve to be reinstated.

 Quantitative research means gathering information on anything you can count or measure. That might be facts about populations, incomes, percentages of people in a particular occupation, or the average age at marriage.

You should fact-check what anybody alleges in your film before you rely on it. Cross-check important facts in at least two authoritative sources; you'll be surprised how oft-quoted "historical facts" have acquired gravitas through exchange and repetition. If several figures are in circulation, use the least extreme. Your credibility rests on information that can't be discredited. Be aware that the Internet is replete with dubious facts, incorrect spellings, and wild accusations of all kinds. Much posted there is a tendentious effort to persuade.

QUALITATIVE RESEARCH

(See definition in box.) Most research for documentaries is qualitative and involves using your intuition and making subjective judgments for which, however, there are some safeguards. The more closely you work with partners, the more you can cross-check your ideas and impressions with other reliable minds.

Pay careful attention to your teammates' impressions and reservations, especially those from the other gender. You should also discreetly cross-check opinions and feelings among those knowledgeable. If, for instance, you are doing a town hall story and someone tells you in confidence that the mayor "is very authoritarian," questions should reflexively pop up in your mind:

 Qualitative research involves what cannot be quantified such as attitudes, aspects of character, motives, methods, goals, outlooks, backgrounds, and so on.

What agenda might the teller have? If you believed him and then found out later that the mayor fired him for incompetence, you'd look really dumb.

How reliable is the informant's source? Was this assessment made first-hand from dealings with the mayor, or is it hearsay from television reporting that was itself recycled from newspaper articles?

Everything and everyone (including yourself) are biased simply because it's human to be subjective. So prolong the conversation with your informant to flush out all the information you can. Tap his views on unrelated issues to see how perceptive and fair he seems across the board and what his attitudes to authority are in general. Talk to other knowledgeable people to see whether, without revealing your source, you can validate or invalidate something potentially important that you've been told.

Avoid leading questions ("Do you think the mayor is authoritarian?") and instead ask open questions (for instance, "What kind of person is the mayor?") that give no hint of what you expect. One person calls him "principled, firm, and a little humorless;" another says he's "loyal to supporters, a bit austere, and not the best listener." A third thinks he's "a rough diamond" and "has done quite a bit of good for the town." A more rounded profile is emerging that is significant for what it omits: Nobody says the mayor is corrupt, a bad manager, or unpopular.

 Leading questions are closed questions because their wording indicates what answer you expect. *Open questions* are value neutral and give no hint of what is most acceptable.

ARCHIVES, FAIR USE, AND BEST PRACTICES

Film archives may be in government, state, local, or private hands and are often very expensive. Material seen extensively on television is held by the company that produced the material and may not be made available to you.

Rick Prelinger of the Prelinger Archives, New York City, has a good article online at www.well.com/gopher/Art/Experimental.Film.and.Video/archival.survival that makes many good points. If your film depends on archive footage, check that it exists and is available for use in your production at a rate you can afford. Negotiate early—don't wait until later. Be sure you declare the media, markets, and rights territory correctly because you are at a disadvantage if you try to renegotiate later. Clear any music rights if music is integral to the footage you want. Anticipate all the extras the library may charge (duplication, research, etc.) Check that you order the duplication in a format that will integrate with your production's workflow. If your film depends on a lot of material from a number of archives, consider hiring experienced archival researchers whose expertise may save you time and money. The article contains much further useful detail.

Just as you can make "fair use" of limited literary material in a publication that discusses or critiques someone else's writing, there is a *fair use doctrine* that can serve as an advisory for what you can and can't do with segments of screen material taken without permission. It is "advisory" because it has yet to be tested in court. If you want to avoid becoming a test case, check the latest developments at these two Web sites: http://fairuse.stanford.edu (Stanford Copyright and Fair Use Center) and www.centerforsocialmedia.org/about/staff/paufder (Pat Aufderheide at The Center for Social Media, School of Communications, American University).

APPROACHING PARTICIPANTS

Starting research, you have little idea what your film will say or whom you will ask to participate. Least of all do you know what part any individual might play in the filming. Emphasize that you're there to gain understanding from those who know and that filming evolves from what you learn over time. Be sure, too, that everyone understands how documentaries shoot ten times more than they use. This takes the heat off the idea that they will have to "perform" or even that you will use their contribution.

TRUST

Unfortunately, documentarians have been known to abuse the trust placed in them by participants. A woman factory worker once spoke candidly and trustingly to a colleague about sexual morals among her female coworkers. When the film went out over the air, her fellow workers were outraged and beat her up the next day. The (male) director apparently knew this was a risk and gambled with her safety for the sake of a more sensational film.

Usually nothing comparable is at risk, and reading a standardized list of possible consequences to each

 Many you meet during research imagine that documentaries illustrate a prior thesis and will ask to see your script. You will have to explain the loose, speculative nature of making today's documentaries and that one decides what to shoot quite late.

 We make documentaries by exploiting other people's lives, so achieving mutual trust is very important. Indeed, you cast particular people *because* they show good will and cooperation.

Explain all possible risks to anyone who deserves fair warning. Withholding what you know from vulnerable participants is unethical and can have dire consequences.

potential participant would scare most people away from filming. You should, however, explain possible risks to anyone who deserves fair warning. Investigative filmmaking is a little different since the very existence of an investigation is enough warning to those of mature age and judgment.

When seeking (or not seeking) permission, outright subterfuge is sometimes justified. When someone has butchered defenseless people, you may be amply justified in using deception to get their testimony, as Claude Lanzmann did in *Shoah* (1985, France). He got the testimony of a Nazi officer from Treblinka camp by posing as a French historian wanting to "restore the balance of truth" to the historical record. In the light of what the man had done, most people, like Lanzmann, would have no scruples about deceiving him. Such clarity is rare; usually it's not black-and-white issues we deal with but shades of gray.

OBSERVATION

Depending on circumstances, being an observer can be comfortable or uncomfortable. When you hang out with a local sports team and they accept your aims, you can watch what's going on and concentrate on developing your awareness. However, show up at a union meeting as an unknown with aims that seem uncertain or deceptive, and you will be very unwelcome.

Wherever possible, gain access through someone trusted by the community; otherwise, be prepared to repeatedly explain yourself in broad terms until everybody seems satisfied. Do be sociable and communicative, as this lowers tension. Do join in if you are invited into group activities and be ready to make a fool of yourself as part of your entry test. Standing aside would make you seem judgmental and as though you are withholding your opinions. Shared experience brings people together, although it will fool nobody that you are one of the group. I once made a sponsored film about a body-changing technique. The foundation asked me to take the full 12 sessions with a practitioner, which I did. It gave me the all-important patient's view and led to an exceptional rapport.

 Sometimes as part of breaking the ice—with young people, in particular—you can let your subject handle the camera and experience interviewing you. By demystifying the camera you imply a more level playing field and that control is to be shared, not imposed.

KEEPING NOTES

Making audio or video recordings during your earliest research may put those you are meeting for the first time on guard. It also stockpiles hours of mostly unrewarding watching and listening. Better is to note key phrases that people use to jog your memory. Afterwards, read over your notes, expand them where necessary to make them intelligible before your memory fades, and write out any important thoughts, impressions, and intuitions. These will be helpful if you want to pursue particular issues during an interview.

 Making field notes enables you to look at your notebook and really listen. Your preoccupation in turn frees the speaker to look more naturally within. The alternative is to get sucked into providing facial reactions as support to the speaker instead of listening for subtexts.

Writing is an important structuring activity that enables your mind to develop initial ideas further. Keep interpretative writing separate; should your notes ever be subpoenaed, you need only produce the notes that people saw you writing, not the more revealing and speculative writing you did in private afterwards.

COMPROMISING YOURSELF

Loyalties and obligations develop between yourself and your participants and lead you into thickets of ethical dilemma. A single example: You are planning a film about the victims of a housing scam whom you get to know and like. You also gain the confidence of the perpetrators, wealthy property developers who offer you hospitality. Refusing might tip them off to your disapproval of their practices, so you go out, eat an expensive dinner, and laugh at their jokes. When you next visit their victims, you feel compromised from sleeping with the enemy. Even if you let this be known, it would be unwise to confide more than a sketchy idea of what you learned, or you will turn into a double agent.

CASTING

Choose participants with the utmost care, since mistaken casting can conceivably land you with someone who evades, distorts, or even manipulates the process. The longer you delay recognizing this during a shoot, the more difficult it will be to extricate yourself. Guard against this by deferring casting decisions as long as possible before shooting. The longer you watch people in action, the less chance you will miscalculate. To avoid bad choices, beware of those who:

 During research, a sense of obligation and even loyalties develops between you and those who have been generous with their time. The urge to repay their generosity can, if you aren't careful, lead you into making skewed judgments and unwise commitments. Try to remain interested, noncommittal, and in a learning mode so you can keep your options visibly open.

 Delay casting (choosing final participants) until the last minute. Learn as much as you can before you leap—the consequences of mistakes can be dire.

- Are overly anxious to participate and try too hard to interest you
- Have an ax to grind
- Think you are going to profit from using them and want money for their participation

At the other end of the spectrum is the anxious personality who:

- Fantasizes calamitous consequences from participating
- Is overly dependent on the good opinion of others
- Is fearful of appearing critical about anything or anybody

You choose people for their characteristics and for what they know. Documentaries must often present conflicting accounts, so you choose those whose presence is going to be persuasive.

EVIDENCE, EXPOSITION, AND DRAMATIC TENSION

The language historians and critics use about documentary—witnessing, recording, testifying, evidencing—suggests that the documentary presents its case to an audience rather like evidence to a jury. Perhaps your film is about workers in a scientific laboratory, one running according to safety conventions unfamiliar to the lay person. Giving too much information (exposition) before it becomes relevant will numb the jury, but providing too little will leave them unable to make the right connections. Keep these questions in mind while you research:

 As in the opening stages of a trial, a documentary must give a *setup*—that is, introduce its characters, their special world, and what their problem is.

What world are we in and what does it feel like?

What is this world's main condition, activity, or purpose?

How does this world operate under normal conditions?

What basic information do we need to engage with the main issues?

What has gone wrong?

What is at issue?

Who represents what?

Trials are dramatic when they focus on a conflict. No drama (and no court case) exists when conditions are normal and everyone is friendly and at peace. Gripping documentaries, therefore, focus on people who are trying to get, do, or accomplish something. This doesn't have to be overtly dramatic stuff about trying to win a race or get a man off death row: it can center on a reclusive artist's compulsion to work with natural forces, as in Thomas Riedelsheimer's *Rivers and Tides: Andy Goldsworthy Working with Time* (2002, Germany; Figure 21-2). Goldsworthy makes intentionally ephemeral artworks in natural circumstances knowing that natural forces will quietly destroy them.

 Laudatory films—those that celebrate or proffer role models—nearly always lack dramatic tension. This is because there are no active issues, and nobody is under duress with whose predicament we can engage.

Whatever anyone wills into being involves volition, planning, and expending energy. It means confronting obstacles, struggling, and adapting to overcome obstructions. This applies as much to a shy 5-year-old enduring her first day at school as it does to a Special Forces unit battling an insurgency.

Beauty, atmosphere, and novelty are all important to documentaries, but the audience always looks for some principle at issue or a person whose will is at stake. So:

What is each main person's role?

What are their issues (that is, what is each trying to get, do, or accomplish)?

Who or what is stopping them, and why?

Who supports or opposes whom?

What does each represent?

What stages of the story have already happened, and what is yet to happen?

FIGURE 21-2

Rivers and Tides: Andy Goldsworthy Working with Time—what man creates, time and Nature erase. (Photo by Andy Goldsworthy.)

Evoking strong actions and representations from the different factions helps ensure dramatic tension. You can put everyone's veracity and credibility under scrutiny by encouraging skepticism in your audience.

TESTIMONY AND WITNESSES

By flushing out conflicting accounts, the audience, like any jury, can assess people's motives and decide what "really happened." So:

What qualifies each person to give evidence?

Is testimony coming from direct experience, or only from hearsay?

Is this person's testimony primary (witnessed by themselves) or secondary (someone else's experience reported)?

What do they know from their own experience that is relevant to what's at issue?

How credibly do they convey what they know?

Do other views or facts support or undermine their views?

What loyalties, prejudices, or self-interests may be skewing their viewpoints?

What other evidence might alter, prove, or disprove their testimony?

Is there anything demonstrable from the person's background that puts their motives, preparation, knowledge, and identity in a new light?

Can an opponent interpret key testimony differently?

How authentic and credible are the documents, pictures, memories, or records used in evidence (for instance, are documents originals or copies)?

In the investigative documentary we frequently see testimony by a range of witnesses to support or undermine key allegations. Testimony is strong when:

- It conveys compelling facts or information.
- It is primary evidence that consists of opinions and inferences based on their own firsthand perceptions.
- Witnesses use reliable principles or methods to interpret those facts.

Testimony is weak when:

- The witness has already heard the testimony of other witnesses.
- It involves hearsay.
- It involves specialization that exceeds the witness' competency.

Witnesses:

- Should be open to challenge by others involved in the issue.
- May not get all the facts until just before shooting or during it and on-camera. This can be explosive but also ethically dubious.

Texts and archives as well as material from the camera and sound recorder provide their own kind of testimony. What they demonstrate can be enigmatic or misleading and not appear so. Each is an authored construct that should be open to question:

Under what circumstances was the footage or document compiled?

What intention or sponsorship lay behind its authorship?

Is there more than one hand behind the materials; if so, are the differences or inconsistencies significant?

What variously are its intended, unintended, and received meanings?

What does it exclude?

How will a contemporary audience receive it?

What proof do you have that it is what it's said to be?

What assumptions lie behind its making, of which its makers may have been aware or unaware?

Has original material been edited or reused in a way that changes its meaning?

If the materials originate in another language, can you rely on the translation?

The images, sounds, and speech you collect will provide the evidence for your film's actions, atmosphere, ideas, conditions, and appearances. The audience cannot ask for elaboration, so the filmmaker must anticipate when the jury needs context, confirmation, or interpretation.

MARSHALING YOUR EVIDENCE

During research, group the evidence you have gathered under a series of headings. With a long and involved film, you may need to enter key information in a database. This allows you two important opportunities:

To find material on the basis of a word or phrase (see all the material concerning, for example, "Cape Verde" and "'rhododendrons").

To selectively remove, arrange, or juxtapose material according to different filters (such as time periods, characters, locations, or shooting dates).

Try giving each item a credibility rating. If you can work in the upper half of that hierarchy, the proof will be strong and most convincing. When it comes time to film:

What will you have to arrange, say, or do to put a participant under pressure to reveal the next levels of truth?

How can you raise the pressure so there is more at stake?

Can you evoke verbal or written testimony with existing visual archives?

Will you need to demonstrate unreliability in a participant to ensure your audience watches critically?

GOING FURTHER

For those particularly interested in the proposal process for public broadcasting or other types of documentary that use a didactic, narrated approach and archival materials:

Bernard, Sheila Curran. *Documentary Storytelling: Making Stronger and More Dramatic Nonfiction Films*. Boston: Focal Press, 2007 (includes sample proposals).

Bernard, Sheila and Ken Rabin. *Archival Storytelling: A Documentary Filmmaker's Guide to Finding, Using, and Licensing Third-Party Visuals and Music*. Boston: Focal Press, 2008.

CHAPTER 22

VALUES, ETHICS, AND CHOICES

The thought and planning you invest before shooting and the degree to which you anticipate problems all help ensure a trouble-free and creative shoot. Regularly review your working hypothesis in the light of your mission and its values, and amend it as necessary. Seasoned filmmakers seldom rely on spontaneous inspiration because once you start filming the pace and demand of the work are all-encompassing. Werner Herzog, questioned after a screening about "the intellectual challenge during shooting," replied caustically that "filmmaking is athletic, not aesthetic." Most filming, he told the startled audience, is so grueling that rarefied thought is all but impossible. François Truffaut makes a similar point in his fiction film *Day for Night* (1973, France), whose central character is a director running into a thicket of problems and compromises. Played by Truffaut himself, the director confides that at each film's start he always thinks it's going to be his best, but halfway through shooting can only think about surviving until the finish. My own fantasy, which returns at least once every shoot, is to escape further filming by miraculously turning into the owner of a rural grocery.

CHECKING YOUR EMBEDDED VALUES

Making a documentary is proposing a vision of reality. Films and video games, especially those exploiting the sensational, alter the threshold of what's acceptable—as can be seen in the rash of shootings in places of education. We in documentary also have a moral responsibility for what we put on the screen.

Look back a few decades and you can see that the screen often represents people, roles, and relationships in particular ways. Criminals or gangsters are "ethnic" types; women are secretaries, nurses, teachers, and mothers; people of color are servants, vagrants, or objects of pity with little to say for themselves—and so on. All this is so familiar that it may seem like old hat. Three writers from the University of Southern California film school, who should know, think differently. They call these regressive assumptions *embedded values*—that is, values so natural to the makers of a film that they pass below the radar of awareness. In their book *Creative Filmmaking from the Inside Out: Five Keys to the Art of Making Inspired Movies and Television* (2003, Simon & Schuster), Jed Dannenbaum, Carroll Hodge, and Doe Mayer demonstrate the traps in making art. Their examination of ethics in practice is especially pertinent to documentary, where unexamined assumptions silently guide the outcome of your film. *Creative Filmmaking* is mostly aimed at fiction filmmakers, but it poses some fascinating questions that I have adapted below. Will the world in your film reinforce stereotypes or reflect instead the complexity and injustices of life as it is? Step back to consider how your intended documentary represents these factors:

 All stories include assumptions about the way things are. If your film unconsciously reinforces questionable norms, then your *embedded values* are in the driving seat. The point is not to become politically correct, which is just another orthodoxy, but to avoid supporting what cannot and should not be normal.

Participants:

- *Class*—What class or classes do they come from? How will you show differences? Will other classes be represented and if so, how?

- *Wealth*—Do they have money? How is it regarded? How do they handle it? What is taken for granted? Are things as they should be and if not, how will the film express this?

- *Appearances*—Are appearances reliable or misleading? How important are appearances? Do the characters have difficulty reading each other's appearances?

- *Background*—Is there any diversity of race or other background, and how will this be handled? Will other races or ethnicities have minor or major parts?

- *Belongings*—Will we see them work or know how they sustain their lifestyle? What do their belongings say about their tastes and values? Is anyone in the film critical of this?

- *Emblems*—Do they own or use important objects, and what is their significance?

- *Work*—Is their work shown? What does it convey about them?

- *Valuation*—For what do characters value other characters? Will the film question this or cast uncertainty on the inter-character values?

- *Speech*—What do you learn from the vocabulary of each? What makes the way each thinks and talks different from the others? What does it signify?

- *Roles*—What roles do participants fall into and will they emerge as complex enough to challenge any stereotypes?
- *Sexuality*—If sexuality is present, is there a range of expression, and will you portray it? Is it allied with affection, tenderness, love?
- *Volition*—Who is able to change their situation and who seems unable to take action? What are the patterns behind this?
- *Competence*—Who is competent and who is not? What determines this?

Environment:

- *Place*—Will we know where the characters come from and what values are associated with their origins?
- *Settings*—Will they look credible and add to what we know about the characters?
- *Time*—What values are associated with the period chosen for the setting?
- *Home*—Do the characters seem at home? What do they have around them to signify any journeys or accomplishments they have made?
- *Work*—Do they seem to belong there, and how will the workplace be portrayed? What will it say about the characters?

Family dynamics:

- *Structure*—What structure emerges? Do characters treat it as normal or abnormal? Is anyone critical of the family structure?
- *Relationships*—How are relationships between members and between generations going to be portrayed?
- *Roles*—Are roles in the family fixed or will they be shown developing? Are they healthy or unhealthy? Who in the family is critical? Who is branded as "good" or "successful" by the family and who "bad" or "failed"?
- *Power*—Could there be another structure? Is power handled in a healthy or unhealthy way? What is the relationship of earning money to power in the family?

Authority:

- *Gender*—Which gender seems to have the most authority? Does one gender predominate and if so, why?
- *Initiation*—Who will initiate the events in the film and why? Who is likely to resolve them?
- *Respect*—How are figures with power going to be depicted? How will institutions and institutional power be depicted? Are they simple or complex, and does what you can show reflect your experience of the real thing?
- *Conflict*—How are conflicts negotiated? What will the film say about conflict and its resolution? Who usually wins and why?
- *Aggression*—Who is being aggressive and who is being assertive, and why? Who are you supporting in this, and whom do you tend to censure?

In Total:

- *Criticism*—How critical is the film going to be toward what its characters do or don't do? How much will it tell us about what's wrong? Can we hope to see one of the characters coming to grips with this?

- *Approval/disapproval*—What will the film approve of, and is there anything risky and unusual in what it defends? Is the film challenging its audience's assumptions and expectations or just feeding into them?

- *World view*—If this is a microcosm, what will it say about the balance of forces in the larger world of which it is a fragment?

- *Moral stance*—What stance will the intended film's belief system take in relation to privilege, willpower, tradition, inheritance, power, initiative, God, luck, coincidence, etc.? Is this what you want?

Creative Filmmaking has pertinent questions for every area of screen creativity and asks only that filmmakers take responsibility for the ethical and moral implications in their work.

ADVISE AND CONSENT

Directing a documentary sometimes feels like being a doctor advising patients about the procedure, complications, and consequences of an irreversible operation. Some listen carefully, while others are inattentive or too unsophisticated to absorb the implications. In America during the 1970s, the Loud family consented to have their lives filmed (*An American Family*, 1973, United States; 12 hour-long episodes on PBS). The exposure, first to the camera and then to savage criticism in the press (as though they were performers), tore the family apart. Afterwards the Louds said that Alan and Susan Raymond, the series makers, had not explained the consequences adequately. Maybe so, but the open-ended nature of such undertakings makes comprehensive explanation virtually impossible. Nobody could have known that Bill would leave Pat or that Lance would come out of the closet in this first of all reality shows.

It is, of course, your responsibility to guard those who trust you from consequences that you, not they, can see possible. These may include physical or legal danger or damage to a person's reputation. By including an unguarded remark, your film could damage or sever family relations. This is too high a price to pay unless the person stands by their remark. *Informed consent* is the permission

 True, a signed release means you are legally free, but it doesn't remove you from your moral obligations.

 The best way to get people to participate is by explaining your film's goals and the contribution they can make. After you've filmed them, their signed release only counts as *informed consent* if you warn them of the foreseeable consequences to what they just said or did on camera. Danger to your participants can arise from how you've used something in the completed film. This you can't foresee at the time of filming, but you can surely guard against it during editing, and perhaps seek their agreement.

FIGURE 22-1 ————————————————————————————————

Roger and Me—the first Michael Moore film, and the first to lampoon a haughty national institution using satire. (Photo courtesy of The Kobal Collection/Warner Bros.)

that someone (or that person's guardian, if they are underage) gives after being duly warned of foreseeable consequences.

EVIDENCE AND ETHICS

Another ethical concern should be with the integrity of the arguments you use. Occasionally, the filmmaker employs artistic license to serve a larger purpose— as Michael Moore did with chronology in *Roger and Me* (1989, United States; Figure 22-1)—and finds his methods returning to haunt him. By simplifying and transposing some causes and effects, Moore handed ammunition to his many enemies. His later work, *Bowling for Columbine* (2002, United States), which targets the lethal inanities of gun culture in America, is more careful—and hits harder as a result.

A documentary is always more powerful if its themes and ideas arise out of an unfolding life rather than when you selectively illustrate a narrated thesis.

FIGURE 22-2

Evidence—beginning and end of a shot in which a man demonstrates the price he believes he paid for doing his job (frames from *A Remnant of a Feudal Society*).

Interestingly, the same principle applies to fiction films; it is the difference between *signifying* a situation versus showing it in the act of being. Once again, drama and the documentary share fundamentals.

You may have to take special care to demonstrate that a point in your film is not contrived. In a documentary I made long ago about an English country estate, *A Remnant of a Feudal Society* (1970, United Kingdom; Figure 22-2), a head groom spontaneously held out his deformed hand to demonstrate what happened (as he thought) to horsemen made to ride in all kinds of weather. Because it was unclear what was wrong with the hand in the wide shot, the cameraman zoomed in close. I afterwards kept the zoom. Removing it by making a cut between long shot and close shot, though more elegant onscreen, would have undermined the spontaneity of the groom's action by making it look prearranged. A simple cut in the footage would have demoted its credibility. Showing the origin and authenticity of evidence helps you maintain a good-faith relationship with your audience.

TRUTH CLAIMS

Documentaries usually assert their truthfulness in one of two ways. The traditional approach is to make a film that is honest to the spirit of your best perceptions and trust that the audience can infer the film's honesty.

In participatory filmmaking, you can build into the film whatever doubts and perceptions would otherwise go unacknowledged. This explores perception as well as what is perceived and may include some self-portraiture by the makers.

 Spectators judge a film's contents by instinct and their knowledge of life, so "transparent" films—films that purport to show life happening as though no camera were present—can communicate very effectively. Participatory and reflexive films let you explore not only what you film but also your doubts and perceptions while filming it.

FIGURE 22-3 ————————————————————————————

Robb Moss examines his own image as cameraman and husband in *The Tourist*. (Photo courtesy of Robb Moss.)

Robb Moss's touchingly autobiographical *The Tourist* (1991, United States; Figure 22-3) examines the two currently dominant aspects of his life—his job as a documentary cameraman, often filming in Third-World countries where people have too many children, and his marriage to a nurse specializing in neonatal care, with whom he wishes to have children and cannot. Without falsely reconciling any of

 How one sees, how one connects with others while making a film, is a Pandora's box that cannot be half opened. Autobiography omits or suppresses some truths and, by this subtraction alone, elevates others. Truth, then, is always provisional and verging on the fictional.

the open questions in his life, Moss chronicles the ironies that fate has dealt them. Finally, the film shows the joy of adopting a daughter.

For economy or self-preservation, autobiography never tells everything. By telling some truths and not others we recreate reality as though handling figures in fiction. It's quite a paradox.

BEHALFERS: SPEAKING FOR OTHERS

Speaking on behalf of others is almost a disease among documentarians, and (as I learned through Henry Breitrose, a fine writer on the documentary) documentarians so afflicted have a special name: *behalfers*. Behalfers make it their business to represent those without a voice, which in the end is everyone unable to make films themselves. This should remind us how charity gets dispensed by the privileged, how it can feel to the recipients, and how self-serving it can be to imagine one is promoting someone else's interests.

Offering your participants a share in authorship may be the only way to overcome the distrust that poisons relations between the religions and races, say, or between feminists and well-meaning males. For decades, Europeans filmed indigenous peoples like small children or zoo animals unable to speak for themselves. Missionaries ran roughshod over native populations because they could not imagine that Africans or Aztecs were equipped to hold mature spiritual beliefs. So whenever you get the impulse to do good, be awfully clear about its basis. Participants need accountability when you elect to speak for them and agreement about who has the right to control their image.

 Belief is dangerous when it legitimizes superiority, so being ethical means treating others, their values, and their lives with the respect and humility that you'd like applied to your own.

 As ordinary people learn more about film's processes and purposes, they become less trustful of those electing to speak on their behalf and demand more control over the outcome. This is less a loss of rights for the filmmaker than a maturing in the relationship.

GIVING AND TAKING

So far this discussion makes the documentarian's lot sound burdensome. Luckily, you don't just take from others: You also give. Plato said that "The unexamined life isn't worth living," and your film examination often helps transform the very lives you thought you were capturing intact. Because filming can compromise, subvert, improve, or even create the end result in your film, you face a conundrum. The solution may be to admit the paradoxes to your audience rather than hide them. Today's audiences are sophisticated and very interested in what filming does to the situation under study.

 Documentary often proves its worth by encouraging participants to examine their lives. The changes that follow are frequently because the attention of a film crew made someone feel they mattered and could take action.

WHAT DO YOU BELIEVE?

The two alternatives outlined earlier—transparency and reflexivity—can be described a little differently as either using the camera to look outward at the world (transparency) or using the world as a mirror in which to examine aspects of the art form or of the self that are

 The self is joined to the world, and the world to the self. Documentary filmmaking—the corner of nature seen through a temperament—helps you fully explore the beauty and mystery of this nexus.

reflected back. This difference is supposed to distinguish the classicist temperament from the romantic, but either can be valid and fascinating so long as you recognize your purposes and priorities from the outset. Do you know what you believe? How will your beliefs guide and inform the way you see the world in your film?

The decision about which route to take should arise from the subject and what you want to say about it. Often finding the right approach is a question of emphasis and of how, temperamentally, you function best as a storyteller.

How will you accommodate your human subjects when they make some adaptations for your camera? Do you trust your audience to make its own assessment of your relationship to truthfulness? Will you need to assist this, and if so, how?

The process of recording and interpreting requires justifying to your participants, who need to trust you as you make your recordings. If the complexities of this relationship affect important truths, will you acknowledge this, either implicitly or explicitly? The recording process may be too intrusive to document some intimate occasions or will seem so to the audience. Can you draw a line and if so, where? These seem like theoretical questions until they engender real consequences. Luckily, it is the real that helps us decide—not only what to do but also what we believe and who we are as we do it.

DOCUMENTARY AS EXPOSURE TO LIFE

Most documentary can't be made in retreat from life unless you make premeditated essay films. You create documentary by intruding into some area of life and learning from the consequences. Until you turn on the camera, many issues and aspects of personality (yours as well as those of your participants) are latent and invisible. Once you start, you may have to argue for your rights as chronicler and critic. Some will attack you for daring, as one person, to make an interpretive criticism of another. What do you believe, and can you stand by your judgments?

During filming, you'll often have to defend your right to record and evaluate. You'll do this best when you believe passionately in the worth of your endeavor. Knowing how documentary has helped social change will make you particularly effective.

Aesthetic and ethical decisions are seldom made from a position of cool intellectual neutrality. More often we struggle with conflicting moral obligations. We have an allegiance to people who trust us on the one hand and an allegiance to truths we hold dear on the other. Does obligation to a grand truth allow you to violate someone's trust or legitimize turncoat behavior? Can you let go of a conviction and make a different film if new evidence shows that you were wrong?

Sometimes you are in trouble no matter which way you turn. In these circumstances, I remind myself that my movie is just one little person's view at one little moment in time.

 Don't try making yourself responsible for definitive truth. That's like wanting your children to be perfect. Your films will always be an imperfect attempt to convey the spirit of what's true.

MISSION AND IDENTITY

Luckily each of us carries one or two certainties taught by life. Recognizing this, you can say, "This I know from life, so this is what I'll enjoy showing." It's important to work from this kind of energy because documentaries take months or even years to complete, and work becomes agony if your heart isn't in it. Films, especially "transparent" films that aim to present life in an authorless way, often hide the roots they have in their maker's psyche. Yet most films are displaced autobiography. All the filmmaker has done is search out others' living truths that the filmmaker knows from his or her own deeply felt experience.

 Most documentary is displaced autobiography— though you start from a personal story or conviction, you look for examples unconnected to yourself out in the world. These lead to a film free from the taint of egocentricity.

By finding other people and other situations that somehow convey what you need to say, you put your convictions under test. It's no longer yourself as subject, but how you see things. You do this by identifying your counterparts floating in life's stream. By catching and tethering them in a structured statement, they mirror the truths life has taught you and further refine and develop your convictions.

 Probably we make documentaries to put our convictions under test—to find other people and other situations that somehow convey the heart of what we need to say.

Much of this happens at an unconscious level. Looking at someone else and trying to see through their eyes creates useful restraints on your ego. Seeking your enduring preoccupations in others and outside yourself leads toward filmmaking with overtones of universality. The discipline of such a process brings its own rewards. With growing maturity you can identify the surrogates to your own values and temperament and allow them to achieve a life of their own in your film. Your work quietly alters how you see the fundamentals of your own life—the very source from which your documentary process sprang. In this way, each project is midwife to the next.

CHAPTER 23

PROPOSING AN
ADVANCED DOCUMENTARY

After research and deciding your purposes and options, you can go ahead and develop a detailed proposal. It will help you communicate the film's nature and purpose while during the search for funding, crew, or other support.

 Writing proposals is a good way to develop films. They put your ideas under test, help you review your basic assumptions, and urge you to develop stylistic or structural possibilities that you would otherwise bypass. Whoever thinks and writes well is on track to excel in the more demanding medium of filmmaking.

WHY WRITE A PROPOSAL?

Writing forces you to clarify the organizational and thematic analysis made during research and prepares you to *direct* the film. The sustained thinking it takes to write something acts to prime you. Then you can catalyze and capture materials that really add up to something and not just impulsively collect what may or may not take shape during editing. The proposal also reveals how ready you are to fulfill the conditions of making good documentary. Your film should:

- Tell a good story.
- Make human truths, both large and small, emerge through behavioral evidence, not just opinion or verbal description.
- Present a personal, critical perspective on some aspect of the human condition.
- Inform and emotionally move the audience.

Like gripping fiction, the successful documentary usually incorporates:

- Well-placed exposition of necessary information (facts or context placed not too early or too late).
- Interesting characters that are actively trying to get, do, or accomplish something.
- Events that emerge from the characters' needs.
- Dramatic tension and conflict between opposing forces.
- Suspense—not people hanging off cliffs, but situations that intrigue your spectators and make them anticipate, wonder, compare, and decide.
- Confrontation among conflicting persons, factions, or elements.
- A climax in the tension between opposing elements or forces.
- A resolution (happy or sad, good or bad, satisfying or not).
- Development in at least one main character or situation.

If these criteria may seem too close to fiction, view one of your favorite documentaries and decide what its dramatic ingredients really are.

Write and rewrite your proposal until you have made it succinct, free of redundancy, and effortless to read. Funders know that thin and muddled writing promises thin and muddled filmmaking. A good proposal, on the other hand, demonstrates that you're ready to meet the implicit expectations of documentary itself, that you really understand the genre, and that you know what you are doing as a director.

 Round up the necessary information and ideas easily using **Projects 2-DP-4 Advanced Working Hypothesis Helper, 2-DP-6 Advanced Proposal Helper,** and **2-DP-2 Style and Content Questionnaire** (all in the Appendix).

This chapter and the two that follow cover the work you'll need to do to turn this information into a documentary proposal.

STEPS TOWARD THE FIRST DRAFT

1. **Check your working hypothesis for its currency** (see **Chapter 21, Advanced Research**).
2. **Review ingredients.**
   a. *List the action and behavioral sequences.* Can you envisage a coherent observational film with these alone? This is a litmus test for how cinematic your film is or how much it depends on speech as narrative guidance.
   b. *Audition.* Using video very informally (if you use it at all), talk with those you're considering for the film. Ask no searching questions—keep those for when you shoot.

    c. *Don't push yet.* Avoid being intrusive or divisive. Listen to what your participants suggest and reply in nebulous terms. You want to delay all decisions till as late as possible.

    d. *Casting.* Watch the tape (if there is one) with a few trusted friends to see how well potential participants come across. This is analogous to casting.

3. **Refine the proposal.**

    a. *Rewrite the working hypothesis* if new people and information have altered its basis, and determine where your thematic purpose is leading. Skimping on this will leave you unsure, and you could end up shooting everything that moves.

    b. *Narrow the focus, deepen the film.* Tightly focused films that go deep are better than broad, generalizing films. What's central, and what can you ditch from the periphery?

    c. *List the points your film must make* so you forget nothing important when you come to direct.

4. **Define the premise.**

    a. *Write a three-line description.* If you can summarize your film and its purposes in three lines and people react to it positively, you may be ready to direct it. If you can't, you aren't.

NOTES ON STEPS 1 TO 4

List the Action and Behavioral Sequences (2a)

Expand your list using the three-column approach shown in **Project 2-DP-2 Style** **and Content Questionnaire** (in the Appendix). Its columns deal with (1) what each sequence "is," (2) what you want it to convey, and (3) how you might shoot it to make the most of its inherent qualities. Cut your form up and mount each sequence on a separate index card or sheet of paper. This gives you large playing cards that you can move around on a table. You can now experiment with the order and juxtaposition of your film's content.

 Seek the center of your film by repeatedly assuming you haven't found it. Do this by subtracting everything that the film is *not* mainly about. Now that you have narrowed the film to its center, how can you develop what's there and go even deeper?

NARROW THE FOCUS, DEEPEN THE FILM (3B)

Discarding whatever is not central to a film benefits it by leading you toward expanding its essence. If you can say that the resolution of one scene or situation is pivotal, you can now allow back whatever leads to it or leads away from it by way of resolution.

DOCUMENTARY PROPOSAL ORGANIZER

Using **Project 2-DP-6 Advanced Proposal Helper** (in the Appendix) will now help you flush out the basics that you'll need to write a proposal or develop a prospectus package. Think of its categories like the pigeonholes in a mail sorting office. A well-researched film has something substantial and different in most pigeonholes and, most importantly, nothing duplicated between them. The Proposal Helper is particularly helpful for longer and more complex works, which often contain more plot and developing issues.

 Very important: When similar material turns up in multiple categories, keep writing more drafts until material appears *only once and in its rightful place.*

THE PROPOSAL

You will probably angle your proposal toward a particular fund, foundation, or television channel—that's if they fund at the conceptual stage, which is rare today unless you have a stellar track record. You may instead be canvassing individual investors. Note that a good title for your film is important to signaling your wares and attracting support.

Use the information you collected in the Proposal Helper under the different headings, putting selected information in the order that will work best for the foundation, fund, or channel to which you are applying. Write compactly, informatively, and evocatively. If the submission rules allow, include photographs and make use of colorful graphics so the reader can visualize all the essentials of the film. A long proposal is less effective than one that says a lot in few pages. This means summoning up the essence with maximum brevity, since a complete proposal may have to be no longer than 4 or 5 pages.

You'll need many drafts before your proposal is direct and brief and fuels the imagination of the reader. This is like making an early version of your film. Expect to go through 10 to 20 drafts before you have something worthy of you.

Typically a proposal will include:

- Cover sheet (1 page)
- Film description (3 pages)
  - **Synopsis** of the project, maybe in 25 words or less
  - **Treatment** explaining background information, structure, theme, style, format (16 mm film, DV, HD, etc.), voice, and point of view
  - **Contributors**
  - **Funding already in place,** including the in-kind contributions that you or others are making

- ○ **Target communities** for the program and why this audience is currently not served by television (which is usually trying to fill gaps); how you are known to, and trusted by, the community in which you propose filming
- ○ **Why this series, channel, or program is the right place** for this film
- ○ **Current status** of the project
- Production personnel (2 to 3 pages)
  - ○ **Applicants' résumés** (the initiators of the project)
  - ○ **Key production personnel** names, positions, short biographies
- Previous and current work samples
  - ○ Previously completed **sample work** (either demo reel or completed film— see fund guidelines)
  - ○ **Work in progress** (WIP) of perhaps 5 minutes' minimum length
  - ○ Written **descriptions of prior work,** applicants' creative contributions to it, its relevance to WIP, and what the WIP represents (rough cut, trailer, selects, or a clip)

Funding organizations streamline their process so they get consistent documentation that is easiest to compare. Each has its own proposal forms, expects you to write in specific ways, and wants a specified number of copies with everything properly labeled. A weary reader sifting through a pile of competing applications will see departures from the norm not as charming originality but as indifference to the jury's task.

 Apply early since first applications will make a greater impression than the blizzard of latecomers. Inattention to detail will knock most people out of the race, so check and double-check everything before you put your proposal in the mail.

FUNDING ORGANIZATIONS

The Independent Television Service (ITVS) Web site is a mine of information on how to apply and what independent films have recently been funded (see www.itvs.org and go to "For Producers"). The site gives valuable hints on writing a better application. For information on the PBS series *POV*, go to www

 Funders put passion and innovation high on their list of desirable attributes. Innovate by knowing thoroughly what you're competing against.

.pbs.org/pov/utils/aboutpov_faq.html. Their call-for-entries Web site is www .pbs.org/pov/utils/callforentries.html#callforentriesk. Many important American independent documentaries get made through these program portals, which are inundated with applications. Because of this, they expect makers to initiate documentaries rather than seek funding at the proposal stage. ITVS and *POV* ask producers to apply with a substantial amount of the footage or a long edited version.

Specialized Web sites are also a mine of information on making documentaries for television. Because so many applications are abysmal, what they recommend is intended to parry the most common mistakes and misunderstandings. An ITVS regional jury on which I once sat for 3 days found only 6 out of 140 applications promising. Two of those we chose (which ITVS in the end failed to support) went on by other means to become quite famous independent films. The moral? Organization and vision are as visible on paper as well-meaning muddle.

THE TREATMENT

The *treatment*, like the proposal, is one more salvo in getting a film made. It exists to convince a sponsor, fund, or broadcasting organization that you can make a film of impact and significance. While the proposal presents its argument rationally via categorized information, the treatment evokes how an audience will experience your film on the screen. It's a short-story narrative that excludes any philosophical or directorial intentions. To make one:

- Restructure the information in the proposal as a chronological presentation, allotting one paragraph per sequence.
- Write an active-voice, present-tense summary of *what an audience watching the film will see and hear from the screen*.
- Write colorfully so the reader can easily visualize what you see in your mind's eye.
- Where possible, convey information and evoke your characters by using their own words in brief, pithy quotations. Put supporting material on your DVD "reel."
- Never write anything you can't produce.
- Keep within the specified page count.

 Purge all academic twaddle from film proposals—it's the kiss of death among film people. For a hilarious exposé of academic language, read George Orwell's "Politics and the English Language" at http://orwell.ru/library/essays/politics/english/e_polit.

 Be sure you haven't overlooked any costs or resources by using **Project 3-BP-2 Advanced Budget Worksheet.**

BUDGET PLANNING FORM

In the early stages, it's useful to use a worksheet to compile high and low figures as optimistic and pessimistic approaches (see project box). This should keep you from underestimation. Add a 3 to 5% contingency percentage without fail at the end to cover the unforeseen, such as bad-weather delays, reshoots, additions, or substitutions. Submit your final budget, or a budget summary sheet, using a professional budget software program. The industry standard software is Movie Magic™, which is expensive and overkill for most documentaries. Less pricey and just as good for the independent is Gorilla™ budgeting software. Once you've entered all your information, you can update any element and have the satisfaction of seeing changes reflected straightaway in the bottom line.

> Unusually low budgets, far from seeming attractive to funders, signal inexperience and will get your proposal tossed out.

THE PROSPECTUS

This presentation package or portfolio communicates your project and its purposes to non-filmmaking funders, who may be quite task oriented. The League of Left-Handed Taxidermists wants to know how *Stuffing Badgers* will be useful to them, how much it costs, and (invariably) why it costs so much. The prospectus uses many of the funding proposal categories and should be succinct and professional. It should contain:

1. *Cover letter*—Describe the nature of the film, its budget, the capital you want to raise, and what you want from the addressee. Only if you are targeting many small investors can this be a general letter; otherwise, write a customized letter to each specific individual. Be careful not to promise different things to different people.

2. *Title page*—A good title does more than anything at this stage to arouse respect and interest. Evocative photos or other professional-looking artwork in the prospectus will also improve your presentation's persuasiveness.

3. *One liner*—Provide a simple, compact declaration of the project. Examples:
   - A theater director goes to live as one of the homeless so she can knowledgeably direct a play about homeless people.
   - Marriage is examined as seen in the ideas and play of 7-year-olds from across the social spectrum.
   - Three people of different ages and backgrounds relive their near-death experiences and show how profoundly their lives have changed since.

4. *Synopsis*—Briefly recount the documentary's intended story in a way that captures its flavor and style.

5. *History and background*—Explain how and why the project evolved and why you feel compelled to make it. Here you establish the strength of your commitment to the story—important because nobody finishes a documentary unless they have a strong emotional investment in it.

6. *Research*—Outline research you have done and what it shows. Here you establish the factual foundation to the film, its characters, its context, and

your authoritative knowledge. If special cooperation, rights, or permissions are involved, show you can secure them.

7. *DVD "reel"*—A 3- to 5-minute, specially edited trailer that proves the characters, landscape, style, and other attractions to which you lay claim. This is your chance to let the screen make your argument with a strong sequence or a montage of material. Among the multitude of applications, your "reel" should be of distinguished material and make its points rapidly. Package it attractively, divide the material up into chapters, and include an overview list so users can effortlessly navigate. Make absolutely sure *the disk plays on a standard player from beginning to end.*

8. *Budget*—Provide a summary of expected expenditures. Don't understate or underestimate; it's amateurish and may leave you funding the film's completion yourself.

9. *Schedule*—State the approximate shooting period (or periods, if shooting is broken up) and preferred starting dates.

10. *Résumés of creative personnel*—In brief paragraphs, name the director, producer, camera operator, sound operator, and editor, and summarize their qualifications. Append a one-page résumé for each. Aim to present a professional, exciting, and specially appropriate team.

11. *Audience and market*—Say for whom the film is intended, and outline a distribution plan to show convincingly that the film has a waiting audience. Copies of letters of interest from television stations, channels, film distributors, or other interested parties are very helpful here. Present a plan for educational follow-up so the film can be used by special constituencies. Most funds require this.

12. *Financial statement*—If you have legally formed with others into a company or group, make an estimate of income based on the distribution plan, and say if you are a *bona fide* not-for-profit company or are working through one, because this may offer investors tax advantages that they can claim against their contributions.

13. *Means of transferring funds*—Supply a letter for the investor to use as a model that makes it easy to commit funds to your production account.

Every grant application is potentially the beginning of a lengthy relationship, so your prospectus and proposals should convey the essence of your project and its purpose in a clear, colorful, individual, and impeccable way.

A working documentary maker has many irons in many fires and must often write proposals based on partial research. Master the fine art of minimizing your uncertain-

> You are what you write: Take every available step to expunge spelling errors and typos. Use professional graphics, layout, and fonts. Print on heavy, expensive-looking paper and include professional-looking business cards, which give you the look of substance at little cost.

ties. Once the project is deemed feasible and funds secured, research and development can begin in earnest.

GOING FURTHER

The following book is intended for fiction films, which elaborate documentaries can come to resemble:

Maier, Robert.G. *Location Scouting and Management Handbook*. Boston: Focal Press, 1994.

CHAPTER 24

PREPARING TO DIRECT

Documentaries involve improvisation, so you must often revise as you go. Making a directing plan is useful, however, because it's one more plank in the all-important development work before you leap into the fray. Work on a computer so you can read, think, and revise over a period of time. Don't forget to compile those life-saving "do not forget" lists of tasks and ideas (see this book's Web site, http://directingthedocumentary .com for downloadable reminder lists). Plan to cover expository information, crucial to the coherence of any story, in multiple ways so you have options in postproduction.

 Get all the conceptual help you can by using **Projects 2-DP-4 Advanced Working Hypothesis** and **2-DP-6 Advanced Proposal Helper.**

DIRECTING PLAN OVERVIEW

THE DIRECTING PLAN

1. Decide:
   a. *Casting*—Which people will you use, and who is your central character?
   b. *Who or what is in conflict*—Question your choices rigorously, as it's easy to get this one wrong (see note 1C on page 372)
   c. *Dialectics* of your film—Determining the central point and counterpoint of its argument will help you collect all the materials you need (see note 1D on page 373).
   d. *Confrontation*—How can you ensure that your movie's antithetical forces will collide (see note 1E on page 373)?

e. *Thematic or other goals*—Identify goals for each sequence and for the film as a whole.

2. List:
    a. *Expository information* that the audience needs in order to understand each sequence
    b. *What's typical and atypical* in each sequence, to guide your filming
    c. *Imagery* such as cityscapes, landscapes, and workplaces that are emblematic of your participants' type, place, or condition

3. Define:
    a. *Main point of view*, whose it is, why it matters, and how you'll make us empathize
    b. *Secondary points of view*, as you might tell the story through secondary characters (see Point of View and Storyteller's Angle [3 and 4] on page 373)

4. *Define your own angle* or point of view, codifying what you want to say and with what emphasis so you collect the materials to do it. This is for your private use only (see Point of View and Storyteller's Angle [3 and 4] on page 373).

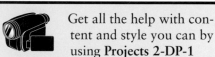

Get all the help with content and style you can by using **Projects 2-DP-1 Dramatic Content Helper** and **2-DP-2 Style and Content Questionnaire.**

ADDRESSING AESTHETIC CONCERNS

5. *Style*—Define:
    a. What best serves *each sequence*
    b. *How point of view* might affect style (in each sequence and in the whole film)
    c. The *stylistic characteristics of the film* as a whole
    d. *Anything to avoid* (negative definition is also creative)
    e. *The genre you are making* (what is it closest to?) (see note 6 below)

6. *Parallel narrative traditions*—What can your film borrow from other forms?

TESTING YOUR ASSUMPTIONS

7. *Pitch* your ideas to anyone who will listen and solicit their reactions. Pitch to different victims until you get a consistently good audience response.

8. *Ask people to read the proposal* and to comment on what it makes them expect. Do they see the film you see?

NEAR SHOOTING

9. *Make the final draft of your intentions.* Even if you have nobody to satisfy but yourself, work over all the considerations prior to shooting. Originality

does not come from talent (whatever that is) but from sustained, determined thought about the tasks and choices that lie ahead.

10. *Obtain permissions.*

a. *People*—Secure a commitment for agreed dates and the amount of time and involvement from those you intend to film.

 People seldom imagine the sheer organization a film takes or see that asking you to switch filming to another week will cause you difficulty.

b. *Places*—Secure written permissions for owners or administrators of non-public locations. Many cities require you to get a permit from the authorities to film in the streets or on public transportation.

c. *Copyright*—If music or other copyrighted material is necessary, now's the time to secure it.

11. *Secure your crew* and put them under contract.

12. Decide what *insurance* you will need.

13. *Make a shooting schedule* and build in options to deal with foreseeable difficulties such as inclement weather or unavailability of a major element or participant.

14. *Do any necessary trial shooting* to:

a. "Audition" doubtful participants.

b. Work out communications with a new crew.

c. Set standards for work you are going to do together.

d. Test new or unfamiliar technology.

NOTES

(Note: Numbering refers to list on page 370.)

WHO OR WHAT IS IN CONFLICT? (1C)

This is fatally easy to decide superficially. Deciding who is in struggle is easy, but deciding *what really is at stake*—for your participants, for those around them, or for society at large—takes a lot of hard, careful thought. It's not enough to list issues—you must decide which is paramount. This is the key to giving your film the definition and clarity it needs to be effective.

 As shooting evolves, the film's purpose and identity often subtly change, so keep watch.

FILM DIELECTICS (1D)

Who and what are pitted against each other? In what hierarchy might these oppositions play out? Their prominence and strength depend very much on how you capture them and how you orchestrate them later during editing. This gives muscle and sinew to your drama. Right now you need to be fully aware of what's available to work with.

CONFRONTATION (1E)

Once you know the main opposi-tional forces in your film, you must ensure they meet in confrontation. A documentary does not reach its potential if its racketeering landlord never meets the tenant association that wants heat in the winter and rats evicted. You may have to fina-gle things to make confrontations happen.

 Documentaries sometimes fail to bring their oppos-ing forces into confronta-tion, and this leaves the audience feeling cheated.

POINT OF VIEW AND STORYTELLER'S ANGLE (3 AND 4)

Who, among those in the film, must we specially understand and sympathize with? How will you take us inside these emotional viewpoints? What changes in thinking and feeling do you want us to experience as we follow the story? What should we feel and think by the end?

Most importantly, what are your attitudes as the Storyteller toward the story you are telling—is it "an endlessly repeating cycle" or "a small-town tragedy"? Is it a "Frankie and Johnnie ballad" or a "defeat snatched from the jaws of victory" type of tale? Is it a tragedy, farce, tall story, or cautionary tale? Don't just give us a record of events and leave your tale to find its own nature. How you shoot and edit your story should give it a clear, exciting identity as a *type* of story. Whichever it is, tell it with style, panache, and gusto. To do this you must adopt a *storytelling role* rather than work from your modest, retiring self. Michael Moore has said he was terrified in *Bowling for Columbine* while confronting Charlton Heston over the National Rifle Association's stance. Taking on social icons comes no more natu-rally to him than it does to you or me; he does it because he feels some-one must. Can you do likewise?

 You alone can give iden-tity to the Storyteller behind your documentary tale. Failing to develop one is like letting a computer read your chil-dren's bedtime story.

GENRE (6)

Every film stands on the shoulders of those before it. Your documentary's ante-cedents will suggest ideas or approaches that can enrich it and take your film farther.

PARALLEL NARRATIVE TRADITIONS (7)

Your film parallels works in other art forms such as music, opera, theater, folktale, or mythology that pursue a similar theme, tell a similar tale, or use a similar form. The parallels you find can help intensify your work and move it toward the universal.

 Documentary's greatest handicap is its tendency toward the parochial. Only if you develop more universal themes will yours cross local boundaries the way fiction films do.

ANTICIPATING THE SHOOT

SCOUTING THE LOCATIONS

During preproduction, the director of photography, sound recordist, and director should check out locations for problems. See **Chapter 9, Camera Equipment,** and **Chapter 10, Lighting,** for the fundamentals.

Camera

Whenever possible the cinematographer scouts locations ahead of shooting. What problems do they pose?

- For an exterior, when is available light at its most useful? (Carry a compass so you can estimate the angle of the sun at different times of day.)
- What setups look promising?
- Is enough electricity available for lighting interiors?
- Can power cables pass under doors when you close windows during shooting?
- Where can lighting stands go so there's maximum freedom to shoot?
- How reflective are the walls and how high is the ceiling?
- Where might the camera go if it's a public event and you must shoot unobtrusively off a tripod using a long lens?

Sound

The first thing a sound specialist does in a new location is to clap her hands, once and loudly. She listens for the *attack* and *decay* of the hand clap. Ideally, they are rapid. If the room is *live* (reverberant) there will be an appreciable comet's tail of sound reflected and thrown around the room. This concerns her greatly, and she may ask for an alternative venue. Take such advice seriously, because sound reflectivity of particular surfaces can make the difference between sound that is usefully dry or not reverberant and one that is unworkably hollow and reverberant (see sound theory in **Chapter 11, Location Sound**).

When in doubt, record representative dialogue in dubious sound locations and roughly edit the results together. You will quickly have the measure of your problems. The sound recordist will also be concerned with:

- Whether drapes, carpet, soft furniture, or irregular surfaces can be legitimately introduced to break up the unwanted movement of sound within the space.
- Alignment of surfaces likely to cause standing waves (sound bouncing to and fro between opposing surfaces, augmenting and cross-modulating the source sound).
- Whether the room has intrusive resonances (mainly a problem with concrete or tile surfaces).
- Whether participants can walk and cameras be handheld without the floor letting out tortured squeaks in dialogue scenes.
- Ambient sound and noise penetrating from the outside.

Typical intermittent sound intrusions might come from:

- Wildlife or domestic animals.
- An airport flight path.
- An expressway, railroad, or subway.
- Refrigeration, air-conditioning, or other sound-generating equipment that runs intermittently and will cause problems unless you can turn it off while shooting.
- Construction sites (you scouted the location on a weekend, not realizing that come Monday morning a pile driver and four jackhammers would compete to greet the dawn and you have no hope of stopping them).
- A school (they have a lot of hue and cry at set times of day).

Be aware that shooting interior dialogue with doors and windows closed can be trying in hot weather.

LOGISTICS AND THE SCHEDULE

Estimating how long each type of scene takes to shoot comes with experience. A 30-minute documentary can take between 3 and 8 working days to shoot, depending on:

- *Distance of travel*—Tearing down much equipment in the old location and setting it up anew is time consuming, so allow plenty of time for transport between the two. Also, a new film unit is slow at the start and faster 10 days later. International travel requires careful planning, as you probably need to comply with customs regulations concerning equipment both going and returning.
- *Amount and complexity of lighting setups*
- *Complexity of sound setups*
- *Amount of randomness inherent in the subject matter*—To film a spontaneous scuffle between boys during a school

 Careful shooting takes longer than you ever imagine possible. Even a simple 20-minute interview may take 3 hours to accomplish, given that you often must socialize with participants when you visit their homes.

yard break, you may have to hang around for days, but to film a postman delivering a particular letter may take no more than 10 minutes.

Schedule two or, at the most, three sequences in a day's work unless you are using available light and are certain that what you want is straightforward. Avoid overly optimistic scheduling by making best-case and worst-case estimates and allotting something in between.

 Give everyone a *printed schedule* before each day's shooting. Time spent planning and informing is time, money, and morale saved later. An under-informed crew stops taking initiative and waits around for instructions.

Whether your shooting is drawn out or compact, make a draft schedule and solicit comment from the crew.

In each schedule include:

➤ Everyone's mobile phone number
➤ A phone contact for each location
➤ Special equipment or personnel required in each location
➤ Clear navigational instructions
➤ Photocopies of maps marked up with locations and phone numbers
➤ The names of people with mobile phones who are allotted to each vehicle whenever it is necessary to converge at a prearranged place and time (to provide for someone getting lost or having car trouble)

Expect trouble and you won't be disappointed. There's a reason why film-making is so often described in the language of military invasion.

ENSURING CHANGE

One luxury peculiar to the independent filmmaker (and there are few) is that you can shoot follow-up material over a long period. Independent filmmakers tend to work as a group and on multiple projects, so occasionally deploying a crew for follow-up is not difficult. Returning at 6-month intervals for a couple of years may capture real changes. Reality shows, which borrow from documentary, accelerate change by putting contestants under extreme tests of endurance, strength, or ingenuity.

PERMISSION TO FILM AT LOCATION FACILITIES

You must secure permission to film in a location in writing *before* you start shooting (Figure 24-1; see also Figure 7-1 in Chapter 7). A film of mine was once held up for a year after getting written permission to film an exhibition in a synagogue. Although I had secured permission for the building, the traveling exhibition's owner, after hugely enjoying himself presenting exhibition items to the camera, later denied he had ever given me permission to film.

All events on private property (which may include a city transportation system) must be cleared by the relevant authority unless you care to risk being

LOCATION AGREEMENT

Location of Property: _____

Description of Property: _____

Dates of Use: _____ Fee for Use: $_____

PICTURE: _____ PRODUCER: _____

       In consideration of the payment of the above-indicated fee, the undersigned hereby grants to Producer, its successors and assigns the right to enter the area located as described above (hereafter "Property") on or about the dates listed above, for the purpose of photographing by motion picture, videotape, and still photography and to make sound recordings and to otherwise use for so-called "location" purposes (the results of which are hereafter collectively referred to as "Photographs"). If such photography is prevented or hampered by weather or occurrence beyond Producer's control, it will be postponed to or completed on such date as Producer may reasonably require. Said permission shall include the right to bring personnel and equipment (including props and temporary sets) onto the Property, and to remove the same therefrom after completion of work.

       The undersigned hereby grants to Producer, its successors, assigns and licensees the irrevocable and perpetual right to use the Photographs of the Property taken by Producer hereunder in connection with motion picture, television photoplays or otherwise, and all the ancillary and subsidiary rights thereto of every kind and nature in such a manner and to such extent as Producer may desire. The rights granted herein include the right to photograph the Property and all structures and signs located on the Property (including the exterior and interior of such structures, and the names, logos and verbiage contained on such signs), the right to refer to the Property by its correct name or any fictitious name and the right to attribute both real and fictitious events as occurring on the Property and to fictionalize the Property itself. The undersigned hereby agrees and acknowledges that any and all Photographs made or to be made by Producer shall be Producer's sole and exclusive property and the undersigned shall have no claims thereto or rights therein or to the proceeds hereof.

       Producer agrees to use reasonable care to prevent damage to the Property and to remove any and all property which Producer may place upon the Property in connection with its use thereof. Producer agrees to restore the Property as nearly as possible to its original condition at the time of Producer's taking possession thereof, reasonable wear and damage not caused by Producer's use excepted.

       Producer hereby agrees to indemnify and hold the undersigned harmless from any claims and demands of any person or persons arising out of or based upon personal injuries and/or death suffered by such person or persons resulting directly from any act of negligence on Producer's part while Producer is engaged in the photographing of said Photographs upon the Property.

       The undersigned hereby releases Producer and its licensees, successors, assigns, all networks, stations, sponsors, advertising agencies, exhibitors, cable operators and all other persons or entities from any and all claims, demands, or causes of action which the undersigned, its heirs, successors or assigns may now have or hereafter acquire by reason of Producer's photographing and using the Photographs taken of the Property, including, but not limited to, all buildings (exterior and interior), equipment, facilities and signs thereon.

       The undersigned hereby represents and warrants that the undersigned is the _____ (fill in: owner, lessee or agent for the owner) of said Property and has the full right and authority to grant the license herein contained. The undersigned hereby indemnifies and agrees to hold Producer free and harmless from and against any and all liability, damages, claims, costs or fees, including but not limited to attorney fees, arising from, growing out of or concerning any breach by the undersigned of this warranty.

FIGURE 24-1———————————————————————————————————

Location Agreement Form from *Clearance and Copyright*, by courtesy of Michael C. Donaldson, who notes that if you are paying this person more than $600, you will need the releaser's Social Security number so you can fill out a W-2 tax form. Otherwise, leave it off. Download this form at www.clearanceandcopyright.com.

taken to court for invasion of privacy. This risk rises as you or your company become worth suing. Sometimes—and this is a great hazard to investigative journalism—a malicious party will initiate legal action as a pretext for obtaining a court injunction that will block your film from showing.

Anything unrestrictedly open to public entry and view (such as the street, markets, public meetings) may be filmed without asking anyone's permission. Handheld cameras count as newsgathering and are protected under freedom of speech; however, cities often restrict street filming from a tripod or other camera support system. This arises from a film crew's potential to become a spectacle that blocks or disrupts traffic flow. Accordingly, you must get police permission and perhaps pay for a cop to control traffic or wave away troublesome bystanders. Once you put up the tripod, you technically speaking cross into the big time, but there may be nobody around who cares. Chicago is still film friendly, while in Paris and New York the honeymoon is long over. To film at any urban location, you must work through a special division of the mayor's office or state film commission. They require proof that you carry the relevant liability insurance in case your activities cause injury.

By tradition, documentary makers often shoot first and ask questions later, knowing that if somebody takes exception, the combination of ideals and poverty will probably lead to nothing more than an irritable dismissal. This solution gets risky in authoritarian countries where the authorities identify cameras as engines of subversion. Moving images from a phone camera can provide powerful, instant, and worldwide evidence of wrongdoing, as the Burmese government discovered after beating up monks who were peacefully demonstrating. The Los Angeles police department went on trial before the world for the Rodney King beating. Years of asserting police brutality had gotten black people nowhere until the evidence was inarguable. Two minutes of footage shot by the alert owner of a camcorder changed history.

THE INDIVIDUAL RELEASE FORM

In this document the signatory releases to you the right to make public use of the material you have shot (Figure 24-2). You ask for the signature immediately *after* shooting. To soften the predatory nature of the request, you may want to give the person, say, 24 hours in which to call you to discuss anything they might want to retract.

 Permission problems or legal hang-ups happen when people imagine you can find fame or fortune from selling footage of them. Practice explaining the reality.

Al Maysles asks people to sign, one after another, under a common declaration in an ordinary notebook. Signing seems less momentous when they can see that others have signed before them. Other documentarians—Fred Wiseman reputedly among them—secure a record of agreement by asking participants to say on-camera that they give permission to be filmed and that their name and address are such and such. A verbal release, however, is no protection against someone who decides at a late hour to pull out, sending an entire project down the drain with a whoosh. Participants know that you can, if challenged, always

INDIVIDUAL RELEASE

Note: This has been prepared in the form of a letter to you, the Producer, to make it less formal and therefore less intimidating.

[date]

To: [your name]
        [your address]

This letter shall confirm that I, the undersigned person, for good and valuable consideration, the receipt and sufficiency of which is hereby acknowledged, has granted permission to you, the producer and your successors, assignees and licensees to use my name and/or likeness as such name and/or likeness appears in photography shot in connection with the Picture tentatively entitled _____ and in connection with advertising, publicizing, exhibiting and exploiting the Picture, in whole or in part, by any and all means, media, devices, processes and technology now or hereafter known or devised in perpetuity throughout the universe. I hereby acknowledge that you shall have no obligation to utilize my Name and/or Likeness in the Picture or in any other motion picture.

        Your exercise of such rights shall not violate or infringe any rights of any third party. I understand that you have been induced to proceed with the production, distribution and exploitation of the Picture in reliance upon this agreement.

        I hereby release you, your successors, assignees and licensees from any and all claims and demands arising out of or in connection with such use, including, without limitation, any and all claims for invasion of privacy, infringement of my right of publicity, defamation (including libel and slander), false light and any other personal and/or property rights.

Very Truly Yours,

[Releaser's signature]
[Releaser's name]
[Releaser's address]
[Releaser's Social Security no.]

FIGURE 24-2————————————————————————————————

Individual Release Form from *Clearance and Copyright*, by courtesy of Michael C. Donaldson, who comments that many individuals will not authorize the use of their likeness in your advertising without substantial extra payment. It is generally not worth the extra money, so you may have to take out that provision. Download this form at www.clearanceandcopyright.com.

play their footage in court. Note that neither a verbal release nor a signed document protects you against charges of slander or deception.

Whichever means you use, get personal releases signed in the euphoria immediately after the participant's filming. No signature is valid without the $1 minimum legal payment, which you solemnly hand over as symbolic payment. Minors cannot sign legal forms themselves and will need the clearance of a parent or legal guardian.

CROWD SCENE RELEASES

You can't get, nor do you need, releases from all the people who appear in a street shot, which contains what anyone in lawful transit might see. So you normally seek signed releases from speaking participants only. Securing the release prevents participants from pulling out arbitrarily or from hitting you up for money once they know that the work you've invested in depends on their contribution.

LEGAL ISSUES

For all film-related legal matters, consult Michael C. Donaldson's highly readable and comprehensive *Clearance and Copyright: Everything the Independent Filmmaker Needs to Know*, 2nd ed. (2003, Silman-James). These aspects are of particular interest to independent documentary makers:

- Copyright and ideas
- Public domain
- Personal rights
- Hiring a scriptwriter and working with a partner
- Provisions common to most agreements
- Registering copyright of the script
- Chain of title
- Others who may have rights in your film
- Title clearance
- Errors and omissions insurance
- All the things that the camera sees
- Clearing music
- Hiring a composer
- Fair-use doctrine
- Parody
- Clearing film clips
- Registering copyright of your completed film
- Copyright infringement
- Copyright on the Internet
- Legal referral services

PAYING PARTICIPANTS

Fiction filmmakers pay actors, but documentary makers don't normally pay their participants, even when they have quite large budgets. This is because paying someone means you are potentially purchasing the truth you want to hear. For

 Documentaries depend on good-faith exchanges captured, not checkbook journalism. Only pay participants for what you've cost them (electricity, say), but do leave something for people in need.

the audience this reduces or disables your film's credibility. There are a couple of exceptions to this.

Celebrities

If you engage a history specialist, such as Harvard's Henry Louis Gates, Jr., to host and help create a series like PBS' *African American Lives* series (2007–2008, United States), you will expect a great deal of his time and expertise and must, of course, compensate him for it. You'd also pay an honorarium to each of the celebrities he interviews in order to reserve some of their precious time and respect their status. The sums involved would all be decided through delicate negotiation during the proposal stage for the series. Some might do it free out of friendship for the host. You would emphatically *not* pay a politician or other public servant. The correct stance is always predicated by the public perception of your action—do you endanger our trust in your film by paying or not paying? Could payments change what we learned? Are they appropriate in the circumstances?

People in Need

If you film destitute hurricane victims telling your camera what their lives are like or if you show the desperate daily life of an African AIDS sufferer who cannot afford medicine, you'd have the heart of a stone if you didn't give a small sum to help out as you left. If you come from the wealthy First World and your career is being enhanced through portraying suffering in the Third World, the least you can do is compensate those with so little to give but who give it in a generous spirit anyway. Ten dollars is little enough to you but may be a week's income where you are filming. What's significant is that you give it freely afterwards; it is not a precondition for filming.

GOING FURTHER

Whatever issues you face, go to The D-Word Web site at www.d-word.com and expect to find your problem discussed in their extensive archives. It's free, and very welcoming.

PART 7B

ADVANCED PRODUCTION

This part looks into the uses of lenses in relation to the perception of space and perspective, which along with image texture has much to do with the look and impact of photography. There is more of the information a director must know on advanced cameras and sound gear, although more elaborate equipment often means that you direct specialists using it, rather than shooting yourself. There is information on the extra personnel in a larger unit and tips on leadership. Because a director must know how to provide the support and challenges and catalyze telling scenes for the screen, there is a comparison between the psychology of acting and that of being a documentary participant. There is information on coverage and shooting with editing in mind. Most importantly, there is a long chapter on interviewing, such an important part of opening people's stories to the audience.

CHAPTER 25

OPTICS

SPACE AND PERCEPTION

The art of the screen involves compromises made to accommodate the fact that the camera sees in two dimensions instead of three and that its field of view is so limited compared with human visual perception. As you'll see in this chapter, we compensate by compressing more into the frame, arranging composition and lighting to create the illusion of depth, and we cram more into screen time than happens in real life.

 Camera lenses have a limited field of view compared with the human eye. Movie compositions compensate for this by artfully compressing more into each frame.

CAMERA EYE AND HUMAN EYE

The eye of the beholder is misleading, for the human eye takes in a huge field of view (Figure 25-1). Check this out by putting your arms ahead, wiggling your thumbs, then gradually stretching your arms sideways. Looking dead ahead, you should still be able to see your thumbs moving with your arms wide apart. This proves that the human eye has 180 degrees of acceptance, but there's nothing like it in cinema optics. In 16 mm filming, a lens of 10 mm focal length is a wide-angle lens, but shooting in 4:3 aspect ratio,

 Train your eye for lighting and composition by doing **Projects 1-AP-3 Analyze Lighting** and **1-AP-4 Analyze Picture Composition.**

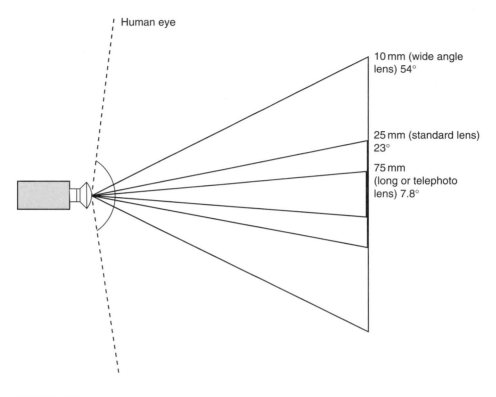

FIGURE 25-1————————————————————————————————————

The human eye's field of vision compared with the much more limited angle of acceptance for 16 mm lenses. Note that vertical angles of acceptance (not shown) are even less, depending on aspect ratio.

it only takes in 54 degrees horizontally and 40 degrees vertically (screen aspect ratios, or height versus width of the image, are explained below).

Understand that a wide-angle lens may have less than a *quarter* of the eye's coverage; this has resounding consequences for dramatic composition. We compensate by rearranging compositions to trick the spectator into seeing the eye's sensation of normal distances and spatial relationships. Characters holding a conversation might stand closer than usual before the camera, yet look normal onscreen. Furniture placement and distances between objects are often "cheated"—that is, moved apart or together to produce the desired appearance onscreen. Even physical movements need adjustment. Someone walking past camera or

 Sometimes you must slow the movement in close-ups so they look normal onscreen.

 "Art is the secret of how to produce by a false thing the effect of a true."—Thomas Hardy (1840–1928), an English novelist

picking up a glass of milk in close-up may have to do it one-third slower if it is to look natural onscreen.

Packing the frame, creating the illusion of depth, and arranging for balance and thematic significance in each composition are all routine compensations for the screen's limited size and tendency to flatten space.

CHOOSING LENSES

PERSPECTIVE

Choosing lenses can seem forbidding, but you don't need a physics degree. Lenses giving the same sense of perspective as the human eye are called *normal*, while departures affecting magnification to either side of normalcy are classified as *wide-angle* or *telephoto*. Analogies from everyday life dramatize the basic differences:

 For each film or video format, a lens that is "normal" is the one that renders foreground and background objects in the same size and relationship as the human eye sees them.

Wide-Angle Lens	Normal Lens	Telephoto Lens
Door security spyglass (diminishes size, makes foreground seem huge compared with background)	The human eye (renders perspective that we consider normal, with foreground sizes relative to background sizes)	Telescope (magnifies and brings everything closer, but compresses foreground and background together)

These domestic devices suggest a range of dramatic possibilities. Compare telescope imagery to that of the security spyglass. The *telescope* brings objects closer; squashes together foreground, middle ground, and background; and isolates the middle-ground object in sharp focus while sending the foreground and background into soft focus. The *security spyglass* brings in a lot of the hallway outside and keeps all in focus, but produces a reduced and distorted image. If your visitor is leaning with one hand on the door, you are likely to see a huge arm diminishing to a tiny, distorted figure in the distance. This exaggerates distance, which is a function of the lens's handling of perspective.

PERSPECTIVE AND NORMALCY

Our sense of perspective comes from knowing the relative sizes of things and thus being able to judge how far apart they are. In a photo with a cat in the foreground and a German shepherd in the background, we judge the distance between them according to their relative sizes. In Figure 25-2 you judge the distance between the foreground and background trucks likewise—by their relative sizes. Many useful lenses, however, depart from this normality. The *focal*

FIGURE 25-2 ————————————————————————————————

Normal lens, where distances appear as the eye sees them.

length of a lens, by the way, is the measurement in millimeters from its optical center to the film plane. Each camera format has its preferred focal length lens for perspective to appear normal:

Format	Focal Length for Normal Lens
8 mm	12.5 mm
16 mm	25 mm
35 mm	50 mm

These are for classic film formats, but those for video image chips (⅓ inch, ⅔ inch, and 1 inch) vary similarly according to target size. There is, as you see, a constant ratio between formats (width of film or image chip in use) and the focal lengths of the lenses. For illustration, the examples that follow discuss only 16 mm-format lenses, whose equivalent you sometimes find (though seldom calibrated) in small-format video cameras. For more on focal length, go to www.dvinfo.net//articles/optics/dofskinny.php.

Normal perspective (Figure 25-2) means the viewer sees an "as-is" size relationship between foreground and background trucks and can accurately judge the distance between them. The same shot taken with a wide-angle lens (Figure 25-3) changes the apparent distance between foreground and background, making it appear greater. A telephoto lens (Figure 25-4) does just the opposite, squeezing foreground and background close together. If someone were to walk from the background truck up to the foreground, the implications of their walk would be dramatically different in the three shots; all would have the same subject, all walks would last the same time, but each lens offers a different dramatic feel.

FIGURE 25-3

Wide-angle lens.

FIGURE 25-4

Telephoto lens, where the foreground to background distances appear different from those in Figures 25-2 and 25-3.

PERSPECTIVE CHANGES WHEN CAMERA-TO-SUBJECT DISTANCE CHANGES

By repositioning the camera and using different lenses, as shown diagrammatically in Figure 25-5, we can standardize the size of the foreground truck, as seen in Figures 25-2, 25-3, and 25-4. Though background distances appear to have changed, the perspective changes actually result from changing the camera-to-subject distance, not from the lens itself.

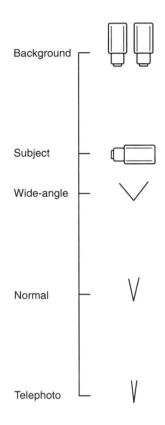

Background

Subject

Wide-angle

Normal

Telephoto

FIGURE 25-5 ————————————————————————————————

Different lenses used from different distances in Figures 25-2, 25-3, 25-4 produced the same size foreground truck but altered the apparent distance to its background. Perspective changes when you alter the camera to subject distance, not because you change lenses.

Now examine Figures 25-6, 25-7, and 25-8. Each is taken with a different lens but from the same camera position. The proportion of the stop sign in relation to the background portico is identical in all three. Perspective (size proportions between planes) has not changed; we simply have three different magnifications. So, we have confirmed that indeed perspective is the product of camera-to-subject distance, for when this remains constant, proportions between foreground and background remain constant, too—even though the image was shot through three different lenses (that is, with three different degrees of magnification).

 Perspective changes result from changing the camera-to-subject distance, not from the lens itself. What you notice about images from a telephoto lens results from being far away and from the depth of field (that is, planes in focus) being shallow.

FIGURE 25-6 ——

Wide-angle lens.

FIGURE 25-7 ——

Normal lens.

LENSES AND IMAGE TEXTURE

Compare Figures 25-6 and 25-8. The backgrounds are very different in texture. Although the subject is in focus in both, the telephoto version—by putting the rest of the image in soft focus—isolates and separates the subject from both its foreground and background. This is because the telephoto lens has a very limited *depth of field* (DOF), with only its point of focus being sharp. Conversely, a wide-angle lens (Figures 25-3 and 25-6) allows deep focus. This is useful if you want to hold focus while someone walks from foreground to background. Deep

FIGURE 25-8————————————————————————————

Telephoto lens. This shot and Figures 25-6 and 25-7 are taken from a common camera position. Notice that the stop sign remains in the same proportion to its background throughout.

focus distracts, however, if it drowns its middle-ground subject in a plethora of irrelevantly sharp background and foreground detail. This has been the characteristic "video" look. Telephotos have a soft-textured background, while the wide-angle shot has one that is hard.

 Depth of field (DOF) refers to the depth before the point of focus, and behind it, in which objects are in acceptable focus. Wide-angle lenses have deep DOF; telephotos have shallow DOF.

LENS SPEED

This deceptive term concerns a lens's light admittance and has nothing to do with movement. A fast lens is one that lets in much light, making it good for low-light photography. A slow lens admits less light. Wide-angles, by their inherent design, tend to be fast (with a widest aperture, say, of $f1.4$), while telephotos tend to be slow (perhaps $f2.8$). In practice this means that, with a two-stop advantage, the wide-angle might give an acceptable exposure at one-quarter the light the telephoto would need. In practical terms, night shooting might be viable with one lens and out of the question with another. Prime (that is, fixed) lenses, having

 For all lenses, DOF increases if you use a small lens aperture (high f-number) and decreases if you use a larger aperture (smaller f-numbers).

 Lens characteristics can either be limiting or have great dramatic utility, depending on how you go about using them.

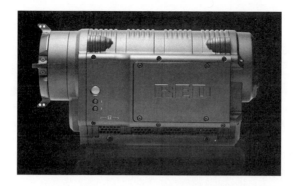

FIGURE 25-9

The RED ONE™ modular digital camera in its basic form and fully equipped. (Photos courtesy of Red Digital Cinema.)

few elements, tend to be faster than zooms, which are multi-element. Primes also tend to have better acuity, or sharpness, because the image passes through fewer optics. The state-of-the-art RED ONE™ modular digital camera (Figure 25-9; *www.red.com*) uses 35 mm lenses and behaves like the feature-film camera it really is, but with none of the bulk.

CONTROLLING THE LOOK

MANIPULATING PERSPECTIVE

Using the magnifying or diminishing effect of different lenses allows us to place the camera differently and yet produce three similar shots (see Figures 25-2, 25-3, and 25-4); when the camera-to-subject distance changes, we can manipulate perspective. Wide-angle lenses appear to increase distance; telephoto lenses appear to compress it.

ZOOMING VERSUS DOLLYING

A zoom is a lens having infinite variability between its extremes (say 10 to 100 mm, which is a zoom with a ratio of 10:1). As we have said, if you keep the camera static and zoom in on a subject, the image is magnified but perspective does not alter. When you dolly in close with a prime (fixed) lens, however, the image is magnified, and you see a perspective change during the move, just as in life. Dollying is movement with a perspective change, zooming is magnification without a change of perspective. By the way, avoid lenses whose image size changes when you alter focus.

GETTING A FILM LOOK

Film stocks and video used to yield differing image aesthetics, but with the more sophisticated high-definition cameras and the control they allow over image black pedestal, contrast, and hue characteristics, it's increasingly difficult to tell which was used. In the latest postproduction software you also have a high degree of control over contrast, gamma (black levels), and color saturation (color intensity).

Differences between film and video images also arise from the relative sizes of each camera's image-collecting area. A film close-up of a man in a park will show his face in sharp focus, but the background and foreground will be agreeably soft. Using selective focus like this helps isolate the subject by sharpness as well as by framing. The same close-up shot with a video camera often has foreground, middle-ground, and background all in similar degrees of focus, and the eye is deluged with detail. Why?

At the root of these differences is the lens's DOF. A 35 mm camera aperture is much larger than most video imaging chips. The larger image size requires more refraction (bending of light through the lens), and the net result is less DOF—that is, less acceptable focus behind and in front of the subject at the focus point. Were you to look at the image produced by a nineteenth-century plate camera, you'd see that because the imaging area is huge, the eyes may be in focus but the nose is out of focus! Now look at the results from a family 8 mm film camera, with its tiny image area. Refraction is so minimal that in daylight hardly anything is ever out of focus.

To emulate the restricted DOF of the 35 mm film camera lens with your camcorder, you can always shoot off a tripod and use the telephoto end of your lens. This will isolate the subject from foreground and background planes, but camera movements must have steady handling, and of course you cannot handhold. Alternatively, you can use an optical attachment such as the P+S Technik's

FIGURE 25-10——————————————————————————————

The P+S Technik Mini35 adapter, which enables the videographer to realize all the depth of field and other qualities of a 35mm film lens. (Photo courtesy of P+S Technik GmbH.)

Mini35 Digital Adapter (Figure 25-10). Using a two-stage optical operation, the adapter accepts different 35 mm lenses to produce an internal image that is then projected into the video camera's imaging path. Now you have the focal length, DOF, and angle of view of the 35 mm format. At a stroke, the videographer has the lens choice and control of the feature film cinematographer. To see which cameras it fits, go to www.pstechnik.de/en/index.php.

COMPOSITION STUDY

The best way to learn composition is to study the work of master photographers—those who produced stills and those who shot for striking documentary or fiction films. How work is composed and how further dimensions can be added during editing are fascinating studies that you can purse in **Project 1-AP-4 Analyze Picture Composition.**

GOING FURTHER

In addition to equipment manuals, consider carrying the *American Cinematographer's Video Manual*, edited by Michael Grotticelli (2005, American Cinematographer) to answer technical questions that come up. The Digital Information Network at www.dvinfo.net is an excellent video technology information site. For image control information, see Gerald Hirschfeld and Julia Tucker's *Image Control: Motion Picture and Video Camera Filters and Lab Techniques* (2005, ASC Press).

CHAPTER 26

ADVANCED CAMERAS AND EQUIPMENT

How your film looks and how to shoot it involves equipment choices. You may want to review basic information in **Chapter 9, Basic Camera Equipment**. As you will see from this chapter, there are currently many video standards and a bewildering array of equipment from which to choose. The higher you ascend in terms of recording quality, the costlier production becomes, but the more marketable your work may become in the future. This doesn't mean, however, that you cannot make significant work inexpensively—only that it's wise to match the medium, material, and market. You can shoot the inside scoop on hazing in the military with the lowest grade camcorder, but anything spectacular like *Winged Migration* merits the best imaging possible. It's a question of what audiences expect.

ARCHIVING ISSUES

Film still captures the highest quality image and is also, paradoxically, the only moving image medium to have physically endured for 100 years. Over time many old acetate-based films turn to dust (when they don't explode), and modern film stocks, though no longer flammable, shrink and their color dyes fade over time. Three-strip dye transfer Technicolor®—now discontinued—is the only medium in which the original color is fully recoverable.

Media stored on high-quality magnetic tape or disk have a relatively long life, perhaps as long as 30 to 50 years, while optical media like DVD and CD are unproven and even unpromising. Pressed disks have a longer life than the ones you burn yourself, which are deteriorating

 Archiving your work presents problems, because everything shot on a film, magnetic, or optical medium deteriorates over time. To know how fast, follow latest discussions in informed circles.

even before you use them and may then only remain readable for 2 to 5 years. The chemical surfaces of discount disks are often so unstable that they become unreadable within weeks or months. Use the best rated disks, and every few years recopy in triplicate anything that you mean to store over time. You will also probably be updating to a new recording standard. For up-to-date information, follow the discussions online.

EQUIPMENT CAUTIONS

GETTING OVERLY ELABORATE

At production meetings, keep lists during discussions so you can research costs before committing yourself. Often, knowledgeable people can suggest simpler, less elaborate ways of getting what you want. Less experienced crew members sometimes try to forestall problems by wanting the "proper" equipment—usually the most expensive. Do you really need three lighting kits and a Steadicam®? True, sophisticated equipment in experienced hands saves time and money and can give wonderful results. But when the person requesting it is using your production to accrue experience, expect long and exasperating delays during shooting.

 Sound personnel know they must often solve unexpected coverage problems at short notice and so need backup equipment for other eventualities.

The sound department often wants a suspiciously large inventory, but this is more justified. When plans change, sound personnel must solve unexpected coverage problems and must be ready for all eventualities. Their backup equipment is probably a wise precaution.

 Pay close attention to software and camera manufacturers' warnings about using associated equipment. Many standards are not compatible.

INCOMPATIBILITY

When a software or camera manufacturer recommends particular associated equipment, follow recommendations assiduously. Some warnings follow.

Planning

- Know and understand each production stage's process.
- Cross-check to find definitive answers before you commit to using particular equipment and methods. Seek specific advice from those who have done what you want to do, and follow it to the letter. Don't reinvent the wheel.
- When possible, stay with a single manufacturer's gear throughout production. If you mix and match equipment, manufacturers are apt to blame breakdowns on the other guy's equipment.

Shooting

- Digital tapes shot on different manufacturers' equipment may not wind up having identical recording specifications or interface properly with other equipment.

- Shooting 24 fps under 50-Hz lighting (especially fluorescents) in Europe or 25 fps under 60-Hz American current will lead to a slow, pulsing illumination effect on-screen. This is because the lighting pulses and the camera frame rates are slightly out of step. If you detect it in the video viewfinder, try different camera shutter-speed settings. You won't see the effect through a film camera eyepiece—but you will see it on-screen, when it's too late.

- If you plan to shoot in non-native format (say, PAL in America or NTSC in Europe), run tests to prove that your equipment and its chargers can meet all likely situations.

Postproduction

- If you edit in PAL in an NTSC country, don't forget the multi-standard players and recorders you'll need. You may, for instance, have a problem transferring 25-fps sound to your otherwise 30-fps editing system.

- Make a roundup of all materials you can possibly need in your postproduction workflow. Integrating the different frame rates, aspect ratios, and video compression codecs can spring produce massive problems on the unwary. See Part 5 and Part 7C for postproduction book references.

DIGITAL ACQUISITION

Digital television has spawned an explosion of competing formats and compression codecs. To decide what format to shoot in, you'll need to research where your final product is aimed and what costs are involved. Googling key words will bring up any number of excellent, detailed explanations. For starters, try www. howstuffworks.com/hdtv.htm. Many cameras, such as the Panasonic® AG-HVX200 (Figure 26-1), work across a range of formats and dispense with tape in favor of recording on P2 plug-in, solid-state memory cards (Figure 26-2). What's available can be bewildering, so following are some salient features, beginning with support equipment.

 Whatever equipment you consider, research professional opinion and experience with extreme care before committing yourself.

 If you need to make controlled camera movements, use the best camera support equipment you can afford.

FIGURE 26-1 ————————————————————————————————————

Panasonic® AG-HVX200 camcorder with one of its two memory cards halfway removed. (Photo courtesy of Panasonic Corp.)

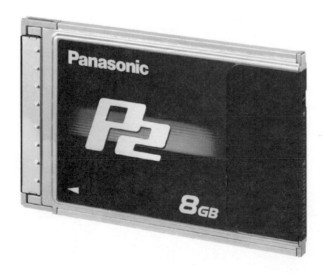

FIGURE 26-2 ————————————————————————————————————

A P2 plug-in, solid-state memory card—no more cassettes, no more real-time download-ing. (Photo courtesy of Panasonic Corp.)

CAMERA SUPPORT

TRIPOD AND PAN/TILT HEAD

Arri, Sachtler, and O'Connor make excellent tripods, but others are less expensive. Be sure the tripod has spikes, not rubber feet alone, because you need a positive engagement with the ground (Figure 26-3). For a superior tripod, look for one that:

- Is made of carbon fiber rather than metal—it's lighter if you are trekking in the wild.

- Can handle a camera 30% heavier than the one you're planning to use—get one that is too small, and it will be flimsy; get one too large, and it will weigh you down.

- Has a tilt head with ball leveling—this allows you to instantly adjust the head according to a bubble level (Figure 26-4).

- Is equipped with a pan and tilt head having a fluid drag, not a friction substitute.

- Has a quick-release plate that you attach to the underside of your camera (Figure 26-5)—this lets you instantly dismount the camera and go handheld.

- Has a carry case and a spreader to go under your "legs," or tripod (Figure 26-6 and Figure 26-7).

- Comes with a baby legs (low tripod, Figure 26-8) and hi-hat or sandbag for low-angle camera support

FIGURE 26-3 ───

Spike feet on a Bogen® tripod ensure a positive engagement with the ground. Rubber feet are kind to floors but allow a sponginess that compromises telephoto shots.

FIGURE 26-4 ──────────────────────────────────

Leveling is quick when your tripod has a ball head.

FIGURE 26-5 ──────────────────────────────────

Quick-release plate mounted on underside of camera.

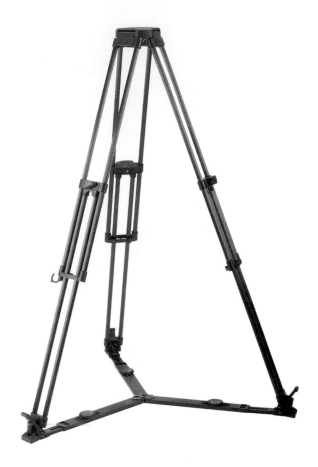

FIGURE 26-6

A light carbon fiber tripod and spreader. For quick relocations, pick up the whole unit, camera and all. (Photo courtesy of Vinten, a Vitec Group brand.)

CAMERA BODY

The columns in the Fletcher Camera comparison chart (Figure 26-9) allow you to compare cameras. Evidently some camera bodies designed for electronic newsgathering (ENG) sit on the shoulder and are ideal for documentary. Others must either be tripod mounted or held in front of one's body. These require a shoulder brace for long duty when shooting handheld. Others, most notably the Arricam ST 16mm film camera included for comparison, are top-heavy and designed to sit on a camera support such as a tripod.

IMAGER

This column displays the various types of image sensing. CMOS (complementary metal–oxide semiconductor) chips are replacing CCD (charge-coupled device) chips whose cameras use a beam splitter. This optically divides incoming light

FIGURE 26-7

Using a spreader can mean safety. Videographer Martin Gremmelspacher and his director, Martin Biebel, are above Moon Valley, Atacama Desert, in Chile awaiting a golden sunset that never materialized. (Photo courtesy of Vinten, a Vitec Group brand.)

between three CCD image chips, each sensing a different complementary color. They must be in alignment, and each gets only one-third of available light, so the cameras are relatively light-hungry. A single CMOS chip (see Figure 26-10) replaces all of this.

LENS MOUNT

The more expensive cameras permit interchangeable lenses, and this column shows the lens mount type.

FIGURE 26-8

Baby legs for low-angle shots. (Photo courtesy of Vinten, a Vitec Group brand.)

IMAGER SAMPLING

This gives the number of pixels (picture cells) generated by the imager—more being better because the image contains more information. See "Pixels" section below.

DIGITAL SAMPLING ON RECORDING MEDIA

Some cameras can record uncompressed or raw data; all offer forms of compression that reduce the amount of digital information flow to more manageable proportions. See "Codecs for Picture Compression" section below.

BASE ASA

A fairly sensitive film stock might have a 500 ASA rating, while a slower (less sensitive) one might rate at 125 ASA. Giving a digital video camera these ratings suggests how it handles low-light filming. Video cameras have gain controls that amplify a low video signal so you can still shoot (with some image degradation) under tiny amounts of illumination.

DYNAMIC RANGE (LATITUDE)

Latitude refers to the difference in stops between the least and the most light in which the imaging system can still register detail. Notice that some film stocks

312-932-2700 Chicago - **FLETCHER CAMERA** - Detroit 248-505-6127

Updated: 11/11/2008 5:29 PM

Imager	Lens Mount	Imager Sampling	Digital Sampling on Recording Media	Base ASA	Dynamic Range	Frame Rates Progressive Only	Recording Format and Load Time	Bit Depth Recorded	Weight Lbs.	Power Draw	VF	Highlighted Positives	Average National Rental
Phantom HD — Single >S35 CMOS	Film PL	2048 × 2048	2048 × 2048 Uncompressed RAW or Selectable Lower	600	10 Stops	5-1052p @ 1920x1080	32G Internal RAM 6m10s @ 24f 60s @150f 30s@300f 8.9s@1000f	14 Bit	12 lbs.	80w	Color	High Speed Capability / Uncompressed RAW / Full Sized Imager / Wide Latitude / Compact Size	$5000 Camera with 2 Cine Mags
Sony F23 — Three 2/3" CCD	Video B4	1920 × 1080	1920 × 1080	320	11-12 Stops	1-60p 4:4:4 (Docked) 1-30p 4:4:4 1-60p 4:2:2 (Undocked)	HDCAM SR 50 Min	10 bit	29 lbs. Docked 11 lbs. Camera Only	106w Docked	Color	Established Workflow / 4:4:4 Color Sampling / Wide Latitude	$3300 with SRW-1 and SRPC-1
Arri D-21 w/ Fiber — Single S35 mm CMOS	Film PL	3018 × 2200	2880 × 2160 Uncompressed ARRIRAW 1920 × 1080 HDCAM SR	200 up to 800	10 Stops	20-60p 4:2:2 20-30p 4:4:4 20-25p RAW	ARRIRAW s.two- d.mag 48 min HDCAM SR 50 min	12 Bit ARRIRAW s.two 10 bit HDCAM SR	16 lbs. Camera 18 lbs. VTR	60w 56w SRW-1 VTR	Optical	4:4:4 4:2:2 and/or RAW Optical Viewfinder S35 mm Imager Allows: - Anamorphic lenses - See outside frame lines - 35 mm Depth of Field	$3000 with SRW-1 and SRPC-1 or S.two
Red one — Single S35 mm CMOS	Film PL	4520 × 2540	2K 3K 4K	320	10 Stops	1-30p @4K 1-60p @3K 1-120p @2K	RedDrive 120 min RedFlash (8GB) 4.5 mins Red-Ram 60 min	12 bit	9 lbs. Camera Only	65 W	Color	Cost vs. Performance S35 mm Imager Allows: - See outside frame lines - 35 mm Depth of Field	$1,200 with Six 8GB Cards
Panasonic HPX-3000 — Three 2/3" CCD	Video B4	1920 × 1080	1920 × 1080	500	10 Stops AVC-I 9 Stops DVCPRO	24p, 25p 30p	5 - P2 Cards AVC-I 100 DVCPRO HD 100 min[1]	10 bit AVC-I 8 Bit DVCPRO	10.5 lbs	43w	B&W	"HD D5" Quality 4:2:2 Color Sampling Full 1920x1080 Cost vs. Performance w/P2 proven workflow	$1,100 with Five 16GB Cards
Sony HDW-F900 — Three 2/3" CCD	Video B4	1920 × 1080	1440 × 1080	320	F900R 9 Stops F900/3 9 Stops F900/2 7.5 Stops	24p, 25p 30p	HDCAM 50 Min	8 bit	F900R 12 lbs. F900/3 17.6 lbs F900/2 17.6 lbs	F900R 34w F900/3 42w F900/2 42w	B&W or Color	Industry Workhorse Proven Easy Workflow	F9C0R $1200 F900/3 $1100 F900/2 $950

FLETCHER CAMERA - Detroit 248-505-6127 · 312-932-2700 Chicago · Updated: 11/11/2008 5:29 PM

Model	Imager	Lens Mount	Imager Sampling	Digital Sampling on Recording Media	Base ASA	Dynamic Range	Frame Rates Progressive Listed Only	Recording Format and Load Time	Bit Depth Recorded	Weight Lbs.	Power Draw	VF	Highlighted Positives	Average National Rental
 Panasonic HPX-2000	Three 2/3" CCD	Video B4	1280 × 720	1280 x 720 AVC-I / 960 × 720 DVCPRO	500	10 Stops AVC / 9 Stops DVCPRO	24p, 25p 30p, 50p, 60p	5 - P2 Cards AVC-I / DVCPRO 100 min⁻¹	10 bit AVC-I / 8 Bit DVCPRO	10 lbs.	43w	B&W Color	HD D-5 quality @ relatively low data and rental rates Also Record 1080	$700 w/ five 16GB Cards
 Panasonic Varicam	Three 2/3" CCD	Video B4	1920 × 720	960 × 720	640 Video Rec / 320 Film Rec	9 Stops	4-60p	DVCPRO HD 32 min	8 bit	16.8 lbs	36w	B&W	Variable Frame Industry Workhorse	$800
 Panasonic HDX-900	Three 2/3" CCD	Video B4	1280 × 720	960 × 720	500	9 Stops	24p, 25p 30p, 50p, 60p	DVCPRO HD 32 min	8 bit	16.7 lbs	36w	B&W Color	Cost	$600
 Sony PMW-EX1	Three 1/2" CMOS	FIXED Cannot Change Lenses	1920 × 1080	1920 × 1080 / 1280 × 720	800	7 Stops	1-60p fps @ 720 / 1-30p fps @ 1080	2 - SxS Cards 100 min	8 bit	6.2 lbs	13w	Color + Color Flipout LCD	Cost 1/2" Imager Full 1920 × 1080 imager and recording	$375 w/two 16 GB cards
 Panasonic HVX-200	Three 1/3" CCD	FIXED Cannot Change Lenses	960 × 540	960 × 720 Using Pixel Shifting	320	7 Stops	6p, 12p, 18p, 20p, 22p, 26p, 30p, 32p, 36p 48p, 60p	2 - P2 Cards 80 min	8 bit	5.3 lbs	14w	B&W	Cost P2 Workflow Most Established Tapeless Workflow	$375 w/two 16GB cards
 for comparison Arricam ST	Single S35 mm Kodak 5219 Vision 3	Film PL	Not Applicable	1920 × 1080 2K 4K 6K Uncompressed	500	14 Stops	1- 60p	3 Perforation 5m55s 400' 14m48s 1000' / 4 Perforation 4m26s 400' 11m 06s 1000'	16 bit (Linear) / 10 bit (log)	25 lbs 400' / 28 lbs 1000'	55w	Optical	Established Workflow Excessive Latitude Proven Archival Value	$2,000 w/2 Mags

Copyright Fletcher Camera 2008 Subject to Correction - Please notify us of any mistakes

FIGURE 26-9

HD 24p camera comparison chart. (Courtesy of Fletcher Camera, Chicago; check www.fletch.com for the latest version.)

FIGURE 26-10 ————————————————————————————————————

CMOS imaging chip. (Photo courtesy of Samsung.)

can hold detail over a 14-stop latitude—twice the latitude of the least evolved digital camera in the chart. The Sony® F23 camera, with 11 to 12 stops of latitude, is snapping at film's heels.

FRAME RATES

Many high-definition (HD) digital cameras now offer variable speed filming so you can speed up action such as clouds passing overhead or slow down vehicle crash tests. The "p" after a number stands for "progressive scan" and means that, unlike television formats that construct each frame from two interlaced frames (odd lines, then even), progressive scan lays down all the information for a frame in a single pass. Fast motion and progressive HD scanning produce a torrent of digital information, so many cameras employ a higher compression codec for the faster frame rates. 24 fps is the standard cinema frame rate; for television, 25 fps is European speed, and 30 fps North American. The cinema frame rate was originally 16 fps but was raised to 24 fps for sound projection; the European and American frame rates are derived from the hertz (cycles per second) of their prevailing electricity supplies (50 Hz, 60 Hz), which in turn dictated television receivers' frame rates. See "Frame Rates" section below.

RECORDING FORMAT AND LOAD TIME

This lists the camera's storage medium and maximum run time before it requires a reload. Notice how run time declines with reduced compression or increased frames per second. All listed cameras record progressive scan, and this permits easier transfer to film for cinema showing. The industry is rapidly moving toward tapeless recording, which means that cameras and recorders have fewer moving parts. *Flash memory* is a form of digital memory that, once activated, requires no power to maintain its storage. See "Codecs for Picture Compression" section below.

BIT DEPTH RECORDED

This refers to the number of bits (units of digital information) used to represent each pixel's color and tonal range. More is better.

WEIGHT

Listed camera weights range from 5.3 to 29 lbs, with the ENG workhorse cameras ranging between 10 and 18 lbs.

POWER DRAW

This rating in watts (a range of 13 to 106 watts for the given cameras) lets you estimate how many batteries you need per working day and what power or recharging arrangements you may have to make.

VIEWFINDER (VF)

This specifies the viewfinder (not the LCD flip-out screen, if the camera has one). Many viewfinders will display *zebra* highlight stripes. These, known colloquially from their appearance as "marching ants," warn the operator that areas of highlight are burning out through overexposure. Often you can set the threshold where zebra stripes start to display; this matters because this is your only reliable warning, viewfinders being unreliable for this. See http://thedvshow.com/faq-pro/?action=article&cat_id=002&id=2&lang= for a movie illustration.

HIGHLIGHTED POSITIVES

These are the camera's most valued features. 1080p represents a high pixel rate. Variable frame means you can set the camera's fps setting and shoot fast or slow motion. A P2 is a flash memory (Figure 26-2) that permits tapeless workflow, but notice that "established workflow" implies there are *un*established workflows—to be shunned like the plague. 4:4:4 refers to the highest possible chroma (color) sampling. Most professional cameras sample at 4:2:2. Raw data is data that is uncompressed in any way and necessarily humungous in quantity.

 The film camera is bow-and-arrow technology but still has reliability, latitude, archival value, and established workflow on its side.

AVERAGE NATIONAL RENTAL

This dollar amount is a useful starting point for budget calculations. Often you can hire a basic shooting package, but hiring equipment is not simple and quick like hiring a car. Read the hire house's terms extremely carefully long in advance of hiring, since you'll need to satisfy, among other things, their credit conditions and apply for

1.33:1 or 4:3 ratio (Early cinema and standard definition TV format)

1.85:1 or 16:9 ratio (High definition television format)

2.4:1 ratio (35 mm anamorphic cinema format)

FIGURE 26-11

Three common picture aspect ratios.

equipment insurance coverage. Both take time to arrange. For typical conditions, see those of Fletcher Camera at www.fletch.com/termsandconditions.html. The good news is that a week's hire is normally computed as three times the daily rate.

SETTINGS AND OPTIONS

ASPECT RATIO

This expresses the width of the frame in relation to its height, which has changed during screen history (Figure 26-11). The aspect ratio and video format you choose will have consequences for equipment and postproduction processes and even how you shoot, since the wider screen demands that you compose a little differently. The cinema and television ratio was traditionally 4:3—that is, a screen of four units wide by three units high. In the 1950s, cinema adopted various widescreen formats (1.85:1, 2.35:1, 2.39:1, 2.55:1). For a short illustrated history, see www.dvdaust.com/aspect.htm. HD video at 16:9 approximates the cinema format of 1.85:1 and is the preferred aspect ratio for HD television. Consumer camcorders mimic this format by using the middle of the imaging chip, leaving an ugly black band of unused video top and bottom. The picture you are left with has fewer *pixels* (individual picture cells, Figure 26-12), more grain, and more *artifacts* (jagged lines or *jaggies* in the image where there should be straight, sharp edges, as shown in Figure 26-13).

 Aspect ratio affects how you compose shots and even how you cover sequences. Widescreen favors horizontal compositions, but when you have vertical ones, think of incorporating camera movements.

As HDTV takes over, 1.33:1 is disappearing. Inherently wide pictorial matter, such as landscape shots and anything making horizontal movement, fills the screen

FIGURE 26-12 ————————————————————————————————————

Artifacts or "jaggies" in a magnified digital image.

FIGURE 26-13

Picture elements (pixels) enlarged.

more satisfactorily. Vertical pictorial matter such as head shots and tall buildings are more difficult to accommodate, but everyone feels that widescreen allows for more interesting filming on balance. The world's archives, however, remain mostly 1.33:1, so postproduction must either show it with black bands at the sides or, content permitting, magnify the original and pare slices from the top and bottom.

FRAME RATES

Because of differing electrical supplies, American analog NTSC (National Television System Committee, who years ago formulated television standards) runs at 30 fps, and the European PAL (Phase Alternating Line) system runs at 25 fps. Which you normally use depends on where you live. NTSC constructs each of its 30 fps from two "i" (interlaced) fields. PAL does the same but records 25i, which in practice is compatible with film's 24p recording. As noted earlier, the "p" stands for "progressive scan," meaning each frame is recorded progressively and in its entirety, rather than being cobbled together from odd and even interlaced frames. Many camcorders now offer variable frame rates so you can over- or under-crank to achieve slow or fast motion at the camera level. Postproduction software allows you to slow footage or speed it up, too, although slowing action footage shot at 1/50th shutter speed is often marred by blurring.

PIXELS

More pixels means more *picture elements* and thus finer detail. Take the standard-definition (SD) NTSC 720 × 480 image: it contains 720 pixels per line and 480 horizontal lines per frame. Its high-definition (HD) siblings do far better and rival 35 mm film in acuity. Video currently used in North America comes in three main formats:

- 1080 24p HD, which records 1920 pixels × 1080 lines at 24p and transfers to film straightforwardly

- 1080i HD, which records 1920 pixels × 1080 lines at 30i
- 720p EDV (enhanced-definition video), which records 1280 pixels × 720 lines at 30i

Enhanced-definition video is currently favored by cable companies because it makes less stringent demands on their transmission systems. Cameras using 720p and 1080i commonly use widely available and inexpensive mini-DV tapes. The trend is to get rid of tape and its associated transport systems and to record straight into P2 memory cards or portable hard drives. Soon you can rejoice in using a camera having almost no moving parts.

 Tapeless workflow is replacing cassettes, which means camcorders with few moving parts.

CODECS FOR PICTURE COMPRESSION

When each frame has more pixels and more lines, your camera, postproduction equipment, and television transmitters all have to process a torrent of digital information. Because much of the information in each new frame repeats what was in the last, engineers have invented compression codecs that, like shorthand, reduce what must be written to the recording medium. A high-compression, "lossy codec," however, will visibly intrude its economies onto the screen, particularly during image movement. For examples and further explanation, see www.cybercollege.com/tvp047.htm. For sound codecs, see the next chapter.

 A *codec* is a formula used by digital equipment to reduce the duplicate video or audio information it makes while recording and thus to make better use of restricted memory.

SHUTTER SPEED

Shutter speed is an old term, left over from photography. It signifies the time during which a digital camera records one full image. Because of interlaced video's 60-fps shooting speed, you can normally shoot a shutter speed of no slower (that is, longer) than 1/60th of a second, but you can select faster shutter speeds—of up to 1/1000th second or faster. When you see whirling helicopter blades that are sharp and moving in an odd, jerky movement, it's because the camera used a fast shutter speed. From cinema feature films we are accustomed to seeing the slight motion blur you get in material shot at 1/50th second or so. If, however, you plan to slow down a racehorse in postproduction, then you must first shoot using a fast shutter speed to get a crisp image.

 Cinema's customary slow shutter speed has accustomed us to slight motion blur during fast action.

TIMECODE

In NTSC you must make a choice concerning *timecode* (TC), the unique time identity assigned to each video frame (Figure 26-14). In NTSC (apocryphally "Never The Same Color") you must choose timecode that is either *drop frame* (DF) or *non-drop frame* (NDF).

Drop frame removes a digit every so often to keep timecode in step with clock time. Whether you choose DF or NDF doesn't usually matter so long as you stay consistent throughout production. Try to use a camcorder with *addressable timecode* (meaning you can set your own starting numbers and letters) so it always writes unique timecode.

Some camcorders reset to zero when you change recording media, with the result that every media item (cassette, hard drive, flash memory) has the same range of numbers, leaving fertile ground for confusion during

 Beware of mixing dropframe (DF) recording with non-drop frame (NDF) recording in your workflow.

7/22/08 9:46 AM

FIGURE 26-14 ——————————————————————————

Timecode—every frame has its own identity number. Generated by the camera, they are vital to an editing program's functioning.

postproduction. Use addressable TC to write a new hour number for each new tape or other media so you have no duplicate numbers to confuse the editing process later.

MATTE BOX, FILTERS, LENS HOOD

If your camcorder allows, fit a *matte box* so you can mount filters professionally in front of the lens (Figure 26-15). Chrosziel and other manufacturers make kits for popular camcorders that include lens hoods, which shade the lens from off-axis light. Absent a matte box, carry filters of the right size to screw onto the front of your lens, such as color conversion #85, #80A, neutral density .3 and .6, graduated neutral density for cooling a hot sky, fog or diffusion filters, and a polarizing filter to reduce surface glare if you plan to shoot over water or certain metal surfaces.

CAMERA AESTHETICS

CAMERA HEIGHT

Directors often accept the tripod as a given and fail to alter camera height. The old adage says that a high camera position suggests domination and a low angle, subjugation, but there are other, less colonial reasons to vary camera height. A high or low camera angle may better accommodate objects or persons in either background or foreground, or may facilitate a particular camera movement. In *On Screen Directing* (1984, Focal Press), the veteran Hollywood director Edward Dmytryk

FIGURE 26-15 ──────────────────────────────────────

Camcorder fitted with a matte box able to carry a range of filters. Notice the movable flag, used to block any strong light arriving at a tangent from hitting the lens. (Photo courtesy of Chrosziel GmbH.)

made a persuasive case for avoiding shots at characters' eye levels simply because they are dull. There's also a psychological reason to avoid them. At eye level, the audience feels itself intruding into the action, rather like standing in the path of a duel. Being a little above or below eye-level position gets us out of the firing line.

ADAPTING TO LOCATION EXIGENCIES

There are no reliable rules for camera positioning and movement because every situation imposes its own demands. Limitations are usually physical: windows or pillars in an interior that restrict shooting in one direction or an incongruity you must avoid in an exterior. A Victorian house turns out to have a background of aerial power lines and must be shot from a high angle to reduce sky. Often you must shelve your expectations and redirect energy into solving the unforeseen. For the rigid, linear personality, this constant adapting is frustrating, but for others it poses interesting and never-ending challenges. Nonetheless, you must plan, and sometimes plans even work out.

 Filming is never less than serendipitous—you are always improvising, always tackling the unforeseen.

BACKGROUNDS

Deciding what part background must play in relation to foreground is an issue of lens choice and camera positioning. For a depressed and hungry character there is a nice irony in showing a huge Ronald McDonald watching her from behind a bus stop. The composition highlights her dilemma and suggests she might blow her bus money on an order of large fries. Sometimes the subject is in the middle ground as in Figure 26-16, where a man looks into the abyss of a giant canyon. The foreground tree branches and the misty depths in the distance help create the third dimension, which is missing from two-dimensional imagery; you use composition, lighting, or perspective to create it.

CAMERA AS INSTRUMENT OF REVELATION

Shots should reveal not just the subject but also the subject's context. Looking down on the subject, looking up at it, or peering between tree trunks all suggest different contexts and different ways of seeing—and therefore of experiencing—the action central to the scene. You could use dialectical editing to make us see that ugly riot police are near a nice bed of tulips, but how much more effective to make the point in a single well-composed frame. Aim to make every frame you shoot contain significant juxtapositions. This will build irony and dramatic tension into every aspect of your filmmaking.

Making the location a meaningful environment and responding to the actions and sightlines of participants in a scene create a more

  Develop your skills and ideas through **Project 1-AP-4 Picture Composition** and then see how compositions add together through **Project 1-AP-6 Analyze Editing and Content.**

FIGURE 26-16 ——————————————————————————————————————

Compositional elements and textures in foreground, middle ground, and background help create the all-important sense of depth.

vivid, spontaneous sense of the scene's unfolding dynamics. Why? Because that way we share the consciousness of someone intelligent and intuitive who picks up all the contextual tensions and ironies.

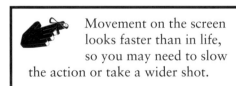 Movement on the screen looks faster than in life, so you may need to slow the action or take a wider shot.

COMPROMISES FOR THE CAMERA

Movement within a frame can look 20 to 30% faster than in life, so you may need to ask participants to slow their movements when shooting action sequences, especially in close-up shots. Even the best camera operator cannot keep a profile in tight framing if the person moves too fast.

How much should you compromise participants' spontaneity to achieve a visually and choreographically polished result? This, of course, depends on the comfort of those you are filming. Sometimes you can ask for changes; other times you'll have to loosen the shot (that is, go wider).

Occasionally, when panning across a repetitive pattern such as a picket fence, you must vary the speed of the camera movement to stop the subject *strobing*. This happens because the frequency of the railings' movement interacts with the camera's frame rate. This is how they won the West with wagon wheels that appeared to turn backwards on the screen. Film camera operators of the day could not see strobing, but those using today's video cameras can. Sometimes patterns in clothing, such as stripes or checks, will cause similar stroboscopic effects.

PRODUCTION STILLS

Carry a digital stills camera so you can shoot high points during your production. Remember to set a policy so everyone knows to freeze on command. Stills should relay the subject and the film's approach, and you'll need at least one superb shot that will make an alluring poster. Compositions should epitomize relationships, thematic issues, the personalities of the participants, and any exotic or alluring situations that might draw audience members into watching. You'll need this when you prepare a publicity package for festivals and prospective distributors.

Persuading people to see your film at a festival is a challenge, so consider equipping yourself with attractive postcards with a promotional still, a brief description of the film's subject, and spaces for place, date, and time. These you press into people's hands as you lock eyes and say, "I hope I'll see you at my film showing." As the occasional target of this technique, I can tell you it works.

PEOPLE AND EQUIPMENT MAINTAINENCE

Something or someone is bound to need mending on location, so plan to bring:

- Equipment manuals, downloaded if necessary from manufacturers' Web sites
- Information on places to hire equipment or get repairs done nearest to the location, especially when abroad
- Basic repair and maintenance tools, such as flashlight, screwdrivers, hex key and socket sets, pliers, wire, solder and soldering iron, and an electrical test meter for continuity and other testing
- A compass for checking the sun's orientation during location spotting
- A radio to check news and weather reports
- Spare batteries for everything that uses them
- Extra cables, which commonly break down where the cable enters the plug body
- Sunblock cream for working outdoors, diarrhea and pain medicines, mosquito repellent, and appropriate first-aid supplies
- Toilet paper in Third World countries (check guide books for other necessities such as water-purification tablets, medical information, shots necessary to guard against local parasites, diseases, etc.)

Also, you will want to:

- Research how to handle bribery demands where you're going.
- Research the cell phone situation if you expect to remain in touch with the outside world.

TRAVEL IN DANGEROUS AREAS

Depending on your citizenship, check with U.S. Department of State (www. usembassy.gov) or your own country's embassy Web site before leaving to go abroad, and take particular note of warnings about dangerous situations. If still in doubt, call your embassy in that country to get their advice. Once you arrive, deposit copies of your travel plans with your embassy and those at home. If advised, keep them apprised of all changes so action can be taken immediately in case of emergencies.

HIRING EQUIPMENT

Before hiring, visit the rental house in an off-peak time, get a guided tour, and learn people's names so you start building a relationship. Knowing who does what will be most important if anything breaks down. Part of their business is to avoid being scammed, so it helps to let them know who you are and what you are doing. They are usually happy to show you their equipment and tell you the relative merits of what they carry. They also know plenty about the common mistakes people make and can give you tips that will help your shoot go well.

 When picking up equipment, the crew must arrive early enough to assemble and run all equipment and prove that it functions correctly. Allow for this in your scheduling.

GOING FURTHER

Video people are mostly young, keen, gregarious problem solvers who like to post material or render help. See the "Getting Information via the Internet" section in the **Book 1** introduction for hints on how to find them.

CHAPTER 27

ADVANCED LOCATION SOUND

This chapter summarizes some of the sound equipment, skills, and approaches that advanced productions need. You may want to review the basic information first in **Chapter 11, Location Sound**. Fortunately, there is now a great deal of expert advice posted on the Internet, and you'll find some links and recommendations at the end of this chapter.

Sound equipment evolves less rapidly than cameras, so I've also listed some industry favorites in the discussions below.

Planning sound coverage poses a number of questions:

 Budget films often take less trouble recording sound than picture. Difficult or impossible to rectify in postproduction, this can disable otherwise good work.

- Will you use the camcorder to record sound or a separate digital recorder?
- What kind of clapper board will you use if you are shooting double system (meaning a camera and sound recorder that are separate)?
- How many types of sound setup can you predict and how will you mike each different situation?
- How many channels of sound will you need to record?
- How many channels does your camera offer, and will you have to incorporate a multiple-channel mixer?
- If you plan to use radio mikes, should you bring wired mikes as backup?
- Should you rent or buy sound equipment?

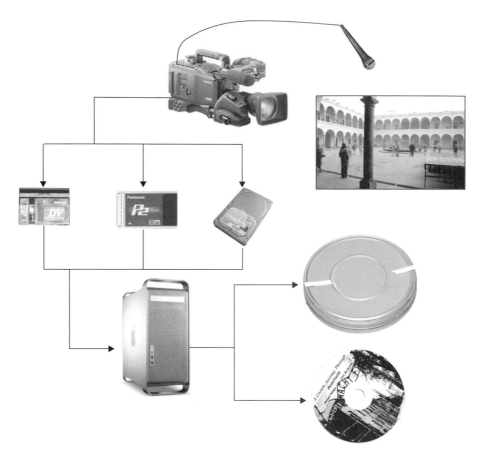

FIGURE 27-1A

Workflow diagram for single system. The camcorder records picture and sound together on DV cassette, P2 flash memory, or hard drive. Not shown is how the edited computer output becomes a DVD or film copy.

SHOOTING SINGLE OR DOUBLE SYSTEM

When you shoot *single system*—that is, with the camcorder recording picture and sound—you have a common though clumsy setup that is hazardous for grab shooting because the camcorder and fishpole operator are linked by cables (Figure 27-1A). Shooting *double system* means using a separate audio recorder so sound and camera operate unattached (Figure 27-1B). This means that you can:

- Move together and separately at will.
- Record better sound than most camcorders.
- Get easier and more representative headphone monitoring.
- Shoot wild tracks as you need them.

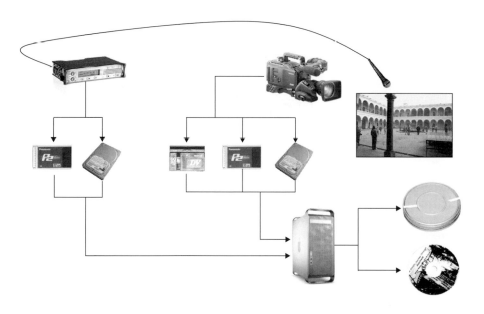

FIGURE 27-1B ——

Workflow diagram for double system, where an audio recorder handles sound separately.

But:

- You'll need one or two extra crew members—to operate more elaborate equipment and keep records. Somebody must log sound and camera media, or bringing them together in postproduction will become a nightmare.
- Sound and picture must be synchronized for each take in postproduction, which is more work but not difficult—*providing* there are consistent sync markers and accurate logs.
- Marking each take with a clapper board makes your operation more visible.
- Recorder and camera inevitably drift out of sync. *Creeping sync* becomes apparent once they are more than 2 frames apart, which means only 1/15th of a second.

Depending on the level of your equipment, sound and picture may drift out of sync in the computer. Creeping sync may show up after 5 minutes of running time or not for an hour or two. Only tests can show whether you're in luck. Shoot a 30-minute take with a clapper at the front and the end, sync sound and picture, then see how far the clappers are apart by the end of the half hour.

USING THE CAMCORDER TO RECORD SOUND

Give yourself a shock and read Dan Brockett's review of consumer camcorders' sound (Internet address at end of chapter). Expect to encounter:

- Flimsy input sockets
- Inaccessible controls for changing input level while shooting

- Poor signal-to-noise ratio
- Ineradicable system hiss
- Occasional hum or buzzing especially when using direct AC (alternating current) power
- Input metering that is indefinite or misleading
- "Hunting" for level when set to automatic level and mike input is low
- Headphone output underpowered, auto level, or poor quality

Though most audience members will think the recording quality is fine, documentary often operates in marginal situations where substandard sound can tip the balance into unintelligibility. A documentary about music would have to be shot very, very carefully.

Safety backup: If you are using a single monophonic mike feeding into a two-channel camcorder, use a "Y" connector to feed its input into both channels. Adjust one channel to peak at –6 dB and the other to peak several decibels lower. Should your main channel overload, you have a second chance in postproduction.

> The largest drawback to shooting single system is that the camera operator, not the recordist, must usually monitor sound levels.

SOUND CODECS

Digital sound recording also uses codecs and varying *sampling rates*. Sampling refers to the refresh rate the system uses as it draws sound waveforms. For sound fidelity set your sound sampling rate to 48k or above (48,000 waveform redraws per second) rather than the slower 32k. Stay consistent throughout your shoot because some editing software won't accept mixed sample rates.

LOCATION RECORDERS AND MIXERS

Using a separate recorder puts the whole job in a sound specialist's hands, where it belongs. Digital audio, like video, can either record full information—which takes up a lot of hard disk or memory card space—or use a codec (compression/decompression, or coder/decoder, software) to condense the signal into less recording space. Your postproduction software must be able to accept the range of codecs—the most familiar being MP3—in which original and library sound are recorded. You will find an article comparing the different codecs and the operating systems that handle them at http://en.wikipedia.org/wiki/Comparison_of_audio_codecs.

RECORDERS

For reliability and high-quality recording, the long-established Nagra range is the classic (Figure 27-2; www.nagraaudio.com). Lower budget productions

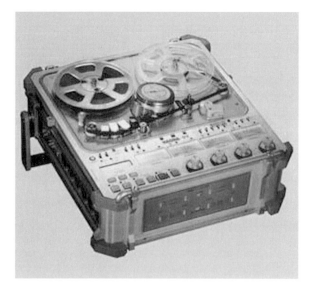

FIGURE 27-2 ————————————————————————————————

The Nagra® D II four-track digital recorder. Tough and reliable, Nagra equipment has long been the industry standard. (Photo courtesy of Nagra, a Kudelski Group Company.)

might use the feature-crammed four-track Sound Devices 744T recorder, which records onto a hard disk or flash card and sells for around $4000 (Figure 27-3; www.sounddevices.com/products/744t.htm). Or they might even consider the highly capable stereo TASCAM® HD-P2 (Figure 27-4; www.tascam.com) for about $1100; this records to flash cards and locks to external time-code for inter-machine syncing.

Robert Altman's pioneering sound recordist built a location sound recorder capable of recording 16 radio microphones simultaneously to eliminate the rigmarole of following individuals with mikes

 Miniature or inexpensive equipment may record fabulous sound but won't be rugged enough to survive a documentary's punishing use.

while shooting. Today you could use a multi-track hard drive recorder intended for music recording such as the Korg® D8888 (Figure 27-5). It has eight XLR inputs, mixing and equalization, and a great deal more. For multi-mike setups (a music or theater production, say) you can handle up to eight mono mikes or four stereo and delay creating an optimal master track later. Multi-track recorders, however, are power hungry and usually require AC power from a wall outlet.

Zaxcom Deva portable state-of-the-art recorders combine 10-track location mixers and recorders and pack many track hours of uncompressed recording into a tough and hermetically sealed hard disk (Figure 27-6; www.zaxcom.com). The 10-second sound buffer is particularly useful for spontaneous shooting, since you always know on startup that the previous 10 seconds come with the

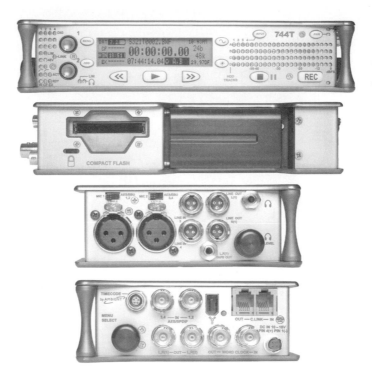

FIGURE 27-3 ————————————————————————————————

Four sides of the feature-packed Sound Devices 744T four-track audio recorder. (Photo courtesy of Sound Devices, LLC.)

FIGURE 27-4 ————————————————————————————————

TASCAM® HD-P2, a stereo recorder that locks to external timecode and writes to flash memory. (Photo courtesy of TASCAM.)

FIGURE 27-5

The Korg® D888 has eight tracks of input and mixing and up to eight tracks out. It records to a hard drive or makes direct data transfer to a computer. (Photo courtesy of Korg USA, Inc.)

FIGURE 27-6

The Zaxcom Deva V is a 10-track recorder using a hard disk, yet is light enough to sling over your shoulder. (Photo courtesy of Zaxcom, Inc.)

recording. The Deva creates DVD backup copies, plugs directly into a computer, and downloads rapidly in the cutting room. With no accessible moving parts, the machine is sealed and immune from grit and dust, as well as extremes of temperature and humidity.

MIXERS

If you want to combine and balance several mike inputs, you'll need a location mixer, because consumer or prosumer camcorders usually have no more than two sound channels. Choose a mixer you can sling over your shoulder rather than one that must lie flat on a table. Professional Sound Corporation (PSC) makes excellent four- and eight-channel portable mixers, as do Wendt (www.wendtinc.net/index.htm) and Shure (www.shure.com/ProAudio/index. htm). Mackie's mixers are favored by music and film productions (Figure 27-7;

FIGURE 27-7

Excellence on a budget—the Mackie® 1402-VLZ3 mixer for 10 microphone/line inputs and two-channel output. (Photo courtesy of LOUD Technologies, Inc.)

FIGURE 27-8

Basic ENG-44 battery-powered four-input, two-channel output location mixer. (Photo courtesy of Sign Video, Ltd.)

www.mackie.com). Sign Video's ENG-44 is a modest and serviceable battery-powered portable mixer with four inputs and two outputs (Figure 27-8; www.signvideo.com/fpamxr.htm). Be aware that the more sound equipment you cobble together, the less mobile you become.

EQ AND ROLLOFF

It is generally not a good idea to adjust equalization (EQ) as you record. You may however "roll off" (reduce) the excessive bass of traffic, since this can misregister in the level meter and lead to distortion. Most microphones have low-frequency attenuator switches for this purpose; otherwise, record "flat" (all frequencies equally) and defer EQ to the postproduction stage.

Volume Unit (VU) Meters

On camcorders and mixers, most VU meters are *averaging* meters; that is, they display average sound level and not peaks, where distortion sets in. Your mixer may have red LEDs that warn of peaking.

Mixer and Camcorder Levels Setup

Use the mixer's inbuilt tone-generator to set a saturation recording level of 0 dB on its VU meter. Feed the mixer output signal into the camcorder's line level input (if it has one, or into the kind of input adapter box pictured in Chapter 11). Manually adjust the camcorder's manual input levels (if you are setting up multiple channels) to also register a 0-dB reading. Record a minute of tone on tape, then check the tape with your editing program's playback to verify that saturation recording is indeed 0 dB. If it's off, lower the camera input until 0 db, and the mixer VU meter will handle a peak of any frequency without distorting.

Peak Tests

In mike recording tests, adjust mixer input levels so normal speech registers at −6 dB and peaks don't stray into the red area. Using editing software, test tracks to check that levels and speech quality hold good. Experiment with deliberate overloads (peaking beyond 0 dB) to discover where audible distortion sets in and which frequencies seem most vulnerable. If necessary, ride gain during recording to keep from peaking into the red. This is difficult or impossible with camcorder-only recording.

Multiple Microphones

 Digital sound compared with its analog predecessor is very unforgiving, and you'll need to learn from experimenting how to record within safe audio limits.

If you keep all mixer channels equally open as you cover several people with several mikes, their ambiences add together to create a dull roar. To minimize this, hold every channel low when nobody is using it, and raise and lower each speaker individually. If, however, each mike records into its own channel of a multichannel recorder, you can record all at full level, then mix them later as needed.

Phasing

Multiple mikes feeding into a common recording channel can create *phasing*. You can recognize this phenomenon when the sound level pulses instead of holding steady. It occurs when further and nearer mikes pick up the same source, but in different phase relationships, and one periodically cancels out the other.

Recording Stereo

Unless you have studied the engineering parameters to stereo or 5.1 recording, don't even attempt setting up multiple mikes. There's even one deadly setup in which one channel cancels out the other when stereo is reduced to mono!

Phantom Power

If a mike mysteriously refuses to work, suspect phantom power problems (see **Chapter 11, Location Sound**).

SMART SLATE

A smart slate is a clapper board containing a crystal-controlled timecode display (Figure 27-9). The numbers move when the bar is opened and freeze when the clapper bar is closed. For double-system shooting, this makes syncing sound to its timecoded picture easy. Camera and recorder must be compatible with the smart slate, and their operators must "jam" (synchronize) the timecode generators every morning, as they drift apart over a period of time. Carry a traditional clapper board if you fear electronic gadgets may break down.

SOUND MONITORING

Good headphone isolation from the surrounding world is a must (Figure 27-10). Widely used professional phones are the Sony® MDR-7506 or MDRV-600 and

FIGURE 27-9 ————————————————————————

The Denecke smart slate electronic clapper board. The timecode numbers are in hours, minutes, seconds, and frames. (Photo courtesy of Denecke, Inc.)

FIGURE 27-10 ————————————————————————

Judging sound depends on headphones that isolate you from surrounding ambience.

FIGURE 27-11 —————————————————————————————————

Sennheiser® HD25 headphones are a location recordist's favorite. (Photo courtesy of Sennheiser Electronic Corp.)

Sennheiser® HD-25 (Figure 27-11). Be aware that any camcorder headphone output that has inadequate level or passes through a compressor circuit will give a false impression of the recording dynamics. Compare what you hear on location with that during playback in the editing suite.

 Monitor all recording *all* the time using professional, ear-enclosing headphones that isolate you from the surrounding world (see Figure 27-10).

MICROPHONE PLACEMENT

Your choice of a boom or fishpole mount for the microphone is between aluminum and carbon fiber, the latter being lighter, which can mean a lot to its handler. A Gitzo™ G1553 is inexpensive and extends to 11 feet. Expect to pay more for the convenience of having the cable pass through the pole's interior. Whenever lighting and composition allow, mike from above. It gives a nice sense of changing sound perspectives, and speech level will be high in relation to the sound effects of body, hand, and foot movements. You can also mike from the sides of frame or from below. In the latter case, body movements can be disturbingly loud in relation to speech.

MICROPHONE TYPES

Most documentary sound is shot using cardioid and hypercardioid mikes, as well as lavalier omnidirectional body mikes. Each has different *pickup patterns* that are related to how much each accepts or inhibits sound coming from off the mike's axis. The cardioid pickup pattern gets its name from its heart-like shape.

SHOTGUN

Microphones have different constructions and sensitivities, but none actually reaches farther, as some people imagine. The hypercardioid or shotgun is ultradirectional and thus discriminates most strongly against off-axis sound. Named for their rifle appearance, shotguns like the Neumann KMR-82i or the Sennheiser® MKH-70 (an industry favorite) use interference tube serrations to suppress off-axis sound. Use this type of mike when you must favor a sound source over others competing from other axes, such as a speaker on a crowded street. The polar pattern (Figure 27-12) for the Sennheiser MKH-70 reveals that its off-axis discrimination varies according to frequency, a feature that is in fact common to all mikes.

> Sorry, but there's no such thing as a zoom mike.

Shorter hypercardioids such as the Sennheiser MKH-416 or MKH-60, Neumann KMR-81i, or Sanken CS-3 have a broader angle of acceptance than their longer brethren. Since the fall-off between on-axis and off-axis sound is considerable for all hypercardioids, you have to be quick panning the mike to a new speaker in a group.

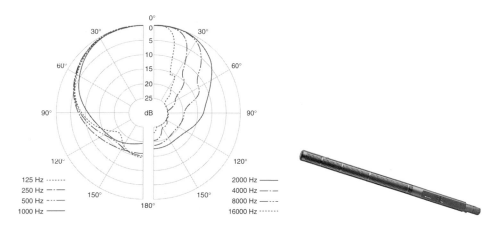

FIGURE 27-12 ⎯⎯⎯⎯⎯⎯⎯⎯⎯⎯⎯⎯⎯⎯⎯⎯⎯⎯⎯⎯⎯⎯⎯⎯⎯⎯⎯⎯⎯⎯

Polar reception pattern for a Sennheiser® MKH-70 microphone showing the slight variations of sensitivity in different frequency bands. (Photo courtesy of Sennheiser Electronic Corp.)

With directional mikes, watch what may be making sound behind the subject since shotguns, like a telephoto lens, tend to squeeze background and foreground together. Angle the mike downward, and perhaps you can get that idling truck motor out of the mike's "line of sight."

CARDIOID

Regular cardioid mikes have an angle of acceptance that is broader still. They are made by the manufacturers already mentioned, as well as well as by AKG, Audio Technica, Beyer Dynamic, ElectroVoice, Schoeps, and Shure—all of whom make a range of mikes. Use cardioids or even omnidirectional mikes for covering a group discussion, as people tend to speak unpredictably from several directions and ultradirectional miking becomes a handicap.

 All microphones register air currents, even indoors, as an intermittent rumble.

Dynamic cardioids are an older design that—unlike sensitive, battery-powered electret condenser mikes—is completely sound-powered. Though less sensitive, they are rugged and will endure the very loud sounds, rough handling, or temperature and moisture extremes that would disable their more delicate cousins.

LAVALIER

The tiny, normally omnidirectional lavalier is usually of an electret condenser design. This allows them to be highly sensitive, full spectrum, and miniature. Some, like the Countryman B6 or the Sanken COS-11 (both waterproof), are tinier than a match head yet give superb sound. Other industry favorites are the TRAM® TR-50B, Sony® ECM-55, PSC MilliMic, or the Sennheiser® MKE 2. Each lavalier comes with a small globular foam windscreen that fits

 The sterile "studio" quality of lavaliers may work for or against you, depending on the needs of your film. Expect a level drop-off if the person turns their head and marked reverberation changes when the person approaches a hard surface.

over the mike to inhibit popping on speech plosives. You can even customize the Countryman B6 by using different caps that alter its audio profile.

If air currents become particularly troublesome outdoors, wrap the lavalier in cheesecloth or bury it in the wearer's clothing (Figure 27-13). Feed a lavalier into its own wireless transmitter or, for minimal interference, wire it direct to the mixer board or camcorder. Tape

 All lavalier mikes suffer from air current and clothing interference sensitivity, with silk, rayon, nylon, and corduroy being among the worst offenders. Pin or tape clothing so it doesn't rub or tap the mike.

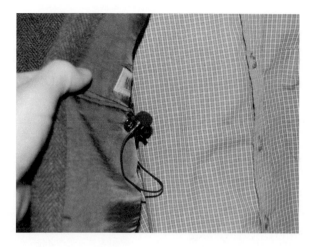

FIGURE 27-13 ————————————————————————————

Lavalier mike hidden under clothing for best protection against air currents.

the XLR connector of the lavalier to the wearer's ankle for easy disconnection between bouts of filming.

WIRELESS MICROPHONES

Imagine lavaliers on several moving participants transmitting to receivers all plugged into a mixing desk. Now you can confidently record several people on the move. Well, yes and no. All wireless mikes, even the very best, are vulnerable to occasional radiofrequency interference, emergency service transmitters, dead spots, and so on. They take setup time, gobble batteries, and need channel changes. This all takes time, especially in cities where radio activity is more extreme. Think of them like cellular phones—

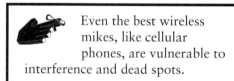 Even the best wireless mikes, like cellular phones, are vulnerable to interference and dead spots.

useful but occasionally treacherous. The Lectrosonics® 210 range has a very good reputation and is an industry standard. Favored among lower price systems is the Sennheiser® Evolution 500 (Figure 27-14).

Check experienced users' comments on the Internet concerning features for particular models—for instance, how many radio channels a system should have and how automatically and seamlessly it changes channels when encountering transmission difficulties.

WHAT TO RENT AND WHAT TO OWN

If you are filming a lot over a long period, it may be worth it to purchase rather than rent the basics such as a fishpole, cables, and digital recorder. Something better

FIGURE 27-14

Sennheiser® Evolution 500 wireless transmitter and receiver. (Photo courtesy of Sennheiser Electronic Corp.)

isn't going to suddenly appear—as happens with camcorders. Having your own basic mike set, a mixer, and a tripod may all make economic sense, too. If you must shoot at short notice, owning your own camera may even be unavoidable, and owning your own editing setup is a must. Better to rent radio mikes, exotic lighting, or camera supports that you use once in a blue moon. If you must shoot at the highest quality for two weeks and then spend many months editing, it's probably wise to rent all of your shooting equipment.

 One of the goals of budgeting is always to foresee whether owning or renting is most economic.

GOING FURTHER

For cost-conscious reviews and practical articles on all aspects of sound, go to Fred Ginzburg's Equipment Emporium (www.equipmentemporium.com). An outstanding 72-page article on sound theory and practice, "Location Sound: The Basics and Beyond" by Dan Brockett, can be found published under the Ken

Stone Index (an offshoot of Final Cut Pro) at www.kenstone.net/fcp_homepage/ location_sound.html. More excellent instructional material is available at the Location Sound Corporation Web site (www.locationsound.com/proaudio/ls/ index.html). For a wide range of up-to-date sound equipment, go to www. thebroadcastshop.com/. The Digital Information Network, at www.dvinfo.net, is excellent for all digital filmmaking matters.

CHAPTER 28

ORGANIZATION, CREW, AND PROCEDURES

Large, well-funded projects have larger crews to make shooting more efficient. A series or feature-length documentary will need a whole production department. In broadcasting these become elaborate organizations as the endeavor takes on a studio dimension.

INTERNS

Organizations of all sizes often take *interns* (unpaid or low-paid assistants) from a nearby film school—a great way to get experience. Some take interns simply to get cheap labor for tedious tasks, but more often internships arise from a laudable desire to teach "the business" to the next generation. An internship can be a capstone to your education and a fine way to get known by local professionals. If they like you and your work, this can lead to a first job and a toehold in professional filmmaking.

PRODUCTION DEPARTMENT

More sophisticated digital technology is allowing crews to do more with less, but the business side of filmmaking is expanding as opportunities to make cost-efficient independent documentaries expand into international markets and coproduction. Today you can't just make and sell a good documentary; it will need publicity, international showings, and "outreach"—that is, you will need to show how, using supplementary publications and showings, you expect the film to lead an active life serving special-interest groups.

PRODUCER

An independent producer might work in an urban area with a number of directors and resemble a literary agent. With ten directors, there might be upward of 30 viable documentary ideas to shop around at any given time. The effective producer is socially adept and a highly articulate salesperson. He or she brings film ideas and sample films and makes pitches at documentary marketplaces such as the Amsterdam International

 Marketing your documentaries—before and after you make them—is vital to your survival. Most film craftspeople hate the business side of filmmaking, so there's a real need for specialized, entrepreneurial producers. Film schools are beginning to train them.

Documentary Festival or the Independent Feature Project (IFP) Market in New York. The producer makes deals with the commissioning editors from cable and television channels at such gatherings, something many filmmakers are diffident about doing. Television representatives who are hunting new ideas and talent scouting for promising filmmakers then compete to develop cofinancing deals for the products they want.

The ideal producer combines the abilities of agent, salesperson, production manager (if he or she works closely with productions), and accountant. She or he knows the changing world of documentary and its audiences, can estimate and monitor costs during production, and can confidently discuss all aspects of proposals and cofinancing. A producer ensures that the finished product gets full publicity, since films sink without a trace if nobody publicizes their existence.

All this takes a special temperament, and a producer should never be a wannabe director. He or she should love documentary and enjoy nurturing production. Anyone with good taste and a stable of impressive production groups will, like a literary agent, become trusted and sought after by overworked commissioning editors, who look to the best producers in search of original work.

In a large organization, producers are often senior administrators with long experience at production, and they can be very supportive and helpful. You may work with assistant producers and a line producer (assigned only to the production and who probably manages the budget and negotiates with vendors), as well as a unit production manager. While producers have creative input and even creative control, the rest of their staff contributes logistical assistance and financial management.

UNIT PRODUCTION MANAGER (UPM)

The unit production manager is responsible for all the arrangements on the shoot and is a necessity for a large, complex project. In a large organization, a UPM may cover several productions and be represented on your production by a line producer. Arrangements they make might include locating overnight accommodations, booking rented equipment at the best prices, securing location or other permissions, making up a shooting schedule (with the director), making travel arrangements, and locating food and accommodations near the shoot.

The UPM's office monitors cash flow, has contingency plans when bad weather stymies exterior shooting, and chases progress. All this lightens the load on the director, for whom this is a burden.

Good production staff are of course organized, compulsive list keepers, socially adept and businesslike, and able to scan and correlate a number of activities. They must be able to juggle priorities and make decisions involving time, effort, and money, and they must not be intimidated by officialdom. Someone good at production management acquires the best experience to become a successful producer.

CREW

SOUND

More sound staff members become necessary once you shoot double system or cover complex situations such as reenactments or large group activities (see **Chapter 27, Location Sound**). There is more gear to handle, greater complexity in the setups, and more records to keep if the production is to remain efficient. If you shoot on a stage, then a boom operator will be necessary—someone able to follow a script and precisely move the mike in time for each incoming line. This is a highly skilled operation.

GAFFER

The gaffer is an expert in rigging and maintaining lighting equipment and knows how to split loads so lighting runs off light-duty household supplies without starting fires or plunging the neighbors into darkness. Good gaffers carry a bewildering assortment of clamps, gadgets, and small tools. Resourceful by nature, they some-times emerge as mainstays of the unit when others get discouraged. During a BBC night-shooting sequence in England, I once saw a boy stumble behind the lights and hurt his knee. Understanding he must remain silent while we were shooting, he doubled over and clutched his knee in mute agony. The kindly electrician (as the gaffer is called in Britain) swooped silently out of the gloom and cradled him in his arms until the shot was finished.

 The gaffer, whose attention is free when the camera is running, is often the only crew member with a whole and unobstructed view. Directors in doubt, therefore, sometimes discreetly ask how the gaffer felt about a certain piece of action.

Usually the director of photography (DP) has a favorite gaffer, and the two work together like Laurel and Hardy. Experienced gaffers know their DP's style and preferences and can prelight ahead of a unit's arrival. Teams of long association gradually dispense with spoken language.

GRIP

Grips fetch, carry, set up (mostly electrical and camera equipment), and have the highly skilled and coordinated job of moving the camera support to precisely worked-out positions when the camera uses a dolly or crane to take mobile shots. Grips need to be strong, practical, organized, and willing. On the minimal crew, they help rig lighting or sound equipment.

 A skilled grip knows something about everyone's job and in an emergency can do limited duty for another crewmember.

PROCEDURES

Some procedures set out below may be needlessly complicated for a one- or two-person shoot. More elaborate procedures become necessary for scripted docudrama or acted historical reconstruction. Others are made necessary whenever you use a double-system setup—that is, a camera and sound recorder that are separate.

SHOT IDENTIFICATION

Keep whatever logs you can of important information as you shoot. Central to recordkeeping is the ability to identify shots and *takes* (repeated attempts at a shot) as you shoot. The traditional marking system is the familiar wooden *slate*, or clapper board, with a closing bar on top (Figure 28-1).

There are many automatic film marking systems, such as the smart slate (see Chapter 27), but many people like the exquisitely low-tech clapper board, which

FIGURE 28-1

Clapper board—necessary whenever you use a double system and must synchronize sound to picture.

has only a piece of chalk and a hinge to go wrong. The clapper board ritual has these functions:

- Visually it identifies the shot number and the production on cassettes, P2 memory, or hard disks as they enter the industrial workflow, which may include a film laboratory as well as the postproduction operation. Some boards have color reference charts attached.

- The operator's announcement aurally identifies the track for sound transfer or digitizing personnel.

- When you record sound and picture separately, they must be synchronized later, so the closing bar provides an exact picture frame against which to align the bang in the recorded track.

When video recording is single system (sound and picture recorded together on the same recording media), sync is not an issue. A clapper board or other marking system becomes essential to precision sync if you are shooting double-system sound. This is because someone must be able to sync picture to its separately recorded sound.

In single-system shoots, log your material simply with a note of content and timecode stopping points. These allow you to review a chosen section during production. On complex productions, the slate, or clapper board, carries not only scene and take numbers but also information for image quality-control experts in film labs or video studios. These include a gray scale, white and black as a contrast reference, and a standard color chart. Video cameras generate an electronic standard color chart called *color bars*, which are recorded for reference purposes at the head of each tape or memory storage.

To summarize:

For single-system (camcorder) video production use a number board for the camera with announcement only. Under pressure, you can dispense with this and simply run the material, logging content and timecode as you go.

For double-system shoots, treat the operation like film and use an announcement and a clapper bar. Keep camera and sound logs.

 The setup is the apparent position of the camera which you change either by making a lens change or by physically moving the camera.

SETUP AND TAKE NUMBERS

What information about the *setup* goes on the clapper board? There are two philosophies of numbering:

- **Method 1**—The *scene/setup/take* system is favored in the Hollywood fiction film industry and might apply to a scripted docudrama. All numbering is based on the script scene number, such as "Scene 104A, shot 16, take 3." Translated, this means script scene 104A, setup 16, attempt number 3. Large organizations making big, highly supervised productions need lengthy factory part numbers. For the small, flexible production, this is overkill. Also, the more elaborate a system is, the more susceptible it is to error and breakdown as people get tired and you depart from the script.

- **Method 2:** The *cumulative setup/take* system is used universally in documentaries and in European feature films. Shooting simply begins at slate 1-1. Each new setup gets a new slate number and a second or subsequent attempt at the same setup will get a new take number (for example, "1 take 2" or "1–2"). This system is ideal for the overstretched small crew because it requires no liaison to coordinate numbers with the script and no adaptation when the inevitable script departures come up. The disadvantage is that it makes life a little busier for the script supervisor, when there is one.

SHOOTING LOGS

Shooting of any elaboration requires two kinds of log. A *camera log* (Figure 28-2) kept by the assistant cinematographer (AC) records content by slate, take, and timecode readings for each new cassette, P2 memory, or hard disk. Its number and information will become vital during editing. A *sound log* (Figure 28-3) kept by the sound recordist records slate and take numbers and whether each track is sync or "wild" (non-sync voice or effects recording). The latter information is important to whomever digitizes into the computer from sound original storage materials (DAT, 1/4-inch master tape, flash memory, hard disk, etc.), since some will need to be synced to picture and some not.

DOUBLE SYSTEM

When sound is recorded separately, camera and sound recorder do not stay in numerical step as they consume memory media. Stock durations are usually different, and additional sound such as wild tracks, sound effects, or atmosphere recordings get added to the sound media as production progresses. On the camera side, shots are sometimes taken silent for convenience. Once sound has been digitized ready for editing, the editing assistant must synchronize each sound take to its picture before the editor can start work.

SINGLE SYSTEM

When shooting single system with a camcorder, a camera log keeps track of both sound and picture, because both are recorded simultaneously on the same media. The camera assistant (if there is one) keeps a master log by timecode readings and briefly notes content with slate and take number and camera setup informa-

 The worst omission is forgetting to mark your recorded media. There's nothing more devastating than to find you've recorded over previous work.

tion. The recorded media, containing both sound and action, goes to the editor for digitizing.

Setup #	Take #	Description and comments	h : m : s

CAMERA LOG Title _____ Page# ____ of total ____
Operator _____ Camera Type/Ser# _____ Job# _____
Location _____ Date Shot _____ Media ID _____

Setup #	Take #	Description and comments	h : m : s
			: :
			: :
			: :
			: :
			: :
			: :
			: :
			: :
			: :
			: :
			: :
			: :
			: :
			: :
			: :
			: :
			: :
			: :
			: :
			: :
			: :
			: :
			: :

FIGURE 28-2

Camera log.

LOGS IN ACTION

Logs help the right material go to the right place in the production chain and to inform everyone what to do with each section of recording. A less obvious log function is to record (by its serial number) which piece of hired equipment made which recording. Should you hear a strange hum or see a picture hue problem, the offending equipment can be quickly identified, withdrawn, and tested.

SOUND LOG	Title _____ Page# _____ of total _____		
Operator _____ Recorder Type/Ser# _____ Job# _____			
Location _____ Date Shot _____ Media ID _____			
Setup #	Take #	Scene description and comments	h : m : s
			: :
			: :
			: :
			: :
			: :
			: :
			: :
			: :
			: :
			: :
			: :
			: :
			: :
			: :
			: :
			: :
			: :
			: :
			: :
			: :
			: :
			: :
			: :
			: :

FIGUE 28-3 ──────────────────────────────────────

Sound log.

THE COUNTDOWN TO SHOOTING

When you shoot double system and need a clapper board as a marking system, there is an unvarying ritual at the beginning of each take:

➢   The director calls, "Stand by to roll camera."

> The clapper operator takes up a position holding the clapper board (also known as clapsticks) in front of the subject, at a height where it is clearly visible. The operator will sometimes direct its placement to ensure that the all-important number and clapper bar are in shot.

> The camera operator turns on the camera, says, "Camera rolling," and calls out, "Roll sound."

> The sound recordist turns on the recorder, waits a few moments for its mechanism to reach a stable speed, then calls out, "Speed."

> The camera operator now says, "Mark it."

> The clapper operator calls out the scene and take number, closes the clapper with a bang, and immediately exits frame.

> The director can now say, "Action" as a cue for the action to begin.

STARTING WITHOUT A CLAPPER

Sometimes, shooting bird mating dances or drug dealers at work on a street corner, you don't want to tell the district that your camera is rolling. You can:

(a) Make a quiet, voice announcement into the mike and tap the mike in view of the camera so subsequent syncing to a mike-tap is easy; or

(b) Simply signal camera and sound to start rolling. After the action is complete, the camera assistant brings the clapper board in to be filmed, but upside down. He or she calls out the scene number, adding, "Board on end," or, "End clapsticks," then claps the bar, after which the director calls, "Cut!" In the cutting room the end-clapped material will have to be end-synced and then backed up for marking at its beginning.

SOCIAL AND FORMAL ISSUES

HAVING OR LOSING AUTHORITY

A major anxiety when you start directing is feeling that you lack authority. It's not, after all, something you can switch on when you need it, especially under what you imagine (not always wrongly) to be hostile scrutiny by those you presume to lead. In a large organization you may, as once I did, find yourself the outsider leading resentful insiders. Simultaneously an information center and parental figure, you will be found wanting, so be prepared to insist on your rights if you sense you are being put to a test. Every situation has its pecking order: A young director should expect subtle challenges from older crewmembers, a woman from male subordinates, a foreigner from the locals. Tiresomely human, but watch your back. Counter these threats—real or imagined—by choosing coworkers carefully and making them partners in all of the conceptual considerations of the film. Stay abreast of your crew's concerns and problems, and make your organizational work impeccable.

Handling people sensitively is part of the director's consensus-building role. How to collaborate is always delicate but is seldom a problem with those fulfilled by their jobs. Most choosing to work in documentary are mature and dedicated people, so it is unwise to try to fool them or make claims beyond your knowledge.

Having authority really means being respected; it means having the humility to ask for help or advice when you genuinely need it and standing by your decisions and intuitions when you should do so.

Ideally, the crew should be present at viewings during postproduction, when the growth and internal complexity of the film come under intense scrutiny. It is here that the comprehensiveness of your work begins to show, and here, too, that crewmembers learn about the contribution they have (or haven't) made. Interestingly, after a long period of segmented, industrialized production, we are returning to the intimate filmmaking of the early twentieth century, which is probably why documentaries are getting better and better. The smaller and more human scale promises films, both documentary and fiction, made in a more individual way—which is surely a significant development.

 When your elevation to director upsets the organization's pecking order, expect subtle or blatant subversion and opportunistic bullying—especially over matters of knowledge. You will have to "fake it till you make it"—that is, carry yourself with more confidence than you feel.

 Only the director can decide what goes into a film. Be open to suggestions but don't let anyone think you're willing to make the film by committee. Handle this delicately.

 Sometimes crews have odd chemistries and react unpredictably to the pressure and intensity of filmmaking when far from home. What happens is always revealing.

USING SOCIAL TIMES AND BREAKS

When you are shooting, a shared intensity of purpose and adventure binds everyone together. Try to keep crew and participants together during meals or rest periods. Relaxing is often the time when more ideas, memories, and associations come tumbling out. Conserved and encouraged, this fellowship makes communication inevitable and energizes even a jaded crew.

 An aware and involved crew acts as an antenna, alerting you to things said or done beyond your knowledge.

GOING FURTHER

Production management becomes a crucial issue on elaborate productions and resembles feature films, for which these books cater:

Cleve, Bastian. *Film Production Management*, 3rd ed. Boston: Focal Press, 2005.

Gates, Richard. *Production Management for Film and Video,* 3rd ed. Boston: Elsevier, 1999.

Hofhaner, Eve. *The Complete Film Production Handbook*, 3rd ed. Boston: Focal Press, 2001 (book and CD-ROM).

Maier, Robert G. *Location Scouting and Management Handbook*. Boston: Focal Press, 1994.

Patz, Deborah S. *Film Production Management: The Ultimate Guide for Film and Television Production Management and Coordination.* Studio City, CA: Michael Wiese, 2002.

CHAPTER 29

ADVANCED DIRECTING

DIRECTING PARTICIPANTS

THE MIND–BODY CONNECTION

To put people at ease means knowing something about how the human mind works under scrutiny. We live our everyday lives comfortably when we can depend on a foundation of assumptions—about our identity, worth, function, and how others regard us. Having an audience destabilizes this in particular ways, as Konstantin Stanislavski, the Russian actor and dramatic theorist, realized. From studying successful actors, he found they had learned to perform naturally and believably by vesting their attention in the thoughts and actions of their characters. Being able to "focus" in this way stilled the anxious, judgmental self and allowed them to function as naturally as if they were alone.

 Make a thorough survey of your intentions before shooting starts using **Project 2-DP-1 Dramatic Content Helper.**

Trained actors therefore maintain focus by keeping up a chain of physical and mental tasks that fit the character they are playing. This foundation is threatened by insecurity of all kinds, even fear of losing focus, since any opportunity for unstructured thought lets the ever-anxious mind take over. An actor losing focus immediately forfeits conviction in everything he says and does. And because no interior state is without its outward manifestation—another Stanislavski realization—the audience knows something is amiss.

Applying this to those participating in making a documentary, we can say that:

- You can tell from a person's body language whether he is unified and focused or divided and troubled.

- You can help. Give participants authentic mental and physical work to do so they relax and feel normal.

- The most intense focus—and thus the greatest relaxation—comes from pursuing their most compelling interests or goals because these shut out all other consciousness.

DOING WHAT COMES NATURALLY

Help your participants by establishing trustworthy reasons for making the film. Involve them in something holding meaning and affirmation for them, and they will take part naturally and spontaneously. A sheltered middle-aged couple, for example, will delightedly fall into a recurring discussion about which food the dog should have. Participants become used to working with you and come to enjoy being who they are in your presence. I once filmed elderly miners describing the bitter days of a strike during which they derailed a train manned by "scabs" or strike breakers. We filmed overlooking their old mine; while they relived the deepest and most divisive issues in their lives, the camera came within 2 feet of their faces. Their emotional involvement left them with no attention to spare for how they might appear to us or to the world beyond our camera.

 Drama and life being lived in the imagination are one and the same thing—consuming. People consumed by the moment are most deeply and revealingly themselves.

SELF-IMAGE AND SELF-CONSCIOUSNESS

The easiest people to work with are those oblivious of their effect on others. Old people and small children are natural because there is no ego, no internal censor at work. Knowing this, you can predict who is at the other end of the scale and will present difficulties. Those compulsively careful of their appearance or with nervous mannerisms are least likely to settle in front of a camera. During a street interview with an elderly lady I saw her completely lose focus. I was puzzled until I saw how, in mid-sentence, she began removing the hair net she realized she was still wearing. The more "proper" someone feels they must look for the record, the less flexible, impulsive, and openly communicative they will be. But since care and circumspection were this lady's stamp, her action was also wonderfully representative. Her friends, seeing the film, would smile in recognition. Notice that the pressure of the camera's presence did not make her behave uncharacteristically.

"DOESN'T THE CAMERA CHANGE PEOPLE?"

People often say, "But the presence of the camera *must* change people." Yes, but only the aspect or degree of a person's response. This can go either way—toward self-consciousness or toward self-revelation. Indeed, the camera may catalyze an honesty and depth of feeling not seen before by a participant's closest friends. Fulfill the human craving for recognition, and sometimes the floodgates open. So:

- You don't need to be unduly protective of people. Most know their boundaries and will go no further than they feel comfortable.

- Because you film something doesn't mean you have to use it. Later, you and your advisers can thoroughly consider the consequences of using or not using the footage.

 No form of observation, including filming, can make anyone act out of character. That's because nothing can change a person's underlying nature.

 Somewhere in everyone there is a longing to be known and recognized. Without it, there could be no documentary as we know it.

Indeed documentarians sometimes decide not to use material and have even destroyed footage because its very existence endangers someone. One exception:

- Never keep anything you've shot that is injurious if someone else has editorial control. Some people say that if you shoot it, you'll use it. Don't shoot it, if you don't trust yourself to abstain.

OBSTACLES: HABITS OF BEING

Particular jobs attract particular kinds of personality, and some employment seems to generate mannerisms and self-awarenesses that are a liability in filmmaking, unless, of course, that is precisely what you want to show. Officials, unused to making public statements and afraid of crossing superiors, will make excruciatingly boring and self-conscious contributions. Lecturers address invisible multitudes instead of talking one on one as they did during research. Before trying to alter a participant's idea of how he should relate to the camera, estimate what is habit and what is only a misperception about filming. The latter you can alter. You can, for instance, say, "There is only one person, me, listening to you. Talk only to me." Another mistaken notion is the idea that one must project the voice. If the participant

 People under pressure or suffering unusual circumstances fall back on habit, and ingrained habits of behavior are hard or impossible to change.

 Choosing participants is casting, no less than for a fiction film; some imagination expended beforehand can warn of the effect filming is likely to have. It's worth speculating, since your statement on the screen depends on who you use and what they do.

cannot respond to direction, a little playback may do the trick. People are usually shocked to see and hear themselves for the first time. Expose an unsatisfactory "performance" only as a last resort, supportively and in private.

Sometimes you will get someone whose concept of a film appearance is taken from commercials and who valiantly projects *personality*. This is true to some aspect of the individual's character and assumptions, and if you are making a film about stage mothers you could hardly ask for anything more revealing.

KEYS TO DIRECTING PEOPLE

Directing actors in fiction and directing those in a documentary, whom Bill Nichols calls "social actors," is not so very different:

> ➤ When you plan to cut from location to location, consider reminding participants before the new scene where we last saw them and what they were doing and feeling.

> ➤ Give anyone on camera plenty to do, so they aren't stultified by self-consciousness.

> ➤ Ask them to do only what is organic to their regular life.

> ➤ Don't ask them to *be* anything (natural, normal, etc.).

Once, filming a mother and daughter washing the dishes together at night, I saw they were camera conscious. To provoke a real interaction, I asked them to resume a recent disagreement. They went straight in, visibly relaxed and oblivious to the camera. The least helpful thing one can say is, "Just be yourself." It sets people worrying: What did he really mean? How does he see me? And which me does he really want?

When you are making a "transparent" film, tell participants:

> ➤ Not to worry about mistakes or silences, since in documentary, we shoot far more than we use.

> ➤ To ignore the crew's presence and not look at the camera. This relieves participants from feeling they must "play to the audience." The crew helps in this by concentrating on their jobs, avoiding eye contact, and giving no facial or verbal feedback.

 You can remove all sensation of acting for your participants by simply making a reflexive rather than a transparent film. That is, you incorporate the participant's relationship with those behind the camera as part of the movie.

REFLEXIVITY

When making a reflexive film, tell participants that:

> ➤ They can talk to you or to the camera as they wish.

> They can do anything and go wherever they need to go during filming.

> Nothing is off limits, and no thought or subject of conversation is disallowed.

> Filming is to catch things as they happen, and to make filming be part of that happening.

In Nick Broomfield's *The Leader, His Driver and the Driver's Wife* (1991, United Kingdom), the director uses boyish disingenuousness to draw out the South African white supremacist Eugène Terre'Blanche (sic), with hilarious and very revealing results. In other films of this type, the director's manipulation can make the audience uncomfortable, which is sometimes true in Ross McElwee's otherwise sophisticated *Sherman's March* (1989, United States).

CAMERA ISSUES AND POINT OF VIEW

COMPROMISES FOR THE CAMERA

When shooting action sequences, you may need to ask people to slow down or control their movements because movement in general, once it has a frame around it, looks perhaps 20 to 30% faster. The operator's fanciest footwork cannot keep a hand framed and in focus if its owner moves too fast.

How willing are you to intrude to get a result that is visually and choreographically accomplished? The ethnographer shuns such intrusion, and most who make documentary have some of the ethnographer in them. But, as Jean-Luc Godard observed, making fiction sends you toward documentary, and making documentary involves you in fiction. Even the most mechanized Hollywood product contains elements of improvisation and inventiveness that leave the camera documenting a "happening."

 The most important rules for documentary are those you set for yourself. Base them on whatever affects your relationship with your participants and thus with your audience. It is something to think through and to decide using principle and experimentation.

CAMERA AS PASSPORT

In everyday life, people make allowance for a camera. If you are shooting in crowds, don't be afraid to go where you would normally not enter. The camera is your passport; use it to go to the front of a crowd, to squeeze between people looking in a shop window, or to cross police lines. In Western countries, this is part of the freedom of the press, but it may not work in all cultures. A colleague went to film in Nigeria and learned (through having stones flung at him) that taking a person's image without asking is theft. In some political climates, merely holding a camera is holding a weapon. Every year, dozens of brave journalists are injured or even killed while doing their jobs. Knowing the rules and staying lucky can mean life or death.

MOTIVATION FOR CAMERA POSITIONING AND CAMERA MOVEMENT

There are few rules for camera positioning, since every scene has its nature to be revealed, and each has its inherent limitations. These are usually physical: windows that restrict an interior to shooting in one direction or an incongruity you must avoid in an exterior. A genuine settler's log cabin must be framed low in order to avoid seeing, above the ancient trees, an ominous revolving sausage over the neighborhood hot-dog stand. Making documentaries is serendipitous; you are always having to jettison plans to accommodate the unforeseen. Such limitations shape film art to a degree undreamed of by film critics.

SERENDIPITY

Serendipity can work in eerie ways. The British miners I mentioned earlier had sabotaged a scab coal train but without hurting anyone. The day before we visited to film them, an express train derailed close to the original site. The next morning I interviewed a doctor who had participated as a strike-breaker in the original incident. Knowing we were coming the next day, he thought he must be dreaming when summoned to a train crash in the small hours. After some queasy soul searching about voyeurism, I altered our plans to film the wreckage (Figure 29-1). It brought home like nothing else the destruction the saboteurs had risked by their demonstration. Adapting to the unexpected is frustrating for some, while for others it is a challenge to their inventiveness and insight. In the name of spontaneity you will be tempted to make no plans, but plan we must, because plans often work out. Luck favors the prepared mind.

FIGURE 29-1 ———————————————————————————————

Be ready for the unexpected—a train wreck that occurred nearby while filming *The Cramlington Train-Wreckers*.

MULTIPLE ANGLES ON THE SAME ACTION

Each aspect of film language, as we've seen, corresponds to some aspect of every-day human perception, but how to justify covering an action from multiple angles? Think of it this way: Cutting together long and close shots taken from the same camera position suggests an observer's intensified, shifting concentration. Imagine a tense family meal covered from five different angles taken from five different camera positions. It's a familiar film convention and has a corollary in literature where multiple viewpoints imply not physical changes of location but shifts in psychological point of view. The same holds true when you cut multiple views together for the screen. Though film seems to give us "real" events, it really gives us a "seeming" that is not, despite appearances, the events themselves but a human way of perceiving them. Test this out by recalling the experience of being a bystander at a major disagreement. You got so absorbed that you forgot all about yourself. Instead, you went through a series of empathic internal agreements and disagreements, seeing first one person's point and then the other's. You were so subjectively involved that "self" disappeared and you had an out-of-body experience of the protagonists' heated realities.

 Multiple angles on the screen imply not physical changes of viewpoint so much as shifts in psychological points of view.

Screen language evokes this heightened state of subjectivity by using a series of privileged views. Each shot suggests an observer's identification migrating as the situation unfolds—sympathy and fascination, distaste and anxiety, say, taking his attention from person to person. Cutting from angle to angle reproduces this familiar psychic experience, but it doesn't work unless scene, shooting, and editing are "right."

It is "right" and "works" when the *empathic shifts are rooted in a single sensibility*—that of a character or of the invisible Storyteller. Without this grounding, the different angles don't feel integrated. By the way, that state of heightened and embracing concentration is not one we normally maintain for long.

ABSTRACTION

The opposite of probing emotional inquiry is withdrawal into mental stocktaking or a state of temporary detachment. In this mode, we alter our examination from a part to the whole, or we zero in on something distracting. By watching your own shifts of attention you will see yourself escaping to a private realm where you can speculate, contemplate, remember, or imagine. Detail that catches your attention turns out to have symbolic meaning or is a part that stands for the whole. A car's rearview mirror just above a swirling water surface can stand for a whole flood. This much-used principle in film is called *synecdoche* (pronounced sin-ek-duh-kee). As you direct or shoot, keep an eye open for anything expressive or symbolic, such as the scale that represents justice or the flower growing on an empty lot to suggest renewal.

Abstraction may not signify withdrawal or refuge, but instead a moment of looking inward to find the significance of a recent event. Selective focus is a device used to suggest this state. When an object is isolated on the screen, and its foreground and background are thrown out of focus, it strongly suggests abstracted vision, as does abnormal motion (either slow or fast).

These are some of the ways to represent how we routinely dismantle reality and objectively distance ourselves from the moment. We may be searching for meaning or simply refreshing ourselves through imaginative play.

SUBJECTIVITY VERSUS OBJECTIVITY

The world we know is full of dualities, oppositions, and ironic contrasts. For instance, you drive your car very fast at night, and then, stopping to look at the stars, become aware of your own insignificance under those little points of light that took millions of years to reach earth. Human attention shifts from subjectivity to objectivity, from past to present and back again, from looking at a crowd as a phenomenon to looking at the tense profile of a woman as she turns away. Screen language exists to replicate every aspect of what an Observer notices and what a Storyteller uses to retell it.

 Model the point-of-view shifts in your films on a consistent stream of human consciousness, and your audience will feel it is sharing an integrated being's presence—that of our invisible, thinking, feeling, all-seeing Storyteller.

FRAMING IMPLICATIONS

Framing can change implications. Isolating people in separate close shots, for instance, and intercutting them will have a very different feel than cutting between two over-the-shoulder shots (OS) or showing the whole scene in medium long shot (MLS). In the single shots, the spectator is always alone with one of the contenders, and editing creates the relationship. In the OS and MLS shots, however, we always see one in relation to the other, and our relation is with the two of them, not each separately. This feels different.

 If learning from life seems slow and ambiguous, remember that if you imitate other filmmakers, you may lose your own "voice" and authenticity.

There is nothing arcane here; your guide to how an audience responds always lies in making astute use of common experience.

USING CONTEXT

How do different backgrounds work with a particular foreground action? If a participant is in a wheelchair and you angle the shot to contain a window with a vista of people in the street, the composition unobtrusively juxtaposes her with the freedom of movement she so poignantly lacks.

Looking down on the subject, looking up at the subject, or looking at it between the bars of a railing can all suggest ways of seeing—and, therefore, of experiencing—the action that makes the scene. True, you can manufacture this through editing, but it's labored. You accomplish far more by building observation and juxtaposition into the shooting. Make yourself respond to each location's particularities; make your camera respond to how participants' movements and actions convey the scene's subtext. The difference is between sharing the consciousness of someone intelligent and intuitive who picks up the event's underlying tensions and sharing the consciousness of a dull eye that swivels dutifully toward whatever moves.

 Don't let the camera be a passive recorder; make it an instrument of ironic juxtaposition or disclosure.

 Rehearse making documentary every spare moment; that is, investigate how you *inhabit* events rather than looking on them like an uncommitted outsider.

HANDHELD OR TRIPOD-MOUNTED CAMERA?

Emotional Effect

As we have said earlier, different camera mountings produce either the steadiness of a settled human view or the unsettled movement associated with quest, uncertainty, excitement, flight, etc. The two kinds of camera presence—one studied, composed, and controlled and the other mobile, spontaneous, and physically reactive to change—contribute a quite different climate of involvement, imply quite different relationships to the action, and alter the film's storytelling "voice."

Practical Concerns

A tripod-mounted camera can zoom in to hold a steady close shot when the camera is distant, but it cannot quickly move to a different vantage should the action call for it. The handheld camera gives this mobility, but at the price of unsteadiness and vulnerability. Going handheld may be the only solution when you cannot predict the action or know only that it will take place somewhere in a given area. Some camcorders are equipped with image stabilizers that compensate (sometimes quite successfully) for the kind of operator unsteadiness that comes from the occasional need to breathe.

The tripod-mounted camera is always "seeing" from a fixed point in space, no matter which direction the camera pans or tilts. Even when zooming in, the perspective (size of foreground in relation to background) remains the same, reminding our subconscious that the observation is rooted in an assigned place. This feeling would be appropriate for a courtroom, because the positions of judge, jury, witness box, and audience are all symbolic and ritually preordained. Because no court would tolerate a wandering audience member, it is logical that the camera/observer should also be fixed.

Covering a conversation handheld, the camera may reframe, reposition itself, and change image size many times to produce all the shots you would expect in an edited version: a long shot, medium two-shots, complementary over-the-shoulder shots, and big close-ups. Covering a spontaneous event with a well-balanced succession of such shots is a rare skill calling for the sensibility of editor, director, photographer, and dramatist all in one person. Because human life generates so much redundancy, you can often edit these shots down to an approximation of the feature film's elegant access to its characters. However, if you make the cutting too elegant, then your technique will cast doubt on the spontaneity of the scene.

 The handheld camera is a questing human intelligence on legs.

 Good handheld camerawork conveys dramatic tension between two entities: spontaneously unfolding events on the one hand and a questing intelligence busy assessing their meanings on the other. This manifestly daring improvisation unfolds on the run and in the teeth of actuality.

Great camerawork is a matter of utter concentration and astute sensitivity to underlying issues. Why else would a veteran Hollywood cameraman such as Haskell Wexler call documentary "real filmmaking"?

COVERAGE

SCENE BREAKDOWN AND CRIB NOTES

When filming a scene you must have ideas about what it establishes and what it might contribute to your intended film. List your goals so you overlook nothing in the heat of battle. If, for instance, you are shooting in a laboratory, you might make a reminder, or *crib note*, on an index card as shown in Figure 29-2.

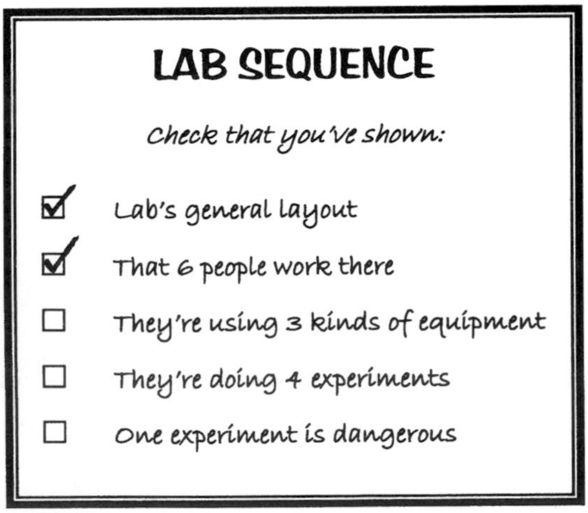

LAB SEQUENCE

Check that you've shown:

☑ Lab's general layout

☑ That 6 people work there

☐ They're using 3 kinds of equipment

☐ They're doing 4 experiments

☐ One experiment is dangerous

FIGURE 29-2

Crib note—goals for a laboratory sequence.

Say your bottom line is showing that the lab workers are dedicated and even heroic, and you must get shots to establish these things. Then, treating the camera as an observing consciousness, you imagine in detail *how you want the scene to be experienced.* If you were shooting a boozy wedding, you'd perhaps want the camera to adopt a guest's point of view. Going handheld, peering into circles of chattering people, it could legitimately bump into raucous revelers, quiz the principals, and even join in the dancing. To shoot in a dance studio, with its elaborate ritualized performances, takes a placing and handling of the camera that is formal and grounded. So how to show lab workers as heroic? The answer might lie in studied shots emphasizing the danger and painstaking rigor of the work they do and thus the human vulnerability of each worker. Perhaps you show a face near a retort of boiling acid. You make us see that each person has his own world and risks destruction in order to investigate significant problems. You see the calm, concentrated eyes above their masks, the elaborate equipment, the dedication.

Whatever the shooting situation, always ask yourself:

➤ What factual or physical details must I shoot to imply the whole?

➤ What will be each essential stage of development that I must cover?

➤ Is elapsed time important, and if so how do I imply it?

➤ What signals the start and end of each developmental stage?

➤ Where does the majority of the telling action lie? (In the courtroom, for example, does it lie with judge, plaintiff, prosecutor, or the jury?)

➤ Who is the central character and how does he or she act on the situation?

➤ When is this likely to change, and what makes the next person become central?

➤ Who changes during this scene?

INSERTS AND CUTAWAYS

Before allowing the crew to wrap, cast your mind back over the events you have just filmed and itemize possible *cutaway shots* or *inserts* (sometimes called *cut-ins*) that you need to shoot for possible ellipsis or cross-cutting. What is the difference?

• A *cutaway* is a shot of something outside the frame, such as the wall clock that somebody looks at. Shoot it from that person's eyeline as safety coverage.

• An *insert shot* is an enlargement of something in the main frame, such as a page in the book that someone is reading.

During a scene I once directed of a carpenter in his workshop, he folded and unfolded something below frame with a clicking noise all the time he was speaking to the camera. The cutaway we took of his hands holding his ruler enabled me to bridge together two separate sections of the interview and also to visually explain the off-screen noises.

EYELINE SHIFTS AND MOTIVATING CUTAWAYS

Frequently, a person you are shooting will hold out a picture, refer to an object in the room, or look off-screen at someone or something. In each case, his action directs our attention to something we need to see. This becomes an insert shot or cutaway. The corollary is that to legitimately use an insert, cutaway, or any cut at all, an editor must find a motivation—whether it emanates from a character or the needs of the story that is being told. Sometimes a cutaway or insert conveys a Storyteller attitude. For example, in the kitchen of a neglected elderly man, the tap drips incessantly. You film a close shot of it and of the dusty, yellowing photographs on his shelf in the background because it speaks volumes about long-standing disregard. Such shots, drawing the viewer's eye to significant detail, arise from (and are motivated by) the Storyteller's narrative intentions. They express an authorial point of view about this man and his life.

 Often in editing you'll use eyeline shifts to motivate cutaways. This is because we are always looking where others look to see what's caught their eye. Eyeline cutting mimics this habit and *motivates* a cut.

SHOOT REACTION SHOTS

Make your editor happy after you've covered two or more people in conversation by getting them to prolong the conversation while you shoot *reaction shots*. These can be listening, watching, or waiting close-ups of each individual when he is not talking. Catch (or even ask for) eyeline shifts; they are worth their weight in gold to the editor.

COVER ALTERNATIVE VERSIONS OF ISSUES

Try to *cover each important issue in more than one way* so you have alternative narrative vehicles later. You could, for example, cover a political demonstration with footage showing how the demonstration begins, close shots of faces and banners, the police lines, the arrests, and so on. But you might also acquire coverage through photographs, a television news show, participant interviews, or street interviews. This would produce a multiplicity of attitudes about the purpose of the march and a number of faces to intercut (and thus abbreviate) the stages of the demonstration footage. You now have multiple and conflicting viewpoints and narrative materials that you can greatly compress through parallel storytelling.

 The key to producing dialogical rather than monological films is to get plenty of coverage and to shoot it from multiple, differing, or even opposing viewpoints.

SPECIAL PHOTOGRAPHY

Documentaries may require special material such as graphics on a rostrum camera, mountaineering on a sheer rock face, coral reefs underwater, cities from a helicopter, or insect life seen through a high-power lens. At such times you are in the hands of a specialist. This may be pleasantly instructional or uncomfortable and even humiliating. Experts can use their knowledge to intimidate—as you know from trying to buy a double-ended whatsit in a hardware store—or they can happily share their knowledge. Research the process and the personnel beforehand so you don't lose control.

CHAPTER 30

CONDUCTING AND SHOOTING INTERVIEWS

The documentary interviewer sets out to draw people's stories from them, and the interviewee either wants to fulfill the interviewer's purpose or to resist and deflect it. As the human presence whom the interviewee addresses, the interviewer functions as a catalyst on behalf of the audience. This can produce fascinating results, so this chapter describes how to go about it. Sometimes, though, you'd like to get an inner monologue that is unmediated and free of your catalyzing influence. To this end, you'll find another method of initiating spoken thought near the chapter's end. Both methods aim to get people speaking from the heart.

 Watching an interviewee describe something important can be magical, and speech becomes action. Profound interchanges like this are at the heart of making documentary. Even in documentaries without dialogue, the director's listening and interactional skills make the film possible.

PRELIMINARIES

INITIAL INTERVIEWING DURING RESEARCH

The research interview is mostly an exercise in listening to see what you might build on subsequently. Refrain from pressing any question since you want to open it up later on camera. Often you'll stop someone, saying, "Don't tell me! Let's hold on to that in case we want it for the camera." Make notes, and if the potential interviewee questions you about the project, describe it in broad generalizations only. This lets you keep your options open and prevents you from creating impressions that subsequently prove misleading.

During research conversations, you often hear something that makes you think, "I must have this in the film." Note it down. Later you'll prepare questions that will elicit all this as naturally as possible. After listening to a number of people, you usually know by instinct who has the best experiences and the best way of telling them.

WHO INTERVIEWS

Busy directors often rely on a researcher, who runs ahead digging up facts and locating likely participants. They become trusted creative colleagues, and when it's time to shoot, the question arises: Should researcher or director conduct the interview? Each may have advantages. The researcher is continuing a relationship already begun, and this will put a hesitant participant at ease. If the director interviews, however, the interviewee is addressing a fresh listener and may be more spontaneous and comprehensive. The team often decides on the spot.

TYPES OF SITUATIONS

Setting

Shoot interviews anywhere significant to the participant, but consider the likely effect of each. In their home, workplace, or a friend's home, the interviewee is more at ease and will likely give more intimate responses. In public places, such as streets, parks, or the beach, he or she will feel more exposed and like one of many. Depending on the topic, this can be productive. Settings such as an old battlefield, childhood home, or first workplace may shake loose many emotion-laden memories.

The fact is that we are not fixed in whom we are. Ray Carney, writing about John Cassavetes' method of characterization in his improvised fiction films, rightly argues that we are constantly negotiating our identity through interaction with others.[1] The context to each exchange and the personality of each interlocutor always draws something a little

 A documentary film is the sum of relationships—those that you and your crew forge with participants and those they negotiate with each other.

different. So expect different settings and different approaches on your part to catalyze different facets of your interviewee.

When you interview someone for whom you can expect little valid cutaway material, you can shoot the interviewer using a second camera. This, of course, makes the interviewer a featured player in the film, but you can get around this

---

[1] Carney, Ray. *The Films of John Cassavetes*. Cambridge, U.K.: Cambridge University Press, 1994, pp. 21–22.

by using participants to interview each other, coaching them beforehand as necessary—and as ethical.

Presence of Others

Whoever is present but off-camera affects an interviewee. Imagine you are interviewing a gentle, older woman whose peppery husband is forever correcting her. You wisely arrange for the husband to do something in another room so she feels free to tell her own story. On the other hand, their unequal relationship may be an important and visible aspect of what they represent. I once shot an interview of a farm manager sitting next to his wife. As he spoke, she interrupted and modified everything he said to make it "nice." Of course this was funny, but it made you suspect her version of what paragons their employers had been.

Groups

Interviewing need not be one on one. A married couple, separately inarticulate through shyness, may prod each other into action and reaction very well. Friends or workmates can likewise provide mutual support. Putting two people together who disagree and interviewing them can be a highly productive strategy because antipathy reduces inhibitions. If you are lucky they will turn to each other and forget all about you. That's ideal. To interview a whole group, try one of two ways:

➤ "Recognize" each new speaker from among those who want to speak.

➤ Encourage them to begin speaking to each other.

➤ Use more than one camera so you always have reaction shots and cutaways.

When you bring a camera and talk to anyone in a public place—say, at a factory gate—others will gather to listen and join in. By not imposing control it often turns into a spirited conversation or dispute. The interviewer, now on the sidelines, can at any time interpose a new question or make a request, such as, "Could the lady in the red jacket talk about the company's attitude toward safety?" And talk she will. You can remain happily silent because your task—to catalyze people's thoughts and feelings—needs no further input.

Vox Pops

Person-in-the-street interviews (called *vox pops*, short for *vox populi*, or "voice of the people") are sometimes useful. You put the same few questions to a range of people and then string their replies together in a rapid and instructive sequence. Entertaining and useful for demonstrating a Greek Chorus of opinion, you can orchestrate diversity or homogeneity, thesis or antithesis. Sections of *vox pop* can lighten something essentially sober and intense, such as a film about political developments. They can also function as legitimate parallel action. When I had to compress the salient points of a 3-hour peace speech into less than 12 minutes, I used *vox pops* as a dialectical counterpoint between the man at the podium and people in the street. Each gave piquancy to the other—and we made virtue come out of necessity.

PREPARATION AND BASIC SKILLS

Before you interview, decide where each interviewee fits in with your film's central purpose. That way you can politely set limits on what each contributes. I don't mean prepare a script or anticipate specific statements, since that would mean treating a participant like an actor. Just say what areas you want to explore and ask the right questions. Ask ahead of time if you may redirect the conversation when it gets away from the areas you want to tackle.

 Decide who represents what in your film's spectrum of issues, then choose who makes the best case for each issue and who best represents each underlying value.

METAPHORICAL THINKING

Making a film usually means delineating a set of forces, each championed by one of your film's personalities. Your job is to gather the material to articulate these archetypal forces. Is this a good versus evil situation? The one against the many? The righteous against the doubters? Decide what archetypal situation you are handling and what role each "actor" might play in your film.

Earlier we said that "plot" represents the rules of the universe, and the protagonist is often the person challenging those rules. There is usually an antagonist, as well as a major conflict. You'll want to question in your mind whether the protagonist is fighting against timeless universal law or only societal norms that shift from generation to generation. All human situations have the kind of constants expressed in myths, folktales, fables, and ballads—for example, "Frankie and Johnny were lovers, but he done her wrong." Their modern equivalencies march on in contemporary films, books, stories, and celebrities. Such sources, when you plumb them, help remind you what's missing from your story. Finding the right analogies and metaphors (that you probably don't share with anyone) helps you decide what role each player occupies in the framework of your story.

BEFORE THE INTERVIEW

REHEARSING

Before interviewing:

> ➤ Work out how to phrase your questions so they become direct and unambiguous.
> ➤ Speak each aloud and listen to your voice. Does it sound direct and natural?
> ➤ Could anyone interpret any question in the wrong way?
> ➤ If the answer is "Yes," alter the question until only the intended understanding is possible.
> ➤ Listen to your questioning again for signs of manipulation and eradicate it.

FREEING YOURSELF TO LISTEN

Because you must maintain eye contact and give facial reactions during the interview, you can't bury your face in notes. List your questions on an index card and keep it for security on your knee when you interview. With it, you won't be afraid of drying up, and you'll probably cover everything without ever needing the prompts. At the end, use it as a checklist to ensure you've forgotten nothing.

 Good interviewing comes from really listening—to what people mean as well as to what they say or don't say. Work intuitively in the moment, dig deeply, and always ask for stories and examples.

BRIEFING THE CAMERA OPERATOR

Some notes on camera placement appear in **Chapter 29, Directing Participants.** You're going to set up a signaling method so you can determine when to zoom between shot sizes. Directors with plenty of material to edit in parallel will often shoot an interview in a one-size shot. Others incorporate different sizes of shots according to the speaker's intensity, because varying shot sizes offers a greater prospect for seamless ellipsis (shortening) of the results. To prepare for this, you'll need to develop an understanding with your camera operator about zooming in and out. Varying the image size allows the possibility of:

- Cutting between different sized shots and thus a good chance of abbreviation
- Restructuring an interview
- Removing what's redundant
- Eliminating the interviewer's questions
- Longer stretches of uncut interview on the screen—when the camera intensifies and relaxes scrutiny, it answers the spectator's need for variation.

Preparing for Image Size Changes

While you are lining up, look through the camera viewfinder and agree with your operator on three standard image sizes and framings. Place the compositional center (in interviews it is the subject's eyes) in the same proportionate spot in each composition's frame, so cuts will look balanced (Figure 30-1). From your interviewing position under or next to the camera, you are going to signal when and how you want each shot to change. I press different parts of the operator's foot. Typically, for:

➢ Wide shot (to cover each question), I press the ankle.
➢ Medium shot (used after the answer has got under way), I touch the top of the foot.
➢ Close shot (for anything intense or revealing), I press the toe.

During a lengthy answer, alternate between medium and close shots. During a new question, however, drop back to wide shot. I try to change image size whenever a speaker shows signs of repeating something. Since repetition is normal, the

FIGURE 30-1

Three sizes of image. Note that each compositional center—the subject's eyes—must be in the same part of the frame if any two compositions are to cut together well.

subsequent versions are often more succinct. Then, if it's in a different image size, you can cut between the two versions.

Zoom Speeds

Ask the operator to match the speed of zoom-ins and zoom-outs to the speaker's current rhythm, but never to make them long and lingering. Cutting into a slow-moving zoom looks hideous, so they should either be usably elegant or fast and functional during throwaway moments such as when you are asking a new question.

PREPARING THE INTERVIEWEE

SAY WHAT YOU WANT

You have the right and even the obligation to say what you want. It helps put the interviewee at ease and guards against digression if you describe the *general subject areas you want to cover and those you don't*. You can, after all, only cover what fits your film. Even though you may feel apologetic, make the limitations you want to impose sound reasonable—because they are.

 Rookie interviewers are often timid about setting limits and allow interviewees to range far and wide. Ultimately, this is unkind, as interviewees sense when they aren't fulfilling the interviewer's hopes.

ESTABLISH YOUR RIGHT TO INTERRUPT

Another way to lower the interviewee's anxiety is by explaining that you may occasionally interrupt or redirect the conversation. I usually say:

> This is a documentary, and we always shoot ten times as much as we use. So don't worry if you get anything wrong because we can always edit it out. Also, if I feel we're getting away from the subject, I may rudely interrupt, if that's all right with you.

Nobody ever objects; indeed, interviewees seem reassured that I take responsibility for where the conversation will go. This will only work if you have oriented the interviewee to the overall purpose of the film in the first place.

RELAXING INTERVIEWEES

Put people at ease by giving them exploratory work in areas that interest them and by being relaxed and interested yourself. Don't hurry, and don't change your manner when the camera rolls because this signals tension. Give the interviewee whatever permission they seem to need and give your undivided attention.

Rarely has this ever failed to work, though inevitably one sometimes runs into trouble. In an interview I began with the pediatrician Dr. Benjamin Spock,[2] he became visibly uncomfortable, though he had been fine throughout the days when we were shooting him in political action. I needed a long interview as a bank of voice-over to explain all the footage we'd shot before returning to the United Kingdom, but his to-camera manner was now so strangely stiff and inhibited that we stopped the camera to ask what was wrong. He realized that he was used to talking to women. Someone suggested we put our production assistant, Rosalie Worthington, in my position under the camera lens. I then posed the questions, and Spock answered to Rosalie, his manner now relaxed and avuncular. Had reflexivity been an option (and had I possessed the imagination to use it) I could have included this oddly revealing information in the film.

 Practice shooting a sophisticated interview using **Project 4-SP-11 Advanced Interview: Three Shot Sizes.**

CAMERA AND EDITING CONSIDERATIONS

INTERVIEWER AND CAMERA PLACEMENT

There are two approaches to setting up the nexus among camera, subject, and interviewer. Each carries different implications and reflects a different philosophy. The interviewee's eyeline tells you which is in use in any film. Either he or she is looking directly on-axis into the camera and addressing you, as Dr. Spock is doing in Figure 30-2, or he or she is talking off-axis to the left or right of camera, as the young man is doing in Figure 30-3. Another off-axis example showing the full crew is provided in Figure 9-13 in Chapter 9.

On-Axis Interview

I like this approach because I prefer to edit out the interviewer and leave the audience face-to-face with the speaker (Figure 30-2). The interviewer's role, as I see it, is to *ask questions the audience would ask if it could.* Once the interviewee is

---

[2] Dr. Benjamin Spock, in "We're Sliding towards Destruction," *One Pair of Eyes* series on BBC.

FIGURE 30-2

On-axis interview—the speaker looks into the camera because the interviewer's head is just below the lens. Once the interviewer's voice is removed, the speaker seems to be talking directly to the audience.

FIGURE 30-3

Off-axis interview—speaker looking off to one side of the camera.

talking, my presence becomes irrelevant and distracting, so I edit it out. To interview on-axis, sit on something low with your head just under the camera lens. The interviewee who converses with you effectively talks directly to the audience.

Off-Axis Interview

In the more traditional approach, the interviewer sits to left or right the camera and in or out of frame. Even when all trace of the interviewer and her questions is removed, the interviewee's eyeline shows he is addressing an invisible interlocutor

(Figure 30-3). The farther the interviewer is from the camera-to-subject axis, the more insistent this impression becomes. Removing the interviewer's voice does not alter this state of affairs; if anything, it magnifies an unseen, unheard presence.

When the Interviewer Should Be On-Camera

If the questioner's pressure and reactions are integral to the exchange, you need his/her presence on camera with the interviewee. Many television interviewers are masterly at this, and so the off-axis interview

 Watching film is inherently passive, so you must do all you can to mobilize your audience's involvement. During on-axis interviewing the interviewee speaks directly to the spectator, who responds with a dialogue in his or her mind. When the interviewee talks off-axis to a third party, especially an interviewer who is a celebrity, the spectator is more an onlooker than a participant.

complements the interviewer's function, especially when they interject appropriate reactions and questions as pressure.

PREPARING TO EDIT OUT THE INTERVIEWER

When you intend to edit out your questions, prepare interviewees by telling them how to include your questions in their answer. Many will look puzzled, so you give an example: "If I ask, 'When did you first arrive in America?,' you might answer '1989,' but the answer '1989' wouldn't stand on its own, so I'd be forced to include my question. However, if you said, 'I arrived in the United States in 1989,' it's a whole and complete statement and that's what I need."

Everyone understands but most forget. So, while you interview, listen like an editor at the beginning of every answer. Is it freestanding or does it depend on the question to make sense? If it depends on the question, get your interviewee to start again. Sometimes you must even feed the appropriate opening words. You'd say, "Try beginning with 'I arrived in America. . . .'" That usually solves it.

VOICE OVERLAPS

Note that if you do remove the questioner, you can use no section where voices overlap. As an interviewer, then, you must consciously *listen to ensure that each new answer starts clean.*

VOX POPULI INTERVIEWS

When you shoot *vox populi* street interviews, off-axis interviewing is unavoidable because the camera, mobile and handheld, is not something you can sit under. Remember to alternate the sides from which you interview, since more interviewees facing one way rather than the other will set the audience wondering what this means.

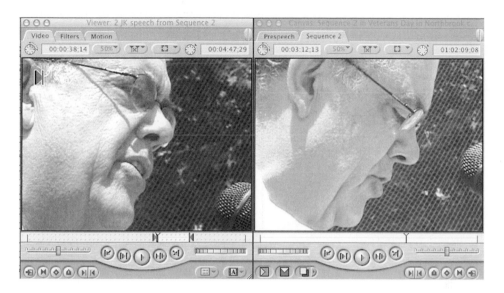

FIGURE 30-4

A jump cut is when two similar images mismatch so footage between them appears to have been removed.

SHOOTING FOR ELLIPSIS

You will need to shoot so you can abridge interviews in editing. If you shoot your interviews in a single size (as Errol Morris does), then you can only bridge different sections together by jump cutting. This is fine if you use such abridgements boldly and consistently as a style. Used intermittently they can be disconcerting; a subject's face suddenly changes expression, or a head jumps to a slightly different position (Figure 30-4). Particularly in a transparent film—that is, one that hides editorial processes under the guise of continuity—the odd jump cut rudely breaks the illusion. You can mask potential jump cuts by cutting away to something pictorially relevant, but again, unless it's a consistent style, it will reek of "cutaway." Likewise, using a nodding interviewer as a cutaway reaction shot will seem equally bogus.

There are two other solutions. One is to run multiple interview strands in parallel, cutting between them and abbreviating each as you go. If you can sustain story momentum, this is an elegant solution. However, the other solution— varying shot sizes during the interview—leaves you with more options.

VARYING SHOT SIZES

In this approach, the camera operator uses the zoom lens to make periodic image size-changes (see operational description in the "Briefing the Camera Operator" section, previously discussed). You can often cut different sections together (as in Figure 30-1) because the chances are good that what you want to use is in different image sizes. Screen conventions allow you to cut them together, providing:

- There is a bold change of image size, either larger or smaller.
- The subject is in a roughly similar physical attitude in the two shots.
- Speech and movement rhythms flow uninterrupted across the cut.

 Minor action mismatches go unnoticed when (1) you have a bold enough change of image size between the incoming and outgoing frames, and (2) talk or action flows uninterrupted across the cut. Be aware that the eye fails to register the first three frames of any new image.

Because of large image size difference between the three frames in Figure 30-1, minor mismatches will pass unnoticed, especially since persistence of vision means *the eye does not register the first three frames of a new image* anyway.

THE INTERVIEW BEGINS

INTERVIEWING AND DIRECTING

To face another human being while making a documentary means to probe, listen, and obliquely reveal oneself and one's purposes as you follow up with further questions. Often, by challenging someone to deeply explore an experience, you become a sounding board to realizations that lead to change. Thus, the interviewer subtly *supports* and *directs*—quite a responsibility. This should never mean manipulating the interviewee into exhibitionism,

 Working to challenge documentary participants is like narrowing and raising the banks of a river. You help the water run deeper and faster. Such shaping pressures help make visible—to both participant and the audience—issues that might otherwise have stayed hidden and unaddressed.

but rather providing the special occasion, assistance, and creative resistance that allows another person to explore—sometimes for the first time—paths that are truly their own.

LEAD BY EXAMPLE

If you are formal and uptight, your interviewee will be more so. You'll only get spontaneity by being relaxed and natural yourself. I try to lower pressure on interviewees by making my first questions deliberately slow and bumbling. That way I show my expectations are totally unlike the manic brightness of the live television show, where hosts chivvy people into performing.

FRAMING QUESTIONS

In commercials that masquerade as documentary you often see a pseudo-sincerity that reeks of manipulation. Sometimes documentary interviewers inadvertently get the same effect. Either through anxiety or the need to control, the interviewer has unconsciously signified the reply he wanted by using a *leading question*. Look at the difference:

Leading question: "Do you think early education is really a good thing?"

Open question: "What do you feel about early education?"

A leading question corrals the interviewee into a particular response. "Did you feel angry coming home to an empty house?" is fishing for a particular answer. As the participant deals with it, he is embarrassed to find himself answering to prescription. His resulting staginess and self-consciousness devalue the film. An open question would be, "Talk some more about the feelings you mentioned when you came home as a kid to an empty house." You are asking him to elaborate on something already mentioned in private. Open questions hand control to the interviewee and ask only for a sincere reply.

FOCUSING QUESTIONS

Some interviewers go fishing with catchall questions: "What is the most exciting experience you've ever had?" Devoid of preparation or focus, they throw out a big, shapeless net. Another habit, rampant in town hall meetings, is the rambling multipart question. The person answering can only tackle what she remembers— usually the last thing on the list. To lead your interviewee into a chosen area rather than trail him, make your questions specific and address one issue at a time.

THE RIGHT ORDER FOR QUESTIONS

To make an easy start, ask first for information. Facts are safe, while opinions or feelings take a more confident, relaxed state of mind. These you keep for later when your subject has become used to the situation and is even enjoying it. There's no point in posing questions in the order you need for your film because you will reorganize everything in editing anyway. The only logical order for questions is that which your participant finds easy and natural. Listen to your instincts so you can maintain the pressure and flow.

Highly sensitive issues can be difficult. Preparing for a film I made with Alexandra Tolstoy, the twelfth and most controversial child of the great novelist Leo Tolstoy, I read in her autobiography that she had been an unwanted child. Worse, she had learned in childhood that her mother had tried to abort her. Understanding that such grievous knowledge would have affected her whole life, I hoped I could touch on it without offending or hurting her. Nervously, I delayed broaching this to the end. Her reply, when it came, was full of dignity and honesty and patently from the heart. In editing, however, I placed it early because it illuminates everything she says subsequently.

In my naïveté, I hardly supposed that an elderly lady of 86 could still feel the anguish of childhood so keenly. What emerges about a person's private pain always leads to deeper appreciation of their strengths. There would be little justification for intruding otherwise.

MAINTAIN EYE CONTACT AND GIVE BEHAVIORAL FEEDBACK

During the interview, maintain eye contact with your subject and give visual (*not* vocal!) feedback as the interviewee talks. Nodding, smiling, looking puzzled, and facially signifying agreement or doubt all contribute the kind of feedback we normally give vocally. They sustain the interviewee in what might otherwise feel like an egocentric monologue. Errol Morris claims to get his extraordinary interviews by keeping expectantly silent and just letting the camera roll.

AIM TO ELICIT FEELINGS

If an interviewee gives you objective fact or measured opinion when you need his feelings, he may be afraid of appearing self-indulgent. People will often give a general answer—for example:

Q: What was your experience in the submarine service like?

A: Oh, it was all right, you know, nothing great.

An older man, he belongs to the No Complaints school in which drawing attention to yourself and your needs is contemptible. You must draw this speaker out by asking for the specific. He answers, "Well, it was hard, and I didn't much like the leadership in my company." Now you need some color. By asking "Can you tell me a story about that?" he produces something you can see and feel. Success.

Turn interviews toward feelings every time. A question such as, "You said you had strong feelings about the fears suffered by latchkey kids?" works well because it signals your interest in how he *feels*. Narratives need specifics. Many people (men particularly, I have to say) produce not the stuff of experience but a wad of arid conclusions. The emotions attached to their memories are buried deep in a filing cabinet, each sealed in a folder inscribed with a contents summary. The buttoned-up interviewee gives you the summary, not the more photographic stuff within. If there is a way to break in, it's by gently refusing generalizations and asking for stories, stories, stories.

GOING WHERE ANGELS FEAR TO TREAD

Making documentary faces us with a precarious duality: We can create a liberating arena for discovery and growth, or we can intrude and exploit by violating invisible boundaries. The danger of exploiting participants is never quite absent, since without access to people and their lives documentaries are not possible. Much documentary making, thank goodness, takes place at a light-hearted level, but in this chapter we must examine the most demanding end of the spectrum.

TEMPTATIONS WHEN INTERVIEWING

As early as the research period, interviewing poses ethical responsibilities. The thrill of the righteous chase can at any time delude you into unfairly demolishing a person's defenses. Although you have a second chance in the cutting room to recognize and prevent this from becoming public, the damage to your relationship with your subject (and your coworkers) may remain. More dangerous is when you don't have editorial control. In spite of your objections, your superiors may use something that you regret shooting.

Here is another interviewing dilemma. You take a participant up to an important, perhaps unperceived, threshold in his life. In a revealing moment, the interviewee crosses into new territory. You see what Rouch calls a "privileged moment," where all notion of film as an artificial environment ceases for participant and audience alike. It is a wonderful moment, but it hinges on the revelation of some fact whose consequences might become damaging if made public. Do you now lean on the person to permit its inclusion in the film? What if the participant is so trusting that you alone can make the decision whether or not it will damage him? Here, wise and responsible coworkers can help you carry the burden of decision. If, however, you decide to suppress the revelation, do you carry on as though you don't know this important but confidential truth? Only you, guided by your own values and knowledge of the circumstances, can finally decide.

 There's always some risk in any relationship where you look for truth more than comfort. In filmmaking the danger is that the relationship is not one of equality.

HAVING POWER

Simply by arriving with an instrument of history called a camera, the interviewer has the upper hand. You may use it to intimidate or liberate, depending on how you handle your role. Your best safeguard is to find participants who appreciate your values and aims and are ready or even eager to make a journey of exploration with you. In return, you make yourself emotionally accessible and ready to give as well as take.

 Good interviewing is a form of displaced authorship. Even with the questions removed, the interviewer's ability as catalyst, selector, and organizer remains written all over the screen.

WITNESSING

You aspire to create a partnership with your interviewee like the "poet as witness" that Seamus Heaney describes in a discussion of World War I poets. To Heaney, those writing about the appalling carnage of that war represent "poetry's solidarity with the doomed, the deprived, the victimized, the underprivileged." The witness, he says, "Is any figure in whom the truth-telling urge and the compulsion to identify with the oppressed becomes necessarily integral with the act of writing itself."[3] Those heroic souls who have since faced tanks in Tiananmen Square, stood in solidarity with Palestinian villagers in the Occupied

---

[3] Heaney, Seamus. *The Government of the Tongue*. London: Faber, 1988, p. xvi.

Territories, or who, as members of Voices in the Wilderness, made themselves human shields during their country's bombing of Iraq in 2003, are courageous people ready to live their convictions to the ultimate. I first met such people among World War I "conchies" (conscientious objectors). Said one, a Quaker, "We felt very strongly that we would rather be killed than kill other people." Forty years later, this—said so quietly and matter-of-factly—still gives me the shivers. What courage it takes to live by this belief! Young though I was, I knew what he meant; it was an honor to record for posterity what he and the others did, which is the witnessing that Heaney asks us to do.

As documentary makers we try to find ordinary people living extraordinary lives and then to act as witnesses to what is special.

THE INTERVIEWER'S NIGHTMARE

Every interviewer dreads the person who can't or won't talk:

Q: "You weren't satisfied when you moved into this apartment?"
A: "Nope."

Try asking, "Talk to me a little about how that happened." If he doesn't respond, it may be wise to abandon the attempt. He may be stonewalling or resolved not to speak of this or any upsetting experience. An old and dear friend, a pilot at 18 in World War II who crashed and suffered innumerable surgeries afterwards, told me almost with pride that he has never spoken of his fighter pilot experiences. When I tried pressing him to give details for history's sake, he sent me an (excellent) autobiography—written by someone else. Some people simply won't revisit emotions. Their experiences have left terrible marks that they can't imagine revisiting.

DUMMY RUN

Very occasionally it happens that you need to stop an interview because the interviewee is, for whatever reason, hopelessly unsatisfactory. Every crew sometime pretends the camera is running in order to avoid hurting the participant's feelings.

INTERVIEWING IN DEPTH

CROSSING THRESHOLDS

In a memorable interview you will see someone cross an emotional threshold and break new ground. This gives what all stories need—a central character who is visibly in movement and developing—and it delivers the emotional content or even shock that we expect of dramatic art.

You confront the caretaking daughter with her contradictory

 The best interviewers really *listen* and press for specifics and examples. Simple rejoinders—such as "How?" or "Why was that?" or "How did that make you feel?" or "Talk some more about that, would you?"— liberate the sentient being from the stoic observer. Asking the interviewee to take time and talk about pictures in his or her mind's eye can also elicit a better kind of telling.

feelings for her mother, and before our eyes she says she recognizes for the first time that she despises aspects of someone she thought she only loved. A man crossing a similar threshold might admit to himself that he was unequal to the job in which he suffered a humiliating demotion.

Both times the interviewee *is experiencing an important realization for the first time.* This is a breakthrough, and the suspense and sense of sharing it is electrifying. Under such circumstances your job is to remain expectantly silent. Wait and wait, if you need to—the silences will be full of drama onscreen.

YOUR MOST POWERFUL TOOL

Moments occur in interviewing when you sense there is more to tell, but the person is wondering whether to risk telling it. A gentle "And?" or simply "Yes, go on" signals that you support her in continuing. After this, stay silent and wait. That silence becomes gripping because imaginatively we enter the interviewee's mind as she visibly and dramatically grapples with a vital issue.

 The expectant silence is the interviewer's most powerful tool for inducing the interviewee to go deeper.

To the insensitive or inexperienced interviewer, silence is failure, so they come crashing in with new questions. The underlying cause is not listening for the subtext and not trusting intuition, but there's no risk to waiting because it is not live television. Your material is going to be edited, so you take no risks by trusting your hunches and waiting in silence.

DON'T CATCH THEM WHEN THEY FALL

Neil Sandell of *Outfront* (see end of this chapter) warns not to break out of your role and comfort someone who becomes emotional or distraught during an interview. To stem suffering is commendable, but it turns the interviewing relationship into something different. Often, the reflex to comfort comes from being embarrassed and wanting to slam a door on what you've precipitated. But people simply don't go where they can't cope. Let them handle it, Sandell advises, and just remain quietly present and supportive.

 People in interviews don't go where they can't cope. If someone breaks down, be quietly present and supportive. It's something that needs to happen, so don't rush in to stop the flow.

 The anthropologist Jean Rouch summed up the moments of naked discovery a person sometimes makes as "privileged moments."

PRIVILEGED MOMENTS

The most impressive windows on human life come as detonations of truth—what the anthropologist Jean Rouch called "privileged moments," when someone on camera suddenly manifests a new awareness. You see these not only during action but sometimes also in an interview. In a film of mine it was a father realizing that, for all his love of country, he would leave it rather than let his sons go off to risk death in a foreign war the way his brother had done in Vietnam.

BEING ADVERSARIAL WITHOUT BEING OFFENSIVE

Here are a couple of nonthreatening ways to open up a delicate area:

1. **The devil's advocate approach**—If you say, "*Some people would say* it's not frightening for a kid to get home before his mother," then you are playing the devil's advocate. The words I've italicized invite the interviewee to discharge his feelings about those who don't realize how scared a young kid can be when he must enter an empty house. Tim Russert used this approach notably when he asked President Bush, "How do you respond to critics who say you brought the nation to war under false pretenses?"

2. **Starting with generalized comment**—Let's say you want an interviewee to say on camera what she's told you in private, that she opted to nurse an ungrateful mother instead of getting married. You'd like to ask, "Didn't you resent your mother's demands when you saw the love of your life marry someone else?" But this is too brutally direct, so you start more generally and at a safe distance: "Our society seems to expect daughters more than sons to make sacrifices for their parents, doesn't it?" She nods and starts talking. She can stay with an impersonal opinion or, when you invite her to tell an illustrative story, she can get closer and closer to the injustice that ruined her life. When she ventures an opinion, you simply ask for an example. By mutual and unspoken agreement, you steer toward the poignant testimony that both you and she want to put on record. How did this work? By starting with general questions, you help frame her situation as a sad injustice that overcomes women unprepared for a societal trap. This is an easier place to start than asking her to flaunt a sense of personal victimization. The distinction matters: Many who are too proud or realistic to admit pain will do so when it might save someone else from the same fate. Without this beautiful and generous human impulse, much documentary would be impossible.

GETTING BRIEFER VERSIONS

Facing an unexpected question, the human memory yields its contents in stages, so interviewees often recount the same events in more than one way. It works like this: Your interviewee searches and struggles to explain. For emotionally loaded events, this is attractively spontaneous and dramatic. She goes back to explain, then to question herself forms a firmer picture and tells the whole episode again.

When it's a matter of getting a few facts in order, this can be tiresomely slow. Many people sense this and spontaneously repeat their explanation in a more orderly and rapid form. When this should happen but doesn't, you can ask, "Maybe you'd just like to go over that once more and give me a shorter version." Usually the interviewee is grateful, and you get a nice short version. In editing you can choose or even combine the best versions.

 Most participants enjoy collaborating in the making of a documentary and are just as sincere when redoing something a second or third time.

BELIEVING IN YOUR AUTHORITY

As you work with a central character in a documentary, you can often sense what their unfinished business is. Novice directors are often hesitant, fearful of rebuff, or too self-conscious to act on their intuitions in this direction. It takes no mystical powers to sense which way a person leans, only careful observation. It's far easier, in fact, to see other people's unfinished business than one's own. If you elect to play a role—that of investigating and making a record—you must expand enough to become assertive and politely demanding in a way that people in regular life (wrongly, I think) might deem invasive. The more stoic and repressive of feeling a person (or culture) is, the more extreme are the pressures they hold behind the mask and the more your function as a catalyst can matter. People usually defer to this right if you act on your belief in it. They will journey inward and take you and your camera along to a degree that is surprising, moving, and humbling.

 In your role as director you sometimes probe on behalf of the audience, on behalf of history, or even on behalf of humanity. This is both frightening and exhilarating.

GIVE AND TAKE

When you have qualms about acting on your instincts, remember that it's normal to doubt one's authority. To the participant, your attention, your invitation to make a record, confirms that he or she exists and matters. What you give is recognition, something we all crave, and this entitles you to invite a partnership that is seldom denied. Why is this?

Perhaps documentarians are the village conscience, the village storyteller, whose job is to remember the village's history, reflect its opinions, and validate each person's worth. When you begin, this role is hard to believe in and harder to act out. At first you ask favors

 The camera is a little engine of history and a magnet to confession. Those who use it often get treated like priests or doctors.

with a groveling sense of apology and obligation, but you find you are welcomed and assisted openheartedly. If you press a little as you shoot, you will find not only that you are allowed to make incursions into your subjects' lives but also that it is *expected*. This you must treat responsibly, naturally, but you must also

FIGURE 30-5

Legacy chronicles a family making it out of the notorious public housing projects—with the belief and support of a film crew. (Photo courtesy of Tod Lending.)

resist those feelings of obligation that will skew your editorial decisions. Sometimes this too is painful.

Occasionally, filmmaking helps people make changes they never imagined possible. Tod Lending's *Legacy* (2000, United States; Figure 30-5) chronicles an African–American family he followed for five years after the murder of a beloved family member. In a postscreening discussion I attended, family members said frankly that it was Tod's support and filming that helped them work their way out of Chicago's notorious Cabrini Green projects (public housing). A film crew that began as witnesses became believers and supporters and upheld their subjects' sometimes hesitant progress through an uncaring world. You can see the opening of this film at http://directingthedocumentary.com.

CONCLUDING THE INTERVIEW

Before ending the interview, check your topic list to make sure you covered what you intended. Then, *while the camera is still running*, ask, "Is there anything else you want to add, anything we forgot to cover?" This records the fact that you handed the last word to the participant, should any dispute arise later. After you cut the camera, thank your participants and briefly appreciate whatever was successful about the exchange. Keep everyone in place so the recordist can shoot a minute or two of presence track.

THE RELEASE

When everyone rises to start dismantling equipment, give each participant a token sum (often the minimum $1) and the *individual release form* (see Figure

24-2 in Chapter 24), so you obtain a signed permission form for your records that explicitly allows you to use the material publicly. This is always an uncomfortable moment. I confess that, when I could, I gave this ghastly ritual to an assistant with instructions to carry it out as a necessary formality. It is normal, even mandatory among many organizations, *not* to pay any significant sum for interviews, since that would open you to charges of checkbook journalism.

  Apply the self-rating checklist to your interviewing results in **Project 5-PP-1 Assess Your Interviewing.**

INTERVIEWING ASSESSMENT

In the Appendix you will find a self-rating checklist to help you assess your performance as an interviewer (see project box). What did you forget? What do you need to work on? Confronting the blind spots and artificiality in your behavior helps you reach for the next level of interviewing. You see there are spontaneous moments of humor, inspired questions, and well-judged pauses, but also self-consciousness, persuasion tilting into manipulation, haste disguised as enthusiasm, and timidity masquerading as respect. What a rendezvous with the ego!

GOING FURTHER: INWARD JOURNEY MONOLOGUES

In most interviews, people speak in the past tense about events already concluded. They face an interviewer and give—or resist or deny—what the interviewer seems to want. The limitation is obvious: that it's interviewer centered, and at some level inherently adversarial. Once I tried to break out by asking an interviewee to see a scene in her mind's eye and describe in the present tense what she saw. It failed because she kept reverting to the past tense— she was an Auschwitz survivor and had every reason to thrust memories back into the distance. Probably the crew, the camera, the lighting, and my presence as an interviewer all made pursuing an inner monologue difficult.

 The limitation of conventional interviewing is that it is interviewer centered and unavoidably adversarial.

However, the approach wasn't completely misguided. The Canadian Broadcast Corporation's radio story program *Outfront* (www.cbc.ca/outfront/) does something similar and gets superlative results. Of themselves they say, with winning moxy, "*Outfront* is where we hand you the microphone. You make a radio documentary, with our help. Then CBC broadcasts it—and you'll even get paid!" Producer Neil Sandell described methods they use in the National Public Radio (NPR) Third Coast Audio Festival broadcast of February 2, 2008 (http://

thirdcoastfestival.org/resound_february_2008). "Ironing Man" and "One Blue Canoe" are examples that will leave you with a lump in your throat.

An *Outfront* producer might say:

- Close your eyes so you can begin seeing things in your mind's eye.
- Use this sentence to begin (interviewer gives a prompt; see samples below).
- Describe in the present tense what you see. Wait for the pictures to form and take as long as you need.

The radio producer's prompts, spoken as necessary, might sound like this:

- I am in my bedroom choosing what to wear. . . .
- I am driving on the highway and there's a large white van coming toward me. . . .
- As I return to consciousness, the first things I hear and see in the hospital emergency room are. . . .

This can produce remarkable, freestanding description from which an editor can extract a spontaneous inner journey—very different from the conventional interview.

Radio documentary is resurging and even showing the way forward for filmmakers. NPR's Third Coast Audio Festival puts out wonderful work drawn from all over the world. Try the Australian work on Show #57 at www.thirdcoastfestival.org/re-sound.asp (rebroadcast February 23, 2008). For depth of social comment, listen to Claudia Taranto's "A Tale of Two Townsvilles," and for unforgettable sound design and sheer gut-wrenching emotion, listen to Kyla Brettle's "000 Ambulance." Before becoming an independent radio producer her training was in literature and music.

The *Outfront* approach is a wonderful way to generate film narration or voice-over. For more adventurous radio work and offbeat treatments, also try listening to Ira Glass and his NPR team in *This American Life* at www.thislife.org. Their forte is funny, quirky, and intimate first-person shows that look deeply into some aspect of popular culture. One show you might enjoy at www.thislife.org is:

Testosterone

Stories of people getting more testosterone and coming to regret it. And of people losing it and coming to appreciate life without it. The pros and cons of the hormone of desire.

PART 7C

ADVANCED POSTPRODUCTION

Editing is procedurally similar for both short and long projects, except that in longer films structure, length, and balance become much more difficult to get right. For one containing interviews you are likely to work from transcripts, so this chapter shows how to select and mark transcript sections and how to assemble them into an initial script for the editor. You are also more likely to need narration, so **Chapter 32, Creating Narration,** describes various methods of creating it. If you are using music you'll need **Chapter 32, Using Music and Working with a Composer. Chapter 34, Editing Refinements and Structural Problems,** deals with methods of balancing your story and testing it on an audience.

CHAPTER 31

FROM TRANSCRIPT TO FILM SCRIPT

The more interviews, the more events, the more elements you must orchestrate in your movie, the more you'll need a paper planning method to stay on top of your material's potential. What follows is a method for carving up transcript copies and narrowing your choices into a workable shape with a minimum of wasted effort. Figure 31-1 is a flow chart to illustrate this. The paper edit method allows you to get selected working materials up on the screen, after which you put documentation aside and work wholly with screen materials.

There's no reason why you can't take the principles that follow and apply them to a database system in which you cut and paste with a computer rather than literally cutting paper. For myself, I like the tactility of looking at hard copy and sliding slips of paper around.

WHAT YOU NEED FOR TRANSCRIPTS

- *Timecode*—Transcripts should include timecode (hours, minutes, seconds) at the beginning of each interview and thereafter, every 30 seconds or so, the numbers interpolated after a convenient period and between sentences or paragraphs.
- *Accurate transcriptions*—These should be made verbatim with any ums, wells, you knows, and all the other verbal curlicues that people use as place markers while their mind assembles what they want to say next. Punctuation should follow the way a person speaks and never be adapted to make his presumed intentions clearer and more literary. The temptation to edit and clarify as you transcribe is ever present, but resist, because it makes extra work for the film editor later. Start a new paragraph when the speaker plainly starts a new thought; otherwise, keep typing in long paragraphs. Remember, it's not literature and you don't lay it out for easy reading. It's a record of how someone spoke.

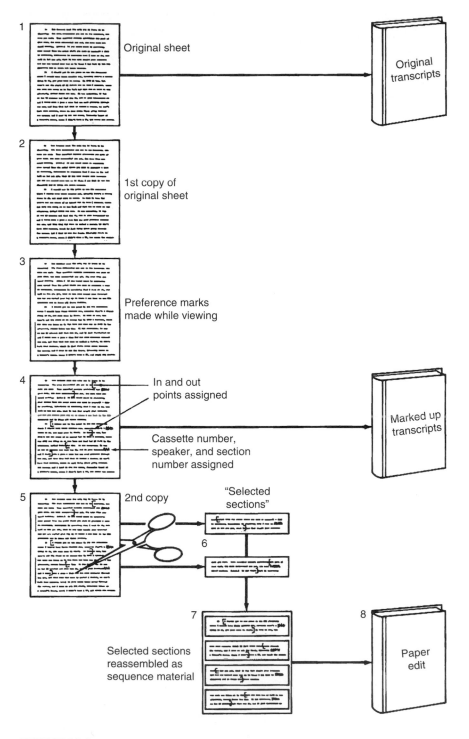

FIGURE 31-1

Flow chart illustrating how to turn transcripts into an assembly script.

- *Line numbering*—Word processing has a line-numbering feature (see box) used in legal documents that I could have used for an oral history film I once made. It had over 20 characters telling the convoluted story of the World War I antiwar conscientious objector movement. Had each interview transcript been line numbered, I could have known where even single lines of cut-up transcript came from—a lifesaver on a really big project.

> *To insert line numbers in Microsoft® Word*, go to **File menu**, click **Page Setup**, click the **Layout** tab. In the **Apply to** box, click **Whole Document**. Click **Line Numbers**. Select the **Add line numbering** check box, and then select the options you want. One allows you to start a second take, say, with a consecutive number. To see the numbers on your screen, select **Print Layout** in the **View** menu.

- *Using a database*—For a film series drawing on a huge base of transcript or archive material, you might want to develop a resource like the one I am using for a large-scale biography. Using an all-purpose database program such as FileMaker® Pro, you can customize it so that, once materials are filed, you can search with incredible speed by key words, time period, or character—or whatever else you nominate as parameters. You can also display the material in different formats (lists, as cards, etc.) and by various priorities such as time period or characters in alphabetical order. Putting the data in the system does take time and effort, but later it hands you a huge information bank that you can use with efficiency and total thoroughness. If you're working with a modest amount of source material, you may get by with yellow highlighter and Post-It® notes, or you can cut copies and paste them according to what follows.

SELECTING THE MATERIALS

Step A. From your typed-up transcript file (Frame 1) make two prints—one we shall designate the Master Transcript and the other the 1st Copy (Frame 2). Amass master copies in a binder titled *Original Transcripts*, and keep them apart. You are going to mark up the first copy of the master.

Step B. Run the film interview on a DVD or editing machine, and follow the speakers' words in the 1st Copy. When a section strikes you as effective—for whatever reason—put a rough vertical "preference mark" in the margin, as in Frame 3. At this stage just *respond* and don't stop to analyze your reactions. There will be a time for that later. Some preferences will be for a story graphically told, others for some well-presented factual information, and still others will be in response to an intimate or emotional moment, be it humor, warmth, anger, or regret.

Step C. Study each preferred section and find its logical in point and out point, using square brackets to indicate the start and finish of the section, as in

```
Q:  What do you remember about the farmer?

Ted:  What do I....?  Oh, well, you know, [he
was all right if you kept your place.  But if
you got smart, or asked too many questions,
he'd be after you.  "Where's that wagon load of
straw?  Why ain't them cattle fed yet?"  And
then he'd say there were plenty of men walking
the streets looking for work if I didn't want
to work.  The only thing you could do was be
silent, 'cos he meant what he said.]  Now his
wife was different.  She was a nice soul, you
know what I mean?  Couldn't see how she came
to marry him in the first place....
```

6/Ted/3
'Ted's descript. of Farmer Wills.'

FIGURE 31-2————————————————————————————

A selected section showing in and out brackets, media origin ID, and tag description.

Frame 4. Figure 31-2 shows an enlarged view of a typical chosen section with its in and out points bracketed. In the margin is written "6/Ted/3." Decoded, this media ID means "Cassette 6, Ted Williams, section 3." Use whatever format you like for section identities, but as with all filing systems *stick with one system for the duration of the project* and make improvements only when you start a new project.

 Whatever system you devise to manage information, stick with it and only make changes and improvements when you are ready to start a completely new project.

Until you replay the selected section you won't know whether you can execute your in and out points as marked. Maybe you can't lose all those verbal warm-ups before the in point; maybe your out point leaves Ted on a rising voice inflection so his statement sounds strange and unfinished.

Section IDs will always allow you to quickly locate the section in the Marked Up Transcripts volume and find it in its parent take. Without some such method, finding where material originated in order to extend it can waste inordinate time during a heavily edited show. You can also of course use a computer search function on the transcript files or search via timecode in the edited version, but searches always take time and effort.

Figure 31-2 has one more notable feature: the handwritten tag description of the section's use, "Ted's descript. of Farmer Wills." When you face dozens of slips of paper, tag descriptions allow you to initially sort and structure them.

Step D. Make a photocopy of the marked sheets (Frame 5). You can now file the parent transcript copy (Frame 4) in shooting order in a binder titled *Marked-Up Transcripts*. Make an index at the front so you can quickly locate each character. Later, during editing, this file will be an important resource.

Step E. Scissor the marked sections (Frame 5) into selected sections (Frame 6), ready for sorting and grouping in pursuit of the paper edit. Because you've identified each slip by subject or intended use and because it carries an ID, you know at a glance what it is, what it can do, and what its context is in the parent sheets, the Marked-Up Transcripts.

Now you are ready to construct a *paper edit*—really, a detailed sketch for the first assembly. The selected sections (Frame 6) will eventually be stapled to sheets of paper (Frame 7) as sequences, and the sequences will be assembled into a binder (Frame 8) holding the paper edit or plan for the first assembly of your movie.

This procedure may seem laborious, but if you are working on an oral history film, say, with a vast bank of spoken material, time spent organizing at the outset (indexes, graphics, guides, color coding, and so on) is effort generously rewarded later. I learned this when hired to edit the final game in the 1966 soccer World Cup documentary, *Goal*. There were 70,000 feet of mostly silent 35 mm film (that's nearly 13 hours) shot from 17 camera positions. The only orientation was a shot of a clock at the beginning of each 1000-foot roll. My assistant Robert Giles and I spent a week up to our armpits in film, making a diagram of the stadium and coding each major event as it appeared in all the various angles. The game had gone into overtime due to a foul, and it was my luck to eventually establish that, during this most decisive moment, *not one* of the 17 cameras was rolling! Then, using sports reports and Robert's far superior grasp of the game, we set about using an assortment of close shots to manufacture a facsimile of the missing foul. No one ever guessed we'd had to fake it.

The project was an editor's nightmare. Had we not first taken the time to invent a decent retrieval system, the men in white coats would have carted us off in the legendary rubber bus.

ASSEMBLING THE PAPER EDIT

To avoid your film turning into solid speech, first deal with your action sequences:

Step F. Prepare to make a rough assembly of action sequences (those that show human processes with a beginning, middle, and end). Make a list of them and design an overall structure that moves them logically through time. Be conservative with your first structure. If you have a film about a rural girl going to the big city to become a college student, stay true at first to the chronology of events (as opposed to the events unfolding according to their importance, say). Afterwards, when you can better see how the material plays, you might intercut her high school graduation, conversations with a teacher, discussions with her father, and leaving home with the development of her first semester as a college drama student. You would then have two parallel

 For a first assembly, follow the chronology of events. Later you may see more compelling ways to organize the story through time.

stories to tell, one in the present and one in the past. It is far too risky at this stage to assume you can do this in one giant step.

Step G. View the action or behavioral material in time sequence more than once to establish its narrative possibilities firmly in your mind. Now you can go on to plan a safe, linear version, beginning from a paper edit that includes speech.

Step H. Take up your chosen transcript sections, as discussed earlier in this chapter (see Figures 31-1 and 31-2. These slips of paper, coded "Jane" for Jane's sequences so you can turn rapidly to parent copies in the marked-up transcripts, might look something like this:

1/Jane/1   Graduation speech

1/Jane/2   Dinner with boyfriend's family

1/Jane/3   Conversation with English teacher

2/Jane/1   Conversation with Dad

You have the many pieces of action made into a preliminary assembly, ready to accommodate the dialogue sections of the film. It's best to represent these as sequences rather than as individual shots, which would be too detailed and cumbersome. Three sequences would go on separate slips of paper, each with a media location (cassette or P2 card number, minutes, and seconds):

1/05:30   Exterior school, cars arriving

2/09:11   Preparations at podium, Jane rehearsing alone

4/17:38   Airport, Jane looking for bus

Kneeling on the floor, move the slips of paper around to try different orders and juxtapositions. Certain pieces of interview or conversational exchange belong with certain pieces of action, either because the location is the same or because one comments on the other. This comment may be literally a spoken comment or, better, implied through ironic juxtaposition (of action or speech) that makes its own point in the viewer's mind.

An example would be a scene in which our student Jane faces having to make a graduation speech before the whole school, a prospect that scares her. To make a literal comment, one would simply intercut the scene with the interview shot later in which she confesses how nervous she feels. A nonliteral comment might take the same rehearsal and intercut her mother saying how calm and confident she usually is. A visual comment during the rehearsal might show that she is flustered when the microphone is the wrong height and that her hands shake when she turns the pages of her speech.

 Conflicting information is always stimulating because it shows contrasting points of view and challenges us to take our own position.

What's the difference? The literal comment is show and tell because it merely illustrates what Jane's thoughts and feelings already give us. The nonliteral comment is more interesting because it supplies us with conflicting information. Her mother rather enviously thinks her daughter can handle anything, but we notice signs that the girl is under a lot of strain. Either the mother is overrating the girl's confidence or she is out of touch with her child's inner life. This privileged insight, discreetly shared with the audience, gives us behavioral evidence that all is not well, that the girl is suffering, and alerts us to scrutinize the family dynamics more carefully.

The order and juxtaposition of material, we can say, have potent consequences. The way you eventually present and use the material signals your ideas about the people and the subject you are profiling and reveals how you intend to relate to your audience. In essence, you are like a lawyer juxtaposing mismatching *pieces of evidence* in order to stimulate the interest and involvement of the jury, your audience. Good evidentiary juxtaposition provides sharp impressions and removes the need to explain.

 Don't waste much time trying to refine the paper edit. Only by working through the nuances of the material onscreen and seeing how it plays can you be sure what really works.

The mobility and flexibility of the paper edit system reveals initial possibilities and gets you thinking. You've moved your slips of paper around on a table or floor like the raw materials for a mosaic. Each juxtaposition gives you ideas and sets you thinking, just as you might from looking at the potent relationships between chess pieces laid out on a board.

Don't worry if your paper edit is vastly too long and repetitious. This is normal; you can only make refined decisions from experimentally intercutting and screening the material. Once you've decided a reasonably logical order for the chosen materials, staple the slips of paper to whole, consecutively numbered sheets and place them in your paper edit binder.

Now that you have a rudimentary story, you can rule lines between sequences and group the sequences into scenes and acts. From this master plan you can begin making a loose, exploratory assembly in your editing computer.

CHAPTER 32

CREATING NARRATION

Nowadays many filmmakers avoid narration because it reminds them of the disembodied, voice-of-God narration associated with traditional documentary. Even so, narration is ubiquitous in natural history, science, government, history, journalistic, and diary film forms. Narration is in fact useful, and there are ways to make it palatable and even highly effective. You will definitely need ways to produce narration for the screen. Perhaps you have a personal or anthropological film and must provide factual links or context. Perhaps you find yourself in difficulties because expositional material is lacking or the film's story line needs simplifying. Narration is the answer.

 Narration is always available to link story materials together. It need be neither dishonorable nor detrimental even though you planned not to use it.

 Analyze your choice of narrated film for its writing and juxtaposing of images and words with **Project 1-AP-1 Analyze or Plan Using the Split-Page Script Form.**

NARRATION

PROBLEMS IT CAN SOLVE

Let's say that during shooting you remembered to elicit all relevant expository information from participants. You assembled the movie to see how it stood on its own feet but you face some problems:

- You are having difficulty getting the film started (convoluted and confusing setup).

- The origin and therefore authenticity of the materials are in doubt (it might be reconstruction, for instance).
- The film is too long and lacks momentum (material that links the best sequences is clumsy and slow).
- The audience needs more information on a participant's thoughts, feelings, choices.
- Overcomplicated storyline requires simplifying.
- Getting from one good sequence to the next takes too much explaining by the participants.
- Film's resolution lacks focus so film fails to resolve satisfyingly.

Your film has expository problems when a lukewarm trial audience becomes enthusiastic because you added comments after the viewing. Narration may be the only way to supply the missing information succinctly, but you will have to tread carefully.

DRAWBACKS

Narration that is less than first rate is intrusive and hampers rather than advances your movie. You'll have to decide whether any narration may pose problems because the disembodied voice adds a mediating presence between the audience and the film's "evidence." Unless the narration comes either from the filmmaker or one of the characters, viewers are apt to assume that a narrator's voice is *the voice of the film itself*. This means they base their judgments not just on what the narration says but also on the quality and associations of the voice. This is why finding a suitable voice is extraordinarily difficult. In effect, the search is for a voice whose words and quality convey your attitudes toward the subject.

If you choose the male "radio voice" and write too commandingly, your narration will seem like the voice of *authority* with all its connotations of condescension and paternalism. Audiences wait wearily to discover what product or ideology the film is touting. The intelligent documentary, on the other hand, uses narration sparingly and neutrally, inviting audience members to use their own judgment, values, and discrimination.

POSITIVE ASPECTS

Narration is a lifesaver when it rapidly and effectively introduces a new character, summarizes intervening developments, or concisely supplies a few inarguable facts. Especially when a film must fit much into a short duration, time saved in one place is time won for more useful purposes elsewhere. Narration:

- Supplies brief factual information.
- Makes you take responsibility for the identity of your film.
- Avoids emotional manipulation.
- Avoids value judgments, unless first established by evidence in the footage.

- Avoids predisposing the viewer in any direction.
- May indicate visual or verbal aspects of the evidence that we might otherwise overlook.
- Lets the audience draw conclusions from the evidence.

A narration can draw on existing traditions of stylized voice already established in literature, ballad, and poetry. Documentaries may, therefore:

- Use a character's voice-over as narration because he or she has insider knowledge and a right to an opinion.
- Take a historical view, as in films that omnisciently survey immigration, war, slavery, etc.
- Adopt the guise of a naïvely inquisitive visitor (as in films by Nicholas Broomfield, Michael Moore, and Morgan Spurlock).
- Take a what-if, suppositional voice, as in Cayrol's commentary for Alain Resnais' *Night and Fog* (1955, France). Its authority—and whether you know it or not seems to make no difference—comes from Cayrol being himself a Holocaust survivor.
- Express a poetic and musical identification with the subject, as in Basil Wright and Harry Watt's *Night Mail* (1936, United Kingdom).
- Radicalize the audience by using a bland or understated way of looking at an appalling situation, as in Luis Buñuel's *Land Without Bread* (1932, Spain).
- Use a letter- or diary-writing voice, as in the authentic war letters from which Ken Burns builds much of the narration for his series *The Civil War* (1990, United States).
- Write a diary for the next generation, as Humphrey Jennings imagined a war pilot doing in *A Diary for Timothy* (1946, United Kingdom). The narration (by the novelist E.M. Forster) projects the hopes of a war-weary generation.

TWO APPROACHES TO CREATING NARRATION

Practically speaking, documentary narration generally fails unless it uses the direct, clear language of everyday speech. Following are two ways to create a narration:

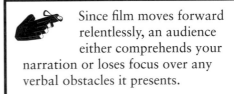 Since film moves forward relentlessly, an audience either comprehends your narration or loses focus over any verbal obstacles it presents.

METHOD 1: READ FROM A SCRIPT

This, the traditional method, can work well if you base your film's verbal narrative on a *bona fide* text such as letters or a diary, when the unavoidable formality present in anyone's reading will feel right. But, if you want spontaneity or a one-to-one tone of intimacy, written narration almost always fails. Just think how often the narration is what makes a film dull or dated. Common faults include:

- Verbosity (a writing problem)
- Heavy or literary writing (a writing problem)
- Doubt over who or what the narrator represents (a question of the narrator's authority)
- Something distracting in the narrator's voice—dull, condescending, egotistic, projecting, trying to entertain, trying to ingratiate, or that holds distracting associations (a performance or casting problem)

Recording a read narration is inherently risky, so do it well in advance and to picture (described later). Expect to record scratch (temporary) narration and keep changing it until you get it right. Never assume it'll be all right on the night. It never is.

METHOD 2: IMPROVISATION

Improvised narration can rather easily strike an attractively informal, one-on-one relationship with the audience. Examples include:

- When a participant serves as narrator
- When you use your own voice in a diary film that must sound spontaneous and not scripted
- When you want to create a composite poetic voice, say, of a Japanese woman carrying out a tea ceremony (a highly questionable "speaking for" ploy but formerly more acceptable)

Let's look at what's involved with each method.

 In search of a direct and simple narration, be prepared to write upward of 20 drafts. There should not be a single redundant syllable.

THE SCRIPTED NARRATION

WRITING

Signs of bad narration include:

- The pseudo-scientific passive voice
- Sonorous, ready-made phrases and clichés
- Convoluted sentences
- The syntax of writing or literary discourse
- Jargon or other language used to impress
- Over-information (constant talking, which robs the audience of time to imagine or guess, is often inflicted by films for children)

- Description of what is already evident
- Condescending humor

Signs of good narration include:

- The direct, active-voice language of speech
- The simplest words for the job
- Language free of cliché
- The most meaning in the fewest syllables
- Language that is balanced and potent to the ear

As you edit and re-edit your film, keep rewriting in search of the power of simplicity. Exult when you find a way to reduce a sentence by even one syllable. Test your writing by reading it aloud to one or more listeners. For some reason, this makes one acutely aware of all that's still wrong.

THE TRYOUT

Now read your words aloud against each film section. The narration must:

- Pick up its sense from the words of the last speaker and feed into those of the next.
- Match them rhythmically.
- Be the right length so the narrator doesn't have to speed up or slow down to fill the space.

Expect to go through many drafts before everything feels right and falls into place. Sometimes the needs of narration require you to adjust ends and beginnings of scenes.

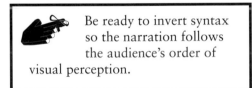 Be ready to invert syntax so the narration follows the audience's order of visual perception.

ALTER SYNTAX TO MATCH SCREEN LOGIC

Sometimes it helps to invert the syntax so the narration follows the order in which the audience notices things. For instance, if you have a shot of a big, rising sun with a small figure toiling across the landscape you might write, "She goes out before anyone else is about." But, the viewer notices the sun long before the human being, and your writing negates the order of perception, so that the viewer, unaware at first of any "she," loses the rest of the sentence. Reconfigure the syntax to follow the order of perceptions (sun, landscape, woman) and you get: "Before anyone else is up, she goes out." This complements the viewer's perceptions instead of swimming against the tide.

ACCOMMODATE SOUND FEATURES

Sometimes you alter phrasing or break sentences apart to create spaces for featured sound effects, such as a car door closing or a phone beginning to ring. Effects can create a powerful mood that drives the narrative forward, so don't

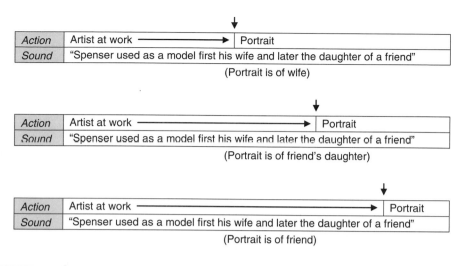

FIGURE 32-1

Different cutting points imply different identities for the portrait's subject.

obscure them. They also help to mask the bane of documentary—too much talk, impolitely known as verbal diarrhea.

THE POWER IN EACH FIRST WORD

Here's a little-known fact that will make you a great editor: During a flow of images, *the first word to fall on a new image influences how the audience interprets it.* For example, suppose we have two shots cut together, as shown in Figure 32-1. The first, outgoing shot is a still photo showing an artist at work at his easel, and the second, incoming shot shows a painting of a woman. The narration says, "Spencer used as a model first his wife and later the daughter of a friend."

Different juxtapositions of words and images actually yield quite different meanings, and the crux lies in which word hits the incoming shot, as illustrated in the diagram. By using a single, unchanging section of narration and positioning it differently we can in fact identify the person in the portrait three different ways, depending on how it sits against the three images.

In another situation, illustrated in Figure 32-2, a simple shift in word positioning may alter only the emotional shading attached to an image rather than its basic identity. For instance, you see two shots, each of a piece of sculpture, and you hear the narrator say, "His later work was provocatively different."

By altering the relationship of narration to incoming image by a single word, the second sculpture becomes either just "different" or "*provocatively* different." Skillful writing and sensitive word placement gives you a potent tool of communication.

OPERATIVE WORDS

Though you often write to images, in editing you must often do the opposite and place images against dialogue or preset narration. There is a little-known

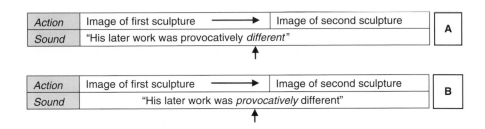

FIGURE 32-2

The first word on each new image affects how we interpret its meaning. Such operative words are italicized to demonstrate how emphasis can change. In (A) the later sculpture seems like a departure in the artist's work, while in (B) the second sculpture evoked an excited reaction.

secret to doing this effectively. In any section of speech, there are **strong** and *weak* points against which to lay a picture cut. To spot the strong ones, listen to the stress patterns in the speaker's language. They indicate dominant intentions by stressing—in slightly higher volume and note—the key syllables. Suppose a mother says this to a recalcitrant teenager: "I want you to wait right here and don't move. I'll talk to you later."

Different readings suggest different subtexts, but a likely one is: "I want you to **wait** right here and **don't** move. I'll **talk** to you later." Stressed words represent the dominant intention, so I think of them as *operative words*. We would design images to this piece of dialogue in a split-page script like this:

Picture	Sound
Wide shot, woman and son	"I want you to …
Close shot, boy's mutinous face	**wait** right here and …
Close shot, her hand on his shoulder	**don't** move. (pause) I'll …
Close shot, mother's determined face	**talk** to you later."

By cutting to a new image on the operative words, you punch home the mother's determination and imply the boy's stubborn resistance. This principle and the rhythms that accompany it permeate the editing of fiction and documentary films. Use **Project 1-AP-6 Analyze Editing and Content** on a fine feature film dialogue sequence, and you will come to understand all the thinking behind the editing. In great part, it responds to the nuances in the playing, not something theoretical or imposed. It is highly structured by the inherent rhythms of physical movement and dialogue.

A potent way to use language when you are editing is to listen like a foreign musician. This makes you listen for clues to meaning within the verbal music people make while conversing. Within a single sentence you hear rising and sinking tonal changes, rhythmic patterns in the stream of syllables like percussion, and dynamic variations of loud and soft. Now your editing, shot selection, and placement begin taking place inside a musical structure and form a new, larger structure. Here film, music, and dance coincide.

Good narration adds to the image, never duplicates its message.

COMPLEMENT, DON'T DUPLICATE

When you write for film, never describe what we can already see. Narration must add information to what we see, never duplicate it. For example, don't say that the child in the shot is wearing a red raincoat (blatantly obvious) nor that she is hesitant (subtly evident), but what you can say is that she has just had her sixth birthday. This is outside what we can see or infer and is legitimate additional information.

TRYING IT OUT: THE SCRATCH RECORDING

Once you have written your narration, record a scratch (quick, trial) narration using any handy reader or your own voice. Lay in the scratch narration and watch it several times dispassionately. Improved versions will jump out at you. You'll see where you need pacing and emotional coloration changes and that you must thin the narration out where the narrator is forced to hurry. Elsewhere the narration may seem perfunctory because it needs developing. You can now more easily imagine what kind of voice you'd prefer. Keep writing and rewriting until you've got every sentence and syllable just right. Now you are ready to think about auditioning and recording the final narrator.

A SCRIPT FOR THE NARRATOR

The script prepared for the narrator should be a simple, double-spaced typescript, containing only what the narrator will read. Set blocks of narration apart on the page and number them for easy location. Try not to split a block across two pages, because the narrator may turn pages audibly during the recording. Where this is unavoidable, lay both flat during the recording so no handling is required. Putting pages inside plastic page protectors will keep them from rattling. If you write a contract for the narrator, stipulate a proportion of call-back time in case you need additions at a later stage.

Writing well is one art, and finding someone to speak it is another. Even professional actors can seldom read a commentary without making it sound canned.

NARRATION: AUDITIONING AND RECORDING

The fact is that speaking and reading aloud are utterly different. Speak to a listener, and your mind is occupied finding words to act on him and ensure that he comprehends. Reading from a script turns you into an audience for your own voice. A few highly experienced actors can overcome this predicament, but they are very rare. Now think of documentary participants; they are going to have far more difficulty speaking from a script, even when the words or ideas were originally their own.

VOICE AUDITIONS

To test native ability, give each person something representative to read. Then ask for a different reading of the same material to see how well the narrator responds to direction. Sometimes the reader focuses effectively on the new interpretation but is unable to hold onto what was previously successful. Another reader may be anxious to please and can carry out instructions but lacks a grasp of the larger picture. This is common with actors whose main experience is commercials.

After you make audition recordings, thank each person and give a date by which you will get back in contact.

Because choosing a narrator is choosing a voice for the film, you will reject many types of voice because of their associations. For any number of reasons, most available voices simply won't sound right. As with any situation of choice, you should record several, even when you believe you have stumbled on perfection. Select the speaker by trying his or her recordings against the film until you are satisfied. Your final choice must be independent of personal liking or obligation. Make it solely on what makes the best narration voice.

 Even if you think you've got the right narrator, do not commit until you have listened carefully to other candidates. Listening to a disembodied, recorded voice is usually a lesser experience than you had in the actor's presence.

RECORDING AND DIRECTING THE NARRATOR

Show your chosen narrator the whole film and listen to his or her ideas about what it communicates and what the narration adds. Encouraging the narrator to find the right attitude and state of mind has much to do with getting the words to sound right. When we speak, we speak from thoughts, experiences, memories, and feelings; invoking the whole person of the narrator gets better results than imagining that everything is on the page.

Record in a professional fashion—that is, with the picture running so the narrator (listening on headphones) can key into the rhythms and intonation of adjacent voices in the film. As you go to record each section, the narrator should cease watching the picture (that is the job of the editor and director) and his or her headphones should be cut off from

 Some filmmakers record *wild*—that is, they shoot narration with no picture and without regard for synchronization or intonation. This is risky. You can be sure of nothing until you fit the narration to see if it works. By then the artist has long gone.

track in and out points, which would be distracting. No access to a studio? Set up your own rig with video playback and original sound available to the artist via headphones. It will be more than worth the trouble.

Large organizations have access to landlines, conferencing facilities, and so forth that make it economically feasible to record a narrator who is distant. This may work for history, science, or journalism, but a narrator in a remote location is difficult to engage emotionally for films that require a personal tone. No fiction director would choose to work miles apart from their actors, nor should you.

ACOUSTIC SETTING

Your best voice recording will probably come from having the speaker about 1 to 2 feet from the microphone. Surroundings should be acoustically dead (not enclosed or echoey), and there should be no background noise. Listen through *good* headphones or through a good speaker in another room. It is critically important to get the best out of your narrator's voice. Watch out for the voice trailing away at ends of sentences, for "popping" on plosive sounds, or distortion from overloading. Careful mike positioning and monitoring sound levels all help.

The narrator should read each block of narration and wait for a cue (a gentle tap on the shoulder or a cue-light flash) before beginning the next. Rehearse first and give directions; these you should phrase positively and practically, giving instructions on what feeling to aim for rather than why. Stick to essentials, such as "Make the last part a little warmer" or "I'd like you to try that a bit more formally." Name the quality or emotion you are after. After rehearsing each block, record it and move on to rehearsing the next.

Sometimes you will want to alter the word stressed in a sentence or change the amount of projection the speaker is using— "Could you give me the same intensity but use less voice?" or "Use more voice and keep it up at the ends of sentences." Occasionally, a narrator will have some insurmountable problem with phrasing. Invite her to reword it while retaining the sense, but be on guard if this starts happening a lot. Sometimes narrators want to take over the writing. Let the narrator do it only if you can hear definite improvement.

Once you have recorded all the narration, play all the chosen parts back against the film so you can check that it all works. If you have any doubtful readings, make additional variants before letting the narrator go. These you audition later and use the best.

CREATING THE IMPROVISED NARRATION

You can achieve a spontaneous and informal narration, one sounding like person-to-person conversation, quite easily through interviewing. Now the speaker's mind is naturally engaged in finding words to act back on you, the interviewer—a familiar situation that unfailingly elicits normal speech. Ways to create an improvised narration include:

1. *Improvising from a rough script*—In this relatively structured method, briefly show your narrator a list of ideas just before recording. You ask

interview questions, and he or she then replies in character, paraphrasing because you have not allowed any learning of lines. Finding the words to express the narration's content reflects what happens in life; we know what we want to say but must find the words to say it.

2. *Improvising from an identity*—This method is good for creating, say, a historical character's voice-over. It develops from a character or type of person the narrator has "become." Together you go over who the narrator is and what this character wants the listener to know. Then you "interview" him, perhaps taking a character role yourself in order to ask pertinent and leading questions. Replying from a defined role helps the narrator lock into a focused relationship.

3. *Simple interview*—From interviewing you can afterward extract a highly spontaneous-sounding narration in the cutting room. In the most common method, the director interviews the documentary's "point of view" character carefully and extensively. Probably it will be done in spare moments during shooting while the chase is on. When you interview, *make sure the replies stand on their own as statements*. Replies that lack self-contained starts won't make sense unless you retain your question, which defeats the interview's purpose. For instance:

Q   "Tell us about how you make your catch in the bay."

A: "With pots, and a boat."

If you remove the question, "With pots, and a boat" doesn't mean much. So amend your question and ask again:

Q: *"Tell us what your work is, what you catch, and how you go about it."*

A: *"Well,* I'm a lobster fisherman and we use lobster pots, and a boat to get from one ground to the next.*"*

Remove everything I've italicized, and suddenly you have a nice, affirmative statement that makes perfect first-person narration. As you interview, listen carefully to make sure you cover all your bases. Keep a list handy of what information you must elicit so nothing gets forgotten, and for anything at all important make sure you get *more than one version from more than one person* so you have options in the cutting room later.

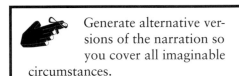 Generate alternative versions of the narration so you cover all imaginable circumstances.

If you've shot sync interviews you can use mostly voice-over and cut to the speaker's image at critical moments. Overused, this can become the slippery slope to a "talking head" picture. You can also interview people while they are at their normal activities. *The House*, a 1996 series about London's deteriorating Royal Opera, had wigmakers and set designers talking to the camera about the management's failings as they powdered wigs or arranged props. Today you aren't bound to make transparent films—that is, ones that pretend we are seeing real life with no camera crew present. Nowadays, we happily share the whole reality with the audience.

When you need to narrate your own film, get a trusted and demanding friend to interview you.

SUMMARY

All three methods produce a narration that can be edited down, restructured, and purged of the interviewer's voice. The results will be fresh and strike a consistent relationship with the audience. Of course, this takes more editing than a written narration, but the results more than justify the labor. Recording and then fitting the improvised narration to picture are editing procedures similar to those for the scripted narration, so use what follows.

RECORDING THE PRESENCE TRACK

Whenever you record a voice track, record some recording studio presence or location atmosphere. As we've said in relation to location recording, this provides the editor with the right quality of "silence" to extend a pause or add to the head of a narration block. Even in the same recording studio and using the same mike, no two presence tracks (also called *buzz tracks* or *room tone*) are ever exactly alike.

FITTING THE NARRATION

Lay narration carefully against picture so the stressed syllables in operative words hit each new image to maximum effect. This often takes small picture-cutting changes, though altering the natural pauses in the narration will often stretch or compress a section of unsuitable length. Be very careful, however, not to disrupt the natural rhythms of the speaker. By paying attention to operative words and their potential, you will see that patterns of pictures and words become receptive to each other and fall into mutually responsive patterns. Magically effective, they drive the film along with an exhilarating sense of inevitability. Good editing is the art that disguises art.

GOING FURTHER

This is a good book for those aiming to make work for public broadcasting:

Bernard, Sheila Curran. *Documentary Storytelling: Making Stronger and More Dramatic Nonfiction Films*. Boston: Focal Press, 2007.

CHAPTER 33

USING MUSIC AND WORKING WITH A COMPOSER

WHEN AND WHEN NOT TO USE MUSIC

Documentaries, like fiction films, commonly use music to build tension, facilitate a transition, or lighten material that would otherwise be dull. Most interesting is when music *suggests what cannot be seen*, such as a character's expectations, interior mood, or the feelings that he withholds. In Pernille Rose Grønkjær's lyrical and delicate *The Monastery: Mr. Vig and the Nun* (2006, Denmark), the 82-year-old Mr. Vig remarks that during all his long life he has never known love. As recounted in Chapter 17 (Figure 17-7), he's a former parish priest trying to donate his rural castle as a future monastery. To his dismay, the nun who comes from Moscow to accept it wants to make extensive repairs. She is 50 years his junior, and they are formal with each other, but she begins to look after him. Johan Söderqvist's music suggests what is happening inside these two tough and reserved characters. One critic described the score of guitar and string orchestra as "exquisite and ... a living, breathing character all on its own."[1]

Study how your favorite film uses music with 1-AP-1 Analyze or Plan Using the Split-Page Script Form, or script out your own film prior to using music.

---

[1]Kirby Dick interviews the director in *Still in Motion*, May 14, 2007, at http://stillinmotion.typepad.com/still_in_motion/2007/05/interview_perni.html.

Hear it for yourself on the film's web site www.themonasterymovie.com/onastery.html, and try to see the film, which has truly beautiful imagery.

MISUSING MUSIC

Music, sad to say, is often used to stir emotions that should arise from the film's content but doesn't. Other times it duplicates what's already evident on the screen; summer music followed by snow music during one of those "and the seasons passed"

 Music, rather than trying to enhance a scene, becomes potent when it adds new elements. When it suggests characters' expectations, interior moods, or the feelings they withhold, it conveys interior dimensions. Music can even do this for landscapes or manmade objects—anything, in fact, to which music can give a soul.

montages would be gilding the lily. Music should never "picture point" the story by commenting too closely. Walt Disney was infamous for "Mickey Mousing" his films—the industry term for making scores into sonic strait-jackets around the minutia of action. The first of his "true-life adventures," *The Living Desert* (1953, United States) was full of extraordinary documentary footage that Disney disfigured by making scorpions square-dance and supplying a different note, trill, or percussion roll for everything that dared to move. Used like this, music becomes a smothering form of control that aggressively bars the audience from making its own emotional judgments. Many documentaries of an older generation suffer in this way, as they also suffocate under patronizing, omniscient narration. Ethnic scenes in documentary pose particular problems and the riskiest solution is to make a poor facsimile of Thai music for a film set in Thailand.

 Music is often made to inject what a film lacks—drama, tension, exoticism, surprise, or magnitude.

USING MUSIC WITH A LIGHT HAND

Luckily, fashions change, and today less is considered more. A rhythm alone without melody or harmony can sometimes supply the uncluttered accompaniment that a sequence needs. Better illustrative music is that used to counterpoint the visible so it provides unexpected emotional nuance. In a story with fine shading, a good score can supply the sense of integrity or melancholy in one character and the interior impulsiveness that directs the actions of another. Music can enhance not just the "givens" of a character (what we already know about him or her) but also the interior development that leads to an action, thus implying moods, motives, or interior processes not otherwise accessible. Music can

 An indifferent sequence suddenly comes to life when music gives it a subtext that boosts the forward movement of the story.

supply needed phrasing to a scene or help create structural demarcations by indicating transitions.

Frequently a succession of scenes constitutes a narrative building block, and music can unite them under a single thematic identity. It can also indicate a new act or other narrative departure. Short *stings* or fragments of melody are good when they belong to a larger musical picture. Stings are a well-established convention in fiction film, but use them cautiously in documentary unless the style of the film and its sound design have been boldly set up to allow it.

Good music can prompt the audience to investigate emotional aspects to the film that are not obvious. Errol Morris does this master-

 Music can help unify material, bracket what's similar, point to common denominators, or accent transitions.

 Music should not substitute for anything but should complement action by offering access to the inner, invisible lives of the characters or their situation.

fully in *The Thin Blue Line* (1988, United States). The bleak and beautiful repetitiousness of Philip Glass's minimalist score underlines the nightmarish conundrum in which a man, trapped on death row for a crime he claims not to have done, must eternally relive the fateful events that led to his incarceration. Morris is quite justified in calling his film a documentary *noir*.

WHERE TO USE MUSIC

Films usually provide their own clues about where to use music. Often it seems natural during periods of tension, exhilaration, and in journeys or other bridging activities—a montage of a character driving across country to a new home, for instance. Transitions of any kind often benefit from music, especially when the mood changes as well as the location. Music can concentrate an emotional change when, for instance, an aspiring football player learns he can join the team, or when someone newly homeless must lie down in shame for her first night in a doorway.

Music can summon the spirit of an age or heighten the residual emotion in a landscape or city vista. It can help a film modulate from realism to a more prophetic mood, as Godfrey Reggio does in his *Koyaanisqatsi* (1982 United States), a long and grandiloquent parable about man's rape of the natural world. It can supply ironic comment or suggest alternative worlds. Hanns Eisler's score plays a major part in Resnais' superb Holocaust documentary, *Night and Fog* (1955, United States) as noted in **Chapter 5, Documentary Language.** Instead of picture-pointing the deportation trains or playing an emotionally loaded accompaniment to the mountains of human hair and eyeglasses, his score plays against the obvious with a delicate, ghoulish dance or by sustaining a tense, unresolved interrogation between woodwind instruments.

STORYTELLER VOICE

Now used more freely as documentaries dare to become subjective and lyrical, music is an aspect of the Storyteller's voice. The best music doesn't illustrate; it seems to give voice to feelings and an emotional point of view, either that of a character or of the Storyteller. It can even function like a Storyteller's aside by expressing an opinion or alternative idea, implying what cannot be seen or commenting on what can.

STARTING AND STOPPING MUSIC

Film music, like debt and smoking, is easier started than stopped. Music being addictive, it can be a real problem to end a section without withdrawal pains. The panacea is to supply something in its place. This can either be a commanding effects track (a rich train-station atmosphere, for example—really a composition in its own right), or a new scene's dialogue, or yet again an inciting moment of action that lugs the spectator's attention forward into a new domain.

 Ending a music section without leaving a void can be difficult. The best solution is to supply something in its place—either strong action or a new and commanding sound element.

When using music not designed to fit your film, section ends can either be faded out or, better, come to a natural finish. In the latter mode, you would back-lay the music from the picture finish point, arranging to fade music up at the picture start or adjusting the scene length to make the picture fit the music from composer's start to composer's finish. With music that is overly long, you can frequently cut out repeated phrases. Composers like to milk good musical ideas, so most pieces are replete with repeated segments.

If you need something from the recorded classical repertoire, enlist the advice of a knowledgeable enthusiast. You can never tell if a piece really works until you play it against the sequence in question. Be careful not to select something overused or fraught with existing film associations, such as Vivaldi's *Four Seasons*, or Wagner's *Also sprach Zarathustra*.

SPOTTING SESSION

Spotting for music is the process of viewing the fine cut, deciding where it needs music and where that music might come from. Some may be popular music or music from a particular era used for atmosphere. Unless it's spontaneously coming from a radio in the street market and a legitimate part of the atmosphere, you will have to acquire the right to use it. The rest will need a film composer.

LIBRARIES AND COPYRIGHT

Music libraries exist that will license a range of music at affordable prices and with a minimum of difficulty. I am assured that their offerings have improved in the last decade.

The copyright situation for using other previously recorded music is complicated. It requires fees and clearances involving any or all of the following: composer, artists, publishers, and record company. Students can often get written clearance for a manageable fee but only for use in festivals and competitions. If you then sell your film or receive rentals for showings, you may find yourself at the sharp end of a lawsuit.

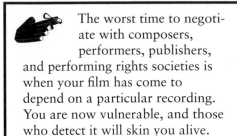 The worst time to negotiate with composers, performers, publishers, and performing rights societies is when your film has come to depend on a particular recording. You are now vulnerable, and those who detect it will skin you alive.

Never assume that the recorded music you want to use will be available when you get around to inquiring. Find out about clearing music for your film from Michael C. Donaldson's *Clearance and Copyright: Everything the Independent Filmmaker Needs to Know* (2003, Silman-James Press) or Phillip Miller's *Media Law for Producers* (2002, Focal Press).

WORKING WITH A COMPOSER

Commissioning original music solves the clearance problem and gives you music unique to your film. Film composers are usually last to be hired in the creative chain and must work fast and efficiently in pressured circumstances. That said, the more time you can give them, the better. For most of what follows I am indebted to my son Paul Rabiger of Cologne, Germany, where he makes music for television and film. Like many involved in producing music economically, he works largely with synthesizer programs, using live instruments when the budget allows. Software favored by composers includes Digital Performer®, Steinberg Cubase, and Emagic Logic® Audio. Such programs permit many tracks, integrate MIDI with live recording, and support video in QuickTime® format so a composer can build music to an accurate video version of the film.

WHEN THE COMPOSER COMES ON BOARD

The composer who comes on board early will read the proposal and see the first available version of the edited film. He or she then mulls over the characters, the settings, and the film's overall content, taking time to develop basic melodic themes and to decide what instrumental texture works best within the budget. Particular characters or situations often evoke their own musical treatment or *leitmotif* (recurring themes), and this takes time especially if the music must reflect a particular era or ethnicity and some research is necessary.

 An experienced composer finds out what the director wants the music to do and avoids coming with preconceived ideas.

WHEN THERE'S A TEMPORARY TRACK

Sometimes while editing, the editor drops in *temp* (temporary) or *scratch track* music that nobody expects to keep but which helps assess the movie's potential during editing. The unlucky composer is then confronted at a screening with a Beatles song or a stirring passage from Shostakovich's *Leningrad Symphony*. Certainly it shows what great music can do for the scene and demonstrates a preferred texture or tempo. Now the unfortunate composer must extract whatever the makers find valuable (say, in rhythm, orchestration, texture, or mood) and try to reach for his or her own musical solutions.

DEVELOPING A MUSIC CUE LIST

Once you have more or less locked down your film's content, screen it with the composer, director, editor, and producer. A DVD or tape version given to the composer should have timecode identical to that displayed in your editing software, since you need a cumulative timing for the whole film as a common reference. The group will break the film down into acts and where these occur on the film's timeline. They will discuss where music seems desirable, what it should achieve, and what seems most appropriate. When music's job is to set a mood, it should do its work and then get out of the way, only to return and comment later. Sometimes a composer will point out just how effective, even loaded, a silence can be. The rhythms of action, camera movement, montage, and dialogue are themselves a kind of music and may require no enhancement. Typical questions center on how time is supposed to pass and whether or not you want music to shore up a weak scene, as it often must. The composer finds out (or suggests) where each music section starts and stops, aiming to depart the discussion session with a music cue list in hand and full notes as to the music's function, with beginnings and endings defined as timecode in and out points. Start points may begin from particular cues in the imagery or dialogue.

If the editor compiles the music cues, sections should be logged from point to point in the cumulative timecode. If there are tightly fitting sections, then log them to the nearest half second. Figure 33-1 shows what this looks like. Because music is easy to start but hard to end, ending cues will take careful planning. As we've said, the rule of thumb is to conclude (or fade out) music under cover of something more commanding. You might take music out during the first seconds of a noisy street scene or just before the dialogue in a new scene. For best practice examples, study fiction films that successfully integrate music with the kind of action you have in your film.

> In the course of hands-on composing, music cues are occasionally added, dropped, or renegotiated when initial ideas meet actuality. Poorly placed or unjustified music may be worse than no music at all.

The computer-savvy composer then takes the DVD or tape copy and either creates a traditional score to be performed and recorded or, working with computers and MIDI-controlled synthesizers, creates music sections directly.

	Music Section 4
00:59:43	Begin music over long shot of Drottningholm Palace
00:59:59	Medium shot actors crossing courtyard and entering theater building
01:00:22	Interior theater, long shot
01:00:31	Backstage, actors enter
01:00:40	Stage manager tests primitive wind machine (make space in music here)
01:00:51	Actors getting into costumes (bring music up between 00:54 and 01:05)
01:01:24	Curtains opening on dress rehearsal
01:01:34	Lose music under first lines from cast

FIGURE 33-1

Typical scene measurements for a music cue segment.

UNIFYING THROUGH TIME

Given that a long film is a progression of scenes whose longitudinal relationships often need strengthening, your composer may use special coding to help group scenes, characters, or situations into musically related families. In a 90-minute film there may be many music cues, from a *sting* or short punctuation to passages that are extended and elaborate. The composer may develop a theme for a main plot, then employ other themes for two subplots. Keeping these from clashing during cross-cutting can be problematical, and their relationship in key is important. Using a coding system keeps the composer aware of the logical connections and continuity that the music must underpin.

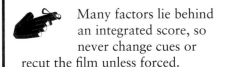 Many factors lie behind an integrated score, so never change cues or recut the film unless forced.

KEYS: DIEGETIC AND NONDIEGETIC MUSIC

Any sound that is a part of the film characters' world, as you may recall, is called *diegetic* sound. The film's own music is something the characters can neither hear nor react to, since this is part of the film's authorial commentary and addressed to the audience, so this is *nondiegetic* sound. In the planning stage the composer decides what progression of keys to use through the film, based on the emotional logic of the story itself. Especially when nondiegetic, composed music takes over from diegetic music on a radio, say, the transition between keys must not clash. This is true for all adjacent music sections, not just original scoring.

CONFLICTS AND COMPOSING TO SYNC POINTS

An experienced musician composing for a recording session will write to very precise timings, paying attention to track features such as dialogue lines and spot effects such as a door slam or tire screech. Instrumentation must not fight dialogue, and the arrangement cannot be too busy at points where it might compete with dialogue or effects. Music can successfully displace a diegetic track that is overloaded. Musical comment in place of a welter of naturalistic sound is more impressionistic and effective.

 An overloaded sound track leaves the audience too tired to respond to other aspects of the film.

If the composer must work around dialogue and spot effects, he or she should have an advanced version of the sound track rather than the simple dialogue track used during editing. This is particularly true for tracks due for a cinema setting. There the sound system may be powerful and sophisticated, and your film's track will come under greater scrutiny.

CONDUCTOR NEEDS

If a written score is played to picture, the score is marked with cumulative timings so the conductor can make a running check that sync points line up while the music is being recorded. Normally you do this to picture as a safeguard. Low-budget film scores make more use of MIDI computerized composing techniques. The composer builds the music to a QuickTime scratch version of the film, so music fitting is done at the source.

HOW LONG DOES IT TAKE?

An experienced composer likes to take upward of 6 weeks to compose, say, 15 minutes of music for a 90-minute feature film but may have to do it in 3 weeks or less, with a flurry of music copyist work at the end if musicians are to play from scores.

THE LIVE MUSIC SESSION

Higher budget productions using live musicians record to picture with the editor present. The editing crew makes the preparations for live music recording. The director and editor supervise the session because nobody else can say for sure whether a shot can be lengthened to accommodate the slight mistimings that always appear during recording. Be prepared anyway for conductor, composer, and soloists to pursue a degree of perfection invisible to anyone else.

 Adjusting picture cutting points is usually easier and more economical than paying musicians to pursue perfect musical synchronicity.

POSTPRODUCTION

FITTING MUSIC

After a live recording session, the editor fits each music section and adjusts picture and sound where necessary. If the music is appropriate, the film takes a quantum leap forward in effectiveness. In the feature world, some editors specialize in cutting and fitting music. Such expertise could be a lifesaver for a documentary about music.

THE MIX

The composer may want to be present at any mix session affecting the functionality of the music. When music has been composed using MIDI, the composer can return to the musical elements with minimal delay and summon a new version that incorporates changes of balance or content.

GOING FURTHER

These are books about the use of music in films that are accessible to non-musicians:

Adorno, Theodor W., Hanns Eisler, and Graham McCann,. *Composing for the Films*. Minneapolis: University of Minnesota Press, 2006.

Prendergast, Roy M. *Film Music—A Neglected Art: A Critical Study of Music in Films*. New York: W.W. Norton, 1992.

Schelle, Michael. *The Score: Interviews with Film Composers*. Los Angeles, CA: Silman-James Press, 1999.

Thomas, Tony. *Film Score: The Art and Craft of Movie Music*. Burbank, CA: Riverwood Press, 1992.

CHAPTER 34

EDITING: REFINEMENTS AND STRUCTURAL PROBLEMS

Long, complex films present two main kinds of problem during editing. There is the familiar one of achieving integrity and flow in individual sequences, and then there's the more intangible problem of adjusting the architecture. By this I mean the support structure that allows the film to carry the audience over a long distance and to experience an exhilarating impact. Let's first explore some analogies that illustrate how way things work at the scene or microcosmic level.

HOW EDITING MIMICS CONSCIOUSNESS

Throughout I have insisted that film language reproduces processes familiar from the way our perceptions process events around us. Our senses collect information, and our mind seeks meaning and then tells the body what it must do by way of action. The eyes are the camera, the ears are sound recording, and camera movements and editing signify the reactions and expectations within the stream of consciousness running in parallel with those life events.

Most people have unexamined ideas about how human consciousness works. You see this when non-actors play lovers having an important conversation. Invariably they lock eyes as they speak, but this is an *idea* of how people converse. The reality is more subtle and interesting and extremely significant for your editing. Observe people in earnest conversation for yourself, and often you'll see that neither person makes eye contact more than fleetingly. Eye-to-eye exchange is intense, draining, and reserved for special moments. Why is this?

During any interaction we are either *acting on* the other person or *being acted upon*. In either mode we glance only at crucial points into the other person's face to see what she means or to judge what effect our words have just had. The rest of the time, because we are gazing inward, our gaze rests on some object or jumps around the surroundings. Then at key junctures in our inner process, our eye returns to the other person.

Take any intense get-together scene from a favorite fiction film and use **Project 1-AP-1 Analyze and Plan Using the Split-Page Script Form** to decide how eyelines and point of view work together.

Now let's look from an external, observing point of view. Watch any two people talking, and then ask yourself what makes *your* eyeline shift back and forth between them. Sometimes it's movements in their eyelines that trigger your eyeline shifts. Each change in the other person's sightline alerts you to significance elsewhere, and your eye goes hunting for it. You'll find a rhythm and motivation to their shifts of eyeline (controlled by the shifting contours of the conversation itself). But see how as you observe them your eyes, moment to moment, *make their own judgment about where to look*. You choose where to look according to the pair's action and reaction, their changes of eyeline, and according to one more thing, which has immense significance. Did you notice how often your eyes leave a speaker in mid-sentence to monitor his effect on the listener? Why? *You were looking for evidence of developing feelings.* You were trying to sniff out subtexts from their effect.

Instinctively, from a lifetime's practice, we "edit" (that is, search with our eyes) as we try to *extract the most subtextual information from any situation*. It's deeply ingrained in our psyche: Always and forever we assemble frameworks of meaning from available clues.

Editing mimics this process and some careful observation will confirm how the search for meaning and subtexts affected the development of editing as we know it. You'll see that the best editing reproduces how our observing, judging, questing minds work when we are closely watching an interaction.

LOOKING AT AND LOOKING THROUGH

To reflect how we watch two people interact in a conversation, a film version must relay three different points of view: one for each of the participants and a third for the observer. The observer's point of view (POV), being outside their enclosed consciousness, tends to look at them from a more detached, judging vantage but is susceptible to empathically entering each protagonist's viewpoint when the observer feels called to do so.

The camera eye and ear observe and collect the memories of the Observer. The Storyteller artfully reworks these memories and finds a special voice to tell the tale.

Depending on what the editor shows, the audience will identify either with one of the characters or with the more detached perspective of the Observer—who in film becomes the Storyteller once the camera observations have become a tale. While character A talks, for instance, the Observer (through whose eyes and mind we see) might look at either A or B in search of ideas, expectations, suspicions, etc., that A has of B or vice versa. Or the Storyteller might show them both in a long shot. The Observer on the spot sees, reacts, and remembers, while the Storyteller uses this material stored in memory to instruct and entertain an audience—functions with an important difference.

These possibilities of viewpoint allow the Storyteller not only to construe privileged viewpoints but also to demonstrate what anyone observing sees (and therefore feels) at any particular moment. This probing, analytic way of seeing develops from the way that we, unconsciously and in the moment, delve into any situation that interests us.

The film process thus mimics the interpretive quest that *both accompanies and directs* human observation. It's complicated to grasp, and you'll understand it best from discovering how you first (passively) observe and then (actively) decide what action to take. There are many nonverbal signs that help—in body language, eyeline shifts, voice inflections, and particular actions—and to which we all ascribe similar meanings.

 Your best teacher of cinema is always going to be what you see, what you hear, what acts on your feelings, and how this input makes you feel, think, then act. Human beings do these things similarly in every culture or there could be no cinema.

 Making documentary, you are forever in a living laboratory and learning about human nature and human behavior.

EDITING RHYTHMS: AN ANALOGY IN MUSIC

Music makes a useful analogy if we imagine, for a moment, an edited conversation between child and grandparent. We have two different but interlocked rhythms going: First, there is the rhythmic pattern of their voices in a series of sentences that ebb and flow, speed up, slow down, halt, restart, fade, and so on. Set against this, and taking its rhythmic cue from speech rhythms, is the visual tempo set up by the interplay of cutting, image compositions, and camera movement. The two streams, visual and aural, proceed independently yet in rhythmic relationship, like the music and the physical movements in a dance performance.

Harmony

When you hear a speaker and see his face, sound and vision are in an alliance like musical harmony. We could, however, break the literalness of always hearing and seeing the same thing (*harmony*) by making the transition from scene to scene into a temporary puzzle.

Counterpoint

We cut from a man talking about unemployment to a somber cityscape. First the speaker is in picture and then we cut to the cityscape while he is still speaking, letting his remaining words play out over the cityscape. It is as if we did the following: While our subject talked to us about growing unemployment, we glanced out of the window to see all the houses spread out below us, the empty parking lots, and the cold chimneys of closed factories.

The film version mimics the instinctual glance of someone sitting there listening; the speaker's words are powerfully counterpointed by the image, and the image lets loose our imagination as we ponder the magnitude of the disruption, of what it must be like to be someone living in one of those houses.

This *counterpoint* of a sound against an unlike image has its variations. One usage is simply to illustrate the actuality of what words can only describe. We might cut from a bakery worker talking about fatigue to shots taken through shimmering heat of workers in a bread factory moving about their repetitive tasks like zombies. Another usage is to create tension and force the viewer into evaluating.

Dissonance

Another usage exploits *discrepancies*. For instance, we hear a teacher describing an enlightened and attractive philosophy of teaching but see the same man lecturing in a monotone, drowning his yawning students in a torrent of facts and stifling any discussion. This discrepancy, to pursue the musical allusion, is like a *dissonance* that spurs the viewer to crave a resolution. Comparing the man's beliefs with his practice, the viewer resolves the discrepancy by deciding that here is a man who does not know himself.

USING YOUR INSTINCTS WHILE EDITING

As you watched your inner process of inquiry and empathy unfold while a couple conversed, so you can expect similarly authentic reactions to a piece of editing. Where is the dream state of high consciousness broken? What breaks it? What is missing, or too long, or too short? What is needed? Your instincts will tell you, if you ask them and wait while your thoughts coalesce. You are looking for an authentic stream of consciousness, and just as you'd recognized a wrong note or wrong chord in a musical composition, so you recognize where things go awry in a piece of editing.

 As you sense a wrong note in music, so you recognize wrong notes in editing. Instinct helps you put them right.

TRIAL AUDIENCES

You'll need to use trial audiences so you get feedback from newcomers—your eventual audience being *only* newcomers. By this stage everyone associated with the film, particularly the director and editor, are hugely fatigued and encumbered from the experience of working on it. You know what the audience should see and feel, and it's easy to assume this is happening. Sitting through each viewing and relating the audience's body language to each part, you'll see from movement or stillness which sections are gripping and which aren't. You ask the same kind of questions but focus on the parts where the audience shows signs of restlessness.

SUBTEXTS: MAKING THE VISIBLE SIGNIFICANT

A baffling problem that often emerges during editing is that, for some reason, nobody *gets* the underlying reason for something. They don't understand that a bank official feels bad when he can't give the small business owner a loan. Your audience sees him as heartless. The problem is one of subtext; for some reason, they don't notice what you notice. Why?

In Chapter 5 of his *Literature and Film*, Robert Richardson goes to the heart of the filmmaker's problem:

> Literature often has the problem of making the significant somehow visible, while film often finds itself trying to make the visible significant.[1]

It's simply difficult to drive the film audience's awareness beyond what is literally and materially in front of the camera. For instance, we may accept a scene in which a mother makes lunch for her children as simply that. So what, you ask, mothers make lunch for kids all the time. But there are nuances: One child has persistent difficulty choosing what she wants. The mother is trying to suppress her irritation. Looking closely, you see that the child is manipulating the situation. Food and eating have become their battleground, their frontier in a struggle over who controls whom. The mother's moral authority comes from telling her daughter she must eat right to stay healthy, while the child asserts her authority over her own body by a maddening noncompliance.

> So often in filmmaking your problem is that of showing that a family meal may be more than food, that it may in fact be a combat zone with deadly serious subtexts.

If the audience had first seen child and mother in some other, more overt conflict over control, they would read the scene correctly, and of course there may be several other ways to channel the audience's attention. But without the proper structural or contextual support, the significance and universality of such a scene could easily pass unnoticed. What you start to see happening on the fourth viewing won't necessarily strike even the more perceptive of first-time viewers. They lack your commitment, your deepening insight that comes from behind-the-scenes knowledge and your repeated exposure.

However your knowledge evolved, you must now evolve your audience's in the same way. You may have to restructure the film or add shots or scenes that

---

[1]Richardson, Robert. *Literature and Film*. Bloomington: Indiana University Press, 1969, p. 68.

alert the audience to that power struggle. You may have to show an additional scene with the bank manager to show that he is a compassionate man.

 You will need **Project 1-AP-5 Diagnosing a Narrative** whenever you need to understand the inner workings of the latest cut and perhaps, in stubborn cases, **Project 1-AP-6 Analyzing Editing and Content**, too.

LONG-FORM STRUC-TURE: WHERE INSTINCTS AREN'T ENOUGH

Long-form films are frequently baffling because in their earlier forms they nearly always fail to deliver. All the sequences work at a local level, yet the totality is a disappointment. You sense that the film is anticlimactic or you miss a certain character who leaves the film early. Instincts tell you a lot of things, and of course you should act on them. But once you've done all that, you must switch strategies and use a more analytic approach. You need to get at the cumulative effect of the film's parts. These won't stop misfiring without a lot of adjustment. And without some special tools, you won't figure out how or why.

USING THE EDITING DIAGNOSTIC FORM

Take a look at **Project AP-3 Editing Diagnostic Form** (in the Appendix). As a prelude to digging into your film's hidden aspects, it invites you to log your film sequence by sequence. You identify each by a content tag title such as "Terry's first confrontation with his supervisor" and briefly describe each sequence's contribution to the film's developing argument, such as "We see the resurgence of Terry's old problem with authority figures."

You'll find it helpful later if you number the sequences and log their cumulative timecode. Use the elapsed time facility in your editing software to determine the length of each sequence. Then, quite subjectively, give each sequence an impact rating of between 0 and 5 stars.

You'll find that merely filling in the form will help you decide:

- Each sequence's identity—because you had to name it (the tag title).
- Its function (experience, facts, or impressions, etc.) and what it contributes to the audience's stream of consciousness. Placing a sequence elsewhere won't change its content but often alters its function.
- Whether its length and impact rating are consonant. Lengthy sequences that contribute little are prime candidates for the ax.
- What the progression of impact ratings looks like, from the film's beginning to its end. By laying it out horizontally, you can build a characteristic curve for the entire film. Does it peak early or sag in places?

Now divide your film into acts and rule colored lines between acts:

- Is all material in its right act?
- Do the length and complexity of each act look proportionate? (Act II is normally longer and more complex than Acts I and III.)

- Does the film imply a contract in its first minute so the audience can judge what lies ahead?

- Do the introduction and development of the film proceed logically? (Often there are back doubles or repetitions, or sequences that seem long delayed.)

- Can you see redundancy? (Showing the same basic situation twice is redundant unless the second raises the stakes in some way.)

- Are there any significant holes in the film's argument?

- Is there too much exposition before there is any action? (Explanations are sometimes better *after* the action.)

- Can exposition be apportioned better?

- Do the characters appear when you are ready for them?

- Looking at the argument, whose film is it?

- Does the film's resolution fall in the right place and occupy the right amount of time?

Some aspects of your film will be limited to where their chronology allows them to go. Other aspects are moveable and may deliver better if you move them. Here's how.

FILM INTO PLAYING CARDS

Photocopy your completed form and cut the copies into discrete sequences. Paste them onto large index cards so you have a set of playing cards that you can group into Acts I, II, and III.

Now move material around to see the potential in using the material differently. This is good to do in a group discussion, with each participant arguing for changes and illustrating his ideas by moving sequences around, narrating the new order, and describing the impressions it creates.

In playing-card form, everyone has a reminder of what the film holds and can take a bird's eye view of its potential. Each sequence you eliminate carries a number and a note of its length so you can compute time saved. The numbers enable you to return the cards to the film's existing form.

Without turning your long film into movable representations, it's almost impossible to explore how its contents might function differently. Use the "playing card" method of discussion and overview.

Without such an overview and discussion of movable parts it's almost impossible to decide where material might belong in a film series. This method is good for surveying each film's dramatic development and deciding where it gets hung up, goes in circles, or otherwise shoots itself in the foot. The longer and more convoluted the work in hand, the more essential a method like this becomes.

MULTIPLE ENDINGS

When your film has several endings, you have a problem whose cause is nearly always the same: You haven't decided what your film is really about. You are hanging on to multiple intentions and hoping you can cover them all. Probably you can't.

 If your film has multiple endings, it's because you haven't decided your film's central purpose. Your film is still sitting on the fence—several fences, perhaps.

To escape the labyrinth, write a fresh working hypothesis for your film and a revised premise. This will help clarify priorities so you can jettison the outriders. Go on, grit your teeth and kill your darlings . . . sorry, but one must. It's the last stage in the artistic process.

MORE TRIAL AUDIENCES

Particularly with a long film, you must use a series of trial audiences to see what effect each round of changes has had. You'll know what information you're seeking and can structure the Q & A session accordingly. If you think some of your audience—say, other filmmakers—would be amenable to discussing the film's working parts in detail, have a set of sequence cards ready. A lot of new ideas arise when people with open minds look at your layout.

LENGTH

Is your film standing up at its present length? A common mistake is to set a length and then resist trimming the film because you always intended it to be, say, feature length (90 minutes) or an hour (58 minutes). It's disappointing when your film doesn't hold up, but if your audiences are telling you it's dragging, then you must bite the bullet and make a good film from the long one. You won't regret it.

TALKING ABOUT YOUR WORK

You may have guessed from the foregoing that talking too much about your work sets up concentric circles of expectation among family, friends, and associates. This will inhibit them from telling you what you need to know. By all means pitch ideas—do that all the time. But once you start filming, shut up and get on with it. Your film will always emerge differently than you expect.

 People who talk a lot in defense of their films are usually trying to ward off insecurity. Keep quiet, listen to your critics, and conserve valuable energy.

Every film you'll ever make is a crap shoot. You will have successes and failures, too. For an inspiring and touching primer on the importance of failure, watch J.K. Rowling's address to the Harvard graduating class at http://harvardmagazine.com/

go/jkrowling.html. She's the single mom who came close to homelessness but still put her energy into writing, because that's what she loved and could do well. The *Harry Potter* books galvanized a whole generation into discovering the joy of reading. Her speech is long, but it's the fullest and most inspiring explanation I've ever heard about what you must endure to become yourself and do the best work, *your* work.

 Try neither to exult nor despair over what your reviewers say. Sometimes they are hasty and superficial. What matters is to keep learning, growing, and getting better at what you care about.

PART 8

EDUCATION AND STARTING YOUR CAREER

How and where you learn to make documentaries depends on your resources and learning style. Every so often someone writes to say they have just won an award and this book was their main teacher. So you may be holding all the academy you need in your two hands. Most, however, will prefer schooling for its structured educational path, equipment, and teammates. The subject of this part is choosing the right institution, making the most of your educational path, and getting established in a film career. For this you can lay the groundwork from the very beginning:

> Use the teaching and facilities above what the college demands for a passing grade.

> Read everything you can about those whose work inspires you.

> Read novels, newspapers, and nonfiction in pursuit of the subjects that fire your imagination.

> Write and write until it becomes a pleasure. Only in this way can you dump out what's in your head and improve it. Write academic papers, criticism, a blog, whatever you can.

> Talk about your film ideas with anyone who'll listen.

> Cram in all the filmmaking experience that you can handle as a student.

> Use teachers and contemporaries by actively seeking help, ideas, and criticism. Don't let shyness or sensitivity to the opinions of contemporaries hold you back.

> Ask all the questions you need answered, even the really stupid ones.

> Find which festivals interest you and plan films you're going to make as entries.

> Compile a show reel of your best work to prove your employability.

On graduating, few emerge as fully fledged documentary directors. Most realize that directing professionally depends on acquiring more experience in the field. Prepare for this during your schooling by developing a specialty such as camerawork, sound, or editing. Then you'll have marketable craft skills and can gain a foothold in the industry. For more on this see **Chapter 36, Getting Work**.

At school and beyond, festival awards represent the clearest path to your future, but you must plan for this. The last chapter in this part is about leveraging yourself into employment. Your success depends heavily on what you've planned to accomplish during your schooling.

CHAPTER 35

EDUCATION

PLANNING A CAREER

How do you get started as a documentary filmmaker? And, after, say, 3 to 5 years of work, where can you expect to be? Parents ask, "Is it responsible to feed young people's hopes when there are so few positions in filmmaking?" The answer is that there are as many positions as there are exceptional filmmakers and storytellers. Documentarians, like actors, musicians, and dancers, are part of an entertainment industry, and there are no limits to what the world needs that is entertaining. And even if those documentarians are good rather than exceptional, there is much today that people will pay to have documented. In my open admissions college we learned that, with few exceptions, it is neither fixed nor predictable who will grow and flourish while learning to make films. Those who do so are always those who persist because they like the process. Once you've got the bug, it's something you must do. Doing anything from enthusiasm is always what makes you excel.

How risky is it to learn filmmaking? Even if you end up taking another direction, an education in filmmaking represents as broad and encompassing a liberal education as you can find. What else incorporates mission, imagery, sound, light, characters, narrative, choreography, music, technology, teamwork, project management, and audiences?

 Documentary makers are like actors, musicians, and dancers; they belong to an entertainment industry that exists to give the public what it finds interesting and relevant.

 Education—institutional or self-administered—is your investment in your future. All investment involves commitment and risk.

If you can scrape together the funds to buy a car, you can instead start going to film school or buy the equipment to learn making documentaries on your own. You can do without a car, but you can't do without a life of meaningful work.

You first need to find out where your tastes and abilities lie. No matter which educational path you take, success depends on actively planning and executing your intentions. It's not enough to plunk yourself down in an educational setting and wait for them to form you. Sadly, this is what the majority do, even though it's no secret that filmmaking is the most entrepreneurial calling under the sun. The next chapter elaborates on how to plan and how to use your schooling.

 To get ahead you will need, like everyone else in the arts, some ability, energy, flair, and lots of persistence. Luck and sociability play some part, but what you need most of all is desire and perseverance.

 Where you go as a filmmaker depends on planning your education and single-mindedly carrying your plans to fruition. No school can make you do this.

When you leave school to start working professionally, you may for some time have to make wedding videos, drive a cab, wait tables, or work construction to keep bread on the table. Doug Block, the maker of *51 Birch Street*, mentioned earlier in this book, still makes his living by wedding videos; they aren't at all easy to make well, and they are hedged around with dynastic politics.

If you gain a modest name and start netting grants and commissions, you'll never have to wonder why you go to work every day. In what other line of work could Morgan Spurlock (*Super Size Me*, 2004, United States; Figure 35-1) take the McDonald's® corporation at its word and convulse the world with horrified laughter? What other job lets you entertain by setting out to find Osama bin Laden?

LEARN ON THE JOB OR GO TO SCHOOL?

Taking the "industry route" and getting into a ground-level apprenticeship situation—always supposing there's one to be had—can be a good deal or a bad deal. Maybe some kindly person (probably a relative) takes you on and happily teaches you all they know, but more likely you're cheap labor so that five years later you're still the company peon who drives the wagon and answers the phones. Why? Most employers are under pressure to survive, and expanding Junior's horizons is not their job. Most, in fact, will take steps to *avoid* enlightening you, so you don't become a competitor.

The on-the-job film training I got, then three decades of teaching, left me convinced that education is a bargain. A single example: In a 15-week editing class, students can use techniques and insights that took me a decade to work out for myself. Arrive at your first job overprepared, and you can always assume more complex duties as the need arises. And it will.

FIGURE 35-1

Morgan Spurlock in *Super Size Me*, taking McDonald's® at their word. (Photo courtesy of The Kobal Collection/Roadside Attractions/Samuel Goldwyn Films.)

Good schooling provides:

- A cultural and intellectual overview of your medium
- Knowledge and history and ideas about the role you want
- Technical training in the use of the tools, techniques, and concepts
- Disinterested help in uncovering your talents, abilities, and energies
- A safe environment in which to experiment at expressing individual vision
- Aspirations to use your professional life to its fullest extent and for the widest good
- Collaborators with whom to face adversity, of which there is plenty in school and after it

 A good film program is like a structured obstacle course. You get history, aesthetics, technical facilities, skilled teachers, and lively contemporaries with whom to discover the medium. Its benefits continue to surface for years after you graduate.

FILM SCHOOLS

Film schools send you through all the roles in filmmaking so you can settle on that which suits your temperament. Discovering your strengths and weaknesses, you acquire confidence and self-knowledge and learn how to remain true to yourself under pressure and criticism. On the debit side, schools have to concern themselves with fairness and equal opportunity, so they teach to the common denominator—to the frustration of fast learners, slow learners, and from time to time everyone else.

Locate good teaching at film festivals by noting which institutions produce the work you like. A sure sign of energetic and productive teaching, even in a small and impoverished facility, is student work that is receiving awards. The school should offer a thorough conceptual, aesthetic, and historical framework allied with strong production expectations.

A SCHOOL'S IDENTITY

Depending on its faculty's interests and traditions, a school that says it teaches documentary may in fact lean toward television journalism, visual anthropology, social documentary, oral history, sociology, or some other form of nonfiction filmmaking. Faculty résumés and honors lists will reveal what the school promotes and whether its students are currently getting recognition.

Many schools teach at both the undergraduate and graduate levels, and there's no guarantee they are equal. A school may practice selective admissions to a graduate division and concentrate resources on a chosen few in the hope of getting festival recognition. Their undergraduate school may be under-resourced and oversubscribed. Or the opposite can be true—the energetic work is coming from undergrads, and the grad school never has its act together. Schools are human institutions, with all that this implies.

STUDENTS AND STARS

What matters is not how the school picks and accelerates its stars (which may follow some odious patronage system) but what it does

 Film schools are supermarkets that stock the shelves with what the majority consume. Documentary is still in the exotic aisle. "Humankind," wrote T. S. Eliot, "cannot bear too much reality."

 Most important to a production department are faculty energy, student morale, and what's expected in the curriculum. Students should prove their knowledge in practical ways, not in film theory as a precursor to touching the equipment.

 Read carefully what a department says about its attitudes and philosophy, and compare several institutions' statements. Usually you have to push past a smokescreen of pious platitudes and self-congratulation.

Everyone who applies to film school identifies with winners and assumes they will follow those who've gone on to greatness. It's important, however, to check out what the majority of students achieve, because you may be among them.

for the majority, the average student. As a learner, sorry to say, you are probably nearly as average as I am, so you need a school committed to realizing the average student's enormous potential. So:

- If the school cites famous names, are they actively connected with the institution? (Some schools shamelessly parade names who passed thankfully from their gates eons ago.)
- Of the distinguished faculty and alumni in the school's literature, how many are recent and how many from previous decades? (Some schools coast on their reputation.)
- Where do most of their students go after graduation?
- What do its former students say about it—both for and against?

LARGE OR SMALL SCHOOL

In the small school, the curriculum may be inspirational or limited to generalist "communications" courses that are overenrolled. It can be an ideal community with brilliant teaching or dominated by self-absorbed personalities who have turned their bailiwick into a dysfunctional family. Smaller institutions or departments, unless expensive, may lack vital resources and offer less choice of coursework, fewer faculty among whom to find a mentor, and less choice of film form to work in.

 A large film school usually runs a core curriculum that fans out into a comprehensive array of specialization tracks; a small school cannot do this, so it might only be good for some initial work.

Large schools, though initially overwhelming, do offer choices in course times, teachers, professional paths, and mentors for advanced projects. You also get a wide choice of student partners and a greater chance to develop professional levels of expertise. My school, Columbia College Chicago, starts every-one out in fiction, but this is under review (www.filmatcolumbia.com). The student can choose to go into screenwriting, cinematography, audio, editing, directing, producing, alternative forms, animation, critical studies—and, of course, documentary.

TOWN OR COUNTRY

Rural schools can be comfortably bucolic and profess all the right sociological and nutritional principles but remain distant from the film community you must eventually join. In an established urban film school, successful former students return as teachers wanting to give back to the next generation. Students and teachers criss-cross the dividing lines. Mentors give advice, steer projects, and exemplify the way of life that students are trying to make their own. Students work on professional projects, then get recommendations or even employment from their teachers. This regenerates the apprenticeship system of old and is very significant to learning. Even in the world's largest cities the filmmaking community is a village where personal recommendation is everything. So consider:

- Where is the school located, and what filmmaking opportunities does the setting offer?
- What does the place feel like? (Visit at all costs.)
- How do the students regard the place? (Talk with your own choice of students.)

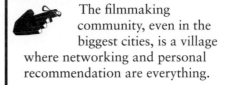 The filmmaking community, even in the biggest cities, is a village where networking and personal recommendation are everything.

CLASS SIZE

Learning to make documentaries is like becoming a musician. No academy would run classes for 40 clarinetists, yet administrators of large institutions often think 40 film students is quite acceptable. Used to history, chemistry, or engineering, they assume education is about students mastering a body of knowledge and taking tests. There are, indeed, body-of-knowledge lecture classes (film history, theory, technology), and these can sometimes be reasonably large (25 to 40 students). If so, don't expect much feedback on your expertise or ideas. How well do you manage under those conditions? Some people prosper, others (like me) need dialogue, not a monologue.

 You'll learn to make documentaries best in a conservatory atmosphere, if you can find it at a price you can afford.

DOCUMENTARY IS A CONSERVATORY ART

Becoming a creative artist takes place best in a conservatory atmosphere—that is, you learn from master practitioners and in small groups using intensive interaction as the mode of learning. Art schools, theater schools, and music schools all know this, but film schools often seem in denial—maybe because film classes are so expensive to run. As attendance exceeds 12 in film craft classes, they decline in effectiveness, although using a well-developed curriculum and assistants can mitigate this. Simply seeing a dozen sets of film tests, dailies, or projects—let alone trying to give an adequate and democratic critique—slows everything to a crawl.

TEACHERS AND WORKLOAD

Wealthy schools that charge high tuition can afford to hire celebrity filmmakers and give them light teaching schedules in exchange for real productivity. Less affluent schools often lack sufficient full-time faculty and use underemployed graduate students for entry-level teaching. You learn from young, enthusiastic teachers, but inevitably they lack real-world experience. Upper level classes, peopled by seasoned students, may however function well and absorb all the full-time faculty's effort. So sift through the department's Web site information and faculty biographies to assess:

- What is the ratio of full-time to part-time faculty?
- How experienced are those teaching the majority of beginning classes?

- What do the senior and most influential faculty teach? (Another irony of film school life is that senior teachers' energies are dissipated in administration duties that non-teachers could do.)

- Are faculty producing?

- Did a suspicious number of the faculty get their education in this same institution?

 Film schools hire filmmakers as teachers, then impose such extravagant teaching and administrative duties that they cannot make films. How active and accessible are faculty in the schools you like?

- Is there a diversity of ethnicity, nationality, gender, and age among the faculty?

GRADUATE OR UNDERGRADUATE?

UNDERGRADUATE DEGREE

If you are seeking an undergraduate degree, you may want to pursue either a B.A. (Bachelor of Arts) or B.F.A. (Bachelor of Fine Arts) degree. Institutions that teach technology to high levels sometimes offer a B.S. (Bachelor of Science) degree. As degrees in general go upmarket, the B.A. seems likely to fall before the B.F.A., which is a few more semester hours but likely to contain more specialized film classes. So:

 Some high-reputation film schools make students compete for whose work gets produced. You enroll, thinking you're going to direct, only to discover several years later that because your project didn't get the votes you are now recording sound for the winner.

- How many hours of general studies are you expected to complete, and how germane are they to your focus in film or video?

- Can you specialize (as a cinematographer, editor, etc.), or does everyone emerge as a generalist?

Schools in the long shadow of Hollywood tend to promote (or are unable to prevent) pernicious ideas about success, ones that blight some students' potential. The moral? A hard-to-enter, expensive school is not necessarily a good school, nor may it fit your profile as a learner. Look well before you leap. For either graduate or undergraduate programs, try to establish:

- Number of students in the department and whether size translates into choice

- Whether you study with students of other ethnicities and nationalities (a huge advantage)

- Length of the program (4 years for a B.A., 3 years M.F.A., and 2 years M.A. are average)

- Graduation rate, if it's made available
- Number of courses the department offers, and what their structure reveals (documentary may be the poor cousin)
- Average class sizes at entry and advanced levels
- How often upper-level courses are offered (some, especially when taught by glitterati, may remain on the course list as a lure to the unwary)

Film school is like medical school; it takes some years of very hard work. This is an intense, shared experience that leaves few aspects of relationship untouched. Lifelong friendships and partnerships develop out of it. Film people often work much of their lives with those they met in film school.

- Whether upper-level courses strive for a professional level of specialization
- Whether your particular interests are treated as a specialty (speak to students studying in this area)
- Whether students own the copyright to their work (many schools retain copyright)
- Who among the faculty is making the kind of films you'd like to make
- What proportion of those electing to direct in school actually get to do so
- What the school's record is like for placing its students in internships and jobs

You will direct documentaries after school only if you plan to be productive and fulfill your goals.

GRADUATE DEGREE

With schools competing for graduate students, there is now a plethora of graduate film study programs, some new and untried. A book packed with good advice and information is Tom Edgar and Karin Kelly's *Film School Confidential: An Insider's Guide to Film Schools* (2007, Perigee). You'll see that entry to graduate school is competitive and based on academic record; acceptance usually depends on what you can substantiate creatively and what you have to say about yourself in writing and in person during an interview. Grad schools are usually small and selective. They give students lots of personal attention but may suffer from small school syndrome, where a few personalities dominate and a combination of airlessness and high expectations induces neurosis among their students.

A graduate student is presumed to be specializing and to have sophisticated interests and work habits, which are a great advantage; however, he or she may not learn some of the technical material as easily as someone younger with a greater natural aptitude. If you already have a bachelor's degree and want an advanced degree, your choices are:

- M.A., which usually has a short syllabus meant to extend an undergraduate degree. It may not lead anywhere useful unless it concentrates on production, as Stanford does to great effect.

- M.F.A., which is a terminal studio arts degree and equivalent to a Ph.D. This is a good qualification for production and vital for teaching, though to seek teaching at the university level you will need several years of independent production and some prize-winning films under your belt.

 Film undergraduates and graduates often learn similar things, and in mixed classes undergrads sometimes outshine grads.

- Ph.D., which signifies a scholarly emphasis generally precluding production. Since you're unlikely to get any production experience, the work you might eventually get would be as a reviewer or, after extensive publishing, as a teacher of history and aesthetics.

Inquire:

- What is the degree's focus? Different institutions specialize differently and aim to prepare you for different kinds of work.
- What proportion of graduates work professionally in the field?
- What kind of internship and job placement program do they offer?

Look for departments that are experienced, taught by filmmakers, and affiliated with a sizeable undergraduate school so there's enough equipment and expertise to draw on. Best known for teaching documentary production in the United States are:

 The best indicator of a quality program is when their students' films win recognition at festivals.

- American University, Washington
- Columbia College Chicago
- New York University
- School of Visual Arts
- Stanford University
- Temple University
- University of Texas at Austin
- University of Southern California

EQUIPMENT

If you know something about equipment, this can be a good indicator of where the department puts its emphasis. During a visit see what you can find out about:

- Quantity, quality, and modernity of equipment
- Who gets to use it
- How up to date the school is in newer technologies

- What backgrounds key faculty members have and what they have produced using the new technology

COSTS AND VISITING

With every school you consider, ascertain what the costs are going to be. Consider:

- How much equipment and what materials are supplied
- What the student must fund along the way
- What financial aid the school offers
- Whether the school has competitive funds or scholarships to offset production costs
- How available dormitories are and how expensive local accommodation is
- What medical and other insurance will cost

Always visit a school you're thinking of attending and talk to students, teachers, and technical staff. The most reliable recommendation will always be that coming from someone you respect who recently attended the school.

 You are going to spend a lot of time and money while at film school, so be sure you know its pros and cons. There are always lots of both.

MOSTLY NORTH AMERICAN SCHOOLS

Any institution you attend should be educationally accredited, but there is no accreditation specifically for film departments or even for their teachers. So it's buyer beware. The schools listed below are affiliated with North American professional associations, but use your detective skills to cross-check a school's reputation and what its education is supposed to deliver. Very few treat documentary as more than a side dish to the main meal of Hollywood fiction.

The Web site www.filmschools.com contains many film school links, while www.filmmaking.net also lists schools in many countries besides the United States that claim to teach filmmaking. Many are private and possibly quick-fix. The film school survey Web site www.filmmaker.com includes pungent comments on particular film schools. These are often by the disgruntled, so read lots of reports, scanning them gingerly for common denominators and peripheral information. Discount whatever lacks spelling or punctuation. Being free and anonymous, it's a great arena for malcontents to unload spleen, but frequent and similar complaints about a school may head you away from a costly mistake.

The first list below is of mostly North American schools affiliated with the University Film and Video Association (UFVA), so you can see if there is a school near you. See the most up-to-date version at www.ufva.org under "About UFVA."

All reputable film schools have Web sites that give a great deal of pertinent information as well as e-mail inquiry addresses. Google® any school you're interested in by name and location. Facilities and expertise will vary. Check curricular offerings, since many don't offer documentary as a specialization. Many American schools allow students in good academic standing to work for their tuition within the department, which offsets some of the high costs.

FILM DEPARTMENTS IN UNIVERSITIES AFFILIATED WITH THE UFVA

Allan Hancock College, Santa Maria, California
Baylor University, Waco, Texas
Bob Jones University, Greenville, South Carolina
Boston University, Boston, Massachusetts
Brigham Young University, Provo, Utah
Brighton Film School, East Sussex, United Kingdom
Brooks Institute, Ventura, California
California Institute of the Arts, Valencia, California
California State University, Fullerton, California
California State University, Long Beach, California
California State University, Los Angeles, California
California State University, Northridge, California
Carnegie Mellon University, Pittsburgh, Pennsylvania
Central Missouri State University, Warrensburg, Missouri
Chapman University, Orange, California
Colorado College, Colorado Springs, Colorado
Digital Filmmaking Institute, Albuquerque, New Mexico
Drexel University, Philadelphia, Pennsylvania
Duke University, Durham, North Carolina
Fairleigh Dickinson University, Madison, New Jersey
Florida State University, Tallahassee, Florida
Framingham State College, Framingham, Massachusetts
Georgia State University, Atlanta, Georgia
Grand Valley State University, Allendale, Michigan
Haywood Community College, Clyde, North Carolina
Hellenic Cinema and Television School, Athens, Greece
Hofstra University, Hempstead, New York
Houston Community College Southwest, Stafford, Texas
Humboldt State University, Arcata, California
Ithaca College, Ithaca, New York
Lamar University, Beaumont, Texas
Lawrence College, St. John's, Newfoundland, Canada
Long Island University–Brooklyn Campus, Brooklyn, New York
Loyola Marymount University, Los Angeles, California

Mel Oppenheim–School of Cinema, Concordia University, Montreal, Canada
Messiah College, Grantham, Pennsylvania
Mills College, Oakland, California
Montana State University, Bozeman, Montana
Montclair State University, Upper Montclair, New Jersey
Morehead State University, Morehead, Kentucky
Morningside College, Sioux City, Iowa
North Carolina School of the Arts, Winston-Salem, North Carolina
Northwest Nazarene University, Nampa, Idaho
Northwestern College, Orange City, Iowa
Northwestern University, Evanston, Illinois
Nova Scotia Community College, Halifax, Nova Scotia, Canada
Ohio University School of Film, Athens, Ohio
Piedmont Community College, Roxboro, North Carolina
Pittsburgh Filmmakers, Pittsburgh, Pennsylvania
Quinnipiac University, Hamden, Connecticut
Rhode Island School of Design, Providence, Rhode Island
Rochester Institute of Technology, Rochester, New York
Rock Valley College, Rockford, Illinois
Rockport College, Rockport, Maine
San Antonio College, San Antonio, Texas
San Francisco State University, San Francisco, California
San Jose State University, San Jose, California
Smith College, Northampton, Massachusetts
Southern Alberta School of Technology, Calgary, Alberta, Canada
Southern Illinois University, Carbondale, Illinois
Syracuse University, Syracuse, New York
Temple University, Philadelphia, Pennsylvania
Texas A&M University, Corpus Christi, Texas
Towson University, Towson, Maryland
UCLA, Los Angeles, California
UNIACC–La Universidad de las Comunicaciones, Santiago, Chile
University at Buffalo, Buffalo, New York
University of Arizona, Tucson, Arizona
University of Chicago, Chicago, Illinois
University of Colorado, Boulder, Colorado
University of Hartford, West Hartford, Connecticut
University of Iowa, Iowa City, Iowa

University of Kansas, Lawrence, Kansas

University of Michigan, Ann Arbor, Michigan

University of Missouri–Kansas City, Kansas City, Missouri

University of Nebraska, Lincoln, Nebraska

University of New Orleans, Lakefront, New Orleans, Louisiana

University of North Carolina, Greensboro, North Carolina

University of North Carolina, Wilmington, North Carolina

University of North Texas, Denton, Texas

University of Oklahoma, Norman, Oklahoma

University of Southern California, Los Angeles, California

University of Southern Mississippi, Hattiesburg, Mississippi

University of Texas–Arlington, Texas

University of Texas–Austin, Texas

University of Toledo, Toledo, Ohio

University of Toronto, Toronto, Ontario, Canada

University of Windsor, Windsor, Ontario, Canada

Valencia Community College, Orlando, Florida

Vassar College, Poughkeepsie, New York

Wayne State University, Detroit, Michigan

Widener University, Chester, Pennsylvania

William Patterson University, Wayne, New Jersey

WORLDWIDE FILM SCHOOLS

For those living in other parts of the globe, you can find information on international film schools affiliated with CILECT, the international association of film schools based in Brussels, at www.cilect.org. They are organized by country; clicking on a film school will give you either a standard form that cross-lists information or a link direct to the school's own Web site. The + sign before a phone or fax number indicates the overseas telephone code that you must first dial in your own country to make an international call. Many schools do not specialize in documentary, but many more are adding it. National schools have very competitive entry requirements, and private schools may be costly depending on the cost of living in the country.

NATIONAL FILM SCHOOLS

National film schools are flagship operations that are usually funded handsomely by the country's government and that work hand-in-hand with whatever film industry they have. The Czech national school in Prague, for instance, runs excellent summer courses in English open to anyone; it has a fine tradition of cinematography and animation. Many schools in wealthy areas of Europe, North America, and the Antipodes are very good. Entry procedures can be lengthy and excruciating, and the chosen few, though undoubtedly smart, become the handpicked racehorses of a particular faculty. In Sweden, the documentary intake has been five students every other year—from a population of 5 million! It does not seem a very productive approach, but that's what the government thinks the country needs. Don't give up if your national film school rejects you. Mike Figgis was rejected by his, so he found another way—and so can you. People accomplish what matters to them.

PRIVATE AND OPEN SCHOOLS

Many large cities now have private film schools, some very good. The London Film School is long established and has an excellent reputation, but as yet lacks a documentary strand. The Documentary Filmmakers' Group Web site offers guidance to resources in Britain (www.dfgdocs.com/Resources/About_Us.aspx). To find private schools in your own country, do an online search by entering your country's name + "film school." For Denmark, I found seven schools this way under www.filmaking.net, which lists schools by countries.

OTHER ROUTES TO EDUCATION

SHORT COURSES

These give useful initial exposure so you can decide whether documentary is for you. The best known facilities in the United States are the Maine Media Workshops (www.theworkshops.com/filmworkshops) and the New York Film Academy (www.nyfa.com), which also makes courses available in other countries. Look critically at course content and cost, and don't be bowled over by glossy hype. For high-cost places like London and New York, compute housing, living, and medical insurance expenses, which can hike costs astronomically. Britain has many short film and television courses in the regions, which may provide better value, and there is an explosion of similar courses in many developed countries. Short courses are usually equipment or procedure oriented rather than conceptual, so expect them to be taught by technicians. They usually aim to inspire beginners, rather than take you to the upper reaches.

STUDY ABROAD

People sometimes assume that work and study abroad will be an extension of conditions in their own country and easily arranged; however, since the September 11 attacks, international students wanting to study in the United States have found entry slower and more difficult. Here are a few pointers:

- Apply far ahead, since obtaining visas has become a longer process.
- The school usually applies for your visa once they accept you.

- You will probably need to take a TOEFL test of English proficiency. Arrange this in your own country (see www.toeflgoanywhere.org).
- Medical insurance is mandatory but may often be purchased through the university at reduced cost.
- Supporting yourself through part-time work is not legal.
- Though you graduate in the United States, you probably can't work there. Like most countries, the United States excludes foreign workers when natives are underemployed.
- Check local costs and conditions very carefully before committing yourself.

Many who consider studying abroad come from countries where education is supplied free by their government. Don't let your affront at the idea of *paying* for education stop you from investing in your future, if you can afford it. You'd pay for a car, so why not buy the skills for a lifetime's work? The stimulation of studying in another culture is itself a valuable education.

If you speak Spanish or Portuguese, Latin American film schools represent very good value. Though they may have little equipment, they often manage to give a wonderful and spirited education. The University of Buenos Aires, Argentina, and the University of Saõ Paolo, Brazil, are two such schools. The International School of Film and Television in Cuba, the Communications University in Santiago, Chile, and the Mexico City schools are all well-equipped and thriving centers of filmmaking and are excellent values for the money. The Cuban school in particular sends out a stream of original and award-winning work.

 Werner Herzog once said that anyone wanting to make films should waste no more than a week learning film techniques. This seems a little brief, but I fundamentally share his "can do" attitude.

SELF-HELP AS A REALISTIC ALTERNATIVE

If you cannot afford film school, then you must acquire knowledge and experience another way. Making films is practical and experiential, like dance or swimming, and you can tackle it with other motivated do-it-yourselfers. This book exists to encourage you to learn through doing. Do lots of the projects, and you will be on your way. Get criticism and participation from others—soliciting whatever specialists you can lay hands on and the nonspecialists for whom you make films. Along the way you will need a mentor or two, people to help solve problems and give knowledgeable and objective criticism of your work. If none is in the offing, don't worry. It's a law of nature that you find people when you are ready for them.

CHAPTER 36

FROM SCHOOL TO FILM INDUSTRY

LOOKING AHEAD WHILE YOU'RE IN FILM SCHOOL

By thinking ahead during your schooling, you can amass the necessary experience, sample work, and survival skills that you'll need once you graduate. Early in your schooling, decide what sort of films you can make with passion and which festivals to aim for, then work to assemble the associates you need to make your films, and work with them so they make theirs. If your school has a producing track, make an aspiring producer into one of your partners.

INTERNSHIPS AS A SENIOR

Well-established schools have an internship office that places senior students, when they have demonstrated their competency, with local media employers. At my school, senior students get work as a grip, assistant editor, production assistant, or camera assistant, and a great many other positions. Via these internships an employer can, at low risk, try people out in places where they can't do much harm. An internship may turn into a graduate's first paid work, and even if it doesn't, it can provide the all-important professional reference when you need it. Albert Maysles is actively involved with passing on his experience and skills, and the Maysles Institute actually offers internships with a small stipend (see www .mayslesfilms.com and look under "Internships"). Maybe take his example and approach a local documentarian you respect who works in your vicinity. Suggest that he or she consider you for a similar learning internship.

 Graduation is on the horizon, and the scary prospect of supporting yourself is hurtling closer. How to go from film student to paid worker in the medium? You will need a well-developed craft in addition to your directing skills and aspirations.

ON GRADUATING

Let's fast-forward to a point where you have knowledge and some experience in filmmaking. First-rate skills in one or more of the following will help you earn a living:

- Camera operating, lighting, or gaffer skills
- Sound recordist, microphone operator, or sound design
- Editor, sound editor
- Producer, production manager, production secretary, or assistant director

Make your production skills tangible by leaving school with a respectable *demo reel* (see page 546) on a DVD. It serves as a portfolio of your work as well as that done for others. With your craft skills and networking through all the contacts you made in film school, you should be able to earn short-term money at crewing while you deploy a longer term plan to gradually establish yourself as a director.

 Enter your best work in a number of festivals, and perhaps you'll win some awards. These are the very best résumé credentials.

 Aspiring directors seldom find work awaiting them; they have to make jobs for themselves.

MAKING A JOB FOR YOURSELF

The film and television industries are downsizing permanent staffs and employing freelancers, so in principle there are more opportunities for small, self-starter companies, but work goes to those with a track record of accomplishment, which is a catch-22 for the beginner. The films you made at school or have made since at your own expense are your investment in your future. If you have a passion for some special subject, then you must show this as your area of expertise embodied in short film work. That area might be anything—ornithology, teaching science, the politics of water supply in Third World countries, or the subculture of bicycle messengers. Now you can use the work you've done to seek commissions from individuals or organizations whose work is in your subject area and who will quickly recognize one of their own. Sometimes, before you know it, you're in another country doing the kind of useful work you dreamed of. Maybe you're doing it unpaid, but you're racking up demonstrable experience for your demo reel, which is what counts.

 If you do get commissioned directing straight out of school, it will probably be sporadic and ill paid for some time.

While you pursue further directing you will need crewing work so you can pay your bills, consolidate your skills, and build up your résumé with film-related jobs.

 To gain acceptance in the film industry, you need *professional-level skills*, *professional discipline*, and *good references*. Initially the latter will come from your teachers.

ENTERING THE FILM INDUSTRY

At an internship, a temporary (and usually unpaid) position may turn into your first paying job. My college has an extension in the CBS studios and thus many connections in Los Angeles, where a great many documentary series are made. Our students find internships in Hollywood as well as in Chicago and other places. Similar arrangements exist in most established film schools, and it's something to look for in any school you're considering. If job channels don't materialize through interning, then you will need other approaches.

NETWORKING

The film industry, of which making documentaries is a part, is a set of linked villages. You get work by networking through personal connections with friends, associates, and any professional contacts acquired during your schooling and internships. Established film schools have alumni associations or other, less formalized networks in the major film centers. Through warm recommendations by your teachers you should be able to use these networks to get interviews and advice.

 Your degree means little in the production world; it is your awards, production work, and recommendations that count.

CRAFT WORKER

Though there are regional and national differences in the film and television industries, developing a track record as a freelancer is similar everywhere. For quite a long time your work will probably be fulfilling mundane commercial needs; that is, you will be expending lots of imagination and effort crewing for industrial, training, or medical films or shooting conferences, graduations, and weddings. Learning to do this reliably, inventively, and to high standards will teach you a great deal. A similar training served Robert Altman and many another director well.

Do good work with a friendly and positive spirit and stay on schedule and budget, and your reputation as an okay person will slowly percolate through the grapevine. In the meantime, aim to stay solvent and invest your spare time in making films with those contemporaries who are also struggling to gain experience and recognition.

This emphasis on becoming known and fitting in may seem like the slipway to compromise, but it need not be. Each new level of accomplishment brings recognition, and this equips you and your group to eventually seek more interesting and demanding work. Once you and your associates have concrete, proven results, you really do have something to offer an employer, fund, or sponsor.

Some interesting facts emerged in a colloquium given by former students at my institution. All were now working in various capacities in the film industry. It transpired that everyone:

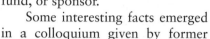 The long time it takes to gain professional acceptance excludes the immature personality impatient for recognition. The top of film school leads to the bottom of the working world. So be open to any kind of (legal) work, and do it reliably and with a good heart. Aim to be in good standing when "something opens up." Something always does.

- Took about the same (long) time to get established and to begin earning reasonable money
- Had moved up the ladder of responsibility at roughly the same (slow) pace
- Found that greater responsibility came suddenly and without warning
- Was scared stiff when it came, feeling they were conning their way into an area beyond their competence
- Grew into their new levels of responsibility
- Loved their job and felt privileged to have work in such an important area of public life

 The change and democratization in filmmaking is producing more filmmakers and a glut of unsold product. Your films must be better than other people's; the keys to this are scattered throughout this book.

THE SEARCH FOR SUBJECTS AND A MARKET

Documentary markets are evolving, and audience appreciation for the genre is growing. Television networks now show independently produced documentaries but increasingly rely on international coproductions to spread the high cost of "big" series meant for worldwide audiences. To enter the race at any level, you must find subjects and treatments that call to a sizable audience.

DOCUMENTARIES THAT CROSS BOUNDARIES AND BUCK TRENDS

Finding large audiences means aiming to make films whose subject, treatment, or thematic intensity carries them across national and linguistic borders. Unlike fiction films and novels, few documentaries achieve this, and few films travel beyond the parochial, linguistic, or cultural enclosure of their makers. This is something to think about long and hard. It's not necessarily a matter of budget, but more of tapping into universal themes and interests.

Films that transcend boundaries are often made by those who, voluntarily or otherwise, have migrated to another country or culture and ingested larger ideas about humanity.

Getting the audience to notice fragile and transient moments in obscure lives is not easy or common in films, yet should be more common in documentary. The uncertainty about meriting an audience's attention makes documentarians play it safe by resorting to exotic or sensational subjects. War, murderers, family violence, urban problems, eccentrics, deviants, demonstrations, revolts, and confrontations all promise something reliably heightened. Less often do documentaries penetrate the heart of everyday subjects with the ease and precision of literature. For the minutia of small-town life or the anguish in a middle-class family, we look instinctively to fiction rather than the documentary. This is not inevitable, as you see in such notable American examples as Ira Wohl's *Best Boy* (discussed in **Chapter 5, Documentary Language**) or David Sutherland's *The Farmer's Wife* (discussed in **Chapter 18, Dramatic Development, Time, and Structure**). Sutherland's films result from the kind of long and close involvement that brought Flaherty his first fame; you can read about his methods at www.davidsutherland.com/bio.html. Of similar intensity, and arising from a similar immersion, is Doug Block's film about his parents' half century of unsatisfactory marriage, *51 Birch Street* (discussed in Chapter 18), and Deborah Hoffmann's bittersweet *Complaints of a Dutiful Daughter* (Chapter 18), which chronicles her reactions while her mother declines gently into Alzheimer's disease. Documentarians wanting to buck the trends, as these films do, will always face difficulties getting access to their subjects and will have difficulty raising money for a film about subjects considered minor. Yet, their intensity of regard, passion, and courageous truthfulness makes the more average documentary look shallow and perfunctory.

Filmmaking is a market commodity that thrives or dies according to audience figures. Complaining about this is futile and unproductive because there are plenty of other obstacles to discourage the fainthearted. Luckily, making a small-canvas documentary no longer requires much of a budget, so now—if you can sustain life by other means—you can simply make a film you believe in rather than trying to get airborne with written proposals.

Creative form is probably more important than finding unique content, which gets more difficult as more films explore more areas of life. *How* a film sees is as important and significant as *what* it sees. Find out where you stand by pitching possible subjects to filmmaking colleagues; argue them out and discover all their possibilities, depths, and difficulties. Pitch to non-film-

> The best way to locate original subjects and approaches (pardon my refrain) is to *pursue what you are passionate about and to shun everything stereotypical.*

makers, too; they need only be the kind of person who's interested by human life and endeavors. Pitching speeds up the evolution of your projects and ideas and doesn't cost a dime.

Go through Netflix® and distributors' Web sites to check out your areas of special interest. Make a study to see where holes exist in the existing commercial structure, holes that you might fill and where you could show an audience is waiting. See everything you can.

USING FESTIVALS

How do filmmakers present themselves at festivals, and what do TV networks and distributors seem interested in buying among your kind of films? The Independent Feature Project Web site is a mine of information on all aspects of producing as an indie (www.ifp. org), especially the financial

Find out what others are producing by attending festivals and conferences. You'll find it energizing to be among aficionados.

aspects. It even advertises job openings and requests for partnerships.

At pitching sessions, such as those that the International Documentary Film Festival Amsterdam (IDFA; www.idfa.nl/iprof_home.asp) holds annually, hopeful producers pitch ideas and are publicly grilled by a panel of commissioning editors, who may or may not buy into the project. You will see a separation between producers and buyers/backers akin to that between authors and publishers. Newcomers can only expect funds from a distributor if they already have a commercially marketable product, and that's hard to prove without a visible track record. Because you are unlikely to get distributors' or television money for a film in the planning stages, you may want to make a superb first five minutes as a demonstration. If you have cornered the rights to a hot subject, you might get offers of partnership from established concerns, which can be a good deal. Be careful not to get swallowed up.

Competition is high, yet most prospective filmmakers represent themselves poorly in writing. Many even overlook aspects of the fund's guidelines. If you were a fund, would you give money to someone who can't follow a few simple rules?

DOCUMENTARY PROPOSALS

You are what you write, so study the sections of this book on writing proposals. Draft and redraft proposals until they are your very best, then try your luck and keep trying, seeking all the critical feedback you can get. Grantwriting is an art all on its own. Volunteer to read and critique other people's proposals—you'll be astonished at how much you learn. Read everything you can lay hands on concerning grants, funds, and grantwriting. Think of applying for grants not as begging but as rehearsals for communicating your vision and originality. Really good proposals are rare, and they do get recognized with funding. Top-notch proposals don't just happen by luck—the people who make them have practiced heart and soul.

FUNDS AND FOUNDATIONS

There is a lot written by filmmakers about funding, but documentary funding conforms to no set pattern. Read about their serpentine paths, and maybe you'll learn something useful. Everyone wants to know the "secret of how you got the money" to make the film, but all the secrets are different, particular to the seeker and the project, and are unlikely to unlock your particular problem. It takes originality to make exceptional films, and the same originality to find resources. When funding organizations do make an award, they usually grant no more than 50% of the budget. The proposal has to be well written, businesslike, and focused on the special area that the fund or foundation supports.

THE DEMO REEL

When you apply for a job or submit a grant application, prepare an edited demonstration reel of *around 5 minutes maximum*. From your bank of the best and most applicable work you've done, custom build DVDs for different application purposes and include a descriptive outline to help users navigate. Make sure each copy plays faultlessly from beginning to end. The demo reel evidences what you can do and who you are. It might contain three 30-second quotations from your camerawork and three of your directing. If you are applying to fund a documentary idea, the demo reel is a trailer that shows material already shot. If your proposed film has great landscapes or a gritty industrial setting, then include a montage of the best shots. If it is character driven, assemble material to establish in a minute or so how attractively interesting and unusual your central character is. A really professional reel argues powerfully and *briefly* for your proficiency and can clinch a jury decision in your favor. The long-established Independent Feature Project (IFP) has good funding ideas and information on its Web site (www.ifp.org).

FUNDS

The United States has a complex and shifting system of *federal, state, and private funding agencies*. Each has guidelines and a track record in funding some special area. As a rule, private grant foundations prefer to give *completion money* to films that are self-evidently good, while government agencies are a little more likely to fund research and preproduction. They may, however, stipulate that you work with a board of academics. This may or may not be productive, so protect yourself by writing this on your cuff: *A camel is a horse designed by a committee.*

 Usually only local organizations will fund local student work or first films. Fund money is good money because you don't usually have to repay it.

If your track record is slender (perhaps a short film that has won some festival awards), and you are seeking preproduction, production, or completion money, investigate your state or city arts council. Each state in the United States has a state humanities committee that works in association with the National Endowment for the Humanities (NEH). This agency works to fund groups of accredited individuals (usually academics) producing work in the humanities. National guidelines can be obtained from The National Endowment for the Humanities, 1100 Pennsylvania Avenue, Rm. 406, Washington, D.C. 20506. (www.neh.gov). The Web site is a mine of information on state humanity and other funds.

Many states and big cities have a film commission or film bureau that exists to encourage and facilitate filmmaking (because it's good business). These offices (see www.studio1productions.com/Articles/FilmCommission.htm) develop formal and informal relationships with the whole local filmmaking community and can be an excellent source of information on all aspects of local production. A full list of those in the United States, as well as a wealth of other documentary-related information, used to be published in the invaluable International Documentary Association (IDA) Membership Directory and Survival Guide, and its successor is expected to arise soon, phoenix-like, on IDA's Web site (www.documentary.org).

Congress proposed $400M in 2009 to budget the Corporation for Public Broadcasting (CPB), which redistributes the money to a number of funds, including the Independent Television Service (ITVS; www.itvs.org). See how the CPB money has been used at the Web site of the newly revived Association of Independent Video and Filmmakers (AIVF; www.aivf.org), an organization dedicated to the independent filmmaker. Additionally, you can always use online searches to dredge up large quantities of information on the Internet. Simply enter the words you want associated together, such as *documentary, fund, festival, pitching, proposal, investors,* etc.

A couple of survey organizations exist to help you find the appropriate private fund or charity to approach. Chicago has the Donors Forum, a clearinghouse that periodically publishes local information (www.donorsforum.org). New York has the Foundation Center (http://foundationcenter.org), a source for nationwide reference collections for those wishing to approach donors and donor organizations. As you might expect, many people compete for funding, so the hoops you must jump through almost amount to a new career.

For funding about subjects pertaining to Latin America, many countries of which now have thriving documentary-making cultures themselves, there are foundations such as the John D. and Catherine T. MacArthur Foundation (www.macfound.org/programs/index.htm), which underwrites projects on subjects they wish to see covered, such as human and community development and global security and development.

JOURNALS AND ASSOCIATIONS

The International Documentary Association (www.documentary.org), mentioned above, is based in Los Angeles and has a strong program of local events. It publishes *International Documentary,* an important quarterly journal with featured articles on new films, filmmakers, trends, festivals, and technology. In the back pages is an updated directory of festivals and competitions; funding; jobs and opportunities; classes, seminars, and workshops; distributors looking for new films; new publications; and classifieds. In Europe, the English language documentary maker's journal, published in Copenhagen, is *Dox* (www.dox.dk). It's the journal of the European Documentary Network (www.edn.dk), whose Web site is a mine of information on funds, festivals, workshops, and recent films.

Another good move is to take out a subscription to *American Cinematographer*, a monthly publication mainly for feature fiction workers but which publishes occasional articles on documentaries. It will help you keep abreast of the latest digital methods and technical innovations, especially in lighting. The journal includes news, interviews, and a lot of "who's doing what" information (see www.theasc.com). Like many such organizations, they also send out material online.

Videomaker is an excellent monthly magazine that reviews new equipment in the prosumer range (i.e., high-end consumer, low-end professional). It is particularly good for accessible explanations of techniques and technical principles, and it lists conferences and workshops (see www.videomaker.com).

Digital Video, or *DV* as it calls itself, is the journal for tools and technique for the independent professional and contains a wealth of information and reviews (see www.dv.com).

JOB INFORMATION

The Internet makes a good labor exchange, and an example of a film job search site is www.media-match.com. Such sites exist to make money for their organizers and aren't necessarily a sure passport to employment, but you may be the only filmmaking vulcanologist or mining safety expert in your area and have skills that get you work. Tim Curran's FAQ, which speaks autobiographically, may be helpful (www.timcurran.com). I found it, and a great deal else, by entering *documentary* and *career* in Google®. Most film career guides focus on Hollywood, but there is information about the general structure and expectations for independents in www.ifp.org/jobs. The Salt Institute, which specializes in documentary stills and sound work for sociologists, lists useful documentary links at www.salt.edu/alumni/jobs_resources.html. You may also find that some of the diary and blog items stimulate your ideas.

What should hearten you is that broadcast organizations now recognize that they have more demand than supply and are soliciting films or ideas for films (Figure 36-1). They are not short of documentaries but are short of *different* documentaries that reach beyond the norms. You can see what the Public Broadcasting Service (PBS) or the BBC and British television expects of producers by going to:

- PBS, www.pbs.org/producers
- BBC, www.close-upfilm.com/features/Filmmaking/documentary.htm
- Interdoc, www.initialize-films.co.uk/what-we-do.htm

If you find the term "business plan" intimidating, now is the time to hunt down the information to educate yourself. PBS has become far more open to independent production—see their application form for *Independent Lens*, a program that consistently puts on interesting shorter material.

FIGURE 36-1

The well-respected PBS documentary series *POV* puts out an annual call for entries. Countless festivals worldwide do the same.

Whomever you plan to approach, learn all you can about the individual, business, or organization that you aspire to join. People who deal with job seekers distinguish rapidly between the hardworking realist and the dreamer floating in alien waters. They make this judgment not on who you are but on how you present yourself—on paper and in person. You will do this well by resourceful reading and lots of networking.

When you send your résumé to an individual or company, send a brief, carefully composed, *individual* cover letter describing your goals and how you might be an asset to the company. Call after a few days to ask if you can have a brief chat with someone just in case something opens up in the future. If you are called for that chat, or better, for a formal interview:

➢ Dress conservatively.

➢ Be punctual.

➢ Know what you want and show you are willing to do any kind of work to get there.

➢ Let the interviewer ask the questions.

➢ Be brief and to the point when you reply.

➢ Say concisely what skills and qualities you have to offer. This is where you can demonstrate your knowledge of (and therefore commitment to) the interviewer's business.

➢ Never inflate your abilities or experience.

➢ Leave an up-to-date résumé and demo reel.

Interviewers often finish by asking if you have any questions, so have two or three good ones ready so you can again demonstrate your knowledge of the company or group.

If shyness holds you back, do something about it. Get assertiveness training or join a theater group and force yourself to act, preferably in improvisational material. Only you can liberate your abilities. Almost all human problems boil down to a matter of courage. Courage, like power, is not given—it's taken.

DOCUMENTARY AS A PREPARATION FOR DIRECTING FICTION

Taking the relatively small British cinema as an example, it's instructive to see who first worked in documentary before moving to fiction: Lindsay Anderson, Michael Apted, John Boorman, Ken Loach, Karel Reisz, Sally Potter, Tony Richardson, and John Schlesinger. Is this a stellar list by chance? Now add those coming from painting, theater, and music or who espouse improvisational methods, and further distinguished names appear, such as Maureen Blackwood, Mike Figgis, Peter Greenaway, Mike Leigh, Sharon Maguire, and Anthony Minghella. Not all are household names, but they do suggest that vibrant fiction cinema often has someone from a documentary background at the helm.

In this book's sister volume, *Directing: Film Techniques and Aesthetics*, 4th ed., (2008, Focal Press, pp. 62–63), I advocate the value to aspiring fiction directors of making documentaries. If this is you, know that documentary experience can give you:

- Rapid, voluminous training in finding and telling screen stories.
- Confidence in your ability to use the screen spontaneously and adaptively.
- A proving ground for your intuitive judgments.
- An eye for a focused and truthful human presence.
- A workout in a genre that requires great narrative compression and poses the same narrative problems as fiction.
- A chance to show real characters in action as they struggle with real obstacles.
- Experience seeing how a person's identity is constructed through interactions and that it's not a fixed commodity functioning similarly under varying circumstances.
- A laboratory for character-driven drama (character is fate!).
- A benchmark for when people are simply being rather than acting.
- Experience at catalyzing truth from participants in preparation to do the same with actors.
- Exposure to shooting in real time, thinking on your feet, and plucking drama from life.
- The risk, confrontation, and chemistry of the moment, which are central to both documentary and improvisational fiction.

A PERSONAL MESSAGE

Documentary is an evolving field in which the levels of inventiveness, humor, courage, and productivity are all going up. As I said in Chapter 1, documentary people are remarkable for their conviviality and helpfulness, and you'll experience this right away at your first conference or festival. They have chosen documentary film—be it ecological, political, humanitarian, or historical—as the work that matters most to them in all the world. I hope that you, dear reader, join this community and use the wonderful art of the screen to help make a better world.

Thank you most sincerely for using this book, and if you have any comments that can help make the next edition better, write me via e-mail at mrabiger@aol.com. I will try to reply. Please don't send unsolicited proposals or films—I simply don't have time to review them (or to do lots of other good things).

May you have good luck, good filming, and good friends.

APPENDIX

NOTES

The 32 projects that follow anticipate most situations that you will meet as a documentary maker. Some are analytic or developmental tools; others are exercises in a particular technique or style of filmmaking. They represent a thorough preparation in concepts and technique, as well as many opportunities for you to find satisfaction expressing ideas and feelings while you work to gain mastery over your craft.

If possible, make no film that fails to express something, however minor, that you feel or believe. That way, you can always fulfill the task in hand *and* inject it with something from your heart and soul.

Where necessary, projects may have explanatory notes and pictures. For teachers, the book's Web site (http://directingthedocumentary.com) will contain assessment forms to help assess students' performances.

APPENDIX TABLE OF CONTENTS

ANALYSIS PROJECTS (AP)
(1-AP-1 TO 1-AP-8)
PROJECT 1-AP-1 ANALYZE OR PLAN USING THE SPLIT-PAGE SCRIPT FORM

Project

Make a split-page script (also called a TV script) either to log an existing film for analysis or to script the precise relationship between words and images in an intended film.

Goals

- Show a film's content and the precise relationship between words and images.   ❏
- Give an overview of a film's editing style.   ❏
- Make how the film presents its content accessible to a reader   ❏
  or fellow filmmaker.

Steps

1. Handwrite your first notes double-spaced on the Split-Page   ❏
   Script worksheet. You can then interpolate additional
   information later. See model in Figure 1-AP-1A below.
2. Write all shot descriptions in the LH action column using   ❏
   present-tense, active voice.
3. Write all words, sound, or music descriptions similarly in the   ❏
   RH sound column.
4. Space them to show the exact point where each relationship   ❏
   between sound and picture changes.
5. Make a finished version using a computer for a really profes-   ❏
   sional look.

Notes: The point of using this format for logging or planning a film is to be precise about shot descriptions, the actual words used, where music starts and stops, and so on. Particularly important is to log overlaps where, for instance, a synchronous speech shot cuts to a new picture with the old sound trailing on as voice-over. No other scripting form can show such subtleties, which are particular to screen language and replicate the way our eyes and ears process the events going on around us.

Action	Sound
Fade in L.S. FARMHOUSE. EXT. DAY	Fade up birdsong, (music fades in.)
MS Farmhouse, burned out barn in B/G	Karen's V/O: "But I thought you said that whole business was being put off! When we last talked about it, you said. . ."
Cut to KITCHEN, INT., DAY CU Ted	Ted: "Everything's changed." K: "Everything's changed?" T: "We're not to blame. You know that."
2S Ted & Karen CU Karen, worried, shocked MS Karen moves L-R to stove MS Ted moves slightly after her	T: "There's a buyer. . . (Music fades out) someone's interested."
Karen turns sharply to face him BCU Ted, eyes waver & drop Cut to O/S on to Karen Cut to O/S on to Ted	K: "Ted, Ted! What are you telling me?" K: "You told me. . . (dog begins barking) . . . you promised me. . . (V/O) you said you'd never let the lawyer swindle us out of this place. . . You said. . ."
Cut to OTHER SIDE KITCHEN DOOR Anna, 4, clutching Raggedy Ann doll, looking frightened.	Ted's V/O: "The agent said it's now or never. We've got to make up our minds."

FIGURE 1-AP-1A ———————————————————————

Example of script in split-page format.

Notes, Example, and Worksheet Form

The goal during analysis is to extract the maximum solid information about an interesting passage of film language, so it's better to precisely log a short sequence (say, 2 minutes) than a long one superficially. Deal first with the picture and dialogue, shot by shot and word by word, as they relate to each other. Handwrite your initial version using wide line spacing on numerous sheets of paper so there's space to insert additional information on subsequent passes. Write down only *what anyone can see and hear*; be eloquently descriptive, but avoid subjective thoughts or feelings. Make several passes dealing with one or two aspects of content and form at a time. Your split-page script should resemble Figure 1-AP-1A.

Once basic information is on paper, consider ruling between sequences, recording shot transitions, screen direction, camera movements, opticals, sound effects, and the use of music.

SPLIT-PAGE SCRIPT for _____ [Title] Page #_____	
Action	**Sound**

PROJECT 1-AP-2 MAKING A FLOOR PLAN

Project

Make a floor plan either for an existing sequence or as a planning tool to help you anticipate your camera and lighting placement in relation to the expected action.

Goals

- Sketch the contents and layout of a space such as a room, workshop, or sports arena. ❏
- Show key positioning of human action through the span of a sequence. ❏
- Show lighting, both ambient and that which is added. ❏
- For analyzing, it is useful to log what camera placement was used to cover the action. ❏
- For planning, use the floor plan to help decide camera and lighting placements and to get the most coverage from the least number of setup changes. ❏

Steps

1. Sketch space and its contents. Use graph paper if you need help keeping to scale. ❏
2. Sketch path of human action. ❏
3. Add in arrows for direction of ambient light or that of lights you mean to add. ❏
4. Put a "V" symbol for each stationary camera angle. ❏
5. Prove your camera positions by drawing a series of key comic-strip frames. Draw stick figures if you have to—they're fine for this. ❏

Notes: A floor plan can also contain electric outlets and the direction of ambient light at different times of day to help schedule a shoot effectively.

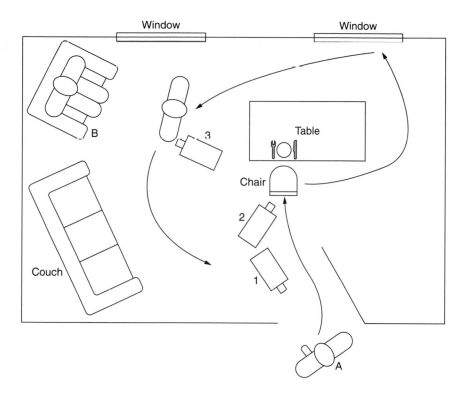

FIGURE 1-AP-2 ─────────────────────────────────────

Floor plan showing entry and movements of Character A in relation to seated Character B. Three camera positions cover all the action. A tripod-mounted camera would require you to repeat portions of the action, making actors of participants. But a handheld camera could move between the three positions without impeding the action's flow.

PROJECT 1-AP-3 ANALYZE LIGHTING

Project

Analyze a film for the elements of lighting. In documentary you can't always control lighting; instead, you control camera angle, composition, and exposure parameters to capitalize on what's present. Here is an exercise in recognizing the elements you must work with. In controlled documentary—a historical recreation, say—you would have the time and facilities to deliberate over using such lighting techniques.

Goals

- Identify examples of:
  a. High contrast, low contrast images ❑
  b. Graduated tonality image ❑
  c. Practical lights ❑
  d. Fill light ❑
  e. High-key and low-key lighting situations ❑
  f. Hard (specular) light and soft light ❑
  g. Portrait shot with frontal lighting ❑
  h. Portrait shot with broad lighting ❑
  i. Portrait shot with narrow lighting ❑
  j. Portrait shot with backlighting ❑
  k. Portrait shot in silhouette ❑

Preparation

1. Pick a documentary with a variety of lighting situations (interior/ ❑ exterior, day/night, artificial light/sunlight, etc.). My choice is _____ [title].
2. Identify one or more of the facets specified in (a) to (k) above. ❑ If possible, use a computer frame-grab facility to collect samples that you integrate into a piece of explanatory writing.

Writing

1. Describe:
   a. In brief, what the film delivers as mood, message, meaning ❑
   b. What makes each of your shots qualify in (a) to (k) lighting ❑ categories
   c. Where the key light originates in each shot (for example, a ❑ window or a fluorescent overhead light or supposedly from a table lamp "practical")
   d. What feeling the particular lighting contributes to each scene ❑
   e. What progression the lighting follows through the film ❑

> 2. **Discuss what you learned from making this analysis and what**   ❏
> **resolutions you formed in relation to your own filmmaking.**
>
> **Notes:** Shooting spontaneously means taking advantage of the lighting and com-
> positional potential of any scene. You'll need a practiced eye and a keen mind to
> realize all that's on offer. During your analysis try to distinguish between lighting
> applied by the filmmakers and shooting that makes artful use of circumstances.
> Shooting under available light is mostly the latter, although a fill light mounted on
> the camera sometimes makes a vital contribution to lighting.
> *Alternative:* Using a digital camera, shoot documentary stills as examples.

Lighting Notes

This project challenges you to categorize types and combinations of lighting situation, become familiar with the look and effect of each, and be able to use the
appropriate terminology in describing them. The aim is to recognize the emotional associations that all the different possibilities of lighting and image control bring to our art.

When you do your lighting study, turn down the color control on your monitor
until you have a black-and-white image uncomplicated by chrominance. What follows is a just a brief rundown; you will need a lighting text to go deeper. YouTube®
and other Web sites offer many lighting demonstrations, but mostly for still photography. I like www.youtube.com/watch?v=9KZe7Xbi6DM for the way it works
in black and white and demonstrates the effect of each source light as it goes.

My illustrations are frame grabs from Tod Lending's *Omar and Pete* (2005,
United States; www.nomadicpix.com), shot by the masterly Slawomir Grunberg. The
film's first 12 minutes are available to watch on this book's Web site, http://directingth-
edocumentary.com. It chronicles attempts by the prison system to rehabilitate recidi-
vists—the hard core who keep returning to prison. Through two such men it examines
the Gordian knot of social disadvantage, racism, poverty, poor education, and dysfunctional family life that lies behind the tragedy of so many African–American men
self-destructing. Grunberg's camera handling and special picture quality set us deep
within a grim world from which there is little escape.

Light Sources: Key, Fill, Backlight, Practicals

Key light is the source casting the shot's shadows. The key light on Omar's sister
in her office comes from the window behind her and off to the left. The rest of her
face is illuminated by *fill light*.

FIGURE 1-AP-3A

Fill light illuminates shadow areas so a
camera can record their detail. In Figure
1-AP-3A, fill comes from *soft light* cast
either by a fixture close to the camera
or by window light reflecting from the
office's white walls. In exterior shots,
you often throw fill light on the subject
using handheld reflectors of silver or
matte white. Fill is necessary because

highlights under sunlight are often so bright that important shadow details, such as in a person's eye-sockets, remain in deep shadow. By adding light to the shadow areas you lower the *contrast* (see following page) between highlight and shadow areas so the recording medium can record detail in each.

FIGURE 1-AP-3B

FIGURE 1-AP-3C

FIGURE 1-AP-3D

FIGURE 1-AP-3E

Backlight is a source shining on the subject from behind and often from above (Figure 1-AP-3B). Also called a *hair* or a *kicker light*, it casts a rim of light around a subject's head and shoulders and creates a separation between the subject and background, as seen here with the two men on Omar's parole board.

A *practical* is any light source that appears in frame as part of the scene, such as a bedside light, miner's lamp, or traffic signal. The fluorescent fixture above Omar and his guard is a practical (Figure 1-AP-3C). Most practicals don't supply light for exposure, but *Omar and Pete* was shot in prison under available light, so they supplied most of the lighting.

Set lighting is that needed to adjust a scene's background to a proper illumination level.

Tonality

A *high-key picture* looks overall bright with small areas of shadow (Figure 1-AP-3D). Any shot, interior or exterior, can be overall bright and thus qualify as high key. Comedies are mostly high key, while *film noir* is by definition low key. Every film needs relief from its predominating mood, and exteriors provide the audience with reprieve in *Omar and Pete*.

A *low-key picture* is one that looks overall dark with few highlight areas (Figure 1-AP-3E). Low-key images, often interiors or night shots, predominate in

FIGURE 1-AP-3F

FIGURE 1-AP-3G

FIGURE 1-AP-3H

FIGURE 1-AP-3I

Omar and Pete. This is the cage of steel surrounding Omar. The system offers him the opportunity to work his way out, but can he do it?

Graduated tonality shots have neither very bright highlights nor deep shadow but consist mainly of midtones—a term referring not to colors but the tonal range between dark and light (Figure 1-AP-3F). Here, Omar seems to blend into the detention facilities that contain him.

Contrast

High-contrast pictures have a big difference between highlight and shadow illumination levels (Figure 1-AP-3G). Here, birds have the liberty that an imprisoned man can only dream of, and their world is in stark contrast to his own.

Low-contrast pictures can be either high or low key, but their highlight levels are not far above their shadow illumination (Figure 1-AP-3H). Notice how selective focus in this case isolates and separates Omar from his background, unlike Figure 1-AP-3F.

Light Quality

Hard lighting describes light quality in terms of its shadow (Figure 1-AP-3I). Hard light or *specular* light creates hard-edged shadows (for example, a studio spotlight, a candle flame, or sunlight as in the prison yard). Hard light is not necessarily strong light, just light coming from an effectively small source whose rays cast distinct shadows.

FIGURE 1-AP-3J ————————

Soft light comes from an effectively large source and creates soft-edged shadows (for example, fluorescent fixtures, sunlight reflecting off a matte finish wall, light from an overcast sky, studio soft light). In Figure 1-AP-3J, there is some shadow under the subject's chin and beard, but it's very indistinct.

Types of Lighting Setup

Photography's limitation is that you must use a two-dimensional medium to present a three-dimensional world. What's missing is depth, so in portraiture you use angled lighting to reveal the third dimension. The basic portrait lighting setup is called *three-point lighting*, and its components are diagrammed in Figure 1-AP-3K. It uses a fill light, a key, and a backlight. There's also *set lighting*, which illuminates the background and which we'll leave aside.

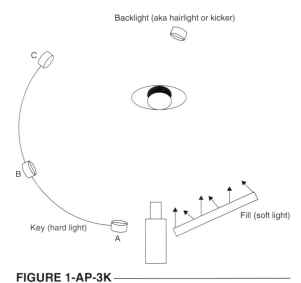

FIGURE 1-AP-3K ————————

In the diagram only the fill light is turned on; it emits disorganized light rays from a broad source that casts little shadow. Keeping it close to, and above, the camera means that any shadow it does cast is largely thrown behind the subject and out of sight of the camera.

Figure 1-AP-3L shows a face lit by fill light alone. Once you turn on the key, it will illuminate the other side of the face and cast definite shadows. By moving the key through positions A, B, and C

FIGURE 1-AP-3L ————————————

FIGURE 1-AP-3M

FIGURE 1-AP-3N

FIGURE 1-AP-3O

FIGURE 1-AP-3P

we create three classifications of lighting.

Frontal lighting setups have the key light in position A, close to the camera/subject axis, so shadows are largely thrown backward out of the camera's view (Figure 1-AP-3M).

Broad lighting setups have the key light in position B so a broad area of the subject's face and body is highlighted by the key (Figure 1-AP-3N).

Narrow lighting setups have the key light in position C to the side of the subject and perhaps even beyond, so only a narrow portion of the face receives highlighting (Figure 1-AP-3O). Most of the face is in shadow and depends on fill for an exposure.

Calculate *lighting ratio* by measuring light reflected in the highlight area and comparing it with that from the fill area. When taking measurements, remember that fill light reaches the highlight area but not vice versa, so you can only take accurate readings with all of the lights on.

In *silhouette lighting*, the subject reflects no light at all and shows up as an outline against raw light (Figure 1-AP-3P). This setup is useful when the subject's identity must be withheld.

PROJECT 1-AP-4 ANALYZE PICTURE COMPOSITION

Project

Analyze pictorial composition, which is a powerful tool for attracting the audience's eye, directing their attention, organizing elements that are in conflict, and suggesting subtexts. Composition is static, dynamic, internal to a shot, and external between shots. All involve point of view and meaning.

Goals

Identify:

a. How the eye travels differently within different kinds of composition ❑
b. What patterns the eye follows and how you would classify that movement ❑
c. The strongest elements in particular compositions ❑
d. Different ways to organize space around human subjects ❑
e. How and why people or objects can be on the edge of frame or even cut off ❑
f. Different ways that the third dimension—depth—can be created ❑
g. How the film's dramatic problem and resulting dramatic tension are implied ❑
h. How compositions draw attention to oppositional forces ❑
i. Variations in visual rhythm through the film and the reason for them ❑
j. Examples of dynamic composition ❑
k. Examples of external composition ❑

Preparation

1. Pick a documentary with a strongly visual style and with a bold use of composition. My choice is _____ ❑
_____ [title].
2. Use a computer frame-grab facility to collect samples that you integrate into a piece of explanatory writing. ❑
3. Find one or more examples of the facets specified in (a) to (k) above, illustrating each with a frame quotation ❑

Writing

Describe in brief:

1. What the film delivers as mood, message, and meaning ❑
2. Why you picked each of your compositional examples to illustrate (a) to (k) above ❑

3. What the film's compositional trends contribute to its overall impact ❏
4. What progression the composition follows through the film ❏
5. What you learned from making this analysis and what resolutions you formed in relation to your own filmmaking ❏

Notes: Shooting to extract, meaning from documentary situations, means you can capitalize on the drama in a scene. This means you've developed a point of view on the tensions, issues, and personalities you are recording and have a dramatist's sensitivity to developing subtexts. You use composition's organizing potential to imply meanings and highlight relationships. Afterwards, you view your work with a keenly critical awareness of what you missed and why. You want to hone your sensitivity for future work.

Notes on Composition

Form is how content is presented, so visual composition is not just embellishment—it's a vital element in communication. Composition can interest and even delight the eye, but in wise hands it becomes *an organizing force that dramatizes relationships and projects ideas*. It makes the subject (or "content") accessible, heightens the viewer's perceptions, and stimulates critical involvement—like language in the hands of a good poet.

Static Composition

Some questions to help you see more critically:

1. *Why did your eye go to its particular starting point in the image?* Was it the brightest point, the darkest, an arresting color, or a significant junction of lines that created a focal point?

2. *When your eye moved away from its point of first attraction, what did it follow?*

3. *How much movement did your eye make before returning to its starting point?*

4. *What specifically drew your eye to each new place?*

5. *Are places in your eye's route specially charged with energy?* Often these are sightlines, such as between two field workers, one of whom is facing away.

6. *If you trace out the route your eye took, what shape do you have?* A circular pattern? A triangle? An ellipse? What else?

7. *How do you classify this compositional movement?* Translating from visual to verbal helps you see what's truly there. Is it geometrical, repetitive textures, swirling, falling inwards, symmetrically divided down the middle, flowing diagonally . . . ?

8. *What parts do the following play in a particular picture?*
    a. Repetition
    b. Parallels
    c. Convergence
    d. Divergence
    e. Curves
    f. Straight lines
    g. Strong verticals
    h. Strong horizontals
    i. Strong diagonals
    j. Textures
    k. Non-naturalistic coloring
    l. Light and shade
    m. Depth
    n. Dimension
    o. Human figures

9. How is depth suggested? It's never present unless created. Is it by angling to make the action take place in the screen's depth instead of its width; by composing a foreground, middle-ground, and background; by creating pools of light receding in a darkened space?

10. *How are the individuality and mood of the human subjects expressed?* By making juxtapositions between person and person, person and surroundings? By framings that suggest meaning or subtext? A good camera operator *sees in terms of relatedness* and uses composition to further the ends of the film.

11. *How is space arranged around a human subject, particularly in portraits?* Often there's more space in front of a person (called *lead space*) than behind. Framing sometimes cuts off the top of a head or does not show a head at all in a group shot.

12. *When are people and objects placed at the margins of the picture so that parts are cut off?* Does a restricted frame make you supply what is missing from imagination?

Visual Rhythm

The film spectator must interpret each shot within a given time. It's like reading the side of a passing bus; if you don't get the words and images in the given time, the bus leaves and you've lost its message. If, however, the bus crawls, you see its message to excess and become critical or even rejecting.

I make this analogy to suggest that there is *an optimum duration for each shot*. This depends on its content and complexity and also on how fast or slowly we think we must work. This was set by the expectations signaled during preceding shots. The principle by which you determine each shot's duration—by content, form, and audience expectation—is called *visual rhythm*. This can be relaxed or intensified according to how you want the film to develop.

Dynamic Composition

Working with moving images means you are handling *dynamic composition*. For instance, a balanced composition can become disturbingly unbalanced if someone moves or leaves the frame. Even a movement by someone's head in the foreground may posit a new sightline and a new scene axis (more about this later) and demand a compositional rebalance. A zoom into close shot usually demands reframing because compositionally there is a drastic change, even though the subject is the same. You might see:

1. *Reframing because the subject moved.* Look for a variety of camera adjustments.

2. *Reframing because something/someone left the frame.*

3. *Reframing in anticipation of something/someone entering the frame.*

4. *A change in the point of focus to move the attention from the background to foreground or vice versa.* This changes the texture of significant areas of the composition.

5. *Different kinds of movement (how many?) within an otherwise static composition.* Across the frame, diagonally, from the background to foreground, from the foreground to background, up frame, down frame, and so on.

6. *What makes you feel close to the subjects and their dilemmas?* This concerns point of view and is tricky, but in general the nearer one is to the axis of a movement, the more subjective one's sense of involvement is.

7. *How quickly does the camera adjust to a figure who moves to another place in frame?* Usually subject movement and the camera's compositional change are synchronous. The camera move looks clumsy if it either anticipates or lags behind the movement.

8. *How often are the camera or the characters blocked (that is, choreographed) in such a way as to isolate one character?*

9. *What is the dramatic justification for zeroing in on one character in this way?*

10. *How often is composition more or less angled along sightlines, and how often do sightlines extend across the screen?* This often marks a shift from subjective to more objective point of view.

11. *What does a change of angle or a change of composition make you feel toward the characters?* Maybe more or less involved and more or less objective.

12. *Find a dynamic composition that forcefully suggests depth.* An obvious one would be where the camera is next to a railroad line as a train rushes up and past.

13. *Can you locate shots where camera position is altered to include more or different background detail in order to comment upon or counterpoint foreground subject?*

Internal and External Composition

Beyond *internal composition* (that is, composition internal to each shot), there is *external composition*. This is the compositional relationship at cutting points between an outgoing image and the next or incoming shot. Seldom do we notice how much it influences our judgments and expectations. Use your slow-scan facility to help you assess compositional relationships at cutting points. Find aspects of internal and external composition by asking yourself:

1. *Where was your point of concentration at the end of the shot?* Trace with your finger on the monitor's face where your eye travels. Its last point in the outgoing shot is where your eye enters the next shot's composition. Interestingly, the length of the shot determines how far the eye gets in exploring the shot—so shot length influences external composition.

2. *Is there symmetry and are shots complementary?* Some shots are designed to intercut.

3. *What is the relationship between two same-subject but different sized shots that are designed to cut together?* This is revealing; the inexperienced camera operator often produces medium and close shots that cut together poorly because proportions and compositional placing of the subject are incompatible.

4. *Does a match cut, run very slowly, show several frames of overlap in its action?* Especially in fast action, a match cut (one made between two different size images during a strong action) requires *two or three frames of the action repeated* on the incoming shot to look smooth, because the eye does not register the first two or three frames of any new image. Think of this as accommodating a built-in perceptual lag. The only way to cut on the beat of music is thus to place all cuts two or three frames before the actual beat point.

5. *Do external compositions make a juxtapositional comment?* Cut from a pair of eyes to car headlights approaching at night, from a dockside crane to a man feeding birds with his arm outstretched, and the like.

PROJECT 1-AP-5 DIAGNOSING A NARRATIVE

Production title _____   Length _____
Editor _____ Date _____   Page # _____

Sequence Content Tag Title	Contribution to Film's "Argument"
_____ _____ _____ _____ Seq #_____ Ends at TC ___:___:___	_____ _____ _____ _____ Impact ☆☆☆☆☆ Length __:__:__
_____ _____ _____ _____ Seq #_____ Ends at TC ___:___:___	_____ _____ _____ _____ Impact ☆☆☆☆☆ Length __:__:__
_____ _____ _____ _____ Seq #_____ Ends at TC ___:___:___	_____ _____ _____ _____ Impact ☆☆☆☆☆ Length __:__:__
_____ _____ _____ _____ Seq #_____ Ends at TC ___:___:___	_____ _____ _____ _____ Impact ☆☆☆☆☆ Length __:__:__
_____ _____ _____ _____ Seq #_____ Ends at TC ___:___:___	_____ _____ _____ _____ Impact ☆☆☆☆☆ Length __:__:__
_____ _____ _____ _____ Seq #_____ Ends at TC ___:___:___	_____ _____ _____ _____ Impact ☆☆☆☆☆ Length __:__:__
_____ _____ _____ _____ Seq #_____ Ends at TC ___:___:___	_____ _____ _____ _____ Impact ☆☆☆☆☆ Length __:__:__

PROJECT 1-AP-6 ANALYZE EDITING AND CONTENT

Project

Analyze a representative section of a documentary to examine relationships of images, words, sound effects, and music. Develop your ideas about what these do for the segment and for the film as a whole.

Goals

- Make a precise split-page script log ❑
- Write about the progressions and juxtapositions you find ❑
- Describe how these assist the segment's function in the overall film ❑

Steps

1. Pick a visually inventive documentary that interests you, and write a 3- to 4-paragraph summary of its content and impact. ❑
2. Pick an approximately 5-minute section that contains challenging film language and that contributes markedly to the film's development. ❑
3. Make a split-page script, precisely logging sound in relationship to picture. ❑
4. Write about the function of picture editing you can see that is:
    a. Structural (builds the scene, directs our attention to significant detail) ❑
    b. Relational (indicates parallel, contrast, symbol, etc.) ❑
    c. Conflictual (differences, oppositions, tensions, conflicting forces, etc.) ❑
    d. Jump cutting (elision of time or space) ❑
5. Write about the function of any sound editing, that you can show is:
    a. Sync (sound and picture seen together) ❑
    b. Overlap (sound leading or trailing its accompanying picture) ❑
    c. Diegetic (sound audible to participants in the movie) ❑
    d. Nondiegetic (sound imposed for authorial reasons by filmmakers) ❑
    e. Dialogue used as voice-over ❑
    f. Narration (either created by filmmakers or using a character's voice-over) ❑
    g. Featured sound effects (used to make a point, create an atmosphere, etc.) ❑
    h. Using music (diegetic or nondiegetic) ❑

6. Write about:

   a. The intentions that seem to lie behind using these   ❏
      techniques

   b. What they made you feel   ❏

   c. What they seem to contribute to the statement you find the   ❏
      film makes

   d. What you learned, making this close study   ❏

Notes: Don't be afraid during analysis to work backward from a feeling. Often you'll find it was triggered by a particular juxtaposition of images, sounds, or ideas. It's important to recognize this and not to hold onto notions about what's right or wrong. Filmmakers rely on their hearts and minds to make their films, trusting that you'll rely on yours.

PROJECT 1-AP-7 ANALYZE STRUCTURE AND STYLE

Project

Analyze a documentary for its acts, structure, style, and thematic statement.

Goals

- Log the contents of a documentary. ❑
- Write about the way its structure and style deliver its content. ❑
- Describe what thematic statement it makes. ❑

Preparation

1. Pick a documentary of about 30 minutes, preferably one you are passionate about. ❑
2. Using the Project 1-AP-6 form, make a rapid overall log. Give each sequence a tag description and calculate its length. ❑

Writing

1. From your preparation, briefly describe:
   a. The film's content ❑
   b. What one feels about its characters and their situations ❑
   c. How you would divide the film into acts, justifying the divisions you chose ❑
   d. The film's style and what seems to have determined it ❑
   e. What principle or factor you think the makers used to determine the film's narrative structure ❑
2. Explain the film's outcomes:
   a. What the film made you feel ❑
   b. The impact and thematic statement the film makes ❑
3. Discuss what you learned from making this analysis and whether you formed any resolutions in relation to your own filmmaking. ❑

Notes: When you look in this kind of depth at a film, you often see what its makers included that previously escaped you. Writing about films well is usually a prelude to making them well.

PROJECT 1-AP-8 ASSESS A DIRECTOR'S THEMATIC VISION

Project

Assess the themes from a director's body of work, and relate these to the director's life and emerging philosophic vision.

Goals

- Compare two or more films by a director whose work excites you. ❑
- Note your reactions, thoughts, and feelings. ❑
- Do bibliographical research on films and on the director's biography. ❑
- Work out your own analysis of themes in relation to the director's life. ❑

Steps

1. View two or more films by the same director. ❑
2. Note what feelings and thoughts the films evoked. ❑
3. Make a bibliographical search and compile articles and essays on the films and director. ❑
4. View your chosen films again, this time making notes of each sequence's content so you have a complete running order list. ❑
5. Research the director's biography and write a 7- to 10-page, double-spaced essay assessing the themes of the two films and how they fit into the director's life and emerging philosophic vision. Demonstrate the connectedness of his or her themes and vision to two or more of the following, noting in your essay which of these parameters you have chosen:
    a. The director's personal and professional history ❑
    b. The intention implicit in the films to change the audience's perspectives in a particular direction ❑
    c. The degree to which the films' "social awareness" component is (or isn't) revealed organically from within the subject ❑
    d. The degree to which the films correctly or incorrectly anticipate audience reactions, especially ones that are biased ❑
    e. Visual, aural, or other special considerations of cinema form that are successfully or unsuccessfully employed ❑
    f. The way your own attitudes to the subject evolved as a result of seeing the films and writing the paper ❑
    g. Other (specify) _____ ❑

Notes: Where a director works in both features and documentary, consider comparing films from both genres.

DEVELOPMENT PROJECTS (DP)
(2-DP-1 TO 2-DP-6)
PROJECT 2-DP-1 DRAMATIC CONTENT HELPER

For each intended scene . . .

1. Who/what/when/where/why (exposition)

a. Who are the main characters?	Types, personalities, background each has?	❏
	Who is the main character and why?	❏
b. What is their situation?	What is it, what led to it, where will it go next?	❏
c. When is this happening?	Era, season, month, time of day or night?	❏
d. Where is this taking place?	War-torn Sierra Leone or sleepy Nebraska; city or village; in a train, car, mansion, or slum; kitchen or bedroom; upstairs or down?	❏
e. Why should anyone care?	What in your subject and approach ensures that your audience will give a damn?	❏

2. Action and character (character is best developed through what people do)

a. What is routine and characteristic?	What's necessary and normal in this activity?	❏
	How little can you show to render it concisely?	❏
	What's especially revealing in each main character's actions of his/her/its temperament and nature?	❏
b. What is surprising or special?	What's behind the surface or goes unnoticed by the casual onlooker?	❏
c. What patterns lie in the situation?	What characteristic movement and cycles of repetition does the place or situation have (by people, traffic, machines, animals, natural phenomena, etc.)?	❏
	What obstructs or conflicts with these patterns?	❏

3. Will and conflict (worthwhile drama depends on active, aspiring characters)

a.	Volition: What's your main character trying to get, do, or accomplish?	In life generally?	❏
		In this intended scene?	❏
b.	Obstructions: What in general stops him/her/it?	Overall?	❏
		In this likely scene?	❏
c.	Conflict	What conflicts will occur in the film?	❏
		What's the single, central conflict in your film?	❏
d.	Strategies: How might he/she/it deal with each new obstruction?	By reflex and without thought?	❏
		Creatively?	❏
		In panic, surprise, disbelief, (you name it)?	❏
e.	Resolution	What do you see as possible outcomes for the scene?	❏
		Which is most likely?	❏
		How will you go forward with shooting if a change becomes necessary?	❏

For the film as a whole . . .

4. Structure (a well-structured story gives a sense of movement and purpose)

a.	Hook: How will you engage your audience?	How will you immediately seize your audience's attention?	❏
		How will you signify the "contract" (what your film is going to deal with and how it will do this)?	❏
b.	Momentum: What will structure your sequences and drive your film forward from beginning to its end?	The steps of a process, event, or journey?	❏
		The emotional order of memory? (In retrospect?)	❏
		The needs of a character? (Character-driven movies?)	❏
		A series of orchestrated contrasts?	❏
		A series of graduated moods?	❏
		Other _____?	❏

c. Time: How will you order it?	According to the chronology of the original events?	❏
	As someone remembers the events?	❏
	According to a storytelling logic for telling the events (for instance, showing a court case conclusion before reconstructing all the steps to get there)?	❏
	Other _____?	❏
d. Apex or crisis	Can you see a pivotal event, moment, scene, situation as your film's likely high point? (You may not.)	❏

5. Change, growth, and resolution (a satisfying story reflects change and growth)

a. Who has the potential for change?	Who or what is under pressure?	❏
	Who is taking risks?	❏
	Who or what needs to change?	❏
	Who or what is really stopping that change?	❏
b. Confrontation	How will your audience see the main conflicting forces meet and collide?	❏
	How will you ensure that this happens onscreen?	❏
c. Growth	Who or what might grow?	❏
	Can you legitimately help that growth by intercession?	❏
	What intercessionary temptations must you resist?	❏
d. Resolution	What outcomes seem possible?	❏
	Which is most likely?	❏
	How will you handle each so your film ends meaningfully?	❏

6. Audience, impact, theme

a. Target audience: Who in particular are you addressing? (Don't say "Everyone!")	A kind of person in the film?	❏
	An authority or institution?	❏
	A section of the public, and if so, which?	❏
	Other _____?	❏

b. My audience must feel . . .	What emotions must you awaken in your audience?	❏
	What emotions must you avoid awakening?	❏
c. My audience must think about . . .	What issue, idea, contradiction, conflict, etc., should your audience be left thinking about?	❏
d. The theme of my film will be . . .	Recall your "In life I believe that . . ." statement and restate the theme your film will establish.	❏

PROJECT 2-DP-2 STYLE AND CONTENT QUESTIONNAIRE

Title _____   Page # _____

Sequence Name and Content	What It Should Convey	Style

PROJECT 2-DP-3 BASIC WORKING HYPOTHESIS HELPER

Film Title _____

Project

Define the basic dramatic essentials for your proposed documentary.

Goals

Define:

- A conviction that you hold and mean to express through a film topic ❑
- The main characters, their agendas, and the obstacles they face ❑
- The film's structure ❑
- Its emotional and intellectual impact ❑
- Its theme and premise ❑

Steps

1. In life I believe that . . . (your life-principle concerning this subject). ❑

2. My film will show this in action by exploring . . . (situations). ❑

3. My central characters are . . . (their characteristics). ❑

4. What each wants to get, do, or accomplish is . . . ❑

5. The main conflict in my film is between . . . and . . . ❑

6. I expect my film's structure to be determined by . . .   ❏

7. Ultimately I want my audience to feel . . .   ❏

8. . . . and to understand that . . .   ❏

Notes: Step 5 is often misconstrued as a resistant difficulty when it should be a major opposition of principles. Wrong would be "between John and the pile of work." Right would be "between his ambition and the farmer's prejudice against hiring foreigners" or "between the depression Jenny so often feels and her need to prove herself to her husband" or "between the highly visible occupying army and the invisible insurgency."

PROJECT 2-DP-4 ADVANCED WORKING HYPOTHESIS HELPER
Film Title _____

Project

Define the dramatic essentials of an advanced documentary.

Goals

Define:

- A conviction that you hold and mean to express through a film topic ❑
- The main characters, their agendas, and the obstacles they face ❑
- The film's point of view ❑
- Its structure and style ❑
- Its emotional and intellectual impact ❑
- Its theme and premise ❑

Steps

1. In life I believe that . . . (your life-principle concerning this subject). ❑

2. My film will show this in action by exploring . . . (situations). ❑

3. My central characters are . . . (their characteristics). ❑

4. What each wants to get, do, or accomplish is . . . ❑

5. The main conflict in my film is between . . . and . . . ❑

6. My film's POV, or its POV character, will be . . .   ❑

7. I expect my film's structure to be determined by . . .   ❑

8. The subject and POV suggest a style that is . . .   ❑

9. The theme my film explores is . . .   ❑

10. The premise of my film is . . .   ❑

11. Ultimately I want my audience to feel . . .   ❑

12. . . . and to understand that . . .   ❑

Notes: Step 5 is often misconstrued as a resistant difficulty when it should be a major opposition of principles. Wrong would be "between John and the pile of work." Right would be "between his ambition and the farmer's prejudice against hiring foreigners" or "between the depression Jenny so often feels and her need to prove herself to her husband" or "between the highly visible occupying army and the invisible insurgency."

PROJECT 2-DP-5 BASIC PROPOSAL HELPER

Project

Compile intended dramatic contents ready for expansion into a proposal.

Goals are to

- Find something for each category, but nothing in more than one category ❏
- Develop your ideas and intentions ❏

Steps

Write a brief paragraph on each of the below:

1. TOPIC and EXPOSITION—Write a paragraph that includes:
   a. Your film's *subject* (person, group, environment, social issue, etc.) ❏
   b. *Expository information* (necessary factual or other background information) ❏

2. OUTLINE SEQUENCES—Write a brief paragraph on each sequence that shows characters, an event, or an activity. Include:
   a. How the expected sequence starts, what its action is, and how it finishes ❏
   b. What information or persuasion it contributes to the film ❏
   c. The agendas or conflicts you expect it to evidence ❏

3. MAIN CHARACTERS—Write about each main character, including:
   a. The person's identity—name, relationship to others in film—and their qualities ❏
   b. What he or she contributes to your film's story ❏
   c. What this character wants to get or do in relation to the others or to the situation ❏

4. CONFLICT—What is being argued or worked out in this film? Define:
   a. What conflict the characters know they are playing out ❏
   b. What other important conflict you can see ❏
   c. Developments you see likely to emerge ❏

5. TO-CAMERA INTERVIEWS—Try not to rely on "talking heads." Well-recorded voice tracks however provide good voice-over narration or interior monologue. Give:
   a. Name, age, gender ❏
   b. Job, profession, or role ❏
   c. Main elements that your interview will seek to establish ❏

6.   STYLE—Shooting or editing style. Comment on:
     a. Type of documentary you are making, and how this might ❑
        affect the film's style
     b. Narration (if there is to be any, and by whom) ❑
     c. Style of camerawork and what it suggests ❑
     d. Lighting moods and what they suggest ❑

7.   STRUCTURE—Describe:
     a. What elements (process, event, journey, seasons?) might ❑
        structure the film
     b. What will probably constitute the climactic point in your story ❑

8.   RESOLUTION—Film endings determine most of their final impact,
     so describe:
     a. Changes your characters will probably undergo, and your ❑
        film's possible endings
     b. What meaning each ending would hold for the audience ❑

9.   YOUR MOTIVATION FOR MAKING THE FILM—What, in your ❑
     background and interests, impels you to make the film? (This
     is your chance to argue that you have the energy, passion, and
     commitment to stay the course and make an outstanding film)

Notes: See Chapter 7 for more information.

PROJECT 2-DP-6 ADVANCED PROPOSAL HELPER

Project

Compile intended dramatic contents ready for expansion into a proposal.

Goals

- Find something for each category, but nothing in more than one category. ❏
- Develop your ideas and intentions. ❏

Steps

Write a brief paragraph on each of the below:

1. TOPIC and EXPOSITION—Write a paragraph that includes:
   a. Your film's *subject* (person, group, environment, social issue, etc.) ❏
   b. *Expository information* (factual or other background information) so the reader can see the enclosed world into which you are going to take us ❏

2. ACTION SEQUENCES—Write a brief paragraph on each sequence that shows characters, an event, or an activity:
   a. The sequence's start, expected action, and finish ❏
   b. What information or persuasion it contributes to the film ❏
   c. The agendas or conflicts you expect it to evidence ❏
   d. Any useful metaphors it will suggest ❏
   e. Any special, symbolic, or emblematic imagery it will contain ❏
   f. What structures the events (especially through time) ❏
   g. What the sequence will contribute to the film as a whole ❏

3. MAIN CHARACTERS—Write about each main character, including:
   a. The person's identity (name and relationship to others in film) and their qualities ❏
   b. What he or she contributes to your film's story ❏
   c. The metaphoric role this person occupies in relation to what else is in the film ❏
   d. What this character wants to get or do in relation to the others or to the situation ❏
   e. Any direct speech quotations that freshly and directly convey this person's essence ❏

4. CONFLICT—What is being argued or worked out in this film? Define:
   a. What conflict the characters know they are playing out ❑
   b. What conflict you see them playing out (of which they may be quite unaware) ❑
   c. What other principles (of opinion, view, vision, and so on) you see at issue ❑
   d. How, where, and when one force will confront the other in your film (the *confrontation*, which is very important) ❑
   e. Possible developments you see emerging from this or other confrontations ❑

5. TO-CAMERA INTERVIEWS—"Talking heads," though overused, make good safety coverage, and their tracks, if well-recorded, provide excellent voice-over narration or interior monologue. For each intended interviewee, list:
   a. Name, age, gender ❑
   b. Job, profession, or role ❑
   c. Metaphoric role in your film's dramatic structure ❑
   d. Main elements that your interview will seek to establish ❑

6. STYLE—Shooting or editing style that might augment or counterpoint your film's content. Comment on:
   a. Documentary genre you are using and how this affects the film's style ❑
   b. Point of view and how this affects shooting and editing styles ❑
   c. Narration (if there is to be any, and by whom) ❑
   d. Lighting moods ❑
   e. Visual and other rhythms ❑
   f. Any intercutting or parallel storytelling ❑
   g. Intended juxtaposition of like or unlike materials to create comparison, ironic tension, etc. ❑

7. TONE—Describe the progression of moods of the film as you see them and the film's prevailing tone.

8. STRUCTURE—Outline how you might structure your film. Consider:
   a. How will you handle the progression of time in the film? ❑
   b. How and through whom will the story be told? ❑
   c. What elements (process, journey, seasons, etc.) might structure the film? ❑
   d. What will probably constitute the climactic sequence or "crisis" in your story? ❑
   e. Where in the intended structure might the "crisis" occur? ❑

9. RESOLUTION—Film endings determine most of their final impact, so describe:
   a. What will become the resolution (or falling action) after the "crisis"? ❑
   b. Your film's possible endings ❑
   c. What meaning each would have for the audience ❑

10. SOCIAL SIGNIFICANCE—What will this film:
    a. Say about the lives it portrays? ❑
    b. Suggest is the social significance of this? ❑

11. YOUR MOTIVATION FOR MAKING THE FILM—What in your background and interests impels you to make the film? (This is your chance to argue that you have the energy, passion, and commitment to stay the course and make an outstanding film.)

12. WHY GIVE A DAMN? You care about this, but how will you make your audience do so?

13. AUDIENCE KNOWLEDGE AND PREJUDICES—What are the expectations (right and wrong) of your audience? Your film must be in dialogue with these so it can extend, subvert, or endorse them. Complete the following:
    a. My intended audience is _____ (don't write "Everyone!"). ❑
    b. I can expect the audience to know _____ but not to know _____. ❑
    c. Positive audience prejudices are _____ and negative ones are _____. ❑
    d. Countervailing facts, ideas, and feelings my audience must experience are _____. ❑

14. THEMATIC PURPOSE—The main idea the film imparts to its audience is _____. ❑

15. PREMISE—Your film's content and purpose summed up in a single sentence (such as you'd see in a TV listing) ❑

Notes: See Chapter 23 for more information.

BUDGETING PROJECTS (BP)
(3-BP-1 TO 3-BP-2)
PROJECT 3-BP-1 BASIC BUDGET

Item	Amount	Total

Preproduction

Researcher	_____ days × $_____ per day	_____
Director	_____ days × $_____ per day	_____
Travel	$_____ to cover _____ journeys	_____
Accommodation and subsistence	_____ days × $_____ per day	_____
Also _____	_____	_____
_____	_____	_____
_____	_____	_____

Production

Camcorder rental	_____ days × $_____ per day	_____
Camera support and equipment rental	_____ days × $_____ per day	_____
Sound equipment rental	_____ days × $_____ per day	_____
Camera operator	_____ days × $_____ per day	_____
Sound recordist	_____ days × $_____ per day	_____
Director	_____ days × $_____ per day	_____
Travel	$_____ to cover _____ journeys	_____
Subsistence and accommodation	_____ days × $_____ per day	_____
Expendables: cassettes or memory	_____ Cassettes/memory chips @ $___ each	_____
Stills camera (for publicity shots)	_____ days × $_____ per day	_____
Also _____	_____	_____
_____	_____	_____
_____	_____	_____

Postproduction

Editor   _____ days × $_____ per day   _____

Postproduction computer and   _____ days × $_____ per day   _____
software

Expendables: DVDs, etc.   _____ × $_____ each   _____

                Extra hard drives   _____ × $_____ each   _____

                  Other _____   _____ × $_____ each   _____

Materials to make up press kits

_____   _____ × $_____ each   _____

_____   _____ × $_____ each   _____

_____   _____ × $_____ each   _____

Festival entry materials

_____   _____ × $_____ each   _____

_____   _____ × $_____ each   _____

_____   _____ × $_____ each   _____

Also _____   _____   _____

_____   _____   _____

_____   _____   _____

                                                        GRAND TOTAL   _____

PROJECT 3-BP-2 BUDGET WORKSHEET

Working Title: _____ **Length** ___m __sec **Date** _____

Crew Member	Address	Phone Numbers
(Director)		Home _____ Work _____ Mobile _____ e-mail _____
(Camera)		Home _____ Work _____ Mobile _____ e-mail _____
(Sound)		Home _____ Work _____ Mobile _____ e-mail _____
(Editor)		Home _____ Work _____ Mobile _____ e-mail _____
Format (circle all that apply)	DV/digital Betacam/HD Type _____ Other _____	Film: B&W/color 16 mm/35 mm

Schedule	Preproduction	Production	Postproduction
From (date)			
To (date)			
Brief description of subject			
Film's working hypothesis is			

Preproduction		
Item	Lo Estimate	Hi Estimate
Director/researcher @ _____ per day for __ /___ days		
Travel		
Phone		
Photocopying		
Food		
Accommodation		
Tests		
Research (library, etc.)		
1. Preproduction SUBTOTAL		

Production					
Role	**Daily Rate**	**Min Days**	**Max Days**	**Lo Estimate**	**Hi Estimate**
Director					
Camera operator					
Sound operator					
Gaffer					
Other					
2a. Production Personnel SUBTOTAL					
Equipment					
Camera (film)					
Camcorder					
Magazines (film)					
Changing bag (film)					
Clapper board (film)					
Lenses					
Filter kit					
Exposure meter					
Color temperature meter					
Tripod					
Baby legs					
Hi-hat					

Tilt head						
Spreader						
Video monitor						
Sound recording package (film)						
Headphones						
Mike boom						
Extra mikes						
Mixer						
Batteries						
Sun gun						
Lighting package						
Tie in cables						
Extension cords						
Other _____						
Other _____						
2b. Production equipment SUBTOTAL						

Materials	Type	Cost per Unit	Min Days	Max Days	Lo Estimate	Hi Estimate
Camera raw stock						
Sound rec. stock						
Develop negative						
Make workprint						

Sound transfer						
Sound stock						
Videocassettes						
Other _____						
Other _____						
Miscellaneous	**Type**	**Per day**	**Min**	**Max**		
Insurance						
Transport						
Food						
Accommodation						
Location or other fees						
Other _____						
2c. Production miscellaneous SUBTOTAL						
Postproduction						
Role	**Cost per Day**		**Min Days**	**Max Days**	**Lo Estimate**	**Hi Estimate**
Editor						
Assistant editor						
Narrator						
3a. Postproduction personnel SUBTOTAL						
Materials	**Type**	**Amount**	**Min**	**Max**		
Archive footage						

Editing equipment						
Music						
Titling						
Sound mix						
Hard drives						
DVD disks						
Other expendables						
3b. Postproduction materials and processes SUBTOTAL						
Production office						
Legal						
Insurance						
Phone/fax, assistance, and other production office expenses						
Production manager						
Other _____						
Other _____						
4. Production office SUBTOTAL						

Budget Summary				
Phase	**Category**	**Subtotal**	**Minimum Estimate**	**Maximum Estimate**
1. Preproduction	1. Personnel and materials			
		TOTAL		
2. Production	2a. Personnel			
	2b. Equipment/materials			
	2c. Miscellaneous			
		TOTAL		
3. Postproduction	3a. Personnel			
	3b. Materials/processes			
	4. Production office			
		TOTAL		
	FINAL SUBTOTAL			
	Contingency (add ___% of final subtotal)			
	PRODUCTION GRAND TOTAL			

SHOOTING PROJECTS (SP)
(4-SP-1 TO 4-SP-14)
PROJECT 4-SP-1 SKILLS PRACTICE: HANDHELD CAMERA STEADINESS

Project

Accomplish a steady hold, tracking shot, hold, walking so smoothly past a brick wall that the camera could be on a dolly. This takes a lot of practice.

Goals

- Handhold a camera at a 45° angle to a brick wall about 3 feet away while walking. ❑
- Produce a stable image that neither bobs nor sways. ❑
- Anticipate changes in the surface as you walk. ❑
- Use your non-viewfinder eye to see ahead or around. ❑

Steps

1. Hold for 5 seconds on the wall, then make a smooth start to your tracking shot. ❑
2. Try to make the camera a solid unit with your head and shoulders. ❑
3. Walk with knees a little bent so you can glide, not bob. ❑
4. Make your footsteps fall in a straight line, so you don't sway. ❑
5. Transfer your weight smoothly from one foot to the other with no pounding action. ❑
6. Slide the leading foot over the surface ahead so it can deal with irregularities as it encounters them. ❑
7. Check composition and open your other eye occasionally to see where you are going. This is nauseating until you get used to it. ❑
8. After a 20-second track, make a smooth stop. ❑
9. Hold your composition steady for 5 seconds, then cut the camera. ❑

Creative Limitations

1. The smaller and lighter the camera, the more difficult this is. ❑
2. The closer you are to the wall, the more noticeably unsteady your movement. ❑
3. The wider the angle lens, the less your irregularity shows. ❑
4. With a walking person in the foreground, our eye is less aware of motion irregularities (try it!). ❑

Notes: Using the wide-angle end of your zoom, stand at a 45° angle to a brick wall about 3 feet away (see Figure 14-2). Hold a static shot for 5 seconds, then move forward maintaining distance and angle. The bricks should slide past, neither bobbing up and down nor swaying nearer to and further from camera. Come to a smooth stop, hold for 5 seconds. See your work on a good-sized screen.

PROJECT 4-SP-2 SKILLS PRACTICE: HANDHELD TRACKING ON MOVING SUBJECT

Project

Walk behind a stranger on the street, staying about 8 feet away and at a 45° angle to the person's forward axis.

Goals

- Handhold a tracking shot in busy, unpredictable surroundings. ❑
- Reflect an awareness of the subject's changing background and ❑
  its significance.
- Be ready to recover from being discovered acting as a voyeur. ❑

Steps

1. Have something friendly to say in explanation if your subject ❑
   becomes aware of you!
2. Shoot sound and have mike handler "spot" you (that is, watch ❑
   out for your safety).
3. Follow for perhaps 3 to 4 minutes, up and down stairs and ❑
   through doors, if possible.

Notes: Keep your subject steady and appropriately composed in the frame. Compose for the background as well as for the subject's movement. Remember to give compositional "lead" space (more space ahead of subject than behind).

PROJECT 4-SP-3 SKILLS PRACTICE: HANDHELD TRACKING BACKWARD WITH MOVING SUBJECT

Project

Handle a camera while walking backwards, shooting someone out walking.

Goals

- Handhold a camera while walking backwards with assistance. ❑
- Shoot three different sizes of someone walking that can be edited together. ❑
- Maintain consistent "lead" space ahead of the walker from shot to shot. ❑
- Reduce subject's self-consciousness. ❑
- Shoot sound coverage of footsteps of the walker. ❑

Steps

Production

1. *Version A.* Arrange for a subject to start walking, facing you as shown in Figure 4-SP-3A. The camera operator walks backward, guided for safety's sake by a light touch from assistant or mike operator.
   a. Frame the subject in a wide shot, and hold that shot for about 15 seconds, then . . . ❑
   b. Let the subject gain on you until you have a medium shot; hold this for 15 seconds, then . . . ❑
   c. Let the subject gain on you again and hold for 15 seconds of big close-up, then . . . ❑
   d. Stop the camera so the subject walks out of the shot. ❑
2. *Version B.* Now do the same thing again but this time, as shown in Figure 4-SP-3B, with the camera shooting at about a 30° angle to the subject's axis. ❑

Postproduction

3. Make the transitions between the three different image sizes as cuts, being very careful to preserve the footstep rhythm. Where you cut in the footstep cycle matters. ❑

Creative Limitations

1. You'll find that people are camera conscious when you shoot on-axis as in Version A. ❑
2. Version B will be more comfortable for the subject, gives a better view of background, and allows the operator partial sight of what's behind. ❑

> **Notes:** As mental work for your subject to do to lower his or her self-conscious-
> ness, ask the subject to mentally run over some recent event in which he or she
> was involved. Experiment with the framing and background to find the most
> acceptable shot. Remember to include "lead" space (more space ahead of a mov-
> ing subject than there is behind him) in the composition.

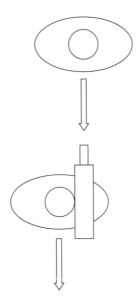

FIGURE 4-SP-3A ————————————————————————————————

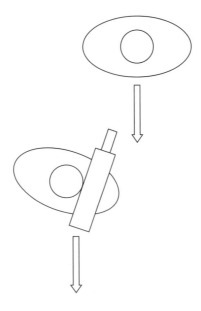

FIGURE 4-SP-3B ————————————————————————————————

PROJECT 4-SP-4 FLAHERTY-STYLE FILM (4 MINUTES)

Project

Cover a human process as a silent movie, constructing narrative through reenacted but natural-looking behavior. Block the action in static frames, directing your participants in reenactments, as in *Nanook*'s hunting, fishing, and teaching sequences. Add music and titles.

Goals

- Say something about the human condition. ❏
- Reveal the temperament of someone handling a demanding human process. ❏
- Tell a story in silent action with musical accompaniment only. ❏
- Explore directing a reenactment in which action is broken into steps and carefully directed. ❏

Steps

Preproduction

1. Make a floor plan and storyboard each scene, using stick figures if you have to. ❏
2. Choreograph action within fixed frames. Plan different angles and shot sizes, varying camera height and using different focal lengths for image variety. ❏

Production

3. Direct participants to do familiar actions. If they are self-conscious, give them mental and physical work to occupy their attention. ❏
4. Ask for actions to be slowed, repeated, etc., when the camera needs it. ❏
5. Get eyeline shots, close shots, reactions, inserts, cutaways. ❏
6. Overlap major action in different-sized shots so you can make nice action match cuts. ❏

Postproduction

7. (Optional) For a black-and-white movie, remove color and adjust contrast. ❏

Creative Limitations

1. No spoofs or mockumentaries, but make a "period" film with inter-titles, if you wish. ❏
2. Shoot from tripod using fixed frames and no zooms or camera movements. ❏

3. Shoot no sound whatever.   ❏

4. Use fade-ins or fade-outs in postproduction, if you wish, but no   ❏
   slow or fast motion.

5. Fit accompanying music but use no vocals.   ❏

Notes: Pick a nonroutine human process that challenges your main character. Emulate Flaherty's spirit, but not the limitations of his techniques; you can, for instance, use modern action match cutting techniques.

Sample Topics

Servicing a piece of large, heavy machinery

Training a dog

Learning to walk on a tightrope or use a trapeze

Going through the stages of an elaborate makeup or hairdo

PROJECT 4-SP-5 VERTOV-STYLE MONTAGE FILM (4 MINUTES)

Project

Cover a place containing many activities as an observational montage, giving particular attention to movement and screen direction, and varying camera height and placement as much as possible. Aim to capture atmosphere and patterns of activity rather than tell a story. Add music and titles.

Goals

- Say something about the human condition. ❏
- Reveal the stages of multiple activities that are happening simultaneously. ❏
- Shoot silent and use musical accompaniment only. ❏
- Use all possibilities that the camera and editing can offer. ❏

Steps

Preproduction

1. Spend time at the location observing and taking notes on what to shoot and how. ❏
2. Arrange your notes as a script to help you organize your thinking before you shoot. ❏

Production

3. Shoot only long-lens material from a tripod; do the rest handheld. ❏
4. Concentrate on capturing movement and in using camera movement meaningfully. ❏
5. Don't forget establishing shots. ❏
6. Try to juxtapose differing activities in the same frame so relativity isn't wholly manufactured in editing. ❏

Postproduction

7. (Optional) For a black-and-white movie, remove color and adjust contrast. ❏
8. Pay careful attention to the beat and transitions of the music as you edit. ❏

Creative Limitations

1. Shoot from tripod for long shots; shoot everything else handheld. ❏
2. No zooms. ❏

3. Shoot no sound whatever.   ❏
4. Use opticals in postproduction and slow or fast motion.   ❏
5. Fit accompanying music but use no vocals.   ❏

Notes: Try to capture the spirit of the place and its activities and try to characterize it as distinctively you would if you were able to visit some vibrant place in history, such as a medieval marketplace or Roman forum.

Sample Topics

A large railway terminus
A heavily used public park
An exercise center with many people and machines
An outdoor festival or show

PROJECT 4-SP-6 DOCUMENT A PROCESS
(4 MINUTES)

Learn

Learn how to cover a process using single-take, handheld coverage. Profile a person or several people, and show the steps of the process, its difficulties and challenges, and the goals and personalities of those involved.

Goals

- Show each step in the process, clearly revealing its nature, pur-   ❑
  pose, and challenges.
- Show how character emerges through action and difficulties.   ❑
- Cover each step imaginatively and with elision editing in mind.   ❑
- Say something about the human condition.   ❑

Steps

Preproduction
1. Choose a process lasting about 20 minutes.   ❑
2. Study it and make notes of its stages—how each starts and   ❑
   ends.
3. Note how you'll boldly cover the process to help elision (shoot   ❑
   reactions and cutaways!).

Production
4. Once you set the process going, you cannot stop the camera or   ❑
   direct participants.
5. You may do more than one take and choose the best in its   ❑
   entirety.

Postproduction
6. Use best take only, then edit down to 4 minutes exactly.   ❑
7. You can add nonvocal music, if you wish.   ❑

Creative Limitations

1. You may not direct participants during the take; you must adapt to what they do.
2. Use the wide-angle end of your zoom only; create different-sized shots by moving the camera.
3. Shoot sound coverage for effects and dialogue.

Notes: This is one of the most useful exercises, since you'll often be covering processes of all kinds. Doing it imaginatively and revealingly is a special talent that requires you to watch for beats and for anything revealing the inner lives of the participants.

Sample Topics

Changing a car tire
Moving a beehive
Clearing a house's gutters of leaves
First parachute or bungee jump

PROJECT 4-SP-7 DOCUMENT AN EVENT
(6 MINUTES)

Learn

Learn how to profile an outdoor event using handheld coverage. Include a central character and incorporate parallel story lines. Include normal contours of the event, but include what's unexpected too. Make the central character and his or her special qualities, values, and conflicts interesting.

Goals

- Show each step in the event, clearly revealing its nature, purpose, and challenges. ❑
- Show your main character's personality emerging through his or her participation. ❑
- Cover each step imaginatively and with elision and parallel storytelling in mind. ❑
- Say something about the human condition. ❑

Steps

Preproduction
1. Choose an event lasting perhaps 2 hours maximum. ❑
2. Research probabilities. Note how stages start and end, and decide how to cover them. ❑
3. Decide angles to help abbreviate processes; plan to shoot plentiful reactions and cutaways. ❑
4. If there are people, animals, or vehicles in movement, plan for backgrounds, meaningful juxtapositions, and consistent screen directions. ❑

Production
5. Once the event starts, you can stop and start the camera but not direct participants. ❑
6. You may shoot up to 2 hours of material (a ratio of 20:1). ❑
7. Cover the event with one or more cameras, but brief each to shoot particular material. Look for the unexpected, the accidental, the eccentric (humor). ❑
8. Shoot central character interview where there's no background interference. ❑
9. You may shoot street interviews. Look for local color and eccentricity (humor). ❑
10. Shoot good dialogue tracks and extra sound effects. ❑

Postproduction

11. Use the best material to make an edited version of 6 minutes ❏ exactly.

12. Use central character's voice-over as narration, but eliminate ❏ all talking-head picture.

13. You may use street interviews as talking heads, but eliminate ❏ the interviewer's voice.

Creative Limitations

1. You may not direct participants; you must adapt to shoot what ❏ they do.

2. Make this a "transparent" film—one that looks more like life ❏ than a film.

3. Let the main character's POV rule the film, although you can ❏ imply other POVs.

Sample Topics

An agricultural show, following one animal or competitor

Beauty pageant or other competition, following a chosen participant

Political demonstration, preferably with police presence

Behind the scenes in a city fireworks display

PROJECT 4-SP-8 DRAMATIZE A LOCATION
(5 MINUTES)

Project

Make a "character study" of a place of your choice. Show its mood, nature, characters, and dramatic tensions entirely through imagery and music.

Goals

- Create a strong mood and a transition to a different, equally strong mood. ❑
- Shoot uncontrolled events in an unobtrusive way. ❑
- Show cycles in the location's evolution throughout a period such as a day. ❑
- Use a montage of visuals to tell the story and shoot to facilitate ellipsis. ❑
- Reveal characters' patterns of behavior and agendas. ❑
- Express a conviction or idea about the human condition. ❑

Steps

Preproduction

1. Research events, personalities, shots, and available light so you are prepared. ❑
2. Find out all you can about the personalities likely to participate. ❑
3. List expository material and arrange your notes into a script that you intend to shoot. ❑
4. Define your film's likely crescendo and conclusion. ❑

Production

5. Shoot silent off a tripod and under available light; be ready to exploit the telephoto lens. ❑
6. Shoot plenty of parallel action to help with ellipsis in editing. ❑
7. Cover the items in your script and grab any gifts that come your way. ❑

Postproduction

8. Edit to make all the film's exposition and plot emerge spontaneously. ❑
9. Edit out whatever shows your participants are aware of the camera. ❑

Creative Limitations

1. Avoid impinging on your subject—you are a fly on the wall. ❑
2. No lighting; use whatever is indigenous to your location. ❑

3. No preparing, manipulating, or even contact after you've got the   ❏
   relevant permissions.
4. Your filming, after editing, must look as though no film unit was   ❏
   present.
5. No words, no songs—let the events, augmented by music,   ❏
   explain themselves.

Notes: Success depends on finding an evocative location with plenty of visually interesting action that you can shoot without making people self-conscious.

Sample Topics

Train or bus terminus, plaza, street market, video games arcade

Truck stop, all-night café, restaurant kitchen, hairdresser's beauty shop

Place at river where wild animals come to drink

Health club, boxing or martial arts training center, dance school

PROJECT 4-SP-9 MAKE AN ESSAY FILM
(5 MINUTES)

Project

Design a film composed of images and narration. Write the narration in a distinctive voice (whose will it be?) that talks to the audience in a particular and personable way. This form favors the diary, retrospective, or survey, so feel free to use it playfully.

Goals

- Conduct your audience stage by stage through an experience or set of special events. ❏
- Narrator directs the audience's attention to anything we should notice. ❏
- Explore the power of language to unlock the connotative potential of images. ❏
- Say something about the human condition. ❏

Steps

Preproduction

1. Make a split-page script, with the images in the left-hand column and words and sound effects in the right-hand column. ❏
2. Designate relationship between words and images accurately to the syllable. ❏

Production

3. Use family photos, archives, stills, text, or live action that you direct. ❏
4. Shoot from tripod with minimal camera movements or zooms. ❏
5. Shoot sound atmospheres and effects but no synchronous sound. ❏
6. Direct participants to do what you need. ❏

Postproduction

7. Read narration against assembled images. Rewrite as required, then record in quiet conditions. Remember to shoot presence track. ❏
8. Fit narration, altering shot lengths and cutting points so everything dovetails. ❏
9. Use music, featured effects, and atmospheres. Make the track neither bare nor overloaded. ❏
10. Vary motion speed or use freezes, if you wish. ❏
11. Overlay front and end titles on imagery. ❏

Creative Limitations

1. Shoot all images off tripod, but you may pan and tilt. ❑
2. Use a live central character or use, say, archive footage in which ❑
   one appears.
3. Do not use synchronous sound. ❑
4. Music must contain no words. ❑

Notes: Don't forget to shoot close-ups and long shots as well as medium shots. Vary the camera height and compose memorable images. Edit on the operative words so you polarize our attention as new images come up. The ending will be important, so consider what thoughts and feelings you want to leave us with.

Sample Topics

Woman visits the grave of a grandmother she wishes she had bothered to know

Soldier assailed in daily life by visions that he or she can't tell anybody

What life looks like the first day you find yourself homeless

What a cat thinks when her people bring home a puppy

PROJECT 4-SP-10 BASIC INTERVIEW, CAMERA ON A TRIPOD (4 MINUTES)

Project

Interview one person, getting that person to describe his or her life before an important, life-changing event, then afterward. What was the event? What was the person like before, and how was he or she changed after? (*This can be shot with sound and picture or using sound alone.*)

Goals

- Put the interviewee at ease.   ❏
- Shoot the interviewee in a single-sized shot in a pertinent   ❏
  location.
- Get the interviewee to speak with intensity and focus.   ❏

Steps

Preproduction

1. Choose your interviewee and discuss what he or she might talk   ❏
   about.
2. Decide where to shoot the interview and what effect you want   ❏
   from the surroundings.

Production

3. Shoot the interview in a single medium shot (head and top of   ❏
   shoulders).
4. Sit next to the camera and interview from out of the shot.   ❏

Postproduction

5. Remove the interviewer's questions so we hear only the inter-   ❏
   viewee talking.
6. Restructure the interview to make it develop logically and   ❏
   meaningfully.
7. Edit to maintain natural speech rhythms of speaker. You can   ❏
   dissolve between sections if jump cuts seem intrusive.
8. Structure the final film to tell the critical event, what the inter- ❏
   viewee was like before it, and how the event left him or her
   changed afterward.

Creative Limitations

1. Interview for no longer than 6 minutes.   ❏
2. Redo the interview from scratch if the first version beats around ❏
   the bush.

3. Avoid editing difficulties by having no voice overlaps between ❑ the interviewer and the interviewee.

4. If the interviewee has stills, mementoes, or video of the event ❑ in question, use those to illustrate the interview. Cutting away to them will help bridge pieces of interview.

Notes: Use the camera mike if you must or, better, place a separate mike close for a more intimate voice quality. No need to mike the interviewer, because the questions will be edited out.

Sample Topics (expect pivotal events such as these)

A life-changing illness or accident

Someone special who made the interviewee see and feel differently

A major test or obstacle that the interviewee overcame—or did *not* overcome

The loss or gain of something or someone important

PROJECT 4-SP-11 ADVANCED INTERVIEW, THREE SHOT SIZES (4 MINUTES)

Project

In a single-person interview, produce a seamless, questionless, and "transparent" flow of on-screen narrative by eliminating all trace of the interviewer's voice. Use this technique for tripod interviews and also for handheld *vox populi* street interviews. In the latter case, move the camera in and out rather than zooming.

Goals

- Put the interviewee at ease and talking directly to the tripod-mounted camera because the interviewer is under the camera lens. ❏
- OR: Shoot handheld street interviews using off-axis interviewing. ❏
- Shoot interviewee in different-sized shots whose compositions cut well together. ❏
- In finished result, interviewee speaks with intensity and focus throughout. ❏

Steps

Preproduction

1. Decide where to shoot the interview and what effect you want from lighting. ❏

Production

2. Wide shot (top of head to knees), medium shot (head and top of shoulders), big close-up (forehead to chin). For *vox pop*, cover with close and medium shots only. ❏
3. Use wider shot for new subject matter and cover moments of intensity in close-up. ❏
4. When changing image size, recompose simultaneously and smoothly. ❏
5. Produce compositional proportions that match on cuts between different-sized images. ❏

Postproduction

6. Make the interviewee's body position and expression match at cuts. ❏
7. Restructure the interview to make it develop logically and meaningfully. ❏
8. Edit to maintain the natural speech rhythms of the speaker. ❏
9. Edit the story to arrive at a climactic moment and resolution. ❏

Creative Limitations

1. Interview for no longer than 6 minutes. ❏
2. Each answer must work on its own without the question. ❏
3. If a voice overlap happens, immediately ask the interviewee to ❏
   start again in the clear.

Notes: Good edited interviews require compact expository information, a center or focus that develops, some significant change, and an outcome or resolution. A lavalier mike is ideal for a tripod setup; use a boom mike for street interviews. Don't mike the interviewer, as the questions are due for elimination during the edit. For tripod work, arrange a touch signal between the director/interviewer and camera operator so you can request particular zoom changes. Image size changes must be considerable for compositions to cut together well.

Sample Topics

How a special person helped the interviewee to resolve a major conflict in his or her life

The worst period in the interviewee's life, how it came about, and how it ended

A moment of enlightenment in the interviewee's life and what it helped decide

PROJECT 4-SP-12 MAKE AN OBSERVATIONAL FILM (6 MINUTES)

Project

Cover a central character in a spontaneously unfolding event, shooting unobtrusively and on the run. Make a "transparent" film that condenses a long process into something short and which says something about the quality and purpose of a human life.

Goals

- Work closely with one or, better, two other crew members. ❑
- Cover all relevant sides of spontaneous exchanges with a single mobile camera. ❑
- Show all relevant stages of the event and reveal the characters' agendas. ❑
- Say something about the human condition through the resulting edited final version. ❑

Steps

Preproduction

1. Research what to expect (events, locations, available light) so you aren't unprepared. ❑
2. Find out all you can at a distance about the personalities likely to participate. ❑
3. Define the film's likely crescendo so you know what you are shooting for. ❑

Production

4. Shoot under available light only, and use a single mike on a short pole. ❑
5. Practice as a unit so you can adapt quickly no matter what happens. ❑
6. To help ellipsis, shoot material that can serve as parallel action. ❑

Postproduction

7. Edit out whatever shows that your participants are aware of the camera. ❑
8. Classify your material into bins—there's going to be a lot of it. ❑
9. Edit to make all the film's exposition and plot emerge spontaneously. ❑

Creative Limitations

1. You can't impinge on your subject at all—you are a fly on the wall. ❑

2. No preparing, manipulating, or even contact after you've got ❑ the relevant permissions.
3. Your filming, when you've finished, must look as though no film ❑ unit was present.
4. No interviews, voice-over, or narration; the events must explain ❑ themselves.

Notes: Much of the success of this type of filmmaking lies in finding an appropriate subject. People busily in action are better than those immobile and aware of the camera. Someone going through an ordeal (say, a test or competition) will be too occupied to care about your presence. Make an open-ended film whose subject's failure may be the heart of a good film.

Sample Topics

Local girl entering a beauty pageant

Male high school friends going out for the evening to hunt, successfully or otherwise, for girls

Amateur theater group's dress rehearsal

Learner-driver who practices and then takes the dreaded driving exam

PROJECT 4-SP-13 MAKE A PARTICIPATORY FILM
(10 MINUTES)

Project

Gather a core sample of attitudes and feelings from a range of interviewees on a contemporary issue, interview best two in depth, then shoot illustrative material to flesh out the narrative that emerges from your questioning. The resulting investigative documentary should use multiple participants and a range of techniques.

Goals

- Introduce, link, and conclude the inquiry with a narration, if you have to. ❏
- Include different genders, ages, and demographic viewpoints. ❏
- Do *vox populi* interviews in two very different areas. ❏
- Conduct two probing interviews with the most interesting street interviewees. ❏
- Use stills, live action footage, or brief quotes from other films. ❏

Steps

Preproduction

1. Write a hypothesis from intuition and research. You are trying to say something! ❏
2. Work out standard questions and follow-ups for the *vox populi* sequences. ❏

Production

3. Shoot *vox pop* interviews, learning and improving questions as you go. ❏
4. Get signed clearances with addresses and contact information. ❏
5. Keep a scorecard so you get proportional coverage of desired demographics. ❏
6. Decide who you will invite to interview in depth and where and what you aim to get. ❏
7. Decide and shoot visual material to juxtapose with interviewees. ❏

Postproduction

8. Assemble the best of the visual material as freestanding sequences. ❏
9. Summarize each interview's contents, so you can find their content easily. ❏

10. Make a list of topics, an order, and roughly assemble.   ❏

11. Integrate the visual, archive, textual, and the interview materials.   ❏

12. Refine until you have a good dramatic arc and the right screen time (10 minutes).   ❏

Creative Limitations

1. Do street interviews handheld, and alternate interviewees L–R, R–L.   ❏

2. Interviewers should stay off-camera and try not to let their voices overlap interviewees' voices.   ❏

Notes: Guess likely answers people will give to your questions, so you can follow up intelligently. Go wherever the interview leads once it starts. You are trying to lead ordinary people into speculation and self-revelation and give your audience a cultural perspective.

Sample Topics

Are you happy? (the question behind Rouch and Morin's *Chronicle of a Summer*)

If there is a life after death, how would you like to spend it?

What makes somebody become a terrorist?

What would a really green life be like for you?

PROJECT 4-SP-14 MAKE A DIARY FILM (12 MINUTES)

Project

Design a diary composed of images and narration. Write narration in your own voice, talking as you would to a diary. This form favors an introspective, intimate conversation with the self. The film's central character may be you, a self-caricature, or other mask.

Goals

- Conduct your audience stage by stage through experiences or events. ❏
- Narrator shares feelings about what we see that are denied to other characters. ❏
- Use sync scenes with interpolated voice over from the diarist. ❏
- Explore the power of words to interpret images and actions. ❏
- Say something about the human condition. ❏

Steps

Preproduction

1. Make a split-page script, with the images in the left-hand column and sound in the right-hand column. ❏
2. Designate likely relationship between words and images. ❏

Production

3. Use photos, archive footage, text, or observation-type live action. ❏
4. Shoot handheld or tripod as seems appropriate. ❏
5. Shoot sound atmospheres and effects. ❏
6. Do not direct participants; simply observe their actions and behavior. ❏

Postproduction

7. Read narration against assembled images. Rewrite as required, then record in quiet conditions. OR: Record improvised "thoughts voice" and edit accordingly. This will sound more spontaneous. Remember to shoot presence track. ❏
8. Fit narration, altering shot lengths and cutting points so everything dovetails. ❏
9. Use music, featured effects, and atmospheres. Make the track neither bare nor overloaded. ❏
10. Vary motion speed or use freezes, if you wish. ❏
11. Overlay front and end titles on imagery. ❏

Creative Limitations

1. Ask someone to shoot occasional and appropriate shots of you, ❏ the diarist, but don't feel bound to use them.
2. Alternate synchronous sound with "thoughts voice"—exterior ❏ with interior realities.
3. Music, if you use it, must have no words. ❏

Notes: Deciding on the persona, or mask, that you proffer will be the hardest part. Self-mocking? Outraged? False modesty? Ever-optimistic loser? Be serious or have fun with this, as you wish. Don't forget to shoot close-ups and long shots (not all medium shots). Vary the camera height and compose memorable images for what your central character remarks upon. Edit on the operative words so you polarize our attention as new images come up. The ending will be important, so consider what thoughts and feelings you want to leave us with.

Sample Topics

Being assailed during a present-day gathering by the ghost of past gatherings

Revisiting a school or other place where you lived an intense period of your life

Drawing a map of your childhood surroundings from memory, then visiting them now

Your daily life in contrast to that of people in a contemporary human disaster

POSTPRODUCTION PROJECTS (PP) (5-PP-1 TO 5-PP-2) PROJECT 5-PP-1 ASSESS YOUR INTERVIEWING		
	Did you . . .	**Yes/No**
Preparing	Question in order to evoke responses in specific areas?	Y/N
	Tell interviewee what you do and don't want to cover?	Y/N
Getting expository information	Get information to comprehensively set the scene?	Y/N
	Get it from more than one person, so you have options?	Y/N
	Take a checklist so you forgot nothing vital?	Y/N
Directing and interacting	Maintain eye contact?	Y/N
	Shape and direct the interview by questioning?	Y/N
	Let the interview proceed informally and by association?	Y/N
	Exert control over the substance of the interview? (It's your film and what it says is your responsibility.)	Y/N
	Let the interviewee take control if your intuition told you it would lead to something important?	Y/N
	Press for clarification? (If you don't know what the interviewee meant, your audience won't either.)	Y/N
	Encourage your interviewee to stay with a significant subject until you felt it was fully explored?	Y/N
	Keep exploring until you reached complete factual and emotional understanding?	Y/N
	Refuse to settle for abstractions or generalities?	Y/N
Listening	Listen as if hearing everything for the first time and thus monitor what a first-time audience hears?	Y/N
	Listen to ensure that the answer started comprehensively; if not, did you have the interviewee start over? (Answers shouldn't depend on information in the question.)	Y/N

	Not think about your next question (since it stops you from listening)?	Y/N
	Listen and catch all subtexts, those unspoken meanings lying beneath the surface?	Y/N
Steering	Direct the interviewee by saying, "Could you talk about . . . (subject)?"	Y/N
	Summarize what you understand so far and ask the participant to continue?	Y/N
	Courteously change subject by saying, "Could we move to . . . (new subject)?"	Y/N
Follow-up	Follow up all intuitions and instincts?	Y/N
	Store further points as you listen, and eventually bring the interviewee back to them?	Y/N
	Expand on something by saying, "Can we return to . . .?"	Y/N
	Encourage going further by quoting interviewee's significant words in a questioning tone?	Y/N
	Open an emotional area by saying, "I got the impression that you have strong feelings about . . ."?	Y/N
	Repeat the interviewee's last words in a questioning tone when he or she stopped and needed encouragement?	Y/N
	Name an impression you're getting; for example, "You seem hesitant to tell me something," "You seem amused," etc.?	Y/N
Silences	Correctly interpret an "I'm finished" kind of silence?	Y/N
	Keep the camera running during a silence until he or she carried on?	Y/N
	Believe you were right to interject and move on?	Y/N
Interviewing people in crisis and "doing damage"	Overcome your fear of intruding? (People know instinctively what they can handle. Just go carefully.)	Y/N
	Act on the knowledge that crises are when people most need to talk?	Y/N
	Act on the idea that giving testimony is healing, and being a good listener is part of it?	Y/N

Closure	Find that a good interview left a sense of catharsis?	Y/N
	Remember to say, "Is there anything you'd like to add?" before concluding the interview?	Y/N
	Thank the interviewee at the end?	Y/N
	Check back the next day to see what after-thoughts the interviewee might have had since?	Y/N
	Maintain humility by acknowledging your failures?	Y/N

PROJECT 5-PP-2 STORY STRUCTURE HELPER

Project

Experiment with different story structures, prospect for alternatives, and explore the gains and losses of each. Do this while you plan a film, just before you edit, or after you find you are dissatisfied with the structure of an edited version and want to try another. This technique is also helpful for developing a pitch and for providing "playing cards" for partners and critics so they can demonstrate alternatives they want to suggest.

Goals

- Make story elements into modular parts. ☐
- Try different orders. ☐
- Find the POV that justifies each. ☐
- Pitch your results to listeners and get feedback. ☐

Steps

Preparation

1. Make a set of small index cards, one for each sequence or ☐
   story element (such as archive material, still photos, documents, or interview).
2. Give each card a number and a tag title so you can recognize ☐
   its contents at a glance.

Experimentally Organize

3. Lay cards out on a large tabletop. ☐
4. Arrange them in different orders to find a logical throughline ☐
   for the film.
5. Improvise an oral treatment describing from card to card what ☐
   you'd see and hear from the screen.
6. When an arrangement works, write down the number ☐
   sequence so you can painlessly reassemble them.
7. Try other arrangements, narrating each and noting down their ☐
   numbers, too.
8. Figure out what POV would make each treatment work best. ☐
9. Are there POVs you haven't tried? Try them—leave no stone ☐
   unturned.
10. Rehearse till you can present two or three best versions in 4 ☐
    to 5 minutes each.

Presentation

11. Use each layout to pitch different film versions to an audience ☐
    of 1 to 6 persons.

12. Ask the audience for pros and cons of each version, listening ☐ carefully and taking notes.
13. Encourage your audience to play with the cards and experi- ☐ ment with alternatives of their own.

Notes: What's great about this method is that, quite painlessly, it gets you to step beyond the obvious approach to plumb the well for alternatives, and it makes you explore alternative POVs. It then provides a set of prompts so you can narrate different versions to explore their effectiveness with a new audience.

GLOSSARY

For further information, see index.

A

Adaptation   The unique way each person adapts to the changing obstacles that prevent him or her from gaining his ends. Prime component in externalizing a person's conflicts.

Addressable timecode   A camera or other timecode having a settable starting point.

ADR   Automatic dialogue replacement. *See* Postsynchronization.

AFI   American Film Institute.

Agenda   What a character is trying to get, do, or accomplish—often unconsciously.

Ambient sound   Sound naturally occurring in any location.

Amp   Ampere, a measure of electrical current flow.

Analog recording   Sound or picture recording whose waveforms are recorded as analog voltages rather than in digital representation.

Angle of acceptance (lens)   Height and width of an image, expressed in degrees or as measurements, filmed by a particular lens at a given distance in a given aspect ratio.

Angle of acceptance (microphone)   Narrow or very wide, according to how much the microphone's design discriminates against off-axis sound.

Anticipating   When an actor (or documentary participant) speaks or acts in advance of the appropriate moment.

Anticipatory sound   Sound brought in ahead of its accompanying picture.

Aperture (lens)   Area of lens in use, expressed as an *f*-stop, which determines the amount of light transmitted.

Artifacts   Tendency for digital imagery to render diagonal lines as jagged rather than straight.

Aspect ratio   The size of a screen format expressed as the ratio of the width in relation to the height. Films made for television are photographed at a ratio of 1.33:1. *See also* Angle of acceptance.

Atmosphere track   Sound track providing a particular atmosphere (café, railroad, beach, or rain, for example).

Attack (sound)   The beginning portion of any sound.

Audio sweetening   The adjusting of level and equalization that accompanies sound mixing.

Auteur theory   The misleading concept that one mind controls the creative identity of a film.

Axis   The imaginary line between scene participants that helps determine the direction they face on-screen. *See* Camera-to-subject axis, Subject-to-subject axis, and Scene axis.

B

Baby legs   A miniature tripod for low-angle shots.

Back lighting   Lighting from behind the subject.

Back story   The events stated or implied to have happened prior to the period covered in the story.

Balanced line   A three-wire audio cable incorporating a noise-canceling design.

Bars   Standard color bars generated in video systems, usually by the camera.

BCU   Big close-up.

Beat   Point in a situation where a buildup of pressure produces a major and irreversible change in at least one character's consciousness (theater term).

Behalfer   Someone who makes a film on behalf of someone else and elects to speak for those supposedly without a voice of their own.

BG   Background.

Blocking   Choreographic arrangement of movements by participants and camera in relation to the location.

Boom   Support pole (or fishpole) permitting a microphone to be suspended close to speakers.

Bounce light   Light directed off a reflected surface such as a wall, ceiling, or bounce card.

Boxcar cutting   Method of assembling sound and action segments as level-cut segments for speed and convenience.

Broad lighting   Lighting that produces a broad band of highlight on a face or other three-dimensional object.

Buzz track   *See* presence.

C

Camera left/right   Movement or placement of objects in relation to the camera. Also expressed as *screen left* or *right*.

Camera motivation   Each shot or a camera movement should be justified in terms of the scene or story.

Camera-to-subject axis   The invisible line between the camera and the subject of its composition.

Capturing   *See* Digitizing.

Cardioid microphone   One having a heart-shaped pickup pattern that favors on-axis sound.

Character generator   An electronic program for producing video titles.

Cheating   The practice of moving participants, furniture, or other objects in relation to each other to minimize shadows or other impediments. If this is evident, you are no longer cheating effectively.

Cinéma vérité   Documentary shooting method in which the camera is subservient to an actuality that is sometimes instigated by the director.

Clapper board   Marker board used at the beginning of takes whose closing bar permits easy synchronization with sound. Also called the *slate*.

Climax   The dramatic apex or turning point of a scene.

Closed question   A question that manipulates the person replying into providing a certain form of answer.

Codec   Digital compression formula applied to sound or imagery that saves storage space by removing duplicate information. *See also* Lossy codec.

Color bars   Standard electronic video color test, usually generated by the camera.

Color temperature   Light color quality, measured in degrees Kelvin.

Comm   Commentary.

Committing action   Action that establishes what a character is trying to get, do, or accomplish.

Complementary shot   A shot compositionally designed to intercut with another.

Completion money   Additional funds required to bring a project to completion.

Composite print   A film print combining sound and picture.

Compression   Sound with a wide dynamic range can be proportionately compressed so the loudest and softest sounds are closer in volume.

Concept   A simple, direct statement of a project's contents, purpose, and intentions.

Confrontation   Bringing into final collision those people or forces that represent the dramatic situation's main conflict.

Contingency percentage   A proportion, usually between 3 and 5%, added to a budget to provide for the unforeseeable.

Contingency planning   Alternative shooting scheduled for scenes threatened by weather or other imponderables.

Continuity   Consistency of physical detail between shots intended to match.

Continuity script   Record of a finished film's contents; useful for proving piracy or censorship.

Contrast ratio   Ratio of lightest to darkest areas in an image.

Controlling point of view   The psychological perspective (a character's or the storyteller's) from which a particular scene is shown.

Counterpoint   The juxtaposing of antithetical elements, perhaps between sound and picture, to create a conflict of impressions for the audience to resolve.

Coverage   The different angles from which a given scene is covered in order to allow variations of viewpoint in editing.

Crab dolly   Wheeled camera support platform that can roll in any direction.

Craning   A boom supporting the camera that can be raised or lowered during the shot.

Crawl titles   Titles that scroll across the screen rather then rolling up or down it.

Creeping sync   Mismatch in action and sound speeds that causes sync to progressively deteriorate.

Crib notes   Director's notes listing intentions and "don't forgets" for a scene.

Crossing the line   Moving the camera across the scene axis; can be problematical.

CS   Close shot.

CU   Close-up.

Cutaway   A shot, often a character's physical point of view, allowing you to cut away momentarily from the main action.

D

Dailies   The film unit's daily output, hurriedly synchronized for viewing. Also called *rushes*.

DAT recorder   Digital audio tape recorder.

Day for night   Special photography that allows a sunlit day shot to pass as moonlit night.

Decibel (dB)   Logarithmic unit of sound measurement.

Decay The tapering away of a concluding sound.

Deep focus Photography that holds objects both near and far in sharp focus.

Demo reel Brief assembly of material on a DVD to best support your proposal or application.

Depth of field Depth of the picture in which objects are in acceptably sharp focus; varies widely according to lens and *f*-stop in use.

DF *See* Drop frame (timecode).

Dialogical discourse Narrative incorporating multiple, even contradictory voices and outlooks.

Diegetic sound Sound belonging in the on-screen world and audible to participants.

Diffused light Light composed of disorganized rays that cast an indistinct shadow.

Digitizing (aka *capturing*) Conversion of analog signal, either audio or video, into a digital equivalent for a computer. Usually uses algorithmic formulation to abbreviate recorded information. *See also* JPEG and MPEG.

Direct cinema A low-profile style of documentary shooting that disallows any directorial intrusion to shape or instigate incidents.

Discrimination (microphone) Ability to reduce sound levels coming from off-axis.

Dissolve Transitional device in which one image cross-fades into another. Also called a *lap dissolve*. One sound can dissolve into another, too.

Docudrama Use of dramatic reenactment in service of documentary purposes.

DOF Depth of field.

Dolby® A proprietary electronic recording system that reduces noise in sound recording.

Dolly shot Any shot on a wheeled camera support.

Double-system recording Camera and sound recorder used as separate instruments.

DP Director of photography.

Dramadoc *See* Docudrama.

Dramatic arc The build, crescendo, and decline of dramatic pressure through a scene or whole film. Also called *dramatic curve*.

Dramatic tension The unresolved knowledge, hopes, fears, and expectations that keep us wanting to know "and what happens next?"

Drop frame (timecode) Timecode that stays synchronous with clock time by periodically dropping a superfluous frame number.

Dub To copy from one electronic medium to another; can be sound or picture.

Dutch angle Shot made with camera deliberately tilted out of horizontal.

DV Digital video, or video and sound recorded digitally. Tape may be as small as 6 mm wide.

DVD Digital video disk.

Dynamic character definition Defining a participant like a dramatic character—by what he or she wants and is trying to accomplish.

Dynamic composition Pictorial composition as it changes within a moving shot.

E

Echo Sound reflections that return after a constant time delay.

Edit decision list Sound and picture edit decisions in a movie, defined as a list of timecode or Keykode® numbers.

EDL *See* Edit decision list.

EDV *See* Enhanced Definition Video.

Effects Sounds laid to augment the sound track of a film.

Ellipsis The removal of superfluous footage from a lengthy process to produce a shorthand version whose missing parts can be inferred by the audience.

Embedded values   Deeply ingrained social assumptions that filmmakers manifest unaware.

ENG   Electronic newsgathering.

Enhanced Definition Video   Video superior to standard definition but inferior to HD (high-definition).

EQ   *See* Equalizing.

Equalizing   Using sound filters to reduce the discrepancy between sound tracks that are supposed to match and sound seamless.

Establishing shot   A shot that establishes a scene's geography and contents.

Exposition   The part of a scene or a story that relays basic information to the audience.

Ext   Exterior.

External composition   The compositional relationship between two images (shots) at the point of transition between them—usually a cut.

Eyeline   The visual trajectory of a character in a scene.

F

Fair Use Doctrine   Documentary practitioner's alleged rights in relation to copyright, as yet untested in court. *See* www.centerforsocialmedia.org/resources/publications/fair_use_in_online_video.

Falling action   *See* Resolution.

FG   Foreground.

FI   Fade in.

Fill light   Diffused light used to raise light level in shadows cast by key light.

Fishpole   *See* Boom.

Flash forward   Moving temporarily forward in time; the cinematic equivalent of the future tense. Quickly becomes a new form of the present.

Flash memory   Nonvolatile computer memory that does not require power to maintain its data.

Flashback   Moving temporarily backwards in time; a cinematic past tense that soon becomes an ongoing present.

Floor plan   *See* Ground plan.

FO   Fade out.

Focal distance   Distance between subject and camera's focal plane.

Focal length (lens)   Distance in millimeters between lens's optical center and image plane.

Focus (acting)   Seeing, hearing, and thinking in character. A documentary participant loses focus when he or she becomes self-conscious and aware of participating in a make-believe world.

Foley   Generic name for recreating sound to picture.

Foreshadowing   Narrative technique by which an outcome is hinted at in advance. Helps to raise expectant tension in the audience.

Form   The means and arrangement chosen to present a story's content.

fps   Frames per second.

Frame rate   Frames recorded per second.

Freeze frame   A single frame arrested and held as a still picture.

f-stop (lens)   *See* Aperture.

FTs   Footsteps; sometimes recreated in stylized documentaries.

Fur mini-screen (sound)   Fur cover for a microphone to reduce air current noises.

FX   Sound effects.

G

Gaffer   Works with director of photography; sets lights and arranges their power supply.

Generation   Camera original is the first generation; copies become subsequent generations.

Genlock   External signal allowing multiple cameras to remain in exact synchronization.

Genre   A kind or type of film (for example, essay, reflexive, direct cinema in documentaries and horror, sitcom, cowboy, domestic drama, etc., in fiction).

Givens   Drama term referring to the given circumstances within which a scene or drama takes place.

Grading   *See* Timing.

Graduated tonality   An image mostly of midtones with neither very bright nor very dark areas.

Gray scale   Test chart useful to camera and lab technicians that shows the range of gray tones and includes absolute black and white.

Grip   Technician expert in handling lighting and set construction equipment.

Ground plan   Diagram showing placement of objects and movements of actors on a floor plan.

Gun mike   Ultradirectional microphone useful for minimizing invasive, off-axis noise.

H

Halation   Image degradation resulting from bright light reflecting internally between lens elements.

Hard light   *See* Specular light.

HD   High-definition digital video.

Headroom   Compositional space left above heads.

Hertz   Unit of electrical or audio frequency that is synonymous with cycles per second.

High angle   Camera mounted high, looking down.

High contrast   Image containing large range of brightnesses.

High down   Camera mounted high, looking down.

High-key picture   Image that is overall bright with few areas of shadow.

Highlight   Brightest area in an image.

Hi-hat   Ultra-low camera support resembling a metal top hat.

Holdover sound   Sound in an overlap cut that persists into the next scene.

Hypercardioid   Microphone with narrow pickup pattern that discriminates strongly against off-axis.

Hz   *See* Hertz.

I

Ideation   Vital phase during which the filmmaker conceives the idea and purpose for a narrative work.

Image stabilization   Mechanical or electronic system compensating for camera unsteadiness.

Imaging chip   The electronic receptor that converts a visual image into digital form.

Improv (improvisation)   Interaction producing a spontaneously determined outcome.

Individual release form   An agreement the participant signs assigning you specific rights and responsibilities.

Informed consent   Permission given by those appearing in your film after you explain the consequences to them of doing so. You do this in terms that each person understands.

Insert   A close shot of detail inserted into a shot providing a more comprehensive view.

Int   Interior.

Interior monologue   Interior "thoughts voice" used as narration.

Interlace recording   Some video systems only draw a complete frame after two interlaced passes—first of odd lines, then of even. *See* Progressive recording.

Intern   Temporary worker, often unpaid, who learns on the job much like an apprentice.

Internal composition   Composition within a given frame.

Irony   The revelation of a reality different from that initially apparent.

J

Jaggies   *See* artifacts.

Jam sync   (1) Copy method transferring all video, audio, and timecode data in one frame-accurate pass. (2) Synchronizing the clocks of, say, a smart slate board with a camera.

JPEG   An electronic algorithm standard used to compress video up to a 20:1 ratio for recording. JPEG allows editing to any particular frame, but MPEG compression may not.

Jump cut   Transitional device in which two similar images taken at different times are cut together so the elision of intervening time is apparent.

Juxtaposition   The placing together of different pictorial or sound elements to invite comparison, inference, and heightened thematic awareness by the audience.

K

Kelvin Scale (deg K)   Light color-reference scale based on thermodynamics of heating a theoretical black body.

Keykode®   Kodak's proprietary system for barcoding each film frame. This facilitates digitizing by assigning each frame its own unique timecode identity.

Key light   A scene's apparent source of illumination that creates the intended shadow pattern.

kW (kilowatt)   One thousand watts of energy.

L

LA   Low angle.

Lap cut   *See* Overlap cut.

Lap dissolve   *See* Dissolve.

Latitude   The ability to record detail in widely separated levels of illumination. Film currently has greater latitude than most video systems.

Lavalier mike   A type of neck or chest microphone.

LCD   Liquid crystal display panel.

Lead space   The additional compositional space allowed in front of a figure or moving object photographed in profile.

Leading question   One whose wording implies the expected answer.

LED　Light-emitting diode.

Legal release　A legally binding release form signed by a film participant that gives permission to use footage taken.

Leitmotiv　Intentionally repeated element (sound, shot, dialogue, music, etc.) that helps unify a film by reminding the viewer of its earlier occurrence.

Level　Sound volume.

Lighting ratio　The ratio of highlight brightness to shadow illumination.

Limiter　Electronically applied upper sound limit, useful for preventing distortion of transient sounds such as a door slamming.

Line of tension　Invisible dramatic axes, or lines of awareness, that can be drawn between important elements and protagonists in a scene.

Lip sync　Recreated speech that is in complete sync with the speaker.

Location release form　Signed document permitting you to shoot at a given location.

Locking picture　The moment when you decide that editing decisions are now complete.

Longitudinal study　A study that follows its subjects and their development over an appreciable length of time, possibly decades.

Looping　*See* Postsynchronization.

Lose focus　*See* Focus.

Lossy codec　One whose degree of compression impinges noticeably on sound or image fidelity.

Low angle　Camera looking up at subject.

Low-key picture　A scene that may have high contrast but that is predominantly dark overall.

Low cut (filter)　Facility allowing reduction of low frequency levels during recording.

LS　Long shot.

M

Macro (focusing)　Additional range of focusing that permits a lens to focus extremely close.

Magazine　Removable lightproof film container for a film camera.

Mannerisms　An actor or documentary participant's idiosyncratic habits of behavior that are difficult to change or suppress.

Marching ants　*See* Zebra stripes.

Master mix　Final mixed sound, first generation.

Master shot　Shot that shows most or all of the scene and most or all of the characters.

Match cut　Transition between two different angles on the same action using the subject's movement to facilitate the transition.

Matte box　Device holding filters in front of camera lens. Usually incorporates a lens hood to shield lens from extraneous light sources.

MCS　Medium close shot.

Memory stick　Solid-state memory, about the size of a stick of chewing gum, plugged into a camera to store settings, information, or even whole images.

MIDI (Musical Instrument Digital Interface)　A standardized digital control for electronic musical instruments.

Midtones　The shades of gray lying between the extremes of black and white.

Mise-en-scène　The totality of lighting, blocking, camera use, and composition that produces the dramatic image on film.

Mix　The mixing together of sound tracks.

Mixer (location)　Portable sound mixer allowing you to combine multiple sound channels.

MLS　Medium long shot.

Mockumentary   Fake documentary intended to amuse.

Modulations   Any electrical or electronic waveforms by which sound or picture are relayed and recorded.

Monological (discourse)   Narrative that speaks with a single unified outlook, unlike dialogical discourse.

Montage   Originally meant editing in general but now refers to the kind of sequence that shows a process or the passage of time.

Montage sequence   *See* Montage.

MOS   Short for "mit out sound," which is what the German directors in Hollywood called for when they intended to shoot silent. In Britain, this shot is called *mute*.

Motif   Any formal element repeated from film history, or from the film itself, whose repetition draws attention to an unfolding thematic statement. *See also* Leitmotiv.

Motivation   Whatever logic impels a character to act or react in a particular way.

MP3   Widely used digital encoding format for sound files.

MPEG   An algorithm standard that maintains quality and achieves up to 100:1 compression. Unlike JPEG compression, each frame is not discrete; you may thus be unable to edit to a particular frame.

MS   Medium shot.

Murphy's Law   "Whatever can go wrong will go wrong." Applies also to people.

Mus   Music.

Music sync points   Places in a film's action where music must exactly fit. Also called *picture-pointing* and can be overdone.

Mute shot   *See* MOS.

N

Narr   Narration.

Narrative compression   Storytelling techniques used to highlight narrative essentials by abridging time and space.

Narrow lighting   Lighting that in portraiture produces a narrow band of highlight on a face.

ND filter   Neutral-density filter. These cut all colors of light equally.

NDF (timecode)   Non-drop-frame timecode. Gives new number to each frame, but because NTSC video is slightly slower than 30 fps, it slowly departs from clock time. *See* Drop frame.

Negative cutting   *See* Conforming.

Networking   The process of going from person to person, using the roots and branches of human networks, in search of particular information or contacts.

Neutral density filter   *See* ND filter.

Noise (sound)   Noise inherent in a sound recording system itself.

Noise (picture)   Image degradation that sets in when a low-light image must be amplified.

Noise reduction   Recording and playback technique that minimizes system noise. *See also* Dolby.

Nondiegetic sound   Authorially applied sound (such as theme music) that is inaudible to the film's characters.

Non-drop-frame (timecode)   *See* NDF.

Normal lens   A lens of a focal length that, in the format being used, renders distances between foreground and background as recognizably normal.

NTSC   Television standards developed for North America by the National Television System Committee.

O

Obligatory moment   In documentary, as in drama, the moment of maximum dramatic intensity in a scene, for which the whole scene exists.

Observational cinema   Filming observationally like an anthropologist and trying to keep equipment and personnel from intruding upon (and thus altering) what one is filming.

Off-axis sound   Any sound arriving at a directional microphone away from its optimal pickup axis.

Omniscient point of view   A storytelling mode in which the audience is exposed to the author's capacity to see or know anything going on in the story, to move at will in time and space, and to freely comment upon meanings or themes.

On-axis sound   That arriving from the direction of a mike's axis.

One-liner or **tagline**   A phrase that sums up the premise and intention of your film in a single line.

Open question   A value-neutral question that avoids implying the reply you may expect. *See also* Closed question.

Operative words   In editing, when language is set against images, the word hitting the beginning of each new image tends to play a big part in how we interpret it. A trained editor will pick important words in speech or narration and make cuts against them, knowing that they have a reinforcing effect.

Optical   Visual device, such as a fade, dissolve, wipe, matte, or superimposition.

OS   Off-screen.

Overlap cut   Any cut in which picture and sound transitions are staggered instead of level cut.

P

Parallel storytelling   Two intercut narratives proceeding in parallel through time.

Pan   Short for *panorama*; horizontal camera movement.

Participant   Someone taking part in a documentary who, in a fiction film, would be an actor.

Personal release form   Signed form by which a participant allows you to use their voice and image.

Perspective   Size differential between foreground and background objects, causing us to infer receding space.

Phantom power   Mike operation power (usually 48 volts) delivered through mike cable as a tiny current from the camera or mixer board.

Phasing (sound)   Sound picked up by two microphones at unequal distances will in some frequencies be out of phase. This causes some sound to cancel itself out—with disconcerting results.

Pickup pattern (microphone)   Design determining whether a microphone picks up all incoming sound equally or discriminates against sound arriving off-axis.

Picture lock   *See* Locking picture.

Picture pointing   Making music fit picture events. Walt Disney films used the device so much that its overuse is called *Mickey Mousing*.

Picture texture   A hard image has large areas in sharp focus and tends toward contrastiness, while a soft image has areas out of focus and lacks contrast.

Pitching   The oral presentation of a film proposal in a brief, comprehensive, and attractive form.

Pixels   Picture elements, the individual cells of the picture that emerge under enlargement.

Playwriting   In drama, one actor's tendency to take control of a scene, particularly in improv work, and to manipulate other actors into a passive relationship. Happens in documentaries, too.

Plot   Arrangement of incidents and logic of causality in a story.

PM   Production manager.

Point of view   Sometimes literally what a character sees (e.g., a clock approaching midnight) but more usually signifies the outlook and sensations of a character within a particular environment. This can be the momentary consciousness of an unimportant character or that of a main character (*see* Controlling point of view). It can also be the storyteller's point of view (*see* Omniscient point of view).

Postsynchronization   Dialogue or effects shot to sync with existing action. Abbreviated as "postsync." *See also* ADR and Foley.

POV   *See* Point of view.

Practical   Any light source visible in the frame as part of the set.

Premise   *See* Concept.

Premix   Subsidiary sound elements mixed together in preparation for the final mix.

Preroll   The amount of time a camcorder or video-editing rig needs to reach running speed prior to recording or making a cut.

Presence   Location atmosphere gathered to augment "silent" portions of track. Every location has its own unique presence.

Prime lens   Fixed (non-zooming) camera lens with few elements and superior resolution.

Privileged moment   Jean Rouch's term for a special, unrepeatable moment in documentary when a participant says or does something that is moving and humanly revealing.

Prosumer   Equipment that is somewhere between consumer and professional in capacity and durability.

Progressive recording   Principle by which a complete video frame is recorded in a single pass. "24p" means 24 frames per second of progressive recording. *See* Interlace recording.

Psychoacoustics   A term for the effect on us of a particular sound, as opposed to its literal cause. A sound can have emotional and cultural associations that go far beyond its cause.

R

Rack focus   Altering focus between foreground and background during a shot.

Radio microphone   A microphone system that transmits its signal by radio to the recorder and is therefore wireless.

Raise the stakes   Expression borrowed from betting that signifies raising the importance of whatever a protagonist is struggling to get, do, or accomplish.

Raw data   Torrent of uncompressed information available from some professional cameras.

Reconnaissance   Careful examination of locations prior to shooting. *See also* Scouting.

Reenactment   Practice in documentary of reenacting situations when necessary.

Reflected sound   *See* Reverberation.

Reflexive cinema   Type of film that includes evidence of its own process and the effect, say, on the participants of the filmmaking process.

Release form   *See* Personal release form.

Release print   Final print destined for audience consumption.

Rendering   Process during editing when a computer combines materials such as titles and backgrounds, and overlaps to create new files. Animation files can take hours to process.

Research   Library work and observation of real life in search of authentic detail to fill out one's knowledge of participants, situations, and events.

Resonance   The tendency for recording spaces to resonate to particular vocal or musical frequencies.

Resistance   Human evasion mechanisms that show up in actors under different kinds of stress. Similar situations happen in shooting documentary.

Resolution   The wind-down events following the film's climax that form the final phase of its development. Also called *falling action*.

Reverberation   Sound reflections returning in a disorganized pattern of delay.

Riding gain   The risky practice of manually adjusting levels as the recording proceeds.

Rising action   Documentary story developments, including complication and conflict, that lead to a scene or a film's climax.

Risk   Whatever makes the protagonist's journey more difficult (and therefore more interesting) or whatever makes the film more challenging to its makers (which lends it more dramatic tension).

Rolling off   Reducing the volume of certain frequency bands; for example, you would use a mike's bass cut switch to roll off heavy traffic background during a street interview.

Room tone   *See* Presence.

Rushes   Unedited raw footage as it appears after shooting. Also called *dailies*.

Rushes book   Log of important first reactions to rushes footage.

S

Sampling rate   The speed at which a digital audio system draws new points along an audio waveform. Faster is better; for example, 48k (48,000 redraws per second) produces better sound than 32k.

Saturation (sound)   Level at which signal distortion sets in.

Scene axis   The invisible line in a scene representing the scene's dramatic polarization. In a labor dispute scene, this might be drawn between the plant manager and the union negotiator. Coverage is shot from one side of this line to preserve consistent screen directions for all participants. Complex scenes involving multiple characters and physical regrouping may have more than one axis. *See also* Crossing the line.

Scene breakdown or **crossplot**   In fiction, a chart displaying the locations, characters, and script pages necessary for each scene. Used in complex reenacted documentaries or any film using actors.

Scene dialectics   Forces in opposition, likely in documentary to be externalized through body language, action, and behavior. A sense of the pressures in each scene, even one lacking human presence, is invaluable to documentary makers.

Scene geography   The physical layout of the location and the placing of the participants. *See also* Master shot.

Scouting (locations, etc.)   Reconnaissance to discover location or other characteristics.

Scratch (music)   Temporary music laid in to test its effect.

Scratch (narration)   Written narration recorded quickly to test its effectiveness.

Screen direction   The orientation or movement of characters and objects relative to the screen (screen left, screen right, up screen, down screen).

Screen left/screen right   Movement or direction specifications. See *also* Screen direction.

SD   Standard-definition television (already obsolescent).

Segue (pronounced "seg-way")   Sound transition, often a dissolve.

Self-reflexive cinema   A documentary form that allows not only the process of filmmaking but also the authorial process to come under the film's scrutiny.

Setup (camera)   Combination of lens, camera placement, and composition to produce a particular shot.

Setup (narrative)   Establishing the sequence of events by which the characters have arrived at their present circumstances.

SFX   Sound effects.

Shock mount   Flexible mount that inhibits handling noise from reaching the microphone.

Shooting ratio   Material shot for a scene in relation to its eventual edited length. 8:1 is a not unusual ratio for dramatic film, and 20:1 or above is common for documentary.

Shotgun microphone   *See* Gun mike.

Shoulder brace   Bracket worn on the body to provide support for a handheld camera.

Shutter speed   Rate at which each frame is taken, its duration expressed in fractions of a second.

Side coaching   In drama the director, during breaks in a scene's dialogue, quietly feeds directions to the actors, who incorporate these instructions without breaking character. Rarely used in documentary, but everything is possible.

Sightlines   Lines that can be drawn along each character's main lines of vision that influence the pattern of coverage so it reproduces the feeling of each main character's consciousness.

Signal-to-noise ratio   The level of a desired signal in relation to other background noise.

Silhouette lighting   Lighting in which the subject is a dark outline against a light background.

Single shot   A shot containing only one character.

Single-system recording   Sound and picture recording made by single instrument. *See* Double-system recording.

Slate   *See* Clapper board.

Slate number   Setup and take number shown on the slate, or clapper, which identifies a particular take.

Soft light   Light that does not produce hard-edged shadows.

Sound dissolve   One sound track dissolving into another.

Sound effects   Non-dialogue recordings of sounds intended either to intensify a scene's realism or to give it a subjective heightening.

Sound mix   The mixing of sound elements into a sound composition that becomes the film's sound track.

Sound perspective   Apparent distance of sound source from the microphone.

Specular light   Light composed of parallel rays that cast a comparatively hard-edged shadow.

Speed (lens)   A fast lens can transmit a relatively large amount of light.

Split-page format   Script format placing action on the left-hand side of the page, sound on the right. Enables a precise transcription of relationships among words, sounds, and images.

Spotting session   A session spent deciding where music or other special features are needed.

Spreader or **spider**   Three-armed bracket under a tripod that prevents its legs splaying.

Static character definition   Giving a character static attributes instead of defining him in terms of dynamic volition.

Static composition   The composition elements in a static image.

Steadicam®   Proprietary body brace supporting a camera; uses counterbalance and gimbal technology so the camera floats as the operator walks.

Sting Musical accent to heighten a dramatic moment.

Storyboard Series of key images sketched to suggest what a series of shots will look like.

Strobing The unnatural result on-screen caused by the interaction of camera shutter speed with a patterned subject, such as the rotating spokes of a wheel or panning across a picket fence.

Subjective camera angle An angle that implies the physical point of view of one of the characters.

Subject-to-subject axis Sightlines between two or more scene participants. If you ignore these when blocking a scene, its edited version is likely to be spatially incoherent. *See* Scene axis.

Subtext The hidden, underlying meaning to anything said or done. It is supremely important, and the director must usually search for it.

Superobjective Overarching thematic purpose of the drama director's interpretation. Documentarians make similar deductions, but from life instead of a text.

Synecdoche Showing a part of something as shorthand for the whole.

T

Tagline An irreducibly brief description useful for its focus on essentials.

Take One filmed attempt from one setup. Each setup may have several takes.

TC Timecode.

Telephoto lens Long or telescopic lens that foreshortens the apparent distance between foreground and background objects.

Temp (music) Temporary music laid in to test its effect.

Tension *See* Dramatic tension.

Thematic purpose The overall interpretation of a complete work that is ultimately identified and decided by the director. *See also* Superobjective.

Theme A dominant idea made concrete through its representation by the characters, action, and imagery of the film.

Three-shot/3S Shot containing three people.

Thumbnail character sketch Brief character description useful either in screen writing or in writing documentary proposals.

Tilt Camera swiveling in a vertical arc—for example, tilting up and down to show the height of a flagpole.

Timecode Electronic code number unique to each video frame.

Timing The process of examining and grading a negative for color quality and exposure prior to printing. Also called *grading*.

Tone Constant sound, generated to assist in setting up levels.

Tracking/trucking shot Moving camera shot made from tracks or a truck.

Transition Any visual, sound, or dramatic screen device that signals a jump to another time or place.

Transparent film One minimizing evidence that anyone knew they were being filmed. Transparent documentary is rather like the invisible wall between players and audience in the theater.

Treatment Usually a synopsis in present-tense, short-story form of an intended documentary. It summarizes expected dialogue and describes only what an audience would see and hear. Can also be a puff piece designed to sell the idea rather than to give comprehensive information about content.

Tungsten Light produced by any tungsten filament source.

Two-shot/2S Shot containing two people.

U

Unit   The whole group of people shooting a film.

Unreliable narrator   Point of view character whose observations are limited by youth, age, bias, emotion, inexperience, etc. The diametric opposite is the authoritative, omniscient narrator, whose views we are supposed to trust.

UPM   Unit production manager.

V

VCR   Videocassette recorder.

Verbal release   Practice of filming a participant rendering verbal permission rather than securing a signed individual release form.

Video assist   A video feed taken from the film camera's viewfinder and displayed on a monitor, usually for the director to watch during shooting.

Visual rhythm   Each image, depending on its action and compositional complexity, requires a different duration on-screen to look right and merit the same audience concentration as its predecessor. A succession of images, when sensitively edited, exhibits a rhythmic constancy that can be slowed or accelerated like any other kind of rhythm.

VO   *See* Voice-over.

Voice-over   Practice of using a participant's "thoughts voice" or interior monologue rather than a talking-head interview or narrator.

Volition   The will of a character to get, do, or accomplish something.

VT   Videotape.

Vox populi   Literally, the "voice of the people." Often shot as street interviews and used as a chorus of opinion.

VU meter   Used to monitor volume units in sound. Peak-reading and averaging VU meters give a different picture.

W

WA   Wide angle.

Whip pan   Very fast panning movement.

White balance   Video camera setup procedure whereby circuitry is adjusted to the color temperature of the lighting source and a white object appears white on-screen.

Wide-angle lens   A lens with a wide angle of acceptance. Its effect is to increase the apparent distance between foreground and background objects.

Wild   Nonsync.

Wild track   A sound track shot alone and with no synchronous picture.

Windscreen   Protection around a microphone to prevent air currents from rattling its diaphragm.

Wireless mike   *See* radio microphone.

Working hypothesis   Working definition of one's underlying intentions while making a documentary. To grasp how your film has evolved, periodically revisit what you decide.

Wrap   The end of a shooting session.

WS   Wide shot.

WT   Wild track.

X

XLR   Sturdy three-connector audio plug or socket.
XLS   Extra long shot.

Z

Zebra stripes   Selectable viewfinder facility that displays moving stripes wherever the image is overexposed. Also called *marching ants*.
Zeppelin   Light, rigid windscreen mounted around a microphone to shield it from air currents.
Zoom lens   Lens whose focal length is infinitely variable between two extremes.
Zoom ratio   The ratio of the longest to the widest focal lengths. A 10 to 100 mm zoom would be a 10:1 zoom.

INDEX